CRIMINAL AND QUASI-CRIMINAL ENFORCEMENT MECHANISMS IN EUROPE

This book looks at the interplay between criminal law and other branches of public law pursuing similar objectives (referred to as 'quasi-criminal law'). The need for clarifying the concepts and the interlink between criminal and quasi-criminal enforcement is a topic attracting a lot of discussion and debate in both academia and practice across Europe (and beyond). This volume adds to this debate by bringing to light the substantive and procedural problems stemming from the current parallel or dual use of the different enforcement systems. The collection draws on expertise from academia, practice and policy; its high-quality analysis will appeal to scholars, practitioners and policymakers alike.

Volume 16 in the series Hart Studies in European Criminal Law

Hart Studies in European Criminal Law

Series Editors: Professor Katalin Ligeti, University of Luxembourg;
Professor Valsamis Mitsilegas, Queen Mary University of London;
Professor Anne Weyembergh, Brussels Free University

Since the Lisbon Treaty, European criminal law has become an increasingly important field of research and debate. Working with the European Criminal Law Academic Network (ECLAN), the series will publish works of the highest intellectual rigour and cutting edge scholarship which will be required reading for all European criminal lawyers.

The series is happy to consider both edited and single authored titles. The series defines 'European' and 'criminal law' in the broadest sense, so books on European criminal law, justice and policy will be considered. The series also welcomes books which offer different methodological approaches.

Volume 1: *EU Criminal Law after Lisbon: Rights, Trust and the Transformation of Justice in Europe*
by Valsamis Mitsilegas

Volume 2: *Challenges in the Field of Economic and Financial Crime in Europe and the US*
Edited by Vanessa Franssen and Katalin Ligeti

Volume 3: *Chasing Criminal Money: Challenges and Perspectives On Asset Recovery in the EU*
Edited by Katalin Ligeti and Michele Simonato

Volume 4: *Limits to EU Powers: A Case Study of EU Regulatory Criminal Law*
by Jacob Öberg

Volume 5: *The Needed Balances in EU Criminal Law: Past, Present and Future*
Edited by Chloé Brière and Anne Weyembergh

Volume 6: *Redefining Organised Crime: A Challenge for the European Union?*
Edited by Stefania Carnevale, Serena Forlati and Orsetta Giolo

Volume 7: *White Collar Crime: A Comparative Perspective*
Edited by Katalin Ligeti and Stanislaw Tosza

Volume 8: *Criminal Liability of Managers in Europe: Punishing Excessive Risk*
Stanisław Tosza

Volume 9: *The European Union and Deprivation of Liberty: A Legislative and Judicial Analysis from the Perspective of the Individual*
Leandro Mancano

Volume 10: *The Legitimacy of EU Criminal Law*
Irene Wieczorek

Volume 11: *The Fight Against Impunity in EU Law*
Edited by Luisa Marin and Stefano Montaldo

Volume 12: *Controlling Immigration Through Criminal Law: European and Comparative Perspectives on 'Crimmigration'*
Edited by Gian Luigi Gatta, Valsamis Mitsilegas, and Stefano Zirulia

Volume 13: *The Principle of Mutual Trust in EU Criminal Law*
Auke Willems

Volume 14: *Surveillance and Privacy in the Digital Age: European, Transatlantic and Global Perspectives*
Edited by Valsamis Mitsilegas and Niovi Vavoula

Volume 15: *The External Dimension of the EU's Policy against Trafficking in Human Beings*
Chloé Brière

Volume 16: *Criminal and Quasi-criminal Enforcement Mechanisms in Europe: Origins, Concepts, Future*
Edited by Vanessa Franssen and Christopher Harding

Criminal and Quasi-criminal Enforcement Mechanisms in Europe

Origins, Concepts, Future

Edited by
Vanessa Franssen
and
Christopher Harding

•HART•
OXFORD • LONDON • NEW YORK • NEW DELHI • SYDNEY

HART PUBLISHING

Bloomsbury Publishing Plc

Kemp House, Chawley Park, Cumnor Hill, Oxford, OX2 9PH, UK

1385 Broadway, New York, NY 10018, USA

29 Earlsfort Terrace, Dublin 2, Ireland

First published in Great Britain 2022

A catalogue record for this book is available from the British Library.

A catalogue record for this book is available from the Library of Congress.

Library of Congress Control Number: 2021950506

ISBN: HB: 978-1-50993-286-3
ePDF: 978-1-50993-288-7
ePub: 978-1-50993-287-0

Typeset by Compuscript Ltd, Shannon
Printed and bound in Great Britain

To Chris, an exceptional scholar and a wonderful person who will be in our hearts and minds forever.

Dear Chris, I am deeply grateful for the journey we made together resulting in this rich volume. Thank you for the numerous inspiring discussions as well as for your fatherly encouragements in the early stages of my career. Vanessa

CONTENTS

LIST OF CONTRIBUTORS

Anna Błachnio-Parzych is Associate Professor in the Criminal Law Department at the Kozminski University, Warsaw, and a member of the Studies and Analyses Office in the Supreme Court of Poland.

Johan Boucht is Professor of Criminal Law at the University of Oslo and Professor of Police Law at University of Bergen, Norway.

Dominik Brodowski is Junior Professor of Criminal Law and Criminal Procedure at Saarland University, Germany.

Ana Laura Claes is a part-time Research and Teaching Assistant at the University of Liège, an Affiliated Junior Researcher at the University of Antwerp and a Member of the Antwerp Bar, Belgium.

Ferry de Jong is Professor of Criminal Law and Criminal Procedure at the Faculty of Law, Economics and Governance of Utrecht University, Netherlands.

Sophie De Sanctis holds a PhD in Law from the University of Luxembourg.

Vanessa Franssen is Professor at the Faculty of Law, Political Science and Criminology of the University of Liège and Affiliated Senior Researcher at the Institute of Criminal Law of the KU Leuven, Belgium.

Christopher Harding is Emeritus Professor of Law at Aberystwyth University in Wales, UK.

Marie Horseele is a full-time Research and Teaching Assistant at the Institute of Criminal Law of the KU Leuven, Belgium.

Raimo Lahti is Emeritus Professor of Criminal Law in the Faculty of Law at the University of Helsinki, Finland.

Tamás Lukácsi (PhD law) works in the Legal Service of the European Parliament.

Maria Pichou is Assistant Professor at the Faculty of Governance and Global Affairs at Leiden University College, Netherlands.

Katja Šugman Stubbs is a Judge of the Slovenian Constitutional Court and Professor of Criminal Procedure and Criminology at the Faculty of Law, University of Ljubljana, Slovenia.

Gary Wilson is Reader in Law in the Centre for Business and Insolvency Law at Nottingham Trent University, UK.

Sarah Wilson is Senior Lecturer in Law at York Law School of the University of York, UK.

Nadine Zurkinden is Senior Researcher for Substantive and Procedural Criminal Law at the Faculty of Law of the University of Zürich and Legal Officer in the Road Traffic Department of the Basle Cantonal Police, Switzerland.

Introduction: Criminal versus Quasi-criminal Enforcement – Setting the Scene

VANESSA FRANSSEN AND CHRISTOPHER HARDING

I. Introduction

This collective volume analyses the historical origins of quasi-criminal, punitive enforcement mechanisms in Europe and makes an effort to clarify terminological differences across national systems, with a view to elaborate more appropriate EU-wide criteria for such enforcement mechanisms. Over the past decades, quasi-criminal enforcement mechanisms have become a phenomenon of significance in most European legal systems, in recent years also increasingly so due to the influence of the European Union (EU) and the Council of Europe. Nevertheless, the relationship between such quasi-criminal mechanisms and formal criminal law remains uncertain and, in some respects, poorly understood.

This research is the fruit of continuing scientific exchanges and interactions in the framework of a European research network entitled *Criminal and quasi-criminal enforcement mechanisms (CQEM)*, created in 2014 by the editors of this book, Christopher Harding and Vanessa Franssen. Over the course of the years, the work of the research network has been financially supported by the College of Europe's Natolin Centre in Warsaw (Poland), the Faculty of Law, Economics and Finance of the University of Luxembourg (Grand-Duchy of Luxembourg) and the Faculty of Law, Political Science and Criminology of the University of Liège (Belgium).

This introductory chapter will present the overall research topic, explain the choice of terminology, define the research objectives and provide the reader with an analytical grid for the subsequent parts of this book.

II. Enforcement Mechanisms: 50 Shades of Grey?

Enforcement, in its general meaning, refers to policies, rules and instruments that aim to ensure respect for legal rules and to provide an adequate reaction when these rules are infringed. Therefore, logically, enforcement is ancillary to substantive rules.

The nature and importance of those substantive rules are thus likely to affect the type of enforcement: the more important they are, the more powerful or intrusive the enforcement tools tend to be.

There exists a whole array of enforcement mechanisms and tools. For instance, enforcement may be ensured by public or private actors (ie, public versus private enforcement).[1] It may be of a criminal, administrative, civil or even hybrid nature. Several enforcement mechanisms may co-exist, ideally in a coordinated way, within one and the same sector and, of course, across sectors. Enforcement, particularly public enforcement, can take place at (sub)national, supranational and/or international level. In a number of cases, these levels interact, in which case one refers to 'multi-level' enforcement.[2] The concrete objectives of enforcement vary (eg, compliance, prevention, punishment or reparation) and influence its nature.

Furthermore, the choice of enforcement mechanism is far from neutral. On the one hand, it may depend on the constitutional or institutional framework of a particular system. This explains why, depending on the legal system, there may be a preference for one or the other enforcement mechanism. However, this preference may also be historically or culturally determined. For instance, in common law systems, public enforcement through civil penalties is preferred to administrative enforcement, as the latter tends to have a more restrictive, bureaucratic meaning. On the other hand, the type of enforcement will determine which authorities are competent to investigate, adjudicate and execute, which procedural rules apply, and, to some extent, also which measures or sanctions are legally available (eg, whereas fines are possible under most enforcement regimes, imprisonment is usually impossible under administrative and civil law).[3] Depending on the choice of enforcement, the applicable terminology may also differ. This can be illustrated by the EU legal framework on market abuse: whereas the Market Abuse Regulation uses the term 'disgorgement' with respect to the illegal proceeds obtained through the administrative infringement,[4] the EU legislator prefers the term 'confiscation' in a (formal) criminal law context,[5] even though both measures and their objectives are as such identical.

In an ideal world, the baseline would be: 'different labels, different content', meaning that each enforcement mechanism would pursue its own objective(s) and apply its own

[1] See, eg, R Bowles, M Faure and N Garoupa, 'The Scope of Criminal Law and Criminal Sanctions: An Economic View and Policy Implications' (2008) 35 *Journal of Law and Society* 389, 395–411.

[2] See, eg, A van Hoek, A Hol, O Jansen, P Rijpkema and R Widdershoven (eds), *Multilevel governance in enforcement and adjudication* (Cambridge, Intersentia, 2006); MA Heldeweg and RA Wessel, 'The Appropriate Level of Enforcement in Multilevel Regulation: Mapping Issues in Avoidance of Regulatory Overstretch' (2016) 5 *International Law Research* 16.

[3] On the distinction between 'criminal detention' and detention of non-nationals, see M Pichou, Chapter 9 in this volume, sections I. and II.

[4] Article 30(2)(b) of Regulation (EU) 596/2014 of 16 April 2014 on market abuse and repealing Directive 2003/6/EC of the European Parliament and of the Council and Commission Directives 2003/124/EC, 2003/125/EC and 2004/72/EC, [2014] OJ L 173, 12 June 2014, p 1 (Market Abuse Regulation).

[5] Articles 1(1) and (4) and 2(2) of Regulation (EU) 2018/1805 of 14 November 2018 on the mutual recognition of freezing orders and confiscation orders, [2018] OJ L 303, 28 November 2018, p 1. This Regulation applies to all proceedings in criminal matters, including those regarding market abuse offences as defined by the 2014 Market Abuse Directive. Directive 2014/57/EU of 16 April 2014 on criminal sanctions for market abuse, [2014] OJ L 173, 12 June 2014, p 179 (Market Abuse Directive).

clearly defined procedural rules and standards that match the level of intrusiveness of the measures and sanctions that are at stake. Unfortunately, the legal reality is far from ideal.

In reality, indeed, we are confronted with enforcement tools that belong to different legal categories while (at least some of) their features are (very) similar. Conversely, some enforcement instruments belonging to the same legal category have varied features. Enforcement labels are thus not always used in a consistent manner. What may be regarded as criminal in one legal area or one legal system is labelled administrative or civil in another one. Sometimes the use of a particular label is deliberate, for instance to avoid burdensome procedures or to empower specialised authorities; elsewhere, it is the result of more fortuitous circumstances or legislative choices made at a higher level.

It goes without saying that inconsistent labelling complicates comparisons and entails a risk of unequal treatment (because, for instance, similar types of behaviour and/or persons are treated differently) and legal uncertainty (for instance, because the applicable procedural safeguards are not clearly defined by law).[6] The principles of proportionality and parsimony (or *ultima ratio*) may also be in jeopardy, either because similar tools (powers, sanctions) are used for infringements of different degrees of severity or because the legislature did not opt for the least intrusive enforcement tool that is necessary to achieve its policy objectives (the problem of over-criminalisation).

To overcome these disparities and to ensure that the fundamental rights enshrined in the European Convention on Human Rights (ECHR) are applied correctly, the European Court of Human Rights (ECtHR) has adopted an autonomous definition of the terms 'criminal charge' (Article 6 ECHR) and 'penalty' (Article 7 ECHR), on the basis of the so-called *Engel* criteria.[7] Over the years, this definition has been expanded to the point that the Court felt the need to adopt an additional subdivision, distinguishing between the 'hard core' of criminal law and more peripheral criminal law.[8] Yet, this subdivision has generated quite some uncertainty and shows the limits of the ECtHR's approach.[9] The ECtHR's functional approach, which was more recently followed by the Court of Justice of the European Union (ECJ),[10] focuses on substantive and procedural safeguards applicable to 'criminal law', regardless of national peculiarities or preferences. But it does not offer much guidance as to the characteristics of other enforcement tools, even those that present substantial similarities with criminal enforcement – let alone the reasons why they are favoured or considered more adequate by the legislature in certain situations.

[6] On this subject, see, eg, V Franssen and S Vandeweerd, 'General Nature, Characteristics, and Safeguards of EU Administrative Criminal Law' (2019) 90 *Revue international de droit penal* 13, 77–82.

[7] *Engel and Others v The Netherlands* (App Nos 5100–5102/71, 5354/72, 5370/72) ECtHR, 8 June 1976.

[8] *Jussila v Finland* (App No 73053/01) ECtHR, 23 November 2006. For a more extensive analysis, see V Franssen, 'La notion "pénale": mot magique ou critère trompeur? Réflexions sur les distinctions entre le droit pénal et le droit quasi pénal' in D Brach-Thiel (ed), *Existe-t-il un seul* non bis in idem *aujourd'hui?* (Paris, l'Harmattan, 2017), 76–80.

[9] See K Šugman Stubbs, Chapter 12 in this volume, section IV; A Weyembergh and N Joncheray, 'Punitive Administrative Sanctions and Procedural Safeguards. A Blurred Picture that Needs to be addressed' (2016) 7 *New Journal of European Criminal Law* 189, 195–97.

[10] Case C-489/10, *Bonda*, ECLI:EU:C:2012:319, 5 June 2012.

III. Choice of Terminology: Criminal versus Quasi-criminal Enforcement

These initial findings regarding the complexity and incoherence of enforcement mechanisms constituted the trigger for the creation of the CQEM research network, at a moment where the criminal/non-criminal divide was fiercely debated before European[11] and national[12] courts. In particular, the members of this research group were interested in better understanding, both conceptually and empirically, the distinction in contemporary legal systems across Europe between criminal law and other branches of law that share a number of characteristics with criminal enforcement (eg, the same policy objectives, the same or similar sanctions) and are likely to be considered 'criminal' within the meaning of Articles 6 and 7 ECHR, even if they do not belong to the 'hard core' of criminal law.

Not surprisingly, at the starting point of the discussion, there was some dilemma in the choice of vocabulary. This was evident when a number of the researchers who have contributed to this volume met some years ago to discuss the research topic[13] and debated the most appropriate language to convey the subject and its nuances. Would it be best to describe it, as is often done, as the choice between criminal law rules and sanctions, on the one hand, and those that are 'administrative' in nature, on the other hand? But the word 'administrative', certainly its English language version, fails to reflect what is actually being posited as a major alternative to the use of criminal law in continental legal systems. To describe rules or sanctions as administrative runs the risk of suggesting something that is bureaucratic, regulatory and 'non-juridical', and perhaps even of a lower order than criminal law. Moreover, as indicated, in common law systems, the objectives of prevention and punishment are rather pursued through civil penalties than through administrative sanctions. Criminal law, it will be readily agreed, is a matter of 'top-level legal control', constitutionally significant and of high personal and social impact. Administrative, in contrast, is suggestive of the more mundane aspects of life, suitable for bureaucratic resolution. Was the latter what those researchers had in mind when they confronted, for instance, the emergence of *Ordnungswidrigkeiten* in the German legal system, or the administrative/non-criminal law investigations and sanctions in the field of EU competition law? Assuredly not, judging by the scale of legal enforcement actually taking place and its 'mimicking' of criminal law.

Others have suggested the terms 'punitive administrative law'[14] or 'administrative criminal law'[15] (or even 'administrative penal law').[16] While the first suggestion is

[11] See, eg, *Grande Stevens v Italy* (App No 18640/10) ECtHR, 4 March 2014; Case C-617/10, *Åklagaren v Åkerberg Fransson*, ECLI:EU:C:2013:105, 26 February 2013; Case C-60/12, *Baláž*, ECLI:EU:C:2013/733, 14 November 2013.

[12] 'Lisbon' judgment of the German Federal Constitutional Court, BVergG, 2BvE 2/08, 30 June 2009, para 355.

[13] Research seminar entitled '*Quasi-criminal enforcement mechanisms in Europe: Disentangling historical origins and concepts*', University of Luxembourg, 16 September 2015. An earlier exploratory discussion took place at the Second Natolin Seminar on *EU Criminal Law and Crime Policy 2014*, organised by the College of Europe in Warsaw, on 3 October 2014.

[14] See, eg, P Caeiro, 'The influence of the EU on the "blurring" between administrative and criminal law' in F Galli and A Weyembergh (eds), *Do labels still matter? Blurring boundaries between administrative and criminal law – The influence of the EU* (Brussels, Editions de l'ULB, 2014), 174; Weyembergh and Joncheray

interesting because the adjective 'punitive' highlights one of the key features this branch of law has in common with criminal law and is fairly well established at EU level,[17] the combination of 'administrative' and 'criminal' (or 'penal') essentially emphasises the hybrid nature of the enforcement mechanism at hand. It indicates that the applicable procedures, competent authorities, and sanctions provided by law formally belong to the field of administrative law, but share some characteristics with criminal law. Still, the reference to 'administrative' remains less convincing from a common law perspective.

Therefore, rather than using existing terms that have very different connotations depending on the legal tradition one comes from, the researchers involved in this research network agreed on using the term 'quasi-criminal enforcement mechanisms', as it more accurately reflects the phenomenon under debate: It suggests there is a set of rules whose characteristics resemble those of 'traditional criminal law', without however fully corresponding to the latter ('quasi', almost). The focus of the discussion indeed extends to various branches of law that copy (at least) some aspects or functions of criminal law, in particular its preventive and punitive objectives. Furthermore, the novelty of this vocabulary[18] conveys the absence of a well-grounded and systematic approach to the subject, as a matter of both wider European and comparative law, and adds to the justification for the present collective volume.

IV. Defining Borders and Concepts for a More Coherent European Approach

While there is a lot research and literature on enforcement, a common understanding of what separates criminal enforcement from other types of punitive enforcement mechanisms is still lacking. What makes criminal enforcement different, distinctive, unique? What characterises other punitive enforcement mechanisms and, most of all, what sets them apart from criminal enforcement? At present, the distinction between criminal and quasi-criminal enforcement is usually made from a positive law perspective, on the basis of ad hoc jurisprudential developments. Unmistakably, the case law of the ECtHR and the ECJ plays an important role in this field. Yet, the case law of both European courts is determined by a specific institutional and constitutional context (the principle of attribution defines the EU's competences, which are limited by traditional national concepts such as 'criminal law' and 'criminal procedure';[19] the ECtHR

(n 9) 194–200; International Association of Penal Law, 'Section III: Resolutions on Prevention, Investigation, and Sanctioning of Economic Crime by Alternative Enforcement Regimes', *Criminal Justice and Corporate Business*, 20th International Congress of Penal Law, Rome, 13–16 November 2019, available at: http://www.penal.org/sites/default/files/files/XX%20Congress%20Res%20Sec%20III%20EN.pdf (last accessed 23 July 2021), para C.

[15] Franssen and Vandeweerd (n 6) 16.

[16] A Nieto Martín, 'General Report on Food Regulation and Criminal Law' (2016) 87 *Revue international de droit penal* 17, 46.

[17] Weyembergh and Joncheray (n 9) 192; Franssen and Vandeweerd (n 6) 16.

[18] Despite its novelty, it is noteworthy that the term 'quasi-criminal' can be found elsewhere in the literature. See, eg, Weyembergh and Joncheray (n 9) 191.

[19] See, eg, Case C-43/12, *European Commission v European Parliament and Council of the EU*, ECLI:EU:C:2014:298, 6 May 2014; Franssen (n 8) 87–88.

only rules in concrete cases, against a particular State Party, taking into account a given national legal framework) and motivated by different legal and pragmatic concerns (to ensure the *effet utile* of EU law;[20] to guarantee the effective protection of the human rights laid down in the ECHR across all State Parties, regardless of national labels). In other words, the role and ambition of these Courts have never been to develop an all-encompassing, conceptual theoretical framework for future policy choices, but rather to give concrete answers to specific problems on the basis of the existing legal framework. Nevertheless, for lack of another European-wide conceptual framework, the case law of these Courts has often been invoked in conceptual discussions and increasingly used as a benchmark at national level, especially over the last two decades.

Therefore, a first and central objective of this collective volume is to develop a better understanding of the origins of quasi-criminal enforcement mechanisms in legal systems across Europe, the role they play in today's society and the interplay of these mechanisms with criminal law. Second, this book aims to analyse the creation of quasi-criminal enforcement mechanisms from a theoretical and substantive law perspective. A third research objective concerns the procedural questions triggered by the development of quasi-criminal enforcement mechanisms and their relation to traditional criminal law and criminal procedure. Fourth, this research intends to offer a better insight into the institutional and constitutional dynamic of the EU – especially at the legislative level when choosing between criminal law and other types of punitive enforcement mechanisms – and the ECtHR in developing its protective case law. Last but not least, the ambition is to flesh out some distinctive criteria for quasi-criminal enforcement as a basis for a future, more coherent European model.

V. Analytical Grid

The foregoing five research objectives constitute the backbone of this collective volume, which is structured in three parts.

Part I centres upon the origins of quasi-criminal enforcement mechanisms in a selection of legal traditions across Europe. The following questions are at the heart of the analysis: When and in which areas did the respective legal systems start using quasi-criminal enforcement mechanisms as an alternative to criminal enforcement? What kinds of quasi-criminal enforcement mechanisms were created and on what conceptual and/or practical considerations are they based? These questions are addressed from a Nordic (by Raimo Lahti in Chapter one), Swiss (by Nadine Zurkinden in Chapter two), German (by Dominik Brodowski in Chapter three), Central-European (by Anna Błachnio-Parzych in Chapter four) and UK perspective (by Gary and Sarah Wilson in Chapter five). Furthermore, a contribution relating to the interplay between criminal and administrative law in Belgian law can be found in Part II, but given its specific focus on customs law – which contains highly derogative rules that are not representative of the entire system – it rather belongs in Part II than in Part I.

[20] See, eg, *Baláž* (n 11) paras 34–35. For an analysis, see Franssen (n 8) 85–86.

Next, Part II takes a closer look at certain aspects of quasi-criminal enforcement mechanisms, and investigates their characteristic features in order to disentangle the different concepts and distinctions that are made. A first sub-part addresses a number of selected topics relating to the general part and principles of criminal law. First, Christopher Harding examines how quasi-criminal enforcement fits into the theory of criminal law (Chapter six). In particular, he questions the normative and policy logic of the quasi-criminal approach, in terms of its justification and intended outcomes. A second contribution (by Ferry de Jong) is dedicated to one of the key principles of criminal law, namely the principle of individual guilt, and studies in a detailed and systematic way how this principle applies, on the one hand, to traditional criminal behaviour and, on the other, to misconduct penalised through quasi-criminal law (Chapter seven). Next, Johan Boucht tackles the thorny issue of non-conviction based confiscation, proceedings for which are based on civil standards, including the standard of proof (Chapter eight). One core objection against such confiscation measures is that they, by simply re-labelling an inherently criminal sanction as civil, circumvent some of the basic standards of the criminal process and therefore jeopardise the rights of the persons concerned.

Subsequently, the second sub-part of Part II is dedicated to specific enforcement mechanisms in legal areas where the distinction between criminal law and other forms of punitive enforcement has raised interesting jurisprudential and/or scholarly debate, that is: migration law (by Maria Pichou in Chapter nine), competition law (by Sophie De Sanctis in Chapter ten) and customs law (by Ana Laura Claes and Marie-Julie Horseele in Chapter eleven). Whereas the latter two involve what could be termed 'regulatory' or 'economic crime',[21] the former, in contrast, is much closer to traditional administrative law, where the State grants (or refuses to do so), in a top-down relation, a specific status and rights to citizens based on both legally defined and more discretionary criteria. In addition, it is worthwhile highlighting that the chapter by Gary and Sarah Wilson also deals with a specific type of economic crime, namely market abuse (Chapter five). Nevertheless, given its strong focus on the UK and because it offers the reader an excellent insight into how punitive 'administrative' law is perceived in this Anglo-Saxon system and how the EU has impacted the national system, it was decided to insert this chapter in Part I.

Finally, Part III focuses on the European legal order, encompassing both the Council of Europe and the European Union, and its ambivalent role in drawing boundaries between criminal and quasi-criminal enforcement. A first contribution (by Katja Šugman Stubbs in Chapter twelve) critically investigates the influence of ECtHR case law on the process of blurring boundaries between criminal and administrative law, and identifies a number of significant consequences following from this process. In Chapter thirteen, Tamás Lukácsi first presents the conceptual framework of the EU regarding criminal law which, in his view, contains strong safeguards against over-criminalisation; and next, he examines the EU's legal and political choices in this field on the basis of a case study, which illustrates how the EU tries to strike a balance between 'criminal law

[21] For a tentative, comparative definition of this notion, see K Ligeti and V Franssen, 'Current Challenges in Economic and Financial Criminal Law in Europe and the US' in K Ligeti and V Franssen (eds), *Challenges in the Field of Economic and Financial Crime in Europe and the US* (Oxford, Hart Publishing, 2017), 2–5.

as an extended arm of internal market creation and criminal law as a matter of national sovereignty traditionally designed to prevent and punish behaviour that is disapproved by society in a certain historical and cultural context.'[22] Third, in a final chapter, Christopher Harding and Vanessa Franssen draw the main conclusions from this research, and endeavour to clarify the aforementioned boundaries based on a number of conceptual criteria and to propose a more coherent European approach.

[22] T Lukácsi, Chapter 13 in this volume, 369.

PART I

The Origins of Quasi-criminal Enforcement Mechanisms: A Comparative Journey Through Europe

1

The Origin and Development of Quasi-criminal Enforcement Mechanisms in Europe: Nordic Perspective

RAIMO LAHTI

I. Introduction

Punitive administrative sanctions (typically administrative fines, also referred to as punitive fees or 'payment penalties') have not been introduced in Finland or other Nordic countries with a cohesive and consistent approach; these sanctions governed by different laws make up a disparate group. This starting point can be explained by a legal tradition in which the scope of criminalised behaviour is kept extensive without clear distinction between crime and other transgressions of law (*Übertretung*). There has been no room for a consistent system of administrative criminal law as developed in Germany (*Ordnungswidrigkeitensystem*), parallel to the proper criminal justice system.

However, in three Nordic countries (Finland, Norway and Sweden) legislative reforms towards more principled administrative penal law systems have been recently prepared and partly implemented. In 2018, a comprehensive comparative legal analysis of administrative punitive fines in these countries was finalised with the economic support of the Nordic Council of Ministers.[1] Two years earlier, in 2016, a new chapter on administrative sanctions was included in the Norwegian Administrative Procedure Act of 1967. In Finland, the Ministry of Justice set up a Working Party (WP) in 2017 to assess the need for the introduction of general legislation on punitive administrative sanctions and the preparation of general guidelines for the legislator (also referred to as 'regulation principles') for these kinds of sanctions. This WP finalised its report at the end of 2018.[2]

[1] See L Halila, V Lankinen and A Nilsson, *Administrativa sanktionsavgifter. En nordisk komparativ studie* (Nordiska ministerrådet, TemaNord 2018:511). See also L Halila and V Lankinen, 'Administrative sanktionsavgifter i nordisk context' [Administrative punitive fees in the Nordic context] (2014) 115 *Tidskrift utgiven av Juridiska Föreningen i Finland* 305.

[2] See the Report of the Working Party of the Ministry of Justice, entitled 'Developing the regulation of punitive administrative sanctions' [*Rangaistusluonteisia hallinnollisia seuraamuksia koskevan sääntelyn kehittäminen*] (Report No 52/2018, Ministry of Justice, dated on 28 November 2018).

The aim of this chapter is to critically analyse the recent legislative developments primarily on the basis of the reforms and reform plans in Finland. A broader Nordic perspective will be provided on the basis of comparative information about the legal situation in the Scandinavian countries of Norway and Sweden and, to begin with and more generally, about the Nordic penal thinking.

II. A 'Nordic Model' for Penal Thinking – Nordic Sub-Region?[3]

There has not been any uniform criminal policy common to the various Nordic countries, but it is nevertheless possible to discern certain essential similarities among them, especially from a distance. Nordics are aware of their common background in legal history, and the work of the Nordic Council and the Nordic Council of Ministers as well as the various forms of co-operation between individual Nordic countries have contributed to the similarity of our legal systems.

Various ways and means of Nordic co-operation have been developed since the Second World War, and these inter-state activities have become still more diversified since the 1960s. The role of Nordic co-operation in penal matters continues to be important, even though these countries have also, to a large degree, acceded to multilateral regional treaties (ie, European conventions) in the field and despite the fact that their membership of the European Union (EU) is divided. There are many reasons for the continued preference for sub-regional co-operation in Scandinavia and for a special model of penal thinking, among them the following.

Co-operation and harmonisation among the Nordic countries in the legal field has ancient historical roots. Even the first statutory provincial laws in the twelfth and thirteenth centuries indicated a considerable Nordic unity in legal thinking. Denmark, Norway and Iceland, on the one hand, and Sweden and Finland, on the other, were politically united for long periods. During the time Finland was incorporated into Russia (1809–1917), it still proved possible to maintain the constitution and codified laws which were inherited from Sweden. Common legal traditions and crucial similarities in economic, social and cultural development can be regarded as the main reasons for the strong mutual *confidence* which prevails between the Nordic states.

Nordic co-operation and harmonisation of legislation are based on a variety of sources. These consist primarily of the treaties between the Nordic countries, of multilateral European conventions, of common basic approaches to crime control and human rights policies, of uniform legislation in relevant areas, and of established practice between state authorities.

[3] Cf. generally, eg, R Lahti, 'Towards a Rational and Humane Criminal Policy – Trends in Scandinavian Penal Thinking' (2000) 1(2) *Journal of Scandinavian Studies in Criminology and Crime Prevention* 141; J Husa, K Nuotio and H Pihlajamäki (eds), *Nordic Law – Between Tradition and Dynamism* (Cambridge, Intersentia, 2007), *passim*.

It is stated in Article 5 of the Nordic Cooperation Agreement[4] (1962) that the contracting parties should aim for mutually consistent provisions on criminal offences and their sanctions. According to the same article it should also be possible, to the broadest extent, for one Nordic country to investigate and judge offences when these have been committed in another.

A precondition for continuing fruitful co-operation lies, as indicated, in a common approach to basic crime control and human rights issues. Essential similarities are discernible in the goals, values and principles governing the reform of Nordic penal codes and the criminal justice systems in these countries. Endeavours to harmonise criminal legislation have led to a number of positive results, particularly in the reform of systems of penal sanctions.

It should, however, be said that there have also been divergent ideological trends in Scandinavia, and that efforts to reform criminal legislation are not always identical in the different Nordic states. When one looks more closely at the differences, they seem striking. But, as a whole, crime control policies in Scandinavia have been essentially similar compared with most other corresponding sub-regions or regions.

A reappraisal of the role of the criminal justice system and the function of penal sanctions were the central themes of the official reports on questions of principle published in 1977 and 1978 in the various Nordic countries: the report of the Finnish Criminal Law Committee; the proposal for a New penal system (*Nytt straffsystem*) of the Swedish Council for Crime Prevention; the Norwegian Ministerial Communication on criminal policy to the Parliament (*Kriminalmelding*); as well as the Danish report on the Alternatives to imprisonment (*Alternativer till frihedsstraf*).[5]

In these official reports, there was widespread agreement that emphasis should be put on justice, legal security and humaneness as leading legal principles in the criminal justice system, at the same time putting emphasis on the general preventive effects of the penal law. The balance of these values and interests varied from one country to another, so that, for example, in the Danish and Norwegian reports the reasoning was pragmatic and consequence-orientated – requiring that the use of punishments be reduced and alternatives to imprisonment developed. The Finnish and Swedish reports gave rise to a new renaissance of general prevention, mainly in the sense of positive general deterrence and reinforcement of morals (the indirect effect of the penal system on morality and the popular attitude towards obeying the law), instead of plain deterrence and repression.

The Finnish, Swedish and Norwegian reports on questions of principle looked at criminal policy as a part of general social policy, even if their main emphasis was on the reappraisal of the system of criminal sanctions. It was important to realise that the criminal justice system has a limited effect on the level or structure of crime, and to be aware of the role of social planning and crime prevention as alternatives or complements to the repressive and reparative measures available under criminal and procedural law.

[4] Treaty of Co-operation between Denmark, Finland, Iceland, Norway and Sweden (the so-called Helsinki Treaty), signed on 23 March 1962.

[5] For a more detailed review, see R Lahti, 'Current Trends in Criminal Policy in the Scandinavian Countries' in N Bishop (ed), *Scandinavian Criminal Policy and Criminology 1980–85* (Copenhagen, Scandinavian Research Council for Criminology, 1985), 59.

The goal of applying the general planning methods of social policy or other similar reasoning models to criminal policy in Finland, for example, was expressed in a more differentiated way of defining the objectives and means of criminal policy. The special goals of criminal policy were clearly laid out: (a) to minimise the suffering and other personal and social costs (injuries, inconvenience) as well as financial costs caused by crime or by the measures of society to control crime, and (b) to allocate these costs in a fair manner among the various parties (society as a whole, real and potential victims as well as real and potential offenders). Hence, the leading principle is that crime should not be minimised 'whatever the cost'. Indicators of damage both from crime and from its control are necessary so that the relative costs can be measured. We should strive for an optimal balance of costs, and for an allocation of costs that is as fair as possible.

A common feature for the reports on questions of principle from 1977–78, as mentioned above, was the sharp criticism against the existing penal system, especially indefinite penal sanctions and imprisonment in general. The requirement of humaneness and the goal of reducing control-caused damage were arguments for more lenient penalties and for alternatives to imprisonment. Nevertheless, the developments of the 1980s and 1990s did not result in the decrease of repression that was envisaged in the reports, with the exception of the drastically reduced prison population in Finland.[6] It is noticeable that the criminal justice system is always a reflection of the structural and cultural aspects of society. If the level of criminal punishments and other punitive sanctions in society becomes higher, we should look for the reasons by examining those structural and cultural factors; seldom is the mere development of crime the adequate explanation for a change.

With regard to criminal law and sanctions policy, the article by the Swedish scholar Nils Jareborg in 1995 in particular was an important basis for debate.[7] He distinguished between *defensive criminal law policy* and *offensive criminal law policy*. These involve two ideal models for decision-making on the system of criminal law (namely: the principles of criminalisation, the guarantees of legal security in criminal procedure, the sentencing principles, as well as the enforcement of criminal sanctions). Jareborg argued for the defensive model, the principles and guarantees of which correspond to the criminal law ideologies of a state governed by the rule of law (ie, it summarises the basic values of a *Rechtsstaat*). The offensive approach represents a socio-technological thinking and sees prevention as the dominant viewpoint. The description of the methods and consequences of this approach shows many of the same traits as the penal law ideology of a social welfare state. Modern criminal law provisions, such as those pertaining to economic crime and environmental offences, drafted between 1990 and 2003 in the course of the overall reform of the Finnish Criminal Code, display many of the characteristics of the offensive approach, making them susceptible to criticism from the points of view of legal security and legitimacy. Increased criminalisation is typical

[6] See T Lappi-Seppälä, 'Penal Policies in the Nordic Countries 1960–2010' (2012) 13(1) *Journal of Scandinavian Studies in Criminology and Crime Prevention Supplement* 85–111.

[7] N Jareborg, 'What Kind of Criminal Law Do We Want?' in A Snare (ed), *Beware of Punishment. On the Utility and Futility of Criminal Law* (Scandinavian Studies in Criminology vol. 14) (Oslo, Pax Forlag, 1995), 17.

for the revised Code, and the statutory definitions are often prone to discretion and unpredictable application.

III. Criminal Law Europeanisation and Evolving Policy on Administrative Penal Sanctions[8]

Since the 1990s, penal law and criminal policy have become more internationalised and more Europeanized. We can also see a comparable, albeit not equally intensive, trend of regionalisation in other parts of the world and not only in Europe. In Europe the regional organisations, the Council of Europe and the EU, and their legal regimes and case law have decisively contributed to this development. In addition to these developments, the reform of basic law in Finland and its increased emphasis on fundamental rights have affected the entire national legal order. The advancement of the mechanisms of administrative penal (quasi-criminal) sanctions as a crucial field of punitive legislation in enforcing the European legal order has been a challenge to the Nordic legal tradition. It has taken a long time for the general awareness about the real relevance of these kinds of non-criminal enforcement regimes to fully develop.

As late as the Report on Decriminalisation (1980) of the Sub-Committee of the European Committee on Crime Problems, the issues of administrative sanctions (*Ordnungswidrigkeiten*) were left out, although it was admitted that in certain cases decriminalisation is combined with other alternative approaches. The concept of depenalisation was also defined in such a way that the forms of 'de-escalation' covered by this term were to be implemented within the criminal justice system.[9] Instead of this kind of narrow definition, preferably larger concepts such as those of penality and control policy could have included penal administrative sanctions, and the analysis of 'other legal systems' would have covered administrative penalties more extensively.

At the level of the European Communities, in 1990 the Commission launched a comparative study of the administrative and criminal penalty systems of the various Member States. As background, it was mentioned that since 1989 the Commission had systematically inserted provisions for controls and penalties in its legislation on agriculture and fisheries to be applied by the Member States. In addition, the study referred to the decision of the Court of Justice in Case C-240/90,[10] where the Court recognised that the Community had power to impose penalties in common agricultural policy matters. As a background factor reference was also made to Case 68/88, according to which the applicable penalties when incorporating Community norms into the national legal systems must be effective, dissuasive and proportionate.[11]

[8] Cf. generally R Lahti, 'Towards a principled European criminal policy: some lessons from the Nordic countries' in JB Banach-Gutierrez and C Harding (eds), *EU Criminal Law and Policy. Values, Principles and Methods* (London, Routledge, 2016), 56; A Suominen, 'The Characteristics of Nordic Criminal Law in the Setting of EU Criminal Law' (2011) 1(2) *European Criminal Law Review* 170.

[9] *Report on Decriminalisation* (Council of Europe, Strasbourg, 1980), esp. p 11.

[10] Case C-240/90 *Germany v Commission* [1992] ECR I-5383.

[11] Case 68/88 *Commission v Greece* [1989] ECR 2965. See *The system of administrative and penal sanctions in the Member States of the European Communities. Volume I – National reports* (Commission of the European Communities, 1994), esp. p 5 (Foreword).

That comparative study revealed a great dispersion in the definition, content and use of administrative sanctions among the Member States. The same was true when a corresponding comparison was made in relation to the candidate countries of the EU in 2000–2001.[12] As for the Nordic countries, the Danish report told that there was no basis for instituting separate statutory provisions on administrative criminal law and even that term was not a sharply defined legal concept.[13] In a separate Swedish report, it was similarly stated that it was not possible to define administrative criminal law or to find an established definition or any assembled provisions on administrative offences in general.[14] The Finnish situation was equivalent to the Danish and Swedish legal regimes.

In 2011, the Commission published a communication aimed at presenting a framework for the principled development of an EU criminal policy under the Lisbon Treaty.[15] This communication also took account of the role of administrative sanctions. Considering that criminal law should be a means of last resort (*ultima ratio*), it stated that the EU legislator needs to analyse whether other tools than criminal law, eg, sanctioning regimes of an administrative nature, could sufficiently ensure the policy implementation. According to the Commission, administrative sanctions may in many cases, of which examples are given, be sufficient or even more effective than criminal sanctions.[16] Although the communication acknowledges the role of administrative sanctions as a part of an overall control policy view, it leaves open how the assessment of its pros and cons in relation to criminal policy measures should be made.

IV. Towards More Principled Legislative Models for a Control Policy in Three Nordic Countries

In the overall reform of the Finnish Criminal Code (1990–2003), the main focus was to concentrate all severe punitive sanctions within the criminal justice system. Nevertheless, there was a trend toward creating punitive administrative sanctions alongside criminal sanctions.[17] The reasons underlying this trend in favour of administrative fines were presented. Primarily in case of minor offences, such as wrongful parking, there was little sense in spending valuable criminal justice resources on the determination of guilt and the ability to pay of the party liable to pay. Therefore, petty offences of low penal value should be consistently depenalised and administrative fines systematically put in

[12] See Study on Penal and administrative sanctions, settlement, whistleblowing and Corpus juris in the candidate countries: Christine Van den Wyngaert, 'The Protection of the Financial Interests of the EU in the Candidate States. Perspectives on the Future of Judicial Integration in Europe' in (2001) 3 *Special Issue of ERA-Forum*, 2–60.

[13] V Greve and C Gulmann, 'Denmark' in European Commision, *The system of administrative and penal sanctions in the Member States of the European Communities. Vol I* (n 11), 68.

[14] M Arnholm (ed), *The System of Administrative and Penal Sanctions in Sweden* (Uppsala, Swedish Society for European Criminal Law, 1997), 7.

[15] European Commission, 'Towards an EU Criminal Policy: Ensuring the effective implementation of EU policies through criminal law', COM(2011) 573 final, 20 September 2011.

[16] See COM(2011) 573 final (European Commission), esp. pp 11–12.

[17] Cf generally R Lahti and M Rainiala, 'Alternative Investigation and Sanctioning Systems for Corporate and Corporate-Related Crime in Finland' (2019) 90 *Revue Internationale de Droit Pénal* 131, 145.

place. Still, the idea to create a general system of administrative penal law for minor offences was not implemented during the overall reform of the Criminal Code; it was reconsidered by a task force in the 2010s (see section V. below).

In cases where sanctions were not to be incorporated into the criminal justice system, basic principles, such as those of legality and proportionality – which are applied when imposing criminal punishments – should also govern the determination of penalties in the administrative procedure. This approach was applied to sanctioning cartels in 1992 in the revision of competition legislation, which was modelled on the European Communities legislation. It was argued that an administrative penalty would be more suitable to sanction cartels and this for several reasons. The sentences imposed for restrictive, anti-competitive practices had thus far been light fines, and the threat of punishment was deemed to lack general preventive effect. The administrative process would provide greater flexibility and effectiveness. Furthermore, competition law matters call for specialised expertise. More important than the subjective culpability of the offender's actions is the harm caused by the act on business in general.[18]

In Norway, a Committee Report entitled 'From fine to remedy' (*Fra bot til bedring*) was published in 2003.[19] It proposed that systematic depenalisation should be strived for in criminal policy, and a cohesive and consistent system for punitive administrative sanctions ought to be created. The European Convention of Human Rights (ECHR) and the case law of the Strasbourg Court (ECtHR) should be taken into account when developing the legal safeguards. The significance of the principles of legality and proportionality was in particular emphasised. The ambitious proposals of the Committee were not systematically implemented. However, on 1 October 2015, a new Criminal Code came into force in Norway, and on 1 July 2017 a new Chapter IX on administrative sanctions was included in the Administrative Procedure Act of 1967,[20] in order to regulate the special characteristics of these types of punitive sanctions.

This new chapter on administrative sanctions comprises provisions on the definition and preconditions of administrative sanctions (administrative fines and loss of rights), provisions determining the types of administrative sanctions applicable to enterprises and individuals) as well as provisions on the principle of *ne bis in idem* and the privilege of self-incrimination.

In Sweden, administrative fines are very common, but there is no unified system on these or other types of administrative sanctions. The latest principled document, a Committee report entitled 'What should be punished?' (*Vad bör straffas?*),[21] includes among other things the following proposals. Firstly, there should be created a systematic

[18] V Hiltunen and R Lahti, *Kartellien kriminalisoiminen Suomessa* [Criminalizing Cartels in Finland] (University of Helsinki, Faculty of Law, 2014), chapter 1. This research report was prepared by order of the Finnish Competition and Consumer Authority.

[19] *Fra bot til bedring*. Et mer nyansert og effektivt sanksjonssystem med mindre bruk av straff [A more differentiated and effective sanction system with reduced use of punishment]. Norges offentlige utredninger (NOU) 2003:15 (Oslo, 2003).

[20] Lov om behandlingsmåten i forvaltningssaker (lov 1967-02-10).

[21] *Vad bör straffas?* Statens offentliga utredningar (SOU) 2013:38 (Stockholm, 2013). For a critical assessment of the report, see I Cameron, 'A Constitutional Perspective on the Criminalisation' in A du Bois-Pedain, M Ulväng and P Asp (eds), *Criminal Law and the Authority of the State* (Oxford, Hart Publishing, 2017) 111, 113.

depenalisation strategy for petty offences: the threat of criminal punishment (by fine) ought to be converted to the threat of a punitive administrative fine. Secondly, a clear distinction should be made between sanctioning petty offences, on the one hand, and transgressions in the economic and financial sectors and corporate activities, on the other. As to the last-mentioned transgressions, administrative penalties should be severe and also have the function of taking away the illegal profit. Thirdly, the Committee report recommends the development of a systematic and coherent system for all kinds of punitive sanction. Fourthly, it is presumed and required that the case law of the ECtHR and the Court of Justice (CJEU) will be applied properly in relation to both types of punitive sanction (criminal and administrative).

V. Reforming Finland's Regulation of Administrative Sanctions

In the overall reform of the Finnish Criminal Code (1990–2003), a new regulation of administrative sanctions which would have created a systematic and coherent system failed to happen due to lack of agreement on the contents and urgency of such a revision. Some years later, in 2005, the Legal Affairs Committee of the Parliament stated in its report that the government should examine possibilities for introducing a more comprehensive and uniform system of administrative sanctions. The Constitutional Law Committee (CLC) of the Parliament has paid attention to the same issue. Accordingly, the Ministry of Justice set up in 2017 a task force, ie, a WP to examine the need for a common regulation of administrative sanctions and for preparing the necessary legal provisions. In addition, the WP had to draft principles and standards for guiding a unified regulation.

In its report of 2018, the WP is moderately cautious in proposing new legislative solutions. Interestingly, its main proposal is to reject the idea of creating a unified general law for administrative sanctions, in line with the majority of the authorities and other stakeholders who had been requested to comment on the draft report of the WP. However, soft-law regulations were regarded as necessary in order to unify procedural principles for handling the imposition and the enforcement of sanctions. The WP states indeed that the preconditions for such legislation are not fulfilled – at least not so far – taking into account the following arguments: First, administrative sanctions are closely linked to the enforcement and supervision procedures and methods of a specific public authority. The sectoral nature of the administrative sanctions and the priority of specific regulation are understandable against the fact that administrative sanctions are part of the sectoral sanctioning scheme: the existing sanction systems vary considerably and there would anyhow be need for specific regulation schemes (eg, for enabling specific penalties tailored to each sector). Therefore, unified legislation would be difficult to formulate as it would easily be of too general nature, inaccurate and unpredictable and so the need for specific legal provisions would not crucially diminish. Secondly, the obligations based on the EU legislation as well as the dynamic case law of the European courts (ECtHR and CJEU) will in any case extensively affect the regulation of administrative sanctions and their enforcement, irrespective of national legislation. Due to the dynamic nature of the practice of the European courts it would be difficult to keep a unified law up-to-date.

To my mind, the reasoning against creating unified general legislation is not convincing. Nevertheless, the proposals of the WP include positive elements. The main innovation in the report of the WP consists in proposing principles and standards which should govern future regulation of administrative sanctions. These proposals are intended as non-binding and non-exhaustive guidelines for the ministries of the Finnish government in their legislative work. These guidelines – as part of the revised Lawmaker's manual (on the website of the Ministry of Justice[22]) – should lead towards more harmonised regulation of the administrative sanctions. The basis for the regulated principles and standards should be their compliance with the provisions of the Finnish Constitution – as interpreted by the CLC – as well as the obligations derived from the ECHR and EU legislation and the case law of ECtHR and CJEU.

VI. Substance of the Regulation of Administrative Sanctions

When looking at these proposals of the WP in detail, they mostly repeat the relevant content of fundamental human and constitutional rights law with some necessary modifications (alleviations), so that what is valid in respect of criminal law and criminal procedural law is, mutatis mutandis, applicable to punitive administrative law. In order to understand the WP's strong reliance on fundamental rights law, one should take into account the change of Finnish legal culture in the 1990s.[23] In what follows, I will first explain that cultural change. Next, I will examine what fundamental rights or their modifications are applicable to administrative sanctions.

Finland ratified the ECHR in 1990, and new provisions on basic rights were incorporated into the Finnish Constitution in 1995 – in the same year that Finland joined the EU. The effects of this ratification of the ECHR and the reform of constitutional (ie, basic) rights in the 1990s were remarkable due to the direct applicability of the individuals' fundamental rights before national courts and public authorities.

Indeed, the ECHR and other important human rights treaties (eg, the UN International Covenant on Civil and Political Rights (CCPR), 1966) have been incorporated through an Act of Parliament *in blanco*. Because of the predominance of the incorporation method, Finland can be said to be a dualist system in form but a monist system in practice when implementing international law in the domestic legal order. This implementation method obviously affects the application of human rights treaties. The CLC has confirmed the following principles: the hierarchal status of the domestic Act of incorporation of a treaty determines the formal ranking of the treaty provisions in domestic law (ie, their rank is normally that of an act of Parliament); incorporated treaty

[22] See http://lainkirjoittaja.finlex.fi/12-yleislait-ja-eraat-yleiset-saantelyt/12-10/ (only available in Finnish) (visited 17 September 2021).

[23] For this change of Finnish legal culture, see in more detail R Lahti, 'Towards Internationalization and Europeanization of Criminal Policy and Criminal Justice – Challenges to Comparative Research' in EW Pływaczewski (ed), *Current Problems of the Penal Law and Criminology* (Wolters Kluwer Polska, 2012), 365, 370.

provisions are in force in domestic law according to their content in international law; and the courts and authorities should resort to 'human-rights-friendly' interpretations of domestic cases, in order to avoid conflicts between domestic law and human rights law.[24]

Comprehensive provisions on the basic rights that were inserted into the Finnish Constitution in 1995 have been essentially inspired by the international human rights treaties. Several of the enacted constitutional provisions make reference to human rights, thus giving semi-constitutional status to human rights treaties. In the legislative works a 'basic-rights-friendly' interpretation, in addition to the above-mentioned human-rights-friendly interpretation, was implied, although the prohibition on courts examining the constitutionality of laws of Parliament was maintained.[25]

The change of Finnish legal culture described above, following its ratification of the ECHR, has had an essential impact on criminal law and criminal procedural law and the doctrines behind them. The legality principle (*nullum crimen sine lege scripta et certa, nulla poena sine lege poenali*) is the leading principle in criminal law, and it has institutional support both in human rights and constitutional law. The principle of culpability and the prohibition of strict liability in criminal law can now be based on human rights norms and constitutional principles which guarantee the inviolability of human dignity.

As for the principles of criminalisation, various human and constitutional rights must be taken into account. In the argumentation, constitutional (and human rights) principles may collide: while the obligation to protect certain rights supports the enlargement of criminal offences, other principles restrict the scope or the method of using criminal law. When dealing with some of the recent government Bills concerning criminal law, there was a general discussion in the CLC on these principles and the tension between certain contradictory arguments but it confirmed the criteria to be fulfilled when criminalising certain conduct: there must be a considerable social need for criminalisation, as well as legitimate reasons from the constitutional rights point of view that it restricts fundamental freedoms in an acceptable way; the benefits of criminalisation must also be proportionate to the extent that fundamental freedoms are restricted; and there must be adequate legal safeguards in limiting fundamental rights and adequate procedural rights translating those safeguards.[26]

In the legal literature, the key criteria for limiting criminalisation have been characterised in the following way: the principle of protection of legitimate interests; *ultima ratio* (criminal law must be used only as a last resort); the rational evaluation of social costs and benefits of criminalisation; the inviolability of human dignity and the legality principle.[27] These criteria correspond with the general preconditions for restricting the fundamental rights that are protected by the Constitution.

[24] See in more detail M Scheinin, 'Incorporation and Implementatipm of Human Rights in Finland' in M Scheinin (ed), *International Human Rights Norms in the Nordic and Baltic Countries* (The Hague, Martinus Nijhoff Publishers, 1996), 257.

[25] There is no Constitutional Court in Finland, but the courts shall give primacy to the provision in the Constitution if the application of an Act would be in evident conflict with the Constitution (section 106).

[26] CLC, Statements nos 25/1994 and 23/1997.

[27] See the pioneering work of S Melander, *Kriminalisointiteoria – rangaistavaksi säätämisen oikeudelliset perusteet* [A Theory of Criminalisation – Legal constraints to criminal legislation] (Helsinki, Suomalainen Lakimiesyhdistys, 2008).

In its report, the WP states that the above-mentioned general preconditions for restricting constitutional rights shall in principle be applied also in the regulation of administrative sanctions, even though the CLC has not made a corresponding assessment of the conditions that must be met for limiting constitutional rights. The legality principle is particularly relevant: the general prerequisites of administrative sanctions must be based on the law laid down by Parliament except when the administrative sanction is based directly on binding EU legislation (ie, an EU regulation). The prerequisites must also be sufficiently precise in defining both the forbidden conduct and the applicable penalty.

It is noteworthy that the WP's proposals mainly emphasise the principles governing legal safeguards in determining administrative sanctions. It is underlined that principles like the presumption of innocence, *ne bis in idem* and the privilege against self-incrimination should be complied with in the administrative procedure in line with the guarantees of fair trial, as interpreted in the case law of ECtHR and the practice of the CLC.

The presumption of innocence is, however, not interpreted by the CLC as an absolute principle and not strictly in the same way as in relation to criminal proceedings. For instance, it is not necessary to adopt the principle of culpability (ie, the prerequisite of intent or negligence) in the legal regulation of administrative sanctions as strictly as it is to be applied to criminal offences. That being said, the threshold for being exempted from liability when there are cogent counter-reasons must not be too high for the respondent. Moreover, in administrative proceedings too, the rights of defence and other legal safeguards should be properly obeyed.

The recent case law of the ECtHR has influenced the significance and content of the *ne bis in idem* principle. A separate legal act (No 781/2013) on the prohibition of double jeopardy (ie, a prohibition against the cumulative application of criminal punishment and administrative fine) was introduced in Finland for tax fraud cases. Accordingly, as a rule, charges may not be brought, nor may a court judgment be passed, if a punitive tax or customs increase has already been imposed on the same person in the same case (Criminal Code 29:11).

However, the WP did not recommend any exhaustive regulation of the prohibition of double jeopardy. It referred to the case *A. and B. v Norway*,[28] in which the ECtHR found that Article 4 of Protocol No. 7 to the ECHR is not infringed even though there are parallel criminal proceedings and administrative proceedings which are criminal in nature. The reasoning behind the decision was that the proceedings were sufficiently closely connected in time and in substance, therefore resulting in the absence of the *bis* element. The WP also referred to Case C-524/15,[29] Case C-537/16[30] and Joined Cases C-596/16 and C-597/16,[31] in which the CJEU considered that there could be a duplication of criminal and administrative proceedings/penalties against the same person with respect to the same acts under certain conditions: national legislation must pursue an

[28] Case *A and B v Norway* App nos 24130/11 and 29758/11 (ECtHR, 15 November 2016).
[29] Case C-524/15 *Criminal proceedings against Menci* ECLI:EU:C:2018:197.
[30] Case C-537/15 *Euro Bank SA v Marek Łopaciński* ECLI:EU:C:2016:143.
[31] Cases C-596/16 and C-597/16 *Di Puma v Commissione Nazionale per le Società e la Borsa (Consob) and Commissione Nazionale per le Società e la Borsa (Consob) v Zecca* ECLI:EU:C:2018:192.

objective of general interest, establish clear and precise rules, ensure that the proceedings are coordinated and ensure that the severity of all of the penalties follows the proportionality principle. In that respect, it is noteworthy that the Finnish Criminal Code (Chapter 6) has provided since 1976 a discretional mitigation of punishment in the cases of accumulative sanctions.

The recent case law of the ECtHR has also strongly influenced the fair trial guarantees of the evidentiary procedure. Explicit provisions have been included in the revised Code of Judicial Procedure (Chapter 17, Sections 18 and 25; No. 732/2015) on the privilege against self-incrimination and on the exclusion of unlawfully obtained evidence in criminal proceedings. As to the administrative proceedings in the administrative courts, similar provisions have been added into the new Act on those proceedings (No. 808/2019, §§ 69, 83). According to the new provision, a person has the right to refuse to testify to the extent that the testimony would subject him or her or a person related to him or her to the risk of prosecution, or would contribute to the investigation of his or her guilt or of the guilt of a person related to him or her. The prohibition against reference to certain evidence includes evidence that is obtained by violating the privilege against self-incrimination or otherwise unlawfully. This rule will not be absolute, but reference to the unlawfully obtained evidence must not result in the violation of the right to fair trial all things considered.

Summarising the proposals of the WP leads to a conclusion that it is a half-way undertaking and its content is near to the results of the Norwegian legislative solution (see section IV above). The WP does not propose a general systematic law on administrative sanctions but rather its proposals rely on the case law of the European courts and entail certain fragmentary legal provisions on the subject. There is a big difference in relation to the legislative strategy in respect of criminal legislation in which a systematic codification of penal provisions is preferred due to its ability to create consistence and coherence in law-making.

To a great extent, it is left open how the relationship between these two types of punitive (criminal and administrative) sanctions should be regulated and what would be the appropriate coordination at the legislative level. This can be regarded as an open wound in the regulatory model proposed by the WP. For instance, Andrew Ashworth has framed the question as follows: how do we decide which forms of anti-social conduct ought to be subjected to civil or administrative regulation, rather than to criminal sanctions? The approach of using administrative sanctions for financial rule-breaking and for corporate wrongdoing may lead to a further widening of the gulf between disadvantaged people and the 'respectable'.[32] Similarly, the fairness in allocating criminal responsibility was emphasised as one of the major values in the Finnish Criminal Code reform.[33]

This starting point is also important in a recent research project commissioned by the Finnish Competition and Consumer Authority on whether individual criminal responsibility of the heads of business should be introduced in addition to the already existing administrative sanctioning of the corporation. In the research report, cartel

[32] A Ashworth, 'Criminal Justice and Civilization' in *Beware of Punishment* (n 7), 13, 16.
[33] R Lahti, 'Towards a principled European criminal policy' (n 8), 65.

activities were considered socially and morally just as reprehensible as traditionally criminalised fraudulent acts.[34] Such a legislative reform would require solutions to the problems in coordinating the administrative procedure under competition law and the criminal process: inter alia, one should clarify the chronological relationship between both processes; the exchange of data between the administrative and judicial authorities, and the effects of criminalisation on the leniency system.

Iain Cameron points out that the alternatives to criminalisation are not always good, typically when a criminal penalty is replaced with severe administrative penalties but without the strong safeguards of the criminal justice process.[35] Therefore, in an acceptable legislative model, one should balance the pros and cons of relying on criminalisation and the strong safeguards of the criminal justice process. Is criminalisation really necessary, or are there more weighty reasons for administrative sanctions instead of criminal punishment?

In a recent statement, the Deputy Ombudsman of the Finnish Parliament presented arguments for the further deliberation of the scope of administrative sanctions.[36] The main emphasis in this interesting reasoning lies on the arguments as to when criminal proceedings are necessary and when administrative sanctioning – at least alone – is insufficient: firstly, when the establishment of the suspected illegal behaviour requires police investigation and coercive measures; secondly, when an erroneous decision on sanctioning cannot go unchallenged, for instance in cases of severe sanctions (eg, unconditional imprisonment); thirdly, when open and public proceedings are needed in order to make the control of exercise of power possible; and fourthly, when the assessment of the suspected illegal behaviour, its circumstances, the suspected person's culpability or the determination of the penalty requires much discretion.

VII. Conclusion[37]

In the prevention of economic and corporate crime, the significance and impact of various kinds of preventive tools and reactive control systems on the achievement of the goals and value aims set by government should be assessed from a comprehensive criminal policy and control policy perspective. The examination of control systems must not be limited only to criminal justice policy or criminalisation principles; the approach to be adopted should instead be one of extensive assessment of control policy and sanctioning policy, wherein the various forms of sanctions, such as punishments under criminal law and economic administrative sanctions of a punitive nature, are subjected to a cost/benefit analysis.

A systematic comparison between administrative sanctions, on the one hand, and criminalisation and criminal law sanctions, on the other, enhances the potential for

[34] Cf above, section IV, text to n 18.

[35] I Cameron, 'A Constitutional Perspective' (n 21), 130.

[36] Statement of Dr Pasi Pölönen, Deputy Ombudsman of the Parliament, for the WP of the Ministry of Justice, dated 2 October 2018.

[37] See also R Lahti, 'Towards a principled European criminal policy' (n 8), 66, 69.

differentiating control systems for economic and corporate crime and the prerequisites for the imposition of sanctions. Underlying this need for differentiation is the fact that the effects of goals and values in the various sectors of control policy and criminal policy pull in different directions and with different forces. Questions for deliberation include, inter alia, whether it is better to differentiate the prerequisites for imposing sanctions and the procedural rules to be complied with in the imposing of sanctions within the criminal justice system in order to increase the efficiency of crime prevention (while at the same time somewhat weakening the fair trial guarantees), or whether such differentiation should be accomplished through the introduction of a parallel system of administrative sanctions.

2

Swiss Peculiarities of the Enforcement Mechanisms in Core, Secondary and Administrative Criminal Law

NADINE ZURKINDEN

I. Introduction

In Switzerland, the enforcement of criminal law is covered by four federal statutes (section II.A. below): the Code of Criminal Procedure,[1] the Administrative Criminal Law Act,[2] the Code of Military Criminal Procedure[3] and the Code of Juvenile Criminal Procedure.[4] This chapter focuses on the Code of Criminal Procedure (in force since 1 January 2011) and the Administrative Criminal Law Act (in force since 1 January 1975).

When the Code of Criminal Procedure entered into force in 2011, it replaced the 26 cantonal criminal procedure laws that had been in force until then. While the Code of Criminal Procedure was being drafted, there were discussions to also include in the Code the procedural rules covered by the Administrative Criminal Law Act. However, this was considered to complicate the drafting even further (it was already difficult to unify 26 different cantonal criminal procedure laws), and therefore the rules governing administrative criminal law procedure remained in the Administrative Criminal Law Act.[5]

While core and secondary criminal law offences (section II.B. and C. below) are prosecuted by public prosecutors, in accordance with the provisions laid down in the Code of Criminal Procedure (section III. A. and B.), administrative criminal law offences are prosecuted by administrative authorities in accordance with the provisions laid out in the Administrative Criminal Law Act (section III.C.). Administrative criminal law offences are prosecuted by administrative authorities because the latter are said to have

[1] Code of Criminal Procedure of 5 October 2007 (*Strafprozessordnung*, SR 312.0).

[2] Federal Act of 22 March 1974 on Administrative Criminal Law (*Bundesgesetz über das Verwaltungsstrafrecht*, SR 313.0).

[3] Code of Military Criminal Procedure of 23 March 1979 (*Militärstrafprozess*, SR 322.1).

[4] Code of Juvenile Criminal Procedure of 20 March 2009 (*Jugendstrafprozessordnung*, SR 312.1).

[5] Botschaft zur Vereinheitlichung des Strafprozessrechts vom 21. Dezember 2005, BBl 2006 1085, 1096.

the expertise needed to conduct investigations in a special field regulated by administrative law (eg, medicine) (section III.C.). It should be noted, however, that even though administrative criminal law offences are prosecuted by administrative authorities they remain criminal law offences. Today's scholars classify administrative *criminal* law as criminal law not only because it has the notion 'criminal' in its name but also because the goals of punishments provided for by administrative criminal law are the same as those for punishments provided for by the Criminal Code: punishment on the one hand and deterrence on the other hand. Consequently, the types of punishment are almost identical to those provided for in the Criminal Code (section II.D.(i)). Furthermore, the Administrative Criminal Law Act declares the general rules of the Criminal Code applicable to administrative criminal law offences unless an administrative criminal law provision provides otherwise (Article 2 Administrative Criminal Law Act).[6]

Bearing in mind that administrative criminal law offences are in truth criminal law offences, the fact that administrative authorities prosecute crimes in place of public prosecutors is in and of itself a Swiss peculiarity, and one that has recently been called into question.[7]

A further – and for lawyers not familiar with Swiss law arguably more shocking – Swiss peculiarity is that both the criminal procedure and the administrative criminal procedure are in most (!) cases, in which defendants get convicted, concluded with a so-called summary penalty order. Such orders are issued by the prosecuting authority (section III.A.(ii). and III.D.(ii)). Furthermore, there is a tendency to expand an even simpler and faster procedure to more and more contraventions: the fixed fine procedure (section III.B.(ii)). Only the fact that defendants can have their case eventually submitted to a criminal court makes the orders (in the sense of proposed judgments) compatible with Article 6 ECHR.[8] However, most defendants do not take their case before a court.

Another Swiss specialty is that apart from criminal punishments there are also administrative sanctions not amounting to criminal punishment in Swiss law but that are in nature similar to punishment. An example with high practical relevance is the withdrawal of the driving licence 'as a warning'. This sanction is imposed by

[6] J Hurtado Pozo, *Droit pénal, Partie générale* (Zurich, Schulthess, 2008) para 96; C Riedo and MA Niggli, 'Verwaltungsstrafrecht, Teil 1: Ein Märchen, eine Lösung, ein Problem und ein Beispiel' in I Häner and B Waldmann (eds), *Verwaltungsstrafrecht und sanktionierendes Verwaltungsrecht* (Zurich, Schulthess, 2010) p 43 with further references. A Eicker, 'Einführung ins materielle und formelle Verwaltungsstrafrecht' in A Eicker (ed), *Aktuelle Herausforderungen für die Praxis im Verwaltungsstrafverfahren, Tagungsband* (Berne, Stämpfli, 2013) pp 11 and 22 et seq; A Eicker, F Frank and J Achermann, *Verwaltungsstrafrecht und Verwaltungsstrafverfahrensrecht* (Berne, Stämpfli, 2012) pp 4 et seq, pp 12, 15, 16 et seq; MA Niggli and S Maeder, 'Verwaltungsstrafrecht, Strafrecht und Strafprozessrecht – Grundprobleme' in Eicker (ed), *Aktuelle Herausforderungen für die Praxis im Verwaltungsstrafverfahren, Tagungsband* (Berne, Stämpfli, 2013) pp 28 et seq. S Maeder and MA Niggli, 'Was schützt eigentlich Strafrecht (und schützt es überhaupt etwas)?' (2011) 4 *Aktuelle Juristische Praxis* 443, p 454.

[7] N Capus, 'La lutte contre la criminalité économique à l'aide du droit pénal administratif', *Jusletter* 8. July 2019 calls the argument into question that in certain areas administrative authorities are preferable to public prosecutors as prosecuting authorities and recommends that an empirical analysis of the implementation of administrative criminal law by the various administrative authorities be carried out before an amendment (which is in preparation) of the Federal Act on Administrative Criminal Law.

[8] M Thommen, *Kurzer Prozess – fairer Prozess?* (Berne, Stämpfli, 2013) p 42.

administrative authorities upon a person who has culpably infringed road traffic legislation and who has already received a criminal penalty for the same conduct. The European Court of Human Rights upheld in recent case law that *ne bis in idem* does not apply to such cases (section IV.). Nevertheless, it is argued in this chapter that in Switzerland fair trial rights are not primarily endangered by a law that is not formally labelled criminal law but includes sanctions with a punitive and deterrent purpose. In Switzerland fair trial rights are rather at stake because (for the benefit of swift completions of proceedings) most convictions for criminal and administrative criminal law offences alike result from a summary penalty order, issued by the prosecuting authority in a preliminary procedure. So these cases are never brought before a court.

In order to give the background knowledge on the Swiss system that is required for the subsequent analysis, this chapter will unravel the different sources of substantive criminal law in Switzerland (section II.), then explain the different types of criminal procedures (section III.), and finally, briefly highlight the withdrawal of the driving licence 'as a warning' as a punitive administrative sanction that complements the criminal punishment a convicted person has already received (section IV.).

II. Different Sources of Substantive Criminal Law

A. Legislative Power: Mainly with the Confederation

Switzerland is a confederation with 26 cantons. Nevertheless, the legislative power regarding criminal law lies mainly with the Confederation (Article 123(1) of the Federal Constitution). The cantons may only legislate on contraventions that are not subject to federal legislation (eg, prohibiting naked hiking,[9] Article 335(1) Criminal Code). Furthermore, they may determine criminal sanctions for offences against cantonal administrative law (eg, violations of cantonal tax law) and cantonal procedural law (Article 123(1) Federal Constitution, read together with Article 335 Criminal Code).[10]

B. Core Criminal Law

The Swiss Criminal Code covers core criminal law; that is, traditional offences such as homicide, assault, theft or fraud. The Swiss Criminal Code entered into force on 1 January 1942. It classifies offences into three categories depending on the severity of the punishment threatened: felonies (punishable by more than three years' custodial detention), misdemeanours (punishable by a monetary penalty or a maximum of three years' imprisonment) and contraventions (punishable by fines only, Article 103 Criminal Code). Examples of felonies are intentional homicide (Article 111 Criminal Code), theft (Article 139) or fraud (Article 146). Examples of misdemeanours are homicide

[9] BGE 138 IV 13.

[10] A Petrig and N Zurkinden, *Swiss Criminal Law* (Zurich, Dike, 2015) p 12.

through negligence (Article 117), assault through negligence (Article 125), failure to offer help in an emergency (Article 128) or coercion (Article 181). Examples of contraventions are acts of aggression that do not cause any injury (Article 126), minor offences against property (Article 172ter) or not complying with official orders (Article 292).

Swiss scholars and courts consider fines (even in the realm of fixed fine procedures, see below section III.B.(ii)) a criminal punishment to sanction a criminal offence, not a mere administrative penalty (as opposed to German scholars who do not consider fines for German *Ordnungswidrigkeiten* to be criminal punishments).[11] Consequently, the general provisions of the Criminal Code apply as a general rule to contraventions (Article 104 Criminal Code). Nevertheless, due to the low degree of wrongfulness of contraventions, Article 105 Criminal Code declares certain provisions not, or only conditionally, applicable. Corporations, for example, do not incur criminal liability for contraventions (Article 105(1) Criminal Code). Furthermore, attempted contraventions or complicity in contraventions are only subject to punishment if expressly stated by the Criminal Code (Article 105(2) Criminal Code).[12]

C. Secondary Criminal Law

In addition to the criminal offences in the Criminal Code, there is an increasing number of criminal offences that are regulated outside of the Criminal Code.[13] Such provisions are referred to as secondary criminal law. They are, for example, found in the Narcotics Act,[14] the Foreign Nationals Act,[15] the Money Laundering Act,[16] the Road Traffic Act[17] and hundreds more: it appears that the legislator feels a need to provide penal provisions for each new act and ordinance. This has been a tendency over the past 20 years.[18]

Secondary criminal law is more relevant in practice than the Criminal Code. Of the criminal provisions covered by the annual statistics on convicted adults,[19] approximately one-third of convictions are based on criminal offences laid down in the Criminal Code, while two-thirds of convictions are based on a provision of secondary criminal law. In particular, offences covered by the Road Traffic Act are of high practical importance.[20]

[11] F Riklin, *Schweizerisches Strafrecht. Allgemeiner Teil I. Verbrechenslehre*, 3rd edn (Zurich, Schulthess, 2007) § 1 paras 23 et seq; BGE 115 IV 137.

[12] A Petrig and N Zurkinden, *Swiss Criminal Law* (Zurich, Dike, 2015) pp 47 et seq.

[13] M Thommen, 'Criminal Law' in M Thommen (ed.), *Introduction to Swiss Law* (Berlin, Carl Grossmann Verlag, 2018) p 376; A Petrig and N Zurkinden, *Swiss Criminal Law* (Zurich, Dike, 2015) p 12.

[14] Federal Act of 3 October 1951 on Narcotics and Psychotropic Substances (*Betäubungsmittelgesetz*, SR 812.121).

[15] Federal Act of 16 December 2005 on Foreign Nationals and Integration (*Ausländer- und Integrationsgesetz*, SR 142.20).

[16] Federal Act of 10 October 1997 on Combating Money Laundering and the Financing of Terrorism in the Financial Sector (*Geldwäschereigesetz*, SR 955).

[17] Road Traffic Act of 19 December 1958 (*Strassenverkehrsgesetz*, SR 741.01).

[18] MA Niggli (ed), *Strafrecht. Sämtliche Erlasse des Bundes zu Kompetenz, Organisation, Prozess, Vollzug, Rechtshilfe sowie das gesamte Nebenstrafrecht*, 2nd edn (Zurich, Orell Füssli, 2006) p 6.

[19] For the statistics see: www.bfs.admin.ch/bfs/de/home/statistiken/kriminalitaet-strafrecht/strafjustiz/jugend-erwachsenenurteile.html (accessed on 7 July 2019).

[20] A Petrig and N Zurkinden, *Swiss Criminal Law* (Zurich, Dike, 2015) p 14. See for statistics: www.bfs.admin.ch/bfs/de/home/statistiken/kriminalitaet-strafrecht/strafjustiz/jugend-erwachsenenurteile.html (accessed on 7 July 2019).

Secondary criminal law comprises (just like the Criminal Code) felonies, misdemeanours and contraventions. For example, racing at more than 100 km/h on a street in a city where the maximum speed limit is 50 km/h constitutes a felony (Article 90(3) and (4)). A gross violation of traffic rules, such as overtaking another car on the right (instead of overtaking it on the left) and causing danger to the safety of others constitutes a misdemeanour (Article 90(2)), whereas driving while intoxicated with a blood alcohol concentration of 0.5–0.79 per mille constitutes a contravention.[21] The majority of road traffic offences concern contraventions (ie are punishable by fines).

D. Administrative Criminal Law

(i) Administrative Criminal Law

Secondary criminal law is labelled administrative criminal law if it is prosecuted by administrative authorities (and not by criminal authorities). The Narcotics Act, for example, provides in its Articles 19–27 for criminal offences. All these offences may be prosecuted by criminal authorities. However, according to Article 28a of the Narcotics Act, offences under Articles 20–22 that are detected by the relevant federal authority (eg, by Swissmedic – the Swiss Agency for Therapeutic Products – in the realm of licensing, production and trade of therapeutic products) are prosecuted by that authority. There is thus a purely formal distinction (depending on the competent prosecuting authority) between criminal and administrative criminal law.[22] The attribution of prosecution power for administrative offences to certain federal administrative authorities is due to their expertise in the respective areas. The administrative authorities have the experts in the field and the expertise needed to conduct the investigation and prosecution in those special areas (eg, medicine), while a prosecutor would have to bring in such experts. When Swissmedic, for example, conducts an investigation the Swissmedic investigating body works closely together with Swissmedic's own scientific experts.[23]

The types of punishment for administrative criminal offences are almost identical to those provided for in the Criminal Code. They are merely supplemented by one 'lower' punishment: the regulatory fine (*Ordnungsbusse*) for regulatory offences (*Ordnungswidrigkeit*). The Swiss regulatory offence is, however, not comparable to the German *Ordnungswidrigkeit* but is a subtype of the contravention.[24] It was introduced

[21] Driving while intoxicated with a blood alcohol concentration of at least 0.8 ‰ constitutes a misdemeanour (Article 91 Road Traffic Act read together with the Ordinance on Alcohol Limits in Road Traffic of 15 June 2012: *Verordnung der Bundesversammlung über Alkoholgrenzwerte im Strassenverkehr*, SR 741.13).

[22] S Maeder and MA Niggli, 'Was schützt eigentlich Strafrecht (und schützt es überhaupt etwas)?' (2011) 4 *Aktuelle Juristische Praxis* 443, p 452; F Riklin, *Schweizerisches Strafrecht. Allgemeiner Teil I. Verbrechenslehre*, 3rd edn (Zurich, Schulthess, 2007) § 1 para 26.

[23] M Burri, 'Swissmedic als Verwaltungsstrafbehörde im "Sandwich" zwischen Verwaltungsverfahren und kantonaler Strafverfolgung: Herausforderungen, Schnittstellen, Zielkonflikte' in A Eicker (ed), *Aktuelle Herausforderungen für die Praxis im Verwaltungsstrafverfahren, Tagungsband* (Berne, Stämpfli, 2013) pp 91 et seq; A Eicker and F Frank and J Achermann, *Verwaltungsstrafrecht und Verwaltungsstrafverfahrensrecht* (Berne, Stämpfli, 2012) p 155.

[24] MA Niggli and S Maeder, 'Verwaltungsstrafrecht, Strafrecht und Strafprozessrecht – Grundprobleme' in Eicker (ed), *Aktuelle Herausforderungen für die Praxis im Verwaltungsstrafverfahren, Tagungsband* (Berne, Stämpfli, 2013) p 31.

because the legislator decided to extend criminal liability for contraventions in administrative criminal law:[25] punishment for complicity in contraventions of administrative criminal law is, for example, generally provided for.[26] Regulatory offences limit criminal liability: eg, complicity as well as aiding and abetting a regulatory offence are not subject to punishment (Article 5 Administrative Criminal Law Act). The most severe form of punishment that can be imposed according to administrative criminal law is deprivation of liberty. Thus the punishments that can be imposed under administrative criminal law are criminal punishments. They are not to be confused with so-called administrative sanctions which have different purposes (eg, there is the Swiss peculiarity of withdrawing driving licences as a warning, which is said to have educational and preventive purposes – as opposed to punitive and deterrent purposes – see below section IV.).[27]

Administrative criminal law provisions (prosecuted by administrative authorities) are included in administrative law Acts that may also include criminal law provisions (prosecuted by criminal prosecution authorities). For example, illegal dispensing of medicinal products is an offence that is prosecuted by criminal prosecution authorities, while illegal advertising of medicinal products is prosecuted by Swissmedic and thus concerns administrative criminal law.[28] The latter remains, however, a criminal provision due to the nature of its sanction (a fine) and purpose (punishment and deterrence from further offending). Furthermore, if deprivation of liberty comes into question, it is mandatory for the sentence to be passed by a cantonal court. This holds also true for other administrative offences outside the realm of medical products (Article 21(1) Administrative Criminal Law Act). In that case the administrative authority (eg, Swissmedic) refers the files to the cantonal prosecutor's office for the attention of the competent criminal court (Article 73(1) Administrative Criminal Law Act). The administrative authority then becomes a party to the proceedings (Article 74(1) Administrative Criminal Law Act).[29]

[25] In core criminal law liability for contraventions is limited due to their low wrongfulness. Eg, attempted contraventions or complicity in contraventions of core criminal law are only subject to punishment if expressly stated by the Criminal Code (Article 105(2) Criminal Code), see section II.B.

[26] A Eicker, F Frank and J Achermann, *Verwaltungsstrafrecht und Verwaltungsstrafverfahrensrecht* (Berne, Stämpfli, 2012) pp 45 et seq with further references.

[27] Withdrawing driving licences as a warning and other so-called administrative sanctions are, however, in nature similar to punishment. Eg, Article 49a et seq Cartel Act, SR 251. Article 50 Cartel Act reads: 'Any undertaking that to its advantage breaches an amicable settlement, a final and non-appealable ruling of the competition authorities, or a decision of an appellate body shall be charged up to 10 per cent of the turnover it achieved in Switzerland in the preceding three financial years'. On the nature of administrative sanctions also see Riedo and Niggli, 'Verwaltungsstrafrecht, Teil 1: Ein Märchen, eine Lösung, ein Problem und ein Beispiel' in I Häner and B Waldmann (eds), *Verwaltungsstrafrecht und sanktionierendes Verwaltungsrecht* (Zurich, Schulthess, 2010) 45 et seq; MA Niggli and C Riedo, 'Quasi-Strafrecht, Strafrecht im engeren und weiteren Sinn und "Sozialethisches Unwerturteil"' in M Amstutz and I Hochreutener and WA Stoffel (eds), *Die Praxis des Kartellgesetzes im Spannungsfeld von Recht und Ökonomie* (Zurich, Schulthess, 2011) pp 91 et seq.

[28] www.swissmedic.ch/swissmedic/en/home/legal/penal-law.html (accessed on 7 July 2019) with references to Articles 86 et seq of the Therapeutic Products Act (*Heilmittelgesetz*, SR 812.21).

[29] www.swissmedic.ch/swissmedic/en/home/legal/penal-law.html (accessed on 7 July 2019) See also below section III.D.(ii).

(ii) History

It is difficult to determine how long exactly administrative criminal law has existed. Of course, there was administrative law before there was administrative criminal law. Administrative law came into existence when the state started to play a more active role in the nineteenth and twentieth centuries, especially when it acquired new tasks such as the administration of services in the areas of social security, grants, social insurance and infrastructure. Furthermore, the state provided basic services regarding transportation, communication, energy, schooling and research. It also became the state's task to protect and promote markets such as agriculture and housing, or to provide for the protection of the environment.[30] Hence, the state, or rather the legislature, set up rules aiming at regulating those areas and imposing penalties (that are criminal in nature as they range from monetary penalties to deprivation of liberty and aim at punishment and deterrence) for non-compliance with those rules.

(iii) Administrative Criminal Law Act

Administrative criminal law provisions have been and still are scattered over many pieces of legislation.[31] In 1975, the Administrative Criminal Law Act partially harmonised them.[32] The Administrative Criminal Law Act applies – as a rule[33] – only to secondary criminal law offences that federal administrative authorities prosecute and adjudicate (Article 1 Administrative Criminal Law Act). It includes substantive and procedural provisions. Its substantive provisions are divided into general rules (eg, on participation) and specific provisions on fraud offences, document fraud offences and assisting offences (ie assisting another person to evade prosecution or the execution of punishment).[34] However, the general rules laid out in the general part of the Criminal Code, as a fall-back option, apply to administrative criminal law (Article 333(1) Criminal Code;[35] Article 2 Administrative Criminal Law Act[36]). That means the Administrative Criminal Law Act may provide for deviations from the general rules laid out

[30] Moor, 'Verwaltungsrecht' in *Historisches Lexikon der Schweiz*: www.hls-dhs-dss.ch/textes/d/D9660.php (accessed on 7 July 2019).

[31] N Zurkinden, 'Criminal liability in companies, associations, and other collective legal entities in Switzerland' in U Sieber and Jarvers and Silverman (eds), *National Criminal Law in a Comparative Legal Context: Special forms of criminal liability* (Berlin, Duncker & Humblot, 2015) p 359 with further references (content available online at infocrim.org).

[32] F Riklin, *Schweizerisches Strafrecht. Allgemeiner Teil I. Verbrechenslehre*, 3rd edn (Zurich, Schulthess, 2007) § 2 para 35.

[33] Some acts explicitly declare provisions of the Administrative Criminal Law Act applicable, even if they are prosecuted by criminal prosecution authorities. See A Eicker, 'Einführung ins materielle und formelle Verwaltungsstrafrecht' in A Eicker (ed), *Aktuelle Herausforderungen für die Praxis im Verwaltungsstrafverfahren, Tagungsband* (Berne, Stämpfli, 2013) p 17.

[34] A Eicker, 'Einführung ins materielle und formelle Verwaltungsstrafrecht' in A Eicker (ed), *Aktuelle Herausforderungen für die Praxis im Verwaltungsstrafverfahren, Tagungsband* (Berne, Stämpfli, 2013) p 17.

[35] 'The general provisions of this Code apply to offences provided for in other federal acts unless these federal acts themselves contain detailed provisions on such offences.' (Translation provided for here: www.admin.ch/opc/en/classified-compilation/19370083/index.html, accessed on 7 July 2019).

[36] 'The general provisions of the Criminal Code shall apply to offences punishable under federal administrative legislation, unless this Act or another administrative law act provides otherwise.' (The translation is the author's own.)

in the Criminal Code.[37] This is the case in Articles 4–11 of the Administrative Criminal Law Act which, for example, provide for the criminal liability of business enterprises if an offence occurs in a business context, the potential fine does not exceed 5,000 Swiss Francs, and detecting the human individual(s) who actually committed the offence in question would involve a *disproportionate effort of investigation* (Article 7 Administrative Criminal Law Act). Dozens of acts comprising secondary criminal law refer to this provision.[38] It should be noted, though, that the rationale behind Article 7 of Administrative Criminal Law Act is to increase the efficiency of prosecution authorities in light of their limited resources. This is different to the criminal liability of corporations as provided for in the Criminal Code where the rationale is not to increase efficiency of prosecution authorities but rather to punish a corporation for its fault. According to Article 102, a corporation may be criminally liable for a *lack of organisation* that made it impossible to attribute the actual offence to a specific natural person (Article 102(1) Criminal Code) or for *failing to take all reasonable organisational measures necessary to prevent* participation in or support of a criminal organisation, financing terrorism, money laundering, or bribery offences (Article 102(2) Criminal Code).[39]

The enforcement of administrative criminal law (see below section III.D.) is also covered by the Administrative Criminal Law Act: Articles 19–103 cover the administrative criminal law procedure.[40] Nevertheless, Articles 6 and 7 of the European Convention of Human Rights remain applicable.[41]

III. Different Types of Criminal Law Enforcement

Depending on the authority designated (in accordance with the relevant law) for criminal prosecution (criminal authorities for core and secondary criminal law; administrative authorities for administrative criminal law) criminal law enforcement is based on different rules.

[37] A Eicker, 'Einführung ins materielle und formelle Verwaltungsstrafrecht' in A Eicker (ed), *Aktuelle Herausforderungen für die Praxis im Verwaltungsstrafverfahren, Tagungsband* (Berne, Stämpfli, 2013) p 16; A Petrig, 'Concept and systematization of the criminal offence in Switzerland' in U Sieber and S Forster and K Jarvers (eds), *National Criminal Law in a Comparative Legal Context: Defining criminal conduct* (Berlin, Duncker & Humblot, 2011) p 104 (content available online at infocrim.org).

[38] N Zurkinden, 'Criminal liability in companies, associations, and other collective legal entities in Switzerland' in U Sieber and K Jarvers and E Silverman (eds), *National Criminal Law in a Comparative Legal Context: Special forms of criminal liability* (Berlin, Duncker & Humblot, 2015) p 359 with further references (content available online at infocrim.org).

[39] A Petrig and N Zurkinden, *Swiss Criminal Law* (Zurich, Dike, 2015) p 127. On the relationship between Articles 6 and 7 Administrative Criminal Act on the one hand, and Article 102 Criminal Code (criminal liability for corporations) on the other, see MA Niggli and S Maeder, 'Verwaltungsstrafrecht, Strafrecht und Strafprozessrecht – Grundprobleme' in A Eicker (ed), *Aktuelle Herausforderungen für die Praxis im Verwaltungsstrafverfahren, Tagungsband* (Berne, Stämpfli, 2013) pp 47 et seq.

[40] A Eicker, 'Einführung ins materielle und formelle Verwaltungsstrafrecht' in A Eicker (ed), *Aktuelle Herausforderungen für die Praxis im Verwaltungsstrafverfahren, Tagungsband* (Berne, Stämpfli, 2013) p 19.

[41] A Eicker and F Frank and J Achermann, *Verwaltungsstrafrecht und Verwaltungsstrafverfahrensrecht* (Berne, Stämpfli, 2012) p 144 with reference to BGE 120 IV 226, consideration 4.a).

A. Core Criminal Law

(i) Enforced by (Cantonal) Criminal Authorities

The Swiss Criminal Code's enforcement is regulated by the Swiss Code of Criminal Procedure that entered into force on 1 January 2011 (prior to that date, every canton had its own criminal procedure law). Criminal law provided for in the Swiss Criminal Code is, as a general rule, enforced by cantonal authorities (Article 123(2) Federal Constitution; Article 22 Code of Criminal Procedure): criminal procedures start with preliminary proceedings, which consist of police inquiries (by members of the cantonal police force) and an investigation by the cantonal public prosecutor. Upon receipt of the indictment by the public prosecutor, the proceedings are handed over to the cantonal criminal court of first instance.[42] In the exceptional case that an offence falls within federal jurisdiction (such exceptions are found in Articles 23 and 24 of the Code of Criminal Procedure and other federal acts, eg, organised crime and terrorist financing if committed abroad to a substantial extent), the Federal Criminal Police and the Office of the Attorney General of Switzerland are responsible for conducting the preliminary proceedings. The main proceedings in the first instance are conducted before the Criminal Chamber of the Federal Criminal Court.

(ii) Summary Penalty Order

It is important to note, however, that most of the offences committed – be they offences of the Criminal Code or of secondary criminal law – are dealt with by summary penalty order (Articles 352 et seq Code of Criminal Procedure). Depending on the source of information (at the cantonal level), this applies to the impressive amount of 80 to 90 per cent of cases. The public prosecutor issues a summary penalty order if the defendant has made a confession or if their criminal responsibility has otherwise been satisfactorily established, provided that the prosecutor considers a fine, a monetary penalty of no more than 180 daily penalty units or imprisonment for less than six months to be appropriate (Article 352(1) Code of Criminal Procedure).[43]

The summary penalty order procedure works as follows: The public prosecutor fixes the sentence. The defendant may either accept or reject it within 10 days. If the public prosecutor decides to stand by the summary penalty order despite its rejection by the offender, the matter is dealt with under the ordinary procedure by the competent criminal court of first instance.[44] If the defendant does not object to the summary penalty order within 10 days, the summary penalty order has the effect of a final judgment; that is, there is no intervention by a court and the decision will be registered in the criminal database.

[42] A Petrig and N Zurkinden, *Swiss Criminal Law* (Zurich, Dike, 2015) pp 32 et seq.
[43] A Petrig and N Zurkinden, *Swiss Criminal Law* (Zurich, Dike, 2015) p 33.
[44] A Petrig and N Zurkinden, *Swiss Criminal Law* (Zurich, Dike, 2015) p 33.

B. Secondary Criminal Law

(i) Enforced by (Cantonal) Criminal Authorities

If not provided otherwise by an Act containing secondary criminal law, the enforcement of secondary criminal law is – like the enforcement of core criminal law – regulated by the Swiss Code of Criminal Procedure. Road traffic offences are thus, for example, enforced by cantonal criminal authorities, too.

(ii) Fixed Fine Procedure

In the realm of minor road traffic offences and other minor offences there is an even simpler, faster and anonymous procedure: the fixed fine procedure. It enables on-the-spot fines and is the basis, for example, for parking and speeding tickets. The Fixed Fine Act[45] formerly provided for the fixed fine procedure only with regard to road traffic contraventions. It entered into force on 1 January 1973.

It has provided the police with the power to impose and collect fines for minor offences listed with their respective fines in an appendix to the Fixed Fines Ordinance.[46] Those fines range from 20 Swiss Francs (eg, for speeding on highways at 1–5 km/h above the speed limit) to 260 Swiss Francs (for speeding on highways at 21–25 km/h above the speed limit).

For a long time, road traffic offences were the only area (at the federal level[47]) to which the fixed fine procedure applied. Only in October 2013 was the fixed fine procedure for the first time extended to a non-road-traffic offence: a person who consumes cannabis is liable to a fixed fine amounting to 100 Swiss Francs.[48]

Given that the fixed fine procedure has proven its worth in sanctioning minor road traffic offences, the Fixed Fine Act, the Fixed Fine Ordinance, and the appended list of fines have been extended to further areas of easily observable and ascertainable minor contraventions outlined in 16 separate Swiss acts.[49] Since 1 January 2020 the fixed fine procedure now applies, for example, to minor offences under the Asylum Act, the Unfair Competition Act, the Weapons Act, and the Environmental Protection Act.[50]

[45] *Ordnungsbussengesetz*, SR 314.1 (since 1 January 2020; until 31 December 2019 it was found in SR 741.03).

[46] *Ordnungsbussenverordnung*, SR 314.11 (since 1 January 2020; until 31 December 2019 it was found in SR 741.031).

[47] The cantons may apply the fixed fine procedure to cantonal contraventions. In Basel-Stadt the Cantonal Ordinance on Fixed Fines (*Baselstädtische Ordnungsbussenverordnung*, SG 257.115) provides, for example, for a fine of 100 Swiss Francs for forbidden billposting if no adhesives were used. With the use of adhesives forbidden billposting is punishable by a fine of 200 Swiss Francs.

[48] This was first provided for by Articles 28b-28l of the Narcotics Act. Those articles were cancelled and the fixed fine can now be found in the appended list 2 of the Fixed Fines Ordinance that entered into force on 1 January 2020.

[49] See press release of the Federal Council (ie Swiss government) of 26 April 2017: www.ejpd.admin.ch/ejpd/de/home/aktuell/news/2017/2017-04-26.html, and: www.bj.admin.ch/bj/de/home/sicherheit/gesetzgebung/ordnungsbussen.html (both accessed on 7 July 2019).

[50] See press release of the Federal Council (ie Swiss government) of 16 January 2019: www.ejpd.admin.ch/ejpd/de/home/aktuell/news/2019/2019-01-16.html (accessed on 7 July 2019).

The fixed fine procedure only applies if the person who issues the fine can determine the minor contravention. Illegal parking, for example, can be easily observed and determined. The contravention must be personally ascertained by a police officer or authorities appointed by the cantons (Article 2(1) Fixed Fine Act). There is one exception to this rule: when radar systems measure excessive-speeding of cars, the fixed fine procedure applies even though it was a machine and not a person who observed the contravention (Article 3(2) Fixed Fine Act).

For those minor offences no other sanctions can be imposed: the driving licence will, for example, not be withdrawn in such cases.

The goal of the fixed fine procedure is to disburden the prosecution authorities.[51] Arguably, the defendant is disburdened, too, because the fixed fine procedure is quick and free of additional administrative costs for the defendant (Article 12 Fixed Fine Act). The latter is – as a general rule – not the case for the other procedures discussed here. In those cases, as a rule, defendants must pay procedural costs if they are convicted (Article 426(1) Code of Criminal Procedure; Article 95(1) Administrative Criminal Law Act).

The fixed fine procedure is also anonymous. This means that the fine is not registered in the national criminal database or anywhere else.

The fixed fine procedure, however, merely supplements the procedural rules for minor contraventions contained in the Code of Criminal Procedure. That means: defendants may either explicitly or implicitly (by not paying the fine) reject the fine. If they do so, the Code of Criminal Procedure applies: the defendants receive a summary penalty order from the cantonal criminal prosecution authority (see above section III.A.) or the cantonal administrative authority (see below III.C), which they can reject and in that case it will be submitted to an ordinary court, as explained above.[52]

C. Criminal Law Prosecuted and Adjudicated by Administrative Authorities

The Confederation and the cantons may delegate the prosecution and adjudication of contraventions to administrative authorities (Article 17 Code of Criminal Procedure). This was already possible before the Swiss Code of Criminal Procedure entered into force and thus allows the state to maintain the historically-grown organisation of authorities in the cantons. If prosecuting and adjudicating of contraventions is delegated to administrative authorities, the simplified contravention proceeding – which is very similar to the summary penalty order procedure (above section III.A.(ii)) – applies (Article 357 Code of Criminal Procedure). In Zurich, for example, the *Statthalteramt* prosecutes and adjudicates contraventions;[53] that is, it issues summary penalty orders that may be rejected by the defendant, whereupon the case is submitted to a court of first

[51] S Maeder, 'Sicherheit durch Gebühren?' *Aktuelle Juristische Praxis* 2014, pp 680 et seq; BGE 135 IV 221.
[52] A Petrig and N Zurkinden, *Swiss Criminal Law* (Zurich, Dike, 2015) p 48.
[53] bezirke.zh.ch/internet/justiz_inneres/stha/de/bezirke/informationen_ueber_die_bezirke/statthalteramt/strafrechtspflege.html (accessed on 7 July 2019).

instance if the authority that issued the summary penalty order decides to stand by it (Articles 355 and 356 Code of Criminal Procedure).[54] The simplified contravention proceeding is in line with the judicial guarantees granted by the Swiss Constitution and Article 6(1) ECHR (right to a fair trial before an independent and impartial tribunal), given that the defendant can access a court competent to review all questions of fact and law.[55]

D. Federal Administrative Criminal Law

(i) Prosecuted and Adjudicated by Federal Administrative Authorities

As mentioned above (section II.D.), federal administrative criminal law is secondary criminal law that is prosecuted and adjudicated by federal administrative authorities. These are, for example, the tax authorities where infringement of tax legislation is concerned, or Swissmedic where infringement of legislation regarding medicinal products is concerned.

(ii) Administrative Criminal Law Procedure

The majority of administrative criminal law cases are dealt with by summary penalty orders or rulings that are issued by the relevant administrative authority. Defendants affected by the summary penalty order may request judicial review (Article 21(2) Administrative Criminal Law Act). The administrative authority issues summary penalty orders when the authority is satisfied it has sufficient proof of the criminal responsibility of the defendant, and provided that the governing ministry considers that the conditions for imprisonment are not met (Article 62(1) read together with Article 21(1) Administrative Criminal Law Act). (If the results of the investigation show that the offender may be liable to imprisonment, the administrative authority concludes its investigation and then submits the case to the cantonal criminal court of first instance.)[56]

The administrative authority fixes the sentence, which the defendant may either accept or reject within 30 days (Article 67(1) Administrative Criminal Law Act). If the administrative authority decides to stand by the summary penalty order despite its rejection by the offender, the administrative authority issues a ruling containing the sentence (Article 70 Administrative Criminal Law Act). The defendant again may either accept or reject it, having 10 days to reject the ruling. If the ruling is rejected, the matter will be dealt with under the ordinary procedure by the competent cantonal criminal court of first instance (Article 73 Administrative Criminal Law Act). By rejecting the

[54] A Petrig and N Zurkinden, *Swiss Criminal Law* (Zurich, Dike, 2015) p 48.

[55] R Hauser and E Schweri and K Hartmann, *Schweizerisches Strafprozessrecht*, 6th edn (Basel, Helbing & Lichtenhahn, 2005) pp 433–34; A Petrig and N Zurkinden, *Swiss Criminal Law* (Zurich, Dike, 2015) p 48; ECtHR 29 April 1988, App No 10328/83, *Belilos v Switzerland*, §§ 61–73.

[56] A Eicker, 'Einführung ins materielle und formelle Verwaltungsstrafrecht' in A Eicker (ed), *Aktuelle Herausforderungen für die Praxis im Verwaltungsstrafverfahren, Tagungsband* (Berne, Stämpfli, 2013) pp 19 et seq.

ruling the defendant risks (as do the defendants who reject a summary penalty order [see above section III.A.2]) having to pay the procedural costs of the ordinary procedure, if they are convicted by the criminal court. Furthermore, the court is not bound by the penalty of the administrative authority's ruling (or the summary penalty order) for punishment. Thus defendants who reject a ruling also risk more severe penalties. What is more, cases tried under the ordinary procedure before the criminal courts are public.

During the investigation conducted by the administrative authorities (eg, Swissmedic), fundamental fair trial rights such as the presumption of innocence, the right to be informed, access to the files, the right to have a defence lawyer present (the latter, however, not for the first hearing, Article 39(3) Administrative Criminal Law Act[57]), the right to participate in investigative acts (eg, inspections or interrogations of witnesses), as well as the right to suggest further evidence taking, are guaranteed.[58] Time and expense are saved by not having a trial before court.

IV. Administrative Procedure

Particularly in the case of road traffic offences (eg, overtaking on the right on the motorway and causing danger to the safety of others), one offence may trigger both criminal and an administrative proceedings.[59] The administrative authority conducts the administrative proceedings. The administrative sanction might be a withdrawal of the offender's driving licence for three months as a 'warning' (*Warnungsentzug*). In Switzerland, such withdrawal of the driving licence is imposed upon a person who has culpably infringed road traffic legislation and has already received criminal punishment for the same conduct. One could say the sanction is a 'collateral consequence' triggered by a criminal conviction. Administrative sanctions such as the withdrawal of the driving licence are not labelled 'criminal sanctions'. They primarily have an educational and preventive purpose – as opposed to a punitive and deterrent purpose: the overall goal is to secure road safety. Nevertheless, the Swiss courts acknowledged that withdrawing a driving licence as a warning is similar in nature to a punishment because the withdrawal is pronounced on the basis of a traffic rule violation committed intentionally or negligently (Article 16(2) and (3) of the Road Traffic Act), its duration depends primarily on the severity of the fault and recidivism can lead to much longer withdrawal periods (eg, Article 16b(2)(e) Road Traffic Act[60]). Furthermore, the withdrawal of a driver's licence

[57] This is criticised by scholars. For example by M Thommen, *Kurzer Prozess – fairer Prozess?* (Berne, Stämpfli, 2013) pp 78 et seq.

[58] A Eicker and F Frank and J Achermann, *Verwaltungsstrafrecht und Verwaltungsstrafverfahrensrecht* (Bern, Stämpfli, 2012) pp 149 et seq and pp 160 et seq; F Frank, 'Zur Verteidigung im Verwaltungsstrafverfahren – Wissenswertes und Ungeklärtes' in A Eicker (ed), *Aktuelle Herausforderungen für die Praxis im Verwaltungsstrafverfahren, Tagungsband* (Berne, Stämpfli, 2013) pp 141 et seq; J Natterer Gartmann, 'Rechte und Pflichten des Beschuldigten im Verwaltungsstrafverfahren' in A Eicker (ed.), *Verwaltungsstrafrecht im Wandel* (Berne, Stämpfli, 2017) pp 103 et seq.

[59] C Riedo and G Fiolka and MA Niggli, *Strafprozessrecht* (Basel, Helbing & Lichtenhahn, 2011) pp 5–6, paras 15–20.

[60] Article 16b(2)(e) Road Traffic Act reads: 'Following an offence of medium severity, the driving licence is withdrawn for an indefinite period, but at least for two years, if the licence has been withdrawn three times in the preceding ten years for at least offences of medium severity [...].' (Author's translation).

is also pursued for punitive (not only preventive) purposes and has a drastic effect on the person concerned.[61] As a consequence Article 6 of the ECHR applies to the withdrawal procedure and the person affected has a right to a public hearing.[62]

The principle of *ne bis in idem*, however, does not apply according to the Swiss Federal Supreme Court because two different authorities with different and each with limited decision-making competences are imposing two different sanctions: the public prosecutor imposes, for example, a monetary penalty but has no authority to withdraw the driving licence, while the administrative authority imposes the withdrawal of the driving licence but has no authority to impose criminal punishments that are provided for in the penal provisions of the Road Traffic Act (Articles 90 et seq). In this respect, the competence of the two authorities deciding the legal consequences of the same offence is always limited: each authority has at its disposal a distinct range of sanctions that do not overlap.[63] This view was supported by the ECtHR in *Rivard v Switzerland*. In that case, the Court emphasised that the missing overlap of sanctions is what distinguishes the circumstances from those of *Sergueï Zolotoukhine v Russia*.[64] Furthermore, it stressed that the Swiss administrative authorities may depart from the criminal judgment only under certain restrictive conditions, for example, findings of fact unknown to the criminal judge. Consequently, there is a link between the proceedings such that the conclusions of one of them have a direct impact on the possible outcomes of the other. The principle of coordination of criminal and administrative procedures is thus applied. Therefore, the withdrawal of the licence in question is similar to a punishment additional to the criminal conviction (the ECtHR refers in particular to *Nilsson v Sweden*,[65] *Maszni v Roumania*,[66] and *Boman v Finland*[67]).[68]

V. Conclusion

In practice, only a minority of the cases in which an accused is sentenced to less than six months of imprisonment are brought before a court – regardless of whether they concern core, secondary or administrative criminal law offences. Such offences are rather dealt with by summary penalty orders and are often accepted by the defendants. With summary penalty orders, the case is not heard in a public, direct and adversarial hearing; that is, no (impartial) judges will establish the facts of the case by hearing

[61] BGE 121 II 22, consideration 3.b).
[62] BGE 121 II 22, consideration 4.d); BGE 133 II 331, consideration 4.2.
[63] BGE 125 II 402, consideration 1.b); 137 I 363, consideration 2.3.2.
[64] ECtHR 10 February 2009, App no 14939/03, *Sergueï Zolotoukhine v Russia*.
[65] ECtHR 13 December 2005, App no 73661/01, *Nilsson v Sweden*.
[66] ECtHR 21 September 2006, App no 59892/00, *Maszni v Roumania*.
[67] ECtHR 17 February 2015, App no 41604/11, *Boman v Finland*.
[68] ECtHR 4 October 2016, App no 21563/12, *Rivard v Switzerland*, §§ 31–34. See for a discussion of *Rivard v Switzerland* and further Swiss literature on the issue: M Schorro, 'Strafverfahren und Administrativmassnahmeverfahren als Teile eines einheitlichen Systems', *forumpoenale* 3/2017, pp 184–89.

the prosecutor and the defendant. The facts of the case are rather established in non-public (Article 69(3)(d) Code of Criminal Procedure) preliminary proceedings by the prosecutors.[69] The more proceedings are completed by a summary penalty order, the fewer ordinary proceedings there are. This increases the efficiency and offence completion rate of the prosecution authorities.[70] Such efficiency increase was explicitly stated as a reason for adopting summary penalty orders in the unified Code of Criminal Procedure that entered into force on 1 January 2011.[71] In fact the summary penalty order was said to be the most effective form of simplification of procedures.[72] Furthermore, there is a tendency to apply the (even simpler and faster) fixed fine procedure to more and more contraventions (ie offences punishable by fines only). In fixed fine proceedings the decision imposing a fine becomes final as soon as the fine is paid. If the defendant does not pay the fine, the case is submitted to the public prosecutor who may issue a summary penalty order or dismiss the case.

One could ask why defendants often accept fixed fine procedures and summary penalty orders.

The advantages of the fixed fine procedure are that it is quick and free of additional cost for the defendant (Article 7 Fixed Fine Act). The latter is – as a general rule – not the case for the other procedures discussed here. In those cases, as a rule, defendants must pay procedural costs if they are convicted (Article 426(1) Code of Criminal Procedure; Article 95(1) Administrative Criminal Law Act). The fixed fine procedure is also anonymous. This means that the fine is not registered in the national criminal database or anywhere else.

The summary penalty procedure spares the defendant from public court hearings and the costs that come with court hearings. Most defendants do not object to summary penalty orders. While one can argue that this means they accepted the punishment for an offence they committed, one may just as well argue that they might not have understood the content of the summary penalty order or their rights to object, or that they simply did not want to risk a public court hearing, a more severe punishment (the court is not bound by the punishment that was set in the summary penalty order) and higher procedural costs. It is thus for good reasons rather shocking for lawyers of other countries that in Switzerland most criminal and administrative criminal convictions result from so-called summary penalty orders – particularly because such orders are issued by the prosecuting authority in a preliminary proceeding.

Especially in road traffic cases defendants are furthermore often not aware of the consequences of accepting a summary penalty order (even if they feel, and maybe are, innocent but just pay the monetary penalty anyhow to get things off the table). They often do not take into consideration that by accepting the summary penalty order the 'collateral consequence' of the withdrawal of their driving licence as a 'warning' may be triggered. Under Swiss law this is an administrative sanction because of its educational

[69] M Thommen, *Kurzer Prozess – fairer Prozess?* (Berne, Stämpfli, 2013) p 323.

[70] M Thommen, *Kurzer Prozess – fairer Prozess?* (Berne, Stämpfli, 2013) pp 46, 233.

[71] Botschaft zur Vereinheitlichung des Strafprozessrechts vom 21. Dezember 2005, BBl 2006 1085, 1111.

[72] Bericht der Expertenkommission 'Vereinheitlichung des Strafprozessrechts', *Aus 29, mach 1. Konzept einer eidgenössischen Strafprozessordnung*, Berne 1997, p 153.

and preventive purpose (as opposed to the punitive and deterrent purposes of criminal sanctions). However, having one's driving licence withdrawn arguably feels like the even more severe punishment for the convicted person. While Article 6 of the ECHR applies to the withdrawal procedure, the ECtHR does not see a violation of the *ne bis in idem* principle.

3

Quasi-criminal Enforcement Mechanisms in Germany: Past and Present

DOMINIK BRODOWSKI

I. Introduction

> The investigation and judgment of all crimes really belongs to the criminal jurisdiction, independent of whether these crimes are large or small – and that is what the Roman jurists had specified. The Germans, however, by differentiating between bloody and non-bloody wounds, have caused very much turmoil.[1]

This quotation originating in 1786 shows how deeply rooted different enforcement mechanisms are in Germany. Before undertaking a more critical discussion of the present situation and its theoretical underpinnings, I will first set the scene by providing an historic overview, beginning with the dark ages of criminal justice in Germany and continuing up to today, where the *Ordnungswidrigkeitenrecht* as *the* legislative alternative to criminal sanctioning more or less also serves as a functional equivalent to corporate criminal liability (section II. below). On this basis, I will analyse common features of this regulatory offence-based enforcement mechanism[2] and its actual and alleged predecessors, in particular its expansion, its flexibility, its efficiency, and its transformative power: as the German scholar Heinz Mattes critically pointed out, such alternative legislative models may especially be found when an old legal order is replaced, or supplemented by a new legal order;[3] over time, as James Goldschmidt argued, quasi-criminal enforcement mechanisms tend to find their way into the core of criminal law

[1] JJ Cella, as cited in J Goldschmidt, *Das Verwaltungsstrafrecht* (Berlin, Carl Heymanns, 1902) 139 (author's own translation): 'Eigentlich gehöret zur Kriminaljurisdiktion die Untersuchung und Bestrafung aller Verbrechen, sie mögen so gross und so klein sein, als sie wollen, und so hatten auch die römischen Rechtsgelehrten die Sache festgesetzt. Die Teutschen haben aber mit ihrem Unterschied unter blutrünstigen und nicht blutrünstigen Wunden die Sache sehr verwirret.'

[2] For alternatives *within* criminal justice and alternatives *to* criminal (and quasi-criminal) justice, see D Brodowski, 'Alternative Enforcement Mechanisms in Germany' in M Dyson and B Vogel (eds), *The Limits of Criminal Law* (Cambridge, Intersentia, 2018) 365 ff and below section III.B.

[3] Cf H Mattes, *Untersuchungen zur Lehre von den Ordnungswidrigkeiten. Erster Halbband: Geschichte und Rechtsvergleichung* (Berlin, Duncker Humblot, 1977) 41.

(section III.A.).[4] Then, I will provide a brief overview on other quasi-criminal or alternative enforcement mechanisms beyond the *Ordnungswidrigkeitenrecht* (section III.B.). On a more theoretical level, I will continue to discuss the different so-called qualitative and quantitative theories proposed in Germany to distinguish criminal law from the *Ordnungswidrigkeitenrecht* (section IV.), and finally set out the conclusions of this contribution (section V.).

II. Background, Core Features, and Current Trends of the Act on Regulatory Offences[5]

In the German legal order of today, the Act on Regulatory Offences (*Ordnungswidrigkeitengesetz* – OWiG)[6] provides for a comprehensive and extensive legal framework for quasi-criminal enforcement. It is applicable in a wide range of contexts ranging from road traffic law to cartel law (below at section II.D.). Imprisonment is not at stake for violations of regulatory offences. Instead, its default sanction is a specific form of monetary penalty, a so-called 'regulatory fine' (*Geldbuße*). This aspect is, however, only one of several distinctions when compared to the separate but intertwined 'classic' criminal law[7] governed by the German Criminal Code (*Strafgesetzbuch* – StGB) and the German Code of Criminal Procedure (*Strafprozessordnung* – StPO). The tales on the historical roots of this Act on Regulatory Offences differ, but should nonetheless be told to provide an overarching picture of the features and theoretical underpinnings of quasi-criminal enforcement in Germany.

A. Regulatory Offence-Based Enforcement from the Dark Ages to the Modern Era?

Some scholars – especially Goldschmidt – trace a distinction between regulatory and criminal offences back to the Frankish Empire, specifically to the banning powers of the kings of old, as they consider these powers to be responses to regulatory matters but not to legal wrongdoing.[8] Other scholars point out, however, that such a distinction was an alien concept to those times, as the king and his actions were seen as a source of

[4] J Goldschmidt, *Das Verwaltungsstrafrecht* (Berlin, Carl Heymanns, 1902) 7.

[5] As I am no legal historian myself, I rely heavily on secondary sources on the historical developments of quasi-criminal enforcement in Germany, in particular the treatises by Mattes (n 3) and Goldschmidt (n 4).

[6] Gesetz über Ordnungswidrigkeiten, as amended. An English version is provided by the German Ministry for Justice and Consumer Protection at: www.gesetze-im-internet.de/englisch_owig/index.html. For coherence with other English-language publications on German criminal law, I will rely on this translation and the terminology used therein wherever possible.

[7] German terminology also uses the term '*Kriminalstrafrecht*' – a term which cannot be translated into English ('criminal criminal law') – to distinguish 'proper' criminal law from the legal regime formed by the Act on Regulatory Offences.

[8] Goldschmidt (n 4) 1 ff.

law, and the only differentiation known back then distinguished between high crimes and misdemeanours, and the people or bodies responsible for adjudicating when these crimes were alleged.[9]

In medieval towns, villages, and settlements, local authorities – be it the chief farmer (*Bauermeister*) or town councillors – increasingly were given and utilised powers to enact local police statutes (*Polizeiordnungen*) and to adjudicate on violations of these laws.[10] These powers reflected the struggle between local (partial) autonomy and the territorial rulers.[11] Local governance – combining what we now differentiate into legislative, executive and adjudicatory powers – covered topics such as minor assault, fraud (market manipulation), and theft offences, as well as other matters of local security.[12] Speaking more broadly, these statutes were a flexible tool to address specific and new aspects of living closely together in a town or settlement.[13] Sentencing powers, however, excluded – at least – the death penalty, and were largely limited to monetary punishment.[14]

At the beginning of the modern era, the (largely failed) attempt to strengthen German unification in the so-called Holy Roman Empire lead to a unified imperial police statute (*Reichspoliceyordnung*) in 1530, amended in 1548 and 1577.[15] It was not a mere summary of previous case law, but indeed the (first?) attempt at a codification of a 'criminal' statute in this territory[16] and preceded the major criminal law statute of that time, the *Constitutio Criminalis Carolina*, by two years. While the 'historic' crimes were included in the penal code *Constitutio Criminalis Carolina*, 'new' crimes enacted in more recent years in local and regional police statutes mostly found their way into the imperial police statute.[17] The imperial police statute 'was created in reaction to social problems of a rapidly changing societal reality',[18] and was amended and supplemented rapidly in the following years.[19] At least in some areas, both the penal code and the imperial police statute were closely intertwined, and both addressed (c)ommissions and harms deemed to be intolerable for public order.[20]

The evolvement of absolutism led to the creation of new and strengthened 'administrative' structures within the German states. Only similar in bearing the label of 'policing' and quite distinct from the modern concept of German police law,[21]

[9] Mattes (n 3) 39 ff.

[10] Mattes (n 3) 42 ff, 44 ff.

[11] Mattes (n 3) 45, 50.

[12] Mattes (n 3) 43, 45.

[13] Mattes (n 3) 45.

[14] Mattes (n 3) 42, 49 f.

[15] K Härter, 'Entwicklung und Funktion der Policeygesetzgebung des Heiligen Römischen Reiches Deutscher Nation im 16. Jahrhundert' (1993) 20 *Ius Commune* 61, 61 f.

[16] Härter (n 15) 62.

[17] Mattes (n 3) 52.

[18] Härter (n 15) 66 (author's own translation): 'entstanden in Reaktion auf gesellschaftliche und soziale Probleme einer sich rasch verändernden sozialen Wirklichkeit'.

[19] Härter (n 15) 86 ff; K Härter, 'Policeygesetzgebung und Strafrecht: Criminalpoliceyliche Ordnungsdiskurse und Strafjustiz im frühneuzeitlichen Alten Reich' in S Kesper-Biermann and D Klippel (eds), *Kriminalität im Mittelalter und Früher Neuzeit* (Wiesbaden, Harrasowitz Verlag, 2007) 189, 195 ff.

[20] Mattes (n 3) 52 ff; Härter (n 15) 63; Härter (n 19) 193 f.

[21] See Brodowski (n 2) 385 for an outline of current police law in Germany and its intertwinement with criminal justice.

authorities executed and upheld the monarch's absolute sovereignty by enacting police criminal laws (*Polizeistrafrecht*), enforcing, *and* sanctioning violations of them.[22]

It is still unclear whether these various forms of 'police' or 'policing' statutes may actually be considered to be a predecessor of current regulatory offences, and to what extent these bodies of law and their enforcement should be seen as distinct from the criminal justice of old.[23] The terminology is – at best – unclear, as the labelling as *police* powers back then referred to public order in general,[24] and the imperial police statute contained offences labelled as *criminal*.[25] A hierarchy of different forms or types of offences did not exist.[26] A separation into (criminal) justice on the one side, and regulation or administration on the other side was evolving, at first, only slowly.[27] In any case, these approaches provided for more flexibility both in defining illegal conduct *and* with regard to sanctioning, compared to the historical penal order.[28]

It would be too superficial to conclude that traditional modes of criminal sanctioning existed for violations of natural rights of human beings, and police statutes for the protection and infringement of public welfare, though such attempts to rationalise a distinction occurred later on (see below at section IV.A.).[29] Instead, these police statutes may be better described as a supplement to traditional criminal law.[30] On the one hand, this supplement provided for a flexible and accessible alternative within criminal justice, slowing down a transformation of the historical criminal justice (such as its thorough codification) and its adaption to modern times.[31] On the other hand, the police statutes eventually led to some transformative changes in the 'historic' criminal justice,[32] for example relating to an increasingly inquisitorial trial format, and to flexibility in sanctioning,[33] either when 'historic' criminal justice deferred questions to local authorities,[34] or when an extensive re-codification of 'historic' criminal justice could not be avoided any longer.[35] Therefore, the evolution of modern criminal justice and some of its core features may well be traced to local, regional, and imperial police powers.

B. Evolving Modern Criminal Justice and a Quest for '*Nulla Poena Sine Iudicio*'

At the beginning of the eighteenth Century, as a result of the Age of Enlightenment, demands to limit state powers and to add checks and balances became widespread.

[22] Mattes (n 3) 61 ff; D Klesczewski, *Ordnungswidrigkeitenrecht*, 2nd edn (Munich, Vahlen, 2016) 23 ff.
[23] See, in particular, Mattes (n 3) 44 ff, on the one hand, and, on the other hand, Goldschmidt (n 4) 70 ff.
[24] Klesczewski (n 22) 22.
[25] Härter (n 19) 193.
[26] Härter (n 19) 205.
[27] Härter (n 19) 192; see also Klesczewski (n 22) 22 f; but see Mattes (n 3) 60 f.
[28] Härter (n 19) 205.
[29] See the extensive analysis by Mattes (n 3) 109 ff.
[30] Compare Mattes (n 3) 41.
[31] Härter (n 19) 210.
[32] Goldschmidt (n 4) 7; see also Mattes (n 3) 50, 57.
[33] Härter (n 19) 206 ff.
[34] Härter (n 19) 206 f.
[35] Compare Mattes (n 3) 92 ff.

This not only led to the safeguard that only the legislature could enact criminal statutes ('*nullum crimen, nulla poena sine crimen parlamentaria*'), but also to a demand that all sentencing powers should rest with an (independent) judiciary and not with the administration ('*nulla poena sine iudicio*').[36] This culminated in § 182(2) of the Frankfurt Constitution (*Paulskirchenverfassung*), which failed in its attempt to withhold any criminal jurisdiction from the police and administration.[37] In practice, therefore, the administration retained – at least at a minor level and up to 1851 – limited sanctioning powers, or even expanded their powers, as more and more German states codified police statutes.[38]

Theorists and legislature alike debated heavily whether there is a practical need for separating criminal justice on the one hand, and regulatory, administrative, or police offences on the other hand, and how to distinguish them materially.[39] In particular, some tried to keep the new criminal codes in German states 'pure' to 'true' criminal wrongdoing, and govern menial transgressions in special police statutes (see below at section IV.A.). In particular, the enactment of the Prussian Criminal Code (1851) and of the German Empire Criminal Code (*Reichsstrafgesetzbuch*) – which still forms the basis of the current German Criminal Code – only clarified the situation temporarily. It contained a tripartite structure of felonies (*Verbrechen*), misdemeanours (*Vergehen*), and transgressions (*Übertretungen*), and tried to incorporate or transform all pre-existing police offences as minor but clearly *criminal* offences. The maximum sentence for these transgressions was, at first, a monetary fine of 150 *Reichsmark* or six weeks' imprisonment.[40] Later on, this tripartite differentiation became inconsistent not only in relation to maximum penalties. On the procedural side, the German Empire Code of Criminal Procedure (*Reichsstrafprozessordnung*) of 1877 primarily referred the adjudication and sentencing of these transgressions by local courts. However, it allowed German states to provide for a police penalty order (*polizeiliche Strafverfügung*) for transgressions in their state laws – an opportunity which was widely utilised. Appeals against police penalty orders led to ordinary criminal proceedings (§§ 453 ff RStPO 1877). In view of this police penalty order, the attempts to fully exclude the administration from 'criminal' sanctioning failed – at least at first.

In Nazi Germany, regulation by direct administrative enforcement mechanisms – excluding any judicial or pseudo-judicial oversight – expanded radically. Therefore, police penalty orders, which had become one important tool for radicalisation, were abolished soon after the end of World War II in the British and American Zones of Occupation, and soon thereafter in Western Germany altogether. These police penalty orders were seen as incompatible with fundamental rights, as the administration must not be able to decide on *criminal* sanctions including (short-term) imprisonment.[41] From then on, adjudication and sentencing for transgressions (*Übertretungen*) could

[36] Mattes (n 3) 85 ff.

[37] W Mitsch, 'Einleitung' in W Mitsch (ed), *Karlsruher Kommentar zum Gesetz über Ordnungswidrigkeiten*, 5th edn (Munich, CH Beck, 2018) 4.

[38] Mattes (n 3) 93, 100 f.

[39] Mitsch (n 37) 4.

[40] Klesczewski (n 22) 26; Mitsch (n 37) 6; Mattes (n 3) 102.

[41] BGBl. 1950 I, 455, 629; see further Mattes (n 3) 104.

only take place in court. Notably, however, it was partly the administration (and not the public prosecution offices) which presented the case to the court.[42]

Partly owing to the overburdening of the criminal justice system (an exception to the *Legalitätsprinzip*, which states that all crimes have to be prosecuted and adjudicated, was only introduced in 1924, and was of limited use back then), partly owing to the inflexibility of criminal justice, a new and distinct enforcement mechanism was gaining traction already in the 1920s. Administrative bodies became competent to adjudicate and sanction specific offences and hand out (non- or quasi-criminal) fines labelled '*Ordnungsstrafen*' (rough translation: order-related punishment). At first, these offences related to areas such as tax law, securities law, and the law on emigration. They could be handed out in parallel with criminal sanctions, and were of only marginal importance compared to criminal law transgressions until 1933.[43] A notable particularity of this special sanctioning regime was its application to legal persons. Such sanctions could be handed out against legal as well as natural persons, first based on case law, and from 1939 onward also based on the written law.[44] The first such statutory basis related to offences against state-set prices for goods.[45] In contrast, the concept of corporate criminal liability is still alien to 'classic' German criminal justice up to today. The provisions on *Ordnungsstrafen* and their practical application were expanded greatly in Nazi Germany, in particular in relation to rationing and the management of scarce resources, likely due to the technicality of the provisions and the need for a flexible tool to sanction violations of these provisions. As the economic crisis continued after 1945, many of these rules were kept in force or even amended by or on behalf of the post-War occupying authorities.[46]

C. The Post-WWII Era of Regulatory Offence-based Enforcement

Early in the post-WWII era, the term *Ordnungswidrigkeit* (rough translation: violation of order) and a coherent, partly independent body of law on regulatory offences was created. Its starting point was the Economic Offences Act of 1949 (*Wirtschaftsstrafgesetz* – WiStG), which aimed at strengthening the rule of law by converting the *Ordnungsstrafen* (expressing *sanctioning*) to *Ordnungswidrigkeiten* (merely reflecting the transgression of the law), and which completely reformed the investigation and adjudication procedure.[47] A famous generic rule first framed by Eberhard Schmidt[48]

[42] Cf Mattes (n 3) 104; Mitsch (n 37) 31.

[43] Cf H Achenbach, 'Ahndung materiell sozialschädlichen Verhaltens durch bloße Geldbuße? Zur Entwicklung und Problematik "großer" Wirtschafts-Ordnungswidrigkeiten' (2008) 155 *Goltdammer's Archiv für Strafrecht* 1, 3; HH Jescheck, 'Die strafrechtliche Verantwortlichkeit der Personenverbände' (1953) 65 *Zeitschrift für die gesamte Strafrechtswissenschaft* 210, 215 f; Mitsch (n 37) 16 ff.

[44] Jescheck (n 43) 215; K Rogall, '§ 30' in W Mitsch (ed), *Karlsruher Kommentar zum Gesetz über Ordnungswidrigkeiten*, 5th edn (Munich, CH Beck, 2018) 22.

[45] § 8 (2) Verordnung über Strafen und Strafverfahren bei Zuwiderhandlungen gegen Preisvorschriften (*Preisstrafrechtsverordnung*, RGBl. 1939 I, 999).

[46] Mitsch (n 37) 31; see also E Schmidt, 'Straftaten und Ordnungswidrigkeiten. Erinnerungen an die Arbeiten der Wirtschaftsstrafrechtskommission (1947–1949)' in H Ehmke, C Schmid and H Scharoun, *Festschrift für Adolf Arndt* (Frankfurt a.M., Europäische Verlagsanstalt, 1969) 418 f.

[47] E Schmidt, 'Probleme des Wirtschaftsstrafrechts' (1948) 3 *Süddeutsche Juristen-Zeitung* 225, 228; Mitsch (n 37) 33.

[48] Schmidt (n 47) 225, 230 ff, in particular 236.

and enacted in § 6 WiStG 1949 determined whether a specific case of transgressing §§ 7 to 21 WiStG 1949 (relating to managing the scarce resources in the post-WWII world) was a criminal or a regulatory offence (a so-called 'mixture provision'). A specific violation was qualified to be a criminal offence if and only if it violated 'wholly or in part the state interest in continuing and preserving the economic order', as it was either 'able, by its extent or by its effect, to impair the productivity of the economic order protected by the state', or as 'the violator expresses, by committing the act, an attitude of disobedience against the economic order protected by the state'.[49] If these conditions were not met, the violation constituted a mere *Ordnungswidrigkeit*, to be prosecuted and adjudicated by administrative authorities (§ 54 [1] WiStG 1949); punishment was then limited to 100,000 DM (§ 29 [1] WiStG 1949). The WiStG 1949 neither contained a general part – meaning it did not set out rules on questions such as intent, mistake of law or of facts, attempt, participation or justification – nor did it transform previous criminal law transgressions to *Ordnungswidrigkeiten*.

In 1952, the legislature transferred the procedural provisions of the WiStG 1949[50] into a separate Act on Regulatory Offences (*Gesetz über Ordnungswidrigkeiten* 1952),[51] and modified them slightly. Aside from 'mixture provisions' such as § 6 WiStG 1949 which continued[52] to apply until the end of 1974,[53] the term used by the legislature in the wording of a statute became decisive as to whether a transgression was an *Ordnungswidrigkeit* or a criminal offence: If it provided for a regulatory fine (*Geldbuße*), it was an *Ordnungswidrigkeit*; if it provided for a criminal fine (*Geldstrafe*) and/or imprisonment, it was a criminal offence. Sentencing powers under the Act of Regulatory Offences were limited to a fine of 1,000 DM, unless otherwise specified by law (§ 5 OWiG 1952). The Act clearly stated that *Ordnungswidrigkeiten* should only be prosecuted and adjudicated if there was a public interest in doing so (§ 7 [2] OWiG 1952), in stark contrast to the principle of mandatory prosecution upheld in German criminal procedure which means that *all* crimes need to be investigated thoroughly and be brought to judgment.

The new, yet still evolving framework for regulatory offence-based enforcement and monetary penalties provided for an increased flexibility compared to the more slowly moving 'classic' criminal justice. For instance, the Act on Regulatory Offences contained a rule on mistake of law (§ 12 OWiG 1952) which the German Criminal Code was at that time missing. Procedural flexibility resulted from tasking the administration with the investigation and issuance of the formal administrative decision labelled *Bußgeldbescheid* including a precise sentence (§§ 35 ff OWiG 1952).[54]

[49] See, in more detail, U Sieber, 'Administrative Sanction Law in Germany' in M Dyson and B Vogel (eds), *The Limits of Criminal Law* (Cambridge, Intersentia, 2018) 306.

[50] For follow-up changes to the WiStG, see BGBl. I 1952 I, 188, 189 ff.

[51] BGBl. 1952 I, 177. For a detailed description and analysis of the time, see E Gerner, 'Das Gesetz über Ordnungswidrigkeiten' (1952) 5 *Neue Juristische Wochenschrift* 521 ff; E Schmidt, 'Straftaten und Ordnungswidrigkeiten' (1951) 1 *Juristenzeitung* 101 ff.

[52] The 'mixture provision' in § 6 WiStG 1949 later on became § 3 WiStG 1954, see BGBl. I 1954, 175.

[53] On the changes to the WiStG, see G Dähn, 'Das neugefaßte Wirtchaftsstrafgesetz' (1975) 30 *Juristenzeitung* 617, 617. The 'mixture provision' was abolished by Art. 149 EGStGB 1974 (Introductory Act to the German Criminal Code, BGBl 1974 I, 469) – the same Act which removed transgressions from the field of criminal law (see below section II.D.(i).).

[54] These features were upheld in later reforms of the OWiG and are explained more extensively below in section II.D.(ii).

In the following years, this new framework was widely used to create new offences, and to transform or 'de-criminalise' some criminal law transgressions (see above at section II.B.) into *Ordnungswidrigkeiten*. New criminal law transgressions (*Übertretungen*) were only rarely enacted, as *Ordnungswidrigkeiten* were considered to be a more apt, flexible and efficient approach, and as more and more calls to abolish transgressions altogether could be heard.[55] However, the continuing overlap between transgressions (in the domain of criminal law) and *Ordnungswidrigkeiten* (in the domain of quasi- or non-criminal law) posed an increasing problem.

D. The Basis for Quasi-criminal Enforcement in Germany Today

(i) *Historical Development*

In 1968, the Act on Regulatory Offences was re-enacted,[56] but the academic attention paid to quasi-criminal enforcement in Germany remained limited, due to the heated debates on the extensive reform of the German Criminal Code going on at that time. The OWiG 1968 contained, for the first time, extensive rules on the general part, including distinct rules on participation, jurisdiction, as well as on sentencing in case of multiple transgressions (§§ 3 ff OWiG 1968). It was applicable to all statutes that stated that a specific, unlawful (c)ommission may carry punishment by a regulatory fine or *Geldbuße* (§ 1 [1] OWiG 1968; as distinct from the criminal law-based *Geldstrafe*). It thus continued the formalistic distinction and deference to the legislature already found in the predecessors of this Act.[57]

At the same time, the Introductory Act on Regulatory Offences of 1968[58] converted most (except for the most severe) road traffic transgressions (previously part of criminal law, see above section II.B.) to *Ordnungswidrigkeiten*. Since then, road traffic violations have constituted the quantitatively most important area of *Ordnungswidrigkeiten*;[59] more generally speaking, regulatory offence-based enforcement became *the* mechanism for addressing minor, frequently occurring offences or, to put it in different terms, for offences committed by the masses.[60]

A few years later, in the major criminal law reform of 1974, transgressions were removed altogether from criminal law, with existing transgressions converted to misdemeanours, 'de-criminalised' to *Ordnungswidrigkeiten* (in particular in §§ 111 ff OWiG, but also in a multitude of specific laws and statutes), or abolished altogether.[61]

[55] Mitsch (n 37) 38; F Gürtler, H Seitz and M Bauer, 'Einleitung' in E Göhler (original author), *Gesetz über Ordnungswidrigkeiten*, 17th edn (Munich, CH Beck, 2017) 10.

[56] BGBl 1968 I, 481. For a detailed description and analysis of the time, see E Göhler, 'Das neue Gesetz über Ordnungswidrigkeiten' (1968) 23 *Juristenzeitung* 583 ff (part 1) and 613 ff (part 2); W Patzig, 'Das Ordnungswidrigkeitenrecht – Rückblick und Ausblick' (1967) 82 *Deutsches Verwaltungsblatt* 309 ff (part 1) and 352 ff (part 2); HJ Bode, 'Grundzüge des neuen Rechts der Ordnungswidrigkeiten' (1968) 21 *Neue Juristische Wochenschrift* 1449 ff.

[57] See further Mitsch (n 37) 41 ff.

[58] BGBl 1968 I, 503.

[59] See further Mitsch (n 37) 43.

[60] Sieber (n 49) 307 f.

[61] Klesczewski (n 22) 28.

Since then, the German Criminal Code has only provided for felonies (*Verbrechen*) and misdemeanours (*Vergehen*). To my knowledge, all criminal statutes of today allow for the possibility of imprisonment (see Article 3 [2] No 1 Einführungsgesetz zum Strafgesetzbuch (EGStGB) 1974[62]), while the threat of imprisonment is an alien concept to the German law of *Ordnungswidrigkeiten*.

Besides extensive formal and some substantive changes to its general part in 1974,[63] and a simplification of judicial proceedings in 1986[64] and in 1998,[65] the Act on Regulatory Offences has remained largely untouched.[66] As will be shown below in further detail, it provides *the* legal basis for a quantitatively extensive,[67] but also qualitatively extensive[68] quasi-criminal enforcement mechanism in Germany today.

(ii) Core Features and Safeguards[69]

(a) General Part; Principles of Liability

As already mentioned above, the Act on Regulatory Offences (OWiG)[70] is applicable to all statutes that state that a specific, unlawful (c)ommission may carry punishment by a fine called a regulatory fine (*Geldbuße*, § 1 [1] OWiG; as distinct from the criminal law-based *Geldstrafe*). The OWiG is structured quite similarly to the German Criminal Code, and partly uses the same words and concepts, but makes significant efforts to avoid the terminology of guilt or culpability (*Schuld*) that is central to German criminal law. Instead, the OWiG uses phrases like 'reprehensible actions' or responsibility (*Vorwerfbarkeit*).[71]

Similarly to the German Criminal Code, the OWiG upholds the guarantees of *nullum crimen sine lege* (§ 3 OWiG) and *lex mitior* (§ 4 OWiG) at the very beginning of the codification; what is more, the constitutional protection of these guarantees by Article 103(2) GG[72] is considered to be equivalent in both the OWiG and the German Criminal

[62] Introductory Act to the German Criminal Code, BGBl 1974 I, 469.

[63] Art 29 EGStGB 1974, BGBl 1974 I, 469.

[64] BGBl 1986 I, 977.

[65] BGBl 1998 I, 156; see J Seier, 'Zur Reform des Ordnungswidrigkeitenrechts' (1996) 9 *Neue Zeitschrift für Verkehrsrecht* 17 ff.

[66] For a detailed analysis of the changes to the Act on Regulatory Offences since 1968, see Gürtler, Seitz and Bauer (n 55) 13 ff; Mitsch (n 37) 44 ff.

[67] See below section II.D.(iv).: there are likely far more than 10 million enforcement decisions per year, compared to around 5 million criminal cases and less than a million persons charged in court.

[68] See below section II.D.(iii). For instance, the Act on Regulatory Offences still serves as Germany's functional equivalent to corporate criminal liability, and can provide for extensive fines which have reached 1 billion €.

[69] See extensively Sieber (n 49) 311.

[70] For a more detailled description on the Act on Regulatory Offences and its provisions, see W Mitsch (ed), *Karlsruher Kommentar zum Gesetz über Ordnungswidrigkeiten*, 5th edn (Munich, CH Beck, 2018); E Göhler (founder), *Gesetz über Ordnungswidrigkeiten*, 18th edn (Munich, CH Beck, 2021); D Klesczewski, *Ordnungswidrigkeitenrecht*, 2nd edn (Munich, Vahlen, 2016); J Bohnert, *Ordnungswidrigkeitengesetz*, 5th edn (Munich, CH Beck, 2018); H Blum, K Gassner and S Seith, *Ordnungswidrigkeitengesetz*, 2nd edn (Baden-Baden, Nomos, 2020); J Bülte, *Ordnungswidrigkeitenrecht*, 6th edn (Munich, CH Beck, 2020); G Rosenkötter, *Das Recht der Ordnungswidrigkeiten*, 7th edn (Stuttgart, Boorberg, 2011).

[71] Sieber (n 49) 313.

[72] Grundgesetz für die Bundesrepublik Deutschland, serving as Germany's constitution. An English version is provided by the German Ministry for Justice and Consumer Protection at www.gesetze-im-internet.de/englisch_gg/index.html.

Code.[73] Further similarities, which were strengthened in the late 1960s and early 1970s when both the German Criminal Code and the OWiG underwent large reforms, extend to the requirement of intent unless negligent behaviour is explicitly mentioned in the offence (§ 10 OWiG), to mistakes of fact and law (§ 11 OWiG), to its non-applicability to persons under 14 years of age (§ 12 OWiG), to attempt (§ 13 OWiG), and to self-defence and necessity (§§ 15 f OWiG).[74] Of more interest are the differences: in contrast to the extensive rules on extra-territorial applicability of the German Criminal Code (§§ 3 ff StGB), the jurisdiction to prescribe generally extends only to the German territory for *Ordnungswidrigkeiten* (§ 5 OWiG). In contrast to the German Criminal Code (§§ 25 ff StGB), there is no differentiation between actors, aiders and abettors; instead *all* persons taking part in an offence are held equally responsible (§ 14 OWiG; concept of uniform perpetratorship[75]), though sentencing decisions may vary depending on the level of individual responsibility. For the prosecution of transgressions, there is only a limited window of opportunity due to a quite strict statute of limitations (§§ 31 ff OWiG). In ordinary cases, prosecution becomes impossible if it has not been formally commenced within six months after the commission of the offence.

(b) Sanctioning

The OWiG only provides for one form of punishment, namely a monetary sanction labelled a regulatory fine (*Geldbuße*). Unless otherwise specified by law, the maximum regulatory fine amounts to 1,000 € (§ 17 [1] OWiG), but may be increased by the economic gain the perpetrators obtained through their offence (§ 17 [4] OWiG),[76] allowing for confiscation being included in the 'regulatory fine'. That feature – a sort of quasi-confiscation regime – must be distinguished from 'normal' confiscation, which is available alternatively under the statute (§ 29a OWiG). The sanctions for multiple independent transgressions are added mathematically together (§ 20 OWiG), unlike the digressive approach taken by the German Criminal Code where a 'combined sentence' (*Gesamtstrafe*) is determined by the court in an overall assessment, and where that *Gesamtstrafe* must be lower than the sum of all penalties (§§ 53, 54 German Criminal Code). And in stark contrast to the German Criminal Code, regulatory fines may be handed out against legal as well as natural persons (§ 30 OWiG).[77] As a so-called incidental consequence, transgressions may additionally lead to confiscation and forfeiture (§§ 22 ff OWiG). This is of particular importance in corporate contexts, where oftentimes such a confiscation measure is imposed independently, barring the prosecution of the corporation (§ 29a [5] OWiG).

(c) Investigation and Prosecution

The investigation and prosecution of regulatory offences rests with the administration (including the police, § 53 OWiG), but generally not with the public prosecution offices

[73] Just see German Federal Constitutional Court, Decision of 4 February 1975 – 2 BvL 5/74 = BVerfGE 38, 348, 371 f.

[74] Sieber (n 49) 312.

[75] Sieber (n 49) 313.

[76] Sieber (n 49) 314.

[77] Sieber (n 49) 314 f.

(§ 35 ff OWiG). However, if there are indications of a crime having been committed, the case file has to be transferred to the public prosecution offices (§§ 41 ff OWiG), as criminal prosecutions take precedence (§§ 21, 42 ff OWiG). Like in standard criminal procedure, the administrative authorities are tasked with a thorough investigation of both inculpating and exculpating elements. Moreover, the same safeguards and limitations as in criminal procedure apply to regulatory offences, including the principle of proportionality, the right to a lawyer (and, in exceptional cases, mandatory defence counsel), 'the presumption of innocence, the right to be heard, [...] and the right [at least] of natural persons to remain silent'.[78] Investigation powers extend in particular to the questioning of witnesses and of the accused, but also to search and seizure as well as minor physical examinations of the accused. By contrast, further-reaching investigation powers – such as interception of post and telecommunications, or undercover operations – are not available (§ 46 OWiG).[79]

The administration enjoys wide discretion in whether to investigate and prosecute regulatory offences (§ 47 [1] OWiG). Instead of a formal prosecution, it may opt for a less formal warning notice and a 'cautionary fine' of up to 55 € in minor cases (such as parking violations). If the offender accepts that 'cautionary fine' and pays it either instantly or within a week, the case is closed immediately (§§ 56 ff OWiG). In contrast, German criminal procedure upholds a strong principle of mandatory prosecution: only once a criminal case has been thoroughly investigated, limited exceptions allow for diversion and non-prosecution (§§ 153 ff StPO).[80]

The investigation ends with a formal administrative decision called a *Bußgeldbescheid* which includes a precise sentencing decision. It must at least include the person addressed, the time, place, and content of the offence, the statute which was breached, and a list of evidence. Beyond these elements, there is no requirement for the reasoning behind the decision (§ 65 f OWiG). If the addressed person (*Betroffener*) does not formally object to this decision within two weeks (§ 67 [1] OWiG), the administrative decision becomes final, and the sentence becomes enforceable (§§ 89 ff OWiG). If the regulatory fine is not paid, and the addressed person does not explain why s/he cannot afford to pay the fine, s/he can be detained temporarily (for up to six weeks) to put pressure on them to either pay up or to explain their inability to comply (§§ 96 f OWiG).

(d) Court Proceedings and Appeal

In case of a formal objection (*Einspruch*), the administration first determines whether that objection has been lodged correctly. If not, it rejects the objection (§ 69 [1] OWiG; the offender may appeal against this rejection to the court). Otherwise, the administration may conduct additional investigations and may either uphold the existing administrative decision or decide to abstain from prosecution (§ 69 [2] OWiG). If it upholds its original decision, it sends the case file to the public prosecution service (§ 69 [3] OWiG). It is then up to the public prosecution service to investigate the case further, to close the prosecution (even against the opinion of the administration), or to

[78] Sieber (n 49) 316.
[79] Sieber (n 49) 316 f.
[80] See, more detailed, Brodowski (n 2) 373 ff; Sieber (n 49) 317.

initiate court proceedings before the local court (*Amtsgericht*) which is also competent in criminal matters.

While the German Code of Criminal Procedure is applicable unless the OWiG specifies otherwise, several provisions of the OWiG lead to a substantial simplification of the court proceedings compared to criminal proceedings. The court may make its decision based on the case file in a written proceeding, unless the affected person or the public prosecution office objects (§ 72 OWiG). The public prosecution office is not required to be present in court (§ 75 OWiG), and the affected person may be released from his/her obligation to attend more easily (§ 73 OWiG). Importantly, the rules on evidence are streamlined: the generic requirement that the court has to determine the merits of the case thoroughly by taking evidence in front of the court is limited by the 'importance of the matter' (§ 77 [1] 2 OWiG). Evidence can be admitted to the proceedings more easily and speedily by reading parts of the case file (§ 77a OWiG). The court may reject requests for the additional taking of evidence if it considers this to be unnecessary in light of what it has already heard (§ 77 [2] OWiG). Last but not least, a reasoning of the court's decision is not required if no appeal has been lodged in time (§ 77b OWiG).[81]

An appeal to the Higher Regional Court – where minor cases are decided by a single judge – is only available in non-minor cases (such as for fines exceeding 250 €) and may only address matters of law (including evidence-taking), but not the factual basis of the decision (§§ 79 ff OWiG).[82]

(iii) Emerging Trends of Regulatory Offence-Based Enforcement in Germany

The law on regulatory offences – both in the Act on Regulatory Offences and in special statutes – has evolved beyond this classic model in recent years. The following three areas warrant a closer look: the OWiG still provides the German functional equivalent to corporate criminal liability (1) and may allow for extensive fines (2). It is also applicable in the enforcement of the GDPR (3).

(a) Functional Equivalent to Corporate Criminal Liability

The Act on Regulatory Offences, and especially § 30 OWiG, has emerged to be the functional equivalent to corporate criminal liability in Germany. Its provisions on sanctioning corporations have been expanded over the years and are also applicable to criminal wrongdoing of corporate organs and representatives, leading in such cases to a regulatory fine of up to 10 million € (§ 30 [2] OWiG). Additionally, the Act requires the owners (§ 130 OWiG) as well as the organs and representatives of corporations (§ 9 OWiG) to take supervisory measures. If a lack of supervision enables or facilitates the commission of a crime in the corporate context, they commit a regulatory offence which may then be attributed to the corporation by means of § 30 OWiG.[83] In combination

[81] Sieber (n 49) 317 ff.
[82] Sieber (n 49) 319.
[83] Sieber (n 49) 314 f.

with confiscation and quasi-confiscation measures available under the OWiG (see above at section II.D.(ii).(b)), regulatory penalties as large as 1 billion € have been handed out to corporations,[84] underlining the severity of sanctions that corporations may face in Germany. By keeping the law on (quasi-)corporate criminal liability outside of the German Criminal Code and stressing at every opportunity that this constitutes a non-criminal form of sanctioning under EU law,[85] the legislature avoids all the dogmatic discussions on corporate culpability and the 'nature' of criminal law.[86] Therefore, even recent initiatives to introduce 'real' corporate criminal liability or, at least, to differentiate between severe corporate offences and other, minor (mass) offences covered by the OWiG,[87] have not attempted to incorporate the rules on corporate criminal liability into the German Criminal Code, but intend to introduce a specific statute *besides* or *between* it and the OWiG.

(b) 'Mega-Ordnungswidrigkeiten'[88]

The line between quasi- and 'true' criminal sanctioning of corporations is further blurred in specific laws which increase the maximum fines against corporations to between 10 and 15 per cent of their annual turnover (§ 81 [4] GWB,[89] § 56 [6] to [8] KWG,[90] § 120 [17] to [24] WpHG[91]), mostly in implementing EU legislation. In these areas of cartel law, banking law, and market manipulation and insider trading, the maximum fine is equivalent to that applicable in systems of 'true' corporate criminal liability.[92] The procedure generally does not differ in relation to these 'mega-Ordnungswidrigkeiten', though some provide for additional measures (especially on debarring from business with the state and on public notices of conviction). As a procedural tweak, §§ 83 f GWB assigns

[84] See staatsanwaltschaft-braunschweig.niedersachsen.de/startseite/aktuelles/presseinformationen/vw-muss-bugeld-zahlen-174880.html.

[85] See, as a recent example, Art 11(1) Directive 2013/40/EU of the European Parliament and of the Council of 12 August 2013 on attacks against information systems and replacing Council Framework Decision 2005/222/JHA, [2013] OJ L 218 of 13.08.2013, p 8.

[86] On this topic, just see J Vogel, 'Unrecht und Schuld in einem Unternehmensstrafrecht' (2012) 32(7) *Strafverteidiger* 427.

[87] See, in particular, a (failed) bill on strengthening the integrity of the economy (*Gesetz zur Stärkung der Integrität in der Wirtschaft*), BT-Drucksache 19/23568, available at dipbt.bundestag.de/dip21/btd/19/235/1923568.pdf, which includes a draft law on sanctioning corporation-related crimes (*Gesetz zur Sanktionierung von verbandsbezogenen Straftaten, Verbandssanktionengesetz – VerSanG*), and alternatives proposed by academics, M Henssler, E Hoven, M Kubiciel and T Weigend, *Kölner Entwurf eines Verbandsgesetzbuches*, available at:www.jpstrafrecht.jura.uni-koeln.de/sites/iss_juniorprof/Projekte/Koelner_Entwurf_eines_Verbandssanktionengesetzes__2017.pdf; M Jahn, C Schmitt-Leonardy and C Schoop, 'Unternehmensverantwortung für Unternehmenskriminalität – "Frankfurter Thesen"' (2018) 37 *Zeitschrift für Wirtschafts- und Steuerstrafrecht* 27; F Saliger, M Tsambikakis, O Mückenberger and H-P Huber (eds), *Münchner Entwurf eines Verbandssanktionengesetzes* (Baden-Baden, Nomos, 2019). A previous draft of the bill is discussed by T Grützner, C Momsen and J Menne, 'Draft Bill on German Sanctions Act' (2019) 5(2) *Compliance Elliance Journal* 26.

[88] Sieber (n 49) 308 f, 320 ff.

[89] Gesetz gegen Wettbewerbsbeschränkungen (GWB), as amended.

[90] Gesetz über das Kreditwesen (*Kreditwesengesetz* – KWG), as amended.

[91] Gesetz über den Wertpapierhandel (*Wertpapierhandelsgesetz* – WpHG), as amended.

[92] Cf D Brodowski, 'Supranationale europäische Verwaltungssanktionen: Entwicklungslinien – Dimensionen des Strafrechts – Legitimität' in K Tiedemann, U Sieber, H Satzger, C Burchard and D Brodowski (eds), *Die Verfassung moderner Strafrechtspflege* (Baden-Baden, Nomos, 2016) 146.

cartel cases to the Higher Regional Courts, and to the Federal High Court of Justice for appeals, instead of the local courts for the first instance hearings, and the Higher Regional Courts for appeals.[93]

(c) Mixed-EU and National Regulatory Offences under the GDPR

While the EU General Data Protection Regulation[94] contains a provision on administrative fines in its Article 83 which is directly applicable throughout the EU, it only contains a rough corpus of rules on the general part and on procedural questions.[95] Therefore, the German legislature has specified in its national implementing law that, as a general rule, the rules of the Act on Regulatory Offences shall apply (§ 41 *Bundesdatenschutzgesetz* (BDSG)). Excluded are a few provisions which relate to questions already governed by EU law, and, by way of exception, Regional Courts are competent in first instance if the administrative decision imposes a fine higher than 100,000 € (§ 41 [1] 3 BDSG).[96]

(iv) Practical Application

Unfortunately, no statistics exist on the quantity, quality, and severity of administrative decisions imposing regulatory fines. It is assumed that, per year, more than 10 million such decisions are taken in relation to minor traffic offences,[97] with many more transgressions not even noticed, investigated, and adjudicated. This underlines the practical importance of the legal system of regulatory fines for minor offences committed by the masses.[98] At the other end of the scale, the *Bundeskartellamt* – the federal administration office responsible for investigating and prosecuting cartel offences – concluded between 3 and 17 cases each year between 2007 and 2016, with the sum of fines ranging between 124.6 million € and 1.1 billion € per year.[99] Just like other well-known examples, such as the 1 billion € regulatory fine recently handed out to Volkswagen[100] or Siemens paying several hundred million € in regulatory fines for corruption offences,[101]

[93] Sieber (n 49) 308 f, 320 ff.

[94] Regulation (EU) 2016/679 of the European Parliament and of the Council of 27 April 2016 on the protection of natural persons with regard to the processing of personal data and on the free movement of such data, and repealing Directive 95/46/EC (General Data Protection Regulation), [2016] OJ L 119 of 4.5.2016, p 1, as corrected.

[95] M Nolde, 'Sanktionen nach DSGVO und BDSG-neu: Wem droht was warum?' (2017) 5 *Privacy in Germany* 114, 115; M Bergt, '§ 41' in J Kühling and B Buchner (eds), *Datenschutz-Grundverordnung/BDSG*, 3rd edn (Munich, CH Beck, 2020) para 1; D Brodowski and D Nowak, '§ 41' in S Brink and HA Wolff (eds), *Beck'scher Online-Kommentar Datenschutzrecht*, 34th edn (Munich, CH Beck, 2020) para 3; J Bülte, 'Das Datenschutzbußgeldrecht als originäres Strafrecht der Europäischen Union?' (2017) 37 *Strafverteidiger* 460, 460; S Golla, '§ 41' in M Eßer, P Kramer and K von Lewinski (eds), *DSGVO, BDSG*, 7th edn (Cologne, Carl Heymanns, 2020) 1.

[96] Brodowski and Nowak (n 95) para 36.

[97] Just see www.zeit.de/mobilitaet/2017-11/bussgeldbescheide-blitzer-fehlerhaft-geblitzt-de-behoerden.

[98] See also Sieber (n 49) 307 f.

[99] Bundeskartellamt, *Jahresbericht 2016*, 20, available at: www.bundeskartellamt.de/SharedDocs/Publikation/DE/Jahresbericht/Jahresbericht_2016.pdf?__blob=publicationFile&v=4.

[100] See above at n 84.

[101] See, in particular, LG München I, Decision of 4.10.2007 – 5 Kls 563 Js 45994/07, available at openjur.de/u/748600.html.

these are just the tip of the iceberg of the broad range of administrative decisions on regulatory offences.[102]

A better statistical overview exists with regard to court proceedings at local courts.[103] In 2019, around 388,000 cases concerning regulatory offences were concluded; around 364,000 (93.8 per cent) of those related to traffic offences.[104] More than 188,500 cases were resolved by the affected persons withdrawing their formal objection to the administrative decision (48.6 per cent); around 65,500 cases were dropped by the court under the rules of non-prosecution (17.0 per cent). Only a handful of cases were dropped by the public prosecution service (999 cases, 0.26 per cent) or led to an acquittal (5963 cases, 1.54 per cent). Most cases were resolved within three months (63.1 per cent), and a further 23.9 per cent within three to six months.[105] These numbers are comparable to the situation in criminal cases handled by local (but not by regional) courts (53.8 per cent resolved within three months, and further 26.8 per cent within three to six months).[106]

III. Features of Past and Present German Quasi-criminal Enforcement Mechanisms

What core features may be discerned from this overview of regulatory offences in Germany past and present? And how do these compare to (other) variations or alternative enforcement mechanisms to be found from and within German criminal justice?

A. Features of Regulatory Offences and Their Enforcement

(i) Expansion

The quantitative and qualitative importance of regulatory offences and their predecessors increase steadily over time. Since the first few – in name – *Ordnungswidrigkeiten* were created post-WWII, hundreds if not thousands of regulatory offences have been created by the legislature. Often, the legislature creates many more regulatory offences in specific topical statutes than it creates criminal offences, probably for the flexibility and efficiency they offer. Similarly to criminal offences, regulatory offences are only rarely abolished altogether; and while criminal offences may be 'decriminalised' by transforming them into regulatory offences, no such alternative is readily available for regulatory offences. The same expansive trend may be noted for historic modes such

[102] See also Sieber (n 49) 309.

[103] Statistisches Bundesamt, *Rechtspflege. Strafgerichte. 2019, Fachserie 10 Reihe 2.3, 2020*, 44, available at www.destatis.de/DE/Themen/Staat/Justiz-Rechtspflege/Publikationen/Downloads-Gerichte/strafgerichte-2100230177004.html.

[104] For comparison, around 660,500 criminal cases reached local courts in 2019. See Statistisches Bundesamt (n 103) 24.

[105] Statistisches Bundesamt (n 103) 44, 48; author's own calculation.

[106] Statistisches Bundesamt (n 103) 40.

as police statutes and police criminal law (above section II.A.). As with criminal law, exceptions to the trend of expansion can only be found on rare occasions, such as when large re-codifications take place, or when society and the state are facing transformation, but also when some regulatory offences have stabilised, grown in importance for the wider public, gained publicity and are moved to criminal codes (above section II.B.).

(ii) Flexibility

Criminal justice, especially the general part of criminal law, evolves only comparably slowly. The long history of criminal justice, the extensive dogmatic constructions of criminal law, and also its philosophical underpinnings mean that any modification of the law is seen as a risky endeavour – especially for politicians, who fear that they might decriminalise heinous crimes by accident, and will then be held politically accountable for such a mistake. Also, introducing new criminal law statutes – while sometimes of high symbolic value and with high political gains – seems to take much more time, tends to lead to tedious discussions (in academia and in legislative bodies), and may even lead to an increased need for (political if not legal[107]) justification compared to the introduction of a mere regulatory offence. Regulatory offences are seen (politically, in academia, and also in society as a whole) as a less important matter that is better left to specialists, who are, however, not very numerous. Unsurprisingly, one may find modifications to the general part (such as in relation to the maximum level of the penalty) and also to the procedure in specific statutes; such modifications are generally unheard of in 'normal' criminal law. History also shows that utilising a different approach than classic criminal law has opened the door to limiting if not circumventing the power of the (independent) judiciary. To summarise, enforcement by regulatory offences serves as a flexible, if not volatile, regulatory tool[108] for the legislature.

The practical application of regulatory offence enforcement is also shaped by flexibility. As the administration enjoys wide discretion in the enforcement of regulatory offences – in stark contrast to the application of criminal laws –, it can easily target such situations and persons where it considers an intervention to be necessary, and abstain otherwise. At the risk of inequality, this allows for a sensible investment of the scarce resources available for enforcement. Moreover, the existence of administrative bodies responsible for the investigation and adjudication of violations opens the door for more specialisation than is possible in the public prosecution offices, which are tasked with the investigation and prosecution of all sorts of crimes, and which are staffed by (expensive) law professionals who have broad generalised skills, but often lack specialised knowledge, for example, in (the supervision of) banking, nuclear power, and/or pharmaceutics.

[107] Cf M Jahn and D Brodowski, 'Krise und Neuaufbau eines strafverfassungsrechtlichen Ultima Ratio-Prinzips' (2016) 71 *Juristenzeitung* 969, 977 f; J Pauly, 'Rügemöglichkeiten von Verfassungsverstößen in der Revision' (2016) 22 *Strafverteidiger Forum* 491, 496.

[108] Critically U Weber, 'Die Überspannung der staatlichen Bußgeldgewalt' (1980) 92 *Zeitschrift für die gesamte Strafrechtswissenschaft* 313, 320 ff.

(iii) Efficiency and Effectiveness

From the wide discretion the administration enjoys follows another advantage: cost-efficiency. Quite often, the administration operates in a less costly way than the public prosecution services, as public prosecutors are paid equally to judges in Germany, and about a third higher than other professionals serving in the administration.[109] Costly trials are most often avoided, and even if those against whom administrative sanctioning decisions are made formally object to them, many cases are speedily resolved in streamlined court proceedings (see above sections II.D.(ii).(d). and II.D.(iv).).

The picture, however, becomes much more blurred in relation to effectiveness. In contrast to criminal justice, enforcement by regulatory offences may lead to instant but minor sanction by means of a cautionary fine (above II.D.(ii).(c).). That may have increased preventive effects compared to a sanction handed out long after the fact.[110] However, the severity of cautionary fines (up to 55 €, to be paid instantly or at the latest within a week) and also of regulatory fines is rather limited, at least in common cases including traffic offences. In light of the uncertain application in practice (owing to the wide discretion enjoyed by the administration) that aspect may limit the preventive effects.[111] Furthermore, it is unclear whether only criminal sanctions stigmatise, but not regulatory offences (see below at IV.A.(ii).), and whether that influences the preventive effects or the effects on pacifying society after a crime. In contrast to many German scholars, I am more sceptical of such stigmatising effects, as often the public and the media mix up the terminology anyway. In my opinion, the severity of the sanctioning, the course of the proceedings and their features (public[ity], formality, etc) may be more decisive in terms of effectiveness than the label of a sanction and its dogmatic construction.

Not only the cost-efficiency but also the effectiveness of regulatory offences may increase, however, because of the broad discretion granted to the authorities to decide whether to investigate, prosecute, and/or sanction them. Using this power, authorities may decide – based on political goals, based on public opinion, based on economic needs, but especially based on *regulatory needs* – on what regulatory offences to focus on, and what regulatory offences may appropriately be 'ignored' at times.

[109] Cf German Federal Constitutional Court, Judgment of 5 May 2015 – 2 BvL 17/09 = ECLI:DE:BVerfG:2015:ls20150505.2bvl001709, at 174 and 188 (ruling on the constitutionality of the salary of judges, and taking the difference between their salary and the salary of other professionals into account).

[110] Humans tend to miscalculate risks that lie far in the future, limiting the preventive effect of delayed sanctioning. For time discounting, intertemporal choice and temporal myopia in criminals, see C Mamayek, R Paternoster and TA Loughran, 'Temporal Discounting, Present Orientation, and Criminal Deterrence' in W Bernasco, JL van Gelder and H Elffers (eds), *The Oxford Handbook of Offender Decision Making* (Oxford, Oxford University Press, 2017) 209 ff; DS Nagin and G Pogarsky, 'Time and Punishment: Delayed Consequences and Criminal Behavior' (2004) 20 *Journal of Quantitative Criminology* 295; and already JQ Wilson and RJ Herrnstein, *Crime and Human Nature* (New York, Free Press, 1985) 50.

[111] Already Cesare Beccaria had pointed out that certainty of sentencing is decisive for preventive effects (see Mamayek, Paternoster and Loughran (n 110) 209 with fn 1). On the rational-choice theory which emphasises the cost-benefit ratio of offending and therefore the level of the sanction, just see ME Collins and TA Loughran, 'Rational Choice Theory, Heuristics, and Biases' in W Bernasco, JL van Gelder and H Elffers (eds), *The Oxford Handbook of Offender Decision Making* (Oxford, Oxford University Press, 2017) 10.

(iv) Transformative Power

Last but not least, let us remember Heinz Mattes' critical statement that alternative, non- or quasi-criminal enforcement mechanisms may especially be found when an old legal order is replaced, or is supplemented by a new legal order.[112] This also holds true for regulatory offences, though on a reduced scale.[113] First, many aspects of the present German economic legal order are secured by regulatory offences; criminal offences in the field of economic law have faced and still face an uphill battle, as these, for example, tend to face higher (academic and political) scrutiny.[114] Second, at least some regulatory offences of the past have slowly and partially been re-enacted as criminal law provisions. Third, especially in the field of procedure, the domain of regulatory offence-based enforcement may be seen as a testbed for criminal procedure. For instance, some simplifications relating to taking evidence in court are slowly finding their way into the German Code of Criminal Procedure. More strikingly, an expert group at the *Bundeskartellamt* explicitly mentioned that the far-reaching procedural changes they suggested for the law on cartel fines 'may be of relevance, for example, for criminal proceedings relating to economic crimes',[115] and that new rules on cartel fines 'may be precursor to other areas [of criminal procedure].'[116]

B. Features of Other Alternative Enforcement Mechanisms in Comparison

(i) Features of Other Alternative Enforcement Mechanisms

Besides the *Ordnungswidrigkeitenrecht* outlined above, criminal justice (in a formal sense; that is, relating to the punishment of offences the legislator has labelled as criminal offences[117]) uses several other alternative enforcement mechanisms, as I have analysed elsewhere in detail.[118] They may either relate to deviations *within* criminal justice or, more properly, *within* the criminal process. That is, these alternatives rely on the same set of actors and are governed by the German Criminal Code and the German Code of Criminal Procedure. Typical examples of such alternatives are rules of diversion and non-prosecution, probation and parole. Other alternative enforcement mechanisms are better described as alternatives *to* criminal justice: though a close link to criminal

[112] Cf Mattes (n 3) 41.

[113] For the transformative power of European administrative sanctions, see Brodowski (n 92) 163 ff.

[114] Cf K Tiedemann, *Wirtschaftsstrafrecht*, 5th edn (Munich, Vahlen, 2017) § 1 II.4, and previously K Tiedemann, 'Entwicklung und Begriff des Wirtschaftsstrafrechts' (1969) 116 *Goltdammer's Archiv für Strafrecht* 71–90, 71 ff.

[115] Bundeskartellamt, *Zwischenbericht des Bundeskartellamts zum Expertenkreis Kartellsanktionenrecht. Reformimpulse für das Kartellbußgeldverfahren* vom 12.1.2015, 2, available at www.bundeskartellamt.de/SharedDocs/Publikation/DE/Berichte/AG_Kartellsanktionenrecht_Zwischenbericht.pdf?__blob=publicationFile&v=2 (own translation).

[116] Bundeskartellamt (n 115) (own translation).

[117] On this formal distinction, see above section II.C.

[118] Brodowski (n 2) 365 ff.

justice exists, a different set of legislation applies, and/or different actors take enforcement measures. Typical examples in Germany relate to police law-based investigation gathering, preventive police law-based detention, and preventive electronic tagging. All these mechanisms, both within and outside criminal justice, allow for flexibility in procedure, but also for flexibility in 'the effects or outcome, with far more tailored legal consequences or – in a broad sense – sanctions being available to micro-manage the behaviour of an actual or presumed offender.'[119] Some of these measures

> may well have more effective long-term effects compared to criminal punishment due to the swiftness and harshness of the state intervention. In more general terms, this flexibility also means a shift from the (criminal) offence (and the specific 'price' one has to pay for it) to the offender (and the question of what is 'best' for him or her).[120]

This comes at the cost of equality of application – and therefore requires trust (by the legislature and/or by the public) in the authorities –, and may put safeguards and defence rights at risk.[121]

(ii) Comparison and Conclusion

Regulatory offence-based enforcement therefore seems to play a somewhat similar but also distinct role compared to other alternative enforcement mechanisms present in Germany. First, regulatory offences are an addition to the *legislative* toolbox. It was a (failed) historic experiment to let the administration choose on the basis of ambiguous criteria whether to pursue criminal sanctions or a regulatory fine (above section II.C.); instead, since 1975 at the latest, enforcement is bound by an abstract decision made ex ante by the legislature, so that the administration cannot select ex post in specific situations between criminal and regulatory offence-based enforcement. Second, while enforcement of regulatory offences offers discretion in whether to prosecute, it only offers a far more limited range of legal consequences, in particular fines (normal and cautionary), but not truly targeted interventions (such as orders prohibiting an offender from entering a certain area, meeting certain people, and/or consuming alcohol). Third, all these measures share a risk of unequal application and of a deterioration of safeguards (such as the involvement of the judiciary) present in classic criminal justice. Fourth, the cost-efficiency of regulatory offence-based enforcement may be higher than *any* alternatives within the criminal justice system, but – as outlined above – that may also come at costs in terms of effectiveness. Fifth, both regulatory offences *and* the alternatives within criminal justice are used to mitigate the trend of ever-expanding state regulation and state intervention – both offer, roughly speaking, more lenient alternatives to classic criminal enforcement. In such a sense, regulation today has become dependent not only on alternative enforcement mechanisms in general,[122] but also on regulatory offences in particular.

[119] Brodowski (n 2) 393.
[120] Brodowski (n 2) 393.
[121] Brodowski (n 2) 393 f.
[122] Brodowski (n 2) 393 f.

IV. A Line Between Criminal and Regulatory Enforcement?

In the preceding description and analysis, I have carefully sidestepped one aspect on which much ink has been spilled in Germany: whether there is a theoretical, dogmatic, or constitutional distinction between 'true' criminal law and other modes of sanctioning, such as the regulatory offence-based enforcement under the OWiG. In this section, I will discuss so-called 'qualitative theories' which state that there are clear differences between criminal and regulatory offences (section IV.A.), so-called 'quantitative theories' which only see a difference in the severity of the actual sanctions handed out (section IV.B.), and argue in favour of the latter.

A. Qualitative Theories – From Feuerbach to the Bundesverfassungsgericht

(i) Scholarly Theories in the Nineteenth Century

Many leading scholars of the nineteenth century attempted to discern a qualitative demarcation line between criminal law and other modes of sanctioning.[123] Despite the influence at least some of them had on the legislature – in particular Feuerbach –, their concepts were never fully implemented in law.

According to Paul Johann Anselm von Feuerbach, criminal law must protect unalienable subjective rights; collective interests, the public order and security must not be protected by criminal law, but by police offences.[124] Christian Köstlin differentiated, largely influenced by Hegel,[125] between concrete endangerment and actual harm as violations to be addressed by criminal justice, and mere abstract endangerment.[126] Others argued for a borderline between *malum in se* and *malum prohibita*. James Goldschmidt[127] and Otto Mayer[128] distinguished static law (including criminal law) on the one hand, and the dynamic, forward-looking, welfare-oriented administration (including administrative sanctioning) on the other. Yet others considered crimes to

[123] See the extensive description and analysis by Mattes (n 3) 105 ff; HG Michels, *Strafbare Handlung und Zuwiderhandlung* (Berlin, de Gruyter, 1963) 5 ff.

[124] PJA Feuerbach, *Lehrbuch des gemeinen in Deutschland gültigen peinlichen Rechts*, 14th edn (Giessen, Heyer, 1847) § 432, 703; see also, though with differences in detail, E Wolf, 'Die Stellung der Verwaltungsdelikte im Strafrechtssystem' in A Hegler (ed), *Festgabe für Reinhard von Frank* (Aalen, Scientia, 1969) 560 ff.

[125] Compare Klesczewski (n 22) 23 ff.

[126] CR Köstlin, *System des deutschen Strafrechts* (Aalen, Scientia, 1978) § 18 17; see also Supreme Court of the German Reich, Judgment of 17 April 1888 – 738/88 = RGSt 17, 303, 304 and, though with significant differences in detail and partially more focus on the highly disputed German concept of '*Rechtsgüter*', HL Günther, 'Die Ordnungswidrigkeit – Delikt ohne unmittelbares verletztes individuelles Opfer' in U Sieber and G Dannecker (eds), *Strafrecht und Wirtschaftsstrafrecht: Dogmatik, Rechtsvergleich, Rechtstatsachen – Festschrift für Klaus Tiedemann zum 70 Geburtstag* (Cologne, Heymann, 2008) 166; Klesczewski (n 22) 15 ff; R Hefendehl, 'Ordnungswidrigkeiten: Legitimation und Grenzen. Ein vergleichender Blick auf Deutschland und Chile' (2016) 11 *Zeitschrift für Internationale Strafrechtsdogmatik* 636, 641.

[127] Goldschmidt (n 4) 529 ff.

[128] Cf O Mayer, *Deutsches Verwaltungsrecht*, vol 1 (Berlin, Duncker Humblot, 1961) 30, para 9.

be a rebellion against the legal order, and violations of regulatory offences to be mere disobedience.[129]

Even though Mattes' monograph provides a more extensive and nuanced analysis of these theories and their failures,[130] Werner Rosenberg already showed in a fascinating article published in 1904[131] that all these concepts suffer from flaws and incompatibilities with a modern understanding of criminal justice. The theories which focus on actual versus abstract harm or endangerment cannot explain that the attempt of criminal offences generally leads to criminal punishment, and that illegal handling of highly dangerous substances such as explosives is a criminal offence, even where a concrete victim cannot be known in advance.[132] Those violating criminal statutes are also disobedient, and disobedience cannot be distinguished properly from a rebellion against the legal order.[133] As the German legal system is not – or at least no longer – based on natural laws, there is no place for a borderline between *malum in se* and *malum prohibitum*.[134] The activities of the administration (and especially sanctioning powers of the administration) need to be governed by law as well, rendering such a differentiation between law and administration moot.[135] Last but not least, Rosenberg already argued that a principle of individual guilt(iness) is required not only for criminal wrongdoing, but also in relation to administrative sanctioning,[136] and that it is dangerous to embed morality in criminal law, as there will always be immoral behaviour that is not a crime, and morally endorsed behaviour that is.[137]

(ii) Twentieth-Century Scholarly Theories and BVerfG Jurisprudence

Yet in the quest for regaining inner and outward stability after the Nazi regime, these warnings by Rosenberg were not heeded. Instead, Eberhard Schmidt,[138] and following him and others, the Federal Constitutional Court (*Bundesverfassungsgericht* – BVerfG)[139] engaged in a further attempt to distinguish criminal law from regulatory offences in a qualitative manner. In a first landmark decision in 1959, it held that the principle of individual guilt *also* applies to regulatory offences, but held that the question at stake – the constitutionality of a partial reversal of proof for *respondeat superior* responsibility in § 23 WiStG 1949 that was in force until 1954 – did not raise issues of

[129] Cf F von Liszt, *Lehrbuch des deutschen Strafrechts*, 2nd edn (Berlin, Guttentag, 1884) 102 (but see also 95 f.); A Merkel, *Lehrbuch des deutschen Strafrechts* (Stuttgart, Enke, 1889) 45 f.

[130] Mattes (n 3) 105 ff.

[131] W Rosenberg, 'Die Dreiteilung der strafbaren Handlungen' (1904) 24 *Zeitschrift für die gesamte Strafrechtswissenschaft* 1 ff.

[132] Rosenberg (n 131) 5 f.

[133] Rosenberg (n 131) 7 f.

[134] Rosenberg (n 131) 8 f.

[135] See already, though rudimentarily, Rosenberg (n 131) 6, 9.

[136] Rosenberg (n 131) 12 ff.

[137] Rosenberg (n 131) 9 f.

[138] E Schmidt, *Das neue westdeutsche Wirtschaftsrecht* (Tübingen, Mohr Siebeck, 1950) 44 f, 51 f.

[139] German Federal Constitutional Court, Decision of 4 February 1959 – 1 BvR 197/53 = BVerfGE 9, 167, at 171 f; German Federal Constitutional Court, Judgment of 6 June 1967 – 2 BvR 375,53/60 and 18/65 = BVerfGE 22, 49, at 79 f; German Federal Constitutional Court, Decision of 16 July 1969 – 2 BvL 2/69 = BVerfGE 27, 18, at 29, 33.

human dignity, as regulatory sanctions lack the 'seriousness' of a criminal sanction.[140] A few years later, it held *criminal* sanctioning powers of tax authorities to be unconstitutional, as the Constitution prescribed that 'judicial power shall be vested in the judges' (Article 92 *Grundgesetz* – GG).[141] In another decision, it considered regulatory offences – despite such (alleged) differences – to be 'criminal law' within the meaning of the constitutional law provisions which grant powers at the federal level.[142] Further reiterations and refinements followed in the jurisprudence of the Federal Constitutional Court, most recently in a decision on protecting the constitutional identity in relation to European Arrest Warrants relating to *in absentia* judgments: 'By way of criminal sanction, the offender is reproached of a socio-ethical misconduct';[143] a criminal sanction is an authoritative statement that a behaviour constitutes socio-ethical misconduct, which 'affects the person concerned with regard to his or her right to being valued and respected, a right that is rooted in human dignity'.[144] In contrast thereto, the administrative sphere relates to less serious disobediences which are not really worthy of punishment by criminal law. Regulatory fines are merely a strong reminder of one's duties and obligations, which lack the 'seriousness' and stigma of a criminal sanction.

However, it should be made clear that the Federal Constitutional Court has, so far, never rejected the choice made by the legislature whether to criminalise conduct or whether to merely sanction it by means of a regulatory offence. In other words, the Court's reasoning on a seemingly strict borderline between criminal offences and regulatory offences has never become operative in German jurisprudence, though it would give content to the *ultima ratio* principle of criminal justice.[145] Moreover, as others and I have already discussed extensively elsewhere,[146] such an attempt to distinguish criminal law from other forms of sanctioning is not convincing. Within the borders of the Constitution, questions of sanctioning and culpability are matters for the legislature to decide and to evolve; criminal justice should not be limited to what have 'traditionally' been crimes.[147] Embedding ethics and morality into criminal law opens the door to too

[140] German Federal Constitutional Court, Decision of 4 February 1959 – 1 BvR 197/53 = BVerfGE 9, 167. See further *infra* at B.

[141] German Federal Constitutional Court, Judgment of 6 June 1967 – 2 BvR 375,53/60 and 18/65 = BVerfGE 22, 49.

[142] German Federal Constitutional Court, Decision of 16 July 1969 – 2 BvL 2/69 = BVerfGE 27, 18.

[143] German Federal Constitutional Court, Decision of 15 December 2015 – 2 BvR 2735/14 = BVerfGE 140, 317, at 52 ff, especially 54 = ECLI:DE:BVerfG:2015:rs20151215.2bvr273514 = www.bundesverfassungsgericht.de/SharedDocs/Entscheidungen/EN/2015/12/rs20151215_2bvr273514en.html.

[144] German Federal Constitutional Court, Decision of 15 December 2015 – 2 BvR 2735/14 = BVerfGE 140, 317, at 52 ff, especially 54 = ECLI:DE:BVerfG:2015:rs20151215.2bvr273514 = www.bundesverfassungsgericht.de/SharedDocs/Entscheidungen/EN/2015/12/rs20151215_2bvr273514en.html.

[145] Cf KF Gärditz, 'Demokratizität des Strafrechts und Ultima Ratio-Grundsatz' (2016) 71 *Juristenzeitung* 641, 642 f; Jahn and Brodowski (n 107) 971; M Jahn and D Brodowski, 'Das Ultima Ratio-Prinzip als strafverfassungsrechtliche Vorgabe zur Frage der Entbehrlichkeit von Straftatbeständen' (2017) 129 *Zeitschrift für die gesamte Strafrechtswissenschaft* 363, 372 ff.

[146] Just see H Mattes, *Untersuchungen zur Lehre von den Ordnungswidrigkeiten. Zweiter Halbband: Geltendes Recht und Kritik* (Berlin, Duncker Humblot, 1982) 1 ff; Rosenberg (n 131) 1 ff; Brodowski (n 92) 158 ff; D Brodowski, 'Die Verwaltung darf nicht strafen – warum eigentlich nicht? Zugleich eine Vorstudie zu einer rechts-evolutionären, weichen Konstitutionalisierung strafrechtsdogmatischer Grundannahmen' (2016) 128 *Zeitschrift für die gesamte Strafrechtswissenschaft* 370, 372 f; Jahn and Brodowski (n 107) 972 f.

[147] Just see M Jahn, '"There is no such thing as too big to jail" – Zu den verfassungsrechtlichen Einwänden gegen ein Verbandsstrafgesetzbuch unter dem Grundgesetz' in M Jahn, C Schmitt-Leonardy and C Schoop (eds), *Das Unternehmensstrafrecht und seine Alternativen* (Baden-Baden, Nomos, 2016) 59, 77 ff.

much ambiguity and subjective interpretation.[148] Stigmatisation within and by society – as a factual consequence – needs to be distinguished from the normative decision by the legislature and the sanctioning decision as such:[149] it is not uncommon that media and the wider public mislabel sanctions, contrary to the official nomination of the sanction. And while imprisonment is not available as a sanction for regulatory offences, but seemingly always for criminal offences in Germany, it is this specific sanction which requires a specific constitutional justification.[150] We cannot and should not distinguish two 'kinds' of a monetary fine of equal amount.

Probably the majority of German scholars[151] either follow the afore-mentioned qualitative distinction or variations thereof. In particular, several state that while there may be some middle ground where the legislature enjoys discretion when to decide between regulatory and criminal offences, a qualitative distinction at least allows one to distinguish a core area clearly assigned to each domain (so-called qualitative-quantitative theories).

I remain sceptical, as these 'core areas' already follow from another aspect. In both criminal law and alternative enforcement mechanisms, a system proportionate to the maximum punishment needs to be constructed, as is required by the constitutional principle of proportionality. And as imprisonment is only (but always) at stake in German criminal law, this leads to a formal distinction between criminal and quasi- or non-criminal regulatory offences.[152] This formal distinction can and should open the door for at least *some* constitutional review of legislative choices on criminalisation.[153] However, and as already stated above, the Federal Constitutional Court has not ruled on this matter, or indeed – with the possible exception of the 1959 decision mentioned above – taken *any* decision which was clearly based on a qualitative differentiation between criminal and regulatory sanctioning.

To summarise my opinion, a famous quotation of 1870 still remains valid:

> The attempts, from the legal schools of the dark ages up to our times, to determine the demarcation lines between crimes and police transgressions have been without avail, despite the preference given to discussing this question. Even in most recent times, in which this discussion has been taken up again and has been continued not without ingenuity, there has been no success in determining this distinction reliably and equally, this distinction which reduces jurists to despair.[154]

[148] Jahn and Brodowski (n 107) 972.

[149] Brodowski (n 146) 370, 373.

[150] See Jahn and Brodowski (n 107) 974 ff, in particular 977.

[151] See, in particular, A Eser, *Die Abgrenzung von Straftaten und Ordnungswidrigkeiten* (Universität Würzburg, Dissertation, 1961) 178 ff; Michels (n 123) 59 f; S Gerhold, 'Einleitung' in JP Graf (ed), *Beck'scher Online-Kommentar Ordnungswidrigkeitengesetz*, 28th edn (Munich, CH Beck, 2020) 13; C Roxin and L Greco, *Strafrecht Allgemeiner Teil*, vol 1, 5th edn (Munich, CH Beck, 2020) § 2 at 131 ff; T Weigend, 'Einleitung' in G Cirener, H Radtke, RRissung-van Saan, T Rönnau and W Schluckebier (eds), *Leipziger Kommentar Strafgesetzbuch*, 13th edn (Berlin, de Gruyter, 2019) 19 f; J Wessels, W Beulke and H Satzger, *Strafrecht Allgemeiner Teil*, 50th edn (Heidelberg, CF Müller, 2020) 20; W Frisch, 'Voraussetzungen und Grenzen staatlichen Strafens' (2016) 36 *Neue Zeitschrift für Strafrecht* 16, 17; Sieber (n 49) 323 f; K Tiedemann, 'Die Gesetzgebungskompetenz für Ordnungswidrigkeiten' (1964) 89 *Archiv des öffentlichen Rechts* 56, 72 f.

[152] Brodowski (n 92) 158 in footnote 92.

[153] Jahn and Brodowski (n 107) 976 ff, in particular 978.

[154] Verhandlungen des Norddeutschen Reichstags, I. Reg.-Periode, Session 1870, Bd. 3 (Anlagen) Aktenstück Nr. 5, S. 87; as cited in Rosenberg (n 131) 16 (author's own translation): 'Vergeblich ist von den Rechtsschulen

B. Quantitative Theories

As underlined already by a famous quotation from 1786 mentioned above,[155] an opposing viewpoint is shared by a significant number – but probably the minority – of German scholars. They state that criminal fines and regulatory fines cannot be distinguished conceptually, but that there is – at most – a quantitative difference depending on the amount of the monetary sanction.[156]

Klesczewski disagrees with such an approach and points to a fundamental difference in how the fines are calculated, and what this calculation expresses. Criminal fines are calculated based on a daily rate system, meaning that an offender is sentenced to pay, for example, 30 daily rates of 10 €; each daily rate reflects the offender's average daily income. This sanction, according to Klesczewski, temporarily limits the criminal's financial freedom and their financial capacity to act, just as imprisonment limits their personal freedom.[157] In contrast, regulatory fines are determined based on '[t]he significance of the regulatory offence and the charge' (§ 17 [3] 1 OWiG) and taking the perpetrator's wealth into account (§ 17 [3] 2 OWiG contains an exception for minor regulatory offences). In combination with the quasi-confiscation regime of § 17 [4] OWiG (see above section II.D.(ii).(b).), regulatory fines merely attempt to make it (much) more economical and rational to follow the rules instead of breaking them. Therefore, according to Klesczewski, a regulatory fine does not limit an individual's capacity to act.[158]

That argument, however reasonable it may be from a philosophical perspective, does not convince me as accurately describing the effects and rationality of the law: both criminal and regulatory fines are enforced by taking money away from the perpetrator; in both cases, there are opportunities to spread out the payment in rates. What the perpetrator suffers is just a financial loss, and only the sum of the fine and not its calculation matters to the perpetrator. Depending on the perpetrator's wealth, a financial sanction – small or large – affects their freedoms and capacity to invest, spend or donate money in exactly the same manner, independently of whether it is a regulatory fine or a criminal fine. In terms of general prevention, the broader society does not seem to pay much attention to the number of 'daily rates', but more to the actual sum which has to be paid.[159]

des Mittelalters bis herab auf unsre Zeit trotz der Vorliebe, welche man der Erörterung dieser Frage gewidmet hat, der Versuch gemacht worden, die Grenzlinien zwischen dem kriminell und polizeilich Strafbaren zu finden. Auch in der neuesten Zeit, in welcher die Erörterung wiederum aufgenommen und nicht ohne Aufwand an Scharfsinn fortgeführt worden, ist es nicht gelungen, jenen [...] die Juristen in Verzweiflung bringenden Unterschied mit Sicherheit und Gleichmäßigkeit durchzuführen.'

[155] See section I. above, at n 1.

[156] Brodowski (n 146) 372 ff; W Knapp, 'Das Recht der Ordnungswidrigkeiten' (1979) 19 *Juristische Schulung* 609, 610; A Schoreit, 'Die sogenannten Ordnungswidrigkeiten' (1967) 114 *Goltdammer's Archiv für Strafrecht* 225 ff; W Mitsch, *Recht der Ordnungswidrigkeiten*, 2nd edn (Berlin, Springer, 2005) § 3 at 10 ff; Mitsch (n 37) 113 ff; Mattes (n 146).

[157] Klesczewski (n 22) 13 f.

[158] Klesczewski (n 22) 13 f.

[159] For example, if the prosecution makes use of rules of deviation based on a financial payment by the alleged perpetrator, it sometimes highlights the magnitude of that payment, such as in a US$ 100,000,000

Another argument that is brought forward against the quantitative approach is that it would make administrative sanctioning decisions – which are then qualitatively equivalent – unconstitutional: only courts may exert sanctioning powers in criminal matters (Article 92 GG), as '[t]he judicial power shall be vested in the judges'.[160] Indeed, such a claim of unconstitutionality had been made by Mattes.[161] Upon closer inspection, however, I do not find such a strict constitutional limitation to the sanctioning powers of the administration.[162] A historical interpretation of Article 92 GG, which recalls that traditionally adjudication and sentencing in criminal matters have always been a matter for the courts, simplifies and sets in stone issues too bluntly. Moreover, a criminal case – and also a case under the OWiG in its current form (above section II.D.(ii).(c) and (d).) – is not an adversarial case requiring judicial balancing and decision-making. And, as stated above, criminal law is not so special compared to quasi-criminal enforcement mechanisms.

Instead, greater focus needs to be on the concept of judicial oversight and on the (procedural) protection of human and fundamental rights ('*Grundrechtsschutz durch Verfahren*'). Article 104 GG already makes it explicit that imprisonment requires judicial authorisation. But even beyond that, the severity of a particular (financial) sanction may require – in a quest for an *optimal* rule of law and justice – automatic[163] judicial involvement, and not merely ex-post judicial review.[164] While this standard is more relative and flexible compared to the majority viewpoint, it allows for an explanation of why even under a quantitative approach, *criminal* sanctions require a trial by court, but alternative enforcement mechanisms (both within criminal justice and beyond, such as regulatory fines) may not – especially if the punishment is limited *and/or* if the addressed subjects are able to properly defend themselves in light of a first administrative decision. And this approach highlights what these alternative models mostly deal with: the enforcement, or, more precisely, the *procedural* side.[165]

V. Conclusion

Although most treatises on German criminal law do not contain much text on quasi-criminal enforcement mechanisms in general and on the law of regulatory offences

payment Bernie Ecclestone made, cf J Brüning, 'Die Einstellung nach § 153a StPO. Moderner Ablasshandel oder Rettungsanker der Justiz?' (2015) 10 *Zeitschrift für Internationale Strafrechtsdogmatik* 586, 586.

[160] Klesczewski (n 22) 11; see further Mitsch (n 37) 107.

[161] Mattes (n 146) 465.

[162] See in more detail, Brodowski (n 146) 370 ff.

[163] Interestingly, other criminal justice systems know forms of *automatic review* even for court decisions, just see US Supreme Court, *Gregg v Georgia*, 428 US 153 (1976), 154, 156 ('The Georgia sentencing scheme also provides for automatic sentence review by the Georgia Supreme Court to safeguard against prejudicial or arbitrary factors.'), 198 ('As an important additional safeguard against arbitrariness and caprice, the Georgia statutory scheme provides for automatic appeal of all death sentences to the State's Supreme Court. That court is required by statute to review each sentence of death and determine whether it was imposed under the influence of passion or prejudice, whether the evidence supports the jury's finding of a statutory aggravating circumstance, and whether the sentence is disproportionate compared to those sentences imposed in similar cases. § 27-2537(c) (Supp. 1975).').

[164] See in more detail, Brodowski (n 146) 385 ff.

[165] J Bohnert, 'Die Entwicklung des Ordnungswidrigkeitenrechts' (1984) 6 *Juristische Ausbildung* 11, 11.

(*Ordnungswidrigkeiten*) in particular, this body of law is of high practical and theoretical importance: quantitatively, regulatory offences are the legislative method of choice to address violations committed by the masses, such as (minor) road traffic violations;[166] qualitatively, they are (at least up to now) the legislative method of choice to address corporate wrongdoing.[167] Their appeal results mainly from three features: firstly, the investigation, prosecution and sanctioning of regulatory offences is far more cost-efficient than involving the criminal justice system, with high-paid prosecutors, judges, and defence counsel.[168] Secondly, the investigation and prosecution of regulatory offences is based on discretion, not on a principle of mandatory prosecution – a feature which enables flexibility in enforcement.[169] Thirdly, regulatory offences and the associated investigation, prosecution and sanctioning procedures tend to be far more flexible for the legislature to modify based on specific needs, compared to the more slowly evolving criminal justice system.[170] Thereby, the current law on regulatory offences, just like historical precedents,[171] continues to serve as a sort of 'playground' for the legislature, with some offences, features of the general part and/or procedural provisions later on finding their way into 'classic' criminal law[172] – such as the current discussion on moving corporate 'criminal' liability from the domain of regulatory offences to the criminal sphere, or at least to a sphere between these two domains.[173] Vice versa, historical precedents[174] for 'decriminalisation' transformed several criminal offences to regulatory offences; similar calls can be heard today.[175] As such intermixtures and amalgamation are not historic accidents but a repetitive theme of the relation between criminal and quasi-criminal or regulatory enforcement in Germany, it makes sense that all attempts to define a clear 'qualitative' demarcation line between them have failed.[176] To me, it seems clear that ever-more focus needs to be placed instead on the concept of judicial oversight of enforcement (be it 'criminal' or 'regulatory' in name), and on the protection of human and fundamental rights in all enforcement mechanisms.

[166] See above section II.D.(iv).
[167] See section II.D.(iii).
[168] See section III.A.(iii).
[169] See section III.A.(ii).
[170] See section III.A.(ii).
[171] See section II.A. at the end.
[172] See section III.A.(iv).
[173] See section II.D.(iii).(a).
[174] See section II.C. at the end, and II.D.(i).
[175] Just see, as a recent example, a proposal by the Greens relating to the criminal offence of using a train, tramway or bus without a valid ticket (§ 265 (1) German Criminal Code), BT-Drucksache 19/1690, available at dip21.bundestag.de/dip21/btd/19/016/1901690.pdf.
[176] See section IV.A. and IV.B.

4

Quasi-criminal Sanctions in Central Europe – Their Origins and Evolution[1]

ANNA BŁACHNIO-PARZYCH

I. Introduction

The purpose of this chapter is to present the origins, evolution and contemporary state of affairs of quasi-criminal sanctions in Central Europe, with a particular focus on Poland and the Czech Republic. The comparison of these two Central-European neighbouring countries is interesting because the Polish and Czech legislators have chosen different approaches in that regard. The comparison will also reveal that, besides different approaches, there are some common features.

Before presenting the origins of quasi-criminal sanctions, the research subject should be defined. First of all, these are measures[2] which are not formally criminal, but their character and function are the same as penal sanctions. For the selection of such sanctions in the Polish and the Czech law, I have taken into account the criteria developed in the *Engel* case law of the European Court of Human Rights (ECtHR).[3] Quasi-criminal sanctions are measures that are penal in nature but are not imposed by courts in criminal proceedings. In Poland and the Czech Republic, the field of law where legislators adopt measures that constitute penalties having a punitive character is administrative law. Although some institutions in private law have a punitive character too, they are very rare and therefore they will not be presented here. Disciplinary penalties will be outside the scope of this chapter too.

The comparison of Poland and the Czech Republic is justified because both countries have a lot in common. They belong to the same language group of West Slavs and have a similar culture and history. The description of the genesis of the quasi-criminal sanctions in these two countries will start after the Second World War.

[1] The chapter was prepared within the project financed by National Science Centre, Poland, grant no. DEC-2018/30/E/HS5/00738.

[2] The term 'measure' will be used in the text in a broad sense, as comprising different kinds of legislators' reactions, including sanctions.

[3] The judgment of the ECtHR in the case of *Engel and others v the Netherlands* (App No 5100/71, 8 June 1976, paras 80–82) became the mile-stone for the further jurisprudence of the ECtHR related to the scope of the application of the guarantees laid down in Article 6 the ECHR.

Back then, both countries (the Czech Republic as a part of Czechoslovakia) were in the sphere of influence of the Soviet Union. They belonged to the group of countries that were behind the Iron Curtain. The next important steps in their history occur in the year 1989 when the period of political, economic and social transformations started, and the year 2004 when they became Member States of the European Union. Therefore, one may ask if the similarities between them also relate to the quasi-criminal sanctions and their development.

II. Origins of Quasi-Criminal Sanctions

A. The Period After the Second World War

Right after the end of the Second World War, the pre-War law was still in force, both in Poland and in Czechoslovakia. Gradually, though, regulations similar to those being in force in the Soviet Union were introduced, as will be explained below.

(i) Poland

In 1950, the Polish legislator adopted the Act on 'criminal-administrative' jurisdiction.[4] It was dedicated to the liability for offences called criminal-administrative offences.[5] However, the Act was of a procedural character and it referred to liability for behaviours regulated in other Acts. Many of them were treated before the second World War as breaches of order (for example, removing and damaging written announcements, disturbance of public peace by shouting, noise, alarm or other excesses). However, many new behaviours constituted criminal-administrative offences too. They were, for example, acts that threatened the socialist economy, such as failure by farmers to comply with the obligation to deliver up cereal crops, slaughtered animals, milk or potatoes, or the sale of goods for resale with a profit (ie speculation). The nature of this kind of liability was controversial. Many scholars perceived that, though the liability for the offences was not adjudicated in criminal proceedings, it had a lot in common with criminal liability. The offences did not only include acts that were breaches of order, but acts that threatened more important legal goods. Furthermore, in 1958, the penalties were tightened (one of them became imprisonment called 'arrest'). The influence of Soviet law was not only visible in the competences of administrative officials, but also in the creation of special administrative bodies which decided collectively. Another possible solution was to pass the competencies to directors of different administrative bodies, who could impose

[4] Published in: *Journal of Laws* 1966 No 39, item 283.

[5] To avoid misinterpretation it should be underlined that the term 'criminal-administrative' offence is used in the text as a direct translation of the Polish term '*karno-administracyjny*' used by the legislator in the aforementioned Act. Later in the text of this chapter the terms 'administrative' offence and 'administrative-criminal' offence will be used too. These terms relate to actual categories of offences provided for in Polish administrative law. All of them have an administrative character, because they are regulated as administrative law. However some of them are called 'administrative-criminal' offences, because of their penal character. The name was first used by D Szumiło-Kulczycka (*Prawo administracyjno-karne*, Kraków, Zakamycze, 2004) and the author purposely reversed the order of the words 'criminal' and 'administrative' to distinguish the character of the new offences that developed in the 1990s from the offences that existed in Polish law from 1951.

sanctions for specific infringements. The purpose was to have a stronger educational influence on society. The characterising feature was the tendency to punish behaviours that traditionally belonged to criminal law by quasi-criminal sanctions,[6] which were not imposed by courts, but by special authorities created for that purpose and dependent on the executive. Initially, they were called adjudicative councils, later they became criminal-administrative councils. Furthermore, a new penalty was introduced – a corrective work order.

The next important stage in the development of this kind of penalty started in 1966, when the Act on transferring some minor offences known as '*wykroczenia*' (a term one could translate as 'misdemeanours', although that term is not entirely satisfactory) to the criminal-administrative realm was adopted.[7] The Polish legislator added to the catalogue quasi-criminal behaviours that constituted crimes against property, in which the value of the subject of the acts or of the damage caused by the acts was below a specific amount of money. These acts were called 'bisected offences' and included, for example, theft, handling stolen goods, and destruction of property.[8] The use of the term 'bisected' was justified by the nature of such acts: Depending on the value of property, some behaviours constituted crimes and other '*wykroczenia*'. These '*wykroczenia*' were treated as the most serious compared to other '*wykroczenia*' and were punishable with a maximum of three months of 'arrest' or fines up to 4,500 PLN (Polish zloty). These offences were also subject to specific (ie in comparison to other '*wykroczenia*') liability rules regarding attempt and incitement. Indeed, these rules were the same as those provided for criminal offences.

The further transformation of quasi-criminal liability took place in 1971, as a consequence of decriminalising tendencies. The legislator finally changed the terminology used in the newly adopted legislation: the Code of '*wykroczenia*' and the Code of Procedure relating to '*wykroczenia*'.[9] From then on, the term '*wykroczenia*' was used consequently instead of the term criminal-administrative offences. The nature of this liability became more similar to criminal liability, but it was still treated, formally speaking, as a non-criminal, administrative liability, despite the fact that the applicable rules were similar to those under the criminal law. However, the dominant position was that there are no qualitative differences between the liability for crimes and the liability for '*wykroczenia*'. It was justified especially because of the nature of the bisected acts that were transferred from the Criminal Code to the Code of '*wykroczenia*' (misdemeanours).[10]

(ii) Czechoslovakia

In Czechoslovakia the codes related to criminal administrative liability (substantive law and procedural law) were adopted in 1950.[11] The authorities that were competent to

[6] It has to be noted that before the Second World War the character of this category of liability was controversial, but it related only to acts which constituted breach of order.

[7] *Journal of Laws* 1966 No 23, item 149.

[8] These 'bisected offences' still exist today (see art 119 Code of '*wykroczenia*').

[9] *Journal of Laws* 1971 No 12, items 114 and 116.

[10] A Marek, 'Pojęcie prawa karnego, jego funkcje i podział' in A Marek (ed), *System prawa karnego, vol. 1, Zagadnienia ogólne* (Warszawa, CH Beck, 2010) 38.

[11] Trestní zákon správní, č. 88/1950 Sb.; Zákon o trestním řízení soudním (trestní řád), č. 87/1950 Sb.

impose penalties for '*přestupcích*' (misdemeanours, although the term is, as explained for Poland, not entirely satisfactory) were called national councils. Among the behaviours that constituted '*přestupcích*' in the aforementioned substantive Criminal Code were: offences against public order, offences against nationalisation, offences against mechanisation of agriculture,[12] offences against the implementation of the single economic plan, offences against the flow of production or against the prohibition of production of certain goods, and offences against medical institutions and facilities. The most severe penalties were two years' imprisonment and forfeiture of property. Czech scholars refer to this period as the period of 'legalised unlawfulness'.[13] This figurative term was used to express the unfairness of the law.

An important stage for development of the quasi-criminal sanctions was 1961. In that year, not only was a new Criminal Code adopted, but also the Act on local people's courts[14] and the Act defining the tasks of national councils ensuring socialist order.[15] The severity of penalties was relaxed in comparison to the previous period. This was the result of decriminalisation trends and the choice to put greater emphasis on educational aspects of liability.[16] The last-mentioned Act was dedicated to '*přestupcích*', whereas the Act on the local people's courts introduced a new category of offences called '*provinění*'. They were less serious than crimes, but more serious than misdemeanours. Among them were: minor attacks on socialist (public) or private property and the violation of the rules of socialist co-existence.

Furthermore, there was also an important change in the criminal law. Similarly to Soviet law, a substantial element was added to the formal definition of the criminal offence, which meant that, to trigger criminal liability, the behaviour had not only to be consistent with the offence definition set forth by the criminal law, but also had to be 'socially detrimental'. Without the last requirement, the behaviour could, however, still be classified as a misdemeanour or an infringement of the principles of socialist co-existence and socialist morality. Both misdemeanours and infringements of socialist co-existence and socialist morality were adjudicated by civil organisations.[17] The latter kind of behaviour was not an offence but simply an infringement of social rules. It should be underlined that the same substantial element of crime definition was added in Polish criminal law, but in Poland not only crimes but also '*wykroczenie*' have to be socially detrimental. However, there are differences in the requirements concerning the degree of this feature of behaviour.

The local people's courts were organised next to national councils and workplaces. The penalties for '*provinění*' were public reprimand, financial penalty, deduction of up to 15 per cent of remuneration for up to three months, transfer to a lower function or a lower position of employment.[18]

[12] I.e. the usage of machines to improve work in agriculture. The Code entailed a specific chapter with offences involving hindering this mechanisation.

[13] P Mates et al, *Zaklady spravniho prava trestniho* (Praha, CH Beck, 2010) 9.

[14] Zákon č. 38/1961 Sb. o mistnich lidových soudech.

[15] Zákon č. 60/1961 Sb., o úkolech národnich vyborů při zajišťovaní socialistického pořádku.

[16] P Mates et al, *Zaklady spravniho prava trestniho* (Praha, CH Beck, 2010) 10.

[17] The term 'civil organisations' refers to organisations under the communist regime that were close to the state without formally being state bodies.

[18] This category of offences was eliminated from the legal system in 1969, when the Act on petty crimes was introduced (Zákon č. 150/1969 Sb., o přečinech). Petty crimes ('*přečinech*') were treated as a new

As regards misdemeanours, which appear in §§ 7–19 of the aforementioned Act on tasks of national councils ensuring socialist order, they were defined as culpable infringements of duty prescribed in other legal provisions if the infringements caused an obstruction of the state administration tasks or a violation of public order and socialist co-existence of citizens, but simultaneously constituted no crime. According to the Act, many behaviours that were not described formally as misdemeanours could be treated this way. As mentioned before, in the Acts adopted in 1961, the Czechoslovak legislator put more emphasis on educational aspects of punishment; this was also the case for misdemeanours. Therefore the nature of the liability for misdemeanours changed. Sanctions imposed by national councils were rebuke, public reprimand (more severe condemnation than rebuke), fine, forfeiture and the obligation to repair the damage.

B. The Period of Political, Economic and Social Transformation after 1989

(i) Poland

In the period of transformation that started in 1989, the process of transferring offences from the area of criminal law to the law of '*wykroczenia*' came to an end. First of all, this kind of liability did not develop as quickly as before, because decriminalisation trends had weakened. Instead, the transformation resulted in an increase in crimes. However, this was not the only reason for restraining the '*wykroczenia*' development. At the same time, the proceedings relating to '*wykroczenia*' started to become more judicial.[19] An amendment of 1990 to the Code of procedure relating to '*wykroczenia*' changed the position of the councils competent for adjudicating '*wykroczenia*'.[20] Before, they had been organised at the same level as the local administrative authorities. The amendment of 1990 integrated them into the judicial system, situating them at the level of first instance, alongside the regional courts. Appeals against the decisions of the councils were not lodged before appellate councils, but before the regional courts.

The final step in this judicialisation process was made with the adoption of Article 237 of the Polish Constitution in 1997,[21] according to which the councils competent for adjudicating '*wykroczenia*' would cease to exist four years after the entry into force of that legal provision. This change was made in light of the constitutional right to a court hearing, which was understood in a very strict way, and was also justified by the critique of the previous practice of the councils, which were regarded as biased and abusive of their powers. They were not independent from the executive and

category of criminal offences alongside crimes. The penalties applicable to them were imposed by the courts in the proceedings characterised by some differences in relation to the proceedings regarding crimes. See also: W Radecki, 'Kategoryzacja czynów zabronionych pod groźba kary w prawie polskim, czechosłowackim, czeskim i słowackim. Część 1' (2012) 2 *Ius Novum* 13–14.

[19] W Radecki, 'Kategoryzacje czynów zabronionych pod groźbą kary w prawie polskim, czeskim i słowackim. Część 1' (2012) 2 *Ius Novum* 31.

[20] *Journal of Laws* 1990 No 43, item 251.

[21] *Journal of Laws* 1997 No 78 item 483.

punishment for '*wykroczenia*' was overused in the fight against opposition in the period of socialism.[22] Therefore, according to the new Code of procedure in '*wykroczenia*' cases,[23] introduced in 2001, only criminal courts had adjudicative jurisdiction over '*wykroczenia*'. This change also implied more procedural guarantees, in line with those applicable to criminal charges. Although '*wykroczenia*' were adjudicated in proceedings separate from criminal proceedings, those proceedings were clearly criminal in nature. Therefore, it is assumed that it is a criminal liability in the broad sense of the term.[24]

For the contemporary picture of quasi-criminal sanctions it is important to note that the approximation of liability for '*wykroczenia*' to criminal law was accompanied by the development of the number of administrative offences. While the liability originally referred to as 'criminal-administrative' liability (above, section II.A.(i).) became a part of criminal law (especially with respect to procedure, because the criminal nature of the offences called '*wykroczenia*' was already clear to scholars long before the judicialisation process), the legislator filled the ensuing gap in the spectrum of legal control by introducing a new kind of liability, labelled administrative, that had no formal connection with criminal law. These new administrative offences were thus meant to replace the former '*wykroczenia*', to enable faster and more effective punishment of certain petty offences.

The first administrative offences were adopted at the beginning of the 1950s and they concerned the liability of 'social economic units'[25] and their employees.[26] In the 1950s and '60s, many of the new offences were dedicated to the liability of legal persons.[27] Until the early 1990s, this kind of liability did not play an important role. Finally, it should be noted that, simultaneously with the evolution sketched above, approximating liability for '*wykroczenia*' to liability for crimes, the legislator also converted many '*wykroczenia*' into administrative offences. While this change might be interpreted as decriminalisation, it was only apparent decriminalisation. Indeed, these 'new' administrative offences were punished with the same severity in the administrative procedure as before under the '*wykroczenia*' liability regime.

(ii) The Czech Republic

After the political changes in Czechoslovakia, which culminated in the Velvet Revolution, the country was divided into the Czech Republic and Slovakia. In both countries Acts on

[22] J Jakubowska-Hara, 'Ewolucja modelu kontroli sądowej w sprawach o wykroczenia' (1999) 19 *Przegląd Prawa Karnego* 37.

[23] *Journal of Laws* 2001 No 106, item 1138.

[24] A Marek, 'Pojęcie prawa karnego, jego funkcje i podział' in A Marek (ed), *System prawa karnego, vol. 1, Zagadnienia ogólne* (Warszawa, CH Beck, 2010) 38.

[25] Social economic units (or '*jednostki gospodarki uspołecznionej*' in Polish) were units that operated in the centrally planned economy during socialism period. They belonged to the public sector. Some of them were legal persons, others were not. See J Kruszewska and T Jackowski, 'Jednostki gospodarki uspołecznionej w przepisach części ogólnej kodeksu cywilnego' (1969) 11 *Palestra* 36–37.

[26] The first act in which the administrative offences were enshrined was the decree of 28 January 1953 on securing rational and economical use of electricity and heat (*Journal of Laws* No 9, item 26). The Ministry of Energy was entitled to impose a financial penalty not only on the social economic unit, but also on its manager.

[27] Therefore, some scholars perceived this kind of liability as criminal liability of legal persons. The reason was the severity of sanctions. See generally: L Tyszkiewicz, 'Problemy odpowiedzialności karnej osób prawnych (zakładów pracy) w polskim systemie prawnym' (1974) 5 *Prace Prawnicze* 170–71.

'*přestupcích*' (misdemeanours; above, II.A.(ii).) were enacted in 1990.[28] This legislation contained both substantive and procedural rules. According to the new legal framework, the law of '*přestupcích*' became a part of administrative law. This is why, ever since, '*přestupcích*' have been called administrative offences. Nevertheless, these offences are not purely administrative in nature.

'*Přestupcích*' were punishable by reprimand, financial penalty, prohibition of business activity, and/or asset forfeiture. The maximum amount of the financial penalty was set at 1,000 CZK (Czech koruna) in the Czech Act on '*přestupcich*'. Nevertheless, in other Acts the amounts of the financial penalty were very often much higher. For instance, the financial penalty prescribed by the Food and Tobacco Act can amount to 50 million CZK.[29]

Like in Poland, alongside the '*přestupcích*', which originally had a mixed character (criminal-administrative), a new category of administrative offences emerged. They were called '*jine spravni delikty*' (ie other administrative offences). Yet, in contrast to '*přestupcích*', there were no specific liability and procedural rules for this new category of administrative offences under Czech law. They appeared in 1950 and evolved from solely employees' offences to many different kinds of offences. They could be committed by natural and legal persons.[30] One explanation for their development was the pursuit by existing administrative authorities, other than the national councils which were entitled to adjudicate in '*přestupcích*' or misdemeanour cases, to obtain autonomous sanctioning powers. This hunger for autonomous sanctioning powers was part of a more general striving of the executive branch for more powers. Another reason for the development of new administrative offences was the desire for harsher and more effective punishment than the sanctions applicable under the law of '*přestupcích*', especially higher financial penalties.[31] Finally, the development of the administrative liability can also be explained as influenced by the possibility to impose penalties on legal persons under that liability regime.[32] As we will see in section III, these motifs are still relevant today.

III. The Current Situation

When presenting the current situation in Poland and in the Czech Republic, I will concentrate on the new administrative sanctions that were introduced in the 1950s (above, section II.B.(i) and (ii)). As mentioned before, those sanctions were developed in the 1990s as a separate category of offences, distinct from '*wykroczenia*' in Polish law on the one hand, and from '*přestupcích*' in Czech law on the other. As will be explained below, these sanctions can be characterised as quasi-criminal. The trends in their development at the beginning of the 1990s continued in the years 2000.

[28] In the Czech Republic – Zakon č. 200/1990 Sb. o přestupcich, in Slovakia – Zakon č. 372/1990 Zb. o priestupkoch.

[29] Zákon č. 110/1997 Sb. o potravinách a tabákových výrobcích.

[30] W Radecki, 'Kategoryzacje czynów zabronionych pod groźbą kary w prawie polskim, czeskim i słowackim. Część 1' (2012) 2 *Ius Novum* 24–25.

[31] See also: W Radecki, ibid 24.

[32] Ibid, 25–26.

A. Poland

(i) Development of the Liability for Administrative-Criminal Offences

As explained above (section II.B.(i).), due to the approximation of the procedural rules applicable to '*wykroczenia*' cases to the rules of criminal procedure, '*wykroczenia*' became part of the criminal law in the broad sense of the term. However, whenever the legislator wanted to introduce new sanctions other than criminal punishment on the basis of criminal law, he usually opted for administrative offences, not '*wykroczenia*', as they were subject to a faster and less formalistic procedure.[33] This choice was a conscious one; this way, the legislator wanted to overcome the problem concerning the excessive length of court proceedings in Poland, even in '*wykroczenia*' cases.[34] First of all, administrative proceedings generally take place *in camera*, ie behind closed doors. Second, the proceedings are mainly based on documents. Third, less formal evidentiary rules are provided for in administrative cases.

Examples of such changes can be found in the field of maritime law. With an amendment of 1991 to the Maritime Code, the legislator abolished the provisions relating to misdemeanours and, replaced them by new administrative offences.[35] As a result, directors of maritime offices obtained the power to impose financial penalties. The same evolution could be witnessed in mining law, nuclear power law, environmental law, tax law and customs law.[36]

Importantly, not only did the legislator change misdemeanours and even certain crimes into administrative offences, but he also strengthened the protection against specific misconduct by introducing parallel administrative offences alongside crimes and misdemeanours.[37] Consequently, the number of administrative offences increased very quickly and a lot of double-track enforcement mechanisms were created.

The changes regarding misdemeanours were not the only explanation for the situation. The increase in administrative offences was also caused by the process of approximation of the Polish law to the European law and then the accession of Poland to the European Union. To fulfil the obligation deriving from many EU directives to introduce sanctions that are effective, proportionate and dissuasive, the Polish legislator decided to criminalise certain misconducts but, more often, to introduce administrative sanctions.

Furthermore, the preference for administrative sanctions cannot be explained only by the pace of the administrative proceedings, but also by the nature of these

[33] The proceedings in '*wykroczenia*' cases are very similar to proceedings for crimes. Many provisions of the Code for Criminal Procedure are applied, *mutatis mutandi*, in the proceedings for '*wykroczenia*'. By contrast, the procedural rules applied to administrative offences cases belong to the administrative procedure.

[34] See, eg: Judgments of the ECtHR App No 30210/96, *Kudła v Poland*, 26 October 2000; App No 73191/01, *Wawrzynkiewicz v Poland*, 17 February 2007; App No 56026/00, *Wende and Kukówna v Poland*, 24 September 2007.

[35] Act of 4 January 1991 on changes of the Maritime Code, Journal of Laws No 16, item 73.

[36] For a further analysis of the conversion of criminal liability into administrative liability see W Radecki, 'Wprowadzenie. Miejsce prawa wykroczeń w systemie prawa' in M Bojarski (ed), W Radecki (ed), *Kodeks wykroczeń. Komentarz* (Warsaw, CH Beck, 2016) 20–21.

[37] The descriptions of the proscribed acts differ a little bit, but it can be said that this legislator's practice led to double-track enforcement.

infringements. They needed specialisation and thanks to transferring the cases to the existing administrative regulating authorities, those cases could be handled by specialised authorities.

Yet another reason for the development of administrative sanctions is the lack of an effective system of criminal liability for legal persons. Although the Polish legislator adopted the Act on liability of collective entities for punishable offences in 2002,[38] the premises of the liability were formulated in such a way that it was difficult to punish legal persons.[39] This explains why administrative sanctions continued to play an important role in this area.

The dynamic development of administrative liability raises doubts about its nature. The main reason for this is the severity of the applicable penalties. Indeed, the amounts of financial penalties for administrative offences are higher than the maximum fines prescribed for crimes (see also below, III.A.(ii).). What is more, the personal scope of application of those administrative offences is broad, encompassing not only legal persons and natural persons who serve special functions, but also other natural persons. Therefore, some scholars conclude that these offences are criminal in nature and propose to label the liability criminal or administrative-criminal.[40] Bear in mind that, in the past, the term criminal-administrative liability was used in relation to '*wykroczenia*' or misdemeanours (above, II.A.(i).), before they were approximated to criminal liability.[41]

It is worthwhile pointing out that the Constitutional Tribunal played an important role in the process of recognising the real nature of administrative offences. Although the Tribunal used different terminology and presented different criteria, many of the Tribunal's judgments highlight the compound character of the administrative liability.[42] According to the Constitutional Tribunal, not only the principle of rule of law and the principle of proportionality, but also the constitutional principles prescribed for criminal liability (principle of legality, principle of fault, presumption of innocence, right to a defence) have to be applied accordingly in relation to specific examples of administrative liability. However, the Constitutional Tribunal is not consistent in its judgments and there are also judgments in which the Tribunal interprets criminal liability in a strict manner, that is, by adopting a formal approach rather than an autonomous meaning.[43] Moreover, even the criteria of the 'autonomous meaning' are not understood in exactly

[38] The current version of the Act was published in a consolidated act, *Journal of Laws* 2016, item 1541 with amendments.

[39] W Zalewski, 'Odpowiedzialność podmiotu zbiorowego w prawie karnym w poszukiwaniu racjonalności' (2017) 1 *Gdańskie Studia Prawnicze* 389–404.

[40] W Radecki, 'Kary pieniężne w polskim systemie prawnym. Czy nowy rodzaj odpowiedzialności karnej?' (1996) 14/15 *Przegląd Prawa Karnego* 5–18; M Król-Bogomilska, *Kary pieniężne w prawie antymonopolowym* (Warszawa, Scholar, 2001) 13; D Szumiło-Kulczycka, *Prawo administracyjno-karne* (Kraków, Zakamycze, 2004); A Blachnio-Parzych, 'The Nature of Responsibility of an Undertaking in Antitrust Proceedings and the Concept of "Criminal Charge" in the Jurisprudence of the European Court of Human Rights' (2012) 5(6) *Yearbook of Antitrust and Regulatory Studies* 35–55; M Mozgawa, M. Kulik, 'Wybrane zagadnienia z zakresu wzajemnego stosunku odpowiedzialności karnej i administracyjnej' (2016) 3 *Ius Novum* 31–62.

[41] See: n 5.

[42] See the judgment of the Constitutional Tribunal of 1 March 1994, U 7/93, OTK 1994/1/5.

[43] See as example of such a position of the Constitutional Tribunal in judgment of 7 July 2009, K 13/08, OTK-A 2009/7/105. See also the judgment of the Polish Supreme Court of 4 December 2019, II KK 208/19, OSNKW 2020/1/6.

the same way as the term 'criminal charge' developed in the case law of the ECtHR. The Constitutional Tribunal most often refers to the 'repressive' character or function of the examined liability.[44] The reference is criticised by scholars, because it is not clear how the Constitutional Tribunal understands the criterion.[45] Predominantly, the Tribunal concentrates on the aim of the penalty, but the Tribunal sometimes uses the term for every sanction that constitutes a penalty[46] and sometimes only for those that feature a higher level of severity.[47] However, in some judgments the Tribunal noticed the repressive character of the examined sanction, but the formal classification was more important and decisive for the way legislator assessed the liability.[48] In many judgments the Tribunal even declared that the decision of the legislator on the classification of liability, and consequently the character of liability, does not have to be justified.[49]

(ii) The Characteristics of Administrative-Criminal Liability

The liability for administrative offences is regulated by different Acts. The Code of Administrative Procedure (KPA), indeed, does not contain a General Part detailing the rules of administrative liability, similar to the scope and meaning of the General Part of the Criminal Code. Liability for an administrative offence is treated like other administrative cases; this means that the rules are the same for issuing a decision on a specific permission (for example, a building permit) as for imposing an administrative-criminal sanction. Some special rules are, however, stipulated in separate administrative Acts. Because these special rules relate only to the specific group of administrative offences, the legislator decided to provide for similar rules with respect to administrative monetary penalties that are not regulated in a special way.[50] They are enshrined in the Chapter IVa of the Code of Administrative Procedure titled 'Administrative monetary sanctions', which was introduced in 2017. It may be treated as a general part of the liability for the kind of sanctions. The most important provisions of the chapter concern the principle of *nullum crimen sine lege* and *nullum poena sine lege* (Article 189b KPA) and the rules on the severity of the penalty. They do not contain the requirement of fault, nor of the social harmfulness of the act.[51] Therefore, the liability generally has an objective character.

[44] Judgments of the Constitutional Tribunal of 8 December 1998, K 41/97, OTK 1998/7/117; 19 March 2007, K 47/05, OTK-A 2007/3/27; 12 May 2009, P 66/07, OTK-A 2009/5/65.

[45] P Burzyński, 'Ustawowe określenie sankcji karnej' (Warszawa, Wolters Kluwer, 2008) 65; M Sławiński, Pojęcie tzw. przepisów o charakterze represyjnym – uwagi na tle dotychczasowego orzecznictwa Trybunału Konstytucyjnego' (2013) 5 *Przegląd Sejmowy* 75, 93.

[46] Judgment of the Constitutional Tribunal 1 March 1994 r., U 7/93, OTK-A 1994/1/5.

[47] Judgment of the Constitutional Tribunal of 18 April 2000 r., K 23/99, OTK-A 2000/3/89.

[48] See Judgment of the Constitutional Tribunal of 7 July 2009, K 13/08, OTK-A 2009/7/105 with dissenting opinion of Judge W Hermeliński.

[49] Judgment of the Constitutional Tribunal of 15 January 2007, P 19/06, OTK-A 2007/1/2; judgment of the Constitutional Tribunal of 14 October 2009, Kp 4/09, OTK-A 2009/9/134. For analysis of the criteria, see A Błachnio-Parzych, 'Zbieg odpowiedzialności karnej i administracyjno-karnej jako zbieg reżimów odpowiedzialności penalnej' (Warszawa, Wolters Kluwer, 2016) 51–66.

[50] Act on the novelty to the Code of Administrative Procedure and other acts of 7 April 2017, published in *Journal of Laws* 2017, item 935.

[51] The person responsible for the conduct is not punished if the infringement of law occurred due to *force majeure* (art 189e KPA).

It is also important to notice that the legislator provided for the *ne bis in idem* principle, but the principle is confined to the rule regarding the cumulation of penalties. However, the regulations of Chapter IVa do not constitute a complex solution to the problem of ensuring an adequate level of guarantees regarding all administrative-criminal offences.

Due to the fact that there are many administrative offences scattered over different Acts, it is difficult to describe, in a general way, the sanctions that can be imposed for administrative offences. The most severe administrative sanctions are administrative monetary sanctions. They are, however, not always labelled this way in the law; the Polish legislator sometimes uses the term of increased payment (Article 276 of the Environmental Protection Act of 27 April 2001[52]) or additional tax liability (Article 111, paragraph 2 of the Act on Goods and Services Tax of 11 March 2004[53]). Their upper limits are also described in different ways. The maximum penalty may be defined as a precise amount of money (eg 50 million EUR in Article 106, paragraph 2 of the Act on Competition and Consumer Protection[54]), or as the share of some economic values (up to 10 per cent of the entrepreneur's takeover gained in the previous year in Article 106, paragraph 1 of the Act on Competition and Consumer Protection).

Other administrative sanctions are specific prohibitions and orders, for example:

- the withdrawal of a concession by the concession-granting authority when an entrepreneur breaches in a serious way the conditions of the concession, or any other conditions adopted for the economic activity covered by the concession, as provided for in the law (Article 58, paragraph 2.1 of the Freedom of establishment Act of 2 July 2004[55]),
- the withdrawal of the permission for investment funds when the fund infringes law regulations or fails to fulfil the conditions defined in a permission (Article 228 paragraph 1 of the Investment Funds Act of 27 May 2004[56]),
- the prohibition of publication (or transfer) by the management of information concerning the investment fund that may be misleading and the order of appropriate corrections to it (Article 229, paragraph 5 of the Act on Investment Funds Act),
- the obligation to refrain from a specific activity (Article 337 of the Act on the Bank Guarantee Fund, deposit guarantee system and forced restructuring of 10 June 2016[57]),
- the prohibition of offering a retail collective investment product, or the issuing of a public warning indicating the person responsible for the violation of the law and the nature of the violation (Article 3c, paragraphs 1.1 and 1.3 of the Act on Financial Market Supervision of 21 July 2006[58]).

[52] Consolidated text published in *Journal of Laws* 2017, item 519, with amendments.
[53] Consolidated text published in *Journal of Laws* 2017, item 1221, with amendments.
[54] Consolidated text published in *Journal of Laws* 2017, item 229, with amendments.
[55] Consolidated text published in *Journal of Laws* 2017, item 2168, with amendments.
[56] Consolidated text published in *Journal of Laws* 2018, item 56, with amendments.
[57] Consolidated text published in *Journal of Laws* 2017, item 1937, with amendments.
[58] Consolidated text published in *Journal of Laws* 2017, item 196, with amendments.

B. The Czech Republic

(i) Development of Liability for 'Jine Spravni Delikty'

The reasons for the development of administrative sanctions in the Czech Republic were the same as in Poland. Its consequence was the dominance of this form of administrative punishment. Although misdemeanours were treated in the Czech Republic as a kind of administrative punishment, the legislator more often decided to introduce new types of administrative offences other than misdemeanours. According to data presented by H Praškova in 1993 there were 100 Acts containing descriptions of so-called '*jine spravni delikty*' (other administrative offences), and 10 years later 200 Acts.[59] The comparison of the number of crimes and administrative offences is even much more surprising. There were about 300 crimes and 800 administrative offences in 2014.[60] Penalties for administrative offences are imposed by administrative authorities. However, the sanctioning decisions are to be appealed before the courts.[61]

In an attempt to categorise this new type of liability in Czech law, it is useful to underline that Czech scholars consider liability for offences (delicts) as the general category of penal liability (*deliktni odpovědnost*).[62] Within this category, different types of offences are distinguished. The main division is between criminal liability and administrative liability (*spravni odpovědnost*). Consequently, judicial and administrative punishments are distinguished. The administrative liability is divided mainly into liability for misdemeanours (*přestupky*) and 'other administrative offences' (*jine spravni delikty*). Next to them, among others, disciplinary offences are stipulated. There are also administrative sanctions that have a compensatory and/or preventive character.

The result of this mosaic was a lack of uniform understanding of the term 'administrative offence'.[63] According to the most often presented classifications found in the literature, the administrative offences constitute: misdemeanours (*přestupky*); so-called other administrative offences of natural persons (*jine spravni delikty fyzickych osob*); administrative offences of legal persons (*spravni delikty pravnickych osob*); administrative offences of mixed character (*spravni delikty smišene povahy/smišene spravni delikty*);[64] public disciplinary offences (*veřejne disciplinarni delikty*); and so-called administrative offence against public order (*pořadkove spravni delikty*).[65] The analysis of

[59] H Praškova, 'Odpowiedzialność za przestępstwa i za delikty administracyjne w Republice Czeskiej' (2016) 5 *Państwo i Prawo* 90, 93.

[60] Ibid. Among them are, for example, behaviours that threaten trust in capital markets (market manipulation, insider trading), offences against the protection of environment, offences provided for in energy law and antitrust law. Like in Poland, many administrative offences were the result of implementation of EU directives.

[61] W Radecki, 'Recenzja książki Heleny Praškovej, *Zaklady odpovědnosti za spravni delikty (Podstawy odpowiedzialności za delikty administracyjne)*, Wydawnictwo C.H. Beck, Praha 2013' (2014) 1 *Prokuratura i Prawo* 152, 156.

[62] Therefore, 'penal liability' is understood as broader than criminal; it encompasses also other kinds of liability which concern punishment. See H Praškova, 'Spravni delikty pravnickych osob a spravni delikty smišene povahy' in P Mates et al, *Zaklady spravniho prava trestniho* (Praha, CH Beck 2010) 164.

[63] W Radecki, ibid, 157.

[64] See H Praškova, 'Spravni delikty pravnickych osob a spravni delikty smišene povahy' in P Mates et al, *Zaklady spravniho prava trestniho* (Praha, CH Beck 2010) 164.

[65] J Staš, 'Možnosti klasifikace spravnich deliktů' in P Mates et al, *Zaklady spravniho prava trestniho* (Praha, CH Beck, 2010) 17–18.

the kinds of administrative offences leads to the conclusion that the categories are not without overlap. Therefore, some of the offences may be categorised into more than one of the above categories of offences. However, such a division is treated as a reflection of actual development of Czech administrative law.[66]

Many scholars appreciate the advantages of administrative punishment. The main advantages are its high effectiveness, lower costs, and the special knowledge of administrative authorities. The last of these is particularly important with regard to administrative offences for infringements of public economic law. Nevertheless, the advantages cannot overcome the risk of the lack of appropriate level of substantial and procedural guarantees. Although they are lower than guarantees in criminal proceedings, the severity of financial penalties is very often much higher than the severity of fines in criminal proceedings.[67] Therefore, scholars underline the need for compliance with the rule of proportionality in legislative decisions and formulate criteria for distinguishing crimes from administrative offences which can be helpful for the legislator in the process of creation of law. These criteria relate to the nature of the protected values, the level of social harmfulness of act, the character of the forbidden behaviour, the nature and the severity of sanctions, and the level of social disapproval deriving from imposition of a specific penalty.[68]

(ii) The Characteristics of the Liability for 'Jine Spravni Delikty'

Whereas rules regarding misdemeanours were contained in special legislation, liability for '*jine spravni delikty*' (administrative offences), similarly to Poland, was not subject to general rules. The legislator prescribed in some separate Acts, in which the administrative offences were laid down, rules relating to specific groups of administrative offences. On the other hand, courts have interpreted many of the rules using analogy to principles of criminal liability.[69] This has led to critical debate on the legal changes.

The new Act on misdemeanours and proceedings related to misdemeanours was introduced in 2016.[70] This Act contains general rules, similar to the general part of a Code, as well as procedural provisions. It was introduced at the same time as 'the Act on selected misdemeanours',[71] which plays the role of the special part of a Code. It deals with selected types of misdemeanour. However, many types of misdemeanour are still dealt with in other separate Acts. Thanks to both new Acts, the general rules regarding liability for the offences that constituted 'other administrative offences' are now clearly defined.

According to this new legislation, the offences that constituted 'other administrative offences' became misdemeanours, and the latter emerged as a more complex category of offences than before. Although the legislator decided to unify administrative offences

[66] J Staš, ibid, 18.

[67] H Praškova, 'Odpowiedzialność za przestępstwa i delikty administracyjne w Republice Czeskiej' (2016) 5 *Państwo i Prawo* 90, 93–94.

[68] H Praškova, ibid, 93.

[69] See among others judgment of the Supreme Administrative Court of 18 April 2007, Č. j. 4 As 10/2006-57; 31 May 2007, Č. j. 8 As 17/2007-135.

[70] Zákon č. 250/2016 Sb. o odpovědnosti za přestupky a řízení o nich.

[71] Zákon č. 251/2016 Sb. o některých přestupcích.

into a single class of offences, namely misdemeanours, the differences between them remained evident. Liability for misdemeanours of natural persons is based on the fault principle. It differs from liability of legal persons for misdemeanours, which has an objective character. As regards the procedure, the legislator has chosen an administrative procedure as the procedure of auxiliary character, namely the procedure to be applied in default of specifically applicable rules. The proposal to refer to *criminal* procedure as an auxiliary one was not accepted because of the traditional perception that this liability is of an administrative nature in the Czech Republic.[72] Czech scholars do not hesitate to label this as liability to 'administrative punishment'. They underline that, although this branch of law is a part of administrative law, it is strongly connected with criminal law.[73] They refer to it sometimes as a kind of criminal law that constitutes a part of administrative law (*trestni pravo spravni*).[74]

IV. Conclusions

The problems related to the administrative liability of a penal character in Poland and in the Czech Republic are similar. This is a kind of liability that developed in a dynamic way at the beginning of the 1990s. Although these two countries had in their legal systems forms of liability that were derived from administrative liability (the origin of '*wykroczenia*' was liability for 'criminal-administrative' offences in Poland)[75] or still were treated as a kind of administrative liability of a penal character ('*přestupcích*' in the Czech Republic), the legislators more often chose the form of liability that is formally administrative, but has a criminal law character (as in Poland), or some other kind of administrative liability (as it was in the Czech Republic). The main reason for this was the need for greater effectiveness, if the pace of the proceedings and the specialisation of administrative authorities are seen as factors of effectiveness. The change in the character of liability for '*wykroczenia*' was yet another reason for their development in Poland. Doctrine now treats misdemeanours in terms of criminal liability in a broad sense. Some scholars use the term 'criminal law *sensu largo*'.[76] Because proceedings in relation to '*wykroczenia*' are dealt with by criminal courts, all the problems that relate to excessive length of court proceedings in Poland now affect misdemeanour cases.

On the other hand, in both Poland and the Czech Republic, administrative liability with a criminal law character is not regulated in a special way. The cases involving administrative offences were, in the Czech Republic, and in Poland still are, treated like any other administrative cases. Guarantees needed from the perspective of fair trial standards are not provided for in such proceedings. However, in the Czech Republic, they constitute now a kind of '*přestupcích*' (misdemeanour); therefore the substantive rules and procedural provisions are provided for in the general legal system.

[72] See also W Radecki, 'Odpowiedzialność za przestępstwa, wykroczenia i delikty administracyjne w prawie polskim, czeskim i słowackim' (2017) 10 *Prokuratura i Prawo* 18, 27.

[73] H Praškova, ibid; P Průcha, *Správní právo, obecná část* (Praha, Doplněk, 2012) 383.

[74] H Praškova, *Zaklady odpovědnosti za spravni delikty* (Praha, CH Beck, 2013) 3–7.

[75] See section II.A.(i).

[76] A Marek, 'Pojęcie prawa karnego, jego funkcje i podział' in A Marek (ed), *System prawa karnego, vol. 1, Zagadnienia ogólne* (Warszawa, CH Beck, 2010) 34.

The liability for '*přestupcích*' is a kind of administrative liability, but of a penal character. As was mentioned before, 'administrative punishment' is accepted by scholars and it is in accordance with the Czech tradition of such liability.

By contrast in Poland, Chapter IVa, entitled 'Administrative monetary sanctions', introduced by the Polish legislator in 2017 into the Code of Administrative Procedure, cannot be regarded as a solution to the problem of the lack of special regulations relating to administrative offences of a penal character. The Code of Administrative Procedure only regulates some of the issues, and the liability for administrative offences is still treated like any other administrative case. The Polish experience with changes in relation to liability for misdemeanours proves that the introduction of procedural guarantees similar to those in criminal proceedings – for example, the right to be heard before a court understood in a very strict way (meaning that the court always has to be the first option), adequate rights of defence, and formal evidentiary rules – would limit the attractiveness of this kind of liability for the legislator. As was presented in section II.A.(i). of this chapter, the approximation of the proceedings in '*wykroczenia*' cases to criminal proceedings led to a search for other ways of punishment. Therefore, the system of penal liability should be organised in such a way as to add necessary guarantees and to preserve the effectiveness of the proceedings. On the other hand, one should wonder whether the approximation to criminal law is necessary in relation to all administrative offences. Furthermore, although there are procedural guarantees that attach to penal liability that must not be sacrificed for the effectiveness of proceedings, many of them may be prescribed in a way that takes into account the fact that the liability is not of a 'core' criminal law kind.[77] However, this thesis requires a careful examination of the applicable guarantees and their scope or specific shape in proceedings regarding administrative offences that have a criminal law nature.

This analysis of the origins and evolution of quasi-criminal sanctions in Poland and the Czech Republic leads to the conclusion that legislators in these countries have avoided comprehensive solutions to the problem of liability that is formally administrative but has a criminal law character. They have ignored duties deriving from the guarantees that should be introduced in proceedings of a criminal law character just by not calling the liability criminal. It appeared easier to develop other ways of sanctioning that are formally situated in the sphere of administrative law. Furthermore, even judgments in which the Polish Constitutional Tribunal underlined that the lack of guarantees in proceedings in administrative-criminal cases was a systemic problem did not bring about a change in the legislators' approach.[78] The reason is that the Constitutional Tribunal did not work out a unified position regarding the new kind of liability in its jurisprudence (above, III.A.(i).). The legislators' activity was limited only to the introduction of specific provisions in some legislation, which the legislator was obligated to enact by the Tribunal's judgment. However, it has to be underlined that these comments

[77] Judgments of ECtHR App No 73053/01, *Jussila v Finland*, 23 November 2006, para 43; App Nos 24130/11 and 29758/11, *A and B v Norway*, 15 November 2016, para 68.

[78] Judgment of the Constitutional Tribunal of 18 November 2010, P 29/09, OTK-A 2010/9/104. The Tribunal ruled that alongside the official modes of adjudicating on responsibility for acts exhibiting features of crimes, a secondary mode of repression is developing through economic sanctions. They are more painful than fines provided for by criminal law, but they are adjudicated without appropriate standards.

refer much more to the Polish legislator. In the Czech system, the legislation on misdemeanours and proceedings related to misdemeanour cases and the Act on selected misdemeanours introduced in 2016 are evidence that the Czech legislator has recently taken action that reveals a more holistic approach to administrative liability of a criminal law nature. In contrast, the aforementioned Chapter IVa introduced into the Code of Administrative Procedure in 2017 in Poland proves that the Polish legislator has still not faced this challenge in an adequate way.

5

The Interplay between Criminal and Quasi-criminal Enforcement Mechanisms in the UK Context Explored through the Prism of 'Market Abuse': Current Approaches and Historical Perspectives

SARAH WILSON AND GARY WILSON

I. Introduction: Background and Context

On 20 March 2018, the Court of Justice of the European Union (CJEU) delivered its preliminary ruling in the joined Italian cases of *Di Puma* and *Zecca*.[1] The ruling followed as a consequence of guidance sought by the Italian state on the provision in Italian law for both criminal and administrative sanctions for insider dealing, with reference to concerns about possible duplication given the potential 'quasi-criminal' status of the latter, and thereby the application of the principle *ne bis in idem*. As is well known, the principle of *ne bis in idem* represents the legal position that a person cannot be criminally prosecuted or punished more than once for the same offence. This position – manifested in the English legal tradition as the rule against double jeopardy[2] – is a fundamental right recognised by both the Charter of Fundamental Rights of the European Union (the Charter)[3] and the European Convention on Human Rights (ECHR),[4] with this case involving the interpretation of both. Interestingly

[1] C-596/16, *Enzo Di Puma v Commissione Nazionale per le Società e la Borsa* (Consob), and C-597/16, *Commissione Nazionale per le Società e la Borsa (Consob) v Antonio Zecca*, Judgment of the European Court of Justice (Grand Chamber) 20 March 2018.

[2] See eg English Bar Council *Response to Commission's December 2005 Green Paper COM (2005) 696 final on: Conflicts of Jurisdiction and the Principle of ne bis in idem in Criminal Proceedings* (London, 29 March 2006).

[3] Charter of Fundamental Rights of the European Union (2000/C 364/01) The Official Journal of the European Communities: http://www.europarl.europa.eu/charter/pdf/text_en.pdf.

[4] Convention for the Protection of Human Rights and Fundamental Freedoms (European Convention on Human Rights, as amended) (ECHR) https://www.echr.coe.int/Documents/Convention_ENG.pdf.

for this analysis, this ruling actually concerned the application of the *ne bis in idem* principle in situations where, following *criminal* proceedings ending in acquittal, an *administrative* fine had been imposed.

In this case, Zecca (together with Di Puma) challenged the legality of an administrative fine imposed by the Italian National Companies and Stock Exchange Commission ('Consob'), because it related to conduct for which they had been tried and acquitted; namely, respectively, unlawful disclosure of inside information by Di Puma and trading with this information by Zecca. Di Puma and Zecca asserted that the subsequent administrative action, brought in respect of these same acts, was unlawful on account of the *res judicata* effect of the criminal proceedings. From this, the referring Italian court – the Court of Cassation – asked the CJEU whether, in meeting its obligation to provide for effective, proportionate and dissuasive penalties for infringements of insider dealing prohibitions under European law,[5] Italian legislation is precluded from permitting administrative proceedings to be brought for acts already subject to criminal proceedings. It was held by the CJEU that where there exists a final criminal judgment of acquittal, finding that there is no offence, the act of bringing proceedings for an administrative fine 'of a criminal nature' (for the same acts) infringes the *ne bis in idem* principle. It was also explained by the CJEU that such an infringement in turn constitutes a limitation of the fundamental right guaranteed by Article 50 of the Charter,[6] and that such a limitation is not easily justified.

On the facts of the case this was found to be so *even* in the light of what is considered necessary for guaranteeing the integrity of the financial markets of the EU and public confidence in financial instruments.[7] In summary, the protection conferred by the *ne bis in idem* principle is not limited to situations in which the person concerned has been subject to a criminal conviction, but extends also to those in which that person is finally acquitted.[8] The ruling helps to frame this analysis of how enforcement pathways and sanctions arising through them which are *not* part of the framework of criminal enforcement might be regarded as 'quasi-criminal'. Here, significance is attached particularly to the guidance sought by the Italian state as to whether, after a court has delivered a final judgment finding a defendant not to have committed the criminal offence alleged, such judgment precludes the pursuit of further formally labelled administrative proceedings based on the same facts with a view to the imposition of penalties which, on account of their *nature and severity*, may be *regarded as* criminal penalties.

In framing this particular consideration of so-called 'quasi-criminal enforcement mechanisms'(QCEM) in the UK, it is important to note that the conjoined case of *Zecca* and *Di Puma* was itself, together with a further conjoined pair *Garlsson Real Estate & Others*[9] and *Menci*, part of a quartet of cases heard by

[5] The law at the relevant time was embodied in the Market Abuse Directive (MAD) 2003, Directive 2003/6/EC of the European Parliament and of the Council of 28 January 2003 on insider dealing and market manipulation (Market Abuse Directive) [2003] OJ L 96/16-25: https://eur-lex.europa.eu/eli/dir/2003/6/oj.

[6] *Di Puma and Zecca*, Judgment of the European Court of Justice (Grand Chamber), above n 1, at para 40.

[7] Ibid, para 46.

[8] Ibid, para 39.

[9] C-537/16, *Garlsson Real Estate SA (in liquidation), Stefano Ricucci, Magiste International SA v Commissione Nazionale per le Società e La Borsa (CONSOB)*, Judgment of the European Court of Justice (Grand Chamber) (EU:C:2018:193).

the CJEU.[10] These cases are considered very important for focusing on UK experiences, notwithstanding the UK's formal departure from the European Union on 31 January 2020, through the process of 'Brexit'. Most obviously, this is because *ne bis in idem* subsists as the rule against double jeopardy in the UK and in the wider common law tradition, and applies across violations of criminal law. These CJEU rulings are authority that the principle applies across different ways in which wrongdoing on the part of individuals can be punished by the state and not just to its pursuit as *criminal* conduct. This position is pertinent for what are known as 'dualist' legal cultures such as the UK, in which the state engages in *non-criminal* enforcement alongside *criminal* enforcement. The former species of legal action is conventionally termed an 'administrative' offence in European legal discourse, and a 'civil' or 'non-criminal' offence in the UK and the wider common law tradition.[11] The UK is properly regarded as a 'dualist' regime on account of the fact that, on occasions, both species of liability can be incurred for substantially the same conduct.

This quartet of cases helps to frame the interest of this analysis in quasi-criminal enforcement mechanisms in many ways. The cases potentially have much to reveal on what QCEMs actually are and how they might be defined. They can also help to expose why we should be concerned about QCEMs in the light of CJEU reflections on how administrative responses are capable of being 'of a criminal nature',[12] on account of the 'nature and severity' of penalties imposed.[13] These rulings have arisen through the very operation of 'dualist' approaches to conduct considered unacceptable, and which the state has an interest in punishing. This suggests that the cases also speak to how it is through the possibilities for responding to the same misconduct in different ways, that the scope for identifying and phenomenalising QCEM arises. The factual setting for the CJEU to examine the interplay between 'criminal' and 'administrative' enforcement in *Zecca* and *Di Puma* and also *Garlsson* is also directly relevant for this analysis. All three cases involved 'market misconduct', which has traditionally given rise to Member States' obligation to provide a regime of *administrative* sanctions which are 'effective and persuasive' as well as 'proportionate'.[14] So-called 'market abuse' is now also subject to minimum criminalisation requirements,[15] thereby making all European Member States inherently 'dualist' to some degree. Fundamentally this quartet of cases frames how this analysis explores the phenomenon of 'quasi-criminal' sanctions through reference to 'market abuse', and by paying attention to how it is commonly considered a type of 'financial crime'.

[10] C-524/15, *Re Luca Menci* Judgment of the European Court of Justice (Grand Chamber) (EU:C:2018:197).

[11] These terms are widely to be found used interchangeably, arising from European emphasis of the language of 'administrative' enforcement and sanctioning, and a cultural tradition of reference to 'civil' and 'non-criminal' in the UK. Contextual sensitivity is also required as the UK also uses the terminology of 'civil' for demarking private law between individuals; and this must also be situated alongside understandings of 'civilian' and 'common law' legal traditions.

[12] *Di Puma and Zecca*, Judgment of the European Court of Justice (Grand Chamber), above n 1, at para 25.

[13] Ibid, para 22.

[14] As evident in many statements within and pertaining to the MAD 2003; see eg MAD 2003 Art 14.

[15] As embodied in the Directive on Criminal Sanctions for Market Abuse, Directive 2014/57/EU of the European Parliament and of the Council of 16 April 2014 on criminal sanctions for market abuse (Market Abuse Directive) [2014] OJ L 173/179, also widely found abbreviated as CSMAD 2014; see https://eur-lex.europa.eu/eli/dir/2014/57/oj.

II. Defining 'Market Abuse' and 'Financial Crime': Understanding Quasi-criminal Enforcement in the UK

All four cases concerned types of financial misconduct which are commonly found referenced as 'financial crime' in key discourses.[16] *Menci* arose in relation to alleged violations of the Value Added Tax (VAT) Directive,[17] and the remaining three cases involved alleged 'market abuse'. 'Market abuse' is a construct applied within European law and wider policy discourse, as an overarching term for conduct regarded as interfering with the effective functioning of capital markets, and which can itself be categorised either as 'market manipulation' or 'insider dealing'. More discussion of this terminology will follow, but at this stage the 'market manipulation' at the heart of the CJEU's consideration of *Garlsson* and 'insider dealing' underpinning *Zecca and Di Puma* help to make a more fundamental point still. By virtue of concerning types of misconduct widely found recognised as types of 'financial crime', these cases provide an interesting context for examining QCEM in the light of CJEU observations on administrative outcomes which are considered to have the nature and severity of criminal sanctions. All the more so, given how generally 'financial crimes' have the reputation of being 'amongst the most difficult crimes' for legal systems to 'deal with … let alone control'.[18] Such viewpoints help to illuminate the arguments which can – and are – made in favour of administrative enforcement. From this general position, reference to 'market abuse' specifically can assist in demonstrating very effectively how administrative enforcement can acquire quasi-criminal characteristics, and why we should be concerned about this.

A. The Complexities of Defining and Problematising 'Financial Crime'

The term 'financial crime' is in many ways a flawed construct.[19] This is because it lacks an agreed international definition and its potentially very wide import has led to carelessness in its use. It *is* however widely used. Furthermore, whilst 'financial crime' can actually be found defined in the UK in law itself, the pertinent Financial Services and Markets Act (FSMA) 2000 definition is not intended to provide a

[16] Key discourses are identified in this reseach as ones arising from key stakeholder interests; mainly academic scholarship, enforcement and regulatory communities, policy-making, and in the wider public sphere.

[17] *Re Luca Menci*, above n 10, in violation of Council Directive 2006/112/EC of 28 November 2006 on the common system of value added tax [2006] OJ L 347.

[18] R Tomasic, 'The financial crisis and the haphazard pursuit of financial crime' (2011) 18(1) *Journal of Financial Crime* 7; 7.

[19] See eg International Monetary Fund (IMF), *Financial System Abuse, Financial Crime and Money Laundering – Background Paper* (Washington DC, 2001); see also the analysis in S Wilson, *The Origins of Modern Financial Crime in Britain: Historical Foundations and Current Problems* (Abingdon, Routledge, 2014).

comprehensive definition, and looks instead to frame the responsibilities of the UK financial conduct regulator.[20] Here, market abuse is 'financial crime' by virtue of being 'misconduct in, or misuse of information relating to, a financial market'.[21] However, it is also the case that reference made to 'market abuse' in the public sphere, including in high-profile discourses in the political sphere, or even by regulators and prosecutors themselves, does not always follow the law's nomenclature. Accordingly, the ways in which the terms 'market abuse' and 'financial crime' are used, and commonly in conjunction with one another are interesting, and highly salient for what the context of market abuse enforcement can reveal about the UK's use of QCEM, and about the concerns which should attach to this. This can be seen for example in reflections from then-Chancellor of the Exchequer, George Osborne MP, who in 2015 insisted that those who committed 'financial crime' and 'fraudulently manipulated' financial markets would be punished severely, and indeed jailed,[22] doing so without any apparent regard for how market manipulation is commonly regarded as a type of financial crime.

More interesting still are reflections from those who are directly involved with enforcement of market abuse legislation. Administrative enforcement of 'market abuse' law in the UK is undertaken by the Financial Conduct Authority (FCA), which in European parlance represents a Member State's 'competent authority'. The FCA can, however, also undertake criminal prosecutions of insider dealing and market manipulation, thus placing this Authority's remit firmly at the heart of examining how administrative sanctions might acquire qualities of criminal enforcement. The FCA has this central role notwithstanding that it is not a 'mainstream prosecutor' of financial crime,[23] with this activity arising directly from the FCA's remit to protect the UK financial system.[24] Notwithstanding this, evidence of regarding market abuse as 'financial crime' *can* be found in reflections from key FCA personnel, and those of its predecessor body, the Financial Services Authority (FSA).[25] That there is a tradition of explicit reference to 'financial crime' within UK financial services legislation, which underpins the regulatory activity of the FCA (and its

[20] Principally concerning protecting the 'integrity' of the UK financial system; see further the FCA's statutory operational objectives underpinning its strategic objective of ensuring the functioning of UK financial markets, which are consumer protection, integrity, and competition. The integrity objective amounts to 'protecting and enhancing the integrity of the UK financial system' in ways which include ensuring that it is not being used for purposes connected with financial crime; see s 1B and s 1D(2)(b) and (c) FSMA 2000 (as amended by the Financial Services Act 2012).

[21] By virtue of s 1H(3)(b) FSMA 2000.

[22] Rt Hon George Osborne MP, Mansion House Speech (London, 10 June 2015): https://www.gov.uk/government/speeches/mansion-house-2015-speech-by-the-chancellor-of-the-exchequer.

[23] The UK's most high-profile prosecutor of financial crime is the Serious Fraud Office, which has jurisdiction in England, Wales and Northern Ireland, with the Crown Prosecution Service also undertaking fraud prosecutions in England and Wales. In Scotland the Crown Office and Procurator Fiscal Service (COPFS) is part of the Scottish Government, with responsibility for a number of core functions, including the prosecution of crime.

[24] See H Sants 'Delivering intensive supervision and credible deterrence', Reuters Newsmakers Event speech, 12 March 2009, archived at: https://webarchive.nationalarchives.gov.uk/20090903063050/http://www.fsa.gov.uk/pages/Library/Communication/Speeches/2009/0312_hs.shtml.

[25] The UK 'Twin Peaks' regime replaced the single 'super-regulator' Financial Services Authority regime in April 2013, implementing the Financial Services Act 2012.

predecessor),[26] makes it unsurprising that key personnel should allude to it.[27] However, this interest from these key post-holders generally lacks any kind of reference to wider conceptualisations of 'financial crime'. This *is* perhaps surprising, given that insider dealing has been described in such spheres as very serious 'financial crime'.[28] It is also surprising because insider dealing – together with market manipulation – also subsists as a *non-criminal* offence, and so thus as *other than* as activity which can be considered 'serious crime'.

It is partly on account of 'dualist' enforcement approaches that the International Monetary Fund (IMF) has expressed its preference for the alternative terminology of 'financial abuse'.[29] But underpinning this preference is also a perception that different approaches to criminalisation between states also reflect different perspectives on the 'wrongfulness' of these activities. Here, UK experiences illustrate how the use of the terminology of 'financial crime' to illuminate 'market abuse' can also be highly normative, and is thereby looking to persuade, constitute, and reinforce particular perceptions of it. This proposition is evident in UK enforcement discourse, as saliently illustrated in reflections from one-time Head of Enforcement at the FSA, Margaret Cole. In insisting that insider dealing is properly regarded as 'serious' crime, Ms Cole acknowledged that it did not attract 'moral outrage' in ways which could be readily identified in other types of crime.[30] On this occasion, Ms Cole also used the terminology of 'white-collar crime' when explaining that insider dealing carried a potential term of imprisonment of up to seven years, albeit doing so without reference to white-collar crime's intellectual heritage and conceptual tradition. Although there was no such reference to 'white-collar crime' in George Osborne's 2015 reflections, or in the subsequent lament from former UK Premier Gordon Brown in 2017 that financial crimes committed by bankers during the crisis remained unpunished,[31] the use of language *does* also appear to have been normative on both of these latter occasions. And in purveying their respective messages that financial misconduct is serious crime, and activity which *should* attract perceptions and responses reflecting this, both George Osborne and Gordon Brown referenced 'fraud' in doing so. This is a term which is commonly found used alongside those of 'financial crime' and also 'market abuse'.

[26] See above n 20.

[27] Reference will be made to reflections from Margaret Cole and Tracey McDermott, both former Directors of Enforcement at the FSA.

[28] M Cole, 'The FSA's approach to insider dealing', Speech to the American Bar Association, 4 October 2007. Ms Cole was at the time the FSA's Director of Enforcement. The speech is archived at https://webarchive.nationalarchives.gov.uk/20090903073700/http://www.fsa.gov.uk/pages/Library/Communication/Speeches/2007/1004_mc.shtml.

[29] International Monetary Fund (IMF) (2001) *Financial System Abuse, Financial Crime and Money Laundering – Background Paper*, above n 19, para 5.

[30] M Cole, 'The FSA's approach to insider dealing', above n 28.

[31] L Elliott, 'Gordon Brown: Bankers should have been jailed for role in financial crisis. Ex-PM warns failure to take tougher stand has made it inevitable that rogue bankers will again gamble with public money' *The Guardian*, London, 31 October 2017: https://www.theguardian.com/politics/2017/oct/31/gordon-brown-bankers-should-have-been-jailed-for-role-in-financial-crisis.

B. The Value of the 'Market Abuse' Case Study

Examining these different terminologies, together with their evident nexuses, particularly as these are evident in the public sphere, can now help us to uncover why financial crimes might be considered to be amongst the most difficult for legal systems to control. In turn this can also speak to the identification and problematisation of QCEM by the analysis here. These propositions are explored through engaging with the 'case study' of 'market abuse'. In UK discourse the term 'market abuse' is found utilised as an overarching construct for the ways in which financial markets can be abused through the occurrence of what is known as 'insider dealing' and 'market manipulation'. The terminology of market abuse itself is a creature of European law and policy which anchors UK law on account of the influence brought to bear by European capital markets law on domestic (UK) law. UK law relating to insider dealing and market manipulation was not always so configured; the earliest criminalisation of insider dealing, which occurred in 1980, was modelled on US fiduciary approaches, whilst the criminalisation of market manipulation pre-dates this by a century or more. In terms of why legal regimes choose to outlaw 'market abuse' at all, we can see concern for behaviours committed within capital markets which are thought to interfere with the proper functioning of these markets.

In proposing that capital markets perform the basic function of a market – to distribute commodities to those who are in need – capital markets are widely regarded as a vital mechanism for ensuring that capital is channelled effectively from those who have it – namely investors – into the sectors of the economy most in need of it, by virtue of being the most dynamic, innovative or otherwise 'important' areas of growth. In European capital markets law, behaviours which are considered capable of undermining the effective capital market function rather than being supportive of it are said to be 'abusive', and thereby to encourage *disorderly* rather than *orderly* market functioning. Any market mechanism is reliant on information and information-flow to promote an effective channelling of capital resources from those who have them towards those in need of them, and on this reasoning many states have legal regimes which acknowledge the importance of information for generating investment activity within financial markets. What becomes apparent from examining different state regimes is that this objective can be pursued in quite different ways, and can subsist in considerably different degrees. For insider dealing specifically, European prohibitions are much more extensive than those found in the US, where US securities law manifests much greater permitted use of information not available to the market. In the pursuit of far-reaching prohibitions, European law underpinning current UK law is premised on the theoretical position that capital will only move in this way, functionally and efficiently, if investors are confident that what appear to be the most promising spheres of economic activity are actually such, and that the securities which facilitate this capital transfer are accurately priced as a reflection of this.[32]

[32] Hence the general emphasis on the need for generating market confidence in European capital markets law policy, see N Moloney, 'Confidence and Competence: the Conundrum of EC Capital Markets Law' (2004) 4 *Journal of Corporate Law Studies* 1.

This 'market-based' rationale brings a wide range of activities within the scope of 'abuse', whereby liability for conduct considered abusive can be incurred potentially by anyone. European capital markets law espouses the idea that requisite 'market confidence' will not arise where there are concerns that information relating to pricing and availability of securities is not disseminated so that it is capable of being accessed by all market participants, or that such information which is available is not accurate. From this, very extensive so-called insider dealing prohibitions look to outlaw improper disclosure of, and dealing which occurs with the benefit of, information about an entity or securities in it which is not available generally in the market, but which if it were available would have a bearing on the market price.[33] Alongside this, prohibitions on market manipulation look to outlaw behaviour which interferes with the accuracy of information underpinning investment decisions. Such interference occurs through making statements to the financial markets about the value of securities in order to create a false or misleading impression about the availability and value of these products, or engaging in conduct designed to give a distorted view of the true market in them or their price or value.[34]

The predominance of European influences in UK prohibitions of insider dealing and market manipulation has been configured as the migration of European capital markets law into UK corporate and securities law.[35] The earliest stages of this migration can be seen in how current criminal law prohibitions of insider dealing pursuant to the Criminal Justice Act 1993 implemented the 1989 Directive coordinating regulations on insider dealing.[36] In the years which followed, the harmonising tendencies of European law would intensify, as is evident in the UK's creation of its first non-criminal 'market abuse' offence in 2000.[37] The Market Abuse Directive (MAD) 2003,[38] obliging Member States to provide a regime of administrative sanctions for market abuse which were 'effective, proportionate, and dissuasive',[39] would provide the basis of the rulings in *Zecca and Di Puma* and *Garlsson*.[40] In 2005 the UK achieved compliance with the MAD 2003 through insertions made to the FSMA 2000 by the Financial Services and Markets Act 2000 (Market Abuse) Regulations 2005:[41] whilst many believed that the market abuse offence as originally drafted was capable of including insider dealing, the 2005 Regulations made explicit provision for this. But it was through the implementation of the 1989 Directive that UK insider dealing law became very *consciously*

[33] Non-criminal liability now arises under the Market Abuse Regulation – Regulation (EU) No 596/2014 of the European Parliament and of the Council of 16 April 2014 on market abuse (Market Abuse Regulation), [2014] OJ L 173/1; also found widely abbreviated as MAR 2014: https://eur-lex.europa.eu/eli/reg/2014/596/oj, with criminal liability arising under (Part V) s 52 Criminal Justice Act 1993.

[34] Non-criminal liability now arises under MAR 2014 (above n 33), with criminal liability arising under (Part 7) ss 89–91 Financial Services Act 2012.

[35] See, eg, P Davies, 'The European Community's Directive on Insider Dealing: From Company Law to Securities Market Regulation' (1991) 11 *Oxford Journal of Legal Studies* 92

[36] Council Directive 89/592/EEC of 13 November 1989 coordinating regulations on insider dealing.

[37] Courtesy of section 118 FSMA 2000.

[38] See above n 5, and see eg G Wilson and S Wilson, 'Market misconduct, the FSA and creating a system of "city grasses": blowing the whistle on whistle-blowing' (2010) 31(3) *Company Lawyer* 67.

[39] See MAD 2003, Art 14(1).

[40] See eg *Di Puma and Zecca*, above n 1, para 19.

[41] See also below n 116, and text thereto.

European in a highly fundamental way. It was at this point that the conceptual basis for UK insider dealing laws shifted away from the US 'micro' relationships-based fiduciary approach,[42] which had characterised the earliest UK criminalisations in 1980[43] and 1985.[44] The Criminal Justice Act 1993 prohibitions marked a replacement of this approach with the 'market egalitarianism' of European capital markets law. This provides a 'macro' or 'market-based' justification for imposing prohibitions on trading with information not generally known to the market;[45] and is underpinned by European single market aspirations,[46] built on the four freedoms of movement, including free movement of capital.[47]

C. The Significance of the UK 'Case Study'

In looking to explore whether any discernible European thinking on and application of QCEMs can be found, and if so, how any identifiable features might be mapped, experiences from Member States are of course generally important. It is also true that distinct cultural contexts could provide an interesting 'off set' for an increasingly harmonised overall regulatory approach. In the light of these considerations, the UK might provide a particularly noteworthy case study. Indeed, the UK is uniquely placed, not only as a former Member State which is currently working through the consequences of leaving 'the Club' of the EU, but also because of how its membership has been characterised by actively seeking to 'ring-fence' European influences in certain key regards, most saliently in negotiated 'opt-outs' for matters relating to crime, justice and security.[48] In turn, several factors make 'market abuse' laws an interesting and effective way to draw out UK experiences of enforcement which might amount to QCEMs. Market abuse provides a clear example of where the three distinct legal systems found within the United Kingdom of Great Britain and Northern Ireland can be viewed as united, rather than showing certain jurisdictional and cultural peculiarities between them;[49] with this position contrasting with laws relating to fraud for example, where Scotland's laws have always been different from those found in England and Wales. Market abuse is also a sphere where the use of both 'criminal' and 'non-criminal' enforcement pathways can be found, thus providing a rich and fertile setting for considering how non-criminal enforcement might be conceptualised as 'quasi-criminal' and might invite perceptions of being 'of a criminal nature'. And whilst Member States are

[42] As explained in N Moloney, *EU Securities and Financial Markets Regulation*, 3rd edn (Oxford, Oxford University Press, 2014) 700–705.

[43] Part V, Companies Act 1980.

[44] Company Securities (Insider Dealing) Act 1985.

[45] See eg N Moloney, *EU Securities and Financial Markets Regulation*, above n 42.

[46] See eg European Commission, *Making the EU Single Market work: Single Market Forum 2014: 20 conferences and workshops across Europe in 2014* (Ref. Ares(2015)5663327 – 08/12/2015), see: https://ec.europa.eu/info/events/single-market-forum.

[47] Ibid.

[48] As part of 'opt-out' provisions negotiated by the New Labour government under Tony Blair as a condition of the UK signing up to the Lisbon Treaty in 2009. In the present context it is pertinent to note that the UK chose to opt out of the CSMAD 2014.

[49] As between the legal systems of England and Wales, Scotland, and Northern Ireland.

now subject to minimum criminalisation obligations arising under the CSMAD 2014 alongside longstanding administrative obligations arising initially under the MAD 2003, the UK can point to a sizable body of criminal enforcement activity alongside considerable regulator enthusiasm for the non-criminal administrative pathway. As will be considered shortly, the UK's position in relation to criminal enforcement appears to be historically rooted, with this appearing also to explain its much more recent adoption of state-focused administrative approaches in this sphere.

III. Phenomenalising QCEMs through UK Enforcement Experiences

Whilst the influence of European capital markets law on domestic UK approaches is manifest, some rhetorical distinctiveness does subsist. Overall the terminology of 'market abuse' is not as widely used in domestic UK discourses as it is in European ones, and where it is, it is used much more readily in relation to 'market manipulation' than for 'insider dealing'. It is also the case that 'financial crime' is much more a trope of common law jurisdictions, with European discourses utilising much more extensively the terminology of 'economic crime'.[50] For the UK, recognising that references which are made to 'market abuse' as 'financial crime' in high-profile discourse in the public sphere by politicians, policy-makers and regulators can be highly normative, might prove valuable for identifying the interest which should be taken in the capability of administrative sanctions to be QCEM. This is evident in George Osborne's insistence that those who manipulate financial markets should be in prison, because in 'any other walk of life' they would, with this view premised precisely on how 'so few individuals have faced punishment in the courts'.[51] For Margaret Cole, insider dealing should be regarded as a very serious crime, though she clearly appreciates that obstacles to this are presented by the lack of 'moral outrage' which attaches to this activity, and certainly so in contrast to perceptions of violent crime.[52] For George Osborne it was right and proper to be tackling financial crime on account of public demand for tough responses,[53] and perhaps unsurprisingly for a regulator rather than a politician, Margaret Cole's references to insider dealing as 'serious crime' are rather less strident. However, it is also the case that Ms Cole's reflections are coming from a place of proximity in understanding that these activities are not readily regarded as 'crimes' in the public consciousness.

[50] The CSMAD 2014 *does* cite the reference, in the de Larosière Group Report (High-Level Group on Financial Supervision in the EU) of 2009, to 'financial crime', but reference to economic crime is more prominent and extensive, see eg the Council of Europe Economic Crime and Cooperation Division: https://www.coe.int/en/web/corruption/home, and there could also be a difference in approach here between the Council of Europe and the EU. For discussion of the meaning and difference between economic and financial criminal law, see eg K Ligeti and V Franssen, 'Current Challenges in Economic and Financial Criminal Law in Europe and the US' in K Ligeti and V Franssen, *Challenges in the Field of Economic and Financial Criminal Law in Europe and the US* (Oxford, Hart Publishing, 2017), 1.

[51] G Osborne, Mansion House Speech 2015, above n 22.

[52] M Cole, 'The FSA's approach to insider dealing', above n 28.

[53] G Osborne, Mansion House Speech 2015, above n 22.

A. Illuminating Enforcement Challenges through the 'Market Abuse' Case Study

Indeed, Ms Cole appears to be acutely aware that convincing the general public that financial market misconduct *should* enjoy wider regard as criminal activity is challenging, and even that such conduct is 'among the most difficult' for legal systems to address. These challenges are themselves rooted in the viewpoint that no jurisdiction has achieved 'great … success' using criminal law in combating 'sophisticated abusive activity on its capital markets'.[54] Views that effective criminal prosecution of financial misconduct crime is wanting are commonly attributed to 'standards and procedures of the traditional criminal justice system, which are necessary to ensure general civil and human liberties'.[55] In domestic UK legal culture, these are most clearly associated with the burden of proof lying with the state, and the standard of proof for criminal proceedings being beyond reasonable doubt, together with the 'cornerstone' British values of the right to a fair trial, and to a trial by one's peers (through the jury system), and protection conferred by the presumption of innocence. The standpoint that the inherent architecture of many legal systems presents 'almost insurmountable barriers' to effective prosecution of market abuse is one that could be applied widely across jurisdictions.

More recently in the UK, a key Treasury Consultation from 2012, in outlining government interest in new criminalisation now embodied in the Banking Reform Act 2013,[56] warned that the use of criminal enforcement is beset with a number of practical obstacles.[57] Concern about the difficulties entailed in using criminal law in response to market abuse clearly underpinned European insistence under the MAD 2003 that Member States *must* have a regime of 'effective, proportionate, and dissuasive' *administrative* sanctions, whilst acknowledging – somewhat grudgingly even – that Member States might also wish to have a regime of criminal responses.[58] In this era of policy-making, European regard for administrative sanctions reflected a wider general appeal for effective enforcement approaches in response to concerns clustering around a perceived 'enforcement gap' arising from the difficulties entailed in achieving criminal convictions, which meant criminal law was unlikely to be an effective deterrent.[59] Administrative actions, in contrast, are underpinned by fewer procedural protections for those subject to them, including a lower burden of proof for the state.[60] They also reflect a different consciousness of wrongdoing evident in the absence of mens rea requirements.

[54] B Rider, 'Civilising the Law – The Use of Civil and Administrative Proceedings to Enforce Financial Services Law' (1995) 3(1) *Journal of Financial Crime* 11, 13.

[55] Ibid.

[56] To give it its full title, the Financial Services (Banking Reform) Act 2013.

[57] HM Treasury, *Sanctions for the directors of failed banks* (London, 3 July 2012), part 4, 15, paras 4.14–4.17.

[58] See MAD 2003, Art 14.

[59] Indeed, the UK secured the first conviction under s 52 Criminal Justice Act 1993 in 2009 (against Christopher McQuiod) see FSA reaction to this in: http://www.telegraph.co.uk/finance/newsbysector/banksandfinance/7696855/FSAs-Margaret-Cole-wages-war-against-criminals-in-the-City.html; see also reflections on criminal enforcement in (the administrative Tribunal ruling) *Hannam v FCA* [2014] UKUT 0233 (TCC), para 186.

[60] As seen discussed in *Hannam* itself, eg para 25.

B. The Market Abuse Case Study: How Enforcement Pathways Might Become 'Blurred'

However, both administrative and criminal proceedings *are* state responses to misconduct. As such, both can be seen to embody reactions to wrongdoing which is considered serious, by virtue of the state's interest in enforcement. This can in turn provide a premise for exploring the similarities as well as evident differences between these actions. In administrative/civil/regulatory actions, in mediating relations between individuals and the state, it is the state rather than individuals undertaking control of particular legal wrongs,[61] here for 'social regulation' reasons.[62] Whilst 'social regulation' justifies government intervention to address specific matters of social importance which would otherwise be unregulated, this is conceptually different from the unique right of the state to punish misconduct considered not simply wrongful but actually 'socially injurious'.[63] The above-mentioned *Zecca* judgment reveals concerns that the theoretical and conceptual distinctions which do subsist between civil regulatory/non-criminal administrative responses and criminal law – and thereby administrative and criminal enforcement – can become blurred.[64] As cases like *Zecca* succinctly demonstrate, the risk of this occurring is perhaps especially acute where regulatory/ administrative offences are in essence counterparts of criminal offences, with different enforcement modes arising from substantially the same unacceptable conduct. European policy-making has now of course changed its emphasis, with an evident much stronger regard for criminal enforcement, but the structurally close interactions between criminal and administrative offences, notwithstanding that these modes of enforcement are functionally different, can be illustrated in the UK's own leading case on administrative enforcement.

C. From 'Blurring' to 'Enforcement Convergence'? The Hannam Case

The case of *Ian Hannam* shows the different ways in which UK administrative control of market abuse might be considered a QCEM. This case concerned an administra-

[61] Hence there is no private action in the UK to sanction market abuse: *Hall v Cable and Wireless plc* [2009] EWHC 1793 (Comm); [2010] 1 BCLC 95.

[62] See A Ogus, *Regulation: Legal Form and Economic Theory* (Oxford, Hart Publishing, 2004), ch 1. For reasons other than those driving 'economic regulation' which largely pertain to monopoly situations; social regulation arises where government intervention is considered necessary to address specific social problems which would be otherwise left unregulated (by economic market-based modes).

[63] See eg classic Glanville Williams' reflections in GL Williams, *Textbook of Criminal Law*, 1st edn (London, Stevens & Son, 1953). And thus requiring the expressive censure unique to a criminal sanction. On this point and how this is central to criminal responses, and thus how the traditional criminal law regime contrasts with broader regulatory enforcement responses such as responsive regulation, see eg A Ashworth, 'Is the Criminal Law a Lost Cause?' (2000) 116 *Law Quarterly Review* 225.

[64] See generally eg JC Coffee Jr , 'Paradigms Lost: The Blurring of the Criminal and Civil Law Models – And What Can Be Done About It' (1992) 101 *Yale Law Journal* 1875 and more specifically in terms of the hybrid nature of regulatory administrative actions see eg S Klein, 'Redrawing the Criminal-Civil Boundary' (1999) 2(2) *Buffalo Criminal Law Review* 679.

tive action brought against Hannam, pursuant to what was then section 118 FSMA 2000, which was the earliest iteration of non-criminal liability for market abuse in the UK. Hannam was a prominent City banker, who as head of Global Capital Markets at JP Morgan Cazenove UK had overseen the merger of JP Morgan and Cazenove. He was also a respected 'rain-maker' whose 'trademark deals' had brought 'businesses from exotic countries to the City'.[65] In 2012 the FSA issued a decision that Hannam had improperly disclosed inside information, breaching section 118(3) FSMA 2000, a finding which was upheld by the Upper Tribunal[66] in 2014. The facts surrounding this action against Hannam originated in his discovery of possible breaches of insider dealing laws involving two of his clients, with the latter occurring in the context of an imminent takeover. It was only once Hannam informed his superiors, who in turn informed the FSA as they were required to do, that Hannam's own breach was discovered. Hannam had disclosed inside information in email correspondence with a longstanding friend, and whilst no trading had occurred as a result of this disclosure, this was a prohibited disclosure through being outwith 'the proper course of the exercise of his employment'.[67] The Upper Tribunal upheld this finding and also the £450,000 fine initially issued.

The prohibited conduct of disclosing inside information, as distinct from using this as a basis for a trade, is also capable of being enforced as a criminal offence pursuant to section 52 Criminal Justice Act 1993. At the time of its initial investigation, it is clear that the FSA actually considered bringing criminal charges against Hannam, and Hannam was expressly found not to have acted dishonestly. Indeed, it was Hannam's prowess in spotting trading activity which appeared to be abnormal between his two clients and his swift internal reporting of this which led to the FSA investigation in the first place, and this was indeed praised by the FSA, as was his cooperation with the authorities once they had been alerted. And whilst Hannam felt his own position was untenable once his emails had been found and resigned so that he could 'clear his name', JP Morgan Cazenove had backed him. It was this narrative of exemplary conduct which enabled Hannam to keep his authorisation to trade in the City,[68] and a number of City people defended his 'rain-making' record.[69] For the purposes of this analysis *Hannam* illustrates how conduct amounting to insider dealing (together with market manipulation) can give rise to dual enforcement possibilities for the same misconduct, by virtue of it being capable of incurring criminal charges and also existing as an administrative offence (with the latter now embodying MAR 2014 provisions).

[65] See J Guthrie, 'Brunch with the FT: Ian Hannam – Fined for disclosing inside information, the City dealmaker has a "Big Boy" breakfast in west London' (London, 4 September 2015): https://www.ft.com/content/90d386b6-523e-11e5-8642-453585f2cfcd.

[66] Specifically the Tax and Chancery Chamber of the Upper Tribunal. For further information on the UK's judicial and tribunal structure see: https://www.gov.uk/courts-tribunals and concerning the Tax and Chancery Chamber of the Upper Tribunal see: https://www.gov.uk/courts-tribunals/upper-tribunal-tax-and-chancery-chamber.

[67] *Hannam v FCA*, above n 59; see eg para 122.

[68] See J Guthrie, 'Brunch with the FT: Ian Hannam', above n 65; see also below nn 75 and 76 and text thereto.

[69] Ibid.

In both enforcement pathways the state bears the burden of proof; but the key difference is the standard of proof, whereby the non-criminal offence is subject to the civil standard of proof on the balance of probabilities rather than the criminal standard of proof beyond reasonable doubt.[70] This position manifests as the requirement that the competent authority is 'satisfied' that market abuse has been committed, with the standard of satisfaction being on the balance of probabilities.[71] By electing to bring a non-criminal action, the competent authority – the FSA and then its successor the FCA – pursued Hannam's misconduct as a matter of social regulation rather than as conduct considered socially injurious and requiring punishment. The Upper Tribunal confirmed that the significant financial penalty awarded against him was considered justified in the light of his serious error of judgement.[72] Indeed, the Upper Tribunal reiterated the FCA's insistence that the conduct alleged against Hannam was 'not tantamount to criminal conduct' in stating that a finding of (non-criminal) market abuse can have 'very serious consequences' for the individual concerned – the penalty of £450,000 imposed on Mr Hannam being an example of such a serious consequence.[73] Such reflections map persuasively onto the strategic emphasis which the FSA and its successor have placed on delivering *deterrence*; namely communicating a warning to the regulated community that enforcement would follow from wrongdoing, and which can be found widely discussed in FSA and now FCA discourse conceptualised as 'credible deterrence'.[74] However, even in the light of a penalty which is regarded as reflecting 'serious' misconduct, and being at the 'exceptional' end of what is likely to be awarded in such circumstances, a distinction between this outcome and punishment arising from the criminal process might be configured in the outcomes for Hannam.

D. *Hannam* and its Significance for Early-Stage Study of QCEMs

Hannam was able to keep his professional authorisation, by being found to have acted in an exemplary manner,[75] and thereby able to continue to work in the financial sphere, and he would not in any case have incurred the custodial penalty available for criminal insider dealing.[76] Nevertheless, there are ways in which what happened to Hannam

[70] This was confirmed in *Hannam* itself (above n 59). Hannam had argued that the criminal standard of proof should apply on account of the allegations being 'tantamount to allegations which constitute criminal offences'; see paras 147 and 150.

[71] Ibid, see eg para 186.

[72] Ibid, with emphasis on such errors with 'serious consequences', eg paras 152, 179, and 492.

[73] Ibid, para 152.

[74] See eg M Wheatley, 'The FCA: the future of conduct regulation', BBA Annual Banking Conference (London: 17 October 2012), available at: https://webarchive.nationalarchives.gov.uk/20130103184105/http://www.fsa.gov.uk/library/communication/speeches/2012/1017-mw.shtml.

[75] This outcome would have been unlikely in the case of a criminal conviction. Whilst criminal insider dealing does not require proof of dishonesty, a criminal conviction would likely cast doubt on an individual being a fit and proper person, the 'benchmark' underpinning the *ex-ante* approval at the heart of the UK authorisation regime (see https://www.fca.org.uk/firms/approved-persons/fitness-propriety). See also discussion of the scope for withdrawing such authorisation in *Hannam*, above n 59, eg para 43 (which also confirmed that there was 'no suggestion that Mr Hannam is not a fit and proper person').

[76] With the statutory maximum being 7 years' imprisonment following conviction on indictment.

speaks to what might represent the characteristics of administrative enforcement which render it capable of amounting to a QCEM. This is framed to a significant degree by the lengthy discussion in the Upper Tribunal prompted by Hannam's – unsuccessful – argument that the correct standard of proof applicable to section 118 FSMA 2000 was the criminal standard of beyond reasonable doubt.[77] Counsel for Hannam had even invited the Upper Tribunal to consider how vesting a public body like the FCA with the power to impose penalties had created a jurisdiction requiring close scrutiny, and one which was appropriately termed a *quasi-criminal* jurisdiction.[78] This use of language is notable in the light of current interest in phenomenalising QCEMs, and whilst the Upper Tribunal insisted that this latter argument lacked appropriate authority,[79] the overall narrative also intimates an appreciation that differences between administrative and criminal enforcement can be difficult to gauge. More is said on this shortly, in explaining how *Hannam* might support a key proposition for early-stage study of QCEMs. This is that whilst non-criminal enforcement which can be considered quasi-criminal does raise important issues for individuals accused by the state of wrongdoing, it does not follow from this that non-criminal enforcement in and of itself amounts to being a QCEM.

IV. Conventional Differences between Criminal and Non-criminal Enforcement

The way in which 'criminal' enforcement has conventionally been differentiated from 'non-criminal administrative' enforcement in the UK reflects how within its traditions the criminal law is the part of the body of law which governs relations between citizens (natural and legal persons) and the state, through which the state responds to behaviour which is considered 'socially injurious'.[80] Rooted in social contract theory,[81] the state is entitled to punish individual wrongdoers for acting unlawfully rather than lawfully, and through doing so prevent further breaches.[82] In this setting the role of the state has evolved from traditions within which a 'community' will accuse an individual of committing an injury to it, and punish this.[83] This is through principles distilled from Enlightenment philosophy, at the heart of which are utilitarian approaches to how citizens should behave – namely, in ways promoting the greatest happiness for the greatest number – and under which crimes should be considered as an injury to society, and the state is justified in punishing such conduct. The right of the state to respond to socially injurious conduct is itself framed by requirements that crimes are to be

[77] *Hannam v FCA*, above n 59, para 14.

[78] Ibid, para 189.

[79] Ibid, para 190.

[80] See eg GL Williams, *Textbook of Criminal Law*, above n 63.

[81] Locke's classic theory was first published as J Locke, *The Second Treatise of Government* in 1690.

[82] The utilitarian basis for this can be seen classically illustrated in the philosophy of British philosopher Jeremy Bentham. This rationale is readily apparent in the influential writings of Cesare Beccaria; see below n 84 and n 88.

[83] D Hay and F Snyder, *Policing and Prosecution in Britain, 1750–1850* (Oxford, Clarendon Press, 1989).

classified according to seriousness, by being measured by the harm inflicted by them; that punishment must be proportionate to the harm inflicted, and must also be swift; and where the goal of punishment is the prevention of crime in society.[84] In non-capital punishment regimes, punishment at its most serious involves loss of liberty, with terms of incarceration commonly recognisably 'tariffed' according to perceived seriousness in offending. But with the very premise of criminal wrongdoing lying in an injury to society, the criminal conviction itself is widely associated with exclusions from civic participation, and also with shame and stigma.[85]

A. Mapping Criminal Enforcement Approaches and Key Criminal Justice Outcomes

The importance of the stigmatising effects of criminal enforcement is deeply embedded in the administration of criminal law in the common law tradition. That this can also be seen across time and across different 'stakeholder' spheres is evident in US sociologist Edwin Sutherland's 1945 reflections on how stigmatising qualities of criminal enforcement are absent from other enforcement modes,[86] and from the Law Commission of England and Wales' observation in 2010 on how a criminal conviction is associated with the imposition of stigma.[87] If one looks at the Enlightenment origins of domestic criminal law then the influence of the European movement is manifest. Especially well known are writings of Cesare Beccaria,[88] setting out the justification for public condemnation of and punishment of acts which are harmful to society. These ideas are also now readily apparent in European policy-making insistence in 2011 that criminal sanctions 'demonstrate social disapproval of a qualitatively different nature compared to administrative sanctions or compensation mechanisms under civil law'.[89] This provided the very basis for minimum criminalisation of market abuse across Member States under CSMAD 2014, with the perceived unique stigmatising qualities of criminal enforcement serving dual punishment and deterrent functions considered to be essential for delivering EU policy on market integrity.[90]

Whilst European policy-making is currently emphasising criminal enforcement, the appeal for non-criminal administrative sanctions amongst enforcement and policy communities is easy to understand. In *Hannam*, and in the context of non-criminal market abuse enforcement, it was suggested by counsel that (what was then) liability incurred under the FSMA 2000 Part VIII, was 'intended to fill a perceived gap between

[84] C Beccaria, *On Crimes and Punishments*, trans H Paolucci (London, Pearson, 1963 [first published 1764]).
[85] EH Sutherland, 'Is "White-Collar Crime" Crime?' (1945) 10 *American Sociological Review* 132; especially 136–37.
[86] Ibid, 137.
[87] Law Commission, *Criminal Liability in Regulatory Contexts: A Consultation Paper*, CP 195, (London, Law Commission, 2010); eg para 1.28.
[88] As evident in Beccaria's proposition that acts committed by citizens which provide greatest happiness for the greatest number should have the status of lawful acts.
[89] European Commission Proposals for a Regulation on Market Abuse and for a Directive on Criminal Sanctions for Market Abuse: Frequently Asked Questions MEMO/11/715 (Brussels, 20 October 2011).
[90] Ibid.

the criminal offences of insider dealing and misleading statements and practices and the regulatory rules applicable to authorised persons'.[91] The FCA explained that this gap arose from how 'obtaining criminal convictions was perceived as too difficult to be an effective deterrent, and disciplinary action could only be brought against authorised persons'.[92] This submission in *Hannam* does acknowledge a longstanding UK tradition for managing the risks presented to financial markets by insider dealing and market manipulation using criminal enforcement. This tradition actually dates back to the nineteenth century, and a very conscious choice made that financial wrongdoing is capable of amounting to a public 'wrong', rather than one existing between 'man and man'.[93] The development of a non-criminal enforcement pathway for market abuse in 2000 was thus a landmark. It marked a very clear point of departure in UK enforcement culture, in which the historical commitment to criminal enforcement which emerged from nineteenth-century reactions to experiences of wide-spread financial dishonesty – which contemporaries themselves termed 'High-art' crime, 'commercial crime' and even 'financial crime'[94] – had persisted throughout the twentieth century. Until 2000 this approach continued to reflect a classic binary divide found in the UK legal tradition between 'private law' and 'criminal law', whereby state enforcement against behaviour considered to be unacceptable (alongside the private actions available to individuals) has historically subsisted as the public interest in punishing and preventing socially injurious behaviour.

B. Criminal Enforcement: Key Justifications … and Obstacles

This strategy of state criminal control of financial misconduct as socially injurious conduct, underpinned by punishment, *is* longstanding, but it has not been an easy pathway for the UK, and this is perhaps not surprising given the viewpoint that no state has experienced much success in this regard.[95] As suggested, this is attributable to a very significant degree to the procedural safeguards arising within criminal law, associated with the burden borne by the state in proving the existence of the offence or/and required mens rea, together with protections conferred on defendants, which *should* properly exist in view of the life-changing consequences which the label of 'criminal' will bring, and which are intended to act generally as a counterpoise for state power.[96] For white-collar criminals the consequences of a criminal conviction can of course be extremely severe, as is readily apparent in narratives of ruined lives[97] and in academic studies of the tensions embodied in judicial decisions on punishment for those who are convicted,[98] and the emotional and 'socio-political' pressures felt by judges in this

[91] *Hannam v FCA*, above n 59, para 186.

[92] Ibid.

[93] See Hansard's Parliamentary Debates, series 3, 146, HC, 8 June 1857, Serjeant Kinglake, col 1363.

[94] See DM Evans, *Facts, Failures & Frauds- Revelations Financial, Mercantile, Criminal* (New York: Augustus M Kelley, 1968 [first published London: Groombridge & Sons, 1859]), see eg 1 and 5.

[95] B Rider, 'Civilising the Law', above n 54, 13.

[96] Ibid.

[97] J Saunders, *Nightmare: Ernest Saunders and the Guinness Affair* (London, Arrow, 1990).

[98] S Wheeler, D Weisburd, and N Bode, 'Sentencing the White-Collar Offender: Rhetoric and Reality' (1982) 47 *American Sociological Review* 641.

setting.[99] Allusion which has been made to the challenges presented by 'sophisticated abusive conduct'[100] also reminds us that capital markets are highly dynamic, and are locations for rapid and often far-reaching innovations – a reflection of how the combination of 'modern sorts of commercial activity, and the modern methods by which dishonest activity may be effected' generate concern that the law can struggle to keep abreast of, let alone ahead of, these challenges.[101]

Criminal enforcement is also a pathway encountering difficulties on account of the very nature of market abuse. Insider dealing and market manipulation have a reputation of being notoriously difficult to discover,[102] by virtue of being concealed in occupational locations and settings which outsiders have limited access to,[103] with information commonly being spread orally within these rarefied sectors (in the case of insider dealing),[104] or transmitted through expert use of technology (in the case of market manipulation).[105] In these circumstances, the attractions of non-criminal administrative enforcement are readily apparent; perhaps particularly those attaching to the absence of mens rea requirements, and the lower standard of proof. As key UK reflections also suggest, for those activities which are discovered, it is by no means certain that they will register in public consciousness even as 'wrongful' behaviour, let alone criminal behaviour.[106] Such viewpoints most obviously have their origins in classic Henry G Manne arguments against the prohibition of insider dealing, clustering around the purported beneficial effects of these activities for ascertaining market availability and assisting in price discovery, and promoting overall liquidity. These assertions together with narratives that no long-term losses are experienced by markets on account of them do continue to persist in certain professional quarters,[107] and can now be found expressed increasingly in relation to market manipulation.[108] The questionable wrongfulness of financial misconduct generally, and market abuse more specifically, can also be found in the wider public sphere. Or certainly the

[99] M Levi, 'Sentencing White-Collar Crime in the Dark? Reflections on the Guinness Four' (1991) 30(4) *The Howard Journal of Crime and Justice* 257, 257.

[100] B Rider 'Civilising the Law', above n 54, 13.

[101] Lord Falconer of Thornton QC, 'Commercial fraud or sharp practice – Challenge for the law' Denning Lecture, 14 October 1997, cited in Law Commission, *Legislating the Criminal Code: Fraud and Deception- A Consultation Paper*, CP 155 (London, 1999), para 1.5.

[102] For reasons very persuasively set out in P Davies et al's 'invisible crime' trope: see P Davies, P Francis and V Jupp, 'The Features of Invisible Crimes' in P Davies, P Francis and V Jupp (eds), *Invisible Crimes: Their Victims and their Regulation* (Basingstoke, Palgrave, 1999) 3–28. These features are analysed utilising six key indices through which (by reference to their absence) the 'contours of invisibility' can be mapped.

[103] See eg S Shapiro, 'The Road Not Taken: The Elusive Path to Criminal Prosecution for White-Collar Offenders' (1985) 19 *Law and Society Review* 179.

[104] See eg G Wilson and S Wilson, 'Market misconduct, the FSA and creating a system of "city grasses"', above n 38. See examples of this in key US case law in *US v Newman and Others* United States Court of Appeals (2d Cir. 2014) Nos 13-1837-cr (L), 13-1917-cr (con) and *US v Salman* United States Court of Appeals (9th Cir. 2015) No 14-10204 DC No 3:11-CR-00625-EMC-1.

[105] This is particularly the case with market manipulation, and is strongly associated with the increasing prominence of automated high-frequency trading (HFT); see eg S Wilson, 'High Frequency Trading and Criminal Liability for "Market Abuse"' [2015] Lloyd's Rep[orts] F[inancial] C[rime] (5) 380.

[106] As evident in FSA reflections on insider dealing enforcement from Margaret Cole, n 28 above.

[107] Manne's arguments are set out in TM Ashe and L Counsell, *Insider Trading* (London, Tolley, 1993) 6.

[108] The benefits of 'layering' practices as well as the scope for abusive 'spoofs' arising in trading practices are evident in FSA, *Market Watch* (August 2009); see also G Wilson and S Wilson, 'Market misconduct, the FSA and creating a system of "city grasses"', above n 38.

perception is that such views are to be found in the public sphere, as can be seen in the need for continued regulator insistence that market abuse is 'serious crime', and as such *should* attract 'moral outrage'.[109]

C. Overcoming 'Obstacles': Explaining the Genesis of Non-criminal Enforcement

It is also the case that those purveying this message of wrongfulness do recognise the need to persuade as well as insist. The strong current of recent domestic (UK) messages in favour of criminal enforcement do have support from Europe, and are also possibly indicative of a broader transnational narrative originating in reactions to the global financial crisis.[110] However, these reflections must also be situated alongside longstanding favour for non-criminal enforcement, evident in the MAD 2003 and practised in the US. Arguments in favour of non-criminal enforcement typically emphasise financial disincentives to market abuse provided by financial penalties and disgorgement of profits rather than typical criminal justice outcomes. In tandem with arguments that hitting pockets is more likely to discourage insider dealing and market manipulation than threats of imprisonment and criminal labelling, support for non-criminal mechanisms is commonly accompanied by suggestions that this *efficacy* argument operates alongside considerations that many 'business crimes' might not even *appropriately* be regarded as 'socially injurious' acts. Thus, the IMF's preference for the language of 'financial abuse' rather than 'financial crime'[111] can capture very different moral positionings found in respect of these activities; including invitations to reverse the demand commonly made to treat white-collar criminals like ordinary criminals, and in doing so, subject ordinary criminals to the pressures and exigencies experienced by businesspeople and professionals.[112]

A system of enforcement placing greater emphasis on administrative action rather than criminal prosecution would also appear to have important endorsement from the Law Commission of England and Wales, which in 2010 opined that, as 'a general statement of principle … The criminal law responds to engaging in seriously reprehensible conduct by imposing the stigma associated with criminal conviction'.[113] In analysing the birth of non-criminal state enforcement for market abuse in the UK, this move was clearly strongly influenced by European capital markets law. But European law demands for administrative sanctions also provided the opportunity for the then FSA to model its activities on the US system, where enforcement reputation is acquired through volume of cases resolved, focusing mainly on administrative actions

[109] Per Margaret Cole, above n 28.

[110] See S Wilson 'Financial Crises and Financial Crime: "Transformative understandings" of Crime, Past Present and Future' in N Ryder et al (eds), *The Financial Crisis and White Collar Crime – Legislative and Policy Responses* (Abingdon, Routledge, 2017).

[111] IMF, *Financial System Abuse, Financial Crime and Money Laundering*, above n 19, para 5.

[112] D Nelken 'White-Collar Crime' in M Maguire, R Morgan, and R Reiner (eds), *Oxford Handbook of Criminology*, 1st edn, (Oxford, Oxford University Press, 1994) 355, 383.

[113] Law Commission, *Criminal Liability in Regulatory Contexts*, above n 87, para 1.28.

and using criminal enforcement only exceptionally for the most serious cases.[114] This development in the UK also finds conceptual support in theorisations of regulation, in which criminal enforcement can be seen as an anachronistic and unsophisticated tool, and where the emergence of different approaches reflects the trajectory of a state which is able to articulate and communicate its expectations through increased resourcing and with greater sophistication in its understandings of the challenges it faces.[115]

The first iterations of the non-criminal offence of 'market abuse' which preceded implementation of the MAR 2014, located in the FSMA 2000 (as amended),[116] were supported by a Code of Market Conduct produced by the FSA, providing guidance for the regulated community on what constituted acceptable 'market practice'.[117] This was in turn underpinned by provision for unlimited financial penalties, or a public censure statement as an alternative; disgorgement of profits made, or losses avoided; and statutory restraining injunctions.[118] From this followed a period of extensive regulator use of the non-criminal pathway. For the UK regulator, the non-criminal pathway would allow very public statements to be made about the 'wrongfulness' of insider dealing and market manipulation, but without the high risks in costs for the state associated with criminal enforcement. As previously discussed, these risks attach particularly to the criminal burden of proof, but they also arise from high levels of uncertainty about whether juries will convict those who are 'respectable' and who 'do not conform to the popular stereotype of "the criminal"'.[119] Thus, non-criminal enforcement might be thought of as serving important conceptual objectives and also more practical ones. For those subject to this enforcement, the remedial outcomes could have significant financial repercussions,[120] and 'public censure' presents the possibility for reputational consequences. But these consequences are regarded as being differently focused from those attaching to criminal enforcement.

V. The Resurgence of Criminal Enforcement, and the Significance for QCEMs

Non-criminal enforcement – purportedly at least – through not restricting civic participation, lacks the stigma attaching to a criminal conviction, and as *Hannam* suggests,

[114] As seen in the activities of the US Securities Exchange Commission; see https://www.sec.gov/.

[115] See generally the discussion in Law Commission, *Criminal Liability in Regulatory Contexts*, above n 87. For the classic responsive regulation model see I Ayers and J Braithwaite, *Responsive Regulation: Transcending the Deregulation Debate* (Oxford, Oxford University Press, 1992) and for an historical perspective see also D Eastwood, '"Amplifying the Province of the Legislature": the Flow of Information and the English State in the Early Nineteenth Century' (1989) 62(149) *Historical Research* 276.

[116] The FSMA 2000 was amended in 2005 by the Financial Services and Markets Act 2000 (Market Abuse) Regulations 2005, SI 2005/381, implementing MAD 2003 into domestic law.

[117] Section 119 FSMA 2000.

[118] Section 123 FSMA 2000.

[119] EH Sutherland, 'Is "White-Collar Crime" Crime?', above n 85, 137.

[120] This can be seen for example in the reaction generated in 2004 to the 'record' penalty awarded against Shell for the market manipulation concerning statements relating to hydrocarbon proved reserves and reserves replacement ratios from 1998 to 2003; see eg PLC Financial Services, 'Market Abuse: FSA publishes final notice fining Shell £17 million' *Thomson Reuters* (24 August 2004) https://uk.practicallaw.thomsonreuters.com/7-102-9424?transitionType=Default&contextData=(sc.Default).

leaves greater possibility for personal and professional lives to continue uninterrupted. In terms of how this non-criminal pathway generated some excitement about creating the potential for the UK to replicate US enforcement experiences, enforcement undertaken by the US Securities and Exchange Commission (SEC) is highly significant. The SEC's enforcement strategy and culture are underpinned by a very heavy overall emphasis on non-criminal enforcement, and only very occasional recourse to criminal enforcement. From this, perceptions had emerged that the SEC's 'long-standing practice of settling with defendants while allowing them to neither "admit nor deny" the allegations asserted against them',[121] across high volumes of (non-criminal/administrative) actions,[122] produced notable enforcement efficiencies, discouraged 'gaming' on the part of those being investigated, and allowed the regulator to acquire a formidable enforcement reputation.[123]

However, in 2009 the then FSA announced that in pursuit of its policy of 'credible deterrence' it would be engaging in criminal enforcement wherever it was possible to do so.[124] The policy of 'credible deterrence' was, for the Authority, the strategy it would adopt in order to make enforcement visible to the regulated community, and in order to embed a belief that the Authority was a force to be reckoned with, and which would ensure that violators of regulatory rules would be discovered and actions brought.[125] The FSA formally adopted 'credible deterrence' as a policy in 2008.[126] At this time it was presented as an organisational philosophy, underpinning the full scope of the FSA's activities as the UK's regulator of financial services.[127] This philosophy continues to frame the operations of the FSA's successor body, the FCA.[128] It was the following year, in 2009, that the FSA specified that the pursuit of 'credible deterrence' would involve it electing to undertake criminal enforcement wherever possible, and in preference to non-criminal action.[129] This would not just be in the sphere of market abuse – it would cut *generally* across 'financial crime' enforcement[130] – but the salience of this direction

[121] Harvard Law School Forum on Corporate Governance and Financial Regulation, 'White Collar and Regulatory Enforcement' (3 February 2012): https://corpgov.law.harvard.edu/2012/02/03/white-collar-and-regulatory-enforcement/.

[122] See K Wolfe, 'Where Have The SEC Enforcement Actions Gone?' (19 September 2018): https://www.law360.com/articles/1084059.

[123] As is the reputation which has been acquired by the SEC; see eg TO Gorman, 'SEC Enforcement Trends and Priorities 2008: Key Considerations for Issuers and their Employees and Counsel' (7 April 2008): https://www.secactions.com/articles/sec/Article6.pdf.

[124] M Cole, 'Delivering credible Deterrence', FSA Annual Financial Crime Conference speech, 27 Apr 2009, archived at: https://webarchive.nationalarchives.gov.uk/20090903063101/http://www.fsa.gov.uk/pages/Library/Communication/Speeches/2009/0427_mc.shtml.

[125] Ibid.

[126] See H Sants, 'Delivering intensive supervision and credible deterrence', above n 24.

[127] Ibid.

[128] See eg T McDermott, 'Credible Deterrence: here to stay', FSA's Enforcement Conference speech, 2 July 2012; archived at: https://webarchive.nationalarchives.gov.uk/20130103184334/http://www.fsa.gov.uk/library/communication/speeches/2012/0702-tm.shtml.

[129] M Cole, 'Introduction' to the FSA Enforcement Conference speech, 22 June 2010, archived at: https://webarchive.nationalarchives.gov.uk/20130104022658/http://www.fsa.gov.uk/library/communication/speeches/2010/0622_mc.shtml.

[130] FSA Press Notice: 'FSA Managing Director, Margaret Cole, to leave this year', FSA/PN013/2012, 15 February 2012, archived at: https://webarchive.nationalarchives.gov.uk/20130103191431/http://www.fsa.gov.uk/library/communication/pr/2012/013.shtml.

for market abuse, in terms of its rationale, and actually its timing, *does* align in interesting ways with the subsequent European policy shift announced in respect of market abuse *specifically* in 2011.

A. Changing European Emphasis: Part of a Wider (Changing) Enforcement Pattern?

In announcing the importance of 'minimum rules on criminal offences and on criminal sanctions for market abuse' in 2011,[131] the European Commission's emphasis was, not surprisingly, on the importance of harmonisation for delivering EU policy on 'market integrity'.[132] However, a move towards greater use of criminal enforcement can also be seen beyond even EU law and policy-making, extending also to the US, where as noted, securities enforcement is traditionally founded on extensive use of non-criminal enforcement, and more occasional use of criminal enforcement.[133] As such, this possibly 'global movement' accords with predictions that the global financial crisis would produce demands for tough new bodies and heightened enforcement aggression.[134] And whilst formal commitment to criminal enforcement in 2009 could plausibly pass for a 'post-crisis' manoeuvre, it is clear from the FSA's announcement of it, and its application for market abuse specifically, that this was a change in direction which was based on reflections on enforcement occurring sometime prior to the crisis. At a time when European thinking and policy-making was – rhetorically at least – still strongly committed to the ability of administrative sanctions to deliver 'effective, proportionate, and dissuasive' responses to market abuse, the FSA had already commenced its pro-criminal law enforcement approach, and had done so with a conscious regard for what it perceived were the limitations of administrative enforcement.[135]

In 2010 the FSA reported that its experiences of using the section 118 offence were that this administrative pathway was neither significantly less resource-intensive to pursue, nor apparently able to produce the 'real changes in market behaviour'[136] necessary to secure acceptable levels of market integrity through transparency and investor confidence',[137] and also had a 'deterrent effect' which was much diluted in comparison with criminal enforcement.[138] These reflections do of course chime in strongly with

[131] European Commission MEMO/11/715, above n 89.

[132] Ibid, and as evident in the subsequent MAR 2014.

[133] See reflections on the key US insider trading decision in *US v Newman and Others*, above n 104, eg Gibson Dunn, 'United States v Newman: Second Circuit Ruling Portends Choppier Waters for Insider Trading Charges against Downstream Tippees' (15 December 2014): http://www.gibsondunn.com/publications/pages/US-v-Newman--Second-Circuit-Ruling-Portends-Choppier-Waters--Insider-Trading-Charges-Against-Downstream-Tippees.aspx, and also the Supreme Court reaction to *Newman* in *Salman v US* 580 US (2016).

[134] Eg N Ryder, *The Financial Crisis and White-Collar Crime: The Perfect Storm* (Cheltenham, Edward Elgar, 2014).

[135] See G Wilson and S Wilson, 'The FSA, "credible deterrence", and criminal enforcement – a "haphazard pursuit"?' (2014) 21(1) *Journal of Financial Crime* 4.

[136] M Cole, 'Introduction' to the FSA Enforcement Conference speech, above n 129.

[137] Ibid.

[138] Ibid.

emergent European thinking that criminal sanctions are able to demonstrate 'social disapproval of a qualitatively different nature compared to administrative sanctions or compensation mechanisms under civil law'.[139] The challenges presented by criminal enforcement for those undertaking it are very real, as recently reiterated in the UK context in the genesis of the new criminal offence of 'reckless banking'.[140] Those making such statements about the superior qualities of criminal enforcement do appear to recognise that this strategy will present challenges. However, as cases like *Hannam* demonstrate, criminal enforcement is not always a viable option, and in close proximity to proclaiming the virtues of criminal sanctions, the European Commission has also insisted that administrative sanctions would remain an important part of the 'toolkit' available to Member States for delivering 'market integrity' within capital markets.[141]

B. Forecasting Future Possibilities

The continuing importance of administrative enforcement is evident from how the MAR 2014 has intensified the administrative capabilities which were available under the MAD 2003. From this alone, the ruling in *Zecca and Di Puma* should be one of note for competent authorities across Member States. Avoiding infringements of the *ne bis in idem* principle is most easily achieved by Member States electing to undertake either administrative or criminal enforcement but not both, and pursuing both forms of action for substantially the same misconduct does require extreme care.[142] The UK has undertaken to adopt the former approach, and the FCA states that administrative sanctions for market abuse will not be imposed where that person 'is being prosecuted for market misconduct or has been finally convicted or acquitted of market misconduct (following the exhaustion of all appeal processes) in a criminal prosecution arising from substantially the same allegations'; and equally a criminal prosecution will not be commenced where the FCA 'has brought or is seeking to bring disciplinary proceedings for market abuse arising from substantially the same allegations'.[143]

This statement provides a clear model for how the UK, as a dualist regime, avoids duplication which infringes the *ne bis in idem* doctrine. This might interest other Member States, all of whom will now be dualist regimes in response to the implementation of CSMAD 2014. This statement also highlights the way that for the UK, decisions on the pursuit of a particular action – either administrative or criminal – can be made by a single authority. This is not the case everywhere, and in many other states, including the US,[144] a criminal action may only be brought by a prosecuting authority. The position in the UK, should help to promote and achieve an enforcement policy which is

[139] European Commission MEMO/11/715, above n 89.

[140] What is known colloquially as the 'reckless banking offence' appears in s 36 Financial Services (Banking Reform) Act 2013, with the formal title 'Offence relating to a decision causing a financial institution to fail'.

[141] European Commission MEMO/11/715, above n 89; and as embodied in the subsequent MAR 2014.

[142] See the *Lloyds Reports Financial Crime* commentary of the CJEU decision in *Garlsson* (above n 9), written by Sarah Clarke QC in [2018] Lloyd's Rep FC (5) 288.

[143] FCA, *Enforcement Guide* EG 12.3.4. (March 2016).

[144] Eg in the US, whereas non-criminal enforcement of securities violations is undertaken by the SEC, criminal enforcement is within the remit of the Department of Justice.

overall coherent, as well as an effective translation of CJEU *ne bis in idem* case law more specifically. In the light of the efficiencies in resource allocation this is perhaps likely to promote, together with encouraging overall enforcement coherence in a sphere where enforcement challenges abound, this ability to combine both tools in the toolbox given to one single authority might be considered invaluable, if not actually indispensable. Cooperation between different enforcement bodies might present conflicts in resource allocation to a greater degree, and may also require greater emphasis on communication in promoting overall coherence in enforcement strategies, as well as in ensuring compliance with key CJEU jurisprudence. However, there may also be advantages to separation in enforcement functions, including generally promoting greater organisational clarity, and greater transparency in remit and function and in accountability structures.

VI. Criminal and Non-criminal Enforcement: Challenges of 'Blurring' and 'Mimicking'

Perhaps especially the capacity for administrative enforcement to mimic criminal enforcement, and for distinctions between them to become blurred, might suggest that appropriate levels of scrutiny are better achieved through maintaining separations in enforcement decision-making functions. Following from this, the FCA's statement on avoiding enforcement duplication says little about how this duplication is capable of arising, and why we might be concerned about this. It remains important to understand how and why administrative sanctions might be considered capable of 'duplicating' criminal ones at all, and thereby why they might be considered 'quasi-criminal' in nature. The *ne bis in idem* principle can only ever possibly be infringed where multiple proceedings are used, and for substantially the same conduct, be this multiple criminal enforcement, or a combination of criminal and administrative proceedings. From this it does not necessarily follow that no issues of justice and fundamental rights arise from the use of only administrative sanctions, or perhaps even multiple use of administrative sanctions. This analysis proposes that the very use of administrative sanctions which might be considered quasi-criminal makes understanding what might vest them with such characteristics an issue of manifest importance.

Explaining current thinking on the comparative merits of criminal enforcement and administrative enforcement, together with the rationale for the earlier much more pro-administrative enforcement policy, helps to clarify distinctions which are conventionally drawn between 'criminal' and 'non-criminal' enforcement. In turn, doing so can assist in illuminating where these distinctions might have become blurred. In administrative sanctions which can be considered 'quasi-criminal' we can see enforcement mechanisms and their sanctions which are perceived to have acquired qualities akin to criminal penalties on account of their 'nature and severity'. But as noted in *Hannam*, administrative enforcement can properly be considered as providing an alternative to criminal enforcement for the state, and UK non-criminal market abuse enforcement was intended as such. *Hannam* also suggests that this mechanism for promoting acceptable behaviour has benefits for the state and for those subject to its reach: by raising standards through deterring impropriety, whilst also recognising that wrongdoing in the 'commercial sphere'[145] is not always appropriately regarded as 'socially injurious' activity requiring punishment.

A. Continuing Importance of Both Enforcement Pathways for 'Market Abuse'

Administrative alternatives to criminal enforcement also enjoy longstanding and widespread support from those who consider the value of financial consequences (through imposition of financial penalties and/or financial forfeiture) to contrast favourably with the threat of criminal justice outcomes for achieving deterrence through compliance.[146] Such thinking encourages a greater emphasis on the financial consequences of unacceptable conduct than is traditionally associated with the criminal process. This might be considered a particularly useful response to financial misconduct – which is widely configured as crime of 'greed',[147] – and also a reaction which is appropriate.[148] In the light of this, administrative enforcement can be configured as a mechanism which advances state action beyond a crude choice between leaving the enforcement of 'wrongs' to individuals who have been 'wronged' and the state interest in punishing conduct considered socially injurious. In turn, administrative enforcement might properly be configured as a development of a state which has the financial resources to put in place a regulatory regime which lays down rules of conduct for behaviour in the 'commercial sphere', rather than reacting to misconduct by instituting a criminal prosecution. This is especially so given that Britain did not actually develop a system of state public prosecution until into the early twentieth century,[149] and thus sometime after the nineteenth-century 'discovery' of financial crime.[150] It is also possible to see the development of non-criminal enforcement as one which seeks to reflect the realities of misconduct in the commercial sphere, and which is underpinned by intellectual understandings of what this requires, accrued from the state's increased capacity to enlist and engage with pertinent knowledge and expertise.[151]

[145] See Law Commission, *Fraud and Deception*, above n 101, para 1.4.

[146] See arguments made in TM Ashe and L Counsell, *Insider Trading*, above n 107.

[147] Commonly situated alongside and contrasted with so-called 'crimes of need'; see S Wheeler, D Weisburd, and N Bode, 'Sentencing the White-Collar Offender: Rhetoric and Reality', above n 98, 657; and DJ Hessing and H Elffers, 'Needy or Greedy? The Social Psychology of Individuals Who Fraudulently Claim Unemployment Benefits' (1993) 23(3) *Journal of Applied Social Psychology* 226.

[148] Michael Ashe QC is a longstanding advocate of financial penalties for insider dealing; see TM Ashe and L Counsell, *Insider Trading*, above n 107.

[149] See C Emsley, *Crime and Society in England, 1750–1900*, 5th edn (Abingdon, Routledge, 2018).

[150] The state can be found undertaking prosecutions sometime before this, and the office of public prosecutor was created in 1879. Interestingly, the state can also be found undertaking prosecutions in respect of financial crime specifically earlier still, most notably that of the Royal British Bank directors in 1858: see S Wilson, *The Origins of Modern Financial Crime* (above n 19) and J Taylor, *Boardroom Scandal: The Criminalization of Company Fraud in Nineteenth-Century Britain* (Oxford, Oxford University Press, 2013).

[151] See D Eastwood, 'Amplifying the Province of the Legislature', above n 115.

B. Non-criminal Enforcement as the UK's 'Conscious Choice'

Non-criminal/administrative pathways are commonly perceived as promoting greater resourcing efficiencies and successful enforcement outcomes, and as such, as providing a panacea for a number of difficulties associated with criminal enforcement, through being able to overcome the associated costs and uncertainties associated with criminal trial proceedings before a judge and jury.[152] However, it is not readily apparent that administrative enforcement can counter the difficulties of actually detecting market abuse, and instead the differences which can transpire by way of 'enforcement flexibility' attach to how evidentially strong the competent authority considers a case to be. Detecting market abuse *has* become easier on account of heightened emphasis on 'reporting' suspicious trading by stock exchanges and commercial entities, and disclosure requirements, but it remains challenging – even in the case of market manipulation, which is based on actual visible trading activity.[153] And notwithstanding the manifest ineptitude which can be found on the part of those who commit insider dealing,[154] information continues to be transmitted in ways which make its discovery difficult, and with *Hannam* also showing how its discovery by enforcing bodies can be highly fortuitous.

However, there may be other ways in which administrative enforcement assists in the fight against market abuse. Indeed, administrative authorities are widely considered to be more specialised than judicial authorities.[155] Actors within the criminal justice system, and the judiciary more broadly, can become closely associated with distinctive specialisms,[156] but a more specialised and 'professionalised' identity which commonly attaches to administrative authorities can be seen from the composition of the Upper Tribunal which heard *Hannam*. This panel included Judge Colin Bishopp and Mr Justice – Sir Nicholas – Warren. Whilst Sir Nicholas Warren enjoyed a career as a barrister and as a judge sitting in the High Court before becoming President of the Tax and Chancery Chamber of the Upper Tribunal,[157] Judge Bishopp's career profile is altogether different. Colin Bishopp initially qualified as a solicitor and engaged in continuous service on many tribunals following his appointment as a part-time Chairman of the VAT

[152] As evident in the submissions in *Hannam* (above n 59, para 186, and as discussed in the main text above herein). See also the discussion in A Ogus, 'Better regulation – better enforcement' in S Weatherill (ed), *Better Regulation* (Oxford, Hart Publishing, 2007) 107.

[153] As is evident eg from the length of time it took US authorities to identify and extradite UK 'Flash Crash' trader, Navinder Singh Sarao.

[154] Eg in the case of Christopher McQuoid (2009), this could be ascertained through a cheque sent to his father in law for precisely half of the proceeds of their 'deal', and in the case of Matthew Uberoi (also 2009) a trading profit of £110,000 was made by a father through inside information passed from his son in email communications coded numerically as Chinese meals.

[155] See generally TT Arvind, J Gray and S Wilson, 'Financial Elites, Law, and Regulation: A Historical Perspective' in G Telesca and Y Cassis (eds), *Financial Elites and European Banking: Historical Perspectives* (Oxford, Oxford University Press, 2018),

[156] Eg former Law Lord, Lord Leonard Hoffmann is widely associated with Company Law, notwithstanding his rich and varied judicial career.

[157] See Jonathan Gaunt QC (Falcon Chambers), Valedictory Speech for Mr Justice Warren (December 2017): https://www.falcon-chambers.com/images/uploads/news/Validictory_Speech_-_Mr_Justice_Warren_12.17_.pdf.

and Duties Tribunal in 1990. Indeed, until his retirement in 2017,[158] Judge Bishopp's lengthy tribunal career included holding appointments as Chair of the Pensions Regulator Tribunal and of the Claims Management Services Tribunal and VAT and Duties Tribunal, as well as acting as Chair for the (now defunct) Financial Services and Markets Tribunal. In Judge Bishopp's career profile we can see a mixture of substantive expertise and also a professional tribunal service identity, and an overall narrative which supports perceptions that administrative authorities are usually more specialised than judicial authorities.

VII. Conclusion

In essence, administrative sanctions carve out an enforcement pathway which seeks to balance the interests of an individual alongside the interests of society in preventing conduct which is unlawful, but doing so in ways which purport to be different from criminal enforcement. In the case of market abuse specifically, we can see this overlaid with European thinking on the importance of having extensive prohibitions founded on perceived harm to financial investors, financial markets – and society at large, embodied in a macro 'market-based' theoretical framework. We can also see a philosophical acknowledgement that those who engage in conduct which is considered to interfere with capital market function do not necessarily need to incur the punishment and wider stigma which are associated with criminalisation.

However, *Hannam* points to a different observed reality. *Hannam* suggests that care should be taken in appraising the advantages which might flow from non-criminal approaches in response to conduct such as market abuse. Moreover, *Hannam* encourages us to reflect on the complexities belying perceptions of administrative sanctions as a proxy for increased state capacity for making sophisticated enforcement choices and ones which are considered most appropriate. This is because *Hannam* intimates strongly that non-criminal enforcement *can* punish and stigmatise. Ian Hannam was not subject to criminal proceedings and he was praised by all concerned for his exemplary conduct, and he also kept his professional authorisation. Notwithstanding the evident support from the City for him and his track record, he has not remained within the echelons he once occupied. What Hannam terms 'the event' has 'spoiled the tone' of his life, and he feels that his 'gracious resignation' was the least-worst option open to him.[159]

Hannam tells the story of how what happened led to him ending up fronting a boutique business (which he himself has described as) 'at the "go-kart" end of the market' with this contrasting starkly with the JPMC 'Ferrari'.[160] Hannam clearly feels ostracised occupationally and personally, and that the 'place card' that had given him 'a seat at the top table' of those within his industry has been 'torn up'.[161] Clearly there are concerns from those within the City that it is a 'Club' from which outsiders are

[158] See https://www.judiciary.uk/announcements/upper-tribunal-judge-retirement-bishopp/.
[159] J Guthrie 'Brunch with the FT: Ian Hannam', above n 65.
[160] Ibid.
[161] Ibid.

easily excluded. Hannam attributed this partly to his working-class background in a setting where those who attended public school have a 'whip hand'.[162] Such connotations of 'outsider' and 'other'[163] are also evident in Ernest Saunders' account of how the ever-lasting 'Nightmare' following his criminal conviction in 1990 has arisen from him being Jewish.[164] As one account of Hannam's experiences suggests, the 'well-heeled elite of which this rough diamond was temporarily a member was delighted to expel him when it got the chance'.[165] On account of the distinctive occupational context for this wrongdoing, the effects of the repercussions for Ian Hannam cannot necessarily be attributed to administrative enforcement per se. Hannam's conduct *was* wrong, but his case *does* invite us to consider whether administrative enforcement allows persons subject to this to be burdened with what are effectively 'criminal consequences' without a conviction from a criminal court,[166] and without the protections of due process which are associated with this.

Given too that enlightened thinking around stigma speaks of concerns that criminal justice outcomes should allow for rehabilitation and reintegration, rather than permanent exclusion, and that the criminal process should seek to shame rather than stigmatise in order to accommodate this,[167] we should be particularly concerned about the possible effects of non-criminal sanctions being considered capable of delivering outcomes of a 'nature and severity' that they 'may be regarded as criminal penalties'.[168] If there are sanctions from outside the criminal process which are capable of delivering outcomes which we more readily associate with the criminal process then we should be mindful of human rights and fundamental freedoms considerations. Protections which are built into the criminal process are not part of the structural architecture of non-criminal enforcement, precisely because, in part,

[162] Ibid.

[163] With this appearing to embody Edward Said's construct of 'the Other', developed in his analysis of 'Orientalism' in EW Said, *Orientalism*, 3rd edn (London, Penguin Random House, 2003). For Said 'the Other' exposed the binaries which arise from the imposition of values, assumptions, and cultural codes of one social group on another, and where differences are construed through culturally-determined and biased and limited historical perspectives. Indeed, 'Othering' has been described as the process through which a dominant group defines into existence a subordinate group, and where individuals or groups can be 'othered' on account of differences of race or gender and religion etc. For Barter-Godfrey and Taket, it is widely recognised that social exclusion is more complex than a dichotomy of 'inclusion' or 'exclusion', with influences also being brought to bear by other social processes, including being marginalised through being 'the other'. For the authors 'othering' is the 'social, linguistic and psychological mechanism that distinguishes "us" from "them"' with this reflecting the Social Identity Theory proposition that people are aware of, 'recognise and evaluate' others in terms of adherence or belonging to social groups; and from this dynamics which can arise between othering, marginalisation, stigma, and inequality, create rewards for being 'normal' or 'like us', and costs attaching to being 'different'. See S Barter-Godfrey and A Taket, 'Othering, marginalisation and pathways to exclusion in health' in A Taket et al, *Theorising Social Exclusion* (Abingdon, Routledge, 2009), 166–72; especially 166–67. Twenty-first century British society continues to show strong othering tendencies on grounds of race, religion and class.

[164] See M Levi, 'Sentencing White-Collar Crime in the Dark?' (above n 99), and J Saunders, *Nightmare: Ernest Saunders and the Guinness Affair* (above n 97).

[165] J Guthrie, 'Brunch with the FT: Ian Hannam', above n 65.

[166] Which for many is the only mechanism by which an individual can properly be classed as a 'criminal', following the reasoning advanced by Paul Tappan in the 1940s, in reaction to Sutherland's controversial work: see PW Tappan, 'Who Is the Criminal?' (1947) 12(10) *American Sociological Review* 96.

[167] See J Braithwaite, *Crime, Shame and Reintegration* (Cambridge, Cambridge University Press, 1989).

[168] *Di Puma and Zecca*, Judgment of the CJEU, above n 1, paras 25 and 22.

administrative sanctions are intended to avoid at least some of the consequences of criminal enforcement. These considerations alone should encourage caution in how we reflect on current favour for criminal enforcement, but making sense of this trend is far from straightforward. This is firstly on account of continuing support for extensive use of administrative sanctions at European level, as evident in the key directions of the MAR 2014. Furthermore, in the domestic sphere, the Law Commission of England and Wales insisted in 2010 that a strong case could be made for the repeal of 'low level' criminal offences in circumstances where 'the introduction of a civil penalty' is likely to be equally effective.[169]

It *is* nevertheless possible to align these different considerations through how the Law Commission also proposed that it was perfectly proper for the criminal law to respond to wrongdoers 'who deserve the stigma associated with criminal conviction because they have engaged in seriously reprehensible conduct'.[170] It is also helpful to draw on recent allusion from HM Treasury to the long and important role played by the criminal law 'in providing a sanction for improper behaviour in the financial services sphere'.[171] But this requires confronting the very real possibility that stigma can also arise through the operation of administrative enforcement. It is not surprising that the Law Commission used 'deterrence' as a reference point for measuring enforcement effectiveness, and that 'securing punishment' was also part of questioning whether the criminal law was an expensive, uncertain and ineffective strategy in regulatory contexts.[172] However, *Hannam* suggests that criminal enforcement objectives might 'leak' beyond the criminal process, perhaps all too easily. Particularly troublingly it does appear that *Hannam* shows the importation of language which is associated with the criminal process into non-criminal proceedings. This is readily apparent in how the Upper Tribunal confirmed that the FCA shouldered the burden of proving that 'Mr Hannam is guilty of market abuse'.[173] And Hannam's submission that the standard of proof applicable was the criminal standard rather than the lower civil standard *did* result in a much more extended consideration of what the appropriate standard should be than one might expect for proceedings which were very clearly outside the criminal process, with this discussion extending even to how difficulties could arise in drawing a 'distinction between the standard which the tribunal should apply and the criminal standard'.[174]

Thus, this is how *Hannam* illuminates the importance of further work for achieving a fuller understanding of how much similarity and how much difference subsists between these mechanisms, substantively and even linguistically, and from this how much 'blurring' of them is occurring. Above reflections from the Law Commission might help to demystify how administrative sanctions have become capable of conflicting with *ne bis in idem* when situated alongside the criminal process, but together with findings from *Hannam* they also suggest that the very conceptual

[169] Law Commission, *Criminal Liability in Regulatory Contexts*, above n 87, para 1.30.
[170] Ibid, para 1.28.
[171] HM Treasury, *Sanctions for the directors of failed banks* , above n 57, para 4.2.
[172] Law Commission, *Criminal Liability in Regulatory Contexts*, above n 87, para 18.
[173] *Hannam v FCA*, above n 59, para 14.
[174] Ibid, para 176.

nature and operation of administrative enforcement pathways raise important issues. In thinking forward about what we do currently understand about such enforcement modes, and what we need to understand about them, it is at this point suggested that the existence of administrative sanctions per se is not problematic, and should be viewed as a positive aspect of the state's interest in preventing unacceptable conduct. Indeed, whatever one might feel about the experiences of Ian Hannam, at the heart of what Hannam terms 'the event'[175] were emails which he should not have sent because they disclosed inside information. This *is* conduct which others in positions like his should refrain from on account of what is believed necessary to protect the functioning of financial markets, and to protect society from the consequences of disorderly markets.

What this analysis suggests is problematic about administrative sanctions lies in how they are capable of mimicking criminal enforcement, and thereby how they appear to be able to expose those subject to them to some of the consequences of criminal enforcement. Administrative enforcement will not lead to imprisonment, but the operation of financial penalties coupled with adverse exposure can lead to life-changing consequences conventionally associated with criminal justice outcomes. It is through this mimicking that administrative enforcement is transformed into a QCEM. At this point in time, much remains to be understood about the consequences, and even actually the *detail* of the Trade and Cooperation Agreement reached between the UK and the European Union, announced on 24 December 2020,[176] literally days ahead of the end of the 'transition period'[177] on 1 January 2021. In these circumstances, it might be easy for the UK to overlook the continuing importance of the essence of *Zecca*.[178] Like many regimes, domestic policy in the UK *is* very strongly pursuing the position as articulated by former Chancellor of the Exchequer George Osborne, that those who 'manipulate markets and commit financial crime should be treated like the criminals they are – and they will be. For let us be clear: there is no trade-off between high standards of conduct and competitiveness. Far from it …'[179] In the pursuit of such policies, this initial analysis of the operation of UK administrative enforcement highlights the importance of asking whether those who are not pursued through the criminal courts will also be 'treated like the criminals they are [not]'? In setting out some initial thoughts on the interplay between criminal and non-criminal state enforcement in the UK, this analysis has sought to highlight the importance of generating critical discursive space for exploring what might be meant by 'quasi criminal enforcement mechanisms' so as to try to 'map' perceived benefits and concerns about it domestically, in the EU and beyond, in an increasingly integrated global financial system.

[175] J Guthrie, 'Brunch with the FT: Ian Hannam', above n 65.

[176] See 'The EU-UK Trade and Cooperation Agreement': https://ec.europa.eu/info/relations-united-kingdom/eu-uk-trade-and-cooperation-agreement_en.

[177] Following the UK's formal departure on 31 January 2020, and characterised by the continuing operation of EU laws during this time.

[178] Even without the additional complexities and actually distracting forces attributable to the disruptions presented by the Covid-19 global pandemic.

[179] George Osborne Mansion House Speech 2015, above n 22.

PART II

Criminal, Civil, Administrative … What's in A Name? Disentangling Concepts, Selected Topics

A. General Part of Criminal Law

6

Quasi-criminal Enforcement in Criminal Law and Penal Theory: What Would Herbert Packer Say?

CHRISTOPHER HARDING

I. Introduction

While the use of administrative and other 'non-criminal law' procedures and sanctions is now an important reality within a number of European jurisdictions, there is an uncertain grasp and articulation of the theoretical underpinning of this phenomenon and regarding the relationship between the criminal and quasi-criminal fields of normativity and enforcement. Especially in the field of 'regulatory'[1] control, any discussion of the use or non-use of criminal law,[2] of criminalisation or decriminalisation, should be based on a clear sense and understanding of quasi-criminal enforcement as distinct from enforcement through criminal law 'properly so called'. In short, what is the normative and policy logic of the quasi-criminal approach, in terms of its justification and intended outcomes?

The jurisdictional host for much that now passes under the name of 'administrative'[3] or 'quasi-criminal' regulation and enforcement has comprised predominantly legal orders in continental Europe. And it is in that European context that much of the contemporary probing of the distinction between 'criminal' and 'administrative' has

[1] As conceptual vocabulary, the terms 'regulation' and 'regulatory' have been commonly used in British and American contexts to connote legal control through specialised public agencies in the socio-economic field of activity, in particular in relation to trading and business, public health and welfare, and environmental protection – what many would regard as *outside* the traditional domain of criminal law which deals with interpersonal relations.

[2] For instance, in relation to anti-competitive business collusion (cartels), or market manipulation. See elsewhere in this volume the chapters by De Sanctis (Chapter 10) and Wilson and Wilson (Chapter 5). See also the line of argument in the Commission's 2011 Communication on crime policy: European Commission, Communication, 'Towards an EU Criminal Policy: Ensuring the effective implementation of EU policies through criminal law', COM(2011) 573 final.

[3] Again, the vocabulary is problematical. 'Administrative' is widely used in a European context, especially in EU instruments and discussion, but has its functional equivalents in Common Law jurisdictions, such as 'civil penalties' in the UK. See further below on some refinement of this conceptual language.

taken place. Sometimes this probing has been scholarly and theoretical,[4] sometimes (although rarely) it has been the forerunner of some legislative change,[5] sometimes it has been judicial, in particular when prompted by constitutional and legal protection concerns (in the case law of the European Court of Human Rights).[6] But viewed across Europe, the probing process has been haphazard, reactive and not really tied together. Despite the quantitative, theoretical and policy-related significance of the subject, there has been relatively little in the way of a general stocktaking and comparative analysis of the subject.[7] Any attempt now to survey this legal scene and make sense of what is happening variously at the national level, and also at the EU level, is fraught with methodological difficulty and problems of interpretation, and soon creates an impression of messiness on the ground and in the legal mind.[8] Across national jurisdictions, differences appear and origins and motivations seem mixed.

It would be useful at this point, then, to offer a clear template for organising and guiding discussion of the subject, especially if the objective is to gain a clearer sense of what has happened, and why and how the present state of play has come about, in order to prepare the ground for some guidelines for coherence in policy and legal development, and a surer sense of future direction. It will be argued here that the account of the subject will benefit from being placed in a structure of four principal organising concepts and ideas:

- the formal ranking of offending conduct
- the provenance and agency of that conduct
- the feasibility of the criminal sanction
- policies of criminalisation and decriminalisation, in the light of the pervasive role of the penal method and contemporary myths of deterrence.

It is also important to conduct this discussion in comparative terms and in doing so to cast the net more widely to consider the range of possible procedures and sanctions in relation to offending and rule-breaking, both within and beyond Europe. In using that comparative method, it is interesting to recollect some earlier musing on the subject contained in investigation and analysis of such approaches in mid-twentieth-century

[4] For instance, in Germany. See further the discussion in this volume by Brodowski (Chapter 3).

[5] The Federal Republic of Germany in the 1960s (see Brodowski (Chapter 3) and Harding (Chapter 6) in this volume), and Finland more recently (see Lahti (Chapter 1) in this volume).

[6] See the discussion elsewhere in this volume, especially that of Sugman Stubbs (Chapter 12).

[7] One important exception was the study commissioned by the European Commission of the administrative sanctioning systems in the Member States and the influence of Community sanctions on domestic sanctions. (European Commission, in two volumes, 1994, 1995). But this is something of a lost source. See the short overview by JAE Vervaele, 'Towards a System of European Administrative Sanctions?' in John AE Vervaele (ed), *Administrative Law Application and Enforcement of Community Law in the Netherlands* (Deventer, Kluwer, 1994), 193. See also, by way of overview: Mireille Delmas-Marty, *What Kind of Criminal Policy for Europe?* (The Hague, Kluwer, 1996); Frank Zimmermann (ed), *Criminal Liability of Political Decision-Makers: A Comparative Perspective* (Cham, Springer International Publishing, 2017). The Association Internationale de Droit Pénal has more recently turned its attention to the role of different sanctions in its 2018 Conference – see further in the editorial conclusions in this volume (Chapter 14).

[8] As indeed was suggested by the 1990s survey: see Vervaele (n 7 above).

'classical' American writing on criminal jurisprudence, particularly that of Herbert Packer in the 1960s. Addressing the justification for using norms of criminal law, Packer had written in his seminal work *The Limits of the Criminal Sanction*:

> The fact is that we do not have a systematic body of theory about the kinds of sanctions available to reinforce the primary norms of conduct that the law seeks to promote, or about their distinguishing characteristics, their strengths and weaknesses, their anticipated benefits and their use, and the social costs that their invocation incurs.[9]

And then, that:

> There is a vast range of economic offenses, especially those in which a corporation rather than a natural person is the object of the law's attention, where the forms of criminal sanction can be and should be dispensed with.[10]

Packer's argument in favour of an appropriate distinction between criminal law and other forms of legal control and penality rehearses the script for much that is now firmly established as administrative and quasi-criminal in many European jurisdictions. In the same way, it may be said that European non-criminalisation or decriminalisation and the shift towards the quasi-criminal, matches what Packer's fellow American contemporary John Langbein analysed as the 'rehabilitation' of the criminal sanction.[11] At an earlier date still, Sanford Kadish had previewed the distinction between sanctions used to deal with crime and sanctions in response to the violation of economic regulations.[12]

This theoretical and conceptual discussion will recall some of that classic American criminal jurisprudence as a trigger for probing the logical and political justification for quasi-criminal enforcement. In doing so the discussion here speculates about a possible posthumous commentary on the part of Packer:

> When I hear about what is happening now in the world of criminal law, and especially over the pond in Europe, I think that the European Union and its Member States, and also the European Court of Human Rights, should engage seriously with the argument quoted above.

II. The Formal Ranking of Offending Conduct

The ranking and categorisation of offending and rule-breaking conduct for ethical and legal purposes has a long history across many jurisdictions. Lawyers and legal historians will be familiar with the vocabulary of classification: 'crime', 'felony', 'misdemeanour',

[9] Herbert L Packer, *The Limits of the Criminal Sanction* (Stanford, CA, Stanford University Press, 1969), especially Part III, chapters 13–17. Packer (1925–72), who was a professor at Stanford University, is acknowledged as a highly influential writer on the subject.

[10] Ibid, at 252–53.

[11] JH Langbein, 'Controlling Prosecutorial Discretion in Germany' (1973) 41 *University of Chicago Law Review* 439, at 453: 'The *Ordnungswidrigkeit* procedure, by decriminalizing the morally neutral, enhances the distinctiveness of what is genuinely criminal. It rehabilitates the criminal sanction.'

[12] Sanford Kadish, 'Some Observations on the Use of Criminal Sanctions in Enforcing Economic Regulations' (1963) 30 *University of Chicago Law Review* 423. Cf John C Coffee, 'Does Unlawful Mean Criminal? Reflections on the Disappearing Tort/Crime Distinction in American Law' (1991) 71 *Boston University law Review* 173.

'petty offence', 'summary offence', 'indictable' and 'non-indictable' offences, indicative not only of the nature of the offending conduct but also procedure and jurisdiction. Such criminal law gradings have been supplemented by further categorisation, especially relevant to this discussion: 'regulatory offending', '*Ordnungswidrigkeiten*', *Bagatelldelikt*'. Naturally enough, this is an organisational response to the wide range of legally and ethically proscribed behaviour in most societies. It is unavoidable. But the details will always be contestable, and the descriptive language seems almost designed to confuse, as can be seen in Glanville Williams' playful and folksy account:

> The word 'offence' is another name for a crime. Crimes in the broad sense include not only the major crimes (indictable offences) but summary offences, which regulate many trades and special activities (the so-called 'regulatory offences'), as well as the conduct of ordinary people in their daily life. In practice, a summary offence would not be referred to as a crime, which is felt to be too strong a description of it. Indeed, we have become a bit squeamish about the word 'crime' altogether, and it is dropping out of use [in the statute-book].[13]

This quotation, from the late 1970s, can provoke many semantic points in the present discussion, but may serve to illustrate the difficulties of vocabulary and meaning, which may then be compounded when moving from one language or one legal culture to another – for instance, how best to translate the German '*Ordnungswidrigkeiten*' from German into English, or the American 'felony' from English into German, or the French '*droit pénal*' into English? But the main point here is that offending conduct will need to be ordered and ranked, and if the outcome of that is to a large extent a matter of procedure and jurisdiction, the motivation is likely to be a need to qualitatively assess the nature of the offending conduct.

As a historical observation, there appears to be an enduring principal distinction, between that which is 'properly' thought of as 'criminal' ('real crime', '*mala in se*') and that which is cast as offending behaviour in a more technical and utilitarian sense ('*mala prohibita*'). Rather disconcertingly at first sight, the latter offences may well be more quantitatively significant and outnumber the former. As Glanville Williams observes: 'summary offences are legion', as a matter of 'the conduct of ordinary people in their daily life'.[14] The same would be true of the German *Ordungswidrigkeiten*. But quantity may have its own significance: in social and economic terms, the 'less criminal' activities are more widely encountered and personally important as a normative experience in that sense. The social historian Robert Shoemaker wished to emphasise this point in his earlier study of crime and criminal justice in seventeenth- and eighteenth-century England, by choosing, unlike the main run of historians, to focus on misdemeanours rather than felonies, since the former were more representative of actual delinquency and the workings of criminal justice.[15] There may be some important clues in a more

[13] Glanville Williams, *Textbook of Criminal Law* (London, Stevens, 1978), 8–9. The author relishes his reader's perplexity. To the reader's imagined exclamation, 'Oh ho! So civil courts can even send people to prison?' his answer is a jolly 'Yes ….' (at p 21).

[14] Williams, n 13 above, at 8–9.

[15] Robert B Shoemaker, *Prosecution and Punishment: Petty Crime and the Law in London and Rural Middlesex 1660–1725* (Cambridge, Cambridge University Press, 1991). Shoemaker's recent work is also of interest in the context of the present discussion, since it probes the importance of 'plebeian agency' in the shaping of modern social policy: Tim Hitchcock and Robert B Shoemaker, *London Lives: Poverty, Crime and the Making of a Modern City 1690–1800* (Cambridge, Cambridge University Press, 2015).

determined focus on such petty and technical offending, or the *mala prohibita*, to use the vocabulary of classical criminal jurisprudence. Equally, there is something very pregnant in Glanville Williams' depiction of the 'conduct of ordinary people in their daily life', which after all may be linked as well to criminological theorising about 'white collar crime'. A closer examination of the content of regulatory offending or *Ordnungswidrigkeiten* reveals a typical diet of everyday and routine personal and occupational activities carried out by people who are not 'typical criminals' engaged in 'core criminality' (see below). This may help to elucidate what is intuitive in the distinction between 'administrative' and 'criminal'.

Taking an inductive approach, it may be possible to elaborate some principle and theory from an observation of practice, in this context the *practice* of describing conduct as *mala prohibita* and this may prove consistent over time and place – employing Hart's methodology of 'descriptive sociology'.[16] Thus Shoemaker, commenting on his subject for study, offences categorised as criminal misdemeanours in seventeenth and eighteenth century England, states:

> [A] distinctive aspect of misdemeanour prosecutions is the large number of victimless offences which directly harmed no one individual but indirectly could be said to harm the whole community. These include regulatory offences, poor law offences, and vice, and they were typically prosecuted by parish officials or informers.[17]

Then, Glanville Williams, writing towards the end of the twentieth century, may be cited; having provided a colourful list of trivial infractions he comments:

> Odd as these offences may seem on first acquaintance, they mostly have good reasons, or anyway some sort of reason … Most summary offences are the result of prosaic efforts to improve safety standards, or to prevent petty fraud or oppression.[18]

Empirically, this kind of description takes us to the heart of *Ordnungswidrigkeiten* and 'administrative' violations. In Glanville Williams' words, these stand in stark contrast to the domain of *mala in se*, where 'be honest and refrain from violence' are 'almost the sum of it'.[19] Real criminal law is also quantitatively less significant, since problems of evidence and resources may limit the actual resort to what is laid down in the text of the law. Yet that text of what is *mala in se* is of huge qualitative significance, as a confirmation of the fundamental and crucial values of a society and its role in sending a powerful and dramatic normative message. Such 'real' criminal law has a rhetorical and behaviour-shaping force which is crucial in society.[20] Whereas what is *mala prohibita* commands much less attention: 'detailed and systematic information about the mass

[16] HLA Hart, *The Concept of Law* (Oxford University Press, 1961), at vii: 'Many important distinctions, which are not immediately obvious, between types of social situation and relationships may best be brought to light by an examination of the standard uses of the relevant expressions and of the way in which these depend on a social context, itself often left unstated.'

[17] *Prosecution and Punishment*, n 15 above, at 6. The English 'Poor Laws' were a system of relief for indigent persons, in force from the sixteenth through to the early twentieth centuries.

[18] *Textbook of Criminal Law*, n 13 above, at 9.

[19] Ibid.

[20] See, for instance the opinion of the German Bundesverfassungsgericht in its 'Lisbon' judgment of 2009: Case concerning the review of the compatibility of the Treaty of Lisbon with the German Basic Law: BVerfG, 2BvE 2/08 vom 30/6/2009, para 355.

of regulatory offences is outside my purview' (as a doctrinal scholar of criminal law) claims Glanville Williams.[21]

Much of this classification and ranking is almost obvious, easy enough to grasp as a distinction and readily agreed upon, and blessed with Latin labelling. But at which point *mala prohibita* may be transformed into 'administrative/punitive' or 'quasi-criminal' is less easy to identify and justify. The outcome, as a matter of formal law and definition, is clear enough in the shift from a consensual and negotiated procedure to a confrontational, adversarial and juridified one. But the motivation and objective for this may be less transparent and indeed may not be consistent over time and place – and the rationale may then have to be sought in provenance, agency, resources, and ideology, and thus more contingent elements.

It should also be emphasised at this point that what appears to be distinctive about the 'quasi-criminal' categorisation is that which is implied in the language of that label – as Wilson and Wilson stress,[22] the mimicry of the criminal law process. That mimicry is not just a matter of penal element, but a resort to a process that is adversarial and juridical, as a significant shift from a process that is consensual and negotiated. A punitive element is part of the quasi-criminal, but not the whole story. The punitive may occur in a whole range of settings, including what is 'soft' administrative or regulatory, as Wilson and Wilson show in their study of the Ian Hannam case, where part of the penal experience was an unavoidable socially-oriented change of professional circumstances, but not brought about in juridified circumstances.[23]

III. Provenance and the Protection of Interests

Provenance, in the sense of the circumstances of origin, is a significant aspect of this discussion. It may explain much about how legal development takes place, but in a comparative analysis it is not determinative. Put another way, provenance helps us to understand why criminal law may not be used or should not be used, but it does not provide the full story. For instance, it does not necessarily take the matter outside the domain of formal criminal law, as is clearly shown by reference to the legal situation in the UK. Provenance is essentially the basis for the category of infractions referred to as *mala prohibita*, and also often as 'regulatory', and relates to the kind of interest and value which is being protected and reinforced.

Thus we may return to that familiar listing already referred to: broadly speaking, matters of economic regulation and governance, health and social welfare, environmental protection, labour and professional relations, every-day and routine ordering of the public space (road traffic, noise, animals) – the 'conduct of ordinary people in

[21] *Textbook of Criminal Law*, n 13 above, at 9.

[22] See their Chapter 5 in this volume.

[23] Ibid, at section III.C. and D. In an analysis of the *Hannam* case it may be said that the fine imposed by the FCA was quasi-criminal, but other outcomes more loosely regulatory. On the wide resort to penal sanctions in different social contexts, see Christopher Harding and Richard W Ireland, *Punishment: Rhetoric, Rule and Practice* (London, Routledge, 1989).

their everyday life',[24] whether that be in a personal or occupational context. A useful checklist for general purposes could be derived from the conduct covered by the 1968 German legislation, the *Ordnungswidrigkeitengesetz*. The German legislation provides perhaps the best elucidation of the subject in the form of a model code, being based on a long tradition of legal control alternative to criminal law, and a long-term theoretical and policy discourse through successive systems of governance. Since 1968 this legal category has been extensive in the German system, comprising both the regulation of economic and social activities and of the public space (especially road traffic matters). As Daniel Ohana argues in his probing and revealing study of the development of *Ordnungswidrigkeiten*,[25] as a very significant model in this context, the deeper historical origins lay in the role of police, used here in the 'new police science' sense of the administration of the economic and social order with a view to pursuing the welfare of the community as a whole.[26] In this discourse, police stands in contrast to law (and especially criminal law), the basic principle of the latter being the autonomy and self-government of the individual. On this view, therefore, the starting point is a qualitative distinction relating to the rationale and substantive scope of criminal law on the one hand and administrative or police sanctioning on the other hand. But for Ohana, this is just the starting point, and his argument urges an understanding of something more complex and historically contingent, based on the political vicissitudes of the German state over the last one hundred years. On this reading of the subject, in the case of Germany, governance through 'police' has been forged successively though periods of Nazification, post-1945 denazification, 1950s decartelisation, and 1960s decriminalisation as inspired by a surgent movement radically advocating a different inspiration and legitimation in new democracy. Ohana summarises the process in these terms:

> [T]he sanctioning mechanism of administrative penalties proved to be instrumental in many ways as the West Germans revised their political institutions, economic structures and social values. Offering a more efficient, yet less stigmatising and less intrusive alternative to the criminal law, it showed itself to be highly malleable and susceptible to adaptation to a variety of uses, depending on the specific contexts and concerns at hand ... it was through the exigencies and constraints faced by the West Germans in this protracted and precarious process that the contours of the *Ordnungswidrigkeitenrecht* were delineated, and its distinguishing features vis-à-vis the criminal sanctioning process were forged.[27]

The resultant code embodied in the 1968 legislation in Germany can then be seen as having served a number of successive purposes: democratisation through denazification, the negotiation of an alternative to criminal law anti-cartel regulation as advocated by American argument, practically relieving the judicial system of the burden of an escalating road traffic control system, and accommodating political arguments regarding the

[24] Williams, n 13 above.

[25] D Ohana, *Administrative Penalties in the Rechtsstaat: On the Emergence of the Ordnungswidrikeit Sanctioning System in Post-War Germany* (Hebrew University of Jerusalem, Working Paper 134/2014); also published in (2014) 64 *University of Toronto Law Review* 243.

[26] Ibid, at p 6. More generally on this concept, see: M Dubber and M Valverde (eds), *The New Police Science: The Police Power in Domestic and International Governance* (Stanford, CA, Stanford University Press, 2006).

[27] Ohana, n 25 above, at 55.

intrusive and stigmatising over-resort to criminal law. The *Ordnungswidrikeitengesetz* became many things to many people. But as the provenance became complex and varied, the basis in terms of a single qualitative difference, as enunciated by the Federal Constitutional Court in its ruling in 1968[28] became less convincing. Road traffic violations were in the same bag as complex economic and business stratagems and small motoring fines mixed in with huge penalties for anti-competitive infringements. Both, in formal description, were 'police', 'administrative' and 'quasi-criminal', but then as such begged further legal complications and questions. Provenance is thus important and explains much, but does not solve the resulting legal conundrum. And this is a conundrum now to be explored with reference to a number of contemporary jurisdictions, both national and supranational.

IV. The Feasibility and Sensible Use of the Criminal Law Process and Sanction

The question of the feasibility of the resort to criminal law has both theoretical/conceptual and practical dimensions.

A. Counterproductive Effects: *Ultima Ratio*

The principle that criminal law and its associated sanctions should be used sparingly, as a matter of last resort is very well-established in the European context.[29] As Douglas Husak has commented, the greater willingness of European theorists to argue for the limitation of criminal law compared to their common law counterparts presents a 'fascinating question in comparative criminal theory'.[30] Last resort arguments have more recently also been asserted in policy statements at the European Union level.[31] There are theoretical and practical aspects of the principle. *Ultima ratio* finds its most convincing justification in the need to preserve the distinctive expressive force and impact of criminal law in guiding personal and social behaviour and the resulting intrusive quality and power of criminal law sanctions, and then may be linked to attempts to distinguish the respective domains of 'core' criminal law and other modes

[28] Decision of the *Bundesverfassungsgericht*: BVerfGE, 27, 1, 16 July 1969, which reaffirmed the classical distinction between matters belonging to the *core* of criminal law and more peripheral matters. See the discussion by Ohana, n 25 above, at 52. And cf the Court's later 'Lisbon' judgment in 2009 (Case concerning the review of the compatibility of the Treaty of Lisbon with the German Basic Law, BVerfG 2BvE 2/08 vom 30/6/2009, para 355), when it revisited this question.

[29] For an overview of discussion, see: C Harding, 'The Interplay of Criminal and Administrative Law in the Context of Market Regulation: The Case of Serious Competition Infringements', Chapter 9 in V Mitsilegas, P Alldridge and L Cheliotis (eds), *Globalisation, Criminal Law and Criminal Justice: Theoretical, Comparative and Transnational Perspectives* (Oxford and Portland, OR, Hart Publishing, 2015), at 203–08.

[30] D Husak, 'Applying *Ultima Ratio*: A Skeptical Assessment' (2005) 2(2) *Ohio State Journal of Criminal Law* 535.

[31] European Commission, Communication, 'Towards an EU Criminal Policy: Ensuring the effective implementation of EU policies through criminal law', COM(2011) 573 final.

of legal control.[32] This is a theoretical and principled limitation on the use of criminal law, but having also a practical element in the claim that over-use of criminal law sanctions will in the longer term dilute their impact and effectiveness, both in retributive and general deterrent terms.

B. The Responsibility of Corporate Actors: Issues of Agency

There have been both doctrinal and practical doubts regarding the use of criminal law in relation to corporate actors. In some European jurisdictions, the requirement of personal responsibility as an element of criminal liability has hindered the development of criminal liability for non-human, corporate actors, for instance still at the present time in Germany, Italy, Greece, Bulgaria and Latvia.[33] In Germany especially (at least until recently)[34] there has been a dogmatic adherence to the principle of personal fault in criminal law: *Schuldprinzip*, based on the argument '*societas delinquere non potest*', that only a human individual can commit a fault, and deriving from a philosophy of agency that finds it difficult to contemplate a distinct corporate psychology and mentality. Various legal systems have found legal routes to circumvent this objection, for instance identifying a superior/vicarious or supervisory responsibility in relation to the acts of human 'agents', including the imputation of the latter's mental element to a corporate superior (for instance, in the case of England and Wales,[35] and the United States), or the pragmatic Dutch solution in the form of 'intellectual' or 'functional perpetratorship'[36] (there is a somewhat similar approach in Belgium).[37] The German approach has been pragmatic in a different way, laying down a form of corporate liability, and hard-hitting sanctions, in the *Ordnungswidrigkeitengesetz*, thus conveniently side-stepping the dogmatic reluctance to contemplate the principle as a matter of criminal law. This latter approach, however, especially the use of severe monetary sanctions, has contributed to the conundrum of identity for administrative prohibitions and sanctions under discussion here. The longstanding argument that the application of criminal law sanctions

[32] For instance, in the rulings of the *Bundesverfassungsgericht*, n 28 above, and the same Court in its 'Lisbon' ruling of 2009 on the compatibility of the Lisbon Treaty with the German Constitution, n 28 above. See also the rulings of the European Court of Human Rights in *Öztürk v Germany* (App No 8544/79), (1984) 6 EHRR 409, at para 52, and *Jussila v Finland* (App No 73053/01), [2007] ECHR 996.

[33] For an overview, see S Beck, 'Corporate Criminal Liability', Chapter 25 in MD Dubber and T Hornie (eds), *The Oxford Handbook of Criminal Law* (Oxford, Oxford University Press, 2014); M Pieth and R Ivory (eds), *Corporate Criminal Liability: Emergence, Convergence, and Risks* (Dordrecht/Heidelberg, Springer, 2011).

[34] There is now a proposal to introduce corporate criminal liability in German federal law. In 2013 draft legislation was put forward by the Minister of Justice for North Rhine Westphalia to establish a corporate criminal code in federal German law but progress has been slow. It has proven difficult to reach a consensus. A revised draft leaked in 2020 refers not to corporate crimes but corporate 'acts' and it seems that the proposed prosecution would be selective – a 'black sheep' approach.

[35] The so-called 'identification' doctrine.

[36] As worked out by the courts in the 1920s and 1930s and then embodied in the Economic Offences Act of 1950 (section 15); see also the revision of the French Penal Code in 1992 (Articles 121–122).

[37] R Verstraeten and V Franssen, 'Collective Entities as Subjects of Criminal Law. The Case of Belgium and the Netherlands' in A Fiorella and AM Stile (eds), *Corporate Criminal Liability and Compliance Programs* (Maples, Jovene editors, 2012) 253, 272–77, 300–04.

to non-human actors may be practically problematical – 'no soul to damn, no body to kick',[38] it is not possible to imprison or whip a corporation – is less convincing when some imagination is applied.[39]

C. Resources

The point does not have to be laboured that criminal law is resource-intensive.[40] The seriousness of the offending behaviour and of the consequences of involvement in formal criminal proceedings results in the need for careful and more painstaking collection of evidence and higher standards of proof, and the work of a range of agencies and personnel in investigation, prosecution, trial, and penal and other sanctioning. Commonly in practice resources for such a process may be scarce or limited. Such a resource dilemma becomes all the more significant in those systems where it is felt that there is a public interest in using criminal law as a matter of principle so that there is, in formal terms, a need for compulsory prosecution (the so-called 'legality' as distinct from the 'opportunity' principle). *Legalitätsprinzip* evolved as another distinctive feature of the German legal system, as a control on prosecutorial discretion, and in particular non-prosecution – as was laid down in Article 152(2) of the Code of Criminal Procedure: '[The public prosecutor] is required …. to take action against all judicially punishable …. acts, to the extent that there is a sufficient factual basis.'[41] It is unsurprising then that the opportunity was taken during the 1960s in Germany to transfer the huge number of road traffic violations from the category of crime to that of *Ordnungswidrigkeiten* to enable a greater resort to prosecutorial discretion and the use of a process which would be less demanding on resources. Moreover, this has been and continues to be an important incentive in the use of administrative rather than criminal law processes in other systems.[42]

D. Difficulties of Proof

This is then a related matter. In areas of offending behaviour where the evidence may not be easily obtained or subject to difficulties of interpretation, or where complexities of responsibility render proof of the attribution more contestable, resort to the criminal law process and its higher demands in relation to evidence may be all the more problematical. For instance, this may be commonly the case in relation to much contemporary economic and financial crime, when evidence may be of a technical nature, requiring expert investigation and assessment, subject to complex trails of discovery, and located in organisational contexts within which it may not be easy to disentangle corporate and

[38] The phrase used by JC Coffee – '"No Soul to Damn, No Body to Kick": An Unscandalized Inquiry into the Problem of Corporate Punishment' (1981) 79 *Michigan Law Review* 386.

[39] See Christopher Harding, *Criminal Enterprise: Individuals, organisations and criminal responsibility* (Collumpton, Willan Publishing, 2007), at 237–242.

[40] See the discussion by Wilson and Wilson, Chapter 5 in this volume.

[41] See the comparative discussion by Langbein, n 11 above. And also elsewhere: see for instance, L Bachmaier, Winter and A del Moral García, *Criminal Law in Spain* (Alphen aan den Rijn, Kluwer Law International, 2010).

[42] See the discussion by Blachnio-Parzych (Chapter 4), and Zukinden (Chapter 2) in this volume.

individual attributions of conduct. Such factors are likely to raise at an early stage the prospect of a low probability of successful investigation, prosecution and conviction, and so act as a significant disincentive to the use of criminal law. The spectre of 'failed prosecution', with attendant political fall-out, looms large for both criminal law and regulatory authorities, attested by a number of recent and contemporary examples in the area of financial crime and antitrust violations.[43]

In short, resort to criminal law raises the stakes for all concerned, and the costs may be high on both sides of the adversarial fence. 'Softer' procedures, less confrontational and adversarial in nature, and resolving matters by negotiation and settlement, may prove so much less costly for all. In so far as quasi-criminal law mimics and has some of the character of criminal law, a relevant question concerns, then, the extent to which, as an alternative to criminal law, very much is gained from the point of view of resources and other costs. For instance, quasi-criminal process is punitive and there may still be stigmatisation costs, even if relatively lower compared to criminal law – but this remains a matter of argument and for further examination, an important task for criminology. Also, in a contemporary European context, the quasi-criminal has in effect been elevated to criminal for purposes of legal protection,[44] as a result cancelling the intended resource-gain of the quasi-criminal approach. There is a continuing question, therefore: while it is agreed that less criminal law should be used, often for reasons of feasibility, it is less certain how to work out alternative processes that successfully address those concerns of feasibility.

V. Criminalisation and Decriminalisation: The Role of Contingency

It is also important to place this discussion within the contemporary frame of debate regarding criminalisation and decriminalisation, which after all is a way of viewing what has been said above about ethical ranking, provenance and feasibility through another lens. As noted already, the 1968 German legislation was significantly driven by principled arguments of decriminalisation, and now at the EU level, in so far as a guiding hand on crime policy is emerging there – the Commission's 2011 Communication nods approvingly at the concept of decriminalisation.[45] But 'decriminalisation' is itself blanket terminology, and as used to denote a policy, can be employed for a range of reasons, as

[43] For instance, to cite just one or two examples: the UK Serious Fraud Office's investigation of the Tchenguiz brothers for alleged illegal involvement in the collapse of the Icelandic Bank Kaupthing in 2012 (judgment of the High Court of England & Wales, 21 July 2012); and the collapse of the UK prosecution of individuals involved in BA/Virgin price-fixing (*R v Burns and others*, Southwark Crown Court, 10 May 2010).

[44] See the now considerable case law of both the European Court of Human Rights and the EU Courts on the standard of legal protection and the legal nature of processes such as *Ordnungswidrigkeiten* and EU cartel investigations.

[45] It is easy enough for the Commission to do at this general level, falling back on the mantra of what is effective, dissuasive and proportionate. Those criteria may accommodate legal action which is either criminal or non-criminal. The problem, of course, is in the application of such unarguable but general criteria, whether at the level of legislation, judicial decision or enforcement.

indicated just above: the German motivation during the 1960s[46] being more ideological compared to the European Commission's argument deriving from *effet utile* concerns.[47]

Perhaps the pertinent question to pose at this point concerns the direction of flow of criminalisation and decriminalisation, or at least the starting point of such processes. It is useful to recognise and emphasise the historical, cultural, political, economic and ethical/legal contingency of most of the conduct outside the area of 'core' criminality. There may be variations over time and place, and even swings of the pendulum over time. This circumstantial character of the subject-matter is self-evident and a historical test of changing circumstance is helpful in understanding arguments about ethical ranking and provenance. The fact that 100 years ago, motor traffic regulation, environmental protection, and economic practices such as anti-competitive collusion, insider dealing and market abuse were outside the radar of delinquency and illegality, and understanding the reasons for that, enables processes of criminalisation and then perhaps decriminalisation to be tracked as indicators of governance. To take one example, the regulation of road traffic is an obvious historical contingency which is technological in character, as changes in technology lead to new opportunities, but also new risks. But taking another example, anti-competitive collusion, there is a different kind of contingency, of trading developments and economic policy. As Geoffrey Fear has argued in relation to the legal control of business cartels:

> Business historians have shown … that [the contemporary] consensus about cartels as conspiracy is historically the exception to the rule, a product of a post-1945 constellation of ideas and events … historians have shown the varied effects and services provided by cartels (quality standards, technology transfers, or risk management) that extend beyond the conspiratorial motivation to raise prices.[48]

As the discussion of provenance has shown, the arguments and policy regarding the resort to criminal and other forms of legal control may vary across time and space and context. Looking back from an early twenty-first century viewpoint, the wide range of church and morality offences of ecclesiastical jurisdictions some 300 years ago may seem incomprehensible – for instance the offence of bringing an 'unquiet' baby into a church service in 1620[49] – while those in an earlier period might have been astounded if foretold about the criminalisation of insider trading or anti-competitive collusion at a later time.[50]

And so, the discussion returns to the key question of the underlying rationale and justification for resort to criminal law sanctions, and also then for alternative means of

[46] See the discussion by Ohana, n 25 above.

[47] As reflected in the title of the Communication – 'Ensuring the effective implementation of EU policies …' (n 31 above).

[48] G Fear, 'Cartels', Chapter 12 in G Jones and J Zeitlin (eds), *The Oxford Handbook of Business History* (Oxford, Oxford University Press, 2007), at 268.

[49] Archdeacon's Court in Nottingham in August 1620: the wife of George Miriall of Carlton had brought a 'most unquiet child to the church to the great offence of the whole congregation', and refused to take the baby out the service. (RFB Hodgkinson, 'Extracts from the Act Books of the Archdeacons of Nottingham', (1926) *Transactions of the Thoroton Society* 30.

[50] Or equally, how might people in the future regard contemporary statements emanating from US enforcement that price-fixers are the worst kind of criminal deserving the 'inferno' of serving a prison term?

legal control. There has been much discussion but little appears to have been resolved. As Ohana has commented, rather pessimistically:

> the debate about the relationship between the administrative and criminal sanctioning processes did not abate until the early 1970s, when German jurists finally despaired – much like their predecessors a century earlier – of their ability to rigorously delineate the boundaries between the two spheres of the penal law. Developments in legislative practices in other Western jurisdictions since the turn of the twenty-first century have only reinforced and entrenched this pattern, further deepening doubts about whether justificatory grounds for differentiating the law governing criminal offenses from the law governing regulatory offenses can be systematically articulated. Indeed, given the wide range of theoretical explanations of the structure and function of the criminal law, it would be unrealistic to believe in the possibility of offering a determinative account of the differences between the criminal law and the administrative penal law that would be immune to contestation.[51]

But let us not renounce the quest for this grail. From the discussion immediately above it may be argued that a convincing distinction between 'core' criminal prohibition and alternative regimes of prohibition and penal sanctioning resides in *the enduring and non-contingent nature of the former and the contingent character of the latter category.* This follows very much from Packer's persuasive analysis of the limits of the criminal sanction referred to above: noting the special and pre-eminent nature of the criminal sanction and the need to use it sparingly, it should be reserved for gross and immediate harms and threats of harm.[52] Physical and psychological aggression and violence and damage to essential material interests are enduring as matters for prohibition; most else is contingent in its social harmfulness. A steadfast application of that principle would confine the criminal sanction to the 'core', the *mala in se.*

Again, as Packer argued, it is important to be certain about the questions of 'what' or 'why', of where to draw the boundary, before becoming embroiled in the question of 'how'.[53] Arguably, much of the criminalisation debate in so many jurisdictions over the last 50 years or more has been an intoxicated flirtation with the question of 'how', without confidently resolving those prior questions of justification and scope. That has then resulted in a fuzzy resort to the 'administrative penal' or the 'quasi-criminal' as a sub-category of the 'non-criminal'.

Part of the problem has arisen from a dogmatic and exaggerated linkage of 'criminal' and 'penal'. In truth, as an empirical matter of general social and moral usage, the 'penal' is pervasive – an important and necessary element of social and political organisation, whether the context is formal state law, or the family, the tribe, the workplace, organised religion, or any of the host of organisations and institutions, across time and cultures.[54] Acts of reprimand and disqualification ought to be accepted as penal in character, and appropriately used as such outside the scope of criminal law. In that way an

[51] D Ohana, 'Regulatory Offenses and Administrative Sanctions: Between Criminal Law and Administrative Law', Chapter 46 in MD Dubber and T Hornie (eds), *Oxford Handbook of Criminal Law* (Oxford, Oxford University Press, 2014), at 1085–86.

[52] Packer, n 9 above, at 365.

[53] Ibid, at 366, where Packer opined perceptively: 'Our national [American] talent runs much more to how-to-do-it than to what-to-do.'

[54] See the argument presented in Harding and Ireland, n 23 above.

element of penality will not be misguidedly cast as the most important or even exclusive component of criminal law. That tendency has influenced a number of important legal determinations, for instance in applying the European Convention on Human Rights, so obscuring the distinction between 'criminal' and 'administrative' and between 'criminal' and 'quasi-criminal'. In short, a penal element is not problematical for the non-criminal, provided that it accords with the basic objectives of the non-criminal.

Once liberated from the tyranny of sanction and process-led classification, it becomes easier to reassert a distinction and classification based on substantive issues of ethical evaluation and provenance, and to allow the sanctions to follow accordingly. If there is a strong consensus that conduct is ethically objectionable and seriously harmful in its effect then there will be a convincing argument for stigmatisation and appropriately severe sanctions. On the other hand, in response to conduct open to objection on circumstantial or contingent grounds, care should be taken in considering any criminalisation and to think instead about the appropriate and effective resort to non-criminal law processes. Up to a point, this approach is recognised in the European Commission's 2011 Communication on EU criminal policy in its reference to what may be termed the first step in a criminalisation decision, as an evidence-based assessment leading to a cardinal location on a scale of criminal law and other regulatory regimes.[55] In the Commission's view this cardinal location will be informed by principles of last resort and proportionality, but also a consideration of effective response. In regard to the latter, the choice of regime should be based on pre-legislative 'impact assessments', but therein lies the risk of slippage into predictive justifying argument drawing upon notions of deterrence. It has been all too easy to employ a predicted deterrent impact to justify criminalisation or the use of severe penalties to deal with instances of economic offending. It will be sensible at this point, then, to address the impact of deterrence argument and theory in relation to the choice of the criminal law method and different kinds of sanction.

VI. Deterrence and the Choice of Regime and Measures: Myths and Rhetoric

A sizeable amount of criminalisation is driven by argument concerning deterrent effect, and this is especially true in relation to conduct which lies outside the 'core' area of criminality as *mala prohibita*, where a retributive justification would be less persuasive. In the EU context, such argument is usually filtered through the requirements of effectiveness ('*effet utile*') and what would prove 'dissuasive' in terms of the well-established mantra (or 'triad') prescribing dissuasive, effective and proportionate sanctions in relation to the enforcement of EC/EU rules.[56] This has been taken up in EU legislation.

[55] European Commission, Communication (2011), n 31 above, at section 2.2.1; C Harding and J B Banach-Gutierrez, 'The Emergent EU Criminal Policy: Identifying the Species' (2012) 37 *European Law Review* 758, at 764, where it is argued that choice of sanction is then the second step, one of 'ordinal location'.

[56] First formulated by the European Court of Justice in the 'Greek Maize Case': Case 68/88, *Commission v Greece* [1989] ECR 2965. The Court ruled that, while choice of penalties remained within the discretion of

For instance, Directive 2009/123 concerning ship-source pollution[57] requires the use of criminal law penalties to ensure dissuasion. This is justified by the argument, in recital (3) of the Directive, that criminal sanctions express social disapproval of a different nature to that expressed by administrative sanctions, and so strengthen compliance with the legislation on ship-source pollution, and should be sufficiently severe to dissuade all potential polluters from such violations. Referring to specific infringements, Article 5(a) of the Directive requires their criminalisation by Member States, and Article 8 requires that necessary measures be taken to make such infringements punishable by effective, proportionate and dissuasive penalties.

But on closer examination this is both a bold assertion (that criminal sanctions strengthen compliance) and a tall order (that penalties be effective, proportionate and dissuasive). In theory, criminal sanctions have the greatest force. But whether that necessarily translates into compliance is a matter that needs to be tested, albeit with some difficulty, and criminological and empirical research in relation to economic crime is relatively scarce. While many lawyers and economists, following Becker's confident 'rational actor' argument,[58] have assumed on the part of rule-breakers a cost-benefit analysis to inform their decision (especially in the context of business and professional activity), this is predictive assumption rather than a belief based on empirical evidence. Contrariwise, even if there was available extensive data regarding later compliance,[59] such compliance may have come about for a number of reasons other than a deterrent calculation, and that is a truism of criminological research in general. Part of the cost-benefit analysis is the probability of enforcement and it is possible to investigate that further. But that may reveal more about the weakness of the claimed deterrent impact of possible criminal sanctions. As Faure points out[60] in relation to environmental crime, closer study of enforcement patterns may show a higher level of enforcement in the context of German *Ordnungswidrikeiten* compared to criminal law elsewhere, which might then translate into a stronger dissuasive impact arising from administrative penalties. Or, again, in relation to cartel infringements, to what extent do potential rule-breakers turn their minds to a carefully thought-through risk analysis? The evidence from one apprehended and convicted cartelist suggested a natural indifference towards legal risks. Keith Packer, a former British Airways executive convicted and sentenced to a prison term in the US for his role in the Air Cargo Cartel, subsequently explained

Member States, the latter must ensure that infringements of EC rules are penalised under conditions, both procedural and substantive, which render the penalty effective, proportionate and dissuasive. For an earlier discussion of the interpretation and meaning of the mantra, see: C Harding, 'Member State Enforcement of European Community Measures: the Chimera of 'Effective' Enforcement' (1997) 4 *Maastricht Journal of European and Comparative Law* 5, especially at 17–18.

[57] Directive 2009/123/EC of the European Parliament and of the Council of 21 October 2009 amending Directive 2005/35/EC on ship-source pollution and on the introduction of penalties for infringements [2009] OJ L 280/52.

[58] GS Becker, 'Crime and punishment: An economic approach' (1968) 76(2) *Journal of Political Economy* 169.

[59] On the problem of selecting, collecting, and using such data, see C Harding, 'Tasks for criminology in the field of EU criminal law and crime policy', Chapter 8 in C Harding and J B Banach-Gutierrez (eds), *EU Criminal Law and Policy: Values, Principles and Methods* (London, Routledge, 2017).

[60] M G Faure, 'Effective, Proportional and Dissuasive Penalties in the Implementation of the Environmental Crime and Ship-source Pollution Directives: Questions and Challenges' (2010) 19(6) *European Energy and Environmental Law Review* 256.

(in 2010) that competition compliance 'is a very dry, boring subject for commercial people who have much higher priorities'.[61]

Some recent studies of EU-led moves towards criminalisation in the context of economic and financial crime have noted the way in which the 'effectiveness agenda' has driven this policy, assuming a need to use criminal law and stronger, more dissuasive sanctions in relation to activities involving money laundering, counterfeiting and market manipulation. In a detailed and critical study, Ester Herlin-Karnell casts doubt on the constitutional legitimacy of such a policy, and in particular concludes that:

> it has been observed that the fact that a proposed criminal sanction would enhance security if complied with, could be a good reason to enact it. But whilst this rationale is in principle plausible, in practice, it leads to a range of too broadly constructed offences. The problem is that this is in disharmony with the principle of legality (and thereby the principle of strict construction of penal provisions) as also guaranteed by Article 49 of the Charter of Fundamental Rights.[62]

Similarly, Vanessa Franssen has observed in relation to the legal control of market manipulation that:

> the EU legislator should assess more carefully the need for criminal sanctions in light of the criminal law principles of proportionality and subsidiarity (including the *ultima ratio* principle). Such assessment requires an in-depth and evidence-based analysis of the reasons why existing enforcement tools are not effective. It is illusory to think that criminalisation will help solve a lack of resources or expertise, which are often the root cause of ineffective enforcement.[63]

It is striking to note the extent to which EU policy-makers have used an assumed need for deterrence as a response to perceived non-compliance in relation to policies and rules. For example, the European Commission has argued that standard minimum sanctions across the Member States are necessary to ensure deterrence in relation to fraud affecting the Union's budget[64] and counterfeiting,[65] in the light of comparative legal research into existing national minimum sanctions. But this is once again assumption and *non sequitur* argument – De Bondt and Miettenen point out that there is little in the findings of existing research into deterrence to support such an assumption in relation to the adoption of minimum sanctions.[66]

There is thus a tyranny of deterrence-based argument among policy-makers, enforcement agencies, lawyers and economists. Deterrent impact is seen as the final

[61] Quoted in C Harding and J Edwards, *Cartel Criminality: The Mythology and Pathology of Business Collusion* (Aldershot, Ashgate, 2015), 238.

[62] E Herlin-Karnell, *The Constitutional Development of EU Criminal Law* (Oxford, Hart Publishing, 2012), at 177.

[63] V Franssen, 'EU Criminal Law and *Effet Utile*: A Critical Examination of the Union's Use of Criminal Law to Achieve Effective Enforcement', Chapter 7 in C Harding and J B Banach-Gutierrez (eds), *EU Criminal Law and Poicy: Values, Principles and Methods* (London, Routledge, 2017), at 110.

[64] Commission, 'Commission Staff Working Document – Impact Assessment Accompanying the Document Proposal for a Directive of the European Parliament and the Council on the Protection of the Financial Interests of the European Union by Criminal Law, SWD(2012) 195 final.

[65] Proposal for a Directive of the European Parliament and of the Council on the Protection of the Euro and Other Currencies against Counterfeiting by Criminal Law, 7 February 2013, COM(2013) 42 final.

[66] W De Bondt and S Miettenen, 'Minimum Criminal Penalties in the EU: In Search of a Credible Justification' (2015) 21 *European Law Journal* 722, at 727.

solution to whatever is perceived and interpreted as non-compliance with rules and deficiencies in enforcement. But criminological research into actual deterrent impact remains largely inconclusive and there are a number of possible alternative explanations for whatever level of non-compliance might be accepted as fact. In such a situation, the use of such an argument as a main justification for either cardinal (use of criminal law) or ordinal (nature and severity of the sanction) criminalisation is far from convincing. In any case, it should be remembered that the expressive force of the criminal law contains within itself a dissuasive power (especially of general deterrence) in the announcement in such terms of a prohibition, and that the expressive and dissuasive functions of criminalisation cannot be wholly disentangled. Indeed, as Packer urged in his discussion, it is useful to move beyond a simple Benthamite or 'rational actor' view of criminal law and its sanctions, and to see the important and primary role of deterrence as a *component* of the expressive and socialising force of criminal law rather than simply as a predictive tool:

> One need not see man as an isolated atom, intent only upon making rational choices that will advance his own pleasure, to see deterrence at work. Let us expand our view to take account of what we know of man as a creature whose impulses are subject from birth to the manifold processes of socialization and whose reactions to situations in which he finds himself are largely automatic. To deny on that view the reality of deterrence is to call into doubt many of our hypotheses about the socializing capacity of human institutions.[67]

This is a call, then, to understand deterrence and dissuasion as an important social reality, rather than an instrumental bludgeon to be used indiscriminately with a guaranteed effect. To be sure a hammer may be used to strike a nail with force, but there is always a risk that it does not strike the nail in the appropriate way or with the intended effect, if it misses the nail altogether or drives it too far. To put the matter another way, the tyranny of deterrence, like the tyranny of the sanction, is to allow a predicted (and to some extent an immeasurable) consequence to design the intervention.

VII. The Value of Non-criminal Law Processes of Legal Control

The purpose of the argument in the two sections above has been to extricate the discussion from the idea that criminal law is in some way distinctively or even uniquely punitive and deterrent, and in that way is necessary for purposes of bringing about compliance with certain rules. And that brings the discussion back to the value of those options within the spectrum of legal control which are located to one side (the so-called 'softer' side) of criminal law. The important argument being made here is that, within this softer zone of legal control, it is conceivable and right to find a resort to punitive measures.[68] Equally there may be real dissuasive impact within such non-criminal law processes: as long ago as 1990, the Advocate General of the Court of Justice in the *Hansen* case

[67] Packer, n 9 above, at 42.

[68] See for instance, Wilson and Wilson's discussion of the *Hannam* case, Chapter 5 in this volume.

considered that civil liability imposed on employers in relation to tachograph infringements was no less dissuasive than criminal liability.[69] In short, as an exercise in legal control, there may be much virtue in considering non-criminal law options.

It remains then to delineate a clear and justifiable space for quasi-criminal law, such as *Ordnungswidrigkeiten* within that zone of legal control. What is of course distinctive about the quasi-criminal is its mimicry of criminal law, but also logically there should be some meaningful distinction, to qualify as 'quasi'. The essential mimicry resides in a rule-based route to enforcement with a clearly defined procedure: what may be more broadly described as a juridical process, resulting in a judged and binding (as distinct from a discretionary or negotiated) outcome. Then, this looks like criminal law, but logically in some significant ways cannot be the same as criminal law. The sensible distinction should then lie in the more specific nature of the procedure, the agencies involved and the sanctions which may be applied, all of which should be determined by reference to the character of the underlying prohibition and breach – as *mala prohibita*, regulatory, or in terms of the argument above, contingent rather than core delinquency. Most importantly, there should be an accepted and recognised distinction in terms of the stigma associated with 'conviction' or a finding of infringement, whether this is viewed as an absence of stigma or a different kind of stigma. In short, this is the difference between being branded and labelled as a criminal or as a regulatory violator.

All else should follow from that. In the quasi-criminal zone the punitive experience, reputational impact, fact-finding and juridical determination should be coloured by a different perception and qualification of the underlying delinquency and the purposes of its legal control. If that is accepted as a guiding principle, then it would be misleading and confusing to claim that a price-fixer is equivalent to a thief or fraudster,[70] or that proceedings to deal with the breach of technical standards, or the management of road traffic, or business collusion, are closely analogous to criminal proceedings for purposes of legal protection.[71] Nor should the quantum of a sanction be allowed to undermine the distinction, as in the case of an individually incapacitating disqualification or a large financial penalty,[72] in the absence of criminal stigmatisation. While the European Court of Human Rights appears to have accepted the argument that a heavy sanction equals a criminal law sanction, that is to elevate the role of the sanction, and sanctions are only part of the picture (and a part of the picture where impact is still imperfectly understood).

Moreover, this should not be then viewed as a matter of lower standards – of evidence, proof, legal protection of defending parties, or force of sanction – but of different and appropriate standards of legal control. Opting to deal with offending conduct as quasi-criminal is to take on board issues of ethical assessment, provenance and

[69] Opinion of Advocate General Van Gerven, Case C-326/88, *Anklagemyndigheden v Hansen and Soen IS* [1990] ECR 2911, at 2925. But this view seems to have been based on conjecture rather than social scientific examination. On the other hand, subjective experience and anecdote may still lead to a correct conclusion.

[70] There are numerous examples of such claims being made by policy-makers and enforcement agents, often supported by legal and economic analysis.

[71] A philosophy of legal protection that has gained ground under the European Convention on Human Rights, and then mimicked under EU law.

[72] There are many examples of huge corporate fines imposed in cases of cartel collusion and market manipulation.

feasibility, and in that way to work towards an agreed way of dealing more effectively with certain categories of problematical conduct. To take the example of business cartel collusion – its ethical assessment as bad business behaviour remains contested, and the feasibility of its investigation, prosecution and sanctioning is variable. It is then, certainly from European perspectives, a good candidate for quasi-criminal processing, as for instance in the case of Germany and the EU. It is interesting then to reflect on the American commitment to using criminal law (under the Sherman Act) or the German exception concerning bid-rigging. The answer here would seem to lie in differing modalities of ethical assessment and provenance and conceptions of harm to the public interest – the historical circumstances of the American objection to 'trusts', and the frequent public procurement context of anti-competitive bid-rigging. At any rate, both historically and at the present time, responses to anti-competitive business collusion remain contested and so contingent.[73]

Perhaps, finally, we should recall again the argument from an American classic. In the conclusion to his discussion of the use of criminal law in the enforcement of economic regulation, Sanford Kadish[74] offered a checklist of helpful questions to be posed in drawing the boundary between the criminal and the quasi-criminal. The list of questions posed there related essentially to matters of ethical assessment, provenance and feasibility but ultimately indicated the contingency of the underlying prohibition:

> But one can, I think, insist that these are the kinds of questions which must be asked about this [semi-criminal] alternative … if we are to escape the limited options inherited from different days in the use of the criminal sanction.[75]

[73] See the account of the subject presented by Fear, n 47 above.
[74] Kadish, n 12 above.
[75] Ibid, at 449.

7

Four Dimensions of *Nulla Poena Sine Culpa*: The Principle of Individual Culpability in Contexts of Criminal and Quasi-criminal Law Enforcement in Europe

FERRY DE JONG*

Wenn der Stein aus der Hand ist, ist er des Teufels.[1]

I. Introduction

The aim of this contribution is to describe in broad outlines the extent to which the classical criminal law principle of *nulla poena* (or *nullum crimen*) *sine culpa*, or of individual culpability, fulfils a structuring function in constraining liability in European criminal law and in a limited number of adjacent fields within European law which can, and will henceforth, be referred to with the term 'quasi-criminal law'. For the purposes of this chapter, this term is taken to denote legal domains with a European law pedigree that are not formally or officially classified as criminal law, but that are imbued with potentially very severe punitive measures, which qualify as 'penalties' within the meaning of Articles 6 and 7 of the European Convention of Human Rights and Fundamental Freedoms (ECHR). In what follows, examples will be drawn mainly from European competition law, but also from a number of other fields of punitive administrative law. The doctrinal status and the structuring efficacy of the principle of *nulla poena sine culpa* are rather unclear within these quasi-criminal law domains.

* The author is greatly indebted to the editors of this volume and to Professors A Gerbrandy, MJJP Luchtman and JAE Vervaele for their invaluable comments on earlier versions of this chapter.

[1] German saying; cp GWF Hegel, *Grundlinien der Philosophie des Rechts*, H Reichelt (ed) (Frankfurt am Main, Ullstein, 1972 [1821]) para 119 (*Zusatz*) 112: 'Ein altes Sprichwort sagt mit Recht: der Stein, der aus der Hand geworfen wird, ist des Teufels. Indem ich handle, setze ich mich selbst dem Unglück aus: dieses hat also ein Recht an mich, und ist ein Dasein meines eigenen Wollens.' ('An old proverb correctly says: a stone flung from one's hand belongs to the devil. When I act, I expose myself to bad luck; consequently, this bad luck has a right over me and is a manifestation of my own will.')

However, the principle is doctrinally underdeveloped within European criminal law as well, despite its long-standing and deep-seated position within most national systems of criminal law. As is well-known, the Lisbon Treaty has abolished the so-called 'pillar structure' that was introduced in the Maastricht Treaty. All policy areas of the European Union (EU) – including that of judicial cooperation in matters of criminal law in the 'Area of Freedom, Security and Justice' (AFSJ) – were thereby merged into one institutional framework. According to paragraphs 1 and 2 of Article 83 of the Treaty on the Functioning of the European Union (TFEU):

> 1. The European Parliament and the Council may, by means of directives adopted in accordance with the ordinary legislative procedure, establish minimum rules concerning the definition of criminal offences and sanctions in the areas of particularly serious crime with a cross-border dimension …
> 2. If the approximation of criminal laws and regulations of the Member States proves essential to ensure the effective implementation of a Union policy in an area which has been subject to harmonisation measures, directives may establish minimum rules with regard to the definition of criminal offences and sanctions in the area concerned.[2]

Numerous measures that include provisions on definitions of offences and on appertaining sanctioning levels have meanwhile been adopted on the basis of this provision.[3] However, with regard to the *general part* of substantive criminal law – that is, the concepts and principles that apply to all criminal offences or to broad categories of these – the EU has up to now shown considerably less legislative diligence. European legislation generally only *refers* to general concepts such as intention, attempt, or participation, without providing definitions of these concepts. According to Jeroen Blomsma, the general part of substantive criminal law has so far remained 'a blind spot in a Union that focuses predominantly on the special part of substantive criminal law'.[4] This is not to deny that the EU has dealt with aspects of the general part on some occasions. And the Court

[2] The legislative competence created by Art 83(1) TFEU is subject to a *numerus clausus* system, which means that legislative initiatives may only concern offences belonging to one of the offence categories listed. Art 83(2) TFEU provides for an ancillary legislative competence for criminalisation based on considerations of *effet utile*; see V Franssen, 'EU Criminal Law and *Effet Utile*: A Critical Examination of the Union's Use of Criminal Law to Achieve Effective Enforcement' in JB Banach-Gutierrez and C Harding (eds), *EU Criminal Law and Policy. Values, Principles and Methods* (Abingdon, Routledge, 2017) 114–46. It is still unsettled whether Art 325 TFEU contains a separate basis for legislation with respect to fraud and other illegal activities that affect the EU's financial interests; see A Klip, *European Criminal Law. An Integrative Approach*, 3rd edn (Cambridge, Intersentia, 2016) 180–90.

[3] An overview of these measures is provided by J Ouwerkerk and W Geelhoed, 'EU Criminal Law' in PJ Kuijper, F Amtenbrink, D Curtin, B De Witte, A McDonnell and S Van den Bogaert (eds), *The Law of the European Union* (Deventer, Kluwer Law International, 2018) 696–701; and by K Ambos, *European Criminal Law* (Cambridge, Cambridge University Press, 2018) 317–86.

[4] See J Blomsma, *Mens Rea and Defences in European Criminal Law* (Cambridge, Intersentia, 2012) 6. The rather modest or even reluctant attempts at contributing to the forming of a general part of European substantive criminal law can presumably (at least partly) be explained by the respect for the diversity of national criminal law traditions. See V Reding, 'On Substantive Criminal Law of the European Union' in A Klip (ed), *Substantive Criminal Law of the European Union* (Antwerp, Maklu, 2011) 12: 'Criminal law is an area where diversity within Europe is great, and these differences are bound to stay. This is because, like no other area of law, criminal law reflects the basic values, customs and choices of any given society'. The sensitive nature of this diversity is reflected in the so-called 'emergency brake procedure' of Arts 82(3) and 83(3) TFEU; see Klip, *European Criminal Law* (n 2).

of Justice of the European Union (CJEU) has in some cases expressed its view on the meaning of certain concepts from the general part. All in all, however, the general part of substantive EU criminal law can currently at best be said to have a fragmentary and nascent character.[5]

This is saliently exemplified by the main topic of the present contribution: the principle of *nulla poena sine culpa*. According to a critical 'Manifesto on European Criminal Policy' that was published in 2009 by a group of scholars in the field of European criminal justice – united in a 'European Criminal Policy Initiative' – certain aspects of the principle of *nulla poena sine culpa* appear sometimes, erroneously, to be not (or insufficiently) adhered to by the European legislature.[6] The Manifesto identifies six 'fundamental principles' of substantive criminal law policy, the third of which is denoted as 'the principle of guilt (mens rea)'. This principle, according to the Initiative, serves as 'a guarantee that human dignity will be respected by criminal law' and 'is in conformity with the generally accepted perception of guilt within the system of administrative Community sanctions'. Moreover, the principle stipulates that the imposition of penalties must correspond to 'the guilt of the individual' and be 'not disproportionate to the criminal offence'.[7] The Manifesto makes reference to a number of legal acts within the broad field of European criminal law that, according to the members of the Initiative, either respect or fail to respect certain aspects of the principle of guilt. The Manifesto primarily focuses on two aspects: the requirement that offence definitions contain a subjective fault element or mens rea element (typically that of intention), and the requirement that penalties are commensurate with the offender's culpability and the seriousness of his or her offence.

Both these requirements are indeed highly important. It must be noted, however, that these aspects clearly do not provide an exhaustive description of the substance of the principle; its ambit is considerably wider. In this contribution, the principle of guilt – that will hereinafter be referred to as the principle of individual culpability or as the principle of *nulla poena sine culpa* – will be dissected into four normative dimensions. It will be argued that the principle demands that the attribution of criminal liability and the imposition of a criminal sanction are subject to (i) the condition that the liable subject can legitimately be considered the 'author' of the offence,[8] (ii) the condition that the offence was committed intentionally, recklessly, or at least negligently, (iii) the condition that it

[5] See A Klip, 'Towards a General Part of Criminal Law for the European Union' in A Klip (ed), *Substantive Criminal Law of the European Union* (Antwerp, Maklu, 2011) 15–33; Klip, *European Criminal Law* (n 2) 195–96; Ambos, *European Criminal Law* (n 3) 324; Ouwerkerk and Geelhoed, 'EU Criminal Law' (n 3) 695.

[6] European Criminal Policy Initiative, 'A Manifesto on European Criminal Policy' (2009) 12 *Zeitschrift für internationale Strafrechtsdogmatik* 707. The other five principles referred to are: 'the requirement of a legitimate purpose', 'the *ultima ratio* principle', 'the principle of legality', 'the principle of subsidiarity', and 'the principle of coherence'. The group also published a 'Manifesto on European Criminal Procedure Law' (2013) 11 *Zeitschrift für internationale Strafrechtsdogmatik* 430.

[7] European Criminal Policy Initiative, 'A Manifesto on European Criminal Policy' (n 6) 707–08. The Manifesto makes a reservation with regard to legal entities; according to the Initiative, whether or not they can act culpably and be held criminally liable is not to be determined at the European level but should be dealt with at the national level. See sections III.A. and III.C. below.

[8] Vanessa Franssen considers this dimension to be an aspect of a related but separate principle: the principle of 'personal punishment'. See V Franssen, 'Corporate Criminal Liability and Groups of Corporations. Need for a More Economic Approach?' in K Ligeti and S Tosza (eds), *White Collar Crime. A Comparative Perspective* (Oxford, Hart Publishing, 2018) 277–305, 288–89.

can reasonably be assumed that the liable subject could have avoided his or her wrongful action (and that unavoidability must be assumed in cases where generally recognised exculpatory defences apply that annul criminal liability), and lastly (iv) the condition that criminal penalties imposed are proportionate to the liable subject's culpability and to the gravity of his or her offence.

These four dimensions of the principle of individual culpability form the focal points of this contribution. To what extent do these dimensions fulfil a structuring function in constraining liability in both European criminal law and European quasi-criminal law? And to what extent may the principle of *nulla poena sine culpa* be said to constitute a *distinguishing* feature between criminal law, on the one hand, and quasi-criminal law, on the other?[9] A satisfactory answer to these questions requires some preliminary explanation. This is offered in section II, which starts with a discussion of the main historical and philosophical background of the principle of individual culpability, followed by a rough comparative account of the ways in which the principle is incorporated in different contemporary criminal law systems in the EU.[10]

The following sections deal with the different dimensions of the principle of individual culpability individually. Section III addresses the abstract and general issue of who can qualify as a liable person in a punitive context. In this connection, attention is paid to the notions of personal agency and individual responsibility.[11] Section IV is devoted to the important concept of mens rea. It discusses the central subjective fault requirements of intention, recklessness, and (serious) negligence.[12] Section V addresses the concept of personal blameworthiness, which is grounded in the presupposition that the defendant was able to avoid his or her misconduct. In this connection, attention is drawn mainly to two types of exculpatory defences: duress or *force majeure* and mistake of law.[13] Section VI deals with the fourth and last dimension of the principle of *nulla poena sine culpa*: the condition that (criminal or administrative) penalties imposed are proportionate to the liable subject's culpability and to the gravity of his or her wrongdoing.[14]

[9] See Franssen, 'Corporate Criminal Liability' (n 8) 288.

[10] In this connection reference will be made predominantly to the criminal law systems of Germany and the Netherlands as examples of systems from the continental tradition, and to the criminal law system of England and Wales as an example of a system from the Anglo-American tradition (in the realisation that it is still highly uncertain what will be the effects of Britain leaving the EU, on whatever terms are eventually agreed upon, for the content of the criminal law of England and Wales.)

[11] In particular with reference to the judgment of the Grand Chamber of the European Court of Human Rights (ECtHR) of 28 June 2018, *GIEM Srl et al v Italy* (App No 1828/06) and the cases of CJEU 7 January 2004, C-204/00 P *Aalborg-Portland A/S et al v Commission* (EU:C:2004:6) and CJEU 10 September 2009, C-97/08 *Akzo Nobel NV et al v Commission* (EU:C:2009:536).

[12] It does so in view of three cases in particular: CJEU 13 December 2018, C-412/17 and C-474/17 *Touring Tours und Travel GmbH and Sociedad de Transportes SA v Bundesrepublik Deutschland* (EU:C:2018:1005), CJEU 23 December 2009, C-45/08 *Spector Photo Group NV and Chris Van Raemdonck v Commissie voor het Bank-, Financie- en Assurantiewezen* (EU:C:2009:806), and CJEU 3 June 2008, C-308/06 *Intertanko et al v Secretary of State for Transport* (EU:C:2008:312).

[13] With reference respectively to CJEU 11 July 2002, C-210/00 *Käserei Champignon Hofmeister GmbH and Co KG v Hauptzollamt Hamburg-Jonas* (EU:C:2002:440), and CJEU 18 June 2013, C-681/11 *Bundeskartellanwalt v Schenker and Co AG* (EU:C:2013:404).

[14] This discussion is based on a reading of, inter alia, ECtHR [GC] 15 November 2016, *A and B v Norway* (App Nos 24130/11, 29758/11) [2016] ECHR 987, and CJEU 20 March 2018, C-537/16 *Garlsson Real Estate SA et al v Commissione Nazionale per le Società e la Borsa (Consob)* (EU:C:2018:193).

II. Origins and Ramifications of *Nulla Poena Sine Culpa*

A. Introduction: The Concept of a Principle

According to a famous Latin phrase, *actus non facit reum nisi mens sit rea*, which is to say: an act does not make one guilty unless one's mind is (also) guilty.[15] As will be seen in the next subsection, the requirement of a 'guilty mind' can be explained from a historical perspective as a safeguard against basing criminal liability solely on the harmful character of the action performed or of its outcomes. A person may be held criminally liable only if it can be proved, or at least be reasonably assumed, that he or she was able to exercise a sufficient degree of control over his or her actions, in other words: that he or she could have *avoided* the prohibited conduct. As robust as this may sound, different legal traditions have developed rather differing ways of assimilating the principle of individual culpability into the main structure of general conditions for criminal liability. This is hardly surprising, considering that we are dealing here with a *principle* of criminal law. Principles, according to Jeremy Horder and Andrew Ashworth, differ from 'ordinary' legal standards 'in that they have a "supervisory" function. The role of principles is to provide a guide to making, and a critical standard for judging, the shape and character of rules and standards in the rest of criminal law.'[16]

This 'supervisory' function necessarily lends principles a certain measure of generality and abstractness. The Dutch criminal law scholar Antonie Peters emphasised that legal principles are essentially *non-instrumental* in that their meaning may not be made dependent on official state policy, and in that their main purpose is to protect the less powerful or vulnerable legal subjects vis-à-vis the state.[17] Peters argued furthermore that principles are *open-ended* and therefore open to a variety of interpretations, which implies that their normative purport can never be exhaustively captured by any given set of positive regulations.[18] This partially explains why the principle of individual culpability functions in differing ways in different criminal law jurisdictions. It also partially explains why different meanings have been ascribed to the principle in different times. The notion of culpability has certainly not always occupied a (central) position among the conditions for criminal liability. In fact, the principle of individual culpability is a rather modern feature of the criminal law's doctrinal make-up.

[15] See AP Simester, JR Spencer, F Stark, GR Sullivan and GJ Virgo, *Simester and Sullivan's Criminal Law: Theory and Doctrine*, 7th edn (Oxford, Hart Publishing, 2019) 9.

[16] J Horder, *Ashworth's Principles of Criminal Law*, 8th edn (Oxford, Oxford University Press, 2016) 65.

[17] AAG Peters, *Het rechtskarakter van het strafrecht* (Deventer, Kluwer, 1972). A Spanish translation of this lecture is included in the volume: WPJ Pompe and AAG Peters, *La Escuela Penal de Utrecht*, (trans C Estela Teseira and G Hofman) (Buenos Aires, Ediar, 2016) 63–88. See on the non-instrumental nature of principles also J Gardner, 'Ashworth on Principles' in L Zedner and JV Roberts (eds), *Principles and Values in Criminal Law and Criminal Justice. Essays in Honour of Andrew Ashworth* (Oxford, Oxford University Press, 2012) 12–14. And see in the same volume N Lacey, 'Principles, Policies, and Politics of Criminal Law', 19–35.

[18] Peters, *Het rechtskarakter* (n 17). See on Peters' views on principles as non-instrumental and open-ended phenomena: AA Franken and PTC van Kampen, 'Law Like Love' in F de Jong (ed), *Overarching Views of Crime and Deviancy. Rethinking the Legacy of the Utrecht School* (The Hague, Eleven International Publishing, 2015) 183–201; and see in the same volume F de Jong and C Kelk, 'Overarching Thought: Criminal Law Scholarship in Utrecht', 60–66.

Before we can embark on the endeavour of accounting for the ways in which, and the degree to which, the principle of *nulla poena sine culpa* structures issues of accountability in contexts of (quasi-)criminal law enforcement within the EU, it is necessary, therefore, to address a number of preliminary issues. This is what the present section sets out to do. Subsection II.B will discuss the main historical and philosophical origins of the principle of individual culpability in criminal law. To this end, three fields of meanings within the rather labyrinthine notion of 'guilt' will be discerned and discussed, following which attention will be focused on the question: who can qualify as a subject to whom criminal liability may be imputed? Subsection II.C, subsequently, offers a succinct comparative topology of some aspects of the culpability principle in contemporary Anglo-American and continental criminal law systems. The focus in this subsection will be on the doctrinal framework of conditions for criminal liability and on the classification of, and the relations between, the most common fault or mens rea elements in contemporary Anglo-American and continental criminal law systems.

B. Historical and Philosophical Origins: Reception and Development of the Culpability Principle

It is a truism that the notion of culpability plays a pivotal role in determining a person's accountability in criminal law. And one may safely maintain that the principle of individual culpability is firmly entrenched in the contemporary criminal law systems of both the Anglo-American and the continental traditions.[19] Present-day Western criminal law systems are 'culpability-based' in the sense that, for criminal liability to be established, an examination is required not only of the bare facts, actions and/or the results thereof, but also of more complex, internal phenomena, such as the subjective mental state of the defendant at the material time of the offence charged. This feature of contemporary criminal law can safely be regarded as a cultural asset, the origin of which can be traced back to the beginning of the modern era.[20] Dutch philosopher and forensic psychiatrist Antoine Mooij has offered a thought-provoking and highly illuminating analysis of the interdependent positions of the notion of guilt or culpability within the domains of, inter alia, criminal law, psychopathology, our culture, and ultimately the human condition.[21] Following a philosophical tradition stemming from classical antiquity, Mooij distinguishes three basic fields of meanings within the semantically labyrinthine notion of guilt.

Within the first field of meanings, the notion of guilt or culpability is closely tied to the notions of cause and action. Mooij speaks here of culpability in the sense of 'guilt of

[19] GP Fletcher, *Basic Concepts of Criminal Law* (Oxford, Oxford University Press, 1998) 81–85, 99–100; HL Packer, *The Limits of the Criminal Sanction* (Stanford, CA, Stanford University Press, 1968) 103–08.

[20] See eg ER Dodds, *The Greeks and the Irrational* (Berkeley, CA, University of California Press, 2004) 28–64; J Rowbotham, M Muravyeva and D Nash (eds), *Shame, Blame, and Culpability. Crime and Violence in the Modern State* (London, Routledge, 2013).

[21] AWM Mooij, *Intentionality, Desire, Responsibility. A Study in Phenomenology, Psychoanalysis and Law* (Leiden, Brill, 2010) 253–75.

cause' or 'guilt of action'. The ancient Greek term for this type of guilt is *αἰτία* (*aitia*; its Latin equivalent being *causa*). A person is responsible for a certain action or result on account of the fact that he or she has performed that action or has brought about that result. The second field of meanings digs a bit deeper. Here, guilt is intimately connected with a shortfall, default, or failure in relation to a certain objective, aim, or standard (that can, but need not be, of a moral nature). It is not the acting or the causing *as such* that grounds the ascription of guilt, but the finding that a person's action or omission fails to meet a certain standard or to achieve a certain aim. Mooij terms this notion 'guilt by default' (Greek: *ἁμαρτία*, *hamartia*; Latin: *culpa*). The third field of meanings, lastly, is referred to as 'guilt of settlement' (*ὀφειλόμενον*, *opheilomenon*; *debitum*) and concerns guilt in a relational dimension. In this connection, guilt refers to circumstances in which something is owed to another, which is to say: situations in which some form of compensation or settlement (in economic, emotional, spiritual or still other terms) is due.

Without much difficulty, these three basic fields of meaning of the notion of guilt can be traced and identified in the doctrinal make-up of substantive criminal law.[22] Paradigmatically, the main elements of a criminal offence are harm and fault. Offence definitions accordingly and typically[23] comprise two basic ingredients or sets of ingredients, referred to as the actus reus (or in German: *objektiver Tatbestand*) and the requisite mens rea (*subjektiver Tatbestand*) respectively. The requirement of mens rea ('guilty mind') attaches the external and objective actus reus to an internal and subjective, mental condition. This mental condition qualifies an action or an omission subjectively, indicating how an action is performed or how a result is brought about: intentionally, knowingly, recklessly, negligently. Mens rea, in other words, represents a form of guilt that is closely connected to the sphere of actions and results, and that therefore belongs to the semantic domain of 'guilt of action' or 'guilt of cause'. Mens rea denotes an internal quality of a performed action, but this internal quality is generally inferred from, or established on the basis of, the outward appearance of the conduct and the accompanying circumstances.[24]

This is exactly why proof of mens rea is compatible with the idea that a defendant, on further consideration, may not be blameworthy for his or her action or omission. After all, someone who has fulfilled the elements of an offence could have done so under conditions which satisfy the demands of a legally recognised exculpatory defence (such as insanity, duress, or excessive self-defence).[25] In such cases, the law acknowledges

[22] See Mooij, *Intentionality, Desire, Responsibility* (n 21) 257–60; for an application of the three fields of meaning of the notion of guilt within the domains of psychopathology and philosophical anthropology, see 260–64 and 264–66 respectively.

[23] So-called strict liability offences form an important exception; these contain no fault or mens rea requirement. See subsection II.C. below.

[24] See F de Jong, *Daad-schuld. Bijdrage aan een strafrechtelijke handelingsleer met bijzondere aandacht voor de normativering van het delictsbestanddeel opzet* (The Hague, Boom Juridisch, 2009); F de Jong, 'Theorizing Criminal Intent: A Methodological Account' (2011) 1 *Utrecht Law Review* 1.

[25] When an exculpatory (or a justificatory) defence applies, this normally leaves the proof of mens rea untouched. In Dutch criminal law, however, the mens rea element of negligence (*culpa*) forms an exception: an exculpatory defence negates the subjective component of the concept of negligence, which renders the proof of negligence impossible. See Blomsma, *Mens Rea and Defences* (n 4) 195–98; De Jong, *Daad-schuld* (n 24) 388–99; cp Simester et al, *Criminal Law: Theory and Doctrine* (n 15) 168–69, 176; see also n 75 below.

that the defendant cannot reasonably be blamed for not having complied with the behavioural standard that the criminal law expects persons to adhere to in normal circumstances. What is lacking in these exceptional cases is personal *blameworthiness*, which is precisely what Mooij's term 'guilt by default' refers to. Finally, the relational notion of 'guilt of settlement' is at issue at the sentencing stage: in the imposition of a criminal sanction the offender's relational guilt towards society is assuaged.[26] This type of guilt is rather difficult to delineate, since it is generally a composite aggregate of the magnitude of the offender's subjective culpability (in the sense of mens rea and in the sense of personal blameworthiness) and objective factors such as the seriousness of the offence including its negative impact on society.

Now, under what conditions may a criminal law system be said to fully comply with the principle of individual culpability or, in other words, to be truly 'culpability-based'? As appears from the foregoing, the labyrinthine notion of guilt finds expression on at least three levels in criminal law. This explains why the principle of individual culpability is such a multifaceted and consequently complex legal concept. On the level of the furnishing of proof, guilt is manifested in the subjective fault elements or mens rea elements that form part of offence definitions. On this first level, criminal law is a 'culpability-based' system only in a relatively weak sense: mens rea is intimately connected with the actus reus, and proof of mens rea still leaves open the possibility that the defendant, on a deeper level, is not blameworthy. This deeper level of culpability concerns the legally recognised grounds for exemption from punishment. Here the principle of individual culpability is manifested in the stronger sense of 'no punishment without blameworthiness'.

And, finally, it could be argued that a given system of criminal law would be *genuinely* culpability-based if the principle of individual culpability were also to operate undilutedly at the level of sanctioning – which is to say, if the system fully submitted to the 'rule' that a penalty inflicted on a defendant may not exceed the extent of this person's individual blameworthiness.[27] For many, if not all, existing criminal law systems, an unqualified subjection to such a rule is not acceptable, however, as this would imply a too far-reaching curtailment of the court's discretionary powers to determine an appropriate sentence.[28] After all, the inherently 'relational' notion of guilt that is at play in the determination of appropriate penalties is not limited to the rather strict notion of personal blameworthiness; instead, as was mentioned above, it typically encompasses different aspects of subjective culpability, in addition to more objective aspects, like the seriousness of the offence.

[26] Mooij, *Intentionality, Desire, Responsibility* (n 21) 259; see also RA Duff, *Answering for Crime: Responsibility and Liability in the Criminal Law* (Oxford, Hart Publishing, 2007) 23–30.

[27] Mooij, *Intentionality, Desire, Responsibility* (n 21) 260; JF Nijboer, 'Schuldbegrip en schuldbeginsel als oriëntatiepunten in het strafrecht' (1989) 4 *Recht en Kritiek* 363, 366–69.

[28] Which is most probably why the Dutch Supreme Court has consistently taken the view that no rule of criminal law precludes the infliction of a severer punishment than is justified by the measure of the offender's individual culpability. See C Kelk and F de Jong, *Studieboek materieel strafrecht*, 7th edn (Deventer, Wolters Kluwer, 2019) 577–78; see also sub-section VI.A. below. It should be noted, however, that this view is perfectly compatible with the view that the principle of individual culpability demands that the measure of individual culpability or (even) personal blameworthiness is at least always *taken into account* in the determination of the penalty.

The three levels on which guilt finds – or may find – expression in criminal law largely correspond to three dimensions of the principle of individual culpability. These three dimensions will be further discussed in sections IV to VI respectively. At the basis of these dimensions lies an additional, fourth dimension that has not yet been introduced. It concerns the very condition on account of which persons are taken to be *susceptible* to the attribution of culpability (or to any moral judgement). This dimension is directly related to the historical roots of the general concept of responsibility. According to Paul Ricoeur, the concept of responsibility is rooted in the notion of attribution or, by a more technical, Kantian term: 'imputation'.[29] Immanuel Kant famously defined the concept of imputation as follows:

> *Zurechnung* (imputatio) in moralischer Bedeutung ist das *Urteil*, wodurch jemand als Urheber (causa libera) einer Handlung, die alsdann *Tat* (factum) heißt und unter Gesetzen steht, angesehen wird; welches, wenn es zugleich die rechtlichen Folgen aus dieser Tat bei sich führt, eine rechtskräftige (imputatio iudiciaria, s. valida), sonst aber nur eine *beurteilende* Zurechnung (imputatio diiudicatoria) sein würde. Diejenige (physische oder moralische) Person, welche rechtskräftig zu zurechnen die Befugnis hat, heißt der *Richter* oder auch der Gerichtshof (iudex s. forum).[30]

In a very general sense, the criminal law is oriented towards imputing criminal liability to culpable persons. And the very thing that grounds a person's criminal liability is his or her individual culpability. It is on account of his or her individual culpability that an offender can legitimately be said to 'deserve' the infliction of punishment.[31] But the notion of culpability is itself grounded in a very basic human capacity: the capacity to choose and act *freely*. This capacity was placed at the centre of much Enlightenment philosophy and may be regarded as the primal factor to account for the fact that the principle of individual culpability serves as 'a guarantee that human dignity will be respected by criminal law'.[32] It was Kant who most pointedly accentuated the conceptual relation between culpability and freedom. Within Kant's theory of criminal law, crime is essentially a manifestation of a wilfully or inadvertently caused infringement

[29] P Ricoeur, *The Just*, trans D Pellauer (Chicago IL, University of Chicago Press, 2000) 13–19.

[30] I Kant, *Die Metaphysik der Sitten* in *Akademieausgabe. Band VI* (Berlin, De Gruyter, 1968 [1797]) 223 (online: https://korpora.zim.uni-duisburg-essen.de/kant/verzeichnisse-gesamt.html). English translation (taken from I Kant, *The Metaphysics of Morals*, L Denis (ed), trans M Gregor (Cambridge, Cambridge University Press, 2017 [1797]) 22): '*Imputation* (*imputatio*) in the moral sense is the *judgment* by which someone is regarded as the author (*causa libera*) of an action, which is then called a *deed* (*factum*) and stands under laws. If the judgment also carries with it the rightful consequences of this deed, it is an imputation having rightful force (*imputatio iudiciaria s. valida*); otherwise, it is merely an imputation appraising the deed (*imputatio diiudicatoria*). The (natural or moral) person that is authorised to impute is called a *judge* or a court (*iudex s. forum*).' See further A Aichele, 'Grüße von Sam. Zum Verhältnis von Zurechnungsfähigkeit und Menschheitsbegriff am Paradigma der Rechtsphilosophie Kants' in M Kaufmann and J Renzikowski (eds), *Zurechnung als Operationalisierung von Verantwortung* (Frankfurt am Main, Peter Lang, 2004) 247–62; J Hruschka, 'Imputation' (1986) 3 *Brigham Young University Law Review* 669; F de Jong, *Symbolic and Diabolic Forces in Criminal Law* (The Hague, Boom Juridisch, 2016) 3–12.

[31] A Norrie, *Crime, Reason and History. A Critical Introduction to Criminal Law*, 3rd edn (Cambridge, Cambridge University Press, 2014) 20–22, 346–47. In this book, Norrie offers a critical and historical analysis of a persistent ideology of individualism that, according to the author, serves as a façade behind which numerous injustices hide within the criminal law and within the administration of criminal justice. See also Duff, *Answering for Crime* (n 26) 191–93.

[32] See the 'Manifesto on European Criminal Policy' (n 6) that was mentioned in the Introduction.

of the public freedom of one or more citizens. Punishment can only be justified on condition that an offence can be morally imputed to the offender, that is to say, on condition that the offender has freely chosen to perform the criminal act. Only a free human being can possibly *choose* to do evil. This is what Kant has termed the 'demonic side' of freedom: man's '*Hang zum Bösen*' springs from human freedom itself.[33] By virtue of his or her freedom, an acting subject may be regarded as 'author' or *Urheber* of the performed act.[34]

The ability to choose and act freely depends on certain subjective, mental capacities. These capacities – which a subject must be presupposed to possess in order that he or she may be *susceptible* to the attribution of culpability – are described by HLA Hart as 'those of understanding, reasoning and control of conduct: the ability to understand what conduct legal rules or morality require, to deliberate and reach decisions concerning these requirements, and to conform to decisions when made.'[35] According to Hart, these 'most important criteria of moral liability-responsibility' have been given only a partial or tardy recognition as general criteria of legal responsibility in most legal systems.[36] This certainly holds true with regard to criminal law systems during the heyday of the so-called Classical School of criminal law. This School dates back to the eighteenth century work of Cesare Beccaria and strongly emphasised the importance of codification, of the principle of legality as a safeguard for human equality and freedom vis-à-vis the state, and of retrospective retribution.[37] In the rather metaphysical tradition of the Classical School of criminal law, individual culpability and the *freie Willkür* that grounds it were considered indispensable conditions for the imputation of criminal liability, but these notions were generally treated rather abstractly: as a rule, culpability and freedom were rather unproblematically presupposed and not called into question in individual cases.[38]

It was the Modern School (or Positivist School) of criminal law that introduced a far more substantial and 'interiorised'[39] treatment of the notion of individual culpability and its relation to the idea of freedom. The Modern School dates back

[33] I Kant, *Die Religion innerhalb der Grenzen der bloßen Vernunft* in *Akademieausgabe. Band VI* (Berlin, De Gruyter, 1968 [1793/1794]) 28–32 (online: https://korpora.zim.uni-duisburg-essen.de/kant/verzeichnisse-gesamt.html); an elaboration of Kant's notion of human fragility is provided by P Ricoeur, *Fallible Man*, trans CL Kelbley (New York, Fordham University Press, 1986 [1960]). See Mooij, *Intentionality, Desire, Responsibility* (n 21) 330–33.

[34] Kant, *Die Metaphysik der Sitten* (n 30) 223.

[35] HLA Hart, *Punishment and Responsibility. Essays in the Philosophy of Law*, J Gardner (ed), 2nd edn (Oxford, Oxford University Press, 2008 [1968]) 227. See also Mooij, *Intentionality, Desire, Responsibility* (n 21) 305–08.

[36] Hart, *Punishment and Responsibility* (n 35) 227.

[37] C Beccaria, *On Crimes and Punishments*, trans GR Newman and P Marongiu (New Brunswick, NJ, Transaction Publishers, 2009 [*Dei delitti e delle pene*, 1764]). The notion of legality is directly related to that of culpability in that culpability can only be imputed to a person on condition that he or she was previously acquainted with the law by virtue of which a certain action is to be regarded as illicit.

[38] See Norrie, *Crime, Reason and History* (n 31) 21, 26–29; and WPJ Pompe, 'De persoon des daders in het strafrecht' in C Kelk (ed), *Gedachten van Willem Pompe over de mens in het strafrecht* (The Hague, Boom Juridisch, 2008 [1928]) 9–24. A Spanish translation of this lecture is included in the volume: Pompe and Peters, *La Escuela Penal de Utrecht* (n 17) 21–39.

[39] Mooij, *Intentionality, Desire, Responsibility* (n 21) 338–40.

to the work of, among others, Cesare Lombroso, and had its heyday in the late nineteenth and early twentieth century.[40] In its wake, the concrete individual offender and the differing endogenous and exogenous factors that (allegedly) predispose individuals to criminality became the centre of interest. On the one hand, this has led to a subtler and more nuanced approach to the concept of culpability. The idea took hold that culpability or blameworthiness is not something that is either completely present, or completely absent due to exceptional exculpating circumstances; culpability can also be diminished to a certain degree, for example on account of a mental disorder that reduces the offender's culpability without eliminating it completely. On the other hand, the classical emphasis on proportionate retribution was lessened to the advantage of a more prospective focus on prevention of crime and the protection of society against 'dangerous individuals'.[41]

This shift in focus was far-reaching but has not detracted from the classical, Kantian postulate that moral or legal culpability can solely be attributed to the moral phenomenon of a 'person' with certain mental capacities which enable this person to act and choose, at least to some extent, freely – and hence not to a 'thing'.[42] As will be seen in subsection III.A. below, this notion of a liable 'person' has undergone a considerable expansion, particularly during the twentieth century. Many contemporary criminal law systems accept that not only natural persons but also legal or corporate entities can in principle assume criminal liability.

C. A Quasi-Comparative Topology of Aspects of the Culpability Principle

As was mentioned earlier, different legal traditions have developed rather differing ways of assimilating the principle of individual culpability into the main structure of general conditions for criminal liability. Of course, this in no way implies that nothing definite may be said with regard to the contents of the principle. As will be seen in the present subsection, different jurisdictions clearly also *share* a good deal when it comes to the way in which they interpret the principle of *nulla poena sine culpa* and implement the various aspects of this principle within their respective criminal law systems. In what follows, attention will be paid first and foremost to the doctrinal framework of conditions for criminal liability and to the classification of the most common fault or mens rea elements. A crude distinction will be made between the Anglo-American law

[40] C Lombroso, *Criminal Man*, trans M Gibson and N Hahn Rafter (Durham, NC, Duke University Press, 2006 [*L'uomo delinquente*, 1876/1878]). On the Modern or Positivist School, see C Fijnaut, *Criminology and the Criminal Justice System. A Historical and Transatlantic Introduction* (Cambridge, Intersentia, 2017); JR Lilly, FT Cullen and RA Ball, *Criminological Theory. Context and Consequences*, 7th edn (Los Angeles, CA, Sage Publications, 2019) 18–30.

[41] See M Foucault, 'About the Concept of the "Dangerous Individual" in 19th Century Legal Psychiatry' (1978) 1 *International Journal of Law and Psychiatry* 1.

[42] Kant, *Die Metaphysik der Sitten* (n 30) 223. See also Ricoeur, *The Just* (n 29) 16; Hruschka, 'Imputation' (n 30) 674 and 682–84.

tradition that is (partly) based on the common law, on the one hand, and the civil or continental law tradition, on the other.[43]

In the civil law tradition, the conditions for criminal liability are generally structured in a tripartite framework. For criminal liability to obtain it is necessary to establish that the defendant has fulfilled the offence definition, that the defendant's act or omission is wrongful, and that the defendant is personally blameworthy.[44] This three-tiered framework exhibits a neat doctrinal distinction between the conditions for criminal liability that are captured by the elements of the statutory offence definition (including the requirements of both actus reus and mens rea) on the one hand, and two important additional conditions for criminal liability that are (normally)[45] non-statutory and hence unwritten, on the other: the wrongfulness of the defendant's act or omission (German: *Rechtswidrigkeit*; Dutch: *wederrechtelijkheid*), and the defendant's personal blameworthiness (German: *Schuld*; Dutch: *verwijtbaarheid*). When it is established that a defendant has fulfilled an offence definition, it is presumed that he or she has acted wrongfully and that he or she is personally blameworthy. These presumptions can be challenged, however, by invoking a defence. Certain defences, when accepted, cancel the presumption of wrongfulness and *justify* the defendant's act or omission. Other defences, when accepted, leave the presumed wrongfulness of the act or omission intact but cancel the presumption of the defendant's blameworthiness, in other words: they *excuse* or *exculpate* the defendant.[46]

The foregoing means that the fault elements that form parts of mens rea (most commonly arranged under the headings of 'intention', 'recklessness' and 'negligence' – see below) need to be distinguished from the more fundamental notion of 'blameworthiness' (referring to the avoidability of the act or omission that is prohibited by the offence definition).[47] Whereas the mens rea requirements form parts of what Antoine Mooij has termed 'guilt of cause' or 'guilt of action' (*αἰτία*; *causa*), the notion of personal blameworthiness refers to what he has termed 'guilt by default' (*ἁμαρτία*; *culpa*).[48] And while

[43] The distinction is crude in the sense that with regard to the civil law or the continental tradition, reference will be had primarily to the criminal law of Germany and the Netherlands, and with regard to the Anglo-American tradition, reference will be had primarily to the criminal law of England and Wales. The term 'common law' will be mostly avoided, because criminal law in England and Wales is nowadays primarily enacted through parliamentary statutes and subordinate regulations. See Simester et al, *Criminal Law* (n 15) 48–50.

[44] U Kindhäuser, *Strafgesetzbuch. Lehr- und Praxiskommentar*, 7th edn (Baden-Baden, Nomos, 2017) 89–94; Kelk and De Jong, *Studieboek* (n 28) 61.

[45] Sometimes wrongfulness figures as an express element of an offence definition; and the fault element of negligence (culpa) is an exception since (at least according to Dutch criminal law doctrine) it conceptually presupposes both wrongfulness and blameworthiness; see Blomsma, *Mens Rea and Defences* (n 4) 175–79, 193–98; F de Jong, 'Facetten van schuld en gronden voor strafuitsluiting' in MM Boone, CM Pelser and T Boekhout van Solinge (eds), *Discretie in het strafrecht* (The Hague, Boom Juridisch, 2004) 139–58. The principle of 'no punishment without blameworthiness' is, however, codified in the Dutch General Administrative Law Act (*Algemene Wet Bestuursrecht*); see M Feenstra and A Tollenaar, 'Kruisbestuiving tussen straf- en bestuursrecht: de ontwikkeling van de verwijtbaarheid in het bestuursrecht' (2017) 10 *Nederlands Tijdschrift voor Bestuursrecht* 351.

[46] Examples of generally recognised justificatory defences are self-defence and necessity. Examples of exculpatory defences are legal insanity, duress, excessive self-defence, and forms of mistake of law or mistake of facts. See for Germany, Kindhäuser, *Strafgesetzbuch* (n 44) 195–201, 205–07, 213–22, 284–328; and for the Netherlands, see Kelk and De Jong, *Studieboek* (n 28) 323–410.

[47] See Blomsma, *Mens Rea and Defences* (n 4) 46–48.

[48] See subsection II.B; and cp, with regard to the fault element of negligence, n 75 below.

the mens rea requirements, like all 'express' elements of an offence definition, have to be positively proved according to the generally applicable standard of proof ('beyond a reasonable doubt') and are governed by the presumption of innocence, the fulfilment of the 'implied' element of blameworthiness – like that of wrongfulness – is presupposed. As soon as the actus reus of an offence and the requisite mens rea are proved, one can conclude that the defendant has committed a prima facie offence. Typically, this conclusion will lead to a conviction, unless the defendant has a recognised defence. In this connection, a probative onus is generally placed on the defendant. The supposition of blameworthiness can only be rebutted when the defendant can establish ('on the balance of probabilities') that an excusatory defence applies.[49]

The three-tiered framework of conditions for criminal liability that was succinctly discussed above is firmly entrenched in most of the continental criminal law systems within the EU. And although Anglo-American law has for a long time not acknowledged a neat doctrinal distinction between fault or mens rea on the one hand and personal blameworthiness on the other,[50] the three-tiered framework has meanwhile gained footing in the Anglo-American criminal law traditions too, at least in the criminal law system of England and Wales.[51] The prevailing view among writers in England and Wales is that (justificatory or exculpatory) defences are superimposed on – and do therefore not coincide with – the different express elements of offence definitions. Correspondingly, next to the old main elements of harm (or actus reus) and fault (or mens rea), the third basic element of every crime is the absence of a valid defence.[52] Notable differences between both legal traditions do remain, however, with regard to the ways in which different dimensions of the culpability principle are inscribed in the structure of the offence. In Anglo-American criminal law systems, for example, the doctrinal classification of legally recognised defences into the categories of justificatory and exculpatory defences is far less common, and much more controversial, than in the continental criminal law systems.[53]

[49] Hence, one may submit that, in contrast to the different mens rea elements, the fundamental notion of personal blameworthiness is subject to a *presumptio nocentiae*; see Mooij, *Intentionality, Desire, Responsibility* (n 21) 259. See further eg Simester et al, *Criminal Law* (n 15) 712; Kindhäuser, *Strafgesetzbuch* (n 44) 91–92; Kelk and De Jong, *Studieboek* (n 28) 67, 72 and 323–27.

[50] See GP Fletcher, *The Grammar of Criminal Law. American, Comparative, and International. Vol I: Foundations*, (Oxford, Oxford University Press, 2007) 312; Fletcher, *Basic Concepts* (n 19) 99–100; A Eser, 'Justification and Excuse: A Key Issue in the Concept of Crime' in A Eser and GP Fletcher (eds), *Rechtfertigung und Entschuldigung. Rechtsvergleichende Perspektiven*, vol I (Freiburg im Breisgau, Max Planck Institut für ausländisches und internationales Strafrecht, 1988) 17–65; J Keiler, 'Actus Reus and Mens Rea: The Elements of Crime and the Framework of Criminal Liability' in J Keiler and D Roef (eds), *Comparative Concepts of Criminal Law* (Cambridge, Intersentia, 2015) 33–36; Blomsma, *Mens Rea and Defences* (n 4) 46–50.

[51] Simester et al, *Criminal Law* (n 15) 9–12, 18–20 and 709–12.

[52] ATH Smith, 'On Actus Reus and Mens Rea' in P Glazebrook (ed), *Reshaping the Criminal Law. Essays in Honour of Glanville Williams* (London, Sweet and Maxwell, 1978) 98; Simester et al, *Criminal Law* (n 15) 18–20.

[53] See Duff, *Answering for Crime* (n 26) 263–98; V Tadros, *Criminal Responsibility* (Oxford, Oxford University Press, 2005) 265–347; J Horder, *Excusing Crime* (Oxford, Oxford University Press, 2004); J Gardner, *Offences and Defences. Selected Essays in the Philosophy of Criminal Law* (Oxford, Oxford University Press, 2007) 91–139; GP Fletcher, 'The Individualization of Excusing Conditions' (1974) *Southern California Law Review* 1269; J Blomsma and D Roef, 'Justifications and Excuses' in J Keiler and D Roef (eds), *Comparative Concepts of Criminal Law* (Cambridge, Intersentia, 2015) 133–77.

And another important difference concerns the issue of whether or not strict liability offences (that do not contain any fault requirement) are permitted and, if so, to what extent valid defences are available to rebut culpability for these offences. In Germany and Finland, for instance, strict liability offences are permitted neither in criminal law nor in regulatory (quasi-criminal or administrative) law, although some exceptions do exist.[54] Contrarily, strict liability offences are well entrenched, for example, in English and in Dutch criminal law.[55] In these jurisdictions, strict liability is generally limited to minor criminal offences (or misdemeanours) and/or to regulatory offences that attract (relatively) moderate penalties. In accordance with minimum requirements that the ECtHR deduces from the presumption of innocence enshrined in Article 6, paragraph 2 ECHR, strict liability offences must not preclude the availability of generally recognised defences.[56]

Important differences between countries exist, furthermore, with regard to the classification of, and the relations between, the (most common) fault or mens rea elements. In this connection it is first of all noteworthy that a tripartite division is adhered to in Anglo-American criminal law, whereas a bipartite division prevails in continental criminal law systems. In the Anglo-American criminal law tradition offence definitions can harbour a wide variety of terms to refer to specific fault requirements or culpable mental states.[57] Clearly, however, there are three mens rea states that are most commonly required by offence definitions and thus represent the most important fault elements in the Anglo-American law systems. These are, in order of decreasing degrees of moral censure: intention, recklessness, and negligence. In this tripartite framework, the mens rea state of recklessness bridges the interval between the concepts of intention and negligence. In the continental criminal law tradition, by contrast, only two main types of fault are distinguished: intention (*dolus*) and negligence (*culpa*). Between these, no interval is in place.[58]

[54] See for Germany: Kindhäuser, *Strafgesetzbuch* (n 44) 210–13; M Mansdörfer, 'The Treatment of Mere Regulatory Offences in German Criminal Law. Historical Developments, Today's Concepts and General Criticisms' in M Ulväng and I Cameron (eds), *Essays on Criminalisation and Sanctions* (Uppsala, Iustus Förlag, 2014) 103–04. For Finland, see J Rankinen, 'Positive Fault Requirements in EU Criminal Law' (2016) 6(2) *European Criminal Law Review* 117.

[55] See for England and Wales: Simester et al, *Criminal Law* (n 15) 191–215; Horder, *Ashworth's Principles* (n 16) 180–88. See for the Netherlands: Kelk and De Jong, *Studieboek* (n 28) 296–399; EHA van Luijk, *Het schuldbeginsel in het Nederlandse strafrecht. Een verkenning aan de hand van de geschiedenis van het Nederlandse strafrecht, de kentekenaansprakelijkheid en het EVRM* (Groningen, Rijksuniversiteit Groningen, 2015) 212–27.

[56] See ECtHR 7 October 1998, *Salabiaku v France* (App No 10519/83), [1988] ECHR 19; ECtHR 29 June 2007, *O'Halloran and Francis v the United Kingdom* (App Nos 15809/02 and 25624/02), [2007] ECHR 545; Van Luijk, *Het schuldbeginsel* (n 55) 319–65; Blomsma, *Mens Rea and Defences* (n 4) 210 and 224–28. In English criminal law it is controversial whether all generally recognised (common law) defences are available with respect to strict liability offences. See Simester et al, *Criminal Law* (n 15) 205–06; Horder, *Excusing Crime* (n 53) 237–76; Duff, *Answering for Crime* (n 26) 229–69.

[57] Simester et al, *Criminal Law* (n 15) 138, mention: 'purpose', 'intention', 'recklessness', 'wilfulness', 'knowledge', 'belief', 'suspicion', 'reasonable cause to believe', 'maliciousness', 'fraudulence', 'dishonesty', 'corruptness', and 'negligence'.

[58] As a matter of course, among the different legal orders that employ the same basic (bipartite or tripartite) system, smaller and larger variances can be observed with regard to how individual manifestations of a fault element are interpreted and how individual fault elements are demarcated from other fault elements. These differences will be largely ignored here. The following exposition merely seeks to sketch in broad outlines the meaning and substance of the most prevalent fault elements that are distinguished within the Anglo-American tradition and the continental tradition.

In both the Anglo-American and the continental tradition, intention is considered the central and generally also the gravest form of mens rea.[59] The two traditions differ with regard to the ambit that is ascribed to the concept of intention. In criminal law systems of the Anglo-American tradition (only) two varieties of intention are generally recognised. The core variety is termed 'direct intention'; this paradigm version of intention is virtually equivalent to the mens rea gradation referred to as *dolus directus* in the continental criminal law tradition. One speaks of direct intention in cases where it can be established that the defendant downrightly wanted or desired to bring about the criminally relevant outcome or to perform the prohibited action (or to omit the criminally prescribed action). And one equally speaks of direct intention in cases where it can be proved that the defendant has acted in the belief that fulfilling the actus reus of an offence would lead to a certain result which the defendant wished to achieve; in these cases, committing the offence serves as a means to a desired end. In either type of cases, the notion of direct intention presupposes that the defendant has acted *because of* a certain desire or a certain belief.[60]

This is supposed to hold true also for a second and separate[61] variety of intention, which is termed 'indirect' or 'oblique intention'; this gradation is often referred to as *dolus indirectus* in the continental criminal law tradition. Indirect intention obtains when a criminally relevant consequence is foreseen by the defendant as certain or virtually certain to occur as a result of his or her action, and thus not merely as a possible or even probable side-effect.[62] HLA Hart has famously offered the following definition: we speak of intention when a foreseen outcome

> is so immediately and invariably connected with the action done that the suggestion that the action might not have that outcome would by ordinary standards be regarded as absurd, or such as only a mentally abnormal person would seriously entertain.[63]

This is where the Anglo-American criminal law tradition draws the line as far as the fault element of intention is concerned. In the bipartite framework of fault elements that prevails in the continental criminal law tradition, by contrast, intention encompasses an additional, third variety, situated underneath the gradation of indirect intention. Next to *dolus directus* and *dolus indirectus*, the continental criminal law systems typically acknowledge as a third layer within the fault element of intention the concept of *dolus eventualis* (in German: *bedingter Vorsatz*; in Dutch: *voorwaardelijk opzet*).[64]

[59] See MS Moore, 'Intention as a Marker of Moral Culpability and Legal Punishability' in RA Duff and SP Green (eds), *Philosophical Foundations of Criminal Law* (Oxford, Oxford University Press, 2011) 179–205.

[60] See Simester et al, *Criminal Law* (n 15) 141–44.

[61] A question subject to doctrinal controversy is whether indirect or oblique intention can be seen as a separate variety of intention, or that it should rather be seen as an evidential construction that merely facilitates the inference that a certain harm was (directly) intended. See Simester et al, *Criminal Law* (n 15) 146–47. Cp Blomsma, *Mens Rea and Defences* (n 4) 9 and 70–72.

[62] See Simester et al, *Criminal Law* (n 15) 145–50.

[63] Hart, *Punishment and Responsibility* (n 35) 120.

[64] *Dolus eventualis* is often translated as 'conditional intention'. However, in English law the term 'conditional intention' refers to a notion quite different from *dolus eventualis*, namely the idea that a 'real' or 'full-blooded' intention to perform a certain action is conditional upon there being circumstances in place that make it possible to realise the intention. See Simester et al, *Criminal Law* (n 15) 152–53. For this reason, the term 'conditional intention' is avoided in the present contribution.

Doctrinally, *dolus eventualis* marks the lower limit of the general concept of intention in criminal law. One speaks of *dolus eventualis* in cases where it can be established that the defendant foresaw (the cognitive aspect) and also accepted (or reconciled himself or herself to – the volitional aspect) the (considerable) possibility that as a result of his or her action a certain harm would occur.[65] Although it must be noted that the notion of *dolus eventualis* is defined and interpreted in slightly differing ways in different criminal law systems,[66] it is abundantly clear that because of this notion the concept of intention has a considerably wider ambit in the continental tradition than is the case in the Anglo-American tradition.

To be sure, we have to be careful not to overestimate the difference between both traditions in this connection. For the majority of offences in English criminal law it is not necessary to prove intention, because proof of the subjective fault element of 'recklessness' normally suffices. Recklessness is a separate fault element in the Anglo-American criminal law tradition. For recklessness to obtain, it generally needs to be established that the defendant has consciously taken a risk that, in the circumstances known to him or her, was unreasonable. It serves a similar function as *dolus eventualis*, with the difference that recklessness does not require proof of a volitional aspect: it is not necessary to establish that the defendant reconciled himself or herself to the effectuation of the relevant harm.[67] However, there are many cases in which proof of intention is indeed necessary in English criminal law;[68] in these cases the difference between the continental and the Anglo-American legal systems with regard to their definitions of intention therefore really matters.[69]

[65] See J Blomsma and D Roef, 'Forms and Aspects of Mens Rea' in J Keiler and D Roef (eds), *Comparative Concepts of Criminal Law* (Cambridge, Intersentia, 2015) 108–09; Blomsma, *Mens Rea and Defences* (n 4) 99–134; Rankinen, 'Positive Fault Requirements' (n 54) 122.

[66] Different legal orders entertain different views and standards regarding the requisite *magnitude* of the perceived chance that a given action will produce a certain criminally relevant result or outcome. And legal orders differ with respect to the meaning and importance ascribed to the volitional and/or the cognitive components of *dolus eventualis*. See eg Blomsma and Roef, 'Forms and Aspects' (n 65) 108–15.

[67] Simester et al, *Criminal Law* (n 15) 154–55; Blomsma and Roef, 'Forms and Aspects' (n 65) 116; RA Duff, *Intention, Agency and Criminal Liability: Philosophy of Action and the Criminal Law* (Oxford, Basil Blackwell, 1990) 142–49.

[68] For instance, recklessness does not suffice for a conviction for murder in English law, since murder requires an intention to kill or at least an intention to cause grievous bodily harm; and neither does recklessness suffice for attempt (whereas *dolus eventualis* generally does in the continental criminal law systems). See Simester et al, *Criminal Law* (n 15) 138, 362–70 and 399–404; Duff, *Intention, Agency and Criminal Liability* (n 67) 173–79 and 192–206.

[69] A matter that complicates things further is that the notion of recklessness functions in some continental law systems as a specific manifestation of the general fault element of *culpa* (negligence). In the Netherlands, eg, recklessness (*roekeloosheid*) constitutes a separate aggravating manifestation of *culpa* in a limited number of offences, such as negligent manslaughter (Art 307 of the Dutch Criminal Code, *Wetboek van Strafrecht*) and negligent causation of a road traffic accident that results in grievous bodily harm or death (Art 6 of the Dutch Road Traffic Act, *Wegenverkeerswet*). In these cases, recklessness (or *luxuria*) marks the upper limit of the concept of negligence, proof of which leads to an increase of the maximum penalty by 100 per cent. Blomsma, *Mens Rea and Defences* (n 4) 200, rightfully notes that recklessness in these contexts may be seen as a middle ground in between *dolus* (*eventualis*) and *culpa* or negligence proper, 'even though it is generally treated as a qualified form of negligence', and that '*luxuria* also helps to prevent the further enlargement of *dolus eventualis*'. For this form of recklessness to obtain it must be established that the defendant has grossly violated an applicable standard of care that exceeds departure from the standard of care that suffices for 'basic' negligence, as a result of which a very grave danger was created. It is furthermore required that the defendant was aware or ought to have been aware of this danger; see Kelk and

Furthermore, also with regard to the general concept of negligence or *culpa*, there are notable differences between the continental and the Anglo-American criminal law systems. For negligence to obtain in English criminal law, for example, it is irrelevant whether the defendant was aware or unaware of the risks that ensued from his or her action or omission;[70] but the concept is itself limited to inadvertent negligence, which means that there is no such thing as 'conscious negligence' in English law (while the concept of recklessness requires conscious risk-taking). The concept of *culpa* in Germany and the Netherlands, by contrast, encompasses both inadvertent and advertent or conscious forms of negligence (*bewusste Fahrlässigkeit*; *bewuste schuld*).[71] This may partly explain why negligence as a minimum mens rea standard is less popular in Anglo-American criminal law systems that, as noted above, typically recognise recklessness as a *tertium quid* between intention and negligence, than in continental criminal law systems that operate with a more rigid dichotomy between *dolus* and *culpa*.[72]

However, apart from this difference, the concepts of negligence in the Anglo-American and the continental criminal law traditions are very similar. As a general rule, negligence or *culpa* comprises both an objective and a subjective component.[73] Objectively, negligence requires that the defendant *ought* to have foreseen the possibility that his or her action or omission would produce the relevant harmful outcome (because a reasonable person in his or her place would have foreseen this outcome) and that the defendant's behaviour falls short of the standard of conduct that applies in the given circumstances. The applicable standard of conduct or standard of care is normally geared, not to the most prudent or cautious person, but to the reasonable person. We blame the negligent defendant precisely because he or she failed to observe this standard of due or reasonable diligence. It must be noted that not just any form of carelessness can qualify as negligence. In many legal systems, a slight discrepancy between the defendant's conduct and the applicable standard of care (*culpa levis*) will not suffice to establish negligence. In these systems, to qualify as negligence, the carelessness must be considerable, that is, sufficiently serious or substantial (*culpa lata*).[74]

De Jong, *Studieboek* (n 28) 298–99. For the equivalent concept in German criminal law (*Leichtfertigkeit*), see Kindhäuser, *Strafgesetzbuch* (n 44) 188. The concept of recklessness in English criminal law is a broader concept that encompasses *dolus eventualis*, but also *luxuria*, and even some forms of conscious negligent behaviour.

[70] Simester et al, *Criminal Law* (n 15) 167.

[71] See Kelk and De Jong, *Studieboek* (n 28) 296–98; Kindhäuser, *Strafgesetzbuch* (n 44) 187–88; Blomsma and Roef, 'Forms and Aspects' (n 65) 122.

[72] See Blomsma and Roef, 'Forms and Aspects' (n 65) 122; Blomsma, *Mens Rea and Defences* (n 4) 172–74. The question whether or not negligence may suffice as a fault element *at all* is subject to doctrinal controversy. See L Alexander and KK Ferzan (with SJ Morse), *Crime and Culpability. A Theory of Criminal Law* (Cambridge, Cambridge University Press, 2009) 69–85; L Alexander and KK Ferzan, *Reflections on Crime and Culpability. Problems and Puzzles* (Cambridge, Cambridge University Press, 2018) 3–4; Simester et al, *Criminal Law* (n 15) 175–76.

[73] Rankinen, 'Positive Fault Requirements' (n 54) 119–23; Blomsma and Roef, 'Forms and Aspects' (n 65) 121–26; Blomsma, *Mens Rea and Defences* (n 4) 174–98.

[74] In Belgian criminal law, by contrast, *culpa levis* (or: *levissima*) may suffice for proof of negligence; see C Van den Wyngaert, S Vandromme and Ph Traest, *Strafrecht en strafprocesrecht in hoofdlijnen*, 11th edn (Oud-Turnhout, Gompel & Svacina, 2019) 318–20 and 338. In English criminal law there exist negligence offences that require 'ordinary' negligence and ones that require nothing less than 'gross' negligence. Ordinary negligence refers to conduct that falls below what would be expected of a reasonable person. Gross negligence

Blaming the defendant for his or her careless behaviour, however, is only legitimate on condition that the subjective requirement of negligence is also fulfilled. Subjectively, it must be established that the defendant also *could* have foreseen the possibility of the harmful outcome and could have attuned his or her behaviour accordingly.[75] With regard to both the objective and the subjective requirements of negligence, certain individual characteristics of the defendant may be taken into account. The *degree* of diligence that was expected of the defendant, for example, may in part depend on the defendant's profession, education, age, et cetera. In German criminal law doctrine this is referred to as '*Garantenstellung*'.[76]

III. First Dimension: Individual Authorship

A. Introduction: Subjectivity, Agency, and Personal Responsibility

The principle of individual culpability demands that the attribution of criminal liability and the imposition of a criminal sanction be subject to the condition that the liable subject can legitimately be considered the 'author' – or, by a German word that was preferred by Immanuel Kant, the *Urheber*[77] – of the offence. The first dimension of the principle of individual culpability traces the offence to a person who is considered the 'free cause' of the offence. Who or what can qualify as the 'author' of a (criminal) offence? Self-evidently, this question is closely linked with the conceptions of subjectivity and agency that are (implicitly or explicitly) adhered to within a given legal system: how one delineates the assembly of (natural or legal) persons who may qualify as 'authors' of offences, depends in part on rules that indicate what types of (behavioural and/or intellectual) involvement of the would-be liable subject in the offence may suffice to establish liability. In other words: the answer to the question who may and who may not assume culpability and liability for a certain offence depends in part on the answer to the question as to how, and on the basis of what criteria, one evaluates the relation between a subject's action or omission, on the one hand, and the registered harm that triggered the quest for a culpable offender in the first place, on the other.

refers to conduct that falls *far* below this standard, which means that in this type of case a more substantial discrepancy exists between the defendant's conduct and the prescribed standard of care. See Simester et al, *Criminal Law* (n 15) 167–68.

[75] This observation necessitates an elucidation. In the previous subsections, it was maintained that mens rea or fault requirements form parts of what Antoine Mooij (*Intentionality, Desire, Responsibility*, n 21) has termed 'guilt of cause' or 'guilt of action' (*αἰτία; causa*), and that the notion of personal blameworthiness belongs to what Mooij has termed 'guilt by default' (*ἁμαρτία; culpa*). And the type of culpability denoted as 'guilt by default' exactly amounts to the idea of a failure to comply with a certain standard or to achieve a certain aim. The subjective aspect of negligence – ie, the reproach that is grounded on the finding that the defendant could (and hence should) have foreseen and avoided the harmful outcome of his or her action – can therefore fittingly be regarded as a form of 'guilt by default'. Still, it is not contrived to position negligence (along with intention and recklessness) in the domain of 'guilt of action', considering that the emphasis in negligence lies on its objective aspect, ie, the objectively assessed carelessness of the behaviour of the defendant. See Blomsma, *Mens Rea and Defences* (n 4) 175–92; see also n 25 above.

[76] See Blomsma and Roef, 'Forms and Aspects' (n 65) 124–25.

[77] See subsection II.B. above.

Different legal systems can employ widely differing criteria to assess whether the relation between a certain subject's conduct and a certain harm is sufficiently 'direct' or 'firm' to sustain the finding that the subject in question can legally be regarded as the 'author' (or as one of the 'authors')[78] of the offence concerned. When this relation is direct or firm enough, the subject is legally identified as the person who has (or as one of several persons who have) indeed committed the offence. The criteria may differ in the degree of their detailedness or their vagueness; relatedly, and seen from a more formal or adjectival viewpoint, they may either demand a relatively stringent application, or allow for a more relaxed application by the adjudicating court. And on a more substantive level, the criteria may accord preponderant weight to objective, outward, or physical aspects; they may also, contrarily, attach paramount significance to subjective, inner, or psychological aspects; or, of course, they may – as they often do – provide a more or less balanced mixture of physical and psychological aspects to be taken into account.

The criteria that are used to establish a subject's authorship or perpetration furthermore depend on the liability regime that applies to the *type* of offence at issue. In many legal systems a distinction is made between (real) criminal offences, on the one hand, and administrative and/or regulatory offences, on the other. This distinction – which is directly related to the distinction between criminal law and quasi-criminal law – is not clear-cut and is prone to causing confusion. In some jurisdictions, such as the German legal system, there exists a relatively sharp doctrinal distinction between, on the one hand, offences that – by virtue of, inter alia, their objective seriousness, the legal interests at stake, and/or the main rationale behind the punishment inflicted on those who have been found guilty of committing the offences – belong to the criminal law proper (*Straftaten*) and, on the other hand, offences that fall below the threshold of criminal law and that are merely regulatory in nature (*Ordnungswidrigkeiten*). In such a 'dualistic' system the two types of offences are typically governed by rather different legal regimes with regard to, for example, the types of sanctions that may be imposed (and the maximum degrees of their severity), the requisite mens rea element in the statutory offence definition, and the types of subjects to whom culpability and liability can be attributed (ie, solely to natural persons or to both natural persons and legal entities).[79]

Many or even most jurisdictions, by contrast, have a 'monistic' system of criminal law that encompasses both the 'serious' criminal offences and many offences that would be classified as 'merely regulatory offences' (including petty offences) within the dualistic system in Germany. In practice, however, these so-called 'monistic' systems are generally not quite as unified as this term suggests. In many legal systems, the legislator has chosen to simply decriminalise certain groups of offences; these former criminal offences, often of a 'regulatory' nature, have in many cases been subsumed under areas

[78] There is, of course, often more than just one subject who could be called to answer for one offence. This is the case in forms of participation and almost by definition in cases where a legal entity or a group of legal entities is prosecuted for a criminal or an administrative offence, such as an infringement of competition law.

[79] See Mansdörfer, 'The Treatment of Mere Regulatory Offences' (n 54); and see P Asp, 'Principles of Criminalization: What is "Criminal" in Criminal Law?' in M Ulväng and I Cameron (eds), *Essays on Criminalisation and Sanctions* (Uppsala, Iustus Förlag, 2014) 109–23.

of administrative law. In the Netherlands this was done, for example, with many minor road traffic offences.[80] These legislative rearrangements have led to a system that in effect resembles the dualistic model. But not in all respects: a notable difference that remains is that the criminal law systems of monistic models typically harbour many offences that are often denoted as 'regulatory' criminal offences (such as environmental crimes, financial and economic crimes, or tax fraud) and large numbers of petty offences. As a rule[81] – and contrary to the so-called 'merely regulatory offences' within the German dualistic system – these offences are just as much governed by the general principles and regulations of the general part of substantive criminal law as are the 'classical' crimes of, say, murder, rape, and theft.

In many legal systems, accordingly, one can distinguish between at least two types offences that are (as is the case in the dualistic system of Germany) subject to different legal regimes. On the one hand, there are those offences that belong to the criminal law (and that may or may not include 'regulatory' and petty offences) and that are consequently punishable with 'actual' criminal penalties. On the other hand, there are offences that belong to administrative law and to which administrative (mostly pecuniary) sanctions apply. The distinction between criminal and administrative offences is based on both instrumental and theoretical considerations. Compared to criminal offences, administrative offences are often subject to a relatively lenient liability regime. From an instrumental point of view, this is conducive to a more efficient enforcement of the underlying norms, especially with regard to high frequency offences. Mens rea requirements, for example, tend to be less strict – and sometimes even absent – in the definitions of administrative offences.[82] From a more theoretical point of view, the existence of administrative offences may serve the purpose of enabling the attribution of liability to subjects that cannot qualify as 'authors' of criminal offences within certain jurisdictions.

An important example of this concerns the position of corporate or legal entities. Criminal liability of legal entities is recognised in many, but certainly not in all legal systems. Most jurisdictions that currently *do* recognise the general possibility of attributing criminal culpability and criminal liability to (certain) corporate or legal entities have not done so until relatively recently.[83] And partly on account of the (for the most part) relatively recent reception of corporate criminal liability into the

[80] These offences may often involve a form of vicarious liability, because liability for offences that concern motorised vehicles is often categorically attributed to the person on whose name the vehicle is registered (Dutch: *kentekenaansprakelijkheid*). See Van Luijk, *Het schuldbeginsel* (n 55); JHB Bemelmans, *Tot het tegendeel is bewezen. De onschuldpresumptie in rechtshistorisch, theoretisch, internationaalrechtelijk en Nederlands strafprocesrechtelijk perspectief* (Deventer, Wolters Kluwer, 2018) 213. The English Road Traffic Offences Act 1988 contains a similar construction; see Simester et al, *Criminal Law* (n 15) 284.

[81] Unless, eg, a certain statute expressly deviates from a particular rule from the general part.

[82] The same holds true for many regulatory offences that form parts of the criminal law in eg the Netherlands; moreover, the actus reus of these offences often takes the form of a breach of a duty of care.

[83] The Dutch legislator, eg, implemented the statutory provision that introduced *general* criminal liability of legal entities in 1976 (Art 51 of the Dutch Criminal Code); prior to this, it had been recognised since around the early twentieth century that legal entities could assume criminal liability for a limited number of (economic and regulatory) offences. See Kelk and De Jong, *Studieboek* (n 28) 518–34; M Groenouwe and E Baakman, 'Changing Ideas on Corporate Criminal Liability. A Comparison between the Netherlands and England and Wales' in F de Jong (ed), *Overarching Views of Crime and Deviancy. Rethinking the Legacy of the Utrecht School* (The Hague, Eleven International Publishing, 2015) 271–85.

positive criminal law of national legal systems, there are still many intricate doctrinal questions pertaining to this phenomenon that have not yet been satisfactorily resolved and that, consequently, are sometimes strongly disputed.[84] The continued existence of these doctrinal controversies may find a further partial explanation in the fact that the phenomenon of corporate liability *itself* has for a long time been 'taboo' in criminal law scholarship: the phrase *societas delinquere non potest* has functioned as a rock-solid adage for ages – as it seemingly still does in a number of legal systems, such as those of Germany and Italy.[85] It is rather easy to see why jurisdictions that adhere to the view that legal entities cannot possibly commit an offence because they simply cannot *act*, reject the possibility of corporate criminal liability. In this view, corporate liability would necessarily involve a form of 'vicarious liability'.

According to the doctrine of vicarious (or derivative) liability, legal liability for a particular harm can be attributed to another (legal or natural) person than the one who has in fact committed the offence which brought about this harm. This implies that a person is made liable for the conduct (and for the accompanying state of mind) of another person.[86] In tort law it may be well-justified to impose liability on employers for certain torts that are committed by employees in the course of their employment; in criminal law, however, purely vicarious liability is rather controversial: one can normally only be culpable of and criminally liable for one's own conduct. In administrative law, vicarious liability is generally seen as less problematic, which partly explains why jurisdictions that do not recognise corporate criminal liability often *do* accept that legal entities can be liable for certain administrative or regulatory offences.[87] Jurisdictions that entertain the view that an action is something that not only a natural or physical person, but also a legal entity is capable of performing, by contrast, need not resort to constructions of vicarious liability and may hence more readily accept the possibility of imputing criminal liability to legal entities.[88]

[84] One unresolved and disputed matter concerns the question how mens rea elements should or could be doctrinally reshaped or reframed so as to attain a better 'fit' with the everyday reality of legal entities. See on this question M Hornman and E Sikkema, 'Corporate Intent: In Search of a Theoretical Foundation for Corporate Mens Rea' in F de Jong (ed), *Overarching Views of Crime and Deviancy. Rethinking the Legacy of the Utrecht School* (The Hague, Eleven International Publishing, 2015) 287–309; Simester et al, *Simister and Sullivan's Criminal Law* (n 15) 299–304.

[85] Germany has not yet adopted corporate criminal liability, although this might change in the near future. See M Engelhart, 'Corporate Criminal Liability and Compliance in Germany' in A Fiorella and AM Stile (eds), *Corporate Criminal Liability and Compliance Programs. First Colloquium* (Naples, Jovene Editore, 2012) 167–206. See for Italy: A Di Amato and F Fucito, 'Italy', *International Encyclopaedia of Laws – Criminal Law*, F Verbruggen and V Franssen (eds) (Deventer, Kluwer Law International, 2016); F Cugia di Sant'Orsola and S Giampaolo, 'Liability of Entities in Italy: Was it Not *Societas Delinquere Non Potest*?' (2011) 2(1) *New Journal of European Criminal Law* 59.

[86] See Simester et al, *Criminal Law* (n 15) 283–92; V Franssen, 'The EU's Fight Against Corporate Financial Crime: State of Affairs and Future Potential' (2018) 5 *German Law Journal* 1221, 1237–38.

[87] See for Germany eg Mansdörfer, 'The Treatment of Mere Regulatory Offences' (n 54). In the Italian system corporate entities are subject to a *sui generis* regime of administrative liability with certain features of criminal liability, and actual criminal liability is accepted for some offences; see Cugia di Sant'Orsola and Giampaolo, 'Liability of Entities in Italy' (n 85).

[88] The doctrine of vicarious liability is akin to that of strict or objective liability; and like constructions of strict liability, constructions of vicarious liability are not completely outlawed under the ECHR, provided that the 'person' to whom liability is attributed has a reasonable possibility to exonerate him- or herself. A notorious example of vicarious liability in quasi-criminal law – manifestations of which exist in many jurisdictions – concerns the administrative liability of a car owner for a road traffic offence in cases where the actual driver of the car at the material time of the offence cannot be identified. In a case against the Netherlands, the ECtHR

As illustrated above, the question as to who or what can qualify as the 'author' of a (criminal) offence is closely linked with the conceptions of subjectivity and agency that are (implicitly or explicitly) adhered to within a given legal system. The view that holds that corporate entities can (directly) commit offences presupposes that one subscribes to a conception of subjective agency that is considerably more 'spiritual' and normative, and at any rate considerably less 'physical', than any conception that would be needed to sustain the opposing view that *societas delinquere non potest*. Given the variegated approaches across legal systems, the EU legislature typically does not oblige the Member States to provide for the possibility of attributing criminal liability to legal entities within their national jurisdictions. Member States must ensure that legal persons can be held liable for certain offences that are criminal in nature, but it is left to the Member States themselves to decide whether this liability takes the form of criminal, administrative or even 'only' civil liability.[89]

However, irrespective of the liability regime chosen, the Member States must still ensure that their domestic law provides for sanctions that are 'effective, proportionate, and dissuasive'.[90] As a result, there are several areas of European or Europeanised quasi-criminal law – such as European competition law – that clearly involve punitive measures that can be, and often are, imposed on legal entities and that qualify as 'penalties' for the purposes of Articles 6 and 7 ECHR. In the following two subsections it will be explored how the notion of individual authorship is reflected in European (quasi-)criminal law. Subsection III.B will deal with the ECtHR's view of non-conviction based penalties; subsection III.C will focus on corporate liability in European competition law.

B. Individual Authorship under the ECHR: *GIEM et al v Italy*

Constructions of vicarious liability in penal matters are generally prohibited by the ECtHR when the defendant is not granted a reasonable possibility of exonerating him- or herself. Although the ECHR does not contain a provision that expressly guarantees the principle of individual culpability, the ECtHR has recognised several dimensions of this principle as ensuing from Articles 6 and 7 of the Convention. One important dimension is that of individual authorship. Cases before the ECtHR which deal with

did not find a violation of the right to be presumed innocent (enshrined in Art 6(2) ECHR), in part because of the fact that defences had been available for the car owner on the basis of which he or she could challenge the imposed fine at court. See ECtHR 19 October 2004, *Falk v the Netherlands* (App No 66273/01) *Reports* 2004-XI; Van Luijk, *Het schuldbeginsel* (n 55).

[89] This may at least partly be explained by the principle of subsidiarity and the related respect by the European legislature for the diversity of national criminal law traditions; see n 3 above. Cp European Criminal Policy Initiative, 'A Manifesto on European Criminal Policy' (n 6) 708. The EU is nevertheless slowly pushing Member States to provide for criminal liability of legal entities; see Franssen, 'Corporate Criminal Liability' (n 8) 279. For a critical analysis of the EU approach (basing corporate liability on a mixed concept of vicarious, direct, and functional liability), see Franssen, 'The EU's Fight' (n 86) 1228–32.

[90] And what is more, these sanctions must be equivalent to the sanctions that can be imposed for similar offences existing in national law; see CJEU 21 September 1989, 68/88 (*Greek Maize* case) *Commission of the European Communities v Hellenic Republic* (EU:C:1989:339); CJEU 27 February 1997, C-177/95 *Ebony Maritime SA and Loten Navigation Co Ltd v Prefetto della Provincia di Brindisi et al* (EU:C:1997:89).

this dimension often concern the question whether non-conviction based penalties contravene guarantees enshrined in the ECHR. This question was at issue in a case decided by the Grand Chamber of the ECtHR, in which four legal entities – GIEM Srl, Hotel Promotion Bureau Srl, R.I.T.A. Sarda Srl, and Falgest Srl – and one natural person – Mr Filippo Gironda – complained that the Italian government had confiscated their property in contravention of a number of fundamental rights enshrined in the ECHR.[91]

The applicants were the (co-)owners of plots of land on which they had developed several building complexes. Although the local authorities had approved the different site development plans and the building permits, and had also assured the applicants time and again that the plans were in agreement with all relevant legislation, the criminal court later found the development plans and building permits to be illegal. The plots of land and the buildings were consequently ordered to be confiscated, even though none of the five applicants was found guilty of an offence by the criminal court. The fundamental question at issue during the proceedings before the ECtHR was whether (and, if so, to what extent) the legality principle of Article 7 ECHR and the presumption of innocence codified in Article 6, paragraph 2 ECHR forbid the imposition of a penalty on a person if this person has not previously been found guilty of committing, or has not previously been convicted of, a criminal offence with reference to which the authorities wish to inflict the penalty.

In previous judgments against Italy the ECtHR had already decided that the sanction of confiscation of property – although labelled in Italian law as an administrative compensation measure – qualifies as a 'penalty' within the meaning of the ECHR,[92] and that the imposition of such a penalty must be preceded by a criminal conviction. This also implies that cases in which criminal proceedings are precluded by reason of lapse of time lack a sufficient basis for the imposition of a confiscation sanction.[93] However, in 2015 the Italian Constitutional Court criticised these judgments and found that the interpretations on which they are based could not be regarded as 'sufficiently consolidated' within the ECtHR case law (partly because the judgments

[91] ECtHR *GIEM et al v Italy* (n 11). See on this judgment JHB Bemelmans and MAP Timmerman, 'Noot bij EHRM (GK) 28 juni 2018, *G.I.E.M. S.r.l. e.a. t. Italië*' (2018) 11 *European Human Rights Cases* (no 219) 680. Measures that are aimed at the tracing, freezing, seizure, and/or confiscation of proceeds of crime exist in many jurisdictions, which is not surprising considering that several legislative initiatives of the EU have obliged Member States to adopt the necessary means to enable these sorts of measures within their respective national legal systems with an eye to combating a large number of designated crimes. See Council Framework Decision 2001/500/JHA of 26 June 2001 on money laundering, the identification, tracing, freezing, seizing, and confiscation of instrumentalities and the proceeds of crime, *Official Journal of the European Union* (OJ) [2001] L 182/1; Council Framework Decision 2005/212/JHA of 24 February 2005 on confiscation of crime-related proceeds, instrumentalities and property, [2005] OJ L 68/49; Directive 2014/42/EU of the European Parliament and of the Council of 3 April 2014 on the freezing and confiscation of instrumentalities and proceeds of crime in the European Union, [2014] OJ L 127/39. See also K Ligeti and M Simonato, 'Asset Recovery in the EU: Towards a Comprehensive Enforcement Model beyond Confiscation? An Introduction' in K Ligeti and M Simonato (eds), *Chasing Criminal Money. Challenges and Perspectives on Asset Recovery in the EU* (Oxford, Hart Publishing, 2017) 1–21; and ECtHR *GIEM et al v Italy* (n 11) paras 147–153.

[92] ECtHR 20 January 2009, *Sud Fondi Srl et al v Italy* (App no 75909/01). See also ECtHR 5 July 2001, *Phillips v the United Kingdom* (App No 41087/98), [2001] ECHR 437.

[93] ECtHR 29 October 2013, *Varvara v Italy* (App no 17475/09).

were not rendered by the Grand Chamber), so that Italian courts could not be required to follow and apply these interpretations.[94]

In response to this, the ECtHR concisely notes that 'its judgements all have the same legal value' and that '[t]heir binding nature and interpretative authority cannot therefore depend on the formation by which they were rendered'.[95] Furthermore, the ECtHR confirms its previous judgments and ultimately finds that Article 7 ECHR was violated in respect of the four applicant legal entities, that Article 6, paragraph 2 ECHR was violated in respect of Mr Gironda, and that Article 1 of Protocol No 1 to the ECHR (protecting the right to property) was violated in respect of all five applicants. For the purposes of the present contribution, it is worthwhile to take a closer look at the ECtHR's reasoning with regard to the relation between the principle of individual culpability, the presumption of innocence protected by Article 6, paragraph 2 ECHR, and the principle of legality enshrined in Article 7 ECHR.

With regard to Article 7 ECHR, the Grand Chamber considers that, for this provision to apply in the cases at hand, it is necessary to establish that the Italian confiscation measure qualifies as a 'penalty' within the meaning of the provision. As is well-known, the ECtHR employs an autonomous concept of 'penalty'. Referring to the wording of Article 7, paragraph 1 ECHR, the ECtHR notes 'that the starting-point in any assessment of the existence of a "penalty" is whether the measure in question is imposed following a decision that a person is guilty of a criminal offence'.[96] In other words, for Article 7 ECHR to apply it must be assessed whether or not the person upon whom the penalty is imposed has been convicted (French: *condamné(e)*) beforehand. In agreement with previous case law, the ECtHR subsequently notes that this forms a relevant, but not a decisive factor.[97] Other relevant factors include the nature and purpose of the sanction, its characterisation under national law, the procedures involved in the making and the implementation of the measure, and the measure's severity.[98] Unsurprisingly – and in line with its earlier judgment in the case of *Sud Fondi et al* that was referred to above – the Grand Chamber concludes that the Italian confiscation measure qualifies as a 'penalty' within the meaning of Article 7 ECHR.[99]

Next, the Grand Chamber examines whether the imposition of the impugned confiscation measures without a prior (formal) conviction was reasonably foreseeable for the applicants.[100] At this juncture in the ECtHR's reasoning, a noteworthy

[94] See para 133 of ECtHR *GIEM et al v Italy* (n 11); see also para II.2 in the concurring opinion of Judge Motoc; and paras 16–57 in the partly concurring, partly dissenting opinion of Judge Pinto de Albuquerque.

[95] ECtHR *GIEM et al v Italy* (n 11) para 252.

[96] ECtHR *GIEM et al v Italy* (n 11) para 211.

[97] ECtHR *GIEM et al v Italy* (n 11) paras 215 and 217. See eg ECtHR 17 December 2009, *M v Germany* (App No 19359/04), [2009] ECHR 2071.

[98] These are the so-called *Engel* criteria. See ECtHR 8 June 1976, *Engel et al v the Netherlands* (App no 5100/71) *Series A* no 22, paras 80–82. And see ECtHR 26 February 1996, *Welch v the United Kingdom* (App no 17440/90) *Series A* no 307-A. The *Engel* criteria were embraced by the CJEU in its judgment of 5 June 2012, C-489/10 *Criminal Proceedings against Łukasz Marcin Bonda* (EU:C:2012:319); see Klip, *European Criminal Law* (n 2) 190–94.

[99] ECtHR *GIEM et al v Italy* (n 11) paras 220–34.

[100] In paras 243–246 of ECtHR *GIEM et al v Italy* (n 11) the ECtHR argues that Art 7 ECHR requires the existence of a 'mental link' that traces liability to the defendant's conduct. Referring to its case law on Art 6(2) ECHR, the ECtHR further notes that this requirement does not preclude forms of objective or strict liability that stem from presumptions of liability, provided that the defendant is not deprived of every possibility to

distinction is made between the four applicant companies, on the one hand, and Mr Gironda, on the other. None of the five applicants had been formally convicted of a criminal offence in connection with which the confiscation measure was imposed. But in contrast to Mr Gironda, whose prosecution was discontinued because the offence with which he was charged was statute-barred, the four applicant companies were never prosecuted at all. Under the Italian law, corporate criminal liability is not (generally) accepted.[101] Legal entities may, however, be administratively liable for certain offences. One of these offences is unlawful site development. The confiscation of property is an administrative sanction that is automatically imposed by the Italian criminal court when this offence is proved, irrespective of whether the owner of the property is a natural person or a legal entity. From the fact that the four applicant companies never were parties to the proceedings that led to the imposition of the confiscation measures, the ECtHR concludes that the four legal entities incurred a penalty for actions for which third parties (namely a number of legal representatives and shareholders who were indicted in a personal capacity) have been found culpable.[102] This amounts to a form of vicarious liability which is at variance with the prohibition, stemming from Article 7 ECHR, on punishing a person for an offence that has been committed by another. With regard to the four legal entities, the ECtHR therefore concludes that Article 7 ECHR has been violated.[103]

Interestingly, the Grand Chamber arrives at a different conclusion in respect of the fifth applicant, Mr Gironda. As was mentioned earlier, Mr Gironda was prosecuted, but the proceedings against him were discontinued because the offence of which he stood accused was statute-barred. Accordingly, he was not formally convicted of, or found culpable of committing, the offence of unlawful site development. However, the ECtHR notes that, although a 'declaration of criminal liability is often made in a criminal-court judgment formally convicting the defendant, this should not be seen as a mandatory rule'.[104] The ECtHR goes on to note that the demands of Article 7 ECHR may be satisfied when the imposition of a penalty is preceded not by a *formal* finding of culpability, but by a finding *in substance* that the defendant has committed the offence.

exonerate him- or herself; cp n 56 above. See PH van Kempen and JHB Bemelmans, 'EU Protection of the Substantive Criminal Law Principles of Guilt and *Ne bis in Idem* under the Charter of Fundamental Rights: Underdevelopment and Overdevelopment in an Incomplete Criminal Justice Framework' (2018) 2 *New Journal of European Criminal Law* 247, which rightfully notes on p 255 that one should distinguish between 'protection against the absence of a culpability requirement' and 'protection against presumptions of the presence of culpability'. Bemelmans and Timmerman, 'Noot bij EHRM (GK) 28 juni 2018' (n 91) 684, doubt whether Arts 6(2) and 7 ECHR lend themselves to an interpretation according to which they demand that offence definitions satisfy certain substantive requirements; see in this connection also Bemelmans, *Totdat het tegendeel is bewezen* (n 80) 212–13 and 505–06; and MAP Timmerman, *Legality in Europe. On the Principle Nullum Crimen Sine Lege in EU Law and under the ECHR* (Cambridge, Intersentia, 2018) 3–4.

[101] See n 85. And see Cugia di Sant'Orsola and Giampaolo, 'Liability of Entities in Italy' (n 85); F Mazzacuva, 'The Problematic Nature of Asset Recovery Measures: Recent Developments of the Italian Preventive Confiscation' in K Ligeti and M Simonato (eds), *Chasing Criminal Money. Challenges and Perspectives on Asset Recovery in the EU* (Oxford, Hart Publishing, 2017) 101–15.

[102] ECtHR *GIEM et al v Italy* (n 11) paras 265–272.

[103] ECtHR *GIEM et al v Italy* (n 11) para 274.

[104] ECtHR *GIEM et al v Italy* (n 11) para 251.

In the case of Mr Gironda the criminal proceedings were discontinued 'solely on account of statutory limitation', whereas all the elements of the offence of unlawful site development were 'made out'.[105] This, according to the Grand Chamber, can be regarded, in substance, as a conviction for the purposes of Article 7 ECHR. Consequently, it is concluded that there has been no violation of this provision in respect of Mr Gironda. However, the ECtHR immediately connects its finding that a confiscation measure may be inflicted without a prior formal conviction with an important reservation: the domestic courts in question must have 'acted in strict accordance with the defence rights enshrined in Article 6 of the Convention'.[106] And Mr Gironda also complained that the Italian authorities, by imposing the confiscation measure, violated his fundamental right provided by Article 6, paragraph 2 ECHR, that is, his right to be 'presumed innocent until proved guilty according to law'.[107]

It is noteworthy that the phrase 'proved guilty according to law' is interpreted rather strictly by the ECtHR. The broadened, substantive concept of 'conviction' that the ECtHR construed with a view to the applicability of Article 7 ECHR, is not subsequently applied also to Article 6, paragraph 2 ECHR. In agreement with its previous case law on the matter, the ECtHR notes in paragraph 314 of the judgment that the protection offered by the right to be presumed innocent extends beyond the proceedings aimed at establishing the defendant's culpability for a criminal offence: 'individuals who have been acquitted of a criminal charge, or in respect of whom criminal proceedings have been discontinued', may not be 'treated by public officials and authorities as though they are in fact guilty of the offence charged'. The presumption of innocence 'could risk becoming theoretical and illusory' if an acquittal or a decision to discontinue criminal proceedings is not respected. In addition, it is stated that 'guilt cannot be legally established where the proceedings have been closed by a court before the gathering of evidence or the conducting of hearings that would have allowed the court to determine the case on its merits'.[108]

In Italy, Mr Gironda had been acquitted by the criminal court on appeal, and the confiscation measure that was imposed by the first instance court had been revoked. This ruling was subsequently quashed by the Italian Court of Cassation (and not thereupon remitted to a lower court). According to the Court of Cassation, the confiscation measure was indeed justified because it had been proved that Mr Gironda was in fact guilty of the offence charged. Thus, the applicant was declared guilty (not formally, as was seen above, but in substance) by the Court of Cassation, despite the fact that the proceedings were discontinued on the ground that the prosecution of the offence was

[105] ECtHR *GIEM et al v Italy* (n 11) para 261. In para 260 the ECtHR remarkably notes that relatively short limitation periods may – especially when complex offences are at issue – lead to situations in which perpetrators 'systematically avoid prosecution and, above all, the consequences of their misconduct'. The ECtHR interprets the Italian legal rules that are at issue in the instant case as seeking to prevent this impunity. This interpretation seems to be inspired by the case-law of the CJEU with regard to retroactive extensions of national limitation periods on the basis of European law. See CJEU 8 September 2015, C-105/14 *Criminal Proceedings against Ivo Taricco et al* (EU:C:2015:555), and CJEU 5 December 2017, C-42/17 (*Taricco II* case) *Criminal Proceedings against MAS and MB* (EU:C:2017:936).

[106] ECtHR *GIEM. et al v Italy* (n 11) para 261.

[107] The four applicant legal entities also complained that the right to be presumed innocent was violated in their cases. These complaints were declared inadmissible.

[108] ECtHR *GIEM et al v Italy* (n 11) para 315.

statute-barred. This course of events, the ECtHR argues in paragraph 317, 'breaches the right to the presumption of innocence'. The underlying idea seems to be that imposing the penalty of confiscation on a person in respect of whom criminal proceedings have been discontinued is tantamount to treating this person as though he or she is in fact guilty. Accordingly, the ECtHR concludes that Article 6, paragraph 2 ECHR was violated in respect of Mr Gironda.

It can be concluded from the foregoing that the 'first dimension' of the principle of individual culpability is clearly manifested in the ECtHR's case law. The Strasbourg court stresses the importance – indeed, the necessity – of establishing the defendant's *own* misconduct as a condition for individual liability of both natural persons and legal entities. Moreover, the ECtHR attaches much weight to an individualised assessment that concentrates on the defendant's *own* culpability for the offence charged. In paragraph 271 of its judgment in the case of *GIEM et al*, the ECtHR cites from its judgment in the case of *Varvara* 'that a consequence of cardinal importance flows from the principle of legality in criminal law, namely a prohibition on punishing a person where the offence has been committed by another'. The prohibition on constructions of vicarious liability of this kind in criminal law had already been emphasised by the ECtHR in earlier judgments[109] and explains why it was concluded that the imposition of a penalty of confiscation of property on the applicant companies in the case of *GIEM et al* was in violation of Article 7 ECHR.

This does not mean that no criticism can be levelled at the approach of the ECtHR. Its reasoning in the case of *GIEM et al* is at certain points somewhat puzzling. As was seen above, the notion of 'conviction' within the meaning of Article 7 ECHR is broader than within the meaning of Article 6, paragraph 2. It is not quite clear what is the rationale for this difference.[110] The ECtHR (still) holds that the imposition of a penalty is not justified without a prior formal conviction of the punished person. In cases where the defendant's culpability for the offence at issue has not at all been assessed and established during the proceedings, the prohibition on imposing a penalty is founded on Article 7 ECHR. In cases, conversely, where this culpability has been assessed and established ('in substance'), but where this finding has not resulted in a (formal) conviction (for instance due to the fact that the prosecution of the offence was statute-barred), the prohibition rests on Article 6, paragraph 2 ECHR.[111]

[109] ECtHR 29 August 1997, *AP, MP and TP v Switzerland* (App No 19958/92), [1997] ECHR 50; ECtHR 29 August 1997, *EL, RL and JO-L v Switzerland* (App No 20919/92), [1997] ECHR 50. See Van Kempen and Bemelmans, 'EU Protection of the Substantive Criminal Law Principles' (n 100) 254–56; Bemelmans, *Totdat het tegendeel is bewezen* (n 80) 214–15.

[110] See Bemelmans and Timmerman, 'Noot bij EHRM (GK) 28 juni 2018' (n 91) 686. In his highly instructive partly concurring, partly dissenting opinion, Judge Pinto De Albuquerque vehemently criticises the concept of a 'substantive' declaration of culpability. According to Pinto De Albuquerque, this concept is in fact 'a blank cheque for the domestic courts to do as they please' (para 29). He argues that, by introducing the notion of a 'substantive' finding of guilt, the majority of the Grand Chamber has enabled domestic courts to deviously circumvent statutory limitation periods, and has acted as 'a subservient surrogate of the [Italian] Government's interests and policy choices' (para 29). According to Pinto De Albuquerque, the concept is, furthermore, at variance with both the principle of legal certainty and the principle of the presumption of innocence (paras 31–35).

[111] See also Directive 2014/42 (n 91), which obliges Member States to enable confiscation 'subject to a final conviction for a criminal offence' and, subject to certain conditions, also in cases where criminal proceedings do not result in a criminal conviction. See M Panzavolta, 'Confiscation and the Concept of Punishment: Can There be a Confiscation Without a Conviction?' in K Ligeti and M Simonato (eds), *Chasing Criminal Money.*

C. Economic Units in EU Competition Law: *Aalborg-Portland* and *Akzo Nobel*

It still remains to be seen how the requirement of individual authorship is dealt with in areas of European quasi-criminal law; that is, in European law domains that are not criminal in nature, but that are endowed with potentially very severe punitive measures that qualify as penalties within the meaning of Articles 6 and 7 ECHR.[112] One important example of a field of quasi-criminal law is European competition law.[113] Almost by definition, competition law is concerned with legal or corporate entities. And quite unlike a natural person,[114] a legal entity may implement changes in its legal structure and/or in the economic activities it applies itself to. Because of this, the question who or what can (still) qualify as the 'author' of a certain infringement of anti-competitive rules can at times assume particularly complex guises. In order to effectively deal with this and other liability issues, the European legislature has opted, from the very start, for a so-called 'economic approach' instead of a purely 'legal approach': EU competition law addresses economic entities denoted as 'undertakings', not legal persons.[115] The concept of an 'undertaking' in the TFEU has a considerably wider ambit than that of a corporate or legal entity. And this focus on economic rather than legal entities primarily serves to prevent potential mismatches between the socio-economic and the juridical reality in allocating liability for infringements of EU competition law.

According to the CJEU, the concept of an undertaking 'covers any entity engaged in economic activity, regardless of its legal status and the way in which it is financed'.[116] The concept must furthermore 'be understood as designating an economic unit even if in law that economic unit consists of several persons, natural or legal'.[117] This implies that a group of corporations, or a group consisting of natural and legal persons, can constitute a single undertaking – or a single economic unit – for the purposes of EU

Challenges and Perspectives on Asset Recovery in the EU (Oxford, Hart Publishing, 2017) 25–52; Franssen, 'The EU's Fight' (n 86) 1244–46. The ECtHR has considerably fewer problems with cases in which the criminal court's decision on the penalty is based *in part* on offences of which the defendant was not convicted; see ECtHR 1 March 2007, *Geerings v the Netherlands* (App no 30810/03) para 44.

[112] See sub-section III.B. above.

[113] See C Harding, 'The Relationship Between EU Criminal Law and Competition Law' in V Mitsilegas, M Bergström and Th Konstadinides (eds), *Research Handbook on EU Criminal Law* (Cheltenham, Edward Elgar Publishing, 2016) 249–371.

[114] However, in most jurisdictions many or even most offences are subject to certain limitation periods and become statute-barred once these expire. This phenomenon could be interpreted as a legal provision that gives expression not only to the idea that the impact of a crime and the demand for retribution lapse over time, but also to the idea that a human individual is not a static entity but changes over time.

[115] See Arts 101–102 TFEU. See further Franssen, 'Corporate Criminal Liability' (n 8); M Veenbrink, *Criminal Law Principles and the Enforcement of EU and National Competition Law: A Silent Takeover?* (Deventer, Wolters Kluwer, 2020) 169. However, considering that economic entities typically lack the capacity to hold rights and obligations, liability for infringements of competition law must be allocated to the legal or natural person actually in charge. See C Harding, 'Sanction Accumulation in the Context of Business Offending. The Full Force of the Law?' (2017) 25(2) *European Journal of Crime, Criminal Law and Criminal Justice* 163–87, 167–68; MJ Frese, *Sanctions in EU Competition Law: Principles and Practice* (Amsterdam, University of Amsterdam, 2012) 64. Cp also subsection VI.C. below, dealing with problems of double jeopardy.

[116] CJEU 10 September 2009, C-97/08 *Akzo Nobel et al v Commission* (EU:C:2009:536), para 54.

[117] CJEU *Akzo Nobel et al* (n 116) para 55. See W Frenz, *Handbook of EU Competition Law* (Berlin, Springer, 2016) 224–25.

competition law. This is assessed on an ad hoc basis, in light of varying economic and organisational factors.[118] Although the focus on economic entities provides for a rather flexible approach in allocating liability for infringements of competition law, difficult questions of responsibility and liability may still arise, especially in cases where, during or after the infringement, changes have occurred within the legal or business structure of the company or group of companies involved.

In order to establish what economic unit should be held liable for an infringement of competition law in these sorts of difficult cases, the European Commission – which is the prime authority to deal with issues of liability under European competition law and to impose fines in cases where it establishes this liability – employs the so-called doctrine of 'economic continuity'. This doctrine entails the following test: if and to the extent that, following a reorganisation, the 'new' undertaking is economically and functionally equal to the 'old' undertaking liability for infringements of competition law that took place prior to or during the reorganisation is not lost but is assumed by the post-reorganisation undertaking.[119] Economic continuity or discontinuity can often be a rather difficult matter to assess. Difficulties may arise when an undertaking has sold or hived-off certain specific business units. In cases where the relevant infringement of competition law has taken place in one or more of these business units, liability as a rule remains with the transferring entity. This result is mainly grounded on two considerations: first, the buyer should not be liable for infringements over which it had no influence and for which it consequently bears no culpability; and second, the entity in whose sphere of responsibility the infringement of law has occurred should not be able to escape liability by means of selling certain of its business units or by otherwise divesting itself of some of its economic activities.[120]

A different result is reached, however, in cases where, after an infringement of competition law, the entire undertaking either is sold to another undertaking or has merged into a new legal entity. In such cases, application of the doctrine of economic continuity generally results in the transferral of liability to the acquiring undertaking or the new corporate entity.[121] This transferral of liability, it must be noted, is subject to the important condition that the entity that was responsible for the management of the undertaking at the material time of the infringement of competition law has been liquidated or has otherwise ceased to exist for legal purposes after the sale or the merge. This implies that an undertaking which remains in existence after a reorganisation or after having divested itself of (some of) its economic activities, normally retains its liability for prior infringements to the exclusion of the successor.[122] This rule was

[118] See Franssen, 'Corporate Criminal Liability' (n 8) 299; Frese, *Sanctions in EU Competition Law* (n 115) 64–65.

[119] Frenz, *Handbook* (n 117) 233; Commission Decision 94/601/EC of 13 July 1994, *Cantonboard, OJ* [1994] OJ L 243/1 (para 145).

[120] Frenz, *Handbook* (n 117) 234; Commission Decision 89/190/EEC of 21 December 1988, *PVC Cartel*, [1989] OJ L 74/1 (para 49).

[121] Frenz, *Handbook* (n 117) 234; see also CJEU 16 December 1975, Case 40/73 *Suiker Unie et al v Commission* (EU:C:1975:174).

[122] Commission Decision 94/599/EC of 27 July 1994, *PVC Cartel II*, [1994] OJ L 239/14 (para 41); this Decision replaced the previous Commission Decision 89/190/EEC (n 120).

confirmed by the CJEU in the case of *Anic*.[123] Anic had been found to have infringed anticompetitive rules by participating in a polypropylene cartel. The company claimed that, although it still legally existed as a legal entity, it could not be held liable for the infringements because it had meanwhile sold off its entire polypropylene business to another undertaking. To no avail: explicitly referring – interestingly – to the notion of 'personal responsibility', the CJEU dismissed Anic's appeal against the judgment of the General Court that held Anic liable:

> In complaining that [the General Court] attributed responsibility for the infringements to it although it had transferred its polypropylene business to Monte, Anic is disregarding the principle of personal responsibility and neglecting the decisive factor, identifiable from the case-law of the Court of Justice … that the 'economic continuity' test can only apply where the legal person responsible for running the undertaking has ceased to exist in law after the infringement has been committed. It also follows that the application of these tests is not contrary in any way to the principle of legal certainty.[124]

Thus, the continued existence of the infringer normally precludes liability of the transferee or the acquiring company. However, in the case of *Aalborg-Portland et al*, the *Anic* rule did not apply.[125] Although this case is relatively old, it may still be seen as a case in point with regard to the way in which the question of 'individual authorship' is dealt with within the quasi-criminal law context of European competition law. Aktieselskabet Aalborg-Portland Cement Fabrik, a Danish legal entity, was found guilty of infringing Article 101, paragraph 1 TFEU by participating in a cartel in the cement sector. The economic activities of this undertaking were later transferred to a newly-established legal entity going by the name Aalborg in 1990, subsequent to which Aktieselskabet Aalborg-Portland Cement Fabrik became a holding company that held 50 per cent of the shares in Aalborg. The other 50 per cent of the shares were held by another company, called Blue Circle. Aalborg was held liable for the infringements of competition law by the Commission; this decision was upheld by the General Court.

On appeal, Aalborg claimed that it was unjustifiably held liable for the infringements committed by Aktieselskabet Aalborg-Portland Cement Fabrik in light of existing case law arguing that 'the "economic continuity" test can only apply where the legal person responsible for running the undertaking has ceased to exist in law after the infringement has been committed'. In his Opinion, Advocate General Dámaso Ruiz-Jarabo Colomer indeed concluded that Aalborg could not be held responsible for the infringements because these were committed by a corporate entity that continued to exist as a holding company, owning 50 per cent of Aalborg's share capital. According to the Advocate General, attributing liability to Aalborg would contravene the principle of individual culpability for two reasons:

> First, it contradicts the case-law of the Court of Justice, which has held that 'it falls, in principle, to the legal or natural person managing the undertaking in question when the infringement was committed to answer for that infringement, even if, at the time of the decision finding

[123] CJEU 8 July 1999, C-49/92 P *Commission v Anic Partecipazioni* (EU:C:1999:356). See A Jones and B Sufrin, *EU Competition Law. Texts, Cases, and Materials*, 4th edn (Oxford, Oxford University Press, 2011) 1118. Cp General Court (GCEU) 28 April 1994, T-38/92 *All Weather Sports Benelux BV v Commission* (EU:T:1994:43).

[124] CJEU *Anic* (n 123) para 145.

[125] CJEU *Aalborg-Portland et al* (n 116).

> the infringement, another person had assumed responsibility for operating the undertaking'. Second, because the 'one and the same economic entity' test, as the key to the transfer of responsibility from the former cement manufacturer to Aalborg, is based on an objective concept which is open to challenge. Irrespective of the mistake in the assertion, since a third party (Blue Circle) holds 50% of the appellant's share capital, fixing the objective in the activity and not in the person carrying it out, irrespective of the fact that the latter person exists and can answer for its acts, is tantamount to ignoring the principle of culpability and the principle that punishment should only be applied to the offender.[126]

The CJEU, however, rejected Aalborg's claim. It ruled that the fact that Aktieselskabet Aalborg Portland-Cement Fabrik still existed did not preclude 'the Commission from proceeding against Aalborg as being, from an economic and organisational point of view, the *author* of the infringement' (emphasis added).[127] It stated that the Court of First Instance had rightfully concluded that, for the purposes of applying Article 85, paragraph 1 of the Treaty establishing the European Economic Community,[128] the undertaking run by Aalborg from 1990 constituted the same economic entity as the one that was previously run by Aktieselskabet Aalborg Portland-Cement Fabrik. Furthermore, the CJEU ruled that the continued existence of the infringing company normally precludes the attribution of liability to the acquiring company, unless both companies are 'structurally related'.[129] In the present case, both companies were indeed found to be structurally related. This means that:

> [t]he fact that Aktieselskabet Aalborg Portland-Cement Fabrik still exists as a legal entity does not invalidate that finding and did not therefore in itself constitute a ground for annulling the Cement Decision in respect of Aalborg. In that regard, it is true that in *Commission v Anic* (paragraph 145) the Court held that there can be economic continuity only where the legal person responsible for running the undertaking has ceased to exist in law after the infringement has been committed. However, that case concerned two existing and functioning undertakings one of which had simply transferred part of its activities to the other and where there was no structural link between them. As is apparent from paragraph 344 of this judgment, that is not the position in this case.[130]

The principle that punishment should only be applied to the offender – also referred to as the principle of 'personal responsibility' – forms an established part of European

[126] Opinion of 11 February 2003, C-204/00 P *Aalborg-Portland A/S et al v Commission* (EU:C:2003:85) paras 70–71. In paras 63–64 of his Opinion, AG Ruiz-Jarabo Colomer interestingly states: 'the Court of Justice must begin by setting out a general principle of law, developed in order to limit the exercise of *ius puniendi* by the public authorities: the principle that punishment should only be applied to the offender, which complements the principle of culpability, whose first and most important manifestation is that only the perpetrator can be charged in respect of unlawful conduct. That principle, like all the safeguards derived from criminal law, requires great caution when it is applied to administrative proceedings, since, when it comes to imposing penalties or making compensation for unlawful conduct, a system of objective responsibility, or strict responsibility, is unacceptable.' See also Blomsma, *Mens Rea and Defences* (n 4) 224–25; JM ten Voorde, 'Een autonome en uniforme uitleg van opzet binnen de Europese Unie. Een commentaar bij HvJ EU 27 februari 2014, zaak C-396/12' (2014) 6 *Nederlands Tijdschrift voor Europees Recht* 203, 208.

[127] CJEU *Aalborg-Portland et al* (n 116), para 355.

[128] Now: Art 101 TFEU.

[129] See on the concept of a 'structural link' as part of the 'economic continuity test' Frese, *Sanctions in EU Competition Law* (n 115) 67–68; Frenz, *Handbook* (n 117) 235; Jones and Sufrin, *EU Competition Law* (n 123) 1118–20; Veenbrink, *Criminal Law Principles* (n 115) 364–65.

[130] CJEU *Aalborg-Portland et al* (n 116), paras 357–359.

competition law. The CJEU has repeatedly stated that, pursuant to this principle, the legal or natural person answerable for an infringement of competition law is the legal or natural person *actually managing* the undertaking at the material time of that infringement.[131] This principle is somewhat relaxed, however, by the doctrine of economic continuity, which – as may be concluded from the foregoing – is sometimes applied with the effect of attributing liability for infringements of competition law to *another* entity than the one that actually managed the undertaking at the material time of the infringement. The rationale for this relaxation is twofold:

- First, a penalty imposed on an undertaking that continues to exist in law but has ceased economic activity is likely to have no deterrent effect.
- Second, if no possibility were foreseen to impose a penalty on an entity other than the one which committed the infringement, undertakings could escape penalties simply by changing their identity through restructurings, sales or other legal or organisational changes.[132]

This is not to deny that the concept of economic continuity has met with criticism. Its precise meaning (including that of the criterion of a 'structural link') is not very clear, and its application is not always straightforward. The CJEU's judgment in the case of *Aalborg-Portland et al*, for instance, has been criticised in light of the first-mentioned limb of the rationale of the doctrine of economic continuity. According to the criticism, the CJEU has not taken sufficient account of the fact that the entity that was in charge at the time of the infringements (Aalborg-Portland Cement Fabrik A/S) remained in existence after the transferral of its economic activities to the newly established legal entity (Aalborg), and also served as a holding company with no less than 50 per cent of shares in the new company: 'the holding company is likely to be stronger financially than the corporate transferee which would mean that avoidance of liability resulting from the thin capitalisation of the new operating entity could not be ruled out.'[133] Notwithstanding this criticism, it is clear that liability for infringements of competition law that occur during or prior to structural changes within a company may not, as a rule, be established on the basis of constructions of *purely* vicarious liability: an entity cannot be liable for an infringement of another entity if no structural links between the two can be established.[134]

However, the principle referred to as 'personal responsibility' is relaxed further by the doctrine of so-called 'parent liability'. A company may be liable for an infringement of competition law committed by an undertaking that it, directly or indirectly (through a shareholding), owns. This liability of a parent for anticompetitive behaviour of its subsidiary is based on the idea that a parent company normally exercises (decisive)

[131] See Frese, *Sanctions in EU Competition Law* (n 115) 64–67.

[132] Frese, *Sanctions in EU Competition Law* (n 115) 67–68.

[133] Frenz, *Handbook* (n 117) 235. See also W Berg, 'Die Rechtsprechung des EuGH und EuG auf dem Gebiet des Kartellrechts im Jahr 2004' (2005) 2 *Europaïsches Wirtschafts- und Steuerrecht* 49.

[134] Cp paras 63–64 in the AG's opinion (n 126). For a critical analysis of the EU's approach to corporate (criminal) liability, see Franssen, 'The EU's Fight' (n 86) and Franssen, 'Corporate Criminal Liability' (n 8).

influence over the (anticompetitive) behaviour of its subsidiaries. In the important case of *Akzo Nobel et al*, the CJEU concluded:

> that the conduct of a subsidiary may be imputed to the parent company in particular where, although having a separate legal personality, that subsidiary does not decide independently upon its own conduct on the market, but carries out, in all material respects, the instructions given to it by the parent company, having regard in particular to the economic, organisational and legal links between those two legal entities … That is the case because, in such a situation, the parent company and its subsidiary form a single economic unit and therefore form a single undertaking … [This] enables the Commission to address a decision imposing fines to the parent company, without having to establish the personal involvement of the latter in the infringement.[135]

As a rule, liability for an infringement of competition law committed by a subsidiary undertaking may be imputed to the parent company only when the parent company has actually exercised *decisive influence* over the conduct of the subsidiary undertaking. To this extent, the principle of personal responsibility – or the principle that liability should only be incurred on the actual offender – clearly appears to be respected by the doctrine of parent liability. However, in cases where a parent company owns all or virtually all of the shares in a subsidiary company which is found to have infringed EU competition rules, 'there is a rebuttable presumption that the parent company does in fact exercise a decisive influence over the conduct of its subsidiary'.[136] Although this presumption may be rebutted, it appears that this possibility is in fact almost illusory. In order to rebut the presumption, the parent company is required to demonstrate that the subsidiary company acts on its own initiative on the market, independently from the parent company.[137]

It may be concluded from the foregoing that, while it is true that the CJEU clearly defers to the 'first dimension' of the principle of individual culpability in its case law in the field of competition law, the purport of this dimension in competition law deviates from the traditional criminal law approach. This is to say that competition law and criminal law differ in the answers given to the question as to who can legally be designated as the 'author' of a certain infringement. The range of persons who may potentially be designated as infringers of EU competition rules is wider than the range of persons to whom – in accordance with the classical view in criminal law – perpetration may potentially be attributed. In other words, whereas the first dimension of the principle of individual culpability implements evidentiary thresholds in both domains, this threshold is generally higher in criminal law than in the quasi-criminal law domain of EU competition law: compared with the latter, criminal law generally demands a more direct and firm relation between a particular person's conduct and a certain harm in order to sustain the finding that this person can legally be regarded as the 'author' of the offence concerned.

[135] CJEU *Akzo Nobel et al* (n 116) paras 58–59.

[136] CJEU *Akzo Nobel et al* (n 116) para 60. See also GCEU 17 May 2011, T-299/08 *Elf Aquitaine SA v Commission* (EU:T:2011:217), upheld by CJEU 2 February 2012, C-404/11 *Elf Aquitaine SA v Commission* (EU:C:2012:56).

[137] See Frenz, *Handbook* (n 117) 232–33; Frese, *Sanctions in EU Competition Law* (n 115) 66–67; Franssen, 'Corporate Criminal Liability' (n 8) 301; GCEU *Elf Aquitaine* (n 136) para 122.

Allowing of a more flexible and adaptable allocation of liability, the economic approach under EU competition law secures a better 'fit' with socio-economic reality than the more rigid, legal approach to corporate liability that prevails in criminal law. In cases, for example, concerning the anticompetitive behaviour of an entity that has meanwhile been dismantled and liquidated, but whose business activities are continued by another (existing or newly created) corporate entity, it is possible, in principle, to impute liability for the infringement to the successor. This is even possible, as was seen above, in some cases where the infringing company has *not* ceased to exist, provided that there is a 'structural link' between the old and the new company. In a strictly legal approach, by contrast, it is not permitted to hold an entity liable for past offences of its predecessor.[138] And in cases concerning parent-subsidiary relations, the parent company may be vicariously liable under EU competition law for an infringement committed by its subsidiary, even when there has been no personal involvement and no guilt whatsoever on the part of the parent company with respect to the infringement. In criminal law, by contrast, liability of a parent company typically clearly requires more, such as proof of a fault element.[139]

So although the economic approach in EU competition law is opportune from an instrumental point of view, the more exclusive focus in criminal law on legal entities (as opposed to 'economic entities'), conversely, has the advantage of rendering the personal scope of attribution of liability more foreseeable, thereby securing a high(er) degree of legal certainty. Moreover, the criminal law approach is conducive to a more distinct determination of the person whose individual culpability should be established and to whom the sanction should be tailored; the criminal law approach is consequently also more apt to satisfy the requirements of the principle of individual culpability.[140] Holding a person liable for another person's behaviour is at variance with the criminal law's basic principles. In EU competition law, however, this is exactly what happens when a group of persons – constituting an 'economic entity' – is collectively held liable for infringements committed by a subsidiary company.[141] Finally and relatedly, it should be noted that although liability for infringements of Articles 101 and 102 TFEU is established at the level of undertakings or economic entities, the legal consequences of the allocated liability are necessarily borne by legal (and possibly natural) persons against whom the Commission's fining decisions and the Courts' judgments are enforced.[142]

[138] See Franssen, 'Corporate Criminal Liability' (n 8) 291.

[139] See Harding, 'Sanction Accumulation' (n 115) 170; Franssen, 'Corporate Criminal Liability' (n 8) 301.

[140] Franssen, 'Corporate Criminal Liability' (n 8) 290. Franssen argues, however, that a more economic approach to corporate criminal liability would be advisable in EU criminal law, in order, inter alia, to more effectively deal with avoidance strategies of undertakings that are deployed with the aim of indemnifying them against incurring criminal liability.

[141] See Frese, Sanctions *in EU Competition Law* (n 115) 62–68; Franssen, 'Corporate Criminal Liability' (n 8) 302.

[142] See the Opinion of AG Juliane Kokott of 10 September 2009, C-978/08 *Akzo Nobel NV et al v Commission* (EU:C:2009:262) para 36: '[T]he addressees of the competition rules and the addressees of decisions of the competition authorities are not necessarily the same.' And see Franssen, 'Corporate Criminal Liability' (n 8) 303; GCEU *Elf Aquitaine* (n 136) para 122.

IV. Second Dimension: Mens Rea Elements

A. Introduction: Fault Elements in EU (Quasi-)Criminal Law

The different fault or mens rea elements of offence definitions represent the second dimension of the principle of *nulla poena sine culpa*. These requirements belong to the domain that Antoine Mooij has aptly termed 'guilt of cause' or 'guilt of action' (*αἰτία*; *causa*).[143] This dimension also warrants a relatively elaborate discussion. This is due, first of all, to the fact that proof of the requisite fault element underpins the presupposition of personal blameworthiness and lays the foundation for the ultimate imputation of criminal liability.[144] In other words, mens rea helps establish the defendant's guilt. There are, however, still more purposes that are discharged by mens rea elements. Winnie Chan and Andrew Simester identify three additional functions.[145] Mens rea sometimes constitutes the morally wrongful character of a defendant's behaviour in that the fault element is sometimes *integral* to the wrong or harm for which the defendant is called to answer: some offences derive their criminal or wrongful character to a considerable extent from the mental state with which they are committed. Moreover, mens rea elements serve the purpose of securing fair warning to defendants. And lastly, mens rea requirements play a mediating role in the process of criminalisation, in the sense that the level of stringency of a fault requirement that is incorporated into in an offence definition affects the ambit of the offence and, consequently, the level of protection offered to the legal interests for the sake of which the offence is created.

The two last-mentioned additional functions of mens rea are especially relevant within the context of European (quasi-)criminal law, considering the multi-layered patchwork of regulations in certain of its areas, the diverging legal traditions of the many EU Member States into which the European rules have to be integrated, and the interpretative questions, uncertainties or even perplexities to which all of this may give rise. A full and fine-grained picture of the different mens rea elements that can be found in the various domains of European (quasi-) criminal law cannot, as a matter of course, be offered here. The aim of the present section is to provide a broad sketch of the meanings attached to the most common fault elements in European criminal and quasi-criminal law.[146] In that regard some attention will be paid to certain interpretative difficulties that can be encountered in the case law of the CJEU. Such difficulties may easily occur in light of the fact that the terms that denote subjective fault elements in

[143] See subsection II.B. above.

[144] See De Jong, 'Theorizing Criminal Intent' (n 24); and see subsection II.B. above.

[145] W Chan and AP Simester, 'Four Functions of Mens Rea' in M Ulväng and I Cameron (eds), *Essays on Criminalisation and Sanctions* (Uppsala, Iustus Förlag, 2014) 143–62.

[146] The issue whether the European legislator and/or the CJEU would do better to adopt the tripartite classification of fault elements that prevails in the Anglo-American criminal law tradition, or rather the bipartite division of fault elements that one encounters in most continental criminal law systems (see subsection II.C.) will not be dealt with here. See Blomsma, *Mens Rea and Defences* (n 4) 59–204; J Blomsma, 'Fault Elements in EU Criminal Law: The Case for Recklessness' in A Klip (ed), *Substantive Criminal Law of the European Union* (Antwerp, Maklu, 2011) 135–59; in the same volume: T Weigend, 'Comments on Jeroen Blomsma's Case for Recklessness', 161–71; G Taylor, 'Concepts of Intention in German Criminal Law' (2004) 24(1) *Oxford Journal of Legal Studies* 99; G Taylor, 'The Intention Debate in German Criminal Law' (2004) 17(3) *Ratio Juris* 346.

European legislative acts are generally not defined by the European legislature, whereas these terms can have meanings that differ significantly across the legal systems of the different Member States. Furthermore, the different language versions of a legislative act occasionally exhibit notable terminological differences concerning fault elements.

In its judgment in the case of *Rinkau*, the CJEU stated that mens rea elements that form parts of European legislation must be regarded as independent or autonomous concepts 'which must be explained by reference, first, to the objectives and scheme' of the legislative instrument in question and, second, 'to the general principles which the national legal systems have in common'.[147] Although the CJEU seeks to ensure as far as possible that the rights and obligations of the contracting states and of concerned individuals arising from European legislation are 'equal and uniform', the conceptual framework of mens rea elements in European criminal and quasi-criminal law is still rather fragmentary and partly inconsistent. This is partially a result of the fact that the CJEU aims not at providing interpretations of mens rea elements that are uniform for the *whole* of EU law, but rather at providing uniform interpretations of mens rea elements for the purposes of the *particular* legislative acts in which they figure.[148] As a consequence, the exact meaning attributed to a fault element may vary somewhat from one legislative instrument to another.

Unsurprisingly, by far the most frequently used concept of subjective fault in European legislation in fields of (quasi-)criminal law is that of intention. Lesser degrees of fault, such as recklessness or negligence, are much more seldom adopted, at least in specifically criminal law provisions.[149] In the remainder of this section a number of interpretative issues will be discussed with regard to three mens rea elements. The following subsection discusses the concept of intention in European criminal and quasi-criminal law; subsection IV.C deals with the concepts of recklessness and (serious) negligence as offence elements in European legislation.

B. Intention: *Touring Tours und Travel* and *Spector Photo Group*

A judgment of the CJEU of 13 December 2018,[150] concerning a preliminary ruling at the request of the German Federal Administrative Court (Bundesverwaltungsgericht), provides an interesting example of a case regarding a form of quasi-criminal law

[147] CJEU 26 May 1981, Case 157/80 *Criminal Proceedings against Siegfried Ewald Rinkau* (EU:C:1981:120) para 11. The CJEU adds that this is 'all the more necessary where … terminological differences exist between the various language versions' of the legislative instrument at issue. With regard to the concept of 'intentional non-compliance' as referred to in eg Art 51(4) of Council Regulation 1698/2005/EC of 20 September 2005 on support for rural development by the European Agricultural Fund for Rural Development (EAFRD), [2005] OJ L 277/1, the CJEU noted in its judgment of 27 February 2014, C-396/12 *Van der Ham and Van der Ham-Reijersen van Buuren v College van Gedeputeerde Staten van Zuid-Holland* (EU:C:2014:98) para 32, that, 'in accordance with settled case-law, that concept must be given an independent and uniform interpretation, having regard to the usual meaning of those words, the context of those Articles and the objective pursued by the legislation of which they are part'.

[148] See Ten Voorde, 'Een autonome en uniforme uitleg' (n 126) 204; Blomsma, *Mens Rea and Defences* (n 4) 5–15; Rankinen, 'Positive Fault Requirements' (n 54) 139; Klip, *European Criminal Law* (n 2) 222–23.

[149] Rankinen, 'Positive Fault Requirements' (n 54) 124.

[150] CJEU *Touring Tours und Travel* (n 12).

enforcement that evokes questions pertaining to the role of the culpability principle in matters within the grey zone between administrative and criminal law. The Bundesverwaltungsgericht asked the CJEU to decide whether a certain national administrative regulation – the enforcement of which may involve the imposition of administrative monetary penalties – is compatible with existing EU law. The matters raised are interesting because they mark a topical tension within the AFSJ. How, if at all, can a Member State fulfil its duties under European law instruments – including obligations to criminalise certain behaviour – to combat illegal immigration and especially (in the current case) to prevent the intentional facilitation of unauthorised entry, transit and residence of third-country nationals, without jeopardizing the free movement of EU citizens and legally staying third-country nationals across the mutual borders of states that are part of the Schengen area?

Paragraph 63 of the German Law on the Residence of Foreign Nationals (*Aufenthaltsgesetz*)[151] formulates a number of obligations addressed to (international) transport undertakings (*Beförderungsunternehmer*). Section 1 prescribes that a carrier of passengers is not allowed to bring foreign nationals into the territory of the Federal Republic of Germany if these foreign nationals are not in possession of the requisite passport or residence permit. This legal prohibition simultaneously entails an obligation on the part of the transporter to carry out adequate checks of passports and visas.[152] Section 2 states that an infringement of this obligation may lead to a formal prohibition from continuing to bring foreign nationals into the territory of the Federal Republic of Germany in breach of section 1, accompanied by a formal warning that for every recurring infringement a fine (*Zwangsgeld*) will be imposed that can range between one thousand and five thousand euros. Two bus service undertakings – one from Germany and the other from Spain – were faced with the aforementioned prohibition under section 2 of paragraph 63 and were threatened with a penalty payment of 1000 euros for every individual foreign national without a passport or resident permit that they would bring into the federal territory of Germany. Both undertakings brought proceedings against the Federal Republic of Germany.

The undertakings claimed that their obligations under paragraph 63 of the *Aufenthaltsgesetz* are at variance with Article 67, paragraph 2 TFEU and Articles 20 and 21 of the Schengen Borders Code[153] insofar as these obligations involve the requirement to check passengers' documents prior to boarding the coach on routes that only cross an *internal* border within the Schengen area. Article 20 of the Schengen Borders Code, after all, prohibits border controls on persons, irrespective of their nationality, when they cross internal borders within the Schengen area. This general prohibition is subject to a limited number of exceptions, which are stipulated in Article 21. These exceptions predominantly concern security checks on persons and the exercise of police powers by

[151] Law on the Residence, Employment and Integration of Foreign Nationals in Federal Territory (*Gesetz über den Aufenthalt, die Erwerbstätigkeit und die Integration von Ausländern im Bundesgebiet*).

[152] Paragraphs 63(1) and (2) of the General Administrative Provision relating to the Law on the Residence of Foreign Nationals (*Allgemeine Verwaltungsvorschrift zum Aufenthaltsgesetz*).

[153] As amended by Regulation 562/2006 that was applicable at the material time of the facts that triggered the proceedings, but was repealed and replaced by Regulation 2016/399/EU of the European Parliament and of the Council of 9 March 2016 on a Union Code on the rules governing the movement of persons across borders (Schengen Borders Code), [2016] OJ L 77/1.

the appropriate state authorities as long as the exercise of these police measures does not amount to an equivalent of border controls. The claimants argued that their obligations under paragraph 63 of the *Aufenthaltsgesetz* cannot qualify as one of the exceptions enumerated in Article 21 of the Schengen Border Code and hence amount to an unlawful contravention of the freedom of movement within the Schengen area.

Against this, the Federal Republic of Germany submitted that it was authorised to obligate internationally operating coach transport undertakings to perform checks on the required documents of passengers and to threaten any non-compliance with this obligation with an administrative penalty on the grounds that a number of instruments of EU law, most notably Directive 2002/90 and Framework Decision 2002/946, require the imposition of penalties for infringements of transport prohibitions such as those provided for in paragraph 63 of the *Aufenthaltsgesetz*. The Directive and Framework Decision[154] aim at preventing the facilitation of unauthorised entry, transit and residence of third-country nationals in the EU. Paragraph 1(a) of Article 1 of Directive 2002/90 requires each Member State to adopt appropriate sanctions against, inter alia, anyone 'who intentionally assists a person who is not a national of a Member State to enter, or transit across, the territory of a Member State in breach of the laws of the State concerned on the entry or transit of aliens'.

In its preliminary ruling the CJEU circumvented this whole issue of whether or not Germany could legitimately claim to uphold and enforce paragraph 63 of the *Aufenthaltsgesetz* for the purpose of fulfilling its duties to combat (the facilitation of) illegal immigration under Directive 2002/90 and Framework Decision 2002/946 (and Directive 2001/51). The reason for this is that the referring court had expressly stated in its request for a preliminary ruling that it did not seek any clarification from the CJEU regarding the possible implications of these three European law instruments for the replies which had to be given to the questions asked.[155] The CJEU therefore stuck to the questions posed by the referring court, the scope of which was limited to an examination of paragraph 63 of the German *Aufenthaltsgesetz* in light of Article 67, paragraph 2 TFEU and Articles 20 and 21 of the Schengen Borders Code. The CJEU noted, first, that the checks as prescribed by paragraph 63 of the *Aufenthaltsgesetz* do *not* amount to 'border checks' within the meaning of, and (directly) prohibited by, Article 20 of the Schengen Borders Code, but must be seen as 'checks within the territory of a Member State', referred to in Article 21 of that regulation. This is so, according to the CJEU,

[154] Council Directive 2002/90/EC of 28 November 2002 defining the facilitation of unauthorised entry, transit and residence, [2002] OJ L 328/17; Council Framework Decision 2002/946/JHA of 28 November 2002 on the strengthening of the penal framework to prevent the facilitation of unauthorised entry, transit and residence, *OJ* [2002] L 328, 1. The Federal Republic of Germany also referred to Council Directive 2001/51/EC of 28 June 2001, [2001] OJ L 187/45 supplementing the provisions of Art 26 of the Convention implementing the Schengen Agreement (the CISA Convention; Convention of 14 June 1985 between the Governments of the States of the Benelux Economic Union, the Federal Republic of Germany and the French Republic on the gradual abolition of checks at their common borders, signed in Schengen (Luxembourg) on 19 June 1990, [2000] OJ L 239/19).

[155] The CJEU recalls in this connection that 'it is for the referring court alone to determine and formulate the questions to be referred for a preliminary ruling concerning the interpretation of EU law which are necessary in order to resolve the dispute in the main proceedings'; CJEU *Touring Tours und Travel* (n 12) paras 39–42. See also CJEU 18 July 2013, C-136/12 *Consiglio Nazionale dei Geologi v Autorità garante della concorrenza e del mercato* (EU:C:2013:489).

because the checks at issue are carried out, 'not "at borders" or "when the border is crossed", but, in principle, inside the territory of a Member State, in the present case the one in which the travellers board the coach at the start of the cross-border journey'.[156]

The checks referred to in Article 21 of the aforementioned Schengen Borders Code are not automatically prohibited by this provision. As was mentioned above, certain checks within the territory of a Member State are permitted, provided that the exercise of these checks does not amount to an 'equivalent of border controls'. And the CJEU concluded, second, that this condition was not satisfied in the present case: the checks imposed under section 1 of paragraph 63 of the *Aufenthaltsgesetz* must be classified as measures that have an 'effect equivalent to border checks', which are prohibited by Article 21.[157] The CJEU therefore ruled that paragraph 2 of Article 67 TFEU and the Schengen Borders Code preclude legislation of a Member State,

> which requires every coach transport undertaking providing a regular cross-border service within the Schengen area to the territory of that Member State to check the passports and residence permits of passengers before they cross an internal border … and which allows … the police authorities to issue orders prohibiting such transport, accompanied by a threat of a recurring fine, against transport undertakings which have been found to have conveyed to that territory third-country nationals who were not in possession of those travel documents.[158]

Advocate General Yves Bot reached the same conclusion in his Opinion. (He differed, however, in his conclusion regarding the classification of the checks prescribed by paragraph 63 of the *Aufenthaltsgesetz*; according to the Advocate General these checks must be treated as 'border checks' within the meaning of, and prohibited by, Article 20 of the Schengen Borders Code.)[159] Having concluded that the border checks prescribed by the *Aufenthaltsgesetz* are prohibited by the Schengen Borders Code, the Advocate General went on to examine whether, as the Federal Republic of Germany maintained in its observations, those checks may be regarded as being imposed under the provisions of international and European law which have been adopted in order to combat illegal immigration. Although, as was seen before, this question was later left unaddressed by the CJEU in its preliminary ruling, it is worthwhile for the purposes of this chapter to pay some attention to the Advocate General's rather extensive treatment of this issue, not least because Bot makes a number of interesting observations on the meaning of *dolus eventualis*.

[156] CJEU *Touring Tours und Travel* (n 12) para 45.

[157] For the reasoning, see CJEU *Touring Tours und Travel* (n 12) paras 46–73.

[158] CJEU *Touring Tours und Travel* (n 12) para 73.

[159] See his Opinion of 6 September 2018, Joined cases C-412/17 and C-474/17 *Touring Tours und Travel GmbH and Sociedad de Transportes SA v Bundesrepublik Deutschland* (EU:C:2018:671) paras 73–104. AG Bot notes that the sole purpose of the checks is 'to ensure that the persons on board the coach who intend to cross the border of the Member State of destination are indeed permitted to enter the territory of that Member State', and that 'those checks have the effect of preventing passengers from entering the territory of that State if they do not have the required travel documents, in the same way as checks carried out by border guards in connection with the crossing of internal borders' (para 85). In this way, the checks have 'the effect of breaking the direct temporal and spatial link with the crossing of the border, thereby extending territorial borders outwards and introducing what commentators have described as "remote checks" or "outsourced" checks' (para 86). Moreover, the AG concludes that para 63 of the *Aufenthaltsgesetz* introduces 'a systematic obligation to carry out checks, compliance with which is unconditional and infringement of which is unlawful' (para 87).

The Federal Republic of Germany had submitted that as soon as a transport undertaking has been informed by the competent authorities of the finding that it has brought third-country nationals without the requisite papers into the territory of Germany, this undertaking is fully aware of its unlawful (past) conduct. If the undertaking nevertheless refrains from carrying out the required checks, although such checks are practicable and reasonable, any continued failure to comply with the obligations under section 1 of paragraph 63 of the *Aufenthaltsgesetz* would suffice to establish that the undertaking has reconciled itself, at least in part, to the possibility of facilitating illegal immigration, and hence that it has acted with *dolus eventualis.*[160] And this, it was argued, would constitute a form of intentional assistance by the transport undertaking of unauthorised entry of a person within the meaning of paragraph 1(a) of Article 1 of Directive 2002/90. Article 3 of Directive 2002/90 and Article 1 of Framework Decision 2002/946 require that this offence is subject to an 'effective, proportionate and dissuasive' penalty. And the Federal Republic of Germany submitted that such a penalty is provided for in the aforementioned section 2 of paragraph 63 of the *Aufenthaltsgesetz.*

Advocate General Bot disagrees. He acutely observes in his Opinion[161] that the Federal Republic of Germany failed to indicate that the offence of facilitation of unauthorised entry defined in Article 1 of Directive 2002/90 had already been transposed into German law in separate provisions, namely in paragraphs 95 to 97 of the *Aufenthaltsgesetz.*[162] But more importantly, he states furthermore that provisions of criminal law require 'a strict interpretation of the material and mental elements constituting that offence'.[163] He goes on to argue that paragraph 1(a) of Article 1 of Directive 2002/90 seeks to criminalise not a person who takes the risk of helping an illegally staying person to enter the territory, 'but rather a person who has the criminal intention of committing the specific act prohibited by law (specific intent)'[164] – which is to say that Article 1 of the Directive only targets those 'persons who, in a considered and intentional manner, engage in conduct with the aim of performing the prohibited act'.[165] According to Bot, this does not warrant an interpretation that includes *dolus eventualis*:

> In its observations, the Federal Republic of Germany actually refers to a form of intention which it calls '*dolus eventualis*', which it defines as 'indirect intention'. That form of intention covers a person who did not intend to commit an offence in its entirety. In the present case, the person concerned does not have a proven wrongful intent to commit a serious offence of collaborating with a smuggling network, but is acting recklessly, carelessly or negligently. … It must be accepted that a person who 'knowingly' or 'intentionally' facilitates the unauthorised

[160] Mistakenly referred to as 'indirect intent' by the Federal Republic of Germany and the AG; see the opinion of AG Bot (n 159) paras 137–138 and 145; and cp subsection II.C. above.

[161] Opinion of AG Bot (n 159) para 123.

[162] These provisions were examined by the CJEU in its judgment of 10 April 2012, C-83/12 PPU *Criminal Proceedings against Minh Khoa Vo* (EU:C:2012:202).

[163] Opinion of AG Bot (n 159) para 126.

[164] Opinion of AG Bot (n 159) para 137.

[165] Opinion of AG Bot (n 159) para 143.

> entry of a third-country national into the territory does not have the same criminal intent as a person who only negligently takes that risk.[166]

As was mentioned before, the CJEU was able to circumvent this whole issue of whether or not Germany could legitimately claim to uphold and enforce paragraph 63 of the *Aufenthaltsgesetz* for the purpose of fulfilling its duties to combat the facilitation of illegal immigration under Directive 2002/90 and Framework Decision 2002/946. Consequently, it did not express itself on the question whether or not *dolus eventualis* is included in the mens rea element of intention within the meaning of paragraph 1(a) of Article 1 of Directive 2002/90. But if it would have addressed this issue, the CJEU would quite probably have indicated that the Advocate General's reasoning on this issue is unsound. As is self-evident, a person who recklessly or negligently takes the risk of facilitating the unauthorised entry of a third-country national does not display the same state of mind as someone who specifically intends to facilitate this unauthorised entry. However, it would be clearly wrong to conclude from this that the concept of intention within the meaning of Article 1 of Directive 2002/90 (and possibly, for that matter, within the meaning of any other legal provision that contains the concept) could not encompass *dolus eventualis*.

In fact, it is rather likely that it does.[167] It is at least clear that the notion of *dolus eventualis* is not alien to the CJEU's interpretation of intention, as may be illustrated, for example, with the case of *Afrasiaba et al.*[168] The case concerned criminal proceedings in Germany against three men who stood accused of having supplied materials intended for the manufacture of nuclear missiles to the Islamic Republic of Iran. This constituted a criminal offence pursuant to paragraph 34 of the (since replaced) German Law on Foreign Trade (*Außenwirtschaftsgesetz*), which implemented Regulation 423/2007.[169] Article 7, paragraph 4 of this Regulation compelled the Member States to prohibit '[t]he participation, knowingly and intentionally, in activities the object or effect of which is, directly or indirectly, to circumvent' the prohibition of supplying economic resources to Iran. In its reference for a preliminary ruling, the Oberlandesgericht in Düsseldorf asked the CJEU, among other things, to clarify whether or not the mens rea requirement referred to as 'knowingly and intentionally' encompasses *dolus eventualis*. In response, the CJEU stated the following:

> The terms 'knowingly' and 'intentionally' imply, for the purposes of Article 7(4) of Regulation No 423/2007, firstly an element of knowledge and secondly an element of intent. Those two

[166] Opinion of AG Bot (n 159) paras 138 and 142. An additional argument for his contention that the offence of facilitation of unauthorised entry excludes the concept of *dolus eventualis* is derived from the fact that the applicable penalties, as defined in Art 1 of Framework Decision 2002/946 (n 154), must be sufficiently dissuasive. And, according to Bot (para 143), 'it is possible to dissuade only persons who intend to commit the act punishable by law or to re-offend. Moreover, the severity of the penalties, which may take the form of an "extradition" measure or custodial sentences, precludes, in my view, such penalties being imposed on persons who take only the risk of committing the offence.'

[167] Except of course in legal systems (such as English criminal law) that do not recognise the concept of dolus eventualis altogether (see subsection II.C. above).

[168] CJEU 21 December 2011, C-72/11 *Generalbundesanwalt beim Bundesgerichtshof v Mohsen Afrasiaba et al* (EU:C:2011:874).

[169] Council Regulation 423/2007/EC of 19 April 2007 concerning restrictive measures against Iran, [2007] OJ L 103/1. The Regulation was repealed in 2010 by Council Regulation 961/2010/EU of 25 October 2010 on restrictive measures against Iran and repealing Regulation (EC) No 423/2007, [2010] OJ L 281/1.

> cumulative requirements of knowledge and intent are met where the person participating in an activity covered by Article 7(4) of Regulation No 423/2007 deliberately seeks the object or the effect, direct or indirect, of circumvention connected therewith. They are also met where the person in question *is aware that his participation in such an activity can have that object or effect and accepts that possibility* (emphasis added).[170]

The last cited sentence attests to a rather straightforward and univocal recognition of the concept of *dolus eventualis* by the CJEU.[171] It is noteworthy that the CJEU binds this concept to a relatively low evidentiary threshold, even for *dolus eventualis* standards: according to the quoted paragraph, it must be established that the defendant consciously accepted the (mere) *possibility* of a circumvention of the relevant prohibition. With this fairly extensive interpretation, the Court seems to have silently passed over the fact that in many national legal systems *dolus eventualis* presupposes a *considerable chance* – that is, a chance of a certain magnitude or gravity – that the defendant's action would indeed result in the relevant harm.[172] It seems reasonable to assume that the CJEU does not refer to the legal traditions of the Member States with regard to the concept of intention because of the Court's objective to ensure the practicability of its interpretation of the terms 'knowingly' and 'intentionally' in the legal systems of all Member States.[173] It should be remembered, however, that the CJEU first and foremost seeks to provide uniform interpretations of mens rea elements for the purposes of the *particular* legislative acts of which they form parts. This implies that the meaning attributed to a certain fault element may vary somewhat from one legislative instrument to another. Moreover, it is not inconceivable that in some other case, concerning the scope and meaning of intention in some other legislative act, the CJEU may be prompted to *deny* that *dolus eventualis* could suffice to establish intention for the purposes of the particular provision at issue.

In addition to this, one can point to some notable differences between EU criminal law and EU quasi-criminal law. One difference – that will be returned to in the next sub-section – concerns the role of intention. Intention enjoys predominance over other fault elements in both criminal law and most quasi-criminal law areas. Its predominance is clearly strongest, however, in the field of EU criminal law, where

[170] CJEU *Afrasiaba et al* (n 168) paras 66–67. In his Opinion of 16 November 2011, C-72/11 *Generalbundesanwalt beim Bundesgerichtshof v Mohsen Afrasiaba et al* (EU:C:2011:737), AG Bot, contrarily, argues for a narrow interpretation of the concept of intention, which leaves no room for the notion of *dolus eventualis*.

[171] In the case of *Van der Ham* (n 177), the CJEU concluded that *dolus eventualis* is also encompassed by 'the concept of "intentional non-compliance" within the meaning of Article 67(1) of Regulation No 796/2004 and Article 23 of Regulation No 1975/2006' (para 37).

[172] The requisite magnitude or degree of seriousness of the chance of the relevant harm may vary from one Member State to another (see n 66 above). This topic is furthermore subject to doctrinal discussions and disputes in many legal systems; see Blomsma, *Mens Rea and Defences* (n 4) 104–12.

[173] This point will be briefly returned to towards the end of the next subsection. See Ten Voorde, 'Een autonome en uniforme uitleg' (n 126) 206 where it is argued that a possible additional reason for the rather broad interpretation of *dolus eventualis* in the *Afrasiaba* judgment may be the CJEU's wish to ensure that no 'gap' exists between the concepts of intention and negligence; furthermore, it could be speculated that the CJEU may have objections against generally binding the concept of negligence to unduly stringent evidentiary requirements, unless, of course, an aggravated form of negligence is at issue; this is the case where legislation makes explicit reference to such an aggravated form (eg the element referred to as 'serious negligence' in a number of Directives, some of which will be discussed in the next subsection).

intention is, so to speak, the 'default' mens rea requirement. A related difference may be seen in the fact that some provisions in EU quasi-criminal law instruments bearing on liability issues do not expressly refer to a fault requirement (whereas criminal law provisions typically do), so that the question may arise whether or not, for liability to be established, proof of a certain fault element is (nevertheless) necessary. The absence of fault elements is often grounded on considerations of effectivity and enforcement. An example of this is Article 2 of Directive 2003/6 which compelled the Member States to prohibit certain persons in possession of inside information from using that information, and to subject violations of this prohibition to administrative sanctions.[174] One of the questions raised in the well-known *Spector Photo Group* case was whether or not it must be proved, for liability to be incurred, that the inside information was used intentionally or deliberately.[175] The CJEU ruled that this was not the case:

> The fact that Article 2(1) of Directive 2003/6 does not expressly provide for a mental element can be explained, first, by the specific nature of insider dealing, which enables a *presumption* of that mental element once the constituent elements referred to in that provision are present … [and] second, by the purpose of the Directive, which … is to ensure the integrity of Community financial markets and to enhance investor confidence in those markets. The Community legislature opted for a preventive mechanism and for administrative sanctions for insider dealing, *the effectiveness of which would be weakened* if made subject to a *systematic analysis of the existence of a mental element.* … [O]nly if the prohibition on insider dealing allows infringements to be effectively sanctioned does it prove to be powerful and encourage compliance with the rules by all market actors on a lasting basis. The effective implementation of the prohibition on market transactions is thus based on a simple structure in which subjective grounds of defence are limited, not only to enable sanctions to be imposed but also to prevent effectively infringements of that prohibition (emphasis added).[176]

A similar issue was brought up in the case of *Van der Ham* that concerned an entirely different branch of quasi-criminal law: the EU's common agricultural policy.[177] Numerous measures aimed at supporting farmers have been adopted since the launch of this policy area in 1962. Mr and Mrs Van der Ham, owners of an agricultural undertaking in the Netherlands, were beneficiaries of two such support measures (that are financed by the European Agricultural Fund for Rural Development). They received income support as well as aid aimed at furthering environmentally-friendly farm

[174] Directive 2003/6/EC of 28 January 2003 of the European Parliament and the Council on insider dealing and market manipulation, [2003] OJ L 96/16; this Directive was later repealed by Regulation 596/2014/EU of the European Parliament and of the Council of 16 April 2014 on market abuse (market abuse regulation), [2014] L 173/1. See also subsection IV.C. below.

[175] CJEU *Spector Photo Group* (n 12).

[176] CJEU *Spector Photo Group* (n 12) paras 36–37. According to the CJEU, the presumption of intention does not violate the right to be presumed innocent enshrined in Art 6(2) ECHR, considering that the presumption of intention must always be open to rebuttal and that the rights of the defence must be guaranteed (paras 43–44). See Rankinen, 'Positive Fault Requirements' (n 54) 138–39; JAE Vervaele, *European Criminal Justice in the Post-Lisbon Area of Freedom, Security and Justice* (Naples, Editoriale Scientifica, 2014) 81–85; Van Kempen and Bemelmans, 'EU Protection of the Substantive Criminal Law Principles' (n 100) 257; Blomsma, *Mens Rea and Defences* (n 4) 208, 224 and 233.

[177] CJEU judgment of 27 February 2014, C-396/12 *Van der Ham and Van der Ham-Reijersen van Buuren v College van Gedeputeerde Staten van Zuid-Holland* (EU:C:2014:98).

management.[178] Beneficiaries of these types of support schemes are required to comply with a number of obligations related to various aspects of the agricultural practice. Pursuant to a Ministerial Decree (which transposed the relevant EU legislation), a failure to comply with these rules is 'punished' with a reduction of the received support by a certain percentage. In cases of intentional non-compliance, the support is reduced by twenty per cent. During an inspection on the Van der Ham premises, the Dutch authorities observed that a particular rule had not been observed. The rule in question was infringed as an immediate result of the conduct of a third party, an agricultural contractor. His failure to comply with the relevant obligation was attributed to Mr and Mrs Van der Ham, on whose behalf and under whose instructions the contractor had carried out his work.[179]

On top of this, the beneficiaries of agricultural aid were found to be liable for the *intentional* non-compliance with the relevant obligation; in consequence of this finding, their subsidy for environment-friendly farm management was reduced by twenty per cent. Pursuant to a provision in the aforementioned Ministerial Decree, intention should always be assessed in light of six listed criteria, some of which refer to fully objective matters of fact. In practice, this meant that intention could be established on the mere ground that one or more of the listed circumstances obtained in the case at hand. One of these circumstances is the existence of 'a long-established, settled policy', which played a pivotal role in the case of Mr and Mrs Van der Ham. The fact that the infringed rule was part of a long-established, settled policy sufficed to ground the finding of intention.

Inferring intention directly from an objective circumstance is in fact not much different from starting from a *presumption* of intention (as was at issue in the *Spector Photo Group* case). Yet, the CJEU concluded that Member States are at liberty to enact provisions that set criteria for establishing intention in relation to non-compliance with the relevant rules. The Court further stated that the adoption of a national provision that lends a high probative value to the criterion of 'the existence of a long-established, settled policy' is not precluded by EU law, on condition that the accused person has the possibility of adducing evidence to negate the inferred intention.[180] In conclusion: within areas of quasi-criminal law, mens rea elements are generally bound to less stringent requirements, and they are generally assessed in a more 'objectified' way, than is typically the case within criminal law.[181] And in view of instrumental considerations,[182] quasi-criminal law offences are occasionally even made subject to a 'strict' liability

[178] As introduced by Council Regulation 1698/2005 (n 147). The Regulation was repealed by Regulation 1305/2013 of the European Parliament and of the Council of 17 December 2013 on support for rural development by the European Agricultural Fund for Rural Development (EAFRD) and repealing Council Regulation (EC) No 1698/2005, [2013] OJ L 347/487.

[179] The CJEU allows this form of vicarious liability on the condition that it can be established that the beneficiary of aid 'acted intentionally or negligently as a result of the choice or the monitoring of the third party or the instructions given to him, irrespective of the intentional or negligent nature of the conduct of the third party'; CJEU *Van der Ham* (n 177) para 53.

[180] CJEU *Van der Ham* (n 177) paras 40–41.

[181] Which is not to deny that many national criminal law systems contain offences which lack a mens rea requirement altogether; see subsection II.C. above.

[182] See Franssen, 'EU Criminal Law and *Effet Utile*' (n 2).

regime in the sense that intention (or a different form of mens rea) may sometimes be presumed – provided, of course, that the presumption is rebuttable.[183]

C. Recklessness and 'Serious' Negligence: *Intertanko*

On 3 June 2008 the Grand Chamber of the CJEU delivered a preliminary ruling at the request of the (administrative) Queen's Bench Division of the High Court of Justice of England and Wales.[184] The judgment provides an interesting example of a case that evokes questions pertaining to the role of the culpability principle in matters that are dealt with in both international law and European (criminal) law. The claimants in the proceedings that gave rise to the reference for a preliminary ruling comprised a group of five organisations within the maritime shipping industry. They asked the High Court to review the legality of Directive 2005/35 on ship-source pollution in light of international law provisions.[185] The international norms in issue are primarily laid down in the International Convention for the Prevention of Pollution from Ships ('Marpol 73/78'), to which all the Member States are parties, but not the EU itself.[186] In addition, since the relevant standards in Marpol 73/78 are, at least to some extent, incorporated in the United Nations Convention on the Law of the Sea ('UNCLOS'),[187] this Convention also played a notable role in the proceedings.

Directive 2005/35 was negotiated in response to major oil pollution disasters, such as the sinking of the *Prestige* tanker off the coast of Galicia in 2002. It was generally recognised that it was urgent to ensure an appropriate implementation and enforcement of the applicable international rules for the prevention and control of vessel-source pollution. The European Commission noted that

> the implementation of Marpol 73/78 shows discrepancies among Member States and there is thus a need to harmonise its implementation at Community level; in particular, the practices of Member States relating to the imposition of penalties for discharges of polluting substances from ships differ significantly.[188]

In order to remedy this, Article 4 of the Directive obligates Member States to ensure that ship-source discharges of polluting substances into certain maritime areas are 'regarded as infringements if committed with intent, recklessly or by serious negligence'.

[183] See n 56 and accompanying text above. The possibility of rebutting the presumption of culpability is the subject of section V below.

[184] CJEU 3 June 2008, C-308/06 *Intertanko et al v Secretary of State for Transport* (EU:C:2008:312).

[185] Directive 2005/35/EC of the European Parliament and of the Council of 7 September 2005 on ship-source pollution and on the introduction of penalties for infringements, [2005] OJ L 255, 11.

[186] The International Convention for the Prevention of Pollution from Ships, signed in London on 2 November 1973, as supplemented by the Protocol of 17 February 1978.

[187] United Nations Convention on the Law of the Sea, signed in Montego Bay on 10 December 1982, entered into force on 17 November 1994. The Convention was approved on behalf of the EC by Council Decision 98/392/EC of 23 March 1998, [1998] OJ L 179/1.

[188] Explanatory Memorandum, Proposal for a Directive of the European Parliament and of the Council on ship-source pollution and on the introduction of sanctions, including criminal sanctions, for pollution offences, COM(2003) 92 final, [2004] OJ C 92E/77 (recital 3).

Article 5 adds that an infringement does not exist when a discharge of polluting substances satisfies certain conditions mentioned in Annex I and Annex II to Marpol 73/78. And where infringements do exist, Article 8 compels Member States to ensure that these are subject to 'effective, proportionate and dissuasive penalties, which may include criminal or administrative penalties'. However, the Directive was amended in 2009 (that is, after the preliminary ruling in the *Intertanko* case) in order, inter alia, to introduce the requirement that the 'infringement' under the Directive is considered a *criminal* offence.[189]

The contents of Articles 4 and 5 of Directive 2005/35 gave rise to the main questions that were at issue in the *Intertanko* case. With respect to the indication of what actions and whose actions constitute an 'infringement' according to these Articles, it appeared that the Directive does not neatly conform to the relevant international norms but expands their scope in two significant respects. First, whereas Marpol 73/78 limits liability in case of accidental discharges of polluting substances to the shipowner and the master, the Directive stipulates that penalties are to be applicable also to the owner of the cargo, the classification society or any other person involved. Second, the Directive attaches the possibility of imposing a penalty at a (seemingly) lower mens rea threshold. Whereas Marpol 73/78 requires that one 'acted either with intent to cause damage, or recklessly and with knowledge that damage would probably occur', the Directive sets the lower limit of the standard for liability to 'serious negligence'. According to the claimants in the *Intertanko* case, unsurprisingly, Articles 4 and 5 of Directive 2005/35 do not comply with the relevant rules under international law and should therefore be considered invalid.

A complicating factor was the fact that the liability scheme under the Directive and the international rules vary somewhat depending on whether discharges of polluting substances take place in the territorial seas of the Member States or in waters beyond the territorial seas. What complicated matters even further was the interplay between international and European law. Norms that are part of international treaties have primacy over European legal instruments, provided that the EU is bound by these norms. Further, a European legal instrument may be examined in light of an international treaty only if the nature and broad logic of the treaty in question do not preclude this and the treaty's provisions are sufficiently operational (that is, unconditional and sufficiently precise as regards their content). It therefore had to be decided whether the relevant provisions from Marpol 73/78 and UNCLOS fulfil these conditions.

Advocate General Juliane Kokott concludes in her Opinion that although all Member States are party to Marpol 73/78, the European Community (EC; now the EU)

[189] Directive 2009/123/EC of the European Parliament and of the Council of 21 October 2009 amending Directive 2005/35/EC on ship-source pollution and on the introduction of penalties for infringements, [2009] OJ L 280/52. The Directive initially made reference to Council Framework Decision 2005/667/JHA of 12 July 2005 to strengthen the criminal-law framework for the enforcement of the law against ship-source pollution, [2005] OJ L 255/164. In CJEU 23 October 2007, C-440/05 *Commission v Council* (EU:C:2007:625), the Framework Decision was annulled because it was found to violate Art 47 of the Treaty on European Union (TEU). See V Mitsilegas, M Fitzmaurice and E Fasoli, 'The Relationship between EU Criminal Law and Environmental Law' in V Mitsilegas, M Bergström and Th Konstadinides (eds), *Research Handbook on EU Criminal Law* (Cheltenham, Edward Elgar Publishing, 2016) 272–93, 279–83.

is not itself bound by it.[190] The same conclusion is later reached by the CJEU. With regard to UNCLOS, however, the Advocate General and the CJEU arrive at opposing conclusions. According to Advocate General Kokott, the EC/EU is bound by UNCLOS; moreover, she concludes that the nature and broad logic of this Convention do not preclude an examination of Directive 2005/35 in light of the Convention, and that the provisions in this Convention – read in conjunction with the relevant provisions in Marpol 73/78 – are sufficiently clear and unconditional.[191] The CJEU disagrees with this finding, as will be seen later on. The Advocate General then goes on to examine whether the Directive complies with the provisions of UNCLOS and Marpol 73/78. She first considers the alleged extension under the Directive of liability for polluting discharges beyond the territorial seas to persons other than the master and owner. Kokott submits – somewhat sweepingly[192] – that the relevant provisions in Marpol 73/78 refer to the master and owner merely 'by way of example', and that they therefore do not preclude liability of other persons, under the same conditions.[193]

More relevant for the purposes of this chapter is how the Advocate General subsequently examines whether and to what extent the personal liability standard employed in Article 4 of the Directive (requiring infringements to be committed 'with intent, recklessly or by serious negligence') is in conformity with the standard under Marpol 73/78 (requiring that one 'acted either with intent to cause damage, or recklessly and with knowledge that damage would probably occur'). For this examination a distinction is made between discharges that take place in the territorial seas of the Member States and discharges that take place beyond these areas (that is, in international straits, in the exclusive economic zone, or on the high seas). This is done because, according to the Advocate General, different international rules apply to infringements depending on whether they take place in or beyond territorial seas. As regards the territorial seas, the Advocate General argues that UNCLOS does not incorporate liability standards from Marpol 73/78. The international rules that cover the territorial seas are more lenient and permit, according to the Advocate General, more room for European legislation to provide for stricter liability conditions than the international standards which are applicable in straits, in the exclusive economic zone and on the high seas.[194]

Insofar as Article 4 of Directive 2005/35 applies to discharges of polluting substances *beyond* territorial waters, the Advocate General contends that its standard of liability may not be stricter than the standard provided for in Marpol 73/78. This implies, first, that the term 'recklessly' in Article 4 must be interpreted in conformity with the equivalent standard in Marpol 73/78, which means that, for recklessness to exist, it is

[190] Opinion of 20 November 2007, C-308/06 *Intertanko et al v Secretary of State for Transport* (EU:C:2007:689) paras 34–79.

[191] See P Eeckhout, 'Case C-308/06, *The Queen on the application of Intertanko and Others v Secretary of State for Transport*, judgment of the Court of Justice (Grand Chamber) of 3 June 2008, nyr' (2009) 46(6) *Common Market Law Review* 2041; R Pereira, 'On the Legality of the Ship-Source Pollution 2005/35/EC Directive – The Intertanko Case and Selected Others' (2008) 17(6) *European Energy and Environmental Law Review* 372.

[192] See Eeckhout, 'Case C-308/06' (n 191) 2047: 'Tongue in cheek, one could say that international law is interpreted in conformity with EC law. A most convenient way of course to avoid breach of international obligations.'

[193] Opinion of AG Kokott (n 190) para 93.

[194] See the Opinion of AG Kokott (n 190) paras 113–138.

not enough that the perpetrator *ought* to have been aware of the risk that, as a result of his actions, damage would probably occur. What needs to be established is that he in fact *acted with knowledge* of this risk.[195] Secondly, the term 'serious negligence' in Article 4 of the Directive equally needs to be interpreted restrictively so as to conform to the lower standard provided for in Marpol 73/78. According to Advocate General Kokott, this implies that the concept of serious negligence present in the Directive could be interpreted in line with the German concept of *bewusste große Fahrlässigkeit* and could hence be taken to mean exactly 'recklessness in the knowledge that damage will probably occur'.[196] This narrow interpretation would conveniently avoid conflict between the Directive and international law as embodied in Marpol 73/78.[197]

However, insofar as Article 4 of the Directive applies to discharges of polluting substances *within* the territorial waters of the Member States, the Advocate General contends that its standard of liability may be stricter than the standard provided for in Marpol 73/78. This means that the phrase 'serious negligence' may be construed more broadly and be taken to refer to 'a serious breach of duties of care without, however, any need for knowledge that damage is probable'.[198] Finally, it is pointed out by Advocate General Kokott that this interpretation of the concept of serious negligence does not infringe the principle of legal certainty, inter alia, because the actual criminal law provisions are adopted by the Member States in implementation of the Directive, and further case law may gradually clarify the concept of serious negligence, which is permissible under ECtHR case law.[199]

As was mentioned before, the CJEU takes another route. It does not share Advocate General Kokott's conclusion that the legality of Directive 2005/35 is susceptible to an examination in light of the relevant provisions in Marpol 73/78 that have been incorporated in UNCLOS. The CJEU, by contrast, concludes that the EC/EU is bound by UNCLOS but that its nature and broad logic preclude the examination of the validity of Directive 2005/35 in light of its provisions, because 'UNCLOS does not establish rules intended to apply directly and immediately to individuals and to confer upon them rights or freedoms capable of being relied upon against States'.[200] This conclusion enables the Court to circumvent the whole issue of whether or not Directive 2005/35

[195] Opinion of AG Kokott (n 190) paras 97–101. In this connection, the AG makes reference (in para 109) to a survey conducted by the Research and Documentation Service at the CJEU, which shows that the concept of recklessness, thus defined, is treated in the legal systems of many Member States as a form of the 'serious negligence' which Directive 2005/35 (n 185) lays down as a standard for liability.

[196] Opinion of AG Kokott (n 190) para 109.

[197] Opinion of AG Kokott (n 190) paras 110–112.

[198] Opinion of AG Kokott (n 190) para 116. See Eeckhout, 'Case C-308/06' (n 191) 2047: 'Effectively, therefore, Kokott proposes that one and the same concept in Article 4 of the Directive be interpreted differently, depending on whether it is applied to acts of pollution in the territorial sea, or beyond that sea.'

[199] Opinion of AG Kokott (n 190) paras 144–149. According to established case law of the ECtHR, Art 7 ECHR does not rule out gradual clarification by means of judicial interpretation. See eg ECtHR 22 November 1995, *CR v the United Kingdom* (App No 20190/92) [1995] ECHR 51: 'However clearly drafted a legal provision may be, in any system of law, including criminal law, there is an inevitable element of judicial interpretation. There will always be a need for elucidation of doubtful points and for adaptation to changing circumstances. … Article 7 of the Convention cannot be read as outlawing the gradual clarification of the rules of criminal liability through judicial interpretation from case to case, provided that the resultant development is consistent with the essence of the offence and could reasonably be foreseen.'

[200] CJEU *Intertanko et al* (n 184) para 64.

conforms to the rules of international law that were invoked by the claimants in the proceedings giving rise to the request for a preliminary ruling in the case at hand. As a consequence of this, the CJEU makes no comments on the alleged extension under the Directive of liability for polluting discharges beyond the territorial seas to persons other than the master and owner; nor does it assess how the concepts of recklessness and serious negligence as employed in Article 4 of the Directive relate to the relevant rules under international law. The only question then left for the CJEU to answer is the fourth and last question that the High Court of Justice of England and Wales referred for a preliminary ruling: 'Does the use of the phrase "serious negligence" in Article 4 of the Directive infringe the principle of legal certainty, and if so, is Article 4 invalid to that extent?'.

The CJEU acknowledges that Articles 4 and 8 of the Directive oblige Member States 'to punish ship-source discharges of polluting substances if committed "with intent, recklessly or by serious negligence", without defining those concepts'.[201] However, the CJEU goes on to note that these concepts 'correspond to tests for the incurring of liability which are to apply to an indeterminate number of situations' and not to 'specific conduct capable of being set out in detail in a legislative measure', and that these concepts 'are fully integrated into, and used in, the Member States' respective legal systems'.[202] Subsequently, and interestingly,[203] the CJEU provides a rather detailed substantive description of the fault element of 'serious negligence' within the meaning of Article 4 of the Directive. According to the CJEU, the concept of negligence is used in all Member States to refer to 'an unintentional act or omission by which the person responsible breaches his duty of care', and the concept of 'serious' negligence in many national legal systems can only refer to a 'patent' breach of such a duty of care.[204] 'Serious negligence' within the meaning of Article 4 of the Directive must therefore

> be understood as entailing an unintentional act or omission by which the person responsible commits a patent breach of the duty of care which he should have and could have complied with in view of his attributes, knowledge, abilities and individual situation.[205]

The CJEU concludes that no breach of the principle of legal certainty exists, since the Directive in any event needs to be transposed into national law, meaning that the actual definition of the infringements and the applicable penalties 'are those which result from the rules laid down by the Member States'.[206] These rules differ across the Member States. One main difference was extensively discussed in subsection II.C.

[201] CJEU *Intertanko et al* (n 184) para 72.

[202] CJEU *Intertanko et al* (n 184) paras 73–74.

[203] See Rankinen, 'Positive Fault Requirements' (n 54) 132.

[204] CJEU *Intertanko et al* (n 184) paras 75–76.

[205] CJEU *Intertanko et al* (n 184) para 77. In this passage one clearly recognises the notion that was referred to as *Garantenstellung* in subsection II.C. above. Cp ECtHR [GC] 15 November 1996, *Cantoni v France* (App No 17862/91), [1996] ECHR 52, para 35: 'The Court recalls that the scope of the notion of foreseeability depends to a considerable degree on the content of the text in issue, the field it is designed to cover and the number and status of those to whom it is addressed ... A law may still satisfy the requirement of foreseeability even if the person concerned has to take appropriate legal advice to assess, to a degree that is reasonable in the circumstances, the consequences which a given action may entail ... This is particularly true in relation to persons carrying on a professional activity, who are used to having to proceed with a high degree of caution when pursuing their occupation. They can on this account be expected to take special care in assessing the risks that such activity entails.' Also AG Kokott refers to these notions in paras 147–149 of her Opinion (n 190).

[206] CJEU *Intertanko et al* (n 184) para 78.

above: whereas English criminal law distinguishes between different mens rea states according to a tripartite framework, continental criminal law systems use a bipartite framework in which the notion of *dolus eventualis* marks the lower limit of the concept of intention. As a consequence, the concept of intention is typically considerably broader in continental criminal law systems than in the Anglo-American systems. In English criminal law, recklessness fulfils a function similar to that of *dolus eventualis*, but it occupies a position between intention and negligence as a separate and independent mens rea element.

The fact that the offence description in Article 4 of Directive 2005/35 explicitly mentions recklessness in addition to intention and 'serious' negligence, then, might strike one as inconsequential, considering that it was concluded in the previous subsection that *dolus eventualis* is a recognised form of intention in EU criminal law.[207] However, the fact that the EU legislature frequently includes the complete triplet of intention, recklessness and (serious) negligence in definitions of infringements, is quite understandable – and opportune – in light of the CJEU's statement, cited above, that EU Directives need to be transposed into national law. Including all three fault elements may serve to facilitate a uniform transposition of the relevant provisions into differing domestic law systems, irrespective of whether these distinguish between two or three main mens rea elements: legal systems adhering to the bipartite classification can simply refrain from incorporating recklessness as a separate element, since it may be assumed that the concept of *dolus eventualis* sufficiently[208] 'covers' the mental state typically referred to as recklessness in legal systems that adhere to the tripartite framework.[209]

Member States appear thus to enjoy some freedom in transposing EU legislation into national law.[210] Under Directive 2005/35, the Member States were furthermore free to subject the offence of ship-source discharges of polluting substances to either a criminal or an administrative liability regime. One year after the CJEU's judgment in

[207] See paras 66–67 in CJEU *Afrasiaba et al* (n 168) cited in subsection IV.B. above.

[208] As was seen in subsection II.C. above, the concepts of recklessness and *dolus eventualis* are certainly not completely identical in substance. Moreover, legal orders that employ the same basic (bipartite or tripartite) framework may still interpret certain manifestations of mens rea elements somewhat varyingly; see n 58 above.

[209] It should be noted that it can be very difficult, if not impossible, to secure a more or less equal and uniform implementation of EU legislation in the different Member States in cases where a so-called 'dual-track' approach is adopted, ie, an approach in which criminal sanctions apply to an infringement when committed intentionally, and administrative penalties apply when this infringement is committed recklessly or negligently. One and the same act, performed with an identical state of mind, may then be found to constitute an infringement committed intentionally (and hence punishable with a criminal sanction) in one country, and be found to constitute an infringement committed with recklessness (and hence subject to the imposition of an administrative penalty) in another country. However, the fact that Member States apply different liability regimes with regard to offences stemming from EU law is a rather 'natural' phenomenon: as will be seen later on, the EU legislature often only provides for minimum rules for criminalisation, and Member States are free to adopt more stringent criminal law rules.

[210] But not necessarily very much, of course. Art 4 of Directive 2005/35 (n 185), for instance, requires at least 'serious negligence'. And as was seen, the CJEU defined this concept in the *Intertanko* case in terms of 'patent' breaches of the relevant duty to care. This seems to imply that gross negligence (*culpa lata*) is required and, consequently, that minor negligence (*culpa levissima*) will not suffice (cp n 74 on applicable standards for negligence in Belgian and English criminal law).

the *Intertanko* case, this discretionary space was removed. As was mentioned above, Directive 2005/35 was amended by Directive 2009/123 which left the Member States with no other option than to make the offence, under the conditions specified in the Directive, subject to criminal sanctions.[211] The CJEU's ruling in the *Intertanko* case nevertheless remains relevant and important. For one thing, the 2009 Directive – like its predecessor – defines polluting ship-source discharges as infringements 'if committed with intent, recklessly or with serious negligence', so that the CJEU's interpretation of the concept of serious negligence in the *Intertanko* case seems valid still.

And on a far more general note, it seems reasonable to submit that the succession of Directive 2005/35 by Directive 2009/123 testifies to the EU legislature's increased, and still increasing, 'appetite for criminal law'.[212] More than that, Directive 2009/123 may even be seen as a rather *rapacious* manifestation of this appetite, considering that it sets the mens rea threshold relatively low: 'serious negligence' suffices to incur criminal liability. Normally, however, the EU legislature 'only' requires Member States to subject *intentional* misconduct to criminal sanctions. A notable example can be found in the Market Abuse Directive and the Market Abuse Regulation, both of 2014, introducing criminal sanctions against insider dealing and market manipulation.[213] Prior to the adoption of these legislative acts, the EU's framework for market abuse still relied on an administrative enforcement regime. The mentioned Directive and Regulation replaced this framework with a 'dual-track' approach consisting of a combination of an administrative and a criminal liability regime.

Article 30, paragraph 2 of Regulation 596/2014 requires Member States to invest the competent national authorities with the power to impose a large number of differing administrative measures, including several quasi-criminal sanctions.[214] The provisions in Regulation 596/2014 set minimum requirements, which is to say that Member States may also adopt criminal sanctions instead of the mentioned administrative sanctions, if they so desire.[215] With respect to some offences, however, the Member States *must* resort to a criminal liability regime as a means to enforce the EU's market abuse rules. Pursuant to Directive 2014/57, Member States are obliged to apply criminal sanctions to the offences of insider dealing, unlawful disclosure of information, and market manipulation, 'at least in serious cases and when committed intentionally'.[216] The Directive provides for, again, minimum rules, so that Member States are free to subject market abuse to more stringent criminal law rules; for example, they may

[211] See n 189.

[212] Franssen, 'EU Criminal Law and *Effet Utile*' (n 2) 92; Mitsilegas, Fitzmaurice and Fasoli, 'The Relationship between EU Criminal Law and Environmental Law' (n 189) 288–91.

[213] Directive 2014/57/EU of the European Parliament and of the Council on criminal sanctions for market abuse of 16 April 2014, [2014] OJ L 173/179 12 June 2014; Regulation 596/2014 (n 174). See MJJP Luchtman and JAE Vervaele, 'Enforcing the Market Abuse Regime: Towards an Integrated Model of Criminal and Administrative Law Enforcement in the European Union' (2014) 5(2) *New Journal of European Criminal Law* 202.

[214] Such as the disgorgement of profits gained or losses avoided and pecuniary sanctions. See Luchtman and Vervaele, 'Enforcing the Market Abuse Regime' (n 213); Franssen, 'EU Criminal Law and *Effet Utile*' (n 2) 94.

[215] See Art 30(1) Regulation 596/2014 (n 213). This freedom for Member States to choose between administrative and criminal sanctions already existed under the former EU framework for market abuse.

[216] See Arts 3(1), 4(1) and 5(1) of Directive 2014/57 (n 213). Art 7 formulates minimum rules for the maximum term of prison sentences for natural persons. The obligation to impose criminal sanctions does not exist with regard to legal entities; see Arts 8 and 9 and see subsections III.A. and III.C. above.

'provide that market manipulation committed recklessly or by serious negligence constitutes a criminal offence'.[217]

The foregoing illustrates a notable difference between EU criminal law and EU quasi-criminal law.[218] When the EU obliges Member States to subject certain behaviour to criminal sanctions, the obligation nearly always concerns intentional manifestations of that behaviour only. Criminalisation of reckless and/or seriously negligent behaviour, by implication, is only seldom required. Liability for unintentional behaviour is much more common in areas of punitive administrative law; and in some of these areas of quasi-criminal law, liability may even extend to 'mere' or 'ordinary' negligence, whereas at least *serious* negligence is required in EU criminal law.[219] And lastly, it was seen in the previous subsection that for some quasi-criminal offences the requisite mens rea element may rather easily be inferred from certain objective criteria, or may even be *presumed* to be fulfilled (provided, that is, that the presumption is open to rebuttal).

V. Third Dimension: Exculpatory Defences

A. Introduction: Blameworthiness and the Defeasible Concept of Culpability

The present section concentrates on a more fundamental layer of meaning within the labyrinthine notion of guilt: the concept of personal blameworthiness. On this deeper level, guilt is intimately connected with a subjective default or personal failure in relation to a certain aim or standard, which is why Antoine Mooij speaks of 'guilt by default' (*ἁμαρτία*; *culpa*) in this connection.[220] Personal blameworthiness concerns neither a person's acting or causing *as such* (which was the subject of section III.), nor the quality of the mental state that accompanied the acting or causing (the subject of section IV.), even though both of these aspects of culpability are indeed presupposed. Personal blameworthiness is primarily concerned, instead, with the ability to *avoid* a failure to meet a certain standard, such as a criminally (or otherwise legally) enforced behavioural standard. As was seen in section II, the actus reus of an offence and the requisite mens rea or fault element constitute necessary but not sufficient conditions for liability in criminal law. Proof of these elements merely occasions the conclusion that the defendant prima facie committed an offence. The defendant is then presumed to be criminally liable.

This presumption is belied, however, in the exceptional cases where the defendant convincingly argues (or where the court ex officio finds) that a certain exculpatory defence applies. Exculpatory defences concern exceptional circumstances that warrant the conclusion that the defendant cannot reasonably be blamed for not having *avoided*

[217] Recital 21 of the Preamble to Directive 2014/45 (n 213).
[218] The other distinctive feature being the possibility in criminal law of imposing a prison sentence; see Franssen, 'EU Criminal Law and *Effet Utile*' (n 2) 95–96.
[219] See Rankinen 'Positive Fault Requirements' (n 54) 133–35.
[220] See subsection II.B. above.

the act of criminal wrongdoing.[221] Contrary to other conditions for criminal culpability, the condition of personal blameworthiness manifests only relatively rarely; and when it does, it does so 'negatively', that is, by way of a defence put forward with the aim of demonstrating its *absence*. If successful, such a defence nullifies the defendant's culpability and, consequently, precludes the imputation of criminal liability. On account of this, criminal culpability should be understood as the sort of phenomenon for which HLA Hart coined the term 'defeasible concept': even though all positive conditions for its existence are satisfied, this existence may still be altogether refuted, defeated, if certain exceptional circumstances obtain.[222]

It is worth stressing that the concept of personal blameworthiness – in spite of the earlier qualifications that rather attest to its exceptional status – represents a highly important dimension of the principle of individual culpability. Since it entails, in essence, a prohibition on inflicting a criminal penalty when it cannot reasonably be assumed that the defendant could have avoided his or her wrongful action, this dimension can even be said to lie at the very heart of the Latin adage *nulla poena sine culpa*. The indispensability of personal blameworthiness as a condition that curtails (albeit 'negatively') criminal liability, is all the more obvious in view of what has been discussed in the preceding sections of this chapter. It was seen, not only that the general part of substantive EU criminal law can still at best be said to have a fragmentary and nascent character, but also that the distinctions drawn in EU and national legislation between criminal law proper, on the one hand, and areas of punitive administrative law, on the other, are often rather artificial and arbitrary.[223] And especially in these areas of quasi-criminal law, conditions for establishing culpability and liability for infringements tend to be less strict.[224]

Although it is true that the principle of individual culpability is recognised, by and large, in areas of quasi-criminal law, its efficacy in these areas is generally weaker than in traditional criminal law. For this reason, it seems especially pertinent to look more closely into the role of personal blameworthiness as a constraining condition for

[221] The exculpatory defence of an unavoidable mistake of law (discussed in subsection V.C. below) cancels – as all exculpatory defences do – the presumption of personal blameworthiness. Sometimes, however, this defence has an import for the finding of intention or negligence. In cases where the requisite fault element is connected with a normative offence element, that is, an element that expresses an aspect of the prohibited conduct's wrongfulness, an unavoidable mistake with regard to that aspect may preclude the proof of the fault requirement. See Blomsma, 'Fault Elements in EU Criminal Law' (n 146) 155.

[222] See HLA Hart, 'The Ascription of Responsibility and Rights' (1948–49) 49 *Proceedings of the Aristotelian Society (New Series)* 171, 174–76. See also L Duarte d'Almeida, *Allowing for Exceptions. A Theory of Defences and Defeasibility in Law* (Oxford, Oxford University Press, 2015); cp Packer, *The Limits of the Criminal Sanction* (n 19) 105–08; Nijboer, 'Schuldbegrip en schuldbeginsel' (n 27) 372–73.

[223] Or motivated by primarily instrumental considerations. See Franssen, 'EU Criminal Law and *Effet Utile*' (n 2); E Herlin-Karnell, 'Is Administrative Law Still Relevant? How the Battle of Sanctions Has Shaped EU Criminal Law' in V Mitsilegas, M Bergström and Th Konstadinides (eds), *Research Handbook on EU Criminal Law* (Cheltenham, Edward Elgar Publishing, 2016) 233–48.

[224] As was seen, this is partly a consequence of the fact that such offences are often, in effect, primarily addressed to legal entities (in whose respect constructions of vicarious liability are generally more readily used; see subsections III.A. and C.) and/or to professional agents operating on a certain market (to whom generally higher standards of due diligence apply; cp ECtHR *Cantoni v France* (n 205); and see subsections II.C. and IV.C.), and the fact that these offences often have relatively low evidentiary standards for mens rea requirements, or even lack a mens rea requirement (see subsections IV.B. and C.).

liability for quasi-criminal offences.[225] This will be done in the remainder of the present section. More specifically, the discussion in the following pages will focus on two types of generally recognised exculpatory defences and on two areas of European quasi-criminal law. Section V.B. discusses the role of 'force majeure' or 'duress of circumstances' (as it is most commonly referred to in English criminal law)[226] within the sphere of agricultural EU regulations that are generally enforced through administrative law. Section V.C. focuses on the role of the exculpatory defence of an unavoidable and hence excusable mistake of law (or *error iuris*) within EU competition law.

B. Force Majeure in the Context of Agricultural Aid: *Käserei Champignon Hofmeister*

The concept of 'force majeure' is widely recognised as a defence, also in areas other than criminal law. Provisions in EU legislation occasionally make reference to this concept as a valid reason for negating liability for the infringement of a non-criminal nature. An example of such a provision was at issue in a preliminary ruling by the CJEU of 11 July 2002 that concerned a specific EU agricultural aid scheme.[227] In 1996, Käserei Champignon Hofmeister GmbH and Co KG (KCH) – a long-established German trading company that sells cheese products within Germany and internationally – exported a quantity of a certain cheese product. It did so under cover of an export declaration form, on which the product was assigned to a specific number corresponding to a certain category of agricultural products that was listed on a so-called 'Common Agricultural Policy Goods List'. Pursuant to legislation under the EU's common agricultural policy, the export of this specific category of goods gave rise to entitlement to an export refund. Prior to exporting the goods, KCH requested and received this refund as an advance payment (of approximately 30,000 DM – the currency of Germany at the time) from the Hamburg-Jonas Principal Customs Office (Hauptzollamt Hamburg-Jonas).

[225] On the recognition of exculpatory defences in European criminal law, see generally Blomsma, *Mens Rea and Defences* (n 4) 419–506; Klip, *European Criminal Law* (n 2) 229–31. For the role of personal blameworthiness as a condition for liability in international criminal law, see M Krabbe, *Excusable Evil. An Analysis of Complete Defenses in International Criminal Law* (Cambridge, Intersentia, 2014); cp MI Francisco Francisco, *Aspects of Implementing the Culpability Principle both under International and National Criminal Law* (Nijmegen, Wolf Legal Publishers, 2004).

[226] In continental systems of criminal law, duress is generally considered as an exculpatory defence (as opposed to the justificatory defence of necessity). This is also the view taken in the present chapter. It must be noted, however, that in English and American criminal law, there is a long-standing discussion on the issue of whether duress should be classified as an exculpatory, a justificatory, or even a *sui generis* defence. See Fletcher, 'The Individualization of Excusing Conditions' (n 53); Simester et al, *Criminal Law* (n 15) 717, 799–814; Norrie, *Crime, Reason and History* (n 31) 231–33; Horder, *Excusing Crime* (n 53) 48–52, 63–68. This discussion should be seen in light of the fact that the doctrinal distinction, typical of continental criminal law, between justifications (negating wrongfulness) and excuses (negating blameworthiness) is less firmly rooted (or less rigidly applied) in the Anglo-American criminal law systems. See subsection II.C. above.

[227] CJEU C-210/00 *Käserei Champignon Hofmeister GmbH and Co KG v Hauptzollamt Hamburg-Jonas* (EU:C:2002:440). See for another example CJEU 18 December 2007, C-314/06 *Société Pipeline Méditerranée et Rhône v Administration des douanes et droits indirects and Direction nationale du renseignement et des enquêtes douanières* (EU:C:2007:817).

However, at the time of the export a sample of the exported goods was examined by the customs authorities. The examined sample appeared to contain the ingredient of vegetable fat, on account of which the authorities concluded that the shipped products belonged to a category of agricultural goods with respect to which no export refund could be obtained.

This result implied that the goods were wrongly specified on the export declaration form and that the export refund was 'unduly received' by KCH. Pursuant to Article 7, paragraph 1 of Regulation 1222/94,[228] the Hauptzollamt thereupon demanded the return of the amount of the unduly granted export refund, increased by 15 per cent. In addition, the Hauptzollamt ordered KCH to pay a penalty on the basis of Article 11, paragraph 1, point (a) of Regulation 3665/87.[229] KCH challenged this penalty before the Finance Court (Finanzgericht). KCH claimed that it was not aware, nor could have been aware, of the fact that the shipped products contained the said ingredient when it applied for the export refund. It found out only afterwards – having inquired with the supplying manufacturing company – that the responsible production line manager had erroneously added vegetable fat to the product on his own initiative (for the purpose of improving the product's taste). KCH argued that neither the management of the manufacturing company nor that of KCH could have anticipated such a mistake. KCH submitted that it could only have established this mistake by carrying out checks at the undertaking in which the goods were manufactured.

The Finanzgericht rejected KCH's arguments, subsequent to which the case was submitted to the German Federal Finance Court (Bundesfinanzhof). Before the Bundesfinanzhof, KCH argued, principally, that the provision pursuant to which the Hauptzollamt imposed the contested penalty, contravenes the principle of *nulla poena sine culpa* and should therefore be declared invalid. Alternatively, KCH argued that the imposed penalty was unjustified because KCH could not be blamed for listing incorrect data in the export refund application, considering that it had acted in a situation of 'force majeure' within the meaning of Article 11, paragraph 1, subparagraph 3 of Regulation 3665/87.[230] Although the Bundesfinanzhof made clear that it did not share KCH's views, it decided to stay the proceedings in order to submit two questions to the CJEU for a preliminary ruling. The first question concerned the compatibility of Article 11, paragraph 1 of the aforementioned Regulation with, inter alia, the principle of *nulla poena sine culpa* insofar the provision 'provides for a penalty even where,

[228] Commission Regulation 1222/94/EC of 30 May 1994 laying down common detailed rules for the application of the system of granting export refunds on certain agricultural products exported in the form of goods not covered by Annex II to the Treaty, and the criteria for fixing the amount of such refunds, [1994] L 136/5.

[229] Commission Regulation 3665/87/EEC of 27 November 1987 laying down common detailed rules for the application of the system of export refunds on agricultural products, [1987] OJ L 351/1. This Regulation was amended by Commission Regulation 2945/94/EC of 2 December 1994 amending Regulation (EEC) No 3665/87 laying down common detailed rules for the application of the system of export refunds on agricultural products, as regards the recovery of amounts unduly paid and sanctions, [1994] OJ L 310/57. Art 11(1) of Regulation 3665/87 at the material time stated: 'Where it has been found that an exporter, with a view to the granting of an export refund, has requested a refund in excess of that applicable, the refund due for the relevant exportation shall be the refund applicable to the actual exportation reduced by an amount equivalent to: (a) half the difference between the refund requested and the refund applicable to the actual exportation; (b) … Where the reduction referred to under (a) or (b) results in a negative amount, the exporter shall pay that negative amount'.

[230] Stating: 'The sanction referred to under (a) shall not apply: in the case of *force majeure* …'.

through no fault of his own, an exporter has applied for an export refund exceeding that applicable'.[231] The second question concerned the interpretation of the concept of force majeure as referred to in the mentioned Regulation.

In answer to the first question, the CJEU rules, first of all, that the sanction imposed on KCH by the Hauptzollamt is of an administrative and not of a criminal nature. The sanction must be seen in the context of the rules under the common agricultural policy that provide for a subsidy scheme in the form of export refunds. The sanctions mentioned in Article 11, paragraph 1 of Regulation 3665/87 serve the primary purpose of preventing any (fraudulent or other) irregularities that prejudice the common policy's budget and general aims, by encouraging exporters to comply with the relevant rules.[232] Moreover, these rules are addressed to traders or exporters who voluntarily choose to benefit from the agricultural aid scheme and who consequently also voluntarily submit to its different requirements and to the penalties that may be imposed when these are not observed.[233] In view of these considerations, the Court concludes – as did Advocate General Christine Stix-Hackl in her Opinion[234] – that the principle of *nulla poena sine culpa* does not apply to the sanction that was inflicted on KCH in the case at hand.[235]

The Court then moves on to the second question referred to it by the Bundesfinanzhof: may an exporter who – in good faith and as a result of inaccurate data supplied by a contracted manufacturing company – enters false information into an export refund application, be said to do so in a situation of 'force majeure' within the meaning of Regulation 3665/87, if the exporter has no means of ascertaining the accurateness of the data supplied, or at least no other means than performing checks at the undertaking in which the goods were manufactured? With regard to this question, the CJEU first calls to mind that, in conformity with earlier judgments, the concept of force majeure within the context of EU regulations under the common agricultural policy must be taken to refer to 'abnormal and unforeseeable circumstances beyond the control of the trader concerned, whose consequences could not have been avoided in spite of the exercise of all due care'.[236] It is furthermore recalled that,

> [e]ven if the fault or error committed by the contracting partner is apt to constitute a circumstance beyond the control of the exporter, they are none the less an ordinary commercial risk and cannot be considered to be unforeseeable in the context of commercial transactions. The exporter is fully at liberty to select his trading partners and it is up to him to take the

[231] See CJEU *Käserei Champignon Hofmeister* (n 227) para 25.

[232] CJEU *Käserei Champignon Hofmeister* (n 227) paras 36–40. See also the Opinion of AG Stix-Hackl of 27 November 2001, C-210/00 *Käserei Champignon Hofmeister GmbH and Co KG v Hauptzollamt Hamburg-Jonas* (EU:C:2001:645) paras 31–36, where it is also stressed that the punitive aspect of the sanction is relatively unimportant, as it does not express any 'social disapproval'. See also Blomsma, *Mens Rea and Defences* (n 4) 24.

[233] CJEU *Käserei Champignon Hofmeister* (n 227) paras 41–42.

[234] Opinion of AG Stix-Hackl (n 232) paras 27–59.

[235] CJEU *Käserei Champignon Hofmeister* (n 227) para 44. The CJEU furthermore concludes that a regulatory system in which the imposition of a penalty is not conditional upon the finding of a fault element (intention or negligence) is not in itself inconsistent with general principles of European law (paras 47–51). All of this, however, does not mean that persons are bereaved of all legal protection, since any penalty must, in any case, rest on a clear legal basis and comply with the principle of proportionality (para 52).

[236] CJEU *Käserei Champignon Hofmeister* (n 227) para 79 (referring to, inter alia, CJEU 9 August 1994, C-347/93 *Belgian State v Boterlux SPRL* (EU:C:1994:314) para 34). On the requirement of having exercised all due care, see also Blomsma, *Mens Rea and Defences* (n 4) 389.

appropriate precautions, either by including the necessary clauses in the contracts in question or by effecting appropriate insurance ...[237]

For this reason, an exporter cannot simply 'hide' behind the fault of a third party with whom the agricultural aid beneficiary maintains contractual relations so as to escape the incurring of a sanction for an infringement pertaining to that aid, because such a fault on the part of a co-contractor 'cannot be regarded as unforeseeable in the context of commercial transactions'.[238] Considering that an exporter has various means to protect him- or herself against the legal consequences that a fault on the part of a third party may entail, such a fault 'falls more within the sphere of the beneficiary than within that of the Community'.[239] Consequently, the CJEU holds that the Bundesfinanzhof's second question must be answered negatively. It may be concluded, therefore, that the CJEU construes the concept of force majeure (or duress of circumstances) rather restrictively.

However, it must be borne in mind that the Court's considerations on force majeure that were referred to above are limited to this concept's meaning and scope within the field of agricultural regulations.[240] The specific context of these regulations, and the aims and objectives underlying them, may be said to at least partly attest to the reasonableness of confining – in this field – the concept of force majeure within rather narrow limits. In the words of Advocate General Stix-Hackl: 'the exporter should be regarded as a partner in the administration of benefits who has to be induced to fulfil his special obligations ... under threat of penalty'; and this penalty is 'the legal consequence of his status as guarantor of the correctness of the refund application, which would appear to be more akin to the civil law institution of a contractual penalty than to a penal sanction'.[241]

Moreover, the administrative penalties that are provided for by the regulations under the EU's common agricultural policy do not stand out as markedly severe. It is in any case safe to say that sanctions in other fields of non-criminal, regulatory law – such as the field of EU competition law to which we will turn in the following subsection – can clearly be far more punitive in nature. However, this does not render the foregoing exposition redundant: *sensu stricto*, the principle of individual culpability precludes the imposition of *any* sanction on a person in cases where it can reasonably be assumed that this person could not have avoided his or her wrongful action. Pursuant to the third dimension of the principle of individual culpability, personal blameworthiness is a necessary condition for the imposition of a sanction, irrespective of whether the sanction is a severe or a lenient one.[242] And the possibility of rebutting the presumption

[237] CJEU *Käserei Champignon Hofmeister* (n 227) para 80.

[238] CJEU *Käserei Champignon Hofmeister* (n 227) para 86. See likewise the opinion of AG Stix-Hackl (n 232) paras 97–99.

[239] CJEU *Käserei Champignon Hofmeister* (n 227) para 85 (with reference to CJEU 12 May 1998, C-366/95 *Landbrugsministeriet, EF-Direktoratet v Steff-Houlberg et al* (EU:C:1998:216), para 28). See likewise the Opinion of AG Stix-Hackl (n 232) paras 103–104.

[240] See the Opinion of AG Stix-Hackl (n 232) para 95: '[T]he concept of *force majeure* does not have exactly the same scope in different areas of the law and in its various spheres of application, so that its precise meaning must be determined by reference to the legal context within which it is intended to operate.'

[241] Opinion of AG Stix-Hackl (n 232) para 41.

[242] The question as to what level of severity of sanction is appropriate in a given case belongs to the fourth dimension of the principle of individual culpability, which is the subject of section VI. Yet, no sanction, however mild, can be considered appropriate when personal blameworthiness fails.

of blameworthiness – and hence the possibility of invoking exculpatory defences – is especially important in fields of regulation where relatively low evidentiary thresholds apply to mens rea elements, or where there is no mens rea requirement for liability at all.[243]

C. Mistake of Law under EU Competition Law: *Schenker and Co*

EU competition law is reputed to be a complicated field of law where new developments arise in rapid succession and where – consequently – legal errors are rather easily made. In a preliminary judgment of 18 June 2013, the CJEU answered the question whether an 'unobjectionable' mistake with respect to a point of law could or should preclude the imposition of a fine based on the antitrust provision of Article 101 TFEU.[244] The request for a preliminary ruling was made by the Austrian Supreme Court (Oberster Gerichtshof) in proceedings between, on the one side, the Austrian Federal Competition Authority (Bundeswettbewerbsbehörde) and the Austrian Federal Cartel Counsel (Bundeskartellanwalt) and, on the other side, Schenker and Co AG and 30 other freight-forwarding undertakings that were members of an interest group going by the name Spediteur-Sammelladungs-Konferenz (SSK). These proceedings concerned the finding of an infringement of Article 101 TFEU and of national law provisions on cartels, and fines imposed pursuant to these provisions.

The SSK was established in 1994, one year before Austria became a Member State of the European Community. The SSK members made agreements on fixed tariffs for domestic freight-forwarding services throughout Austria with the aim of ensuring freight rates that were competitive with rates for rail and other forms of inland transport.[245] In 1996, the Austrian Cartel Court (Kartellgericht) officially declared the SSK a so-called 'minor cartel', a type of cartel that was allowed under the national Law on Cartels (*Kartellgesetz*) of 1988.[246] Pursuant to paragraph 16 of that law, 'minor cartels' are cartels that have a share of less than five per cent of the entire domestic market. Subsequent to the Kartellgericht's declaration, the SSK members continued to take measures to ensure the SSK's compatibility with Austrian competition law. The members constantly monitored their market shares. Furthermore, they repeatedly consulted their competition counsel from an Austrian law firm in order to obtain up-to-date advice in light of new legal and factual developments. This legal advice, however, concerned the question of how the SSK members could ensure their remaining within the 'minor cartel' exception under Austrian competition law, but failed to consider obligations and prohibitions stemming from EU law that had meanwhile become applicable in Austria.

[243] Art 11(1) of Regulation 3665/87 (n 229) does not require the finding of a fault element for the imposition of a sanction; it does, however, provide for a considerably higher sanction in cases where the relevant infringement is committed intentionally. On the notion of strict liability, see subsections II.C. and III.A. above.

[244] CJEU 18 June 2013, C-681/11 *Bundeskartellanwalt v Schenker and Co AG* (EU:C:2013:404). See on Art 101 TFEU also subsection III.C. above.

[245] SB Völcker, '*Ignorantia Legis Non Excusat* and the Demise of National Procedural Autonomy in the Application of the EU Competition Rules: *Schenker*' (2014) 51(5) *Common Market Law Review* 1497, 1499.

[246] This law was in force until 2006, when it was replaced by the *Kartellgesetz* 2005.

It was only over a decade later that doubts were first raised concerning the lawfulness of SSK's existence under EU competition law. This happened in late 2007, during a meeting of the SSK board with a representative of the law firm that had been issuing the legal advice to the SSK members. In view of the doubts raised, it was decided to dissolve the SSK with immediate effect. One of the freight-forwarding companies involved, Schenker and Co AG, thereupon applied to the Bundeswettbewerbsbehörde within the framework of a so-called 'leniency programme' (which had been introduced in Austria in 2006).[247] The decision on this application came early 2010. On 18 February of that year, the Bundeswettbewerbsbehörde requested the Kartellgericht to declare that Schenker had infringed Article 101 TFEU and national competition rules, but without fining it, and to impose a fine on all remaining former SSK members for their respective contributions to 'a single, complex and multi-faceted infringement of national and European Union law on cartels by agreeing on tariffs for domestic consolidated consignment transport throughout Austria'.[248]

One year later, the Kartellgericht rejected the request. It based the rejection on the argument that its 1996 ruling – in which the SSK was found to be a lawful 'minor cartel' – already 'implied' that the SSK did not contravene European law, as the SSK had no relevant effect on trade between EU Member States; moreover, the SSK members had obtained advice from a reliable legal counsel, specialised in matters of competition law. With regard to the requested 'mere declaration' in respect of Schenker, the Kartellgericht ruled that it was not entitled to find an infringement of Article 101 TFEU without also imposing a fine, arguing that only the Commission is invested with the competence to take such a declaratory decision. The Bundeswettbewerbsbehörde appealed the Kartellgericht's ruling to the Oberster Gerichtshof, after which the Commission decided to intervene in the appeal procedure as an *amicus curiae*. The Oberster Gerichtshof stayed the proceedings and requested a preliminary ruling. One of the two questions referred to the CJEU concerned the possibility of imposing a fine on an undertaking found to have infringed Article 101 TFEU in cases where this undertaking has unobjectionably erred with regard to the lawfulness of its conduct, for example because it has relied in good faith on expert legal advice or on a ruling of a national competition authority.[249]

In her Opinion, Advocate General Juliane Kokott starts from the view that 'although antitrust law is not part of the core area of criminal law, it is recognised as having a character similar to criminal law'.[250] Certain principles stemming from criminal law must therefore be assumed to apply also in competition law. One of these is the principle of *nulla poena sine culpa*, which the Advocate General believes to be intrinsic to the presumption of innocence and to be implicitly contained in Article 48, paragraph 1 of

[247] On compliance and leniency programmes in competition law, see generally Frenz, *Handbook* (n 117) 854–55, 863–65, 1009–20.

[248] CJEU *Schenker and Co* (n 244) para 23.

[249] The second question was whether or not national authorities are entitled to forbear from imposing a fine on an undertaking found to have infringed EU competition, on the ground that this undertaking participated in a leniency programme.

[250] Opinion of 28 February 2013, C-681/11 *Bundeskartellanwalt v Schenker and Co AG* (EU:C:2013:126), para 40.

the EU's Charter of Fundamental Rights (CFR) and in Article 6, paragraph 2 ECHR.[251] The applicability of the principle of *nulla poena sine culpa* within the context of competition law is further evidenced, according to Kokott, by the fact that Article 23, paragraph 2 of Regulation 1/2003 states that fines may be imposed by the Commission only for intentionally or negligently committed infringements of EU antitrust law.[252] The applicability of the principle implies that certain forms of error of law must preclude the attribution of liability and, consequently, the imposition of a penalty. Kokott stresses, however,

> that not every error of law is capable of precluding completely the liability of the undertaking participating in the cartel and thus the existence of a punishable infringement. Only where the error committed by the undertaking regarding the lawfulness of its market behaviour was *unavoidable* – sometimes also called an *excusable* error or an *unobjectionable* error – has the undertaking acted without fault and it cannot be held liable for the cartel offence in question. Such an unavoidable error of law would appear to occur only very rarely. It can be taken to exist only where the undertaking concerned took all possible and reasonable steps to avoid its alleged infringement of EU antitrust law.[253]

The Advocate General then addresses the issue of whether, and under what conditions, an undertaking's reliance on legal advice may exonerate this undertaking from liability. Under Regulation 1/2003, undertakings are themselves responsible for monitoring the compatibility of their market behaviour with EU antitrust law, which impels undertakings to obtain specialised legal advice. Kokott reasons that '[i]f an undertaking relies, in good faith, on – ultimately incorrect – advice provided by its legal adviser, this must have a bearing in cartel proceedings for the imposition of fines'.[254] Under certain conditions, this should result in the conclusion that the undertaking has a valid defence in the form of an excusable mistake of law and that, consequently, liability is barred. The Advocate General advises that, for this result to obtain, six cumulative minimum requirements must be satisfied.[255] Good-faith reliance on legal advice may only result in exoneration, for example, if the advice relied on is provided by a specialist legal counsel, is not manifestly incorrect, and contains a complete and express account of all relevant legal aspects. Moreover, undertakings must always 'be aware that certain anti-competitive practices are, by their nature, prohibited, and in particular that no one is permitted to participate in "hardcore restrictions", for example in price agreements'.[256]

The Advocate General subsequently considers under what conditions an undertaking's reliance on rulings or decisions of national competition authorities may lead to an exoneration. Considering the increased importance of the role of national competition authorities under the decentralised enforcement regime introduced by Regulation 1/2003, Kokott reasons that legitimate expectations may more readily be

[251] Opinion of AG Kokott (n 250) para 41.
[252] Council Regulation 1/2003/EC of 16 December 2002 on the implementation of the rules on competition laid down in Articles 81 and 82 of the Treaty, [2003] OJ L 1/1. See Opinion of AG Kokott (n 250) para 42.
[253] Opinion of AG Kokott (n 250) paras 45–46.
[254] Opinion of AG Kokott (n 250) para 58.
[255] See opinion of AG Kokott (n 250) paras 62–73.
[256] Opinion of AG Kokott (n 250) para 70.

created by decisions taken by national competition authorities than by expert legal advice.[257] Also in this respect, she lists a number of minimum requirements which must be met in order for an undertaking to have a valid defence.[258] Some of these parallel the requirements for good-faith reliance on legal advice. It is furthermore required, inter alia, that the authority's decision concerns 'exactly the same matters of fact and law in respect of which the undertaking concerned invokes an error of law precluding liability'.[259] She ultimately concludes that several of the requirements are not satisfied in the case of the former SSK members and that, consequently, 'the undertakings concerned have not committed an excusable error of law', which means that 'any error regarding the lawfulness of their market behaviour may be held against them'.[260]

The CJEU reaches the same conclusion in its preliminary ruling. Interestingly, however, the CJEU arrives at this conclusion by an entirely different route. Whereas the Advocate General's reasoning centres on the protective role of the principle of *nulla poena sine culpa* in curtailing liability in antitrust law, the Court's reasoning is anchored in an almost diametrically opposed principle, the instrumental principle of *effet utile*.[261] The Court rationalises that, although the Commission may – pursuant to Article 23, paragraph 2 of Regulation 1/2003 – only impose fines for infringements of antitrust law if these are committed intentionally or negligently, the same restriction does not apply to national competition authorities.[262] But *if* a Member State chooses to limit the power of its competition authority to impose penalties to cases of intentional or negligent infringement, the standard of proof for these fault elements must not be higher than the standards which are employed by the Commission, 'so as not to jeopardise the effectiveness of European Union law'.[263] And with regard to errors of law, the CJEU states the following:

> In relation to the question whether an infringement has been committed intentionally or negligently and is, therefore, liable to be punished by a fine in accordance with the first subparagraph of Article 23(2) of Regulation No 1/2003, it follows from the case-law of the Court that that condition is satisfied where the undertaking concerned *cannot be unaware of the anti-competitive nature of its conduct*, whether or not it is aware that it is infringing the competition rules of the Treaty. … Therefore, the fact that the undertaking concerned has characterised wrongly in law its conduct upon which the finding of the infringement is

[257] Opinion of AG Kokott (n 250) para 85.

[258] See opinion of AG Kokott (n 250) paras 87–96.

[259] Opinion of AG Kokott (n 250) para 91.

[260] Opinion of AG Kokott (n 250) para 97. With regard to the second question referred to the CJEU, Kokott concludes that Regulation 1/2003 (n 252) does not prohibit national competition authorities from (merely) finding an infringement of antitrust law without imposing a fine, 'provided that the principles of equivalence and effectiveness enshrined in EU law are respected'; see paras 103–14.

[261] See Völcker, '*Ignorantia Legis Non Excusat*' (n 245) 1504. The CJEU refers to the first sentence of recital 1 of Regulation 1/2003 (n 252): 'In order to establish a system which ensures that competition in the common market is not distorted, Articles 81 and 82 of the Treaty must be applied effectively and uniformly in the Community.'

[262] CJEU *Schenker and Co* (n 244) para 35: 'It is not apparent from the wording of Article 5 of the regulation that conditions relating to intention or negligence have to be met in order for the measures of application which are provided for by the regulation to be adopted.'

[263] See CJEU *Schenker and Co* (n 244) para 36.

> based cannot have the effect of exempting it from imposition of a fine in so far as it could not be unaware of the anti-competitive nature of that conduct (emphasis added).[264]

The Court subsequently concedes that a national competition authority may in exceptional cases refrain from imposing a fine despite the finding of an infringement, in particular when the 'principle of protection of legitimate expectations' is at issue.[265] However, the margins for this possibility seem extremely narrow: according to the CJEU, legitimate expectations cannot, in any event, be derived from expert legal advice, or from a decision taken by a national competition authority.[266] In answer to the referring court's first question, the Court quite unequivocally states that an undertaking which has infringed Article 101 TFEU 'may not escape imposition of a fine' even where the infringement has resulted from an error of law 'on account of the terms of legal advice given by a lawyer or of the terms of a decision of a national competition authority'.[267] This robust conclusion seems to shut the door on any excusable 'mistake of law' defence with regard to infringements of Article 101 TFEU.

Unsurprisingly, many commentators have noted and criticised the CJEU's rather severe or even uncompromising approach in the *Schenker* case, and have questioned the Court's commitment to respecting the principle of individual culpability in matters of antitrust law. Sven B Völcker, for example, states that '[i]n marked contrast to the Advocate General, the Court appears far more interested in establishing the supremacy of the principle of "uniform and effective application of EU competition law" than acknowledging [the principle of] nulla poena sine culpa'[268] (to which the 'principle of protection of legitimate expectations' referred to by the CJEU is not equivalent).[269] Now, of course it could be argued that the CJEU's ruling should be interpreted to the effect that a mistake of law defence is precluded *only* in cases where the anticompetitive behaviour is sufficiently *evident* to sustain the finding that the undertaking in question cannot have been unaware of the anticompetitive nature of its conduct. However, considering the Commission's and the EU Courts' expanding interpretation of the notion of 'anticompetitive conduct', it is not at all clear in what situations – if there are any at all – the

[264] CJEU *Schenker and Co* (n 244) paras 37–38. The Court refers in this connection to its previous judgments of 8 November 1983, Case 96/82 *IAZ International Belgium NV et al v Commission* (EU:C1983:310) para 45; 9 November 1983, Case 322/81 *Nederlandsche Banden Industrie Michelin NV v Commission* (EU:C1983:313) para 107; and 14 October 2010, C-280/08 P *Deutsche Telekom v Commission* (EU:C:2010:603), para 124.

[265] CJEU *Schenker and Co* (n 244) para 40.

[266] See CJEU *Schenker and Co* (n 244) paras 41–43. With regard to the second question that was posed by the Austrian Oberster Gerichtshof, the CJEU concludes that national competition authorities are permitted to confine themselves, by way of exception, to finding an infringement without imposing a fine 'if the undertaking concerned has participated in an national leniency programme'; see paras 44–50.

[267] CJEU *Schenker and Co* (n 244) para 51.

[268] Völcker, '*Ignorantia Legis Non Excusat*' (n 245) 1510. See also Van Kempen and Bemelmans, 'EU Protection of the Substantive Criminal Law Principles' (n 100) 256: 'After all, the culpability then centres on the fact that one did not refrain from certain conduct, although one could assume that one was still operating within the rules of the law. The Court would then thus apply a certain rule of conduct not laid down by law as such.' And see ES Lachnit, 'Laten we geen boete opleggen … Het arrest Schenker: de mogelijkheden voor een beroep op dwaling en afzien van boeteoplegging in het Europese mededingingsrecht' (2013) 8 *Nederlands Tijdschrift voor Europees Recht* 279; P Rojac and O Lynskey, '*Schenker*; Expert Legal Advice Cannot be Relied upon to Exempt an Undertaking from Competition Law Sanctions' (2013) 5(1) *Journal of European Competition Law and Practice* 27; Frenz, *Handbook* (n 117) v, 1020–33.

[269] See Völcker, '*Ignorantia Legis Non Excusat*' (n 245) 1508–09.

anticompetitive nature of conduct is not to be regarded as sufficiently conspicuous so as to preclude an excusable mistake of law.[270]

What seems at any rate a justified conclusion to be drawn is that the role of the concept of personal blameworthiness in curtailing (and sometimes precluding) liability is significantly more modest in the quasi-criminal domain of EU competition law than is generally the case already in criminal law. As was seen in subsection V.A. above, the concept of personal blameworthiness functions as a 'negative' condition for liability in criminal law, in the sense that this condition is, in principle, presumed to be fulfilled, *unless* a recognised exculpatory defence applies that attests to the absence of personal blameworthiness. However, even though the maxim that *ignorantia iuris non excusat* underlies the legal systems of all EU Member States, an unavoidable and therefore excusable mistake regarding the unlawfulness of one's conduct is at least recognised as an exculpatory defence in the criminal law systems of most Member States.[271] The conditions which must be satisfied for such a defence to apply are generally rather strict in criminal law – especially within sub-fields of a 'regulatory' nature, where offences are typically addressed primarily to professional agents.[272]

Seen from the perspective of legal certainty, and considering the generally applicable 'duty to know the law', it is quite understandable that relatively stringent conditions apply for a valid mistake of law defence in criminal law.[273] And in view of the distinctly regulatory character of EU antitrust law and the legitimate interest in a uniform and effective application thereof, one might, moreover, rightfully argue that it would be justified and advisable to raise the evidential threshold for a valid mistake of law defence even a bit higher in respect of antitrust offences. However, to effectively shut the door on virtually any possibility of successfully invoking such a defence in antitrust proceedings is clearly incompatible with the principle of individual culpability. More specifically, it contravenes this principle's third dimension, according to which liability may only be imputed to a person if the presumption that this person could have avoided his or her wrongful action is not defeated by a valid exculpatory defence.

And considering the unmistakably punitive nature of EU competition law, there is much to be said for a more wholehearted commitment to the principle of individual culpability in this field, and thus for a more generous recognition of the exculpatory defence of an unavoidable mistake of law. In fact, it is hard to see how or why the two sets of cumulative minimum requirements for a valid mistake of law defence that were formulated by Advocate General Kokott in her thoughtful Opinion, could not or should not have been gratefully adopted by the CJEU. The requirements show quite

[270] See Völcker, '*Ignorantia Legis Non Excusat*' (n 245) 1510–12. Völcker also points out (at 1512–13) that it is unclear how one should deal with a case in which the undertaking erred in good faith, not with regard to the lawfulness of its conduct, but with regard to the applicability of one of the exceptions of Art 101(3) TFEU.

[271] See Blomsma, *Mens Rea and Defences* (n 4) 464–76.

[272] Conditions for defences tend to be stricter for professional agents or officials on account of their '*Garantenstellung*'; see subsection II.C. above. Issues of *error iuris* are usually dealt with by the ECtHR on the basis of the criterion of foreseeability within the context of the principle of legality enshrined in Art 7 ECHR; see eg ECtHR *Cantoni v France* (n 205) and ECtHR 17 May 2010, *Kononov v Latvia* (App No 36376/04), [2010] ECHR 667. On the concept of 'regulatory criminal law', see subsection III.A. above.

[273] See Blomsma, *Mens Rea and Defences* (n 4) 467–69.

some resemblance to the conditions that usually apply to a defence of an unavoidable mistake of law within criminal law, which may indicate that the requirements listed by Advocate General Kokott should also prove to be sufficiently practicable.[274] Moreover, in light of their concise and stringent formulation, the fear that the adoption of these requirements will jeopardise legal certainty in the field of European competition law seems unwarranted, or at least premature.[275] Lastly, due to its *exculpatory* (and hence not *justificatory*) nature, the potential impact of a mistake of law defence is by definition limited: where it applies, it defeats the presumption of personal blameworthiness, but does not affect the wrongfulness of the behaviour concerned.[276]

VI. Fourth Dimension: Proportionate Penalties

A. Introduction: The Relational Dimension of Individual Culpability

The fourth and last dimension of the principle of individual culpability leads to the domain that Antoine Mooij has denoted as 'guilt of settlement' (*ὀφειλόμενον*; *debitum*). This dimension of the principle is inherently *relational*.[277] Guilt needs to be settled. Culpability within this context means, therefore, that something is owed to another, or is owed to 'the Other' (society). And what is owed is related to the degree of culpability; in this connection, aspects of what Mooij has termed 'guilt of action' and 'guilt by default' also come into play. The culpability principle requires that punishment does not exceed the offender's just deserts, regardless of whether imposing additional or more severe punishment enhances social utility. The proportionality requirement *as such* is a generally acknowledged dimension of the principle of individual culpability. Sanctions must not be disproportionate – but disproportionate in relation *to what* exactly?

This is a controversial matter. It is disputed, for example, whether a penalty may or may not exceed a certain level of severity that is indicated (in whatever mysterious way) by the measure of the offender's guilt. The answer to this question depends, of course, in large part on the answer to a further question, namely: what does 'the offender's guilt' exactly refer to here? If the labyrinthine notion of guilt is taken here in the rather strict sense of the degree of the offender's 'personal blameworthiness', it seems – as was argued in subsection II.B. above – that the principle of individual culpability would overcharge the administration of criminal justice. The fact that the notion of guilt at play in the determination of appropriate penalties (guilt in the sense of 'guilt of settlement') is inherently 'relational' rather indicates that the requirement of

[274] See Frenz, *Handbook* (n 117) 1025–33.

[275] Cp, however, Th von Danwitz, 'Ignorantia Legis Non Excusat' (2013) 4(5) *Journal of European Competition Law and Practice* 389, 390: 'Even if one might not agree with the Court's findings, the clearness of the decision bears an important advantage in terms of legal certainty. Indeed, a different approach would have raised more and rather difficult legal issues regarding the minimum requirements and the assessment of expert legal advice … in what is now twenty-eight national jurisdictions.'

[276] Blomsma, *Mens Rea and Defences* (n 4) 538–39.

[277] See also Duff, *Answering for Crime* (n 26) 23–30.

proportionality has regard to a more extensive notion of culpability that encompasses aspects of 'guilt of action' and 'guilt by default', in addition to more objective factors such as the seriousness of the offence and its impact on society.[278]

To this must be added that the meaning or substance of the requirement of proportionality can vary significantly depending on the context in which the requirement is operative. Within a legislative context, the requirement is relevant in connection with the determination of what types of penalty and what maximum level of severity of the considered penalties (in terms of the duration of the deprivation or restriction of physical freedom, or in terms of the amount of financial deprivation, for example) could be deemed appropriate for a certain offence, taking account of general and abstract factors such as the seriousness of the conduct and the nature and weight of the legal interest the protection of which formed the primary reason for the conduct's penalisation. Evidently, the requirement of proportionality has rather different contours within the more concrete and tangible context of measuring out appropriate penalties in individual cases. The determination of appropriate sanctions in individual cases allows for much more case-specific particularities and subjective factors to be taken into account, such as the measure of the defendant's personal blameworthiness.[279]

All of this, of course, still tells us nothing about the role of the requirement of proportionate penalties in the vast domain of European (quasi-)criminal law. The European Criminal Policy Initiative's 'Manifesto' – that was referred to in section I above – stipulates that 'the European legislator has to justify that the requirements in European legislation as to the sanctions permits [*sic*] the imposition of penalties which correspond to the guilt of the individual and which are not disproportionate to the criminal offence'.[280] With reference to a number of EU legal acts concerning criminal offences, the Initiative states that it is 'alarming that the legislator does not pay attention to the fact that the penalty scale should be proportionate to the dangerousness of the offence'.[281]

[278] See Mooij, *Intentionality, Desire, Responsibility* (n 21) 260; see subsection II.B.

[279] With respect to other (less case-sensitive) dimensions of the principle of individual culpability, the differences between the legislative context of drafting offence definitions and the adjudicative context of hearing and deciding individual cases may of course be considerably smaller. In the determination of the requisite mens rea element for a particular offence, eg, the legislator makes an active and important contribution to the effectuation of the second dimension of the principle of individual culpability.

[280] European Criminal Policy Initiative, 'A Manifesto on European Criminal Policy' (n 6) 708.

[281] European Criminal Policy Initiative, 'A Manifesto on European Criminal Policy' (n 6) 712, referring to Council Framework Decision 2002/475/JHA of 13 June 2002 on combating terrorism, [2002] OJ L 164/3, and to the (then) Proposal for a Council Framework Decision on preventing and combating trafficking human beings, and protecting victims, COM(2009) 136 final. In a recent study by the Initiative, it is concluded that the instrument of 'minimum maximum penalties' – used by the EU legislator in directives adopted under Art 83 TFEU – does not effectively contribute to the harmonisation of criminal sanctions; instead, it leads to an overall increase of the level of punitiveness, and it often has a negative impact on the coherence of national systems and on the proportionality of national rules on sanctions. For this reason, the Initiative proposes an alternative instrument for the harmonisation of sanctions that is based on a model of categories of relative severity; see H Satzger, 'The Harmonisation of Criminal Sanctions in the European Union. A New Approach' (2019) 2 *Eucrim* 115. See also M Kaiafa-Gbandi, 'The Post-Lisbon Approach towards the Main Features of Substantive Criminal Law: Developments and Challenges' (2015) 5(1) *European Criminal Law Review* 3, 10–11 and 18; and HG Nilsson, 'Some Reflections on the Development of an EU Criminal Policy, on Directives in Criminal Law and Sanctions Contained Therein' in M Ulväng and I Cameron (eds), *Essays on Criminalisation and Sanctions* (Uppsala, Iustus Förlag, 2014) 163–84, 178–81.

In the following pages it will be assessed whether this or similar criticism applies to sanctions in fields of quasi-criminal law. The famous *Greek Maize* case may serve as a point of departure. In this judgment the CJEU ruled that Member States,

> whilst the choice of penalties remains within their discretion, … must ensure in particular that infringements of Community law are penalized under conditions, both procedural and substantive, which are analogous to those applicable to infringements under national law of a similar nature and importance and which, in any event, make the penalty *effective, proportionate and dissuasive* (emphasis added).[282]

The phrase that penalties must be 'effective, proportionate and dissuasive' has rapidly developed into a mantra of the EU courts and legislature. The terms have been interpreted in different ways. What seems clear, at any rate, is that the requirement of proportionality places restrictions on the level of dissuasiveness of a given penalty (and perhaps also on its effectiveness). In her Opinion for a number of cases concerning criminal proceedings, Advocate General Juliane Kokott stated that a proportionate penalty is one that is 'appropriate (that is to say, in particular, *effective* and *dissuasive*) for attaining the legitimate objectives pursued by it, and also necessary. Where there is a choice between several (equally) appropriate penalties, recourse must be had to the least onerous'.[283] This definition primarily concerns the notion of proportionality on the abstract level of legislation. On the concrete level of individual cases, however, the principle of individual culpability is generally considered to require that penalties are proportionate to the seriousness of the offence and to the culpability of the defendant. In this connection, Andrew von Hirsch and Andrew Ashworth state the following in their seminal work *Proportionate Sentencing*:

> Once one has created an institution with the condemnatory implications that punishment has, then it is a requirement of justice, not merely of efficient crime prevention, to punish offenders according to the degree of reprehensibleness of their conduct. Disproportionate punishments are unjust not because they possibly may be ineffective or counterproductive, but because they purport to condemn the actor for his conduct and yet visit more or less censure on him than the degree of blameworthiness of that conduct would warrant.[284]

Von Hirsch and Ashworth explicitly relate the level of censure warranted by the 'degree of blameworthiness' of the relevant conduct to the 'seriousness of the offence';[285]

[282] CJEU *Greek Maize* (n 90) para 24. On this judgment see Klip, *European Criminal Law* (n 2) 72–82.

[283] Opinion of 14 October 2004, C-387/02, C-391/02 and C-403/02 *Criminal Proceedings against Silvio Berlusconi, Sergio Aldechi* and *Marcello Dell'Utri et al* (EU:C:2004:624) para 90. Cp K Nuotio, 'A Legitimacy-based Approach to EU Criminal Law: Maybe We are Getting There, After All' (2020) 11(1) *New Journal of European Criminal Law* 20, 23–24: 'Proportionality has, as is generally known, two possible interpretations. There is act-proportionality which requires that the punishment should be proportionate to the gravity of the offence. The second interpretation is means-end-proportionality. This second interpretation of proportionality would obviously be close to the effectiveness test. In criminal law, act-proportionality is particularly significant, since it reveals the penal value of the act in question. It is rather obvious that sentences that are both effective and proportionate may help with the internalization of those values and also give reasons for potential perpetrators not to engage in the forbidden conduct. Proportionality and effectiveness are thus internally linked.'

[284] A von Hirsch and A Ashworth, *Proportionate Sentencing. Exploring the Principles* (Oxford, Oxford University Press, 2005) 134.

[285] See Von Hirsch and Ashworth, *Proportionate Sentencing* (n 284) 137–62; cp M Thorburn, 'Proportionate Sentencing and the Rule of Law' in L Zedner and JV Roberts (eds), *Principles and Values in Criminal Law and Criminal Justice. Essays in Honour of Andrew Ashworth* (Oxford, Oxford University Press, 2012) 269–84.

the notion of blameworthiness in this context, therefore, corresponds with the aforementioned 'extensive' and relational meaning of culpability that appertains to the fourth dimension of the principle of *nulla poena sine culpa*. In the remainder of this section, the focus will be on the meaning and role of the proportionality principle in areas of quasi-criminal law. As a matter of course, it will not be possible to provide a complete and detailed account of this fourth dimension of the principle of individual culpability within European quasi-criminal law; as with respect to the three dimensions that were discussed in the preceding sections, we will have to content ourselves with a rather pointillist sketch. Subsection V.B. contains a brief discussion of the Commission's method of setting fines for infringements of EU competition law. Subsection V.C. revisits the phenomenon of 'dual-track' enforcement systems;[286] it investigates how the requirement of proportionate sanctioning, in conjunction with the principle of *ne bis in idem* as laid down in Article 50 CFR and in Article 4 of Protocol No 7 to the ECHR, serves its purpose of curtailing liability in cases of dual proceedings.

B. Proportionality of Fines in EU Competition Law: The 2006 Fining Guidelines

Article 49, paragraph 3 CFR states that '[t]he severity of penalties must not be disproportionate to the criminal offence'. Although this provision explicitly concentrates on criminal offences, the requirement of proportionality of sanctions is taken to apply to quasi-criminal offences as well.[287] The present subsection discusses the proportionality requirement specifically in relation to pecuniary sanctions that can be imposed for infringements found in EU competition law, a field of quasi-criminal law that was encountered already in many previous subsections in this chapter. Article 49 CFR is referred to, albeit rarely, in judgments of the CJEU and GCEU concerning competition law cases.[288] Pursuant to Article 23, paragraph 2 of Regulation 1/2003, the Commission is authorised to impose fines on undertakings or associations of undertakings found to have intentionally or negligently infringed Article 101 or 102 TFEU.[289] In order to enhance the transparency and impartiality of its decisions, a four-page document containing 'Guidelines on the method of setting fines' in pursuance of the mentioned provision in Regulation 1/2003 ('*Fining Guidelines*') was published by the Commission in 2006.[290] According to these *Fining Guidelines*, it is the Commission's duty

> to pursue a general policy designed to apply, in competition matters, the principles laid down by the Treaty and to steer the conduct of undertakings in the light of those principles.

[286] Touched upon already in subsection IV.C.

[287] See P De Hert, 'EU Criminal Law and Fundamental Rights' in V Mitsilegas, M Bergström and Th Konstadinides (eds), *Research Handbook on EU Criminal Law* (Cheltenham, Edward Elgar Publishing, 2016) 105–24, 122–23.

[288] See Veenbrink, *Criminal Law Principles* (n 115) 206.

[289] Formerly Arts 81 and 82. See Art 23(2)(a) of Regulation 1/2003 (n 252). See also subsection V.C. above.

[290] Guidelines on the method of setting fines imposed pursuant to Article 23(2) of Regulation No 1/2003 (*Fining Guidelines*), [2006] OJ C 210/2. These replaced the Guidelines on the method of setting fines imposed pursuant to Article 15(2) of Regulation No 17 (1962) and Article 65(5) of the ECSC Treaty, [1998] OJ C 9/3.

> For this purpose, the Commission must ensure that its action has the necessary deterrent effect. … Fines should have a sufficiently deterrent effect, not only in order to sanction the undertakings concerned (specific deterrence) but also in order to deter other undertakings from engaging in, or continuing, behaviour that is contrary to Articles [101 and 102 TFEU] (general deterrence).[291]

The rather strong emphasis which is placed on the importance of (specific and general) deterrence, may at least partially explain the already frequently observed fact that the fines imposed by the Commission for anticompetitive behaviour have steadily increased over the last few decades and have reached a very high level.[292] The Commission's *Fining Guidelines* have also been endorsed by the CJEU and the GCEU in their respective case law on antitrust law; the EU courts, however, leave the Commission quite a bit of discretion in applying the guidelines.[293] We are, it seems, impelled, therefore, to look somewhat closer into the meaning and weight afforded to the requirement of proportionate sanctions in this context. Although this requirement is not explicitly mentioned anywhere in the *Fining Guidelines*, some aspects of it are implicitly referred to. This is the case, for example, where it is stated that 'the Commission must have regard both to the gravity and to the duration of the infringement',[294] and where certain mitigating factors are listed on account of which a fine may be decreased in respect of an individual undertaking.[295] These aspects are included in the 'two-step methodology' to be followed by the Commission in setting fines to be imposed on undertakings or associations of undertakings in individual cases.

In a first step, the Commission determines a 'basic amount' for the fine by reference to the value of sales of goods and services, insofar as these sales relate to the anticompetitive behaviour in the relevant market. As a rule, the basic amount is calculated by taking a proportion (of up to 30 per cent) of the value of sales of the preceding full business year,[296] multiplied by the number of years during which the relevant undertaking or association of undertakings has participated in the infringement. In order to ensure the desired deterrent effect, the resultant amount is subsequently further increased by a certain percentage of the sales value.[297] In a second step, the Commission determines the definite amount of the fine to be imposed by taking into account a number

[291] *Fining Guidelines* 2006 (n 290) para 4 (references omitted).

[292] See, eg, W Bosch, 'The Role of Fines in the Public Enforcement of Competition Law' in K Hüschelrath and H Schweitzer (eds), *Public and Private Enforcement of Competition Law in Europe. Legal and Economic Perspectives* (Heidelberg, Springer, 2014) 53–61. In addition to the quasi-criminal EU regulation of cartels (and the possibility of civil damages actions), many Member States have introduced (criminal) offences targeting anticompetitive behaviour of corporate and/or individual actors; see Harding, 'The Relationship Between EU Criminal Law and Competition Law' (n 113) 250–51, and Th Ackermann, 'The Interaction of Public and Private Antitrust Enforcement. The Calculation of Fines and Damages' in K Hüschelrath and H Schweitzer (eds), *Public and Private Enforcement of Competition Law in Europe. Legal and Economic Perspectives* (Heidelberg, Springer, 2014) 63–76.

[293] See Veenbrink, *Criminal Law Principles* (n 115) 207–17.

[294] *Fining Guidelines* 2006 (n 290) para 2. This requirement stems from Art 23(3) of Regulation 1/2003 (n 252).

[295] See *Fining Guidelines* 2006 (n 290) paras 29 and 35.

[296] The percentage taken depends on, inter alia, the harmful nature and geographic scope of the infringement in question; see *Fining Guidelines* 2006 (n 290) paras 22–23.

[297] Namely by an amount ranging between 15 and 25 per cent of the sales value; *Fining Guidelines* 2006 (n 290) para 25.

of aggravating and mitigating circumstances. Aggravating circumstances include, inter alia, continuance or recurrence of infringements after their detection, and refusals to cooperate with the Commission.[298] Mitigating circumstances include, for example, a merely negligent or a substantially limited involvement in the infringement, and an effective cooperation with the Commission.[299] At this stage, the Commission may even increase the amount once more, so as to optimise the fine's deterrent effect.[300] However, the final amount of the fine must not, in any event, exceed 10 per cent of the total turnover in the preceding business year of the undertaking or association of undertakings.[301]

As said, both EU courts have endorsed the Commission's *Fining Guidelines*. With regard to cartel offences, the courts accordingly often distinguish between the stage of determining the 'objective gravity' of the offence and the stage of determining its 'relative gravity'; moreover, room is left for the possibility of adjusting the fine on the basis of circumstances not taken into account in the two previous stages.[302] The objective gravity relates to the overall seriousness of the offence, which is assessed on the basis of circumstances that are common for all undertakings that participated in the cartel; the relative gravity, on the other hand, refers to the seriousness of the contribution of an individual undertaking in relation to that of the other cartelists.[303] In the stage of determining the relative gravity of the offence, the fine is thus individualised with reference to aggravating and mitigating factors that are unique to the conduct of one participating undertaking. Although it seems that this approach corresponds rather neatly with the two-step method of setting fines as described in the *Fining Guidelines*, a recent survey of the relevant case law conducted by Marc Veenbrink has revealed that this case law is rather confusing and is inclined to produce unpredictable or even arbitrary ways of determining fines.[304]

It is shown, for example, that the distinction between the objective and the relative gravity of anticompetitive behaviour is often applied inconsistently where the courts scrutinise the Commission's method of determining the amount of a fine in individual cases. On the one hand, the courts tend to rather benevolently gloss over mistakes pertaining to the manner in which individualising factors are taken into account by the Commission. On the other hand, the case law testifies to a certain formalistic tenor in respect of the courts' assessment of complaints lodged by undertakings. Complaints against a fine imposed by the Commission are occasionally rather easily refuted when the arguments raised in their support are not presented in the correct

[298] See *Fining Guidelines* 2006 (n 290) para 28.

[299] See *Fining Guidelines* 2006 (n 290) para 29. The Commission is required to apply the leniency rules set out in the so-called Leniency Notice (para 34) and it may decrease the fine if the relevant undertaking would otherwise not be able to pay it (para 35). Lastly, the Commission may ultimately decide to impose only a 'symbolic' fine (para 36).

[300] *Fining Guidelines* 2006 (n 290) paras 30–31.

[301] *Fining Guidelines* 2006 (n 290) paras 32–33. This requirement stems from Art 23(2) of Regulation 1/2003 (n 252).

[302] See Veenbrink, *Criminal Law Principles* (n 115) 208; and see, eg, GCEU 15 July 2015, T-418/10 *voestalpine AG and voestalpine Wire Rod Austria GmbH v Commission* (EU:T:2015:516), paras 417–23.

[303] This factor was applied already in CJEU *Suiker Unie et al* (n 121) para 623.

[304] See Veenbrink, *Criminal Law Principles* (n 115) 207–17.

manner or order (for example, when they are not placed under the right 'heading').[305] Moreover, complaints as to the disproportionate character of a fine may be dismissed on the mere ground that the fine in question does not exceed 10 per cent of the relevant undertaking's total turnover in the preceding business year. In other words, satisfaction of the requirement of Article 23, paragraph 2 of Regulation 1/2003 is seen, in some cases, as a guarantee of proportionality.[306]

These examples of formalistic reasoning seem incompatible with the basic rule that the (objective and relative) gravity of an infringement of EU competition law depends on 'the particular circumstances of the case' in question. Accordingly, the assessment of the proportionality of fines imposed for such infringements requires an examination in light of *all* relevant factors which the Commission must take into account.[307] Although these factors are many and varied, there are also factors which, according to the EU courts' case law, do not necessarily need to be taken into account in the determination of an appropriate fine.[308] It may, at any rate, be said that both the GCEU and the CJEU tend to subject decisions of the Commission to impose a fine pursuant to Article 23, paragraph 2 of Regulation 1/2003 to a 'restrained scrutiny'. When the legality of such fining decisions is brought up for review, the EU courts generally confine themselves to verifying whether the Commission considered all relevant factors, that is, whether it followed its own *Fining Guidelines*; aside from this, the courts will

[305] See Veenbrink, *Criminal Law Principles* (n 115) 209–10, with reference to GCEU 15 July 2015, T-413/10 and T-414/10 *Socitrel/Sociedade Industrial de Trefilaria, SA and Companhia Previdente-Sociedade de Controle de Participações Financeiras, SA v Commission* (EU:T:2015:500) paras 297–98.

[306] See Veenbrink, *Criminal Law Principles* (n 115) 215–16, with reference to, inter alia, CJEU 26 January 2017, C-644/13 P *Villeroy and Boch SAS v Commission* (EU:C:2017:59) para 81; GCEU 9 September 2015, T-92/13 *Koninklijke Philips Electronics NV v Commission* (EU:T:2015:605) paras 214–215. In other cases, however, it is – rightfully – stated that satisfaction of the condition laid down in Art 23(2) of Regulation 1/2003 (n 252) does *not* preclude an undertaking from being able to argue that the imposed fine is disproportionate; see, eg, GCEU 12 December 2012, T-410/09 *Almamet GmbH Handel mit Spänen und Pulvern aus Metall v Commission* (EU:C:2012:676), para 228.

[307] For an enumeration of relevant factors and appertaining case law, see Veenbrink, *Criminal Law Principles* (n 115) 220 and 393–405. Cp paras 98–103 of AG Dámaso Ruiz-Jarabo Colomer's Opinion (n 126) concerning the *Aalborg-Portland* case that dates from before the Commission's *Fining Guidelines* of 2006 (n 290) and which was discussed in subsection III.C. above: 'the penalty must be proportionate to the gravity of the infringement and to the further circumstances, both subjective and objective, which are present in each case … The Court of Justice has held that the gravity of infringements has to be determined by reference to numerous factors, such as the particular circumstances of the case, its context and the dissuasive effect of fines, and has further stated that no binding or exhaustive list of criteria has been drawn up. … The requirement that the penalty be proportionate to the gravity of the infringement has the consequence that when an infringement has been committed by a number of persons, it is necessary to examine, using the abovementioned guidelines, the relative gravity of the participation of each. That is a requirement of the principle of equal treatment, which demands that the fine be the same for all undertakings in the same situation and prevents those in a different situation from being punished with a similar penalty.'

[308] Interestingly, the CJEU stated in its ruling of 25 March 1996 (dec) C-137/95 P *Vereniging van Samenwerkende Prijsregelende Organisaties in de Bouwnijverheid (SPO) et al v Commission* (EU:C:1996:130) para 57, that 'the Court of First Instance was not required to verify, in order to determine the gravity of the infringement, whether it had been committed intentionally or negligently, still less to distinguish between the two cases'; see Frese, *Sanctions in EU Competition Law* (n 115) 120–21. Under the Commission's 2006 *Fining Guidelines* (n 290), however, negligence may be a mitigating circumstance 'where the undertaking provides evidence that the infringement has been committed as a result of negligence' (para 29). See further Veenbrink, *Criminal Law Principles* (n 115) 224–25.

normally only find reason to quash or amend the Commission's decision in case of a manifest error.[309]

Although one can certainly point to judgments evidencing a more comprehensive scrutiny of imposed fines by the EU courts,[310] the overall purport of their case law – in conclusion – gives cause for some concern, especially when we recall some of the conclusions that were drawn earlier on. As was seen in subsection III.C., liability for infringements of Articles 101 and 102 TFEU is established at the level of *undertakings*; a fine that is proportionate with reference to the relevant undertaking or association of undertakings may, however, have disproportionate consequences for the legal (and possibly natural) persons in respect of whom the Commission's fining decisions (and the EU courts' judgments) are enforced. It was furthermore seen that, under EU competition law, a parent company may be held vicariously liable for an infringement committed by its subsidiary, even when there has been no involvement or guilt with respect to the infringement on the part of the parent company. And as was mentioned, the average severity of fines imposed by the Commission for anticompetitive behaviour has increased rather spectacularly over the last few decades. As a corollary of the rather dominant focus which is placed on the desired deterrent or 'dissuasive' effect of the fines imposed, the importance of the protective function of the requirement of proportionate sentencing may occasionally be easily disregarded.[311]

C. *Ne Bis In Idem* and Dual-Track Liability Regimes: *A and B v Norway* and *Garlsson Real Estate*

As was seen in subsection IV.C., the EU legislature and the legislatures of certain Member States may subject an infringement to a 'dual-track' approach consisting of a combination of an administrative and a criminal liability regime.[312] Imposing penalties for one and the same offence under both administrative and criminal law is in fact a rather widespread practice in the EU Member States, especially in fields of tax law and environmental law.[313] These dual-track systems allow for a stratified enforcement system, for instance in the sense that the applicable 'track' in concrete cases depends on whether the infringement concerned is committed intentionally, or committed

[309] See B Vesterdorf, 'The Court of Justice and Unlimited Jurisdiction: What Does it Mean in Practice?' (2009) 2 *Global Competition Policy* 2–3; M Baran and A Doniec, 'EU Courts' Jurisdiction over and Review of Decisions Imposing Fines in EU Competition Law' (2010) 3(3) *Yearbook of Antitrust and Regulatory Studies* 235, 238–39; Veenbrink, *Criminal Law Principles* (n 115) 211–17; Frese, *Sanctions in EU Competition Law* (n 115) 123.

[310] See, eg, Baran and Doniec, 'Jurisdiction over and Review of Decisions' (n 309) 245; Veenbrink, *Criminal Law Principles* (n 115) 216.

[311] See generally V Franssen, *The Principles of Corporate Sentencing in EU Law* (Oxford, Hart Publishing, *forthcoming*). On the (increased) focus on punitiveness and *effet utile* in EU competition law, see, eg, Franssen, 'Corporate Criminal Liability' (n 8) 298–303; C Harding, 'The Relationship Between EU Criminal Law and Competition Law' (n 113) 269–70.

[312] See the concluding pages of subsection IV.C. which discussed the EU's dual-track approach with regard to market abuse offences under Directive 2014/57 (n 213) and Regulation 596/2014 (n 174).

[313] See the Opinion of AG Pedro Cruz Villalón of 12 June 2012, C-617/10 *Åklagaren v Hans Åkerberg Fransson* (EU:C:2012:340) para 83.

recklessly or negligently. However, dual-track approaches may also, in certain cases, give rise to parallel or consecutive proceedings – and so possibly to an accumulation of (punitive) sanctions – with regard to what, on balance, constitutes one infringement. Salient examples of such sanction accumulation can be found in a field of quasi-criminal law that has already been referred to multiple times in previous sections of this chapter: EU competition law dealing with antitrust infringements. Referring to the regulation of business cartels in an international context, Christopher Harding states that

> [a] single international cartel, if detected and then subject to legal enforcement action, may attract a range of different measures, across a number of jurisdictions, which may be applied to a number of actors of both a corporate and an individual human nature, either sequentially or simultaneously. The complete programme of sanctions in the case of one cartel may be co-ordinated to some extent, but to an extent is also likely to be haphazard and unpredictable …[314]

In other words, differing 'multiplying factors' may account for sanction accumulation in cases where multiple legal systems with an interest in doing so claim jurisdiction and commence proceedings with regard to a single infringement. The 'multi-jurisdictional patchwork' – consisting of variable rules, policies and interests that appertain to the different proceedings – often renders it difficult or even unfeasible to satisfy the requirements of legal certainty, equality and proportionate sentencing.[315] These cases – like all cases where infringements are subject to multiple proceedings, whether nationally or internationally – are particularly prone to give rise to issues of double jeopardy, and thus of issues regarding the principle of *ne bis in idem*. This principle can be said to be rather intimately connected with the requirement of proportionate sentencing and thus with the principle of individual culpability, at least with respect to proceedings that may lead to an accumulation of (criminal and/or administrative) sanctions.[316]

Quite obviously, the principles of *ne bis in idem* and individual culpability differ significantly, both in terms of their substance and rationale, and in terms of the contexts in which they are operative. The principle of individual culpability serves to secure that no punishment is inflicted on the guiltless, and that the guilty receive no harsher punishment than may be justified on the basis of the measure of their culpability (taken here in the more objective, 'relational' sense that was referred to in subsection VI.A.). The principle of *ne bis in idem*, on the other hand, serves to guarantee that those who, following prosecution, are either acquitted or convicted of a certain offence *once*, are not subsequently submitted to the unpleasant or possibly even tormenting experience of being tried or punished for the same offence *anew*.[317] So, whereas the principle of individual culpability exercises its protective authority during the entire phase

[314] Harding, 'Sanction Accumulation' (n 115) 164.

[315] See Harding, 'Sanction Accumulation' (n 115) 172, 186. Over and against the rather cluttered and unpredictable system currently in place, Harding argues in favour of an internationally or regionally co-ordinated, more exclusive model of regulation for internationally operating cartels, ideally in the shape of 'a one-stop enforcement shop, which could estimate both victimhood and an appropriate quantum and kind of sanction at that level' (at 187).

[316] See Van Kempen and Bemelmans, 'EU Protection of the Substantive Criminal Law Principles' (n 100); Herlin-Karnell, 'Is Administrative Law Still Relevant?' (n 223) 243–44.

[317] Unless the national law allows a reopening of the case 'if there is evidence of new or newly discovered facts, or if there has been a fundamental defect in the previous proceedings, which could affect the outcome of the case'; Art 4(2) Protocol No 7 ECHR. Cp Art 52(3) CFR.

preceding a final judgment on the defendant's liability, the principle of *ne bis in idem* is only operative *as from* the very moment of that final judgment.

We should furthermore note that, in line with this 'temporal' difference, there is a difference regarding the rationale of both principles: it is a concern for *legal certainty* and *res iudicata*, rather than a concern for individual culpability, that primarily grounds the principle of *ne bis in idem*. However, the principles coincide in at least one important respect: both principles serve to protect against the infliction of *undeserved* penalties. Commencing new proceedings in defiance of the principle of *ne bis in idem* infringes on the right of the person involved to legal certainty, and causes undeserved distress. Moreover, new proceedings may (again) culminate in the imposition of a sanction, and may therefore easily render the total amount of punishment inflicted for one and the same infringement *disproportionate* and hence, to that extent, undeserved. The principles of *ne bis in idem* and *nulla poena sine culpa* intersect exactly at the point where both seek to prevent overreaching reactions to a given infringement that lead to disproportionate punishment.

The requirement of proportionate sentencing and the principle of *ne bis in idem* have both found expression in the CFR. The proportionality requirement is found, as was seen before, in Article 49, paragraph 3 CFR. Article 50 CFR contains the principle of *ne bis in idem*, guaranteeing the right of any person not 'to be tried or punished again in criminal proceedings for an offence for which he or she has already been finally acquitted or convicted within the Union in accordance with the law'. The CJEU has adopted this principle also in the quasi-criminal law domain of EU competition law.[318] Article 4, paragraph 1 of Protocol No 7 to the ECHR contains a similar definition of the principle of *ne bis in idem*.[319] There is, however, a notable difference in scope.[320] The protection offered under the ECHR is limited to the right not to be tried or punished more than once *within* one and the same Member State of the Council of Europe. Article 50 CFR, in contrast, applies to both national and transnational situations ('within the Union').[321]

As was mentioned before, dual-track approaches that subject a certain offence to both a criminal and an administrative enforcement and liability regime may in certain

[318] See eg CJEU 14 February 2012, C-17/10 *Toshiba Corporation et al v Úřad pro ochranu hospodářské soutěže* (EU:C:2012:72) para 940: '[T]he principle [of *ne bis in idem*] thus precludes an undertaking being found liable or proceedings being brought against it afresh on the grounds of anti-competitive conduct for which it has been penalised or declared not liable by an earlier decision that can no longer be challenged.'

[319] The principle is furthermore enshrined in Art 54 of the CISA Convention implementing the Schengen Agreement (n 154). On the different versions of the principle of *ne bis in idem* at the European level, see JAE Vervaele, 'Ne Bis In Idem: Towards a Transnational Constitutional Principle in the EU?' (2013) 9(4) *Utrecht Law Review* 211.

[320] Pursuant to Art 52(3) CFR, the level of protection offered by Art 50 CFR may not be lower than the minimum standard of Art 4(1) of Protocol No 7. Accordingly, also Member States that have not (yet) ratified Protocol No 7 (currently: Germany, the United Kingdom and the Netherlands) are bound by this minimum standard (save insofar as these Member States choose to apply a weaker version of the principle of *ne bis in idem* with respect to cases that do not pertain to EU law – cp n 321 below).

[321] Pursuant to Art 51(1) CFR, the scope of Art 50 CFR – and of all other provisions in the Charter – is limited to situations concerning EU law. However, it would seem impractical and – in the long run – untenable for a Member State to apply different standards of the *ne bis in idem* principle depending on whether a case concerns EU law or non-EU law. See Van Kempen and Bemelmans, 'EU Protection of the Substantive Criminal Law Principles' (n 100) 262.

cases unlock parallel or consecutive proceedings and may lead to an accumulation of sanctions. Should such approaches categorically be said to unjustifiably contravene the principle of *ne bis in idem*? And, if not, under what conditions can dual-track approaches be said to sufficiently respect the rights enshrined in Article 4, paragraph 1 of Protocol No 7 ECHR and Article 50 CFR? These questions were dealt with by the Grand Chamber of the ECtHR in its landmark judgment of 15 November 2016 in the case of *A and B v Norway*.[322] The underlying case concerned the offence of large-scale tax evasion with respect to which both an administrative fine pursuant to the Norwegian Tax Assessment Act of 1980 (*Ligningsloven*) and a prison sentence were imposed on the applicants. Before the ECtHR, the applicants complained that they had been prosecuted and punished twice in respect of the same offence under the Tax Assessment Act, and that this amounts to a breach of the principle of *ne bis in idem*.

The satisfaction of the principle's '*idem*' condition was undisputed: the factual circumstances underlying the criminal prosecution and the decision to impose an administrative tax fine were clearly sufficiently similar to sustain the conclusion that the penalties applied concerned the 'same' offence.[323] Nor was it a complicated task for the Court to determine that both sets of proceedings must be regarded as 'criminal' for the purposes of Article 4 of Protocol No 7 ECHR.[324] The arguments presented to the Court primarily concerned the principle's '*bis*' aspect, that is, the question of whether there had been a 'duplication' of proceedings with regard to the one offence at issue. In this connection, the Grand Chamber concedes – caving in to the pressure exerted by several contracting states defending their practice of double-track enforcement systems – that a combination of criminal and administrative procedures with regard to the same offence does not *eo ipso* amount to a duplication of proceedings as prohibited by Article 4 of Protocol No 7 to the ECHR.[325] According to the Court, this provision does not preclude dual proceedings that constitute 'complementary legal responses to socially offensive conduct … provided that the accumulated legal responses do not represent an excessive burden for the individual concerned'.[326]

The Court further notes that, in order to comply with the requirements under Article 4, paragraph 1 of Protocol No 7, the dual proceedings must be shown to satisfy the overarching criterion of being 'sufficiently closely connected in substance and in time'. In an effort to specify the meaning of this rather vague criterion, the Grand Chamber revisits a number of previous judgments in which the criterion has already been

[322] ECtHR [GC] 15 November 2016, *A and B v Norway* (App Nos 24130/11 and 29758/11) [2016] ECHR 987.

[323] See ECtHR *A and B v Norway* (n 322) paras 140–141 and 148. The '*idem*' aspect is defined by both the CJEU and the ECtHR in terms of the identity of factual circumstances underlying the offences, (largely) irrespective of their legal classification or the legal interests protected. See CJEU 9 March 2006, C-436/04 *Criminal proceedings against Leopold Henri Van Esbroeck* (EU:C:2006:165) para 42; and ECtHR 10 February 2009, *Sergey Zolotukhin v Russia* (App No 14939/03), [2009] ECHR 252, para 84. In EU competition law, however, the protected legal interest is (still) a relevant factor in assessing the 'idem' aspect; see CJEU *Toshiba Corporation et al* (n 318); Veenbrink, *Criminal Law Principles* (n 115) 365–67.

[324] See ECtHR *A and B v Norway* (n 322) paras 136–139 and 148. Also in this respect, the ECtHR and the CJEU apply the same set of criteria – the so-called *Engel* criteria – in their respective case law; see n 98 and accompanying text above.

[325] See ECtHR *A and B v Norway* (n 322) paras 94–100, 104 and 117–20. See Veenbrink, *Criminal Law Principles* (n 115) 35–38.

[326] ECtHR *A and B v Norway* (n 322) para 121.

applied.[327] On the basis of these earlier judgments, the Court concludes that the criterion demands that the respondent state convincingly demonstrate, in particular, that the dual proceedings in question form 'an integrated system enabling different aspects of the wrongdoing to be addressed in a foreseeable and proportionate manner forming a coherent whole, so that the individual concerned is not thereby subjected to injustice'.[328] In addition, the Court enumerates certain 'material factors' which must be taken into account when assessing whether a 'sufficiently close connection in substance' obtains. These factors include, inter alia, the following:

> [W]hether the different proceedings pursue complementary purposes and thus address, not only *in abstracto* but also *in concreto*, different aspects of the social misconduct involved … [A]nd, *above all*, whether the sanction imposed in the proceedings which become final first is taken into account in those which become final last, so as to prevent that the individual concerned is in the end made to bear an excessive burden, this latter risk being least likely to be present where there is in place an offsetting mechanism designed to *ensure that the overall amount of any penalties imposed is proportionate* (emphasis added).[329]

The judgment has met with rather sharp criticism. According to Giulia Lasagni and Sofia Mirandola, the Grand Chamber's decision has effectively down-scaled the protection offered by the *ne bis in idem* principle under Article 4 of Protocol No 7 ECHR.[330] Moreover, the judgment has introduced criteria for the assessment of the compatibility of dual criminal and administrative proceedings that 'are either "empty shells" or very ambiguous and difficult to apply in practice, and could possibly lead to arbitrary results'.[331] Subsequent case law of the ECtHR has not remedied these shortcomings. Worse still, in a number of later judgments and decisions, the ECtHR seems to have weakened the importance of some of the 'material factors' that were expressly mentioned in the *A and B v Norway* judgment. Among these, interestingly and tellingly, is the criterion regarding the availability of an 'offsetting mechanism' designed to guarantee the proportionality of the overall amount of penalties that may be imposed in a dual-track system. In other words, even the very factor that was accorded preponderant weight

[327] See ECtHR *A and B v Norway* (n 322) paras 108–134. The Court refers, ia, to ECtHR *Zolotukhin v Russia* (n 323), ECtHR 30 May 2000, *RT v Switzerland* (App No 31982/96), ECtHR 13 December 2005 (dec) *Nilsson v Sweden* (App No 73661/01) *Reports* 2005-XIII, and ECtHR 20 May 2014, *Nykänen v Finland* (App No 11828/11).

[328] ECtHR *A and B v Norway* (n 322) para 122.

[329] ECtHR *A and B v Norway* (n 322) para 132. In applying these factors to the case at hand, the Grand Chamber ultimately finds that Art 4 of Protocol No 7 ECHR has not been breached in respect of the applicants (paras 144–153).

[330] G Lasagni and S Mirandola, 'The European ne bis in idem at the Crossroads of Administrative and Criminal Law' (2019) 2 *Eucrim* 126. See also the dissenting opinion of Judge Pinto de Albuquerque; and see MJJP Luchtman, 'The ECJ's recent case law on ne bis in idem: Implications for law enforcement in a shared legal order' (2018) 55(6) *Common Market Law Review* 1717.

[331] Lasagni and Mirandola, 'The European ne bis in idem' (n 330) 128. These authors argue – with reference also to, inter alia, ECtHR 16 April 2019, *Bjarni Ármannsson v Iceland* (App No 72098/14) para 53, and ECtHR 6 June 2019, *Antoine Nodet v France* (App No 47342/14) para 47 – that, eg, the condition of foreseeability is rendered almost meaningless by the fact that the ECtHR considers this condition satisfied on the mere ground that the national law provides for the possibility of dual proceedings. See also Luchtman, 'The ECJ's recent case law on ne bis in idem' (n 330) 1727.

in *A and B v Norway* appears to have a less decisive meaning than initially assumed.[332] Lasagni and Mirandola conclude that,

> like in other matters, the Court's scrutiny seems to take the form of a global assessment. Although it does verify the observance of each specific condition, neither of them is a *conditio sine qua non*. It is only their combination that decides whether the proceedings are sufficiently connected as a whole or not. Not to mention that such a condition [of an offsetting mechanism] becomes wholly irrelevant where the first procedure has resulted in an acquittal. In this latter case, there will not only be no sanction to offset, but a subsequent finding of guilt in the second set of proceedings will risk violating the presumption of innocence under Art. 6(2) ECHR.[333]

If we consider the rather widespread use of dual-track enforcement systems both in EU law and in the domestic legal systems of many EU Member States, it becomes clearly expedient, indeed pressing, to examine how the CJEU interprets and applies the requirement of proportionate punishment with respect to instances of sanction accumulation in the grey area between administrative and criminal law. It must be noted that already in 2013 – that is, three years before the ECtHR delivered its judgment in the case of *A and B v Norway* – the CJEU ruled that dual-track systems do not, in and of themselves, amount to a violation of the principle of *ne bis in idem*. In its well-known judgment in the case of *Åkerberg Fransson*, the CJEU held that Article 50 CFR does not preclude the successive imposition of an administrative penalty and a criminal penalty for a single offence 'as long as the remaining penalties are effective, proportionate and dissuasive', and provided that 'the first penalty is not criminal in nature'.[334]

The possibilities for Member States to subject offences to dual-track enforcement systems were further expanded five years later. In three judgments, all delivered on 20 March 2018, the CJEU explicitly considers to what extent the fundamental right enshrined in Article 50 CFR may legitimately be *restricted* in light of the requirements set forth in Article 52, paragraph 1 CFR. One of these judgments is the preliminary ruling in the case of *Garlsson Real Estate*.[335] The case concerned offences of market manipulation under (then still) Directive 2003/6.[336] Pursuant to national legislation that

[332] See ECtHR 4 December 2018 (dec) *Matthildur Ingvarsdottir v Iceland* (App No 22779/14), in which case the ECtHR concluded that the dual proceedings were sufficiently closely connected in substance despite the absence of such an 'offsetting mechanism'.

[333] Lasagni and Mirandola, 'The European ne bis in idem' (n 330) 128–29 (references omitted).

[334] CJEU 26 February 2013, C-617/10 *Åklagaren v Hans Åkerberg Fransson* (EU:C:2013:105) paras 36 and 37. See also CJEU 27 May 2014, C-129/14 PPU *Criminal proceedings against Zoran Spasic* (EU:C:2014:586) paras 55–59, dealing with the possibility – under Art 54 of the CISA Convention (n 154) – of a second criminal prosecution in cases where the first prosecution for the same offence had taken place in another Member State and resulted in a conviction and the imposition of a criminal sanction, which was, however, never executed. See JAE Vervaele, 'Schengen and Charter-related ne bis in idem protection in the Area of Freedom, Security and Justice: *M* and *Zoran Spasic*' (2015) 52 *Common Market Law Review* 1339.

[335] CJEU 20 March 2018, C-537/16 *Garlsson Real Estate SA et al v Commissione Nazionale per le Società e la Borsa (Consob)* (EU:C:2018:193). The other two judgments are CJEU 20 March 2018, C-524/15 *Criminal proceedings against Luca Menci* (EU:C:2018:197), concerning market abuse, and CJEU 20 March 2018, C-596/16 and C-597/16 *Enzo Di Puma v Commissione Nazionale per le Società e la Borsa (Consob)* and *Commissione Nazionale per le Società e la Borsa (Consob) v Antonio Zecca* (EU:C:2018:192), concerning tax fraud.

[336] See n 174. This Directive – substituted by Regulation 596/2014/EU in 2014 – was discussed already in subsection IV.B. above. See also Luchtman and Vervaele, 'Enforcing the Market Abuse Regime' (n 213); Veenbrink, *Criminal Law Principles* (n 115) 43–46.

had been adopted by the Italian state in order to transpose this Directive into national law, an administrative penalty of several millions of euros was inflicted on Mr Stefano Ricucci and two companies that stood under his direction (Magiste International SA and Garlsson Real Estate SA) for the offences in question. In addition, Mr Ricucci was criminally prosecuted for the same offences. These parallel criminal proceedings resulted in a final judgment by which the criminal court sentenced Mr Ricucci to a term of imprisonment (which sentence was never executed due to a pardon that was later granted to him).

Before the Italian Court of Cassation, Mr Ricucci submitted that the principle of *ne bis in idem* had been breached in his regard, as he had been tried and punished twice for the same acts. The Court of Cassation thereupon decided to request a preliminary ruling from the CJEU. One of the questions referred to the CJEU was whether or not Article 50 CFR permits the imposition of an administrative penalty on a person in respect of an offence of which this same person has already been convicted by a final judgment of a criminal court.[337] In answer to this question, the CJEU notes, first, that a limitation of the principle of *ne bis in idem* must meet an 'objective of general interest' within the meaning of Article 52, paragraph 1 CFR. This condition is satisfied, according to the CJEU, where Member States, in order to 'protect the integrity of the financial markets of the European Union and public confidence in financial instruments', provide for double-track systems that pursue 'complementary aims relating, as the case may be, to different aspects of the same unlawful conduct at issue'.[338]

It is stated, second, that dual-track enforcement systems that allow for a duplication of proceedings and penalties of a criminal nature must comply with the principle of proportionality referred to in Article 52, paragraph 1 CFR, which is to say that this possibility of dual proceedings and penalties must 'not exceed what is appropriate and necessary in order to attain the objectives legitimately pursued'.[339] In order to satisfy this requirement, national legislation must provide for clear and precise rules that allow individuals to predict which acts or omissions are liable to be subject to a duplication of proceedings and penalties of a criminal nature. By implication, national legislation must ensure an effective coordination between both tracks, so as to reduce the additional disadvantage of dual proceedings for the persons involved above what is strictly necessary for achieving the relevant objectives of general interest.[340] Moreover,

> the duplication of penalties of a criminal nature requires rules allowing it to be guaranteed that the severity of the sum of all of the penalties imposed corresponds with the seriousness of the offence concerned, that requirement resulting not only from Article 52(1) of the Charter, but also from the principle of proportionality of penalties set out in Article 49(3) thereof. Those rules must provide for the obligation for the competent authorities, in the event of the imposition of a second penalty, to ensure that the severity of the sum of all of the penalties imposed does not exceed the seriousness of the offence identified.[341]

[337] A second question was whether or not Art 50 CFR may be directly relied upon by an individual before a national court.

[338] CJEU *Garlsson Real Estate et al* (n 335) para 46.

[339] CJEU *Garlsson Real Estate et al* (n 335) para 48.

[340] CJEU *Garlsson Real Estate et al* (n 335) paras 51–55.

[341] CJEU *Garlsson Real Estate et al* (n 335) para 56.

In other words, national legislation must provide for an offsetting mechanism designed to ensure that the severity of the penalty that was imposed first is fully taken into account when a second penalty is calculated. With respect to the case underlying the request for a preliminary ruling, the CJEU finds that the safeguards against excessive severity of the cumulated penalties were insufficient, because the offsetting mechanism in place under Italian law related only to the duplication of pecuniary penalties but not to the accumulation of a term of imprisonment and an administrative fine of a criminal nature.[342] In respect of Mr Ricucci, the CJEU furthermore notes that the duplication of proceedings can anyway not be considered 'strictly necessary in order to achieve the objective [of general interest]' – and should thus be regarded as prohibited by Article 50 CFR – if, according to the referring court, the outcome of the initial, criminal proceedings was already 'such as to punish the offence committed in an effective, proportionate and dissuasive manner'.[343]

When compared to the approach taken by the ECtHR in *A and B v Norway* and in subsequent case law, it may seem that the CJEU employs a somewhat stricter proportionality requirement insofar as its ruling in the *Garlsson Real Estate* case may be said to indicate that criminal proceedings take precedence over (quasi-criminal) administrative proceedings. This impression is corroborated by the two other judgments of 20 March 2018 concerning the compatibility of dual-track enforcement regimes with the requirements under Articles 50 and 52 CFR. In one of these, the CJEU held that the principle of *ne bis in idem* (also) precludes the initiation of (punitive) administrative proceedings following a final *acquittal* in criminal proceedings with regard to the same offence.[344] In the other judgment, by contrast, the CJEU concluded that the initiation of criminal proceedings *after* the imposition of an administrative sanction (of a 'criminal' nature) does not amount to a violation of Article 50 CFR.[345]

However, the three CJEU rulings of 20 March 2018 do not make entirely clear when and why a duplication of proceedings and penalties should be considered incompatible with Article 50 CFR. Do these judgments imply that Article 50 CFR is to be interpreted as precluding the bringing of administrative proceedings following criminal proceedings with respect to the same offence (only) if these criminal proceedings ended in the imposition of an 'effective, proportionate, and dissuasive' punishment? Or should the principle of *ne bis in idem* rather be taken to prohibit additional administrative proceedings (only) when they follow criminal proceedings that resulted in an acquittal? Although these alternative interpretations are not necessarily mutually exclusive, neither are they, of course, completely congruous.[346] Be that as it may, it appears warranted to

[342] CJEU *Garlsson Real Estate et al* (n 335) para 60.

[343] CJEU *Garlsson Real Estate et al* (n 335) para 57. The fact that the prison sentence imposed on Mr Ricucci was never executed is considered irrelevant in this regard; see para 62. With regard to the second question asked by the Italian Court of Cassation (see n 337 above), the CJEU concludes that the right conferred by Art 50 CFR is directly applicable by individuals before national courts; see para 68. AG Manuel Campos Sánchez-Bordona reached the same conclusions in his Opinion of 12 September 2017, C-537/16 *Garlsson Real Estate SA et al v Commissione Nazionale per le Società e la Borsa (Consob)* (EU:C:2017:668).

[344] CJEU *Di Puma* (n 335).

[345] CJEU *Menci* (n 335).

[346] See Lasagni and Mirandola, 'The European ne bis in idem' (n 330) 131, who argue that 'it appears at least peculiar that the CJEU explicitly highlighted this more demanding meaning of the proportionality requirement precisely in *Garlsson*, that is in the field of market abuse, where the duplication of punitive proceedings is a choice that does not find its legal basis in purely national law (as in the case of VAT examined in *Menci*), but derives from the transposition of Directive 2003/6/EC (the validity of which was not questioned by the Court)'.

conclude that the CJEU has attuned its interpretation of the principle of *ne bis in idem* to that of the ECtHR, and vice versa.

Already for some years, both European courts have acknowledged that, subject to certain conditions, dual-track punitive enforcement systems are not at variance with the principle of *ne bis in idem*, even when these systems may lead to a duplication of proceedings and penalties in relation to one and the same offence. This implies that the protective efficacy of Article 4, paragraph 1 of Protocol No 7 ECHR and Article 50 CFR has been reduced in relation to the level of protection that was upheld still in previous case law.[347] As was expounded before, the principle of *ne bis in idem* overlaps with the principle of *nulla poena sine culpa* insofar as both seek to prevent disproportionate punishment. It was seen that both the ECtHR and the CJEU emphasise that where dual-track systems allow for an accumulation of sanctions, these systems should provide for an offsetting mechanism designed to ensure that the overall amount of penalties imposed is proportionate.

It may be said, insomuch, that both courts at least recognise the importance of the fourth and last dimension of the principle of individual culpability with regard to offences that may give rise to multiple proceedings and to sanction accumulation. The status and the exact meaning of the requirement of proportionality of sanctions, however, remain rather uncertain. For instance, it is not clear what exactly is comprehended by the requirement's *correlative* in contexts of double-track enforcements systems: to what extent does the requirement that an aggregate of sanctions is proportionate to 'the seriousness of the offence' imply that (the measure of) personal blameworthiness must be taken into account?[348] Do considerations of subjective aspects of guilt have a role to play at all in these regulatory contexts? And lastly, it is not clear whether – and if so, under what conditions – *effet utile*-oriented interests may even override the demand of proportionate sanctioning altogether.[349]

VII. Conclusion

This contribution has concentrated on the role of the principle of individual culpability, or *nulla poena sine culpa*, in European criminal law and – especially – in a number of

[347] Such as ECtHR *Zolotukhin v Russia* (n 323). Cp Lasagni and Mirandola, 'The European ne bis in idem' (n 330) 132: '[T]he case law of both European courts on the legitimacy of double-track punitive systems seems … to glide towards a downward competition. Ruling in favour of the admissibility of double-track systems (under certain conditions), both courts have lowered the level of protection previously granted to individuals, and shown that the equivalence clause is in itself insufficient to ensure an adequate level of fundamental rights safeguards.' Cp Luchtman, 'The ECJ's recent case law on ne bis in idem' (n 330) 1748: 'What is important to stress in that regard is that the ECJ – not the ECtHR – has upheld the almost binary status of the ne bis in idem guarantees. A second prosecution or sanction after a final first one is a limitation of the principle, requiring a solid justification. The ECJ has managed to avoid an open conflict with the ECtHR, but has also kept its options open to raise the standards over time. That is quite a remarkable – maybe even an impressive – balancing exercise.'

[348] See subsection VI.A. above. Cp the reference to 'the harm caused … by the offence committed' in CJEU *Garlsson Real Estate* (n 335) paras 59 and 63.

[349] Lasagni and Mirandola, 'The European ne bis in idem' (n 330) 129. See also Luchtman, 'The ECJ's recent case law on ne bis in idem' (n 330) 1755; Nuotio, 'A Legitimacy-based Approach to EU Criminal Law' (n 283).

fields of European punitive-administrative or 'quasi-criminal' law. As is well-known, prior to the entry into force of the Lisbon Treaty in 2009, there was a long and fierce debate on the issue of whether or not the EU was entitled to create punitive enforcement measures regarding matters in respect of which the EU lacked an explicit competence to adopt criminal legislation, that is, matters that fell outside the scope of the intergovernmental 'third pillar'. The dispute dates back, at least, to 1992, in which year the CJEU delivered its landmark judgment in the case of *Germany v Commission*.[350] In this judgment, the CJEU affirmed the EU's competence to provide for administrative sanctions in order to protect the internal market. According to a much-heard criticism, the fact that these sanctions do not officially count as 'criminal' sanctions does not in itself make it any less likely that they satisfy the *Engel* criteria and thereby qualify as 'penalties' for the purposes of Articles 6 and 7 ECHR.[351] Moreover, the adoption of quasi-criminal punitive measures indicated for many a type of 'function creep' that could potentially lead to a supranational system of sanctions throughout the EU.[352]

As is known, however, these and other criticisms have not stopped the EU from expanding its competences. The Lisbon Treaty has significantly expanded the EU's legislative competence in matters of criminal law. Consequently, the EU has increasingly obliged its Member States to criminalise certain conduct in order to enhance the *effet utile* of EU law.[353] This fact has not, however, rendered the function of administrative sanctions less important. As was seen, the EU legislature has in recent years, for example, repeatedly resorted to a 'dual-track' enforcement mechanism consisting of a combination of administrative and criminal liability regimes.[354] Over the past few decades, EU Member States have as a result implemented a vast number of both criminal and quasi-criminal enforcement mechanisms stemming from different subfields of European law. According to Ester Herlin-Karnell, the possibility of providing for administrative sanctions 'played an important role in expanding the competences of the EU and thereby, prior to the Lisbon Treaty, made possible a quasi-criminal law system at the expense of the due process safeguards traditionally associated with criminal law'.[355] Concurrently, it may be asked whether systems of EU quasi-criminal law have also come at the expense of *substantive* criminal law safeguards.

The present contribution has attempted to dig out whether and to what extent the demands ensuing from the classical substantive criminal law principle of *nulla poena sine culpa* are recognised and adhered to in EU quasi-criminal law. The analysis was divided into five parts: after a propaedeutic discussion of the principle's origins and of the ways in which the principle is reflected in contemporary criminal law systems in section II, four dimensions of the principle of *nulla poena sine culpa* were addressed

[350] CJEU 27 October 1992, C-240/90 *Germany v Commission* (EU:C:1992:408); see also the conclusion of AG Francis Jacobs of 3 June 1992, C-240/90 *Germany v Commission* (EU:C:1992:237).

[351] ECtHR *Engel et al v the Netherlands* (n 98). As was seen in subsection III.B. above, the *Engel* criteria were adopted by the CJEU in its judgment in the *Bonda* case (n 98).

[352] Herlin-Karnell, 'Is Administrative Law Still Relevant?' (n 223) 234–35. See also E Herlin-Karnell, *The Constitutional Dimension of European Criminal Law* (Oxford, Hart Publishing, 2012) 10–41.

[353] See Franssen, 'EU Criminal Law and *Effet Utile*' (n 2).

[354] See subsections IV.C. and VI.C. above.

[355] Herlin-Karnell, 'Is Administrative Law Still Relevant?' (n 223) 237.

individually in sections III to VI. The first dimension concerns the condition that a liable subject can legitimately be considered as the 'author' (or *Urheber*) of the offence in question. As appears from the ECtHR's case law, this means that, in principle, one can be held criminally liable only for one's *own* misconduct. It was seen, however, that this requirement applies less strictly in the quasi-criminal law domain of EU competition law. Liability for infringements of Articles 101 and 102 TFEU is established at the level of undertakings or 'economic units'. Under this 'economic approach', a group of persons may in certain cases be held collectively liable for a single infringement. And in parent-subsidiary relations, a parent company may in certain cases be held vicariously liable for an infringement committed by its subsidiary, even when there has been no involvement or guilt with respect to the infringement on the part of the parent.[356]

The second dimension of the principle of individual culpability relates to mens rea; it concerns the condition that the liable subject is found to have committed the offence in question intentionally, recklessly, or at least negligently.[357] Leaving exceptions aside, it was seen that the mens rea requirement of intention marks a notable distinction between EU criminal law and EU quasi-criminal law. When the EU obliges its Member States to criminalise certain behaviour, this obligation normally only concerns intentional manifestations of that behaviour. Criminalisation of reckless and/or seriously negligent behaviour, by implication, is only seldom required. By contrast, liability for unintentional behaviour is rather common in areas of quasi-criminal law; in some of these areas, liability may even extend to 'mere' or 'ordinary' negligence, whereas at least 'serious' negligence is required in EU criminal law. In other words, mens rea requirements are generally less stringent within areas of quasi-criminal law than is typically the case within criminal law. Moreover, it was seen that with regard to some quasi-criminal offences, the requisite mens rea element may rather easily be inferred from objective circumstances, or may even be presumed to be fulfilled – provided, that is, that this presumption is rebuttable.

The third dimension of the principle of *nulla poena sine culpa* concerns the condition of personal blameworthiness. Someone is personally blameworthy for his or her wrongful action if it can reasonably be assumed that he or she could have avoided the action. In criminal law, personal blameworthiness is normally presumed when a subject is found to have fulfilled the elements of an offence definition; this presumption is defeated, however, if a generally recognised exculpatory defence applies. The possibility of rebutting the presumption of blameworthiness – and hence of invoking exculpatory defences – is especially important in fields of quasi-criminal law where relatively low evidentiary thresholds apply to mens rea elements. However, it was seen that the concept of force majeure (or duress of circumstances) is construed rather restrictively by the CJEU in the context of regulation under the EU's common agricultural policy. Moreover, it was seen that the CJEU seems to have effectively shut the door on virtually any possibility of successfully forwarding the defence of an excusable mistake of

[356] In other words: the range of persons who may potentially be designated as infringers of EU competition rules is wider than the range of persons to whom – in accordance with the classical view in criminal law – perpetratorship may potentially be attributed. See subsection III.C. above.

[357] This is, of course, not to deny the existence of (sometimes numerous) strict liability offences in criminal and/or quasi-criminal law systems in different Member States. See subsections II.C. and III.A. above.

law with regard to antitrust offences. It therefore seems that the third dimension of the culpability principle is only very partially recognised in EU quasi-criminal law.

The fourth dimension of the principle of *nulla poena sine culpa*, lastly, concerns the condition that penalties are proportionate to the liable subject's culpability in a 'relational' sense that includes the gravity of the relevant offence. The requirement of proportionate sentencing is laid down in Article 49 CFR, and ever since the CJEU delivered its ruling in the *Greek Maize* case,[358] the EU courts and legislature have persistently demanded that sanctions in areas of EU law are 'effective, proportionate and dissuasive'. With regard to the pecuniary sanctions that are imposed by the Commission for cartel offences, it was seen that the Commission seems to lend preponderant importance to the deterrent or dissuasive effect which these quasi-criminal penalties are intended to produce. Correspondingly, it seems that relatively little attention is generally paid to the requirement of proportionality.[359] It was furthermore seen that, according to both the CJEU and the ECtHR, dual-track liability regimes are not necessarily precluded by the principle of *ne bis in idem*. Where dual-track systems allow for an accumulation of (criminal and administrative) sanctions for one and the same infringement, the national law in question must provide for an offsetting mechanism designed to ensure that the overall level of penalties imposed is proportionate to the seriousness of the offence. What this exactly means in practice, however, is not very clear.[360]

In conclusion: although it is true that the principle of *nulla poena sine culpa* is recognised, by and large, in areas of quasi-criminal law, the efficacy of this principle is generally considerably weaker in these areas than in traditional criminal law. The requirements that ensue from the four dimensions of the principle of individual culpability – and that serve the protective function of curtailing liability for infringements – are generally stronger, and applied more strictly, in criminal law. This need not be an alarming conclusion per se. After all, legal principles were seen to be 'open-ended' phenomena, which is to say that they, by definition, are open to a variety of interpretations.[361] The principle of *nulla poena sine culpa* may accordingly assume slightly different meanings, and be attributed varying degrees of normative force, depending on the type and underlying rationale of the legal (sub)domain in which the principle is operative. Arguably, most areas of quasi-criminal law have a predominantly 'regulatory' character; and given that regulatory legal domains are known to accord much weight to instrumental considerations and *effet utile* concerns, it may seem only natural that correspondingly less weight is accorded to protective requirements, such as those embodied by the principle of individual culpability.

However, the findings that were summarised above may still be a cause for concern. It was seen that the distinctions drawn in EU law and national law between criminal law proper, on the one hand, and punitive administrative law, on the other,

[358] CJEU *Commission v Hellenic Republic* (n 90).

[359] The fact that liability for infringements of Arts 101 and 102 TFEU is established at the level of undertakings implies that a fine may have disproportionate consequences for the legal (and possibly natural) persons in respect of whom the Commission's fining decisions are enforced. Moreover, it was seen that the EU courts tend to subject the Commission's fining decisions to a restrained scrutiny; see subsection VI.B. above.

[360] See, eg, n 332 above.

[361] See Peters, *Het rechtskarakter* (n 17) and subsection II.A. above.

are often rather artificial and arbitrary.[362] For example, the different forms of anti-competitive conduct that are penalised under EU competition law are classified as administrative offences; however, this 'wholesale' allocation to administrative law is hardly self-explanatory (and even less so in light of the EU's increased 'appetite for criminal law').[363] It is at least not contrived to consider 'hard-core' cartel offences as wrongs that are *mala in se* and that are therefore suitable candidates for criminalisation.[364] Moreover, on a far more abstract note: the findings of this chapter may perhaps be said to bear witness to a tendency in contemporary Western societies towards disregarding or even disparaging inner qualities, and towards overrating outward phenomena.[365] In contrast to outward qualities – that have the advantage of being available, at least potentially, for immediate observation – inner qualities are intricate, intangible, and are consequently often considered 'troublesome'. The classical (Kantian) concept of 'imputability' and the appertaining notions of action, fault and culpability have consequently come under increasing pressure.[366] But as Paul Ricoeur reminds us, disregarding inner qualities – and thus disregarding the principle of *nulla poena sine culpa* – comes at a price:

> The recent history of what is called the law of responsibility, in the technical sense of the term, has tended to make room for the idea of a responsibility without any fault ... The perverse effect consists in the fact that, the more we extend the sphere of risks, the more pressing and urgent is the search for someone responsible, that is, someone, whether a physical or a legal person, capable of indemnifying and making reparation. ... When so disconnected from a problematic of *decision*, action finds itself placed under the sign of a fatalism that is the exact opposite of responsibility. Fate implies no one, responsibility someone.[367]

[362] See subsection III.A. above.

[363] See Franssen, 'EU Criminal Law and *Effet Utile*' (n 2) 92, 98–99; and see subsection IV.C.

[364] In the United States, cartel activity has been treated as criminal offending already since the late 19th century. And several EU Member States have introduced criminal offences that target certain aspects of 'hard-core' cartel activity. See Harding, 'The Relationship between EU Criminal Law and Competition Law' (n 113).

[365] See AWM Mooij, 'On (Free) Will' in F de Jong (ed), *Overarching Views of Crime and Deviancy. Rethinking the Legacy of the Utrecht School* (The Hague, Eleven International Publishing, 2014) 421–33; See also Mooij, *Intentionality, Desire, Responsibility* (n 21).

[366] See subsection II.B. above.

[367] Ricoeur, *The Just* (n 29) 25–26.

8

Non-conviction Based Confiscation: Moving the Confiscation of Criminal Proceeds from the Criminal to the 'Civil' Sphere

*Benefits, Issues and Two Procedural Aspects**

JOHAN BOUCHT

I. Introduction

The traditional approach to asset recovery is by way of criminal law. However, confiscating the proceeds of crime within criminal proceedings often requires not only a criminal conviction, but also a causal connection to be established between the offence(s) of which the defendant has been convicted and the assets in question. These requirements limit the availability of asset confiscation in situations where, for example, the criminal conduct from which the assets originate cannot be proved to the required evidential standard or where the defendant has fled or died, even where the assets in question are likely to constitute proceeds of crime. From a policy perspective, this is unfortunate as it inhibits the effective recovery of criminal proceeds.

The criminal law approach to confiscation has subsequently been broadened by rules on so-called extended criminal confiscation that facilitate confiscation also in some of these situations.[1] In extended confiscation proceedings, a triggering conviction will still be necessary, but the causality requirement between the property and the criminal conduct is diluted and the burden of proof concerning the origin of the assets may be reversed.[2] The purpose is thus to facilitate confiscation also in situations where

* I am grateful to the editors, Dan Frände, Ian Smith and Jo Stigen for valuable comments on an earlier draft of this article. All remaining errors are my own.

[1] See eg Article 5 of the EU Confiscation Directive 2014/42/EU.

[2] For an analysis of various regimes of extended criminal confiscation, see J Boucht, *The Limits of Asset Confiscation. On Assessing the Legitimacy of Extended Appropriation of Criminal Proceeds* (Oxford, Hart Publishing, 2017), 30–66. This chapter is in part based on the findings of that book.

the assets in question cannot be causally connected to the offence(s) for which the defendant has been convicted.

In some jurisdictions, the asset recovery regime has been further expanded beyond the domains of criminal law through the introduction of rules on non-conviction based confiscation.[3] Non-conviction based (NCB) confiscation is a measure for depriving an individual of certain identified property that is or represents the proceeds of crime, in proceedings detached from prior or parallel criminal proceedings, and irrespective of whether or not the property can be causally linked to (an) offence(s) of which the individual has been convicted. Proceedings are often conducted using civil procedural rules, but can also take place within a criminal procedural framework.[4]

There is considerable institutional support for introducing NCB confiscation schemes. For example, Article 54(1)(c) of the UN Convention Against Corruption, urges the signatory states to consider 'taking such measures as may be necessary to allow confiscation of such property without a criminal conviction in cases in which the offender cannot be prosecuted by reason of death, flight or absence or in other appropriate cases.' The Financial Action Task Force (FATF) also recommends implementation of such schemes. Its fourth recommendation states, inter alia:

> Countries should consider adopting measures that allow such proceeds or instrumentalities to be confiscated without requiring a criminal conviction (non-conviction based confiscation), or which require an offender to demonstrate the lawful origin of the property alleged to be liable to confiscation, to the extent that such a requirement is consistent with the principles of their domestic law.[5]

At the European level, a proposal for a NCB confiscation scheme could be found in Article 5 of the proposal for the EU confiscation directive (2014/42/EU).[6] However, some Member States found the proposal too far-reaching, and it was therefore taken out of the final Directive (although some remnants can be found in Article 4(2)). The Commission nevertheless still harbours interest for introducing an NCB confiscation scheme at EU level.[7]

[3] A number of European countries have established NCB confiscation schemes, for example the UK, Ireland, Italy, Bulgaria and Slovenia. In Norway, the Justice Department is currently (as of autumn 2019) considering introducing NCB confiscation.

[4] For an overview of the development of asset confiscation schemes, see J Boucht. 'Asset confiscation in Europe – past, present, and future challenges' (2019) 26(2) *Journal of Financial Crime* 526, 529–34. For a brief history of asset confiscation, see M Fernandez-Bertier, 'The history of Confiscation Laws: From the Book of Exodus to the War on White-Collar Crime' in K Ligeti and M Simonato (eds), *Chasing Criminal Money. Challenges and Perspectives On Asset Recovery in the EU* (Oxford, Hart Publishing, 2017), 51–73.

[5] See also TS Greenberg, LM Samuel, W Grant and L Gray, *Stolen Asset Recovery. A Good Practices Guide for Non-Conviction Based Asset Forfeiture* (Washington DC, World Bank, 2009).

[6] Se COM(2012) 85 final. The proposal was criticised, see eg Jon Petter Rui, 'Non-Conviction Based Confiscation in the European Union – An Assessment of Art. 5 of the Proposal for a Directive of the European Parliament and of the Council on the Freezing and Confiscation of Proceeds of Crime in the European Union' (2012) 13 *ERA Forum* 349–60.

[7] See Report from the European Commission to the European Parliament and the Council: Asset recovery and confiscation. Ensuring that Crime does not pay (COM(2020) 217 final, 2.6.2020), 14. See also Commission Staff Working Document: 'Analysis of non-conviction based confiscation measures in the European Union' (SWD(2019) 1050 final, 12 April 2019).

Asset recovery law is particularly tinged by the tension between efficacy arguments (the use of broad draconian regimes) and *Rechtsstaat*-based arguments (protection of individual rights). There is a tendency today to give preference to the former. Moving sanctions and other measures targeting 'dirty money' outside of the criminal domain is indeed a feasible way of making the asset recovery system more effective. However, it is crucial that also the rights of the individuals targeted are duly protected.

A core issue in the legal analysis is therefore what the safeguard regime should look like in NCB proceedings, ie how a fair and proportionate balance between the interests of the state and those of the individual should be struck. When seeking to identify an adequate safeguard regime it would seem more feasible to adopt a functional approach and to identify criteria based on 'the true' nature and consequences of NCB confiscation proceedings.

In this chapter, I will begin by looking at what NCB confiscation is and how it can be justified. After this, I will look at the enforcement needs that may call for NCB confiscation schemes to be implemented and with regard to which such schemes can be controversial. The rest of the chapter is dedicated to a discussion on two important procedural aspects, namely what the proper standard of proof should be in NCB confiscation proceedings and to what extent, if any, reversing the burden of proof may be justified in such proceedings.

II. Non-conviction Based Recovery of Criminal Proceeds – Main Characteristics

A. The Purpose of Confiscation

How can NCB confiscation, and confiscation in general, be justified? Various objectives tend to feature in policy documents, judicial decisions and legal doctrine. Not all of the following are necessarily invoked in every jurisdiction, but one or more normally features:

- *restoration of the status quo ante*: to restore the state of things before the relevant offence was committed (gain neutralisation);
- *deterrence of potential offenders* (general prevention) and *actual offenders* (special prevention) from committing unlawful acts in the future;
- *prevention*: to remove the property in question from the defendant in order to prevent it from being used to further crime (safety measure); or
- *remedy*: compensating either the victim for costs incurred by the crime or the government for the expense of law enforcement activity.[8]

The relationship between these objectives is not always clear. In assessing how asset confiscation is, or should be, justified it may be useful to distinguish, in line

[8] For a more thorough discussion on this, see Boucht *The Limits of Asset Confiscation* (n 2), 95–116.

with Hart's classical distinction, between a general justifying aim and principles of distribution.[9] Why confiscation is a good institution (its overarching purpose) and how confiscation orders should be calculated are separate questions that call for separate justifications. A third important question concerns how confiscated assets are disposed of.

Confiscation – both criminal and NCB – forms part of the criminal justice sanctioning system. As such, it also shares the general justifying aim of that system, which is general prevention (deterrence).[10] It would indeed send an unfortunate message if criminals were permitted to retain the fruits of their crimes. However, deterrence is problematic as a guiding principle of distribution.[11] Confiscating the respondent's assets for the purpose of disincentivising offending is problematic out of principle. Moreover, measuring the proportionality of a confiscation order against its deterrent aims will render it difficult, if not virtually impossible, to impose any substantive limitations on confiscation schemes based on proportionality considerations. In addition, there is empirical uncertainty as regards the factual effects of deterrence in a confiscation context.[12]

The proper purpose of confiscation at the distributive phase, both criminal and NCB, ought instead to be to recover the financial benefit that the respondent has obtained through unlawful conduct.[13] An individual who has obtained assets by way of criminal conduct has no moral right to that property and should therefore not be allowed to retain it. The main distributive principle of asset confiscation should therefore be restoration, or gain neutralisation of (past) criminal conduct, ie to restore the *status quo ante*.[14] An inherent limitation to the quantification of confiscation orders (and to the pursuit of general prevention) will thus be the reference at the quantification stage to particular criminal conduct in the past. A confiscation scheme

[9] HLA Hart, *Punishment and Responsibility* (Oxford, Clarendon Press, 1968), 6. See for this line of reasoning, Boucht (n 2), 96.

[10] On the justification of punishment, see eg Andrew Ashworth and Jeremy Horder, *Principles of Criminal Law*, 7th edn (Oxford, Oxford University Press, 2013), 16–17.

[11] See Boucht (n 2), 98–100.

[12] For confiscation to have a deterrent effect, it must be known to offenders that such a sanction may be imposed on them. Research on the deterrent effects of punishment proper suggests that much less is known amongst potential perpetrators about the consequences of their actions than the law-makers would like to think. As J Ulph, 'Confiscation orders, human rights, and penal measures' (2010) 126 *Law Quarterly Review* 251, 278 rightly observes, it cannot be said with confidence that all criminals understand the current confiscation regime and, foreseeing the consequences of their actions, will take steps to avoid these severe measures. Moreover, research indicates that membership of a group might weaken the capacity to let consequences guide actions, due to group pressure (see PH Robinson and JM Darley, 'Does Criminal Law Deter? A Behavioural Science Investigation' (2004) 24 *Oxford Journal of Legal Studies* 180–81). For a general discussion, see Boucht (n 2), 101–09.

[13] Confiscation measures can of course also be based on, for example, purely preventative considerations. However, this would seem to require particular safeguards to be put in place because of the exorbitant potential of prevention as a principle of quantification.

[14] This is in line with how Lord Walker and Hughes LJ, with whom the other Law Lords agreed, described the aim of asset confiscation in the important UK Supreme Court case *R v Waya* [2012] 3 WLR 1188, para 21: 'Nor is it to be doubted that the severity of the regime will have a deterrent effect on at least some would be criminals. It does not, however, follow that its deterrent qualities represent the essence (or the "grain") of the legislation. They are, no doubt, an incident of it, but they are not its essence. Its essence, and its frequently declared purpose, is to remove from criminals the pecuniary proceeds of their crime.'

based on such restoration principle will still also fulfil the other purposes, for example deterrence, prevention.[15]

At the disposal phase, other objectives become relevant. It is particularly at this stage that remedial considerations are of importance: It is a notable aim of any confiscation regime to facilitate monetary compensation of costs related to the criminal conduct in question. This may involve using the confiscated funds to compensate for damages incurred by the victim of the offence (the victim perspective). It may also involve schemes through which law enforcement agencies may apply for funding from confiscated assets.

B. Main Characteristics of NCB Confiscation

There are different kinds of NCB confiscation schemes, but I wish to look at two types here. One is a so-called hybrid model; it forms part of the criminal confiscation regime, but modifications have been done concerning, for example, the standard of proof and the need to concretise the offences in which the assets allegedly originate. This kind of regime can be found in German law under section 76a(IV) of the German Criminal Code (StGB).[16] The other is the civil recovery model, which operates quite independently from the criminal confiscation regime and the criminal process. This kind of scheme can be found in Ireland under the Proceeds of Crime Act 1995 and in the United Kingdom under the Proceeds of Crime Act 2002, Part V.

What then are the features that distinguish NCB confiscation from criminal confiscation? NCB confiscation proceedings relate to identified illicit property, rather than, for example, estimated benefit in value, ie a certain amount that the respondent has to pay. The proceedings can therefore be said to be *in specie* rather than *in personam* (that is, directed against an individual who is normally the defendant).[17] The aim is to target identified illicit property rather than the holder of it. Therefore, all that in principle is required for confiscation is that a person holds or controls identified property that constitutes or represents the proceeds of crime.

Whereas in criminal confiscation the existence of a predicate criminal conviction is a necessary prerequisite, NCB confiscation schemes facilitate confiscation irrespective

[15] For a discussion on how the restorative aim at the quantitative phase affects the proportionality assessment, for example in the direction of applying a net principle so that costs are deductible, see J Boucht, 'Proportionality in Asset Confiscation Proceedings' in E Billis, N Knust and JP Rui (eds), *Effectiveness and Proportionality. Modern Challenges in Security Law and Criminal Justice* (Oxford, Hart Publishing, 2021).

[16] This kind of scheme has also been proposed in Norwegian law by the Criminal Law Council in their report NOU 2020: 10. However, in the subsequent Bill (Prop. 241 L (2020–2021)), the Department of Justice did not support the introduction of a hybrid scheme into Norwegian confiscation law.

[17] In some jurisdictions, for example the United States, this concept is based on the idea of the primary responsibility of property in certain circumstances, i.e. that the property rather than the owner is liable to the claimant, see SD Cassella, *Asset Forfeiture Law in the United States* (JurisNet LLC, 2013), 29–37. However, Cassella observes (at 34–35) that the modern notion of *in rem* proceedings, rather than being based on the fiction that the property itself has done something wrong, is based on an understanding that they are simply structures to allow the state to acquire title to criminally tainted property in single proceedings. It is noticeable that while NCB confiscation proceedings in the US are actually brought against property (eg *United States v $734,547.82 in US Currency*, 286 F.3d 641, 657 (3d Circuit 2002)), NCB confiscation proceedings in for example England and Ireland are brought in the name of the holder rather than against the property.

of a criminal conviction. Civil recovery proceedings are, moreover, in principle wholly detached from criminal proceedings. NCB confiscation proceedings may thus be brought regardless of whether or not criminal proceedings are pending or have been brought for a criminal offence (for example because of insufficient grounds for prosecution), whether there has been an acquittal, or whether the person suspected of the offence has absconded or died.

Proceedings under the hybrid model are often conducted within the criminal procedural framework, while proceedings under the civil recovery model are often conducted within the civil procedural framework. In both types of confiscation schemes, the burden of proof is on the state. In order to successfully claim recovery, the state will therefore have to prove that the identified assets are liable to confiscation, ie that the individual holds certain identified property and that that property is or represents the proceeds of crime.

The standard of proof in NCB confiscation proceedings varies, but a common feature is that it is lower than that which applies in criminal proceedings. In the civil model, the standard of proof is often the civil standard, ie a balance of probabilities.[18] Some hybrid models operate with a different standard of proof. For example, the proposed Norwegian confiscation scheme requires a 'clear balance of probabilities', ie an enhanced civil standard rather than the criminal standard. The German hybrid model under section 76a(IV) is formally based on the criminal standard, which in German law corresponds to '*Überzeugung*', ie that the judge must be 'convinced' that the assets derive from unlawful conduct. However, section 437 of the German Criminal Procedural Code (*Strafprozessordnung*; StPO) eases this requirement by allowing the judge to reach this decision in view of the disproportionality between the assets and the respondent's legitimate income, the circumstances in which the assets where located, and the personal or economic circumstances of the respondent.

Various civil recovery schemes have been assessed by the ECtHR, but have normally not been considered to be in violation of ECHR Article 6(2), Article 7 or Article 1 of Protocol No 1 to the ECHR (ECHR-P1) (which also includes a procedural aspect in light of Article 6(1)). In a number of rulings the ECtHR has concluded that the fairness of civil recovery proceedings falls to be examined under the civil head of Article 6(1) ECHR.[19]

In order to make the system more effective and to mitigate the effects of the burden of proof in cases where sufficient evidence may be difficult to obtain, some states have taken steps towards reversing the burden of proof in NCB confiscation proceedings, thereby placing the burden of explanation on the respondent. This may require the respondent to produce some explanation as to the lawful origin of the assets in question in order to avoid a presumption of illicit origin to be applied to his detriment (see further below section V.D).

An example of such a scheme is the unexplained wealth mechanism introduced in UK in 2017. An Unexplained Wealth Order (UWO) under Part 8 of the Proceeds

[18] See eg POCA 2002 s 6(7) (UK) and POCA 1996 s 8(2) (Ireland). Also the civil recovery scheme proposed in Norway law is based on a balance of probabilities, see Rui (n 64 below).

[19] See eg *Gogitidze v Georgia*, App No 36862/05 (ECtHR, 12 May 2015) and *Walsh v the United Kingdom*, App No 43384/05 (ECtHR, 21 November 2006).

of Crime Act (POCA) 2002 is an investigatory measure assisting the authorities in the confiscation of assets otherwise difficult to reach.[20] A UWO can be made (section 362B) where the High Court is satisfied that there is reasonable cause to believe that the respondent holds property the value of which is greater than £50,000 and that there are reasonable grounds for suspecting that the known sources of the respondent's lawfully obtained income are insufficient for enabling the respondent to obtain that property.

UWOs target two kinds of respondents. First, so-called politically exposed persons ('PEPs'), ie individuals who are, or have been, entrusted with prominent public functions by an international organisation or by a state other than the UK or another EEA state, a family member or a close associate of such persons, or someone otherwise connected with such persons. A UWO may also be issued where there are reasonable grounds for suspecting that the respondent is, or has been, involved in serious crime (whether in a part of the UK or elsewhere), or a person connected with the respondent is, or has been, so involved. The meaning of serious crime, which is understood in accordance with Part 1 of the Serious Crime Act 2007, is extensive and gives the scheme a far-reaching scope.

A UWO requires the respondent to provide a statement setting out, inter alia, the nature and extent of his interest in the targeted property, and how s/he obtained the property (POCA 2002 sections 362C–D). If the respondent fails 'without reasonable excuse' to comply (or purport to comply) with the requirements imposed by the UWO within the period specified by the court, the property is 'presumed' to be recoverable for the purpose of civil recovery proceedings under Part 5 of POCA. It is not quite clear what a 'purported explanation' is, but it would seem that there is not necessarily any requirement as to the quality of the explanation given. The quality of the explanation may, however, affect the extent to which the court will draw inferences from it.[21]

The ensuing analysis will focus on the civil model ('civil recovery') of NCB confiscation, but some arguments also apply, *mutatis mutandis*, to the hybrid model.

III. Civil Recovery – Enforcement Needs and Advantages

NCB confiscation can be a potent law enforcement tool. Compared to criminal confiscation it is clearly more flexible. Not only can NCB confiscation proceedings be brought

[20] The first case came before the UK courts in 2018. In *National Crime Agency v Hajiyeva* [2018] 1 WLR 5887, a UWO was made on the basis that the respondent held certain property, being the beneficial owner of the company which was the registered proprietor of the property, and that she was a 'politically exposed person' within the meaning of s 362B(4) POCA 2002 (see section IV.D. below), since her husband was a politically exposed person having previously been the chairman of a bank in a non-EEA country.

[21] Moreover, a statement made by a person in response to a requirement imposed by an unexplained wealth order may under s. 362F(1) POCA 2002 not be used in evidence against that person in criminal proceedings. However, this firewall against criminal proceedings (based on the privilege against self-incrimination) can be circumvented according to s. 362F(2)(d) if on a prosecution for some other offence, in giving evidence, the person makes a statement inconsistent with the statement mentioned in subsection (1). This would not seem unproblematic in light of Article 6(2) ECHR.

irrespective of any pending criminal proceedings, but they normally also engage a less stringent procedural framework. It is therefore generally easier for the state to successfully pursue confiscation claims.

NCB confiscation may facilitate the confiscation of identified property suspected of being or representing the proceeds of crime in a number of situations in which criminal confiscation may not be available. Criminal confiscation may, for example, be unavailable where the defendant (who is the holder of the property) is *out of reach* for the criminal justice system, but the property itself is located on the state's territory.[22] The defendant may be deceased or may have absconded. Criminal proceedings against a dead person are problematic in light of ECHR Article 6.[23] In the latter case of abscon-sion, it may be possible to convict a person *in absentia* in some situations, but there may be limitations as to how far this is possible. Even if the respondent is not physically out of reach and does reside on the state's territory, criminal proceedings may be ruled out because of diplomatic immunity.[24]

Civil recovery can further be useful in cases where the state has not been able to *secure a criminal conviction* against the defendant. It may be, for example, that the rules on the admissibility of evidence prohibit certain evidence from being invoked, that the state has not produced sufficiently convincing evidence in order to establish criminal liability beyond reasonable doubt, or (in jurisdictions where such limitations apply) that the application of statutory limitations preclude a criminal conviction. A practical example is that a large amount of cash is found in the possession of a person, but although, in view of the circumstances, it is likely to represent criminal proceeds, there is not sufficient evidence of any criminal wrongdoing whereby criminal confiscation is not available.

Criminal confiscation may also be unavailable because *no owner* can be found of the suspected property. For example, property may be found in connection with a criminal offence, but no owner or holder of the property can be identified.

The extent to which NCB confiscation is necessary as a supplement to criminal confiscation may vary between jurisdictions depending on their legal framework. However, as reforms within an evidence-based and rational criminal justice policy should be knowledge-based, it would be reasonable to expect that states, before new and more far-reaching schemes are introduced, should first clearly delineate the actual need

[22] Greenberg et al (n 5), 31–32. It may be become an issue if NCB confiscation can also target property located abroad. For example, under s 282A of the UK's POCA 2002, a recovery order can be made in respect of property wherever situated, provided there is or has been a connection between the case and the UK.

[23] In *AP, MP, and TP v Switzerland*, App No 19958/92 (ECtHR 28 August 1997), para 48, the ECtHR held that '[i]t is a fundamental rule of criminal law that criminal liability does not survive the person who has committed the criminal act'.

[24] According to Article 31(1) of the Vienna Convention on Diplomatic Relations (1961), '[a] diplomatic agent shall enjoy immunity from the criminal jurisdiction of the receiving State'. According to the same provision, a diplomatic agent shall also enjoy immunity from its civil and administrative jurisdiction, except in the case of, inter alia, a 'real action relating to private immovable property situated in the territory of the receiving State, unless s/he holds it on behalf of the sending State for the purposes of the mission' or an 'action relating to any professional or commercial activity exercised by the diplomatic agent in the receiving State outside his official functions'. The individual would thus be shielded against criminal confiscation proceed-ings, but NCB confiscation proceedings might be possible in these two scenarios.

to do so.[25] The state should thus also clearly demonstrate that any perceived shortcomings of the existing system can be remedied only by implementing more far-reaching methods and that the proposed methods are actually capable of doing so.

IV. … And Issues

The use of NCB confiscation as a way of moving confiscation proceedings outside of the criminal justice framework has proved controversial. Both substantive and procedural issues have been raised. One often expressed criticism concerns the alleged circumvention of due process. For example, Smith, Owen and Bodnar argue, with regard to UK law, that there is 'no doubt that the consequence of civil recovery is to circumvent the staple aspects of due process protection in criminal law'.[26] According to the authors,

> there is no need to allege a specific unlawful act, the need to adduce cogent and persuasive evidence in order to prove an allegation … , and the need to prove the allegation to a respectably high standard, given the serious nature of the allegation, is again diluted in as much as it will not be necessary to prove the matter beyond reasonable doubt.[27]

Another procedurally related criticism concerns the relationship between NCB confiscation and criminal proceedings. Where civil confiscation is available, the question arises whether law enforcement should always prioritise criminal proceedings where this is possible, or whether it can freely choose between the two. In some jurisdictions the focus of law enforcement seems to be on NCB confiscation rather than criminal confiscation, because of the stringent evidential requirements that apply in the latter proceedings. This is not unproblematic. Greenberg et al write: 'criminal prosecutions should be pursued whenever possible to avoid the risk that prosecutors, courts, and the public would view disgorgement of assets as a sufficient sanction when criminal laws have been violated.'[28]

The risk that these authors allude to is that prosecutors, for the sake of convenience, limit their claim to recovering the assets by way of civil recovery when the case should properly have been made the subject of criminal proceedings. However, to downgrade criminal proceedings for such reasons may undermine the effectiveness of law enforcement and the public's faith in it.[29] Arguably, while NCB confiscation may be an alternative to confiscation in criminal proceedings in some situations, it should remain, as a main rule, supplementary and not become a substitute for criminal proceedings for reasons of convenience where the case should properly have been dealt with within the

[25] RT Naylor, 'Wash-out: A Critique of Follow-the-Money Methods in Crime Control Policy' (1999) 32 *Crime, Law and Social Change* 1, 3.

[26] I Smith, T Owen and A Bodnar, *On Asset Recovery: Criminal Confiscation and Civil Recovery*, Binder I (Oxford, Oxford University Press, 2012), para I-1022. See also C King, 'Civil Forfeiture and Article 6 of the ECHR: Due Process Implications for England & Wales and Ireland' (2014) 34 *Legal Studies* 371, 375.

[27] Smith, Owen and Bodnar (n 26), I-1022.

[28] See Greenberg et al (n 5), 29.

[29] Greenberg et al (n 5), 29.

criminal framework. One way of addressing this issue is through legislative steering, such as under the UK's POCA 2002.[30]

Substantive aspects of civil confiscation schemes have also been criticised. One such criticism has related to the protection of innocent owners. As no (clear) nexus to the criminal conduct in question is required from the holder of the property, confiscation may potentially target assets held by individuals in good faith.[31] In light of Article 1 ECHR-P1, it may be questioned to what extent civil proceedings *in specie* may legitimately affect the rights of third parties acting in good faith. Many NCB confiscation schemes today have implemented mechanisms for protecting bona fide third parties and have therefore attempted to deal with this issue.[32]

Another point of concern relates to the structure of NCB confiscation schemes, which do not require that the unlawful conduct from which the assets in question derive is specified. It follows that it can be difficult to assess substantive proportionality of a confiscation order, as such an assessment, which is based on what is required to be confiscated in order to achieve gain neutralisation, requires some clarity as concerns the unlawful conduct in question.[33]

Also how mixed funds are dealt with in some schemes, ie where tainted assets have been co-mingled with legitimate assets, has been criticised. For example, under the German § 76a(4) StGB, if the tainted property has been mixed with legitimate property (eg the property has been obtained in part with tainted funds, in part with legitimate funds), some argue that the tainted assets should be seen as contaminating the entire property (*Totalkontaminationslehre*).[34] Consequently, the identified assets become liable

[30] See eg the UK's POCA 2002 s 2A, prescribing the content of 'relevant authorities' guidance, which holds that 'the reduction of crime is in general best secured by means of criminal investigations and criminal proceedings'. In the *Guidance by the Secretary of State to the Director of the Assets Recovery Agency* (7 February 2005), it is considered (at para 2) inter alia that this point of departure will 'underpin the way in which the Director exercises her asset recovery functions and she must do her best to facilitate and promote criminal investigation and criminal proceedings'. Moreover (at para 5), where a criminal conviction has been obtained, 'criminal confiscation of the proceeds of crime will best contribute to the reduction of crime'. In the Attorney-General's guidance on asset recovery powers for prosecutors issued by the UK Attorney-General's Office (29 November 2012), available at: www.gov.uk/guidance/asset-recovery-powers-for-prosecutors-guidance-and-background-note-2009, criminal proceedings are given primacy over civil recovery proceedings. Para 1 states, 'The reduction of crime is in general best secured by means of criminal investigations and criminal proceedings. However, the non-conviction based asset recovery powers available under the Act can also make an important contribution to the reduction of crime where (i) it is not feasible to secure a conviction, (ii) a conviction is obtained but a confiscation order is not made, or (iii) a relevant authority is of the view that the public interest will be better served by using those powers rather than by seeking a criminal disposal.' This kind of legislative steering would seem important in order not to undermine the primacy of criminal confiscation over civil recovery.

[31] This was, for example, the pre-CAFRA (Civil Asset Forfeiture Reform Act) 1990 situation in the USA. The CAFRA 1990 introduced an 'innocent owner' protection into the federal civil confiscation regime. See Cassella (n 17), 39–44.

[32] See UK law (POCA 2002 ss 308(1) and 266(3)) and Irish law (POCA 1996 s 3) for two alternative arrangements as regards bona fide protections.

[33] See Boucht (n 15).

[34] However, there is some discussion as to whether the entire property (*Totalkontamination*) or only the illicit part (*Teilkontamination*) applies. M-L Marstaller and T Zimmermann, *Non-conviction-based-confiscation in Deutschland? Eine straf- und verfassungsrechtliche Untersuchung zur Legitimität der erweiterten selbständigen Tatertragseinziehung nach § 76a IV StGB i.V.m. § 437 StPO* (Baden-Baden, Nomos Verlag, 2018), 75 argue that the 'Totalkontaminationslehre' applies. T Fischer, *Strafgesetzbuch mit Nebengesetzen*, 66. Auflage (Munich, CH Beck, 2019), § 76a rn. 10 instead argues that the provisions should be applied so that only part of the assets are contaminated.

to confiscation in their entirety. That confiscation would target legitimate property has, however, been criticised as confiscation is a criminal sanction without the prior establishment of guilt.[35]

The *in specie* (or *in rem*) nature of NCB confiscation, which means that it is intended to implicate only the property and not the owner/holder, has furthermore been criticised. The notion of 'guilty property' that underlies *in rem* confiscation has been criticised as a legal fiction.[36] For example, Naylor writes:

> It is impossible for seizure of property to be anything but punitive. It is impossible to declare a car or house or bank account to be the proceeds of cocaine sales, for example, without simultaneously smearing its owner with the accusation of drug trafficking. But with no need for a criminal conviction prior to asset seizure, there is also no need for the state to enter into court proceedings a shred of evidence to substantiate the implicit accusation against the owner.[37]

Some critics also point at the reputational aspect of civil recovery and argue that the potential stigmatising effects on the respondent's reputation should not be underestimated.[38] Even if the confiscation claim, being *in specie*, is not intended to directly implicate the respondent in any unlawful conduct it is far from given that such technical distinctions can be perceived and understood by the public, and media, outside the specialised legal context. The risks of this would seem to be particularly pertinent in the internet and social media society of today.[39]

V. The Standard and the Burden of Proof

A. Preliminary Remarks

Non-conviction based confiscation can be a powerful tool for the state to use in order to recover criminal proceeds where criminal confiscation for one reason or another is not available. However, as the critical discussion in section IV has indicated, it is not an uncontroversial measure. Many of the critical observations are important and should

[35] See T Rönnau and M Begemeier, 'Wider die Entgrenzung der Vermögenseinziehung gemäß § 76a Abs. 4 StGB durch die Geldwäschedogmatik' (2018) 73(9) *Juristenzeitung* 443–50. In this connection, the requirement set out by the ECtHR in the recent Grand Chamber judgment *G.I.E.M. S.r.l. v Italy*, App Nos 1828/06 34163/07 19029/11 (ECtHR, 28 June 2018) that a penalty must be preceded by an establishment of guilt can also be observed. For a contrasting opinion to Rönnau's and Begemeier's, see Marstaller and Zimmermann (n 34), 78–79.

[36] See eg King (n 26), 375.

[37] Naylor (n 25), 41.

[38] On the reputational aspect, see L Campbell, 'Criminal Labels, the European Convention on Human Rights and the Presumption of Innocence' (2013) 76(4) *Modern Law Review* 681, 705. See also Boucht (n 2), 136–37.

[39] Anonymity of the respondent to the proceedings would seem to be an important safeguard for the respondent, which would not be a serious infringement of the interests of a public process. As possible victims ought nevertheless to be made aware of the NCB confiscation proceedings, anonymity might be supplemented by restriction orders that prevent the victim from disseminating this information, for example on social media.

not be dismissed simply by reference to the needs of effective law enforcement. It is crucial for the legitimacy of the criminal justice system that a fair and proportionate balance is struck between the interests of the state and those of the individual, so that the burden placed on the individual is not excessive. However, provided that sufficient safeguards, substantive and procedural, are put in place, NCB confiscation is likely to be a useful and acceptable supplement to criminal confiscation.[40]

I have in a different context suggested that the legitimacy of confiscation schemes, both criminal and NCB, can be assessed in light of the three following parameters:[41]

i) the scope of the 'target area' (inter alia what is targeted, who is targeted and whether bona fide protections are available);
ii) the extent to which a proportionality requirement forms part of the scheme; and
iii) the construction of the procedural safeguard regime (the burden and standard of proof and general procedural safeguards, eg the opportunity to put a case to the responsible authorities and to adduce evidence, to receive a reasoned judgment within a reasonable time, etc).[42]

Achieving a fair scheme is not necessarily about satisfying fixed standards, but rather about appropriately balancing various parameters against one another. One narrowly defined parameter, for example the target area, can make a diluted procedural safeguard less controversial. In other words, certain onerous features may be counterbalanced at other stages of the scheme. What is important is that the restraints seen as a whole provide reasonable safeguards, both substantive and procedural, for the confiscation subject as the holder of the assets.[43]

Ultimately, any normative statement of law depends on a political theory and on the underlying normative conception of the proper relationship between the state and its inhabitants.[44] The normative framework that I adhere to in this context is the perspective of a liberal theory of criminal law, based on the ideals of a liberal *Rechtsstaat* adhering to the rule of law, in European Common Law and Civil Law traditions (with Nordic overtones).[45] The normative arguments in this context depend on the kind of liberal conception of the criminal law that Jareborg refers to as 'defensive'.[46] Such a criminal law not only aims at protecting individual, collective, and public and state interests against infringements, but also serves to protect individuals against the abuse of power, in this context primarily by the state. This kind of criminal law takes seriously, in its pursuit of crime control and the enforcement of criminal sanctions, whether in the form of punishment or by way of civil or preventative schemes, the due protection, both

[40] See eg also P Alldridge, 'Proceeds of Crime Law since 2003 – Two Key Areas' [2014] 3 *Criminal Law Review* 171, 173.

[41] Boucht (n 2), 143–44.

[42] Subsidiarity (as discussed in section 4 *in fine*) is not mentioned as a separate parameter, but is assumed to constitute a general prerequisite for engaging civil confiscation schemes.

[43] For this kind of discussion, see Boucht (n 2), 205–31.

[44] RA Duff, *Answering for Crime: Responsibility and Liability in the Criminal Law* (Oxford, Hart Publishing, 2007), 11.

[45] See Boucht (n 2), 22–23.

[46] N Jareborg, 'What Kind of Criminal Law do We Want?' in A Snare (ed), *Beware of Punishment. On the Utility and Futility of Criminal Law* (Oslo, Pax förlag, 1995), 17, 20–28. See also See also W Hassemer, 'German Legal Philosophy and the Criminal Law' (1990) 10 *Tel Aviv University Studies in Law* 187, 187–92.

procedurally and substantively, of the state's inhabitants from unjustified infringements of their core values.[47]

In this context, I intend to focus on two procedural aspects of civil recovery, namely the standard of proof (in section V.C.) and the availability of a reversed burden of proof (section V.D.) in NCB confiscation proceedings. As indicated in section IV, the structure of NCB confiscation schemes that do not necessarily require that the unlawful conduct from which the assets allegedly derive be specified, makes a substantive proportionality assessment of the magnitude of the confiscation order difficult to conduct. Procedural proportionality, ie the procedures by which the measure in question is imposed, therefore becomes integral in safeguarding the respondent's interest. The standard of proof and the burden of proof are thus both important from a principled perspective, as essential safeguards for avoiding wrongful confiscation decisions, but they are also relevant from a practical viewpoint. However, before these questions are addressed, I will say something about what the evidential requirement relates to.

B. What the Evidential Requirement Relates to

The standard of proof is closely related to the question of *what* circumstances must be proved before a confiscation decision can be made. In confiscation proceedings, a crucial fact that needs to be established is that the assets in question are or represent criminal proceeds, ie that they derive from criminal conduct. Two alternative approaches can be considered here. In the first, there is no requirement to establish causality between the assets and the unlawful conduct from which they allegedly derive. In the second, such a requirement is present.

If there is no causality requirement, the state does not have to prove that the assets derive from any concrete unlawful conduct. There is, in other words, no need to establish a connection between the identified property and the unlawful conduct ('the open model'). This kind of scheme can be found in the German NCB confiscation scheme under section 76a subsection 4 *Strafgesetzbuch* (StGB). According to this provision,

> [a]n object derived from an unlawful act which has been seized in proceedings brought on suspicion of one of the offences referred to in sentence 3 having been committed is, as a rule, to be separately confiscated even in those cases in which it is impossible to prosecute or convict the person affected by the confiscation.

[47] The ECHR embodies many of the values necessary for assessing the legitimacy of a particular confiscation scheme. The normative analysis should nevertheless be independent of the limits set by the Convention. The ECtHR has shown a readiness to display considerable deference towards how states construct and use asset confiscation as a means of crime control. The jurisprudence of the ECtHR is therefore not necessarily as powerful a restraint in the field of confiscation as it may be in other fields of criminal proceedings. See also M Panzavolta and R Flor, 'A Necessary Evil? The Italian "Non-Criminal" System of Asset Forfeiture' in JP Rui and U Sieber (eds), *Non-Conviction-Based Confiscation in Europe. Possibilities and Limitations on Rules Enabling Confiscation Without a Criminal Conviction* (Berlin, Duncker & Humblot, 2015), 111 at 142–45. For a critique of the ECtHR position, see also R Ivory, *Corruption, Asset Recovery, and the Protection of Property in Public International Law: The Human Rights of Bad Guys* (Cambridge, Cambridge University Press, 2014), 250 and the partly concurring and partly dissenting opinion by Judge Pinto de Albuqueque in *Varvara v Italy*, App No 17475/09 (ECtHR, 29 October 2013).

The relevant unlawful conduct that may give rise to NCB confiscation is described in sentence 3 of the provision and includes, inter alia, terrorist-related offences, offences relating to human trafficking, procuring, money laundering, smuggling etc.

Under this provision, it is merely required that the assets have been seized in proceedings relating to a 'suspicion' of a relevant offence. The precise meaning of 'suspicion' (*Verdacht*) is not quite clear and will have to be clarified by the courts. However, provided that the assets are seized in connection with such proceedings, there does not seem to be any requirement (at least not in view of the wording) that the property in question actually derives from these offences. Instead, it would seem that it can derive from any offences and thus that there is no requirement to trace the assets to a relevant type or kind of criminal conduct.[48]

If, on the contrary, a finding of causality is required ('the nexus model'), the state will have to trace the assets back to particular unlawful conduct. It is, therefore, not enough that the state produces (circumstantial) evidence supporting a general conclusion that the assets are or represent proceeds of crime.

This kind of requirement has been established by the courts in regard to section 243 of the UK's POCA 2002, Part 5.[49] The state must therefore describe the unlawful conduct, from which the assets allegedly derive, in such general terms that enable the court to reach a conclusion as to whether the conduct in question might properly be described as unlawful. It suffices that the conduct is described in terms of 'importing and supplying controlled drugs', 'trafficking women for the purpose of prostitution' etc, and it is not necessary to specify the unlawful conduct in detail, for example when it was committed, who participated etc. However, if the circumstances in which the property was handled are such as to give rise to an 'irresistible inference' that it could only have been derived from crime, no tracing is required.[50] In this case, therefore, the evidential burden is mitigated.

Of these two alternative approaches, the nexus model would clearly seem preferable in view of the nature of NCB confiscation proceedings (no trigger conviction is required which means that the inherent likelihood of the assets being unlawful may be weaker).[51] Under this model, the property in respect of which the order is sought has to be traced back to certain criminal conduct. Assets could, in other words, be confiscated as drug proceeds only if it can be proved that they derive from drug trafficking generally, but they would not have be linked to a particular drug offence. The tracing operation may, for example, require the work of forensic accounting and involve following the proceeds through a complex series of steps.[52] From a proportionality perspective, a nexus requirement constitutes an important procedural safeguard. However, the tracing requirement should probably not be interpreted too strictly.

[48] Also under the new provision proposed by the Criminal Law Council in Norway (section 67a of the Criminal Code 2005), no such tracing is required. See NOU 2020: 10: *Inndragning av utbytte fra gjengkriminalitet*.

[49] See eg *R (Director of Assets Recovery Agency and Others) v Green and Others* [2005] EWHC 3168 (Admin) para 17; Sullivan J's conclusions were approved by the Court of Appeal in *Director of Assets Recovery Agency v Olupitan* [2008] EWCA Civ 104. See also *Serious Organised Crime Agency v Bosworth* [2010] EWHC 645 (QB). A tracing requirement also exists under US forfeiture law, see Cassella (n 17), 469–70.

[50] Williams J in *Serious Organised Crime Agency v Gale and Others* [2009] EWHC 1015 (QB) para 17.

[51] See also Boucht (n 2), 214–15.

[52] Cassella (n 17), 467.

However, the assets in question should not necessarily in themselves have to be traced back to unlawful conduct, provided that an increase in the respondent's wealth can be traced back to certain unlawful conduct. For example, say there is strong evidence that the respondent has been involved in armed robbery and obtained £10,000 benefit from the robbery. In light of the restorative aim, property to that value should in principle be liable to confiscation, even if certain property in itself had been legitimately obtained, provided that it can be showed that the respondent did in fact benefit from the offence.

C. The Standard of Proof

The standard of proof refers to the degree of probability to which a factual proposition in a case must be proved in order for the judge to hold it as true.[53] The standard of proof is thus a mechanism for distributing errors, ie for achieving a certain distribution of correct and wrongful decisions.[54] In criminal law, the acceptance of wrongful convictions has traditionally been low (the so-called 'Blackstonian ratio') because of the nature of criminal punishment.[55] A high standard of proof (beyond reasonable doubt), which seeks to ensure that where errors do occur they will result predominantly in false acquittals rather than false convictions, has therefore been considered necessary.

In civil (private law) proceedings, in contrast, what is at stake is two private (horizontal) interests, where the disadvantages from a wrongful decision in one direction normally more or less equal the disadvantages of a wrongful decision in the opposite direction.

A third category is so-called administrative (or regulatory) proceedings. These are vertical proceedings (state–individual), but as they concern issues other than punishment, they are often pursued using civil procedural rules. Administrative proceedings that involve burdensome decisions, for example disciplinary sanctions or administrative fines (for example tax surcharges, withdrawal of driver's licence) have been considered to constitute a criminal charge under Article 6 ECHR, which triggers certain additional safeguards.[56]

The requisite standard of proof other than in criminal proceedings varies between jurisdictions. In some jurisdictions, the standard of proof is set at a 'balance of probabilities'. A balance of probabilities means that 'the tribunal of fact must be able to say, on the whole of the evidence, that the case for the asserting party has been shown

[53] I Dennis, *The Law of Evidence*, 5th edn (London, Sweet & Maxwell, 2013), 440.

[54] L Laudan, *Truth, Error and Criminal Law. An Essay in Legal Epistemology* (Cambridge, Cambridge University Press, 2006), 68.

[55] In Blackstone's seminal work *Commentaries on the Laws of England* (published in 1893) he formulated this ratio as follows: 'It is better that ten guilty persons escape than that one innocent suffer.'

[56] See eg *Öztürk v Germany*, App No 8544/79 (ECtHR 21 February 1984), *Malige v France*, App No 27812/95 (ECtHR 23 September 1998) and *Jussila v Finland*, App No 73053/01 (ECtHR 23 November 2006). For an overview of the concept of a 'criminal charge' under Article 6(2), see Harris, O'Boyle & Warbrick, *Law of the European Convention on Human Rights*, 4th edn (Oxford, Oxford University Press, 2014), 377–81.

to be more probably true than not'.[57] Such a standard of proof in civil proceedings can, in light of the interests involved, be justified as it will over time result in a majority of correctly decided judgments.[58] However, not all jurisdictions apply a pre-defined standard of proof. In some Continental and Nordic jurisdictions, for example Germany, Finland and Sweden, discharging the legal burden of proof requires either that the judge is 'convinced' (*überzeugt*) that the facts exist, or that the facts are '(fully) proved'.[59]

Some jurisdictions operate with a sliding or flexible scale, so that the more serious the allegation, the higher the required standard of proof. This may apply both where a jurisdiction applies a pre-fixed standard and where it does not. For example, in English law courts have traditionally applied a flexible standard depending on the gravity and seriousness of the allegation.[60] However, in *Re B (Children)*, Lady Hale, with whom the other Law Lords agreed, declared 'loud and clear' that the standard of proof in finding the facts necessary to establish the threshold

> is the simple balance of probabilities, neither more nor less. Neither the seriousness of the allegation nor the seriousness of the consequences should make any difference to the standard of proof to be applied in determining the facts. The inherent probabilities are simply something to be taken into account, where relevant, in deciding where the truth lies.[61]

In other jurisdictions, for example Norway, courts operate not only with a balance of probabilities but also with a heightened civil standard as a fixed standard. In cases where the allegation is graver, where the factual circumstances are particularly onerous for the party, or the consequences more severe, the requisite standard is often a 'clear (or strong) balance of probabilities'.[62] In Finnish law, on the other hand, where there is no pre-fixed standard of proof, the amount of evidence required in order for the facts to be 'proved' may vary between types of cases and can in some more serious civil cases even approach the criminal standard.[63]

In this context I will, for reasons of convenience, refer to the 'balance of probabilities' as the civil standard and 'beyond reasonable doubt' as the criminal standard.

What then would a proper standard of proof be in NCB confiscation proceedings? As mentioned in section II, NCB confiscation is pursued in many jurisdictions within the framework of civil proceedings. The standard of proof required for the discharge

[57] R Glover and P Murphy, *Murphy on Evidence*, 13th edn (Oxford, Oxford University Press, 2013), 111.

[58] See eg JE Skoghøy, *Tvisteløsning*, 2nd edn (Oslo, Universitetsforlaget, 2014), 877. Both of these premises have been questioned, see M Strandberg, *Beviskrav i sivile saker* (Bergen, Fagbokforlaget, 2012), chapter 8.

[59] See for German law, Zivilprozessordnung s 286(1), for Finnish law, see J Lappalainen, *Siviiliprosessioikeus II* (Helsinki, Kauppakaari, 2001), 341–47 and for Swedish law, P-O Ekelöf, *Rättegång IV*, 6th edn (Stockholm, Norstedts Juridik, 2008), 69–73. See also K Clemont and E Sherwin, 'A Comparative View of Standards of Proof' (2002) 50 *American Journal of Comparative Law* 243, 254.

[60] See eg *Hornal v Neuberge Products Ltd* [1957] 1 QB 247. In *Re H (Minors)* [1996] AC 563, para 7, Lord Nicholls declared that the civil standard is finite and set at the balance of probabilities, but that the inherent probability or improbability of an event is itself a matter to be taken into account when weighing the probabilities and deciding whether, on balance, the event occurred. He said, '[t]he more improbable the event, the stronger must be the evidence that it did occur before, on the balance of probability, its occurrence will be established'.

[61] *Re B (Children)* [2009] 1 AC 11, para 70.

[62] See, eg, Supreme Court case Rt. 2007 s. 1217.

[63] See Lappalainen (n 59), 347.

of the legal burden of proof is thus the civil standard, often a balance of probabilities.[64] In principle, the risk of a wrongful confiscation decision is thus less than 50 per cent.

The standard of proof should be set at a level at which the expected advantage of ordering confiscation is higher than the expected advantage of rejecting a confiscation claim – in other words, where the risk of a faulty decision is acceptable. This is a policy-related issue.

Using the civil standard in NCB confiscation proceedings is often sought to be justified by the non-criminal nature of NCB confiscation and by pragmatic effectiveness reasons.[65] The latter relates to the potential difficulties for the state to prove circumstances relating to NCB confiscation if the standard is set too high. The penetrative force of these rules in society may thus be decreased.

When assessing the appropriate standard of proof it is important to consider the nature of NCB confiscation proceedings. In ECHR law, the ECtHR has repeatedly held that NCB confiscation proceedings do not constitute a criminal charge under Article 6(2).[66] Recently this was considered by the court in *Gogitidze v Georgia*, a case that concerned the confiscation by the Georgian state of assets belonging to a senior official and his close relatives as the proceeds of corruption.[67] The Georgian confiscation scheme was specifically aimed at recovering wrongfully acquired property and

[64] The standard of proof is set at a balance of probabilities in UK law (POCA 2002, s 241(3)), in Irish Law (POCA 1996, s 8(2)) and under US federal rules (see SD Cassella, *Asset Forfeiture Law in the United States*, 2nd edn (JurisNet LLC, 2013), 456). The Norwegian proposal for an NCB confiscation scheme sets the standard of proof at a balance of probabilities, see JP Rui, *Sivilrettslig inndragning rettet direkte mot formuesgoder* (Bergen, Justisdepartementet, 2016), 117. Also the Italian system of preventative confiscation operates with a standard of proof that is clearly lower than the criminal standard (see M Panzavolta and R Flor, 'A Necessary Evil? The Italian "Non-Criminal" System of Asset Forfeiture' in JP Rui and U Sieber (eds), *Non-Conviction-Based Confiscation in Europe. Possibilities and Limitations on Rules Enabling Confiscation Without a Criminal Conviction* (Berlin, Duncker & Humblot, 2015), 111 at 136–38).

[65] In a hybrid model, where the allegation is made in a criminal procedural context, the argument relating to the non-criminal nature of the measure has little persuasive force.

[66] In this connection, the relevance of Art 7 (whether or not it constitutes a criminal penalty) to NCB confiscation proceedings can be considered. In *G.I.E.M. S.r.l. v Italy*, App Nos 1828/06, 34163/07 and 19029/11 (ECtHR, 28 June 2018), the Grand Chamber assessed the compatibility of certain Italian confiscation measures with Article 7 ECHR. The Court interpreted Art 7 as requiring that punishment must include 'the existence of a mental link through which an element of liability may be detected in the conduct of the person who physically committed the offence' (para 242). An indication of the Court's position in regard to NCB confiscation is found in *Dassa Foundation and others v Lichtenstein*, App No 696/05 (ECtHR, 10 July 2007), a case that concerned the seizure and subsequent confiscation of all assets held by two foundations because of suspicion of bribery by another individual. According to the Court, the confiscation measure in this case did not amount to a penalty under Article 7. In distinguishing this case from *Welch v the United Kingdom*, App No 56054/00 (ECtHR, 10 February 2004), where an extended criminal confiscation order under the English scheme was held to constitute a penalty under Art 7, one important factor emphasised by the Court, which also made the confiscation measure more comparable to a restitution of unjustified enrichment under civil law than to a fine under criminal law, was that the confiscation order was limited to actual enrichment. This is in line with the argument suggested in section II of this chapter. However, if confiscation targets also legitimately acquired property, it is difficult to see how this would not be a penalty (for a similar opinion, see JP Rui and U Sieber, 'NCBC in Europe: Bringing the Picture Together' in JP Rui and U Sieber (eds), *Non-Conviction Based Confiscation in Europe – Possibilities and Limitations on Rules Enabling Confiscation Without a Criminal Conviction* (Berlin, Duncker Humblot, 2015), 245 at 294). To the extent that legitimate assets can be confiscated, for example in the case of co-mingled assets based on a *Totalkontaminationslehre* or denial of the net principle as guiding principle for calculating confiscation orders, a tension would arise with Art 7.

[67] *Gogitidze v Georgia*, App No 36862/05 (ECtHR, 12 May 2015).

unexplained wealth from public officials and certain related persons, even without the prior criminal conviction of the official concerned. The fairness of civil confiscation proceedings was, according to the Court, thus to be assessed under the civil head of Article 6(1). A confiscation order concerning an individual's movable and immovable assets amounts to an interference with the right to peaceful enjoyment of one's possessions Article 1 ECHR-P1.

> [T]he Court reiterates its well-established case-law to the effect that proceedings for confiscation such as the civil proceedings in rem in the present case, which do not stem from a criminal conviction or sentencing proceedings and thus do not qualify as a penalty but rather represent a measure of control of the use of property within the meaning of Article 1 of Protocol No. 1, cannot amount to 'the determination of a criminal charge' within the meaning of Article 6 § 1 of the Convention and should be examined under the 'civil' head of that provision.
>
> the Court reiterates, in the light of its well-established case-law, that the forfeiture of property ordered as a result of civil proceedings *in rem*, without involving determination of a criminal charge, is not of a punitive but of a preventive and/or compensatory nature and thus cannot give rise to the application of the provision in question.[68]

The focus was on the burden of proof, but the Court also touched upon the standard of proof when it assessed whether or not a reasonable balance had been struck between the means employed for the confiscation of the assets in question and the general interest in combating corruption. The Court started by observing that

> common European and even universal legal standards can be said to exist which encourage, firstly, the confiscation of property linked to serious criminal offences such as corruption, money laundering, drug offences and so on, without the prior existence of a criminal conviction.

Concerning the standard of proof, the ECtHR recalled its previous case law relating to the proportionality test under Article 1 ECHR-P1, and found it 'legitimate for the relevant domestic authorities to issue confiscation orders on the basis of a preponderance of evidence which suggested that the respondents' lawful incomes could not have sufficed for them to acquire the property in question.'[69] The Court continued:

> Indeed, whenever a confiscation order was the result of civil proceedings *in rem* which related to the proceeds of crime derived from serious offences, the Court did not require proof 'beyond reasonable doubt' of the illicit origins of the property in such proceedings. Instead, proof on a balance of probabilities or a high probability of illicit origins, combined with the inability of the owner to prove the contrary, was found to suffice for the purposes of the proportionality test under Article 1 of Protocol No. 1.[70]

[68] *Gogitidze v Georgia*, App No 36862/05 (ECtHR, 12 May 2015), paras 121 and 126.

[69] *Gogitidze v Georgia*, App No 36862/05 (ECtHR, 12 May 2015), para 107.

[70] Para 107. The position by the ECtHR in Gogitidze was confirmed in the subsequent judgment *Telbis and Viziteu v Romania*, App No 47911/1 (ECtHR 26 September 2018), which also involved the confiscation of assets from an individual convicted of corruption and his family members.

An NCB confiscation order which only targets assets that are or represent criminal proceeds, and thus only seeks to neutralise illicit gain, is not, arguably, of a punitive nature.[71]

Where the standard of proof is set at the balance of probabilities, the risk of wrongful confiscation decisions is less than 50 per cent. However, it may be questioned if this represents an appropriate allocation of the risk of wrongful confiscation decisions in NCB confiscation proceedings. In fact, a normative claim can be made that the standard of proof should be higher in NCB confiscation proceedings, so that the corresponding acceptable risk of doubt is smaller. There are several reasons for this.

NCB confiscation proceedings are based on an allegation that the property in question is or represents criminal proceeds, ie that the assets originate, directly or indirectly, in unlawful conduct, although there is no direct claim that the respondent has taken part in such conduct. No formal communication of blame concerning any such conduct is involved.[72] Indeed, civil recovery proceedings may to some degree resemble restitution proceedings where the defendant is compelled to give up his gains to the claimant.[73] However, this resemblance does not automatically put civil recovery proceedings on par with private law proceedings. First of all, NCB confiscation, rather than being pursued between two individuals, is pursued vertically, ie, as an exercise of state power against an individual. As such, NCB confiscation forms part of administrative law rather than private law.[74] Indeed, this does not per se require a higher standard of proof; there are administrative proceedings that legitimately can be pursued using the civil standard. However, it is an important starting point.

As argued in section II, NCB confiscation, both the hybrid model and the civil recovery model, pursue the same policy goals as the criminal justice system in general. Even if the objective of NCB confiscation is to neutralise gain by removing illicit assets from circulation, it shares deterrence (or general prevention) as a general justifying aim with the criminal justice system.[75] As these schemes do not require the state to specify any offences that the assets allegedly derive from, the link to the relevant criminal conduct is clearly weaker.

[71] In *Saliba v Malta*, App No 4251/02 (ECtHR, 8 November 2005), para 17, the ECtHR maintained that a measure that merely restores the status quo ante, for example a confiscation order based on a net principle, does not constitute a penalty under Art 7. See also Boucht (n 2), 127, Rui and Sieber (n 66), 261.

[72] Marstaller and Zimmermann (n 34), 70–71.

[73] See eg *Dassa Foundation and others v Lichtenstein*, App No 696/05 (ECtHR, 10 July 2007), where the Court argued that there were several elements that made seizure and forfeiture in that case, 'in the manner in which these measures are regulated under Liechtenstein law, more comparable to a restitution of unjustified enrichment under civil law than to a fine under criminal law.' See also G Virgo, *The Principles of the Law of Restitution*, 2nd edn (Oxford, Oxford University Press, 2006) distinguishes between three different principles upon which restitutionary claims can be based: unjust enrichment, wrongdoing, and proprietary claims. Virgo finds confiscation to be a restitutionary remedy based on wrongdoing. He writes (at 548): '[d]isgorgement of the proceeds of crime to the State should be considered to fall within the law of restitution, since, by committing a crime, the offender has committed a wrong against the State by breaching his or her duty to abide by the criminal law of the land.'

[74] Rui and Sieber (n 66), 301. See also for example the Irish High Court case *Criminal Assets Bureau v J.W.P.L.* [2007] IEHC 177, in which the Court held that civil recovery proceedings were not a civil and commercial matter for the purposes of the EU's Recognition and Enforcement of Judgments Regulation (No 1215/2012).

[75] See for example *Telbis and Viziteu v Romania*, App No 47911/15 (ECtHR, 26 September 2018), where the Court at para 71 noted that confiscation measures form part of 'a crime-prevention policy.' See also Boucht (n 15), 257 and Marstaller and Zimmermann (n 34), 69–71.

Indeed, it would seem that a distinction could be made between two types of NCB confiscation cases. First are proceedings where the unlawful conduct in question is known and would have been dealt with in criminal proceedings, had it not been for the defendant's flight or illness, statutory limitations, or insufficient evidence for a criminal conviction. The second type of cases is where the criminal conduct in which the assets allegedly originate is unknown (or at least unspecified). In the former case, the nexus to an offence is established, whereas not necessarily so in the latter. Arguably, the contextual assumption, or inherent likelihood, of the assets being illicit, depending on the circumstances, can thus be weaker in the second case than in the former case.[76]

The potential implications of a wrongful confiscation decision also point in the direction of a higher standard of proof. A confiscation order may impose considerable economic hardship on the respondent. Moreover, as the confiscation order should only target illicit property, the standard of proof becomes instrumental in deciding that this is in fact the case, and thereby securing that the confiscation scheme is proportionate (for example under Article 1 ECHR-P1). If there is insufficient clarity as to the liability to confiscation of the assets in question, it cannot be necessary to confiscate them.

The state would seem better suited to carrying the risk of a wrongful confiscation decision; a wrongful confiscation decision has considerably different implications depending on whether the losing part is the state or the individual. In the former scenario, the negative impact on the overall legitimacy of the criminal justice system is still likely to be small.

As indicated in section IV, the reputational aspect can also be of relevance in the internet and social media society of today. An NCB confiscation claim formally targets certain identified property (*in specie*) that is considered to be or to represent the proceeds of crime, but is not intended to directly implicate the respondent in any unlawful conduct.[77] Whether or not stigma is nevertheless generated is contingent on the social message of a certain measure (and how it is understood). This social message may vary between jurisdictions depending on, for example, legal traditions.[78] For example, if civil recovery is historically accepted within a jurisdiction, the public blaming of and stigmatising effect on the respondent may be reduced, as 'everyone knows' that no blame is intended. However, not only may a person feel stigmatised, without having any reason to feel so, but a person or a group might project stigma onto someone without any good reason to do so. It should not, for example, be taken for granted that individuals or the media are capable of distinguishing between criminal proceedings *in personam* and civil recovery proceedings *in specie*. In a hybrid model, the stigmatising aspect seems to be even more prevalent.

On balance, these considerations in my view support a prima facie assertion that the standard of proof should be higher than a balance of probabilities in NCB confiscation proceedings, both under the hybrid model and the civil recovery model.[79]

[76] The contextual assumption refers to the inherent probability of the assets' being illicit, which may be inferred either from the existence of prior convictions of acquisitive crime, or from certain other particular circumstances that speak in the same direction. See Boucht (n 2), 135.

[77] Marstaller and Zimmermann (n 34), 73.

[78] See J Stanton-Ife, 'Strict Liability: Stigma and Regret' (2007) 27 *Oxford Journal of Legal Studies* 151, 156.

[79] Boucht (n 2), 226–27. In the *Resolutions on the Prevention, Investigation and Sanctioning of Economic Crime by Alternative Enforcement Regimes*, adopted by The International Criminal Law Association (AIDP)

What then would be an adequate standard of proof to which the state has to satisfy its burden? The criminal standard cannot be necessary as this would defeat the purpose of the measure. The proper standard of proof should therefore sit somewhere between the criminal standard and a balance of probabilities. A plausible formulation might be 'a clear balance of probabilities'.[80] A mere balance of probabilities should not be considered sufficient; it should instead be required that it is clearly more probable than not that the assets in question are liable to confiscation.[81] In other words, the margin of doubt accepted in order to decide on confiscation would be narrower. This standard would, in my view, be appropriate also for the nexus model. It should apply regardless of whether NCB confiscation is pursued following a previous acquittal of criminal charges ('a second bite at the cherry') or as independent proceedings.[82]

D. The Burden of Proof

In section V.C., the discussion dealt with what the proper standard of proof should be in NCB confiscation proceedings where the legal burden of proof is on the state. Some jurisdictions have, however, taken steps towards reversing the burden of proof in NCB confiscation proceedings.

Before moving on, a few words ought to be said about what is meant by a reversed burden of proof.[83] First, a distinction can be made between a legal burden of proof and an evidential burden of proof. A legal burden of proof refers to the burden of convincing the judge of a fact to the requisite standard of proof. The risk in case of insufficient evidence ('a draw') lies thus with the party upon whom the burden is

at the XX International Congress of Penal Law in Rome, 13–16 November 2019, it is held that '[a]n excessive lowering of these standards in non criminal conviction based (civil) confiscation proceedings must, however, be rejected independent of their label, because this would contravene the fundamental right to property and the proportionality principle. This type of confiscation should therefore require a high standard of proof'. The US House Committee on the Judiciary in the House of Representatives also concluded: 'The general civil standard of proof – preponderance of the evidence – is too low a standard to assign to the government in this type of case. A higher standard of proof is needed that recognizes that in reality the government is alleging that a crime has taken place' (House of Representatives, Report 106–92, 18 June 1999, 12).

[80] Boucht (n 2), 226–27. There is some support in national jurisdictions for this standard to apply in confiscation proceedings. A clear balance of probabilities was required by the Norwegian Supreme Court (see cases Rt. 1999 s. 14 and Rt. 2007 s. 1217) in regard to administrative confiscation of unlawful fish drafts. The Swedish legislation on extended criminal confiscation (Penal Code chapter 16 section 1b) also requires that it be clearly more probable than not that the assets in questions derive from past unlawful conduct.

[81] From the perspective of consistency and predictability, a fixed standard would be preferable. However, as mentioned earlier in this section, in some jurisdictions, for example the UK, hybrid standards are not accepted. However, as indicated by Lady Hale in *In re D* [2008] UKHL, the inherent improbabilities can be taken into account when deciding where the truth lies. Where the allegation is inherently improbable, the evidence presented for the court may have to be more cogent, robust and convincing, urging the courts to assess the evidence before them with particular care to safeguard against wrongful decisions. If this requirement is taken seriously, the practical differences from requiring a clear balance of probabilities may not necessarily be so big.

[82] In some jurisdictions, NCB confiscation may also be used in situations where assets are found, for example at a train station or an airport, but no owner can be established. This scenario should possibly be distinguished from the former two; as such a balance of probabilities may be a sufficient standard of proof in such proceedings.

[83] On the burden of proof, see eg *Murphy on Evidence* (n 57), 73–102.

placed. An evidential burden of proof means that the party has to adduce evidence so as to create a prima facie case regarding the issue in question against the other party, but s/he does not have to prove it to the requisite standard of proof. If the party discharges the evidential burden, the burden of proof shifts back onto the party who has the legal burden proof.

Secondly, statutory presumptions may affect the burden of proof. Statutory presumptions mean that provided that a certain fact is proved, the court is mandated to take as proved also another fact (the presumed fact) unless this is rebutted.[84] A presumption may either shift the legal burden of proof, so that the respondent has to prove to the requisite standard that the fact does not exist, or it may shift the evidential burden of proof. In the latter case, the respondent will have to produce enough evidence so as to provide a prima facie case against the presumed fact in order for the normal burden of proof to apply.

There are examples where the burden of proof in practice (although not in law) has been all but reversed. For example under chapter 3 of Part 5 of POCA 2002, cash forfeiture is possible where the court is satisfied that the cash is recoverable property, or is intended by any person for use in unlawful conduct. However, the courts have held that having a very large amount of cash in one's possession may well, in certain circumstances, demand an answer.[85] This would, however, effectively seem to amount to reversing the burden of proof in many cases onto the respondent (although this has been denied by the courts).[86]

A recent example of steps being towards formally reversing the burden of proof in NCB confiscation proceedings is the unexplained wealth mechanism introduced into UK law in 2017 through Part 8 of the Proceeds of Crime Act 2002 (see section I.B). A UWO requires the respondent to provide a statement setting out, inter alia, the nature and extent of his interest in the targeted property, and how s/he obtained the property (POCA 2002 sections 362C–D). If the respondent fails 'without reasonable excuse' to comply (or purport to comply) with the requirements imposed by the UWO, the property is 'presumed' to be recoverable for the purpose of civil recovery proceedings under Part 5 of POCA. A UWO does not reverse the legal burden of proof, but rather has the nature of an evidential presumption; it is sufficient that the respondent provides some explanation but s/he does not have the legal standard of proof to actually disprove the allegation.

[84] *Murphy on Evidence* (n 57), 75–76.

[85] The *R (Director of Assets Recovery Agency) v Green and Others* [2005] EWHC 3168 (Admin.), at para 33. However, Sullivan J distinguished this situation from having other property in one's possession: 'By contrast, conduct consisting of the mere fact of being in possession of other types of property, expensive jewellery, houses, cars and so forth, or the mere fact of having a lavish lifestyle or of living beyond one's apparent means, do not, without anything more, provide reasonable grounds for suspicion demanding an explanation.' Furthermore, under sections 297A–G POCA 2002, authorities may forfeit cash without a court hearing in uncontested cases where a senior officer is satisfied that the cash is recoverable property, or is intended by any person for use in unlawful conduct, provided that a notice is given. If no objection is made within the period for objecting, and the notice has not lapsed, the cash is forfeited.

[86] R Booth, G Bastable and N Yeo, *Money Laundering Law and Regulation. A Practical Guide* (Oxford, Oxford University Press, 2011), 297.

Another example is the German hybrid model under section 76aStGB, subsection 4 (see section V.B. above). This provision is supplemented by section 437 of the German Criminal Procedural Code (StPO). According to this provision, 'the court may, in particular, base its conviction as to whether the object was derived from an unlawful act on the gross imbalance between the value of the object and the legitimate income of the person concerned. When reaching its decision, it may also take into account '(1) the outcome of the investigations into the offence giving rise to the proceedings, (2) the circumstances under which the object was found and secured, and (3) the person concerned's other personal and economic circumstances.' As a result, confiscation can be decided on an evidential presumption of illicit origin where no degree of tracing is required. This also effectively amounts to reversing the burden of proof.

Reversing the burden of proof in NCB confiscation proceedings is a controversial move, which may increase the risk of wrongful confiscation decisions, although to shift the evidential burden of proof onto the respondent is less far-reaching than shifting the legal burden. To require the respondent, in the absence of a criminal conviction of acquisitive offences and upon the threat of confiscation, to prove the legitimacy of his assets, creates a tension in regard to his freedom as an individual.[87] Autonomous people should, in principle, not be subjected to an obligation to act in order to exculpate themselves unless there are good reasons for requiring such action. The legitimacy of NCB confiscation schemes reversing the burden of proof should therefore be assessed meticulously and critically.

The further away one gets from the situation where the assets can directly be shown to constitute proceeds of crime, the weaker the case for making a confiscation decision arguably becomes. For example, to base confiscation on a general presumption concerning the disproportionality between the respondent's legitimate earnings and the assets s/he holds, would seem to disregard too many alternative hypotheses, even if the respondent remains silent.[88] An exception might be made where the circumstances in which the property was handled are such as to give rise to an 'irresistible inference' that it could only have been derived from crime.

However, the difficulty of obtaining sufficient evidence in some situations, and how this may affect efficiency, should of course be acknowledged, although this is not a new dilemma in the context of criminal justice. There may be situations in which calling on the respondent to provide an explanation is not unfair. This might be the case if strong suspicions prevail concerning the illicit origin of certain assets, but sufficient evidence is virtually impossible to obtain and there are particularly pressing policy reasons calling for the confiscation of criminal proceeds. I will return to this point later.

[87] International Covenant on Civil and Political Rights (1966) states: 'All peoples have the right of self-determination. By virtue of that right they freely determine their political status and freely pursue their economic, social and cultural development.'

[88] See eg the English cases *R (Director of Assets Recovery Agency) v Green and Others* [2005] EWHC 3168 (Admin) paras 33 and 47 and *Assets Recovery Agency v Olupitan* [2008] EWCA Civ 104.

It may be useful to first recall how reversing the burden of proof fits in with the requirements set out by the ECHR. In criminal proceedings, the presumption of innocence in Article 6(2) requires as a main rule that the burden of proof is on the prosecution.[89] Certain presumptions are nevertheless permissible provided they are confined within reasonable limits and 'take into account the importance of what is at stake and maintain the rights of the defence'.[90] As observed in section V.B., NCB confiscation is not considered by the ECtHR to represent a criminal charge under Article 6(2) ECHR. As an infringement of property rights, the fairness of the proceedings thus falls to be determined in light of the civil head of Article 6(1).[91]

The question of a reversed burden of proof in NCB confiscation proceedings came up in the case *Gogitidze v Georgia* mentioned in section V.B.[92] The Georgian scheme was constructed so that confiscation proceedings could only be initiated if an official had first been charged with a relevant offence – (including corruption) committed during his or her term in office, against the interests of the public service, the enterprise or organisation concerned – or of one of the following offences: money laundering, extortion, misappropriation, embezzlement, tax evasion or violations of custom regulations, regardless of whether the official in question was still in office or not. Once a public prosecutor had filed a civil action for confiscation, which had to be substantiated with sufficient documentary evidence, the burden of proof would then shift onto the respondent. If the respondent failed to refute the public prosecutor's claim by proving that the property (or the financial resources for the purchase of the property) had been lawfully acquired, the court would order the confiscation of the property in question.

The Court concluded (at paragraph 122) that the reversed burden of proof violated neither Article 6(1) nor Article 1 ECHR-P1. It held that

> there can be nothing arbitrary, for the purposes of the 'civil' limb of Article 6 § 1 of the Convention, in the reversal of the burden of proof onto the respondents in the forfeiture proceedings *in rem* after the public prosecutor had submitted a substantiated claim …

Rather, the Court continued, it was only reasonable to expect the respondents to discharge their part of the burden of proof by refuting the prosecutor's substantiated suspicions about the wrongful origins of their assets.

This is an interesting judgment that goes to the heart of the problem discussed in this section. Although the court concluded that no violation had occurred, the case should, in my view, not be interpreted as providing carte blanche for reversing the burden of proof in NCB confiscation proceedings. Three circumstances are worth observing. First, *Gogitidze* concerned NCB confiscation under a scheme that was specifically aimed at

[89] See *Barberà, Messegué and Jabardo v Spain*, App No 10590/83 (ECtHR, 6 December 1988), para 77.

[90] See *Salabiaku v France*, App No 10519/83 (ECtHR, 7 October 1988), para 28. In *Phillips v the United Kingdom*, App No 41087/98 (ECtHR, 5 July 2001), paras 40–47, the ECtHR analysed the compatibility with Article 6 ECHR of the extended confiscation scheme under the UK's Drug Trafficking Act 1994, a scheme based on far-reaching and sweeping statutory presumptions that reversed the burden of proof onto the defendant. This extended criminal confiscation scheme was considered neither unreasonable, nor to deprive the defendant of a fair hearing under Article 6(1) ECHR.

[91] See *Gogitidze v Georgia*, App No 36862/05 (ECtHR, 12 May 2015), para 121.

[92] *Gogitidze v Georgia*, App No 36862/05 (ECtHR, 12 May 2015).

recovering wrongfully acquired property and unexplained wealth from public officials subsequent to initiation of criminal charges against those officials.

In its assessment (concerning both the legitimacy of the aim and its proportionality), the Court consistently limited its discussion to serious offences and noted that the proceeds in this case indeed were suspected to derive from *serious* criminality entailing unjust enrichment, such as 'corruption, money laundering, drug offences and so on'. This is in line with the limitation in Article 3(4) of the Council of Europe Convention on Laundering, Search, Seizure and Confiscation of the Proceeds from Crime and on the Financing of Terrorism (2005), to which the Court also refers, that urges states to reverse the burden of proof in confiscation proceedings in respect of *serious offences*.

It follows, that the 'target area' of the Georgian regulation was narrowly defined. As suggested in section V.A above, the aim should be to appropriately balance various parameters against one another so that the confiscation scheme, seen as a whole, is efficient not only for removing proceeds of crime from circulation, but also for providing safeguards, both substantive and procedural, for the confiscation subject. Certain onerous features at one stage of the scheme may therefore be counterbalanced at another stage. For example, if the target area is narrowly defined, some reduced procedural safeguards may be less controversial than if applied generally.

Secondly, confiscation proceedings could be initiated only if an official had first been charged with the relevant offences and the prosecutor had made a prima facie case based on a reasonable suspicion that the property in question had been acquired unlawfully. Only then would the legal burden of proving the licit nature of the assets, in order to avoid confiscation, be shifted onto the respondent.

Thirdly, the Court did seem to take into account that there had been a large problem with corruption in the country.[93] Corruption of state officials is a serious offence where policy-based expectations relating to confiscation are, and should be, high. This means that the assessment might not be the same in a case where these circumstances are not present.

Lastly, in support of its decision, the Court (at paragraph 105) referred to 'a common standard' expressed in international instruments.

> Having regard to such international legal mechanisms as the 2005 United Nations Convention against Corruption [UNCAC], the Financial Action Task Force's (FATF) Recommendations and the two relevant Council of Europe Conventions of 1990 and 2005 concerning confiscation of the proceeds of crime (ETS No. 141 and ETS No. 198), the Court observes that common European and even universal legal standards can be said to exist which encourage firstly, the confiscation of property linked to serious criminal offences … without the prior existence of a criminal conviction. Secondly, the onus of proving the lawful origin of the property presumed to have been wrongfully acquired may legitimately be shifted onto the respondents in such non-criminal proceedings for confiscation, including civil proceedings *in rem*.

[93] This is not the first time that the Court has identified certain areas where effective measures have been deemed particularly pressing and where the Court's tolerance would appear to be higher. For example, Panzavolta and Flor (n 47), 146 note, concerning the fact that the ECtHR has dismissed most human rights concerns directed at the Italian confiscation regime, that 'it seems that the ECtHR has done so mostly because it acknowledges the peculiarity of the Italian situation with regard to the pressing need to fight organized crime'.

It is true that these instruments encourage states to further develop their rules on confiscation and suggest that states consider the possibility of reversing the burden of proof in confiscation proceedings. However, the starting point seems to be confiscation in a criminal context, ie where a criminal conviction is necessary in order to initiate confiscation proceedings. For example, Article 31 of the UNCAC concerns confiscation of proceeds derived from criminal offences established in accordance with the Convention, and the suggestion in Article 31(8) that states consider reversing burden of proof relates to this context. That states consider implementing NCB confiscation schemes instead is suggested in Article 54(1)(c) and only in cases in which the offender cannot be prosecuted by reason of death, flight or absence or in other appropriate cases.[94] Reversing the burden of proof in NCB confiscation proceedings is not specifically mentioned.

The FATF's fourth (2021) recommendation, which the ECtHR also refers to (at paragraph 65), urges states *either* to consider adopting NCB confiscation schemes, *or* to require an offender to demonstrate the lawful origin of the property alleged to be liable to confiscation. Reversing the burden of proof in criminal confiscation proceedings is thus presented as an alternative to introducing NCB confiscation. Thus, to assert, as the Court does, that there are 'common European and even universal legal standards' that encourage reversing the burden of proof also in NCB confiscation proceedings would seem to me to be taking it a step too far.

Confiscation proceedings must, in order to be proportionate, not impose an excessive burden on the individual. However, shifting the burden of proof in NCB confiscation proceedings will easily place a considerable burden on the respondent, and should thus be approached with restraint. In assessing whether this may be fair in a particular situation, the perspectives of both the state and the individual should be considered. The consequences of a wrongful decision are crucial in this assessment. For example, even if it intuitively might seem less controversial to reverse the burden of proof in in regard to serious offences, the relatively more serious consequences that normally follow in that situation may still speak against doing so. In view of the burden placed on the respondent, shifting the evidential burden would be preferable to shifting the legal burden.

The legitimacy of a reversed burden of proof should also be assessed in light of the extent to which there are other compensating features of the confiscation scheme, for example by mechanisms that increase the inherent likelihood of the assets in question being illicit. For example in *Gogitidze v Georgia*, NCB confiscation proceedings under the Georgian rules could only be initiated after the respondent had been charged with a relevant offence.

A reversed burden of proof in NCB confiscation proceedings should, if at all legitimate, moreover only apply to a more limited group of respondents. The 'target

[94] See also Article 3(4) of the Council of Europe Convention on Laundering, Search, Seizure and Confiscation of the Proceeds from Crime and on the Financing of Terrorism (2005), which urges states to reverse the burden of proof in confiscation proceedings in respect of a serious offence or offences. Even if the term 'confiscation' in the Convention refers both to criminal confiscation and civil *in rem* proceedings relating to criminal activities (see Explanatory Report to the Council of Europe Convention on Laundering, Search, Seizure and Confiscation of the Proceeds from Crime and on the Financing of Terrorism (2005), para 30) the context would still seem to relate mainly to conviction-based confiscation proceedings.

area' should, in other words, be relatively narrowly defined. A wide scope of application, quickly becomes problematic from the perspective of proportionality, and, thus, legitimacy.

Indeed, as noted above, it may not be unreasonable in some situations to expect the respondent to provide an explanation in order to avoid confiscation. However, requiring the individual to provide an explanation concerning the provenance of his assets would have to be based on strong policy reasons. For example, the mere fact that an individual who is on social benefits also holds certain more valuable property should as such not be sufficient to reverse the burden of proof onto the respondent. Also to reverse the burden of proof merely on a reasonable suspicion that an individual has been involved in serious crime would be to take this approach too far.

An example where it might not be unreasonable to do so would be corruption cases that implicate public officials, in regard to which it may be virtually impossible to obtain evidence for the purpose of a criminal conviction. If such individuals, who are suspected of being involved in serious criminal conduct, also are in possession of disproportionate wealth, it may not be unreasonable to shift the burden of explanation onto them.

VI. Epilogue

NCB confiscation provides a way for states to move the confiscation of criminal proceeds into the non-criminal sphere. This kind of confiscation can be a useful and powerful tool for law enforcement. However, in order to be a fair and proportionate response to acquisitive crime, the interests and rights of the respondent have to be taken seriously. As substantive proportionality may be difficult to assess due to the nature of NCB confiscation schemes, it has been suggested that sufficient procedural safeguards, inter alia requiring a sufficiently high standard of proof and being restrictive with permitting reversals of the burden of proof, become key in ensuring that the operation of such schemes are fair, and thereby also legitimate.

B. Special Part of Criminal Law

9

'Crimmigration' and Human Rights: Immigration Detention at the European Court of Human Rights*

MARIA PICHOU

I. Introduction

The detention of migrants, refugees and asylum seekers is a growing and disconcerting practice of many national migration policies across the world. In Europe, the way in which states have handled emergency situations at their borders has taken its toll on the respect for human rights. The migrant and refugee crisis has obliged states to establish extemporaneous facilities, reception centres and other installations to contain this flow and to detain people arriving in their territories irregularly. As a result of states' unwillingness or inability to respond to the multiple challenges of the crisis – either in material terms due to lack of resources or political will, or in legal terms due to lack of clarity of the applicable legal rules – states have been found responsible for violations of their obligations under human rights law.

Aside from the crisis, however, the power of states to control their borders constitutes a prominent manifestation of their sovereignty, which is reflected in their power to detain non-nationals on the basis of them being 'aliens'. Controlling borders denotes surveilling the entry into the state's territory, and detaining non-nationals who enter irregularly or whose presence on the territory is considered illegal is a complementary aspect of that sovereign power. The question remains, however, whether and under which conditions the mere presence of non-nationals on the territory of a state constitutes a violation of law, and crucially of which branch of law. The response is not simple or uniform across Europe, as the legal basis for the detention of non-nationals varies from country to country in Europe. Several academics have increasingly pointed to the conflation of administrative and immigration law with criminal law since policy-makers connect immigration with the criminalisation of the entry and of the presence of non-nationals on the territory of a state, and consider immigration law through the

*This analysis in this Chapter was made before the ECtHR deliberated on the case *Ilias and Ahmed v Hungary*, App No 42287/15 (ECtHR, 21 November 2019). For other recent developments, see also the Joined Cases C-924/19 PPU and C-925/19 PPU, FMS and others, ECLI:EU:C:2020:367, 14 May 2020.

prism of criminal law and not that of human rights law. This merger between criminal law and immigration law has been classified as 'crimmigration law'.[1] Immigration law is indeed torn, albeit that it should not be, between two paradigms: the administrative law paradigm, which has always been the primary branch of law regulating immigration; and the criminal law paradigm, which is increasingly used to regulate and enforce immigration rules.[2] Immigration detention is generally viewed as a type of administrative internment, different from criminal incarceration. The intersection between immigration law and criminal law and the compatibility of detention of non-nationals with human rights law is the focus of this chapter.

Specifically, this chapter examines how the European Court of Human Rights (ECtHR or the Strasbourg Court) has addressed immigration detention in Europe. It looks at immigration detention through the right to personal liberty of non-nationals of Member States of the Council of Europe (COE). It focuses precisely on the application of Article 5 § 1 (f) of the European Convention on Human Rights (ECHR or the Convention), and this choice is pertinent in the discussion of 'crimmigration', as Article 5 ECHR applies to any case where the person's liberty is at stake regardless of the context and refers to criminal detention (pre-trial and after conviction) and to measures imposed on offenders who are not blameworthy, as well as to preventive measures (for containing the spread of infectious diseases for example).[3] The conflation between criminal and migration policies ('crimmigration') is particularly demonstrated in the cases where detention is used as a deterrent tool, as deterrence constitutes one of the main objectives of criminal law. Moreover, certain states in Europe have criminalised the illegal presence of non-nationals as a crime in their criminal codes. Looking at immigration detention through the lens of the human right to liberty is particularly helpful, as Article 5 of the ECHR, although providing the same procedural guarantees, does distinguish between criminal detention and the detention of non-nationals. While detention is primarily a criminal law enforcement tool, when used in the immigration context on people whose sole 'crime'[4] is their irregular presence in the host state, it becomes a specific human rights issue under the Convention.

Furthermore, Article 5 ECHR introduces six specific limitations to the right to liberty, allowing the state to encroach on this individual freedom, which interestingly are not to be found in the corresponding articles of the Universal Declaration of Human Rights or the American Convention on Human Rights.[5] Remarkably, during

[1] See Juliet P Stumpf, 'The Crimmigration Crisis: Immigrants, Crime, and Sovereign Power' (2006) 56 *American University Law Review* 367. César Cuauhtémoc García Hernández, 'Deconstructing Crimmigration' (2018) 52(1) *U.C. Davis Law Review* 197–253. Maartje van der Woude, Vanessa Barker & Joanne van der Leun, 'Crimmigration in Europe' (2017) 14(1) *European Journal of Criminology* 3–6. See also the indispensable blog: http://crimmigration.com/.

[2] https://www.yalejreg.com/nc/immigration-law-is-torn-between-administrative-law-and-criminal-law-by-michael-kagan/ (accessed 10 June 2020).

[3] For a short history of the drafting of this provision and the negotiations between the states, see William Schabas, *The European Convention on Human Rights: A Commentary* (Oxford, Oxford University Press 2015) 221–26.

[4] In certain countries in Europe, the violation of immigration laws would not only be a violation of administrative law but would constitute also a violation of criminal law (see for example in Italy and France, before the legislative reforms that took place after their condemnation by the ECtHR).

[5] See Articles 9, 10 and 11 of the Universal Declaration of Human Rights; Article I and XXV of the American Declaration on the Rights and Duties of Man (American Declaration), as well as Article 7 of the American Convention on Human Rights (American Convention).

the drafting process of Article 5, when paragraph 1 (f) was proposed by the United Kingdom, and was tailored after a proposal made by five countries (Australia, Denmark, France, Lebanon, and the United Kingdom) to the UN Commission on Human Rights, and in the document prepared by the Secretariat-General of the Council of Europe for the Committee of Experts, it was noted that the General Assembly had not taken into consideration the case of so-called 'administrative internment'.[6] The relevance, therefore, of looking at the case law of the Strasbourg Court is particularly important.

The chapter constitutes a doctrinal legal analysis of the case law of the Strasbourg Court. The classification of the case law on the general question of the detention of non-nationals is based on the HUDOC database and the ECtHR's own classification. During the analysis, the term 'non-national' or 'alien'[7] is employed to signify every person who is not national of the Member State and the term 'irregular', instead of 'illegal',[8] to define the persons who arrive in a Member State either without documents or through irregular means.[9] The chapter first provides an analysis of the relevant legal framework governing the deprivation of liberty of non-nationals under the ECHR, and then proceeds to examine how the ECtHR interpretes the obligations of states when they use detention in the immigration context, whether as an informal or formal administrative border-control tool, as a deterrent technique for new arrivals or even as a penalty for the crime of illegal entry or for not complying with an expulsion order. Apart from the ECHR, EU secondary legislation, although not the focus of this chapter, is also taken into account when related to the detention of third-country nationals.

To address immigration detention as a quasi-criminal enforcement tool from a human rights perspective, two main issues drive the analysis in this chapter. First, it will examine the criteria for the establishment of centres where migrants can be detained and the legal basis for the detention of non-nationals therein. Although, many states have employed the practice of detaining informally non-nationals in an attempt to cope with the migration and refugee flows, administrative practices alone, without a statutory provision or established case law, cannot serve as sufficient legal basis for the detention of people in reception centres. Second, the chapter will investigate whether the exceptional character of a migration/refugee crisis may play a role when adjudicating cases of detention of aliens. The case law of the Strasbourg Court confirms that despite the challenges, states must abide by their obligations under the Convention and

[6] Schabas, *The European Convention on Human Rights* (n 3) 222, where the author refers to the Preparatory Report by the Secretariat-General concerning a Preliminary Draft Convention to Provide a Collective Guarantee of Human Rights, Doc B 22 III TP 2-37, at 28.

[7] The term 'alien' is used in Article 16 of the ECHR, in Article 4 of Protocol No 4 and in Article 1 of Protocol No 7 to the ECHR.

[8] 'Irregular' refers either to the means of entering the host country or to the person's documents (or the absence thereof) when entering the host country. The term 'illegal' denotes a violation of law *a priori*, which may not be the case for asylum seekers, whose refugee status is subsequently recognised. It is also a political choice to not characterise a person as 'illegal', especially when approaching the issue from a human rights perspective.

[9] For an analysis of the terminology in the immigration context, see Stephan Scheel and Vicki Squire, 'Forced Migrants as "Illegal" Migrants' in Elena Fiddian-Qasmiyeh, Gil Loescher, Katy Long and Nando Sigona (eds), *Refugee and Forced Migration Studies* (Oxford, Oxford University Press, 2014) 188.

specifically respect the guarantees of the right to liberty, and, with certain caveats, the right to liberty of movement.

During the analysis, I address the distinction between the right to liberty under Article 5 of the Convention and the right to liberty of movement, enshrined in Protocol No 4, with the aim of investigating whether the latter may be applicable in cases of detention of aliens. I argue that under certain conditions the right to liberty of movement may be applicable in cases of detention of people who enter a Member State irregularly. Finally, this chapter reviews the EU 'Hotspot' approach adopted in 2015 by the European Commission to address emergencies at the European borders.[10] When adopted, this policy raised interesting legal questions regarding the responsibility of EU Member States in the light of the European Convention on Human Rights. Despite these EU coordinating efforts to address the crisis at the time, it is clear, however, that the responsibility for the conditions at detention centres of non-nationals still lies with the individual EU Member States.[11]

II. Detaining Migrants

Migration in Europe is framed by national law, EU law,[12] public international law,[13] and the European Convention on Human Rights. Considering that in many European states the right to bring an individual petition to an international tribunal exists only under the Convention, the ECtHR has an important role to play in safeguarding the rights of both EU citizens and aliens.[14] When it comes to arresting or detaining aliens who attempt to enter European territory irregularly, European states need to abide by the requirements laid down in Article 5 of the Convention:

> Everyone has the right to liberty and security of person. No one shall be deprived of his liberty save in the following cases and in accordance with a procedure prescribed by law: …

[10] In September 2020, the EU Commission proposed a new Pact on Migration and Asylum, covering all of the different elements needed for a comprehensive European approach to migration: https://ec.europa.eu/info/publications/migration-and-asylum-package-new-pact-migration-and-asylum-documents-adopted-23-september-2020_en.

[11] See analysis below in section III.

[12] See Directive 2013/33/EU of The European Parliament and of the Council of 26 June 2013, laying down standards for the reception of applicants for international protection. Particularly Articles 8, 9, 10 and 11. [2013] OJ L 180/96-116, 29.6.2013.

[13] For a comprehensive analysis see: Vincent Chetail, *International Migration Law* (Oxford, Oxford University Press, 2019); Pieter Boeles, Maarten Den Heijer, Gerrie Lodder and Kees Wouters (eds), *European Migration Law* (Cambridge, Intersentia, 2014); Vincent Chetail and Céline Bauloz (eds), *Research Handbook on International Law and Migration* (Cheltenham, Edward Elgar Publishing, 2014); Vincent Chetail (ed), *International Law and Migration*, vols I and II (Cheltenham, Edward Elgar Publishing, 2016); Brian Opeskin, Richard Perruchoud, and Jillyanne Redpath-Cross (eds), *Foundations of International Migration Law* (Cambridge,Cambridge University Press, 2012); Vincent Chetail, 'The Human Rights of Migrants in General International Law: from Minimum Standards to Fundamental Rights' (2013) 28(1) *Georgetown Immigration Law Journal* 225.

[14] As rightly pointed out by Laurie Berg, 'structurally international or regional courts are better placed as international treaty law, to articulate international standards that are responsive to the protection needs of migrants'. Laurie Berg, 'At the Border and Between the Cracks; The Precarious Position of Irregular Migrant Workers Under International Human Rights Law' (2007) 8 *Melbourne Journal of International Law* 19, 20.

Article 5 ECHR provides for the right to liberty and security.[15] The deprivation of liberty under Article 5 ECHR contains an objective and a subjective element. The objective element refers to a person's confinement in a restricted space and for a certain period, while the subjective element corresponds to that person's lack of consent to the confinement in question.[16] The corresponding article in the EU Charter of Fundamental Rights (the Charter) is Article 6, which is identical in wording. As Article 53 of the Charter provides that all EU institutions and Member States are obliged to interpret the Charter in light of existing jurisprudence of the ECtHR, and due to space constraints, the analysis in this chapter will focus only on the case law of the ECtHR on immigration detention.

The guarantees of Article 5 of the Convention are threefold. The article provides for a general right, it lays down the conditions for a permissible deprivation of liberty in exceptional cases, and it prescribes certain procedural safeguards. The general provision protects everyone's right to personal liberty and security. It does not provide a right of entry, nor a right not to be expelled or a general right to asylum for persons whose safety is threatened in their country of origin. The key word in the general part of the article is 'everyone', which entails that all natural persons enjoy the right to liberty, regardless of their nationality, age and status. The substantive content of the right to liberty refers to the right of all people, falling within the jurisdiction of a Member State, to determine their location and change their physical whereabouts freely. The Court's case law has focused mostly on 'liberty', and has not given any clear indication on the distinct or autonomous concept of 'security'.[17] According to the Council of Europe, the word 'security' refers simply to the prohibition of an arbitrary deprivation of liberty.[18]

The article imposes a positive obligation on states not only to refrain from actively violating the right to liberty but also to take appropriate steps to protect everyone and to prevent unlawful interference within their jurisdiction.[19] A procedure prescribed by law must be in place in national law, allowing for an arrest or detention only in specific cases. There are only six limitations to the right of liberty that the state is permitted to impose on this fundamental right. Any deprivation of liberty is automatically unlawful if it does not fall under one or more of these six permitted exceptions laid out in Article 5: post-conviction detention (Article 5 § 1 (a)); non-compliance with a court's order or legal obligation (Article 5 § 1 (b)); detention for criminal prosecution (Article 5 § 1 (c)); detention of minors (Article 5 § 1 (d)); medical reasons (Article 5 § 1 (e)); immigration detention (to prevent entry or for expulsion and extradition) (Article 5 § 1 (f)). This list of limitations to the right to liberty is exhaustive and it must be interpreted strictly. The state must justify that the detention relies on one of these six grounds.

[15] See also: Articles 3 and 9 of the Universal Declaration of Human Rights; Article 9 of the International Covenant on Civil and Political Rights (ICCPR); Articles I and XXV of the American Declaration on the Rights and Duties of Man (American Declaration); Article 7 of the American Convention on Human Rights (American Convention);

[16] *Storck v Germany*, App No 60613/00 (ECtHR, 16 June 2005) [2005] ECHR 406, para 74.

[17] In *Bozano v France* the Court found that there was a breach of both liberty and security without however explaining the distinction. *Bozano v France*, App No 9990/82 (ECtHR, 18 December 1986) [1986] ECHR 16, para 54. See also Schabas, *The European Convention on Human Rights* (n 3) 228.

[18] Nuala Mole and Catherine Meredith, *Asylum and the European Convention on Human Rights* (Strasbourg, Council of Europe Publishing, 2010) 143.

[19] *El-Masri v the Former Yugoslav Republic of Macedonia*, App No 39630/09 (ECtHR, 13 December 2012) [2012] ECHR 2067, para 239.

Article 5 §§ 2–5 provide procedural rights to any person whose liberty has been deprived, namely the right to be 'promptly informed of reasons', 'to take proceedings by which the lawfulness of the detention shall be decided speedily by a court', and an 'enforceable right to compensation for any violation of this right to liberty.[20] These rights are autonomous in that they need to be granted and observed independently from the lawfulness of the arrest or detention. Specifically, the right to be promptly informed of the reasons for the arrest, being applied in accordance with all limitations listed in Article 5 ECHR, constitutes an autonomous concept under the Convention and exceeds that applicable in a criminal law framework. Although it is true that the terms 'arrest' and 'charge' used in Article 5 § 2 imply a criminal law context, the Court held that this procedural right to be promptly informed should be interpreted 'autonomously' so as to expand the notion of 'arrest' beyond the realm of criminal law, and its application to the other limitations to the right to liberty.[21] Consequently, the right to be promptly informed has also been applied in cases of detention for medical reasons and immigration detention, for example.[22] The detainee must be provided with information relating to the purpose and the justification of the detention, and the applicable national law authorising the detention. Moreover, simply providing information about the legal status of a migrant does not meet the requirements of Article 5 § 2 of the Convention. The legal and factual grounds for the deprivation of freedom must be communicated to the person concerned in a language that he understands.[23] Finally, this information must be provided promptly, upon the commencement of the detention and not immediately before the return, deportation or expulsion.

The rights to have the detention speedily reviewed by a court (Article 5 § 4) and to be compensated for any violation (Article 5 § 5) constitute a *lex specialis* to the general right to an effective remedy under Article 13.[24] The legality of the detention is reviewed according not only to domestic law but also to the Convention. The judicial review is limited to controlling the legality of the detention, by an authority which possesses the competence to judge upon this issue. Furthermore, this review must take place speedily, which is a condition stricter than that of 'within a reasonable time', prescribed in Article 6 of the Convention. The judicial review under Article 5 § 4 touches upon issues of liberty of the person, and, thus, it requires a particular standard of diligence.[25]

A. Legal Basis for the Detention of Migrants

Article 5 permits states to arrest and detain people when three general requirements are cumulatively met. First, there must be a legal basis in domestic law, authorising the

[20] Article 5 § 3 provides for the right to be brought promptly before a judicial authority specifically in the context of criminal law.

[21] *Van der Leer v The Netherlands*, App No 11509/85 (ECtHR, January 1990) [1990] ECHR 3.

[22] *X v the United Kingdom*, App No 7215/75 (ECtHR [GC], 5 November 1981) [1981] ECHR 6; *Conca v Belgium*, App No 51564/99 (ECtHR, 5 February 2002) [2002] ECHR 14; *Saadi v the United Kingdom*, App No 13229/03 (ECtHR [GC], 29 January 2008) [2008] ECHR 80.

[23] *Fox, Campbell and Hartley v the United Kingdom*, App Nos 12244/86, 12245/86 and 12383/86 (ECtHR, 30 August 1990) (1990) 13 EHRR 157.

[24] *Garabayev v Russia*, App No 38411/02, (ECtHR, 30 January 2008) para 108.

[25] *Hutchison Reid v the United Kingdom*, App No 50272/99 (ECtHR, 20 February 2003) [2003] ECHR 94, para 79; *Moiseyev v Russia*, App No 62936/00 (ECtHR, 9 October 2008), para 160. *Khlaifia and Others v Italy*, App No 16483/12 (ECtHR, 1 September 2015) [2016] ECHR 757, para 94.

deprivation of liberty. Second, the arrest and detention must comply with a procedure prescribed in national law. Third, state authorities must not act arbitrarily and national law must provide adequate safeguards protecting the detainees from arbitrariness. Looking more closely at the detention of migrants as a border-control tool, the exception provided in Article 5 § 1 (f) is relevant:

> ... the lawful arrest or detention of a person to prevent his effecting an unauthorised entry into the country or of a person against whom action is being taken with a view to deportation or extradition.

This exception rests on two limbs, as it provides two grounds for the detention of aliens. Arrest or detention is permitted either in order to prevent an unauthorised entry into the country or when action is being taken in order to deport or extradite a person. Regarding the first limb, unless a state has authorised entry into the country, by granting, for example, a residence permit or by accepting an application for asylum, any entry is considered unauthorised for the purposes of Article 5.[26] Such a detention must be carried out in good faith and must be closely connected to the purpose of preventing unauthorised entry. The ECtHR noted that the question as to when the first limb of Article 5 ceases to apply, because the individual has been granted formal authorisation to enter or stay, is largely dependent on national law.[27] The second limb is two-pronged, as it introduces the distinction between deportation and extradition. Deportation is the expulsion of a person or group of persons from a place or a country, while extradition is the transfer of criminals or suspects between countries.

Unlike the other limitations to the right to liberty listed in Article 5, there is no requirement that the detention be justified as necessary for detaining non-nationals to prevent their entry or for their expulsion and deportation.[28] In this regard, the right to liberty under the ECHR differentiates from Article 9 of the ICCPR, which requires that any deprivation of liberty must be lawful, necessary and proportionate. That is why under the ECHR the lawfulness of the underlying order for the deportation or extradition is not relevant, neither is the nature of the detention, be it administrative of criminal.[29] The provision only requires the existence of such an order and the Court does not have to look at whether the detention is necessary for the expulsion/deportation (necessity test). There is, however, a caveat to the non-application of the necessity test in this paragraph: when national law prescribes that the detention order must be justified as necessary, the Court will apply this necessity test to the detention under Article 5 § 1 (f).[30] Moreover, the principle of due diligence must be observed during the proceedings for the removal of aliens.[31] Consequently, a deprivation of liberty under

[26] *Saadi v the United Kingdom*, App No 13229/03 (ECtHR, 29 January 2008) [2008] ECHR 80, 31. *Suso Musa v Malta*, App No 42337/12 (ECtHR, 23 July 2013). See also Schengen Borders Code, Article 13.

[27] *Suso Musa v Malta*, App No 42337/12 (ECtHR, 23 July 2013), para 97.

[28] *Chahal v the United Kingdom*, App No 22414/93 (ECtHR, 15 November 1996). See contrary William Schabas, who connects the necessity test for the detention of aliens with the assessment of its arbitrariness. Schabas, *The European Convention on Human Rights* (n 3) 243.

[29] *Nolan and K v Russia*, App No 2512/04 (ECtHR, 12 February 2009) [2009] ECHR 262, para 96. See also Article 1 of Protocol No. 7 to the Convention, which postulates the requirements for a lawful expulsion of aliens.

[30] *Rusu v Austria*, App No 34082/02 (ECtHR, 2 October 2008) para 54.

[31] *Quinn v France*, App No 18580/91 (ECtHR, 22 March 1995). *Singh v the Czech Republic*, App No 60538/00 (ECtHR [GC], 25 January 2005). *M and Others v Bulgaria*, App No 41416/08 (ECtHR, 26 July 2011), paras 75 and 76.

Article 5 § 1 (f) is justified for as long as deportation proceedings are in progress and are conducted with due diligence.

The principle of legal certainty is paramount in assessing the legal basis for the detention of migrants. Either statutory legislation or established case law authorising the deprivation of liberty must be in place.[32] Administrative practices alone, without being based on a legal provision or judicial decision, do not constitute a sufficient legal basis.[33] However, the existence of a legal basis in and of itself does not suffice. This legal basis must be sufficiently precise so that the consequences of a given action are foreseeable. This holds particularly true for diplomatic notes or international treaties between European states and third countries, based on which irregular migrants are returned to these third countries. When there is confusion among the national authorities as to the application of the national provisions, then the national legal basis falls short of the standard under Article 5.[34] Therefore, a lack of clarity of the national rules regulating the substantive conditions for a deprivation of liberty violates Article 5.

Moreover, the detention must comply with a procedure prescribed by law. Specifically, the detention must be compatible with national law, EU law and the ECHR. National law must lay down substantive and procedural rules prescribing the conditions for the detention. No gross and obvious irregularities are permitted in the course of issuing a detention order.[35] In cases of detention of aliens awaiting their deportation or extradition, states are required to apply the principle of proportionality, and the detention should not last for an unreasonable period of time. The length of the detention is reasonable when it does not exceed the time required for pursuing its purpose. A detention is also unlawful when there is lack of recording of the details of the the detainees and their detention.[36]

Finally, a deprivation of liberty is arbitrary where there has been an element of bad faith or deception on the part of the authorities. This holds particularly true when the national provision is not accessible or foreseeable.[37] The notion of arbitrariness, albeit not defined in the Convention, extends beyond the unlawfulness of the detention under national law. A deprivation of liberty may be in conformity with domestic law, and still be unlawful under the Convention, because it is arbitrary.[38] A variety of factors may render the detention arbitrary. Lack of good faith,[39] of due diligence,[40] of a realistic prospect of removal,[41] and no predetermined maximum period of detention[42] have all been regarded by the Strasbourg Court as rendering the detention arbitrary.

[32] *HL v the United Kingdom*, App No 45508/99 (ECtHR, 5 October 2004) [2004] ECHR 720, paras 116 et seq. *Laumont v France*, App No 43626/98 (ECtHR, 8 November 2001) [2001] ECHR 749, para 51. *A and Others v Bulgaria*, App No 51776/08 (ECtHR, 29 November 2011), para 68.

[33] *Baranowski v Poland*, App No 28358/95 (ECtHR, 28 March 2000) [2000] ECHR 120, paras 54–56.

[34] *Nasrulloyev v Russia*, App no 656/06 (ECtHR, 11 October 2007) [2007] ECHR 805.

[35] Such as when the court issuing the detention order is not competent, or the detainee was not provided a hearing.

[36] *Shchebet v Russia*, App No 16074/07 (ECtHR, 12 June 2008). *Kurt v Turkey*, App No 24276/94 (ECtHR, 25 May 1998) [1988] ECHR 44, para 125.

[37] *Nolan and K v Russia*, App No 2512/04 (ECtHR, 12 February 2009) [2009] ECHR 262.

[38] *A. and others v the United Kingdom*, App No 3455/05 (ECtHR [GC], 19 February 2009) [2009] ECHR 301.

[39] *Longa Yonkeu v Latvia*, App No 57229/09 (ECtHR, 15 November 2011).

[40] *Singh v the Czech Republic*, App No 60538/00 (ECtHR [GC], 25 January 2005).

[41] *Mikolenko v Estonia*, App No 10664/05 (ECtHR, 8 October 2009).

[42] *Auad v Bulgaria*, App no 46930/10 (ECtHR, 11 October 2011) para 128. *Mathloom v Greece*, App No 48883/07 (ECtHR, 24 April 2012).

In the light of the aforementioned, the core principles that apply to any deprivation of liberty under Article 5 add 5 § 1 (f) may be summarised as follows:

- the principle of the rule of law;
- the principle of legal certainty, which refers to the legal basis of the detention;
- the principle of due diligence, which relates to the procedure of detention;
- the principle of proportionality, which refers to the measure in question; and
- the principle of protection against arbitrariness, which concerns all the legal standards under Article 5 and goes to the heart of the right of liberty.

B. Interpreting the Right to Liberty of Non-nationals

According to the Strasbourg Court's established case law, states have the right to control the entry, residence and expulsion of aliens.[43] Detention is complementary to that right.[44] Neither the Convention nor its Protocols provide for the right to asylum. However, the treatment of aliens by state authorities may give rise to a series of violations of the Convention. The recent refugee and migration crisis in Europe gave the Court the opportunity to adjudicate upon the protection that member states are obliged to grant not only to refugees and people in need of international protection but also to migrants.

Regarding specifically the right to liberty of aliens, the Court's case law is classified in four categories: a) migrants detained in transit zones, b) violations regarding migrants' detention conditions, c) violations of rights of migrants with specific needs, such as children, and d) violations regarding the procedural safeguards for challenging the lawfulness of their detention.[45] The Court has taken specific notice of the cumulative effects and the specific allegations of the people concerned; that is, the length of their detention, the conditions, the lack of space, access to natural light and open air, private bathroom facilities.[46] Regarding migrants in transit zones, the Court has found that holding people in transit zones constitutes a deprivation of liberty falling within the scope of Article 5.[47] The Court determined in *Riad and Idiab v Belgium* that detention at an airport for more than 10 days amounts to inhuman and degrading treatment.[48] Regarding the detention conditions, they must be appropriate.[49] For example, police stations were considered to be inappropriate premises for the detention of persons who await the application of administrative measures.[50] Detaining children in an adult detention centre, even when accompanied by their mothers, amounts to a violation

[43] *Khlaifia and Others v Italy*, App No 16483/12 (ECtHR, 1 September 2015) [2016] ECHR 757, para 119.
[44] Mole and Meredith, *Asylum and the European Convention* (n 18) 136.
[45] http://www.echr.coe.int/Documents/FS_Migrants_detention_ENG.pdf.
[46] *Khlaifia and Others v Italy*, App No 16483/12 (ECtHR, 1 September 2015) para 123.
[47] *Amuur v France*, App No 19776/92 (ECtHR, 25 June 1996).
[48] *Riad and Idiab v Belgium*, App Nos 29787/03 and 29810/03 (ECtHR, 24 January 2008).
[49] *Dougoz v Greece*, App No 40907/98 (ECtHR, 6 March 2001).
[50] *Dougoz v Greece*, App No 40907/98 (ECtHR, 6 March 2001).

of Article 3 of the Convention.[51] The deprivation of liberty is unlawful when national courts do not review the conditions under which aliens are held.[52] Furthermore, if national laws do not lay down a maximum period for the detention of persons whose expulsion has been ordered by the courts, then the right to liberty of person, guaranteed by Article 5, is contravened.

Regarding the detention of aliens as a border-control technique, the informal detention of migrants in reception centres may violate several articles of the Convention. The Court had the opportunity to determine the lawfulness of the detention of migrants in this context in the case of *Khlaifia v Italy*.[53] This case is interesting as it raised the two legal issues which are the focus of this chapter and demonstrate the tendency towards the criminalisation of immigration law: a) what constitutes a valid legal basis for the detention of aliens in reception centres, and b) whether the crisis was that exceptional to allow deviations from state obligations under Article 5?

The case originated in an application by Tunisian nationals, who were intercepted at sea by the Italian authorities, found not to possess the necessary documents, and were transferred to Lampedusa. Initially, the applicants were placed at a reception and accommodation centre – Centro di Soccorso e Prima Accoglienza – specifically reserved for Tunisian adults. The centre was under permanent surveillance, and the applicants were not allowed to leave the centre or have any contact with the outside world.[54] After a fire and a violent riot between migrants took place at the centre, the applicants were transferred to a sports park, from which they managed to escape, only to be subsequently arrested in the village of Lampedusa during protests. After their placement at the reception centre, and then overnight at the airport, they were finally transferred to the port of Palermo and placed on moored ships. The applicants were not allowed to leave these ships, and the conditions of their detention remained similarly poor to the reception and accommodation centre they were placed in earlier. Around 14 days after their first arrival in Italy, the applicants were finally returned to Tunisia, by virtue of an ad hoc agreement Italy had concluded with Tunisia.

Italy claimed that the facilities in question were not detention but reception centres, where state authorities provided first aid and basic shelter to irregular migrants and asylum seekers. Indeed, the centres where the applicants were initially placed in Lampedusa were called 'initial reception and accommodation centres'.[55] However, national law provided only for the establishment of 'centres of identification and expulsion', where the detainees were provided with the right to have the legality of their detention reviewed by a Court. Consequently, only the detention of aliens in the 'centres of identification and expulsion' had a legal basis under Italian law. According to the

[51] *Mubilanzila Mayeka and Kaniki Mitunga v Belgium*, App No 13178/03 (ECtHR, 12 October 2006) [2006] ECHR 1171.

[52] *Garabayev v Russia*, App No 38411/02 (ECtHR, 30 January 2008).

[53] *Khlaifia and Others v Italy*, App No 16483/12 (ECtHR [GC], 15 December 2016) [2016] ECHR 1124.

[54] According to the Amnesty International reports, the conditions of their detention were appalling, including severe overcrowding, lack of sleeping accommodations and filthy sanitary facilities. Amnesty International Briefing paper, 'Italy: Amnesty International findings and recommendations to the Italian authorities following the research visit to Lampedusa and Mineo', 21 April 2011. *Khlaifia and Others v Italy*, App No 16483/12 (ECtHR, 1 September 2015) [2016] ECHR 757, para 35.

[55] *Khlaifia and Others v Italy*, App No 16483/12 (ECtHR, 1 September 2015), para 7.

defendant state, the placement of the irregular migrants in these reception centres was temporary and to their benefit, until their transfer to 'centres for identification and expulsion'. However, a de facto transformation of the reception centres into detention centres, without providing people with the right to access a court and the procedural rights of Article 5, led to a violation of the Convention.

In the *Khlaifia* case the Court (both the Grand Chamber and the Second Section initially) unanimously found a violation of the migrants' right to liberty, and of all its procedural facets under Article 5 ECHR: the applicants' right to be promptly informed about their detention, their right to have the lawfulness of their arrest and detention reviewed by a court and their right to compensation. The state was condemned because the Italian authorities had detained the applicants in different places without a legal basis in domestic law. Specifically, the Court determined that a) the detention was illegal since there was no domestic legal basis, b) the reasons for the detention were not clearly explained to the detainees, and c) the detainees were not provided with an avenue through which they could dispute their detention.

Regarding the procedural rights of detained migrants under Article 5 §§ 2–5, detention for a period of several days, which has not been ordered by a court or other competent authority with judicial power, cannot be considered lawful within the meaning of Article 5.[56] Moreover, any formal order for detention must refer to the factual and legal grounds of the detention, it must provide clear instructions for a judicial review of the legality of the detention, and this information must be provided promptly, upon the commencement of the detention. Furthermore, the detainees must be informed of the specific legal basis that authorises their detention. Finally, the detained migrants need to be able to exercise their procedural rights while they are still in the Member State. Consequently, this information cannot be provided to detainees just before their expulsion or deportation.[57] An accessible and effective remedy constitutes the substance of the procedural safeguards of Article 5 §§ 2–5.

Following the *Khlaifia* case, the deprivation of liberty of migrants in reception centres has been found compatible with the Convention only when there is a specific legal basis in domestic law. Furthermore, the legal basis for the detention of migrants must be precise and foreseeable. An international treaty between a Member State and a third state on the basis of which irregular migrants are arrested and returned to that third state, does not serve as a valid legal basis for the purposes of the Convention, if the content of the treaty is not public, precise and foreseeable.[58] Additionally, national law must stipulate specifically the establishment of such centres where aliens can be detained. Irrespectively of the nature or the name of the place where aliens are detained by virtue of domestic law, their deprivation of liberty may still be unlawful under Article 5 of the Convention. The detention of each specific individual in these centres must follow a formal decision, and must be subject to a judicial review.[59] In the absence of these

[56] *Shamsa v Poland*, App Nos 45355/99 and 45357/99 (ECtHR, 27 November 2003).

[57] *Khlaifia and Others v Italy*, App No 16483/12 (ECtHR, 1 September 2015), para 97.

[58] The ECtHR found specifically that the international treaty between Italy and Tunisia did not constitute a sufficient legal basis, because the content of the treaty was not public and foreseeable for the applicants.

[59] In *Khlaifia*, the detention was unlawful because no formal decision placing each individual in detention was taken.

requirements, the 'reception' of irregular migrants amounts to a de facto detention and an unlawful deprivation of liberty. Briefly summarised, the de facto detention of aliens at reception centres without a specific and precise domestic legal basis and without a prescribed procedure in law is arbitrary and contravenes Article 5 of the Convention.[60]

III. Human Dignity as a Response to the Crisis

A. The EU's 'Hotspot' Approach to Managing Exceptional Migratory Flows

Due to the flow of refugees and migrants to Europe, states must provide accelerated procedures for the return of people who are not in need of international protection. In order to address the issue, the European Union developed the idea of 'hotspots', where new arrivals in frontline states are to be registered and fingerprinted. Specifically, the European Commission took on the responsibility to draft a roadmap, having been allocated this task by the European Council in June 2015. According to the European Commission's Explanatory note, this approach is destined to provide a platform for four EU agencies – Frontex, EASO, Europol and Eurojust – to intervene rapidly and in an integrated manner in frontline Member States.[61] Hotspots are developed when there is a crisis due to specific and disproportionate migratory pressure at European external borders. It is essentially a coordinating mechanism, which provides operational assistance to EU Member States. This assistance may take multiple forms: registration, screening and debriefing of people, forensic support, asylum support, and coordination of the return of migrants who do not have the right to stay in Europe. These EU agencies already had the mandate to provide Member States with assistance under the existing mechanisms. What the 'Hotspot' approach was envisaged to bring, is coordination between European agencies and, allegedly, a more efficient merging of efforts.

Nevertheless, the responsibility for the detention, for the detention conditions and for the treatment of migrants and refugees at these EU Hotspots still lies with EU Member States. First, the mechanism is triggered upon the request of the Member State and lasts for a limited period of time and for as long as the emergency persists. Second, the EU 'Hotspot' policy does not provide reception facilities to its host Member State but builds upon their existence and functioning. Furthermore, the Commission's Explanatory note on the hotspots spells out that the existence of national reception facilities and 'pre-removal' centres is necessary for the successful implementation of the 'Hotspot' approach.[62] Finally and crucially, according to the 'Hotspot' approach flowchart in the Explanatory note, the relevant EU Member State is responsible for the possible detention of aliens in these centres. Consequently, one could assume that Member States will be accountable for any violation of human rights taking place at these centres.

[60] *Khlaifia and Others v. Italy*, App. No 16483/12 (ECtHR, 1 September 2015) paras 71–72.

[61] Explanatory note on the 'Hotspot' approach, 15 July 2015. Available at: https://data.consilium.europa.eu/doc/document/ST-10962-2015-INIT/en/pdf.

[62] Ibid, para 6.

The issue, of course, remains that the establishment of the EU 'Hotspot' centres should still be compatible with the guarantees of the Convention and with the requirements laid down in Article 5 in case of detention of migrants and asylum seekers. The 'fast-track' character of the EU 'Hotspot' approach is especially problematic in light of the Court's standing in the *Saadi* case, where the Grand Chamber found a violation of the right to be promptly informed under Article 5 § 2, when the applicant's detention was for the purpose of administrative convenience in processing fast-track claims of asylum to ensure the speedy resolution of a considerable number of asylum applications.[63] A clearly identifiable legal regime should be in place for the detention of people at these EU 'Hotspot' centres, along with respect for the all aforementioned criteria for a lawful deprivation of the liberty under Article 5 § 1 (f).

B. Human Dignity and Immigration Detention

The ECtHR acknowledged the multitude of obligations that weigh upon European states because of the migration and refugee flows in Europe. Nevertheless, the Court was firm in asserting that no exceptional factor absolves states from their obligation to apply the guarantees of the Convention regarding the right to liberty. Interestingly, the ECtHR connected the detention conditions of migrants with the protection of human dignity. Providing basic living conditions to people who are deprived of their liberty is a core requirement for the protection of their human dignity.

> The Court does not under-estimate the problems encountered by the Contracting States when faced with exceptional waves of immigration such as that which underlies the present case. It is also aware of the many duties that the Italian authorities had to assume, obliged as they were to take measures to provide, simultaneously, for rescue at sea, for the health and accommodation of the migrants, and for the prevention of disorder on an island inhabited by a small community. Those factors cannot, however, exempt the respondent State from its obligation to guarantee conditions that are compatible with respect for human dignity to all individuals who, like the applicants, find themselves deprived of their liberty.[64]

Human dignity proves to be a useful tool for the Court to underline that the Convention protects human beings and not only citizens, or more specifically nationals, of Member States.[65] Human dignity encompasses the fundamental axiom that human rights originate from the inherent dignity of every human being.[66] Although there is no reference to human dignity in the Convention, the Court has invoked human dignity specifically

[63] *Saadi v the United Kingdom*, App No 13229/03 (ECtHR [GC], 29 January 2008) [2008] ECHR 80, para 76. The number of asylum application of some 13,000 of the approximately 84,000 asylum applications made in the United Kingdom per year at that time. In order to achieve this objective, it was necessary to schedule up to 150 interviews a day and the applicant was selected for detention on the basis that his case was suited for fast-track processing.

[64] *Khlaifia and Others v Italy*, App No 16483/12 (ECtHR, 1 September 2015), para 128. However, when the case reached the Grand Chamber, the Court was unable to declare a violation of Article 3 on the basis of the detention conditions.

[65] A HUDOC search for judgments containing the words 'human dignity' combined with Article 5 § 1 (f) produced 17 results as of February 2016. The words '*dignité humaine*' yielded 22 judgments.

[66] Jane McAdam, 'Human Rights and Forced Migration' in Elena Fiddian-Qasmiyeh, Gil Loescher, Katy Long and Nando Sigona (eds), *Refugee and Forced Migration Studies* (Oxford, Oxford University Press, 2014) 203.

in cases of deprivation of liberty. The Court asserts that the Convention requires the respect of human dignity of people who have lost their autonomy and are deprived of their liberty. In the case *Kudła v Poland*, the Grand Chamber accepted that detention as a measure contains inherently and unavoidably a certain degree of suffering, and that states must ensure that the circumstances and conditions of detention do not exceed that degree.[67] Although this unavoidable level of suffering per se may not infringe the Article 3 prohibition of inhuman or degrading treatment, states must nevertheless ensure that all prisoners are detained in conditions that are compatible with respect for their human dignity.[68] States violate the detainees' human dignity by transferring people to reception centres that have overcome their spatial capacity.[69] The overcrowded conditions in migrants' and refugees' centres particularly have a negative impact on human dignity of the detainees.

Concerning the confinement of foreign minors, the Court ruled that very poor detention conditions of a minor undermined the very essence of human dignity.[70] In the case of *Aden Ahmed v Malta*, the Court elaborated on the concept of human dignity of a detained immigrant. Specifically, the Court ruled that when the detention provokes feelings of anguish and inferiority, humiliating and debasing the person and breaking his moral and physical resistance, his human dignity is diminished, and there is consequently a breach of the Convention.[71] The concept of human dignity is also found in the *Saadi* case. Six dissenting judges found that 'no human being may be used as a means towards an end'.[72] This statement encapsulates the essence of the concept of human dignity.[73] According to the Court's established case law, detention conditions are compatible with respect for human dignity when the detainee's health and well-being are adequately secured.[74] The *Khlaifia* case on the detention of migrants in reception centres is interesting, as the Court employed the concept of human dignity in order to dismiss the crisis as a justification for their detention conditions.

IV. Liberty and Freedom of Movement

The right to personal liberty undoubtedly applies to aliens who enter the territory of Member States and who are subsequently detained. The right to liberty of movement,

[67] *Kudła v Poland*, App No 30210/96 (ECtHR [GC], 26 October 2000) [2000] ECHR 512, paras 92–94. *A and Others v The United Kingdom*, App No 3455/05 (ECtHR [GC], 19 February 2009) [2009] ECHR 301, para 128. *Kim v Russia*, App No 44260/13 (ECtHR, 17 July 2014), para 34, *Alim v Russia*, App No 39417/07 (ECtHR, 27 September 2011), para 40.

[68] *Riad and Idiab v Belgium*, App Nos 29787/03 and 29810/03 (ECtHR, 24 January 2008), [2008] ECHR 1900, paras 99 and 107.

[69] *Rashed v Czech Republic*, App No 298/07 (ECtHR 27 November 2008), para 61.

[70] *Rahimi v Greece*, App No 8687/08 (ECtHR, 5 April 2011), para 85–86.

[71] *Aden Ahmed v Malta*, App No 55352/12 (ECtHR, 23 July 2013), para 99.

[72] Joint Partly Dissenting Opinion of Judges Rozakis, Tulkens, Kovler, Hajiyev, Spielmann And Hirvelä, *Saadi v the United Kingdom*, App No 13229/03 (ECtHR [GC], 29 January 2008), para 34.

[73] Such an idea is pertinent to the 'natural perspective of human rights, whereby human rights are conceived as given entitlements due to every human being qua human being'. Marie-Benedicte Dembour, *When Humans Become Migrants, Study of the European Court with an Inter-American counterpoint* (Oxford, Oxford University Press, 2015), 4.

[74] *Yefimova v Russia*, App No 39786/09 (ECtHR, 19 February 2013), para 234.

however, is more complex regarding its applicability to aliens. The relationship between the right to liberty and the right to liberty of movement under Article 2 of Protocol No 4 is interesting in this respect. The right to liberty of movement is enshrined in Article 2 of Protocol No 4 to the Convention:

> Everyone lawfully within the territory of a State shall, within that territory, have the right to liberty of movement and freedom to choose his residence.

This provision draws directly from Article 12 of the ICCPR.[75] The freedom of movement is combined with the right of people to choose freely their place of residence within the territory of the state. The scope of the right to liberty of movement is limited both territorially and regarding the quality of the right-holder. The scope is limited territorially, as it can only be enjoyed within the specific territory of that state. Moreover, the freedom of movement is guaranteed only to everyone *lawfully present* in a Member State.[76] The lawfulness of the presence is assessed according to domestic law.

The right to liberty and security of person under Article 5 is much wider in scope. It is guaranteed for everyone, irrespective of the lawfulness of his or her presence in a Member State and regardless of residence status. The right-holders of the two provisions, therefore, are different. Equally different are also the bearers of the obligations imposed by the two provisions. Article 5 is binding upon all Member States, while Protocol No 4 is binding on a certain number of states which ratified it.[77] A paradox ensues from the legal requirements of the two provisions. The right to freedom of movement is a qualified right, as it can be limited by the state. Under Article 2 § 3 of Protocol No 4, a restriction of freedom of movement must be justified as necessary in a democratic society.[78] The necessity of the detention measure, however, is not required for the more severe deprivation of liberty under Article 5 § 1 (f). In other words, while a restriction of freedom of movement must be necessary in a democratic society under Article 2 § 3 of Protocol No 4, the more severe deprivation of liberty under Article 5 § 1 (f) does not have to be. This paradox demonstrates why the Court should scrutinise whether the detention is necessary (necessity test) in cases of immigration detention (under Article 5 § 1 (f)) as well.

[75] ICCPR, Article 12:

'1. Everyone lawfully within the territory of a State shall, within that territory, have the right to liberty of movement and freedom to choose his residence.
2. Everyone shall be free to leave any country, including his own.
3. The above-mentioned rights shall not be subject to any restrictions except those which are provided by law, are necessary to protect national security, public order (*ordre public*), public health or morals or the rights and freedoms of others, and are consistent with the other rights recognized in the present Covenant.
4. No one shall be arbitrarily deprived of the right to enter his own country.'

[76] See Article 45 of the Charter, which provides for the right to freedom of movement only for EU citizens.

[77] The total number of ratifications of/accessions to Protocol No 4 is 43 as of January 2021. The United Kingdom, Greece, Turkey, Switzerland are not signatory states to this Protocol.

[78] '3. No restrictions shall be placed on the exercise of these rights other than such as are in accordance with law and are necessary in a democratic society in the interests of national security or public safety, for the maintenance of *ordre public*, for the prevention of crime, for the protection of health or morals, or for the protection of the rights and freedoms of others.'

The nature and the substance of both rights, however, is qualitatively the same. The general right to liberty under Article 5 secures essentially the same substantive elements to people as the right to liberty of movement.[79] Still, there is a difference of degree and severity between the two rights.[80] The Court has found that both Article 5 of the Convention and Article 2 of Protocol No 4 protect essentially the same right and differ only in degree.[81]

In order for the Court to establish whether there is a violation of Article 5 or Article 2 of Protocol No 4, the concrete situation of the individual is taken into account.[82] The Court undertakes an autonomous assessment of the situation and it is not bound by the legal characterisation of the domestic courts.[83] In principle, a restriction order imposing the obligation to reside at a specific place and/or to report to an authority may be a restriction of freedom, but does not amount to a deprivation of liberty under Article 5. When an interference with a person's freedom contains elements of coercion, elements of isolation, or is of significant duration, then the measure in question is considered a deprivation of liberty and not a violation of freedom of movement. In the context of detention of migrants, in *Amuur v France*, the Court found that holding aliens in transit zones constitutes a restriction of their freedom of movement, which is not comparable to that occurring in detention centres for aliens awaiting deportation.[84] Although there was theoretically the possibility for the applicants' to leave the airport to seek refuge to another country, the Court found that their detention in the transit zone amounted to a deprivation of liberty, because practically they did not have the opportunity to go to another country.[85]

A qualification, however, is necessary regarding the applicability of Article 2 of Protocol No 4, to aliens. Since the right to freedom of movement is guaranteed only to people who are lawfully present in a state, this provision, in principle, is not applicable to people entering the territory of a Member State irregularly. Therefore, it can be argued that this right is not applicable to irregular migrants, asylum seekers and refugees who are detained after their arrival. However, 'lawfully within the territory of a state' does not mean 'recognised as lawfully within the territory' of that state. Regarding asylum seekers and refugees, the situation may differ and Article 2 of Protocol No 4 may be applicable to them. A person does not become a refugee because of his recognition as such, but he is granted asylum by the state authorities because he is a refugee. As the determination of refugee status is merely declaratory, during the time that refugees, having entered irregularly a Member State, await the determination of their status, there is some validity in the argument that they may be considered lawfully within the territory of the Member State. In the case of *Hirsi Jamaa v Italy*, the Strasbourg Court

[79] In the *Khlaifia* case, the Italian Senate in its report on the human rights of migrants at the reception centres had criticised the lack of freedom of movement, which was imposed without a judicial or administrative order. *Khlaifia and Others v Italy*, App No 16483/12 (ECtHR, 1 September 2015), para 31.

[80] *Guzzardi v Italy*, App No 7367/76 (ECtHR, 6 November 1980), para 93.

[81] Ibid, para 93.

[82] See the case *Guzzardi v Italy*, where the Court asserted a violation of Article 5 – and not of Article 2 of Protocol No 4 – because it considered all the aspects of the concrete case of detention cumulatively. *Guzzardi v Italy*, App no 7367/76 (ECtHR, 6 November 1980), para 95.

[83] *HL v the United Kingdom*, App No 45508/99 (ECtHR, 5 October 2004), para 90.

[84] *Amuur v France*, App No 19776/92 (ECtHR, 25 June 1996).

[85] Ibid, para 48.

accepted that Article 3 ECHR applies to those who have not yet had their status declared (asylum seekers) and even to those who have not expressed their wish to be protected and to file an application for asylum.[86] Neither the absence of an explicit request for asylum nor the lack of evidence for proving their refugee status may absolve the state of its international obligations vis-à-vis any person in need of international protection.

By parity of reasoning, Article 2 of Protocol No 4 may be applicable to asylum seekers who await the determination of their status because they may be already 'lawfully present' on the territory of the host state, should their refugee status be subsequently recognised. This approach is also corroborated by the fact that EU law considers that every person who has filed an asylum application should be considered as lawfully present (granted the right to remain and the freedom of movement) within the territory of the Member State.[87] Furthermore, according to the revised Reception Conditions Directive, an EU Member State shall not hold a person in detention for the sole reason that he or she is an applicant of international protection.[88] Detention under EU law is allowed, however, when there is a risk of absconding of the applicant or to determine whether the applicant had the right to enter the territory.[89] The Strasbourg Court, from its side, has found that as soon as an asylum seekers surrender to state authorities upon their entry, they effectively seek an 'authorized' entry into the country, and consequently their detention under Article 5 § 1 (f) may not be justified.[90]

In conclusion, international and EU law restrict the possibility of depriving refugees and asylum seekers of their liberty and imposing restrictions on their freedom of movement. There is, however, a gap of protection for irregular *migrants* who are unlawfully within the territory of a Member State, since a restriction of their freedom does not amount to a deprivation of liberty under Article 5. Neither a violation of Article 5 nor a violation of Article 2 of Protocol No 4 can be established in cases of irregular migrants whose freedom is restricted, but which restriction does not reach the threshold of Article 5. By underlining the distinction between the two rights, the Court may have indicated a solution to overcome this gap. According to the Court:

> The difference between deprivation of liberty and restrictions on freedom of movement under Article 2 of Protocol No. 4 is merely one of degree or intensity, and not one of nature or substance. Although the process of classification into one or other of these categories sometimes proves to be no easy task, in that some borderline cases are a matter of pure opinion, the Court cannot avoid making the selection upon which the applicability or inapplicability

[86] *Hirsi Jamaa v Italy*, App No 27765/09 (ECtHR [GC], 23 February 2012) [2012] ECHR 1845.

[87] Article 7 of the Directive 2013/33/EU of the European Parliament and of the Council of 26 June 2013 laying down standards for the reception of applicants for international protection (recast), which provides asylum seekers with the freedom of movement. And Article 9 of the Directive 2013/32/EU of the European Parliament and of the Council of 26 June 2013, on Common Procedures for Granting and Withdrawing International Protection (Recast), which imposes on Member States the obligation to grant every person having filed an application for asylum the right to remain in the Member State.

[88] Directive 2013/33/EU of the European Parliament and of the Council of 26 June 2013 laying down standards for the reception of applicants for international protection (recast), Article 8.

[89] Ibid, Article 8 § 3 (c).

[90] *Saadi v the United Kingdom*, App No 13229/03 (ECtHR [GC], 29 January 2008), para 65. See, contra, the older cases *Paramanathan v Germany*, App No 12068/86 (EComHR), (1986) 51 DR 237 and *Omwenyeke v Germany*, App No 44294/04, where the Court held that people whose asylum claim has not been yet determined, can be detained to prevent 'unauthorised entry'.

of Article 5 depends. In order to determine whether someone has been deprived of his liberty, the starting-point must be his or her concrete situation, and account must be taken of a whole range of criteria such as the type, duration, effects and manner of implementation of the measure in question.[91]

V. Concluding Remarks

It is interesting that the ECtHR insists on commencing its reasoning in most cases concerning the detention of non-nationals in the context of immigration by underlining the right of states to control their borders and their immigration policy.[92] It appears that the Court seeks to reassure the states on their competence in this domain. This observation has led certain scholars to argue that in the eyes of the Court migrants are first aliens, subject to states' control, rather than human beings.[93] Invoking human dignity in migrants' cases may be a way to reverse this.

The detention of irregular migrants is lawful only for the specific purposes of Article 5 § 1 (f). It is neither a criminal detention nor a deterrent tool as a general border management technique. And in any case, reality shows that the detention of migrants as a security tool for border control does not prevent the flow of irregular migrant towards Europe.[94] Furthermore, EU law requires that detention must be the last resort and all alternatives must be exhausted.[95] In *Mikolenko v Estonia*, the Court has also found that the states are obliged to examine alternatives to detention.[96] Back in 2014, the European Migration Network study on the use of detention in the context of migration found that the majority of EU Member States had developed alternatives to detention, including obligations to report, electronic monitoring and residence requirements.[97] On the one hand, these alternatives to detention may still restrict the refugees' right of freedom and must comply with Article 2 of Protocol No 4, when this is applicable to Member States that have ratified it. On the other hand, immigration detention has become the rule after the crisis hit Europe in 2015.

[91] See *Khlaifia and Others v Italy*, App No 16483/12 (ECtHR [GC], 15 December 2016) [2016] ECHR 1124, para 64. *Amuur v France*, App No 19776/92 (ECtHR, 25 June 1996), para 42, [1996] ECHR 25. *Stanev v Bulgaria*, App No 36760/06 (ECtHR [GC], 17 January 2012) [2012] ECHR 46, para 115.

[92] See, however, the '*Tabitha* case', where the Court regarded the applicant as a child rather than as an illegal migrant, and it countenanced the idea that states are entitled to control the entry of aliens into their territory only with regards to Article 8: *Mubilanzila Mayeka and Kaniki Mitunga v Belgium*, App No 13178/03 (ECtHR, 12 October 2006) [2006] ECHR 1171, para 74.

[93] Dembour, *When Humans Become Migrants* (n 73) 5.

[94] A list of possible non-detention measures has been provided by the UN Special Rapporteur on the Human Rights of migrants.

[95] Reception Conditions Directive (2013/33/EU) (n 88), Article 8(2), and Directive 2008/115/EC on common standards and procedures in Member States for returning illegally staying third-country nationals (Return Directive), Article 15(1).

[96] *Mikolenko v Estonia*, App No 10664/05 (ECtHR, 8 October 2009). See also Return Directive (2008/115/EC), Article 15(1) and Reception Conditions Directive (2013/33/EU), Article 8(2).

[97] European Migration network, 'Synthesis Report – The use of detention and alternatives to detention in the context of immigration policies, 2014', available at: http://ec.europa.eu/dgs/home-affairs/what-we-do/networks/european_migration_network/reports/docs/emn-studies/emn_study_detention_alternatives_to_detention_synthesis_report_en.pdf.

The ECtHR case law on detaining irregular migrants in reception centres is important for a number of reasons. First, the Court is clear on the protection of the right to liberty that states need to grant to aliens entering their territory, independently of their status – irregular migrants, asylum seekers or refugees. The Court uses the concept of human dignity as a tool to shift the focus onto protecting primarily human beings. Immigration detention is not allowed unless it has a legal basis in national law. This means that informal, de facto detention of migrants, in the absence of a clear legal basis and without providing all procedural guarantees, violates their right to liberty and contravenes the Convention. The Strasbourg Court is also clear that no crisis can absolve states from their obligations under the Convention.

Interpreting the Convention as living instrument allows for the Court's role to evolve over time and to respond to contemporary challenges. As understandings of human rights evolve, such a progressive interpretation of the Convention may grant greater protection to forced migrants in the future.[98] Although regulating immigration lies still within states' core competence and exercise of their sovereignty, human rights law plays an important role in regulating the circumstances for the detention of aliens, irrespective of their status – irregular migrants, refugees, asylum seekers. Holding them in detention per se may be allowed in the immigration context; the conditions and the circumstances for doing so, however, are under the scrutiny of the Court.

[98] McAdam, 'Human Rights and Forced Migration' (n 66) 204.

10

Cartel Offences: Quasi-criminal Enforcement for Criminal Behaviour?

SOPHIE DE SANCTIS

I. Introduction

There is now universal and strong condemnation of cartels involving price fixing, output limitation, bid rigging or allocation of customers or markets between competitors. Indeed, cartels are often distinguished from other forms of anticompetitive behaviour owing to their high degree of harmfulness to competition. They prevent a basic feature of functioning markets: the behavioural autonomy of market participants and therefore competition between them. Agreements on prices, bids, output or market sharing between competitors allow them to coordinate their behaviour on the market to a very significant degree.[1] Consequently, they are no longer subject to competition and its associated risks and one consequence of this is that prices no longer stem from the meeting of offer and demand on a market. Significantly, cartels are considered to generate only negative effects with no countervailing positive effects. As stated by a former EU Commissioner: 'Cartels differ from most other forms of restrictive agreements and practices by being "naked". They serve to restrict competition without producing any objective countervailing benefits'.[2] They have been described as cancers and compared to viruses.[3] The expression 'fight against cartels' is now commonly used by public officials,[4] thereby equating competition collusion to organised crime.

Such is the presumed harmfulness of cartels that the debate is no longer on whether or not cartels deserve to be sanctioned in the first place but rather on the precise nature

[1] As stated by the Organisation for Economic Co-operation and Development (OECD), 'a "hard core cartel" is an anticompetitive agreement, anticompetitive concerted practice, or anticompetitive arrangement by competitors to fix prices, make rigged bids (collusive tenders), establish output restrictions or quotas, or share or divide markets by allocating customers, suppliers, territories, or lines of commerce': OECD, 'Recommendation of the Council concerning Effective Action against Hard Core Cartels' (1998), C (98)35/FINAL.

[2] M Monti, 'Fighting Cartels Why and How? Why Should We be Concerned with Cartels and Collusive Behaviour?', *Speech at 3rd Nordic Competition Policy Conference* (Stockholm, September 2000).

[3] Ibid; N Kroes, 'Tackling Cartels – a Never-ending Task', *Speech at Anti-Cartel Enforcement: Criminal and Administrative Policy – Panel session* (Brasilia, October 2009).

[4] eg, J Almunia, 'Fighting Against Cartels: A Priority for the Present and for the Future' (Brussels, April 2014).

of the penalties to be imposed against cartelists. Cartels can be subject to both public (administrative and criminal) and private enforcement. Thus Article 101 of the Treaty on the Functioning of the European Union (TFEU) prohibits cartels and, at an EU level, the European Commission is responsible for prosecuting and sanctioning cartels through an administrative procedure. However, this administrative enforcement by the European Commission has evolved over time in such a way that it has become a quasi-criminal form of enforcement (see section II below). The quasi-criminal nature of the procedure and the sanctions imposed by the European Commission raise the question about the real nature of the cartel behaviour. Is it just an administrative infringement or is it also a criminal offence?

The question of the 'criminalisation' of competition law, and more specifically of anti-cartel rules, is an on-going debate. A European and global trend towards the criminalisation of cartel behaviour has been observed, with increasingly severe fines for companies and an ever-growing list of jurisdictions enshrining in their legislation prison sentences for individuals participating in cartels. However, despite this trend, no consensus has been reached as regards its merits either among legislators or in the legal literature. The fundamental question of the legitimacy of the use of criminal law to sanction cartel members still constitutes a relevant and pending issue (section III below).

II. Emergence of a Quasi-criminal Enforcement of the Prohibition on Cartels

The porosity of the boundaries between administrative and criminal enforcement has been observed in different areas of law[5] and competition law offers one significant illustration. EU competition rules (involving a prohibition on cartels) officially belong to the branch of administrative law. However, as will be seen in this section, the enforcement of competition rules has led to the creation of a punitive branch of law, which can be considered, in many ways, as lying between administrative and criminal law. First, due to the severity of the fines imposed on companies, the specific features of the European Commission's investigation and a certain moralisation of the infringement, there has been a movement of administrative competition law enforcement towards the features of criminal enforcement (see section II.A below). This has led to European courts affirming the need for the level of protection of the defence rights of companies facing cartel investigations to be close to that upheld in criminal enforcement (II.B).

A. Evolution of Administrative Enforcement Towards Criminal Enforcement

The choice of an administrative model for the enforcement of EU competition rules could be described as an 'imposed' choice, since the EU did not have any competence

[5] F Galli and A Weyembergh (eds), *Do labels still matter? Blurring boundaries between administrative and criminal law. The influence of the EU* (Brussels, Institut d'études européennes of the Université libre de Bruxelles, 2014).

to impose criminal sanctions at the time when competition law was enshrined in EU law.[6] In any event, it appears a coherent choice since it corresponds to a certain view of administrative law, which is present in German law, and the prohibitions laid down are similar to those provided for in respect of other administrative law infringements. Indeed, the rules prohibiting cartels are part of the 'objective dimension' of competition law,[7] aimed at protecting the market as a whole, and not individual interests (comparable to other administrative law infringements). The protection of the economic public order[8] is at the forefront of the aims of competition law. This is similar to the German conception of administrative infringements, which seeks to maintain public order[9] and to protect general interests without adding any moral dimension. The administrative enforcement implies a certain degree of flexibility and less formality than in the judicial process applicable for criminal law.[10] Most of the EU Member States have also chosen an administrative model of competition enforcement,[11] even if the approach to the administrative sanction varies from one Member State to another in accordance with their legal traditions (this explains why certain differences in terminology exist across Member States, for instance).[12]

However, competition law enforcement has evolved in such a way that its solely administrative nature is in doubt. Indeed, in many ways, competition law has appropriated the features of criminal law proceedings. As stated by one commentator, 'competition law proceedings belong to the darkest "fiftieth shade of grey" insofar as they share more similarities with the prosecution of robbery than with the enforcement of administrative obligations'.[13] Criminal law is often described as the branch of law protecting the most important legal interests against harmful conduct and

[6] Moreover, the recipients of the sanctions imposed by the Commission are undertakings (even if the application to individuals is not theoretically totally excluded, see Opinion of EU Court of Justice (CJEU) Advocate General Lenz in Case 170/83 *Hydrotherm v Compact* EU:C:1984:222). Imposing criminal sanctions on undertakings would have raised the sensitive issue of corporate criminal liability, which was not recognised in all Member States.

[7] G Clamour, *Intérêt général et concurrence. Essai sur la pérennité du droit public en économie de marché* (Paris, Dalloz, 2006). See especially p 86.

[8] The notion of economic public order has been used by the CJEU in the setting of fines: 'the extent of the market affected and the damage to the economic public order must be taken into account'. See Cases C-204/00 P, C-205/00 P, C-211/00 P, C-213/00 P, C-217/00 P and C-219/00 P *Aalborg Portland and Others v Commission* EU:C:2004:6, para 91.

[9] On the notion of *Ordnungswidrigkeiten*, see European Court of Human Rights, (App No 8544/79) *Öztürk v Germany*, 21 February 1984.

[10] C Harding, 'The Interplay of Criminal and Administrative Law in the Context of Market Regulation: The Case of Serious Competition Infringements' in V Mitsilegas, P Alldridge and L Cheliotis (eds), *Globalisation, Criminal Law and Criminal Justice* (Oxford, Hart Publishing, 2015) 199, 208.

[11] European Competition Network, 'Working Group Cooperation Issues And Due Process', *Decision-Making Powers Report* (2012) and European Commission, *Commission Staff Working Document, Enhancing competition enforcement by the Member States' competition authorities: institutional and procedural issues* accompanying the document Communication from the Commission to the European Parliament and the Council *Ten Years Of Antitrust Enforcement Under Regulation 1/2003: Achievements And Future Perspectives* (SWD 231, 2014).

[12] See, eg, the use of the word 'civil' and not 'administrative' in common law jurisdictions; C Harding, 'The Interplay of Criminal and Administrative Law' (n 10), 202–03.

[13] A Bailleux, 'The fiftieth shade of grey. Competition law, "criministrative law" and "fairly fair trials"' in Galli and Weyembergh (eds), *Do labels still matter? Blurring boundaries between administrative and criminal law. The influence of the EU* (Brussels, Institut d'études européennes of the Université libre de Bruxelles, 2014), 137, 151.

establishing penalties with a punitive purpose, applied by a court following a due process.[14] Indeed, the harm to one or several highly valuable legal interests is committed by an offender with a certain degree of intent. As a result, criminal sanctions are the harshest type of penalty available (including the deprivation of liberty through imprisonment) and require a strict protection of procedural rights before the sanction is handed down. It is worth examining, therefore, how competition law enforcement by the EU has adopted some of the features of criminal enforcement, such as the severity of the sanction (i), the coercive nature of the procedure (ii), as well as the importance given to the moral nature of the act concerned (iii).

(i) The Severity of the Sanctions Imposed

As mentioned, since criminal law is designed to protect the most important legal interests in society, the harm done to these interests leads to harsh sanctions. Even if Article 23(5) of EU Regulation No 1/2003[15] stated that the decisions taken by the European Commission relating to fines 'shall not be of a criminal law nature', the high level of the fines reveals the punitive character of the sanction. It generates a material burden which brings the fines imposed closer to the severity of criminal sanctions.

Not only may fines imposed on a company participating in a cartel reach 10 per cent of the company's worldwide consolidated turnover,[16] but the fines imposed have also regularly increased over time. Indeed, record amounts have been imposed by the Commission over the last few years. For example, in July 2016 and September 2017, the Commission fined six truck manufacturers involved in a cartel a record figure of more than EUR 3.8 billion in total.[17] In 2013, eight international banks were ordered to pay EUR 1.7 billion[18] whereas in 2012 the members of the TV and computer monitor tubes cartel received a total fine of more than EUR 1.47 billion.[19] These are very substantial sums of money and a comparison between the total amount of the fines imposed by the Commission from 1990 to 1994 and those imposed during the years 2010 to 2014 shows that the amounts of fines were nearly 15 times higher (when the number of cases were multiplied by only three).[20]

[14] P Caeiro, 'The influence of the EU on the "blurring" between administrative and criminal law' in Galli and Weyembergh (ibid), 187.

[15] Regulation (EC) No 1/2003 of 16 December 2002 on the implementation of the rules on competition laid down in Articles 81 and 82 of the Treaty [2003] OJ L1/1.

[16] The fine shall not exceed 10% of the total turnover in the preceding business year of the undertaking or association of undertakings participating in the infringement (Art 23(2) of Regulation No 1/2003).

[17] Summary of Commission Decision of 19 July 2016, Case AT.39824 – Trucks, [2017] OJ C108/6, and Commission Press release, 'Antitrust: Commission fines Scania €880 million for participating in trucks cartel', 27 September 2017.

[18] Summary of Commission Decision of 4 December 2013, Case AT.39914 – Euro Interest Rate Derivatives [2017] OJ C206/17. After amendment, the fine was reduced to EUR 1.5 billion.

[19] Summary of Commission Decision of 5 December 2012, Case COMP/39.437 – TV and computer monitor tubes [2013] OJ C303/13.

[20] The calculations are based on the figures available on the Directorate-General Competition website, http://ec.europa.eu/competition/cartels/statistics/statistics.pdf.

Different factors can explain the increase in fines. Certainly, the entry into force of Regulation No 1/2003, allowing a de-centralised enforcement of competition law, has enabled the Commission to concentrate its work on larger and more economically significant cartels. However, another central factor is the emphasis placed upon the deterrent effect of fines. Indeed, the stated objective of fines imposed by the Commission is both to punish and deter.[21] Although the hierarchy between these two objectives is not clearly stated by the EU institutions and in EU law, certain indicators appear to show that the deterrent effect is the key objective for the Commission.[22] For instance, its decision-making practice as well as the rules governing fines illustrate that the deterrent effect is substantial and even preeminent (even if the retributive objective is certainly not absent when setting fines). Thus, the guidelines for setting fines of 1998 and 2006 expressly state(d) that the fines imposed should have a sufficiently deterrent effect.[23] The 2006 guidelines for setting fines also explicitly integrate deterrence at two stages of setting fines: in the determination of the basic amount of the fine[24] and in the adjustments to the basic amount where a specific increase for deterrence is possible.[25] Moreover, the guidelines specify that the need to achieve deterrence in a particular case may justify departing from the methodology stated in the guidelines or from the limits of the value of sales taken into account.[26]

The pursuit of deterrence is not just one element of calculating fines; it is also a general requirement presented all along the fine-setting process.[27] Deterrence justifies the inclusion in the calculation of fines of elements increasing the amounts of fines. For example, the dual dimension of deterrence is often put forward. Indeed, general deterrence can justify the imposition of a fine on an undertaking that is no longer active on the market where the cartel took place.[28] Surprisingly, deterrence also influenced the

[21] CJEU, Case 41/69 *ACF Chemiefarma v Commission* EU:C:1970:71, para 173. More recently see, CJEU, Case 289/84 *Showa Denko v Commission* EU:C:2006:431, para 16. European Commission, *Thirteenth Report on Competition Policy* (Brussels, 1983), para 62: 'The purpose of the fines is twofold: to impose a pecuniary sanction on the undertaking for the infringement and prevent a repetition of the offence, and to make the prohibition in the Treaty more effective'.

[22] European Commission, *Report on Competition Policy 2008* (COM(2009) 374 final, Brussels, 2009), para 8: '[w]hen the Commission prohibits anticompetitive behaviour and fines cartel members, its ultimate purpose is not only to punish those members for past behaviour, but above all to deter every company from continuing or engaging in anti-competitive behaviour'. See also P Whelan, *The Criminalization of European Cartel enforcement, Theoretical, Legal, and Practical Challenges* (Oxford, Oxford University Press, 2014), 38.

[23] Para 4 of the Commission Guidelines on the method of setting fines imposed pursuant to Art 23(2)(a) of Regulation No 1/2003 [2006] OJ C210/2 and para 1A of the Commission Guidelines on the method of setting fines imposed pursuant to Art 15(2) of Regulation No 17 and Art 65(5) of the ECSC Treaty [1998] OJ C9/3.

[24] Para 25 of the Guidelines on the method of setting fines 2006.

[25] Paras 30 and 31 of the 2006 Guidelines.

[26] Para 37 of the 2006 Guidelines.

[27] V Giacobbo-Peyronnel and P Singer, 'Quelques réflexions et interrogations au sujet de l'effet dissuasif des amendes en droit communautaire de la concurrence' (2009) 4 *Concurrences* 74. See also EU General Court (GCEU) in Cases T-56/09 and T-73/09 *Saint-Gobain Glass France and Others v Commission* EU:T:2014:160, para 380: 'deterrence is an objective of the fine and a general requirement which must be a reference point for the Commission throughout the calculation of the amount of the fine. Thus, the objective of deterrence does not necessarily require that there be a specific step in that calculation in which an overall assessment is made of all relevant circumstances for the purposes of attaining that objective'.

[28] CJEU in Case C447/11 P *Caffaro v Commission* EU:C:2013:797, para 38.

notion of the gravity of the infringement in the 1998 guidelines.[29] As a consequence, the amounts of the fines for cartel infringements can be very high. Considering that the probability of detection of cartels remains often quite low, increasing the severity of the fines makes the fines even more deterrent, as the EU Court of Justice recognised in the *Musique diffusion française* case.[30]

(ii) Extensive Powers of Investigation

In many ways, the administrative procedure leading to a sanction in competition enforcement mimics the criminal procedure. It is based on an investigative model where the Commission investigates the case and decides to adopt a decision. For this, the Commission has extensive investigatory powers.

In this way, there is a rapprochement with criminal enforcement which can be observed. Firstly, the strengthening of the Commission's investigatory powers gives the administrative enforcement model the features of classical criminal law procedure. Secondly, the negotiating options available to the Commission (leniency and settlement procedures), implying that the proof comes from the offender, demonstrate the influence of post-modern criminal law.

As regards the Commission's investigatory powers, its rights of inspection allow it to conduct all necessary inspections of undertakings and associations of undertakings.[31] In order to improve the effectiveness of the inspections, these can be made without prior notice to create a surprise effect (dawn raids). In addition, Regulation No 1/2003 allows the Commission to enter private homes (the homes of directors, managers and other members of staff of the undertakings and associations of undertakings concerned) to find business records related to the investigation.[32] Thus, the procedure has an intrusive nature (raising issues relating to the respect of privacy)[33] as well as a constraining one. Indeed, the Commission may fine an undertaking if it supplies incorrect or misleading information in response to a request[34] and may impose a periodic penalty payment to compel the undertaking to supply complete and correct information or to submit to an inspection.[35] This is not purely hypothetical: in 2008, the Commission ordered E.ON Energie AG to pay a fine of EUR 38 million for breaking a seal securing documents

[29] V Giacobbo-Peyronnel and P Singer, 'Quelques réflexions et interrogations au sujet de l'effet dissuasif des amendes en droit communautaire de la concurrence' (2009) (4) *Concurrences* 74, 81.

[30] eg 'it was open to the Commission to consider that it was appropriate to raise the level of fines so as to reinforce their deterrent effect', CJEU in Cases 100/80, 101/80, 102/80 and 103/80 *SA Musique Diffusion française and others v Commission*, EU:C:1983:158, para 108.

[31] Art 20 of Regulation No 1/2003.

[32] Art 21 of Regulation No 1/2003. In the *Marine Hoses* case, the Commission conducted a surprise inspection at the private home of the cartel coordinator, see Commission Decision of 28 January 2009 in Case COMP/39406 – Marine Hoses, para 61: https://ec.europa.eu/competition/antitrust/cases/dec_docs/39406/39406_1902_1.pdf.

[33] I Asmal and M Ramsden, 'EC Dawn Raids: A Human Rights Violation?' (2008) 5(1) *The Competition Law Review* 61.

[34] Art 23(1) of Regulation No 1/2003.

[35] Art 24 of Regulation No 1/2003.

seized during an inspection.[36] Moreover, in practice, staff members can be put under pressure to cooperate with the Commission during investigations.[37]

As regards alternative procedural options, it should be recalled that a trial is not always used to establish criminal liability. Negotiated solutions between the offender and the criminal enforcement authorities again demonstrate a postmodern form of criminal law, influenced by an economic analysis of law.[38] The use of negotiated solutions is also well established in competition law. Indeed, enterprises involved in a cartel can cooperate with the Commission through a settlement procedure during which they acknowledge their participation in, and liability for, a cartel.[39] This procedure is inspired by the criminal plea-bargaining process. Another possibility based on a whistleblowing system is the immunity and leniency procedure. Indeed, the corporate members of a cartel can request immunity or a reduction of their future fine if they collaborate in proving the existence of a cartel by submitting information and evidence.[40]

There are many reasons explaining why competition law investigations have taken on the features of criminal investigations with the Commission holding extensive investigatory powers.

First, it should be recalled that competition law proceedings have evolved greatly since their introduction into law in 1962. As described in the work of Christopher Harding and Julian Joshua, the system of cartel regulation has gone from a consensual notification to a repressive mode of control.[41] Indeed, Regulation 17/62[42] established the rules for applying Articles 85 and 86 (now Articles 101 and 102) of the Treaty and created an ex ante control based on the direct applicability of the prohibition rule of Article 85(1) and a prior notification by undertakings of restrictive practices for exemption under Article 85(3). However, the number of cases and the role of the Commission expanded with the development of the EU. Due to the ex ante control system provided for in Regulation 17/62, the Commission's limited administrative resources and the complexity of decision-making system, measures were eventually taken in order to

[36] European Commission, summary of the Commission Decision of 30 January 2008 relating to a proceeding under Art 23(1) of Regulation No 1/2003, Case COMP/B-1/39.326 – E.ON Energie AG [2008] OJ C240/6. Decision confirmed by the GCEU in Case T-141/08 *E.ON Energie AG v Commission* EU:T:2010:516 and by the CJEU in Case C-89/11 *E.ON Energie AG v Commission* EU:C:2012:738.

[37] As stated by certain practitioners, 'it must be emphasised that being subjected to a Commission competition investigation is hardly a pleasant experience. Vast quantities of documents are demanded by the Commission; initial failure to cooperate with investigations (by, for example, invoking the right to silence or legal privilege) regularly results in threats of criminal sanctions at which point individuals will often submit': See D Slater, S Thomas and D Waelbroeck, 'Competition law proceedings before the European Commission and the right to a fair trial: no need for reform?' *The Global Competition Law Centre Working Papers Series*, GCLC WP 04/08, p. 24.

[38] G Royer, 'Analyse économique du droit et traitement négocié de la délinquance d'affaires' in J-P Jean, A Giudicelli and M Masse (eds), *Un droit pénal postmoderne? Mise en perspective des évolutions et ruptures contemporaines* (Paris, Presses Universitaires de France, 2009).

[39] Commission Regulation (EC) No 622/2008 of 30 June 2008 amending Regulation (EC) No 773/2004, as regards the conduct of settlement procedures in cartel cases [2008] OJ L171/3, and Commission Notice on the conduct of settlement procedures in view of the adoption of Decisions pursuant to Arts 7 and 23 of Council Regulation (EC) No 1/2003 in cartel cases [2008] OJ C167/1.

[40] Commission Notice on immunity from fines and reduction of fines in cartel cases [2006] OJ C298/17.

[41] C Harding and J Joshua, *Regulating cartels in Europe*, 2nd edn (Oxford, Oxford University Press, 2010), 149.

[42] EEC Council Regulation No 17 First Regs implementing Arts 85 and 86 of the Treaty [1962] OJ L13/204.

reduce the number of individual notifications, speed up the processing of applications for authorisation and encourage the de-centralised processing of complaints.[43] However, these measures reached their limits and more radical reform was deemed necessary.[44] The will of the Commission was to eliminate the notification and exemption system, to de-centralise the application of EU competition rules and to set up an *ex post* supervision of restrictive practices.[45] In order to act effectively against non-notified (and therefore undisclosed) restrictions of competition, the Commission was in favour of increasing its powers of enquiry.[46] Consequently, Regulation No 1/2003 was adopted and it put in place a new system with an *ex post* control, which allowed the Commission to focus on the most serious cases.

Second, the role and attitude of the Commission has evolved since the 1960s.[47] Indeed, the objective of Regulation 17/62 (ie the removal of cartels by notification or discovery and prohibition) did not result in the end of cartels: many companies continued to be involved in cartels and simply hid their arrangements.[48] This led to an evolution of the role and motivation of the competition authority (the Commission) which had to adopt a 'police role' (and not just a 'regulatory role') because it had to find and uncover cartelists.[49] Thus, competition enforcement entered a domain of quasi-criminal enforcement.

Third, the focus on deterrence since the late 1970s also generated the need for severe sanctions and the creation of an impression on the market that there was a high probability of detection. In such a way, companies would be discouraged from getting involved in cartels. To this end, the competition authority needed 'more invasive powers of investigation'.[50]

Fourth, the Commission faced the issue of its evidential burden. The search for concrete evidence was necessary in order to prove the existence of an infringement. For this, the Commission had to understand the market through economic evidence and factual evidence (proof of meetings or agreements) to assess the circumstances surrounding a potential cartel.[51] Given their often secretive nature, invasive and far-reaching investigative methods and powers were required,[52] permitting the Commission to either collect the information or to encourage/coerce companies to provide it.

[43] European Commission, *White Paper on modernisation of the rules implementing Articles 85 and 86 of the EC Treaty* [1999] OJ C132/1.

[44] Ibid.

[45] Ibid.

[46] Ibid.

[47] Harding and Joshua (n 41), 110 ff.

[48] C Harding, 'The Anti-Cartel Enforcement Industry: Criminological Perspectives on Cartel Criminalisation' in C Beaton-Wells and A Ezrachi (eds), *Criminalising Cartels: Critical Studies of an International Regulatory Movement* (Oxford, Hart Publishing, 2011), 370 ff.

[49] Ibid.

[50] Ibid.

[51] Harding and Joshua (n 41), 150.

[52] 'Thus, cartels are unique among the various types of anticompetitive conduct, and unique investigative methods are required to combat them', OECD, *Hard Core Cartels, Recent progress and challenges ahead* (Paris, OECD Publishing, 2003), 19.

(iii) A Moral Dimension of the Offence?

As part of the analysis of this quasi-criminalisation of competition law enforcement, it is also worth assessing whether or not the administrative infringement encompasses a moral dimension bearing similarities with a criminal offence. In this regard, it should first be recalled that the criminal offence is based upon the willingness to commit the offence (*mens rea*, the guilty mind). Second, criminal liability can be justified by a moral responsibility because the behaviour harms ethical or moral values. By contrast, EU competition rules are based on an 'outcome-oriented' approach where the cartel is regarded as, and sanctioned due to being, an instrument of damage.[53] The focus is not put on the conduct.

Certainly, Article 101(1) TFEU does not include any moral element, in contrast to a criminal offence, which requires a physical and a mental element. The administrative infringement can be described as a material offence (strict liability offence). However, that observation must be qualified, since the will of the undertakings is not totally absent from the cartel infringement. Indeed, the practical element of the cartel infringement requires the existence of an agreement or a concerted practice between undertakings. An agreement is defined as 'a concurrence of wills on the very principle of a restriction of competition'.[54] To this end, an agreement can be proved by demonstrating a joint intention expressed by the undertakings to conduct themselves on the market in a specific way.[55] There is, therefore, some mental component in the cartel prohibition.

The role played by the intention of the undertakings is more prevalent at the stage of setting the fine. Indeed, Regulation No 1/2003 states that the Commission may impose a fine on undertakings where they have acted 'intentionally or negligently'.[56] The principle *nulla poena sine culpa* requires that a violation be established before a fine can be set.[57] As cartels are considered serious infringements,[58] it is very difficult for undertakings to prove that the cartel behaviour has not been committed intentionally.[59] Indeed, the intention can be considered to be irrefutably presumed in cartel cases.[60]

The degree of the fault committed also has an impact on the amount of the fine. Thus, the basic amount of the fine can be increased or decreased where the Commission finds that there are aggravating or mitigating circumstances.[61] These circumstances demonstrate that the intention behind the conduct of the undertaking is indeed taken into account. Consequently, the repetition of the same or a similar infringement is an

[53] Harding and Joshua (n 41), pp 56 ff.

[54] GCEU, Case T-186/06 *Solvay v Commission* EU:T:2011:276, para 86.

[55] Ibid, para 85.

[56] Article 23(2) Regulation No 1/2003.

[57] Opinion of Advocate General Kokott in Case C-681/11 *Bundeswettbewerbsbehörde and Bundeskartellanwalt v Schenker & Co. AG and Others* EU:C:2013:126, para 42.

[58] See the former Commission guidelines on the method of setting fines of 1998 (para 1A) where the cartels are classified as very serious infringements: [1998] OJ C9/3.

[59] For example, see CJEU in Case C-235/92 P *Montecatini v Commission* EU:C:1999:362, para 209.

[60] L Bernardeau and J-P Christienne, *Les amendes en droit de la concurrence. Pratique décisionnelle et contrôle juridictionnel du droit de l'Union* (Brussels, Larcier, 2013), 178.

[61] Commission 2006 Guidelines (n 23).

aggravating circumstance because the undertaking must have been, or should have been, aware of the unlawful nature of its acts given it has already been sanctioned for a prior infringement. Likewise, the refusal to cooperate with, or the obstruction of, the Commission when it carries out its investigation, and the role of the leader in, or instigator of, the cartel are aggravating circumstances.

Therefore, even if at first sight the willingness of the cartel members does not seem to be relevant to the commission of the competition law infringement, the intention is not totally insignificant given its impact at the stage of setting fines.

Since the *Quinine* and *Dyestuffs* cases and as time has gone by, the moral perception of cartels by the Commission has also evolved. Indeed, the investigating powers of the Commission have enabled the EU regulator to become increasingly aware of the harmful nature of these often secretive and well-organised practices.[62] Progressively, the words used to describe cartels show that a moral judgement or a value judgement has been increasingly applied. As mentioned previously, this disapproval is particularly noticeable in the statements of the commissioners responsible for competition. Thus, Mario Monti characterised cartels as 'cancers on the open market economy',[63] whilst Neelie Kroes compared them to viruses[64] and made a parallel between cartels and theft.[65] This rhetoric is a reminder of the one used by the US authorities. Indeed, the US Supreme Court described cartels as 'supreme evil of antitrust'.[66] Moreover, the 'underhand' character of the conduct of cartels' members has been highlighted by the EU General Court:

> the infringement of Article 101(1) TFEU … involves engaging in conduct which is generally regarded as underhand, to the detriment of the public at large, and which entails a clear stigma and a potential fine, for the undertakings responsible, of up to 10% of annual turnover, which is undoubtedly severe.[67]

The administrative sanction imposed no longer maintains a moral neutrality, therefore, but carries a stigma similar to criminal sanctions.[68]

In conclusion, the enforcement of competition law, and more particularly rules prohibiting cartels, involves a stringent procedure conducted by the Commission and heavy fines aimed at punishing cartelists as well as deterring cartels. These severe

[62] J Joshua and S Jordan, 'Combinations, concerted practices and cartels: adopting the concept of conspiracy in European community competition law' (2004) 24(3) *Northwestern Journal of International Law and Business* 647.

[63] Monti, 'Fighting Cartels Why and How?' (n 2).

[64] See, eg 'Our task is made harder because cartels are always changing shape – adapting like viruses to fight our attempts to kill them off', Kroes, *Tackling Cartels* (n 3).

[65] 'I do believe that we need to begin changing general perception of the competition rules. […] It is up to us to show that when we break up cartels, it is to stop money being stolen from customers' pockets': N Kroes, 'Taking Competition Seriously – Anti-Trust Reform in Europe', *International Bar Association Conference* (Brussels, March 2005).

[66] US Supreme Court, *Verizon Communications v Trinko*, 540 US 398, 408 (2004): 'Moreover, compelling negotiation between competitors may facilitate the supreme evil of antitrust: collusion'.

[67] GCEU in Case T-48/11 *British Airways plc v Commission* EU:T:2015:988, para 34, which refers to the Opinion of Advocate General Sharpston in Case C-272/09 P *KME Germany and Others v Commission* EU:C:2011:63, para 64.

[68] '[T]he condemnation ("stigma") associated with the imposition of cartel – i.e. quasi-criminal – penalties against the undertaking', Opinion of Advocate General Kokott in Case C-681/11 *Schenker & Co AG and Others* EU:C:2013:126, para 59.

administrative sanctions result in a quasi-criminal form of enforcement. By adopting some of the features of criminal law, therefore, punitive administrative sanctions imposed on cartel members and the procedure followed by the Commission lead to the creation of a hybrid branch of law. This so-called administrative punitive law or quasi-criminal law, which has also been named 'criministrative law',[69] makes it more difficult to clearly distinguish between criminal law and administrative law.[70] As a result, judges applying core criminal law do not have the monopoly on imposing repressive sanctions. As in criminal enforcement, where the equilibrium between the sanction imposed on the offender and the protection of its rights is also required during the prosecution, repressive competition law calls for a regime applying procedural safeguards.

B. A Quasi-criminal Enforcement Requiring Strengthened Protection

The evolution of the administrative enforcement of competition rules towards criminal enforcement demands a level of protection for punished undertakings similar to and modelled upon that required in criminal law. Already in 1991, Advocate General Vesterdorf underlined the characteristics of criminal law applicable to the cartel case submitted.[71] The establishment of a protective legal regime stems from the case law of the European Court of Justice concerning the application of Article 6 of the European Convention of Human Rights (ECHR) and the scrutiny of competition law sanctions and proceedings, including by the European Court of Human Rights.

(i) Nature of Competition Sanctions Examined by the ECtHR

In order to apply the right to a fair trial and the guarantees offered by Article 6 of the ECHR, the European Court of Human Rights (ECtHR) had to decide whether competition proceedings constituted a 'criminal charge' under Article 6 ECHR. The notion of a criminal charge is an autonomous concept, which has to be understood within the meaning of the ECHR,[72] independently of the domestic laws of the states that are party to the convention. The ECtHR formulated three criteria ('*Engel* criteria') in order

[69] Bailleux, *The fiftieth shade of grey* (n 13).

[70] See, eg, 'Les problèmes juridiques et pratiques posés par la différence entre le droit criminel et le droit administratif pénal' (1988) 59(1/2) *Revue internationale de droit pénal* 27, and European Commission, *Etude sur les systèmes de sanctions administratives et pénales dans les Etats membres des communautés européennes* (Luxembourg, EU Publications Office, 1995). Also, O Jansen (ed), *Administrative Sanctions in the European Union* (Antwerp, Intersentia, 2013) and Galli and Weyembergh (n 5).

[71] 'I have in mind the tension which can clearly be felt – perhaps even more so in the present cases than in any previous competition case which has come before the Court of Justice – between the procedural framework of the cases, consisting of an administrative procedure followed by judicial review of legality, and the substance of the cases, which all broadly exhibit the characteristics of a criminal law case. In many instances, the parties' submissions can only be understood with the help of the terminology and concepts used in criminal law and procedure.' Opinion of Advocate General Vesterdorf in Case T-1/89 *Rhône-Poulenc SA v Commission*, EU:T:1991:38.

[72] ECtHR (App No 6903/75) *Deweer v Belgium*, 27 February 1980, para 42.

to determine whether or not a sanction or a proceeding involves a criminal charge.[73] Firstly, the Court examines whether the provision(s) defining the offence charged belongs, according to the legal system of the respondent state, to criminal law. This criterion has only a formal and relative value. Secondly, the Court looks into a factor of greater importance which is the very nature of the offence. Thirdly, the Court takes into consideration the nature and degree of severity of the penalty that the person concerned risks incurring.

Through its case law, the ECtHR has further developed these criteria. The second criterion, the nature of the offence, has been described as 'the mo[st] important'.[74] In assessing the nature of the offence, the Court takes into account the general character of the legal rule.[75] For instance, in the *Menarini* judgment, which concerned a financial penalty (EUR 6 million) imposed by the Italian Competition Authority against a company for price fixing and market allocation, the ECtHR stated that Italian competition law was aimed at protecting free competition on the market and that the competition authority aims at supervising agreements restricting competition. Consequently, the offence was regarded as affecting the general interests normally protected by criminal law.[76] In a prior case dealing with French competition law, the European Commission of Human Rights reached the same conclusion: the provision of the French law at stake was aimed at protecting free competition on the market and therefore it affected the general interests of society normally protected by criminal law.[77] The Court examined also whether the sanction was imposed by a rule whose purpose was deterrent and punitive. The Court reached this conclusion in the *Menarini* judgment.

Concerning the fulfilment of the third criterion, the ECtHR examines the nature and degree of severity of the penalty. Deprivations of liberty liable to be imposed as punishment belong to the criminal sphere.[78] Regarding fines, the Court takes into account the amount, the entry on the police register and the possible conversion into a term of imprisonment.[79] In the *Menarini* judgment, the Court highlighted that the fine had a preventative as well as a punitive aim, and stressed the severity of the sanction. Consequently, the company was judged as being subject to a criminal charge within the meaning of Article 6 ECHR.

In the *Jussila* judgment relating to tax surcharges, the ECtHR introduced the notion of a 'hard core of criminal law'. However, the concept was not clearly defined in the judgment. The Court stated that 'it is self-evident that there are criminal cases which do not carry any significant degree of stigma' and that '[t]here are clearly "criminal charges" of differing weight'.[80] Moreover, the Court specified that the interpretation of the notion of a criminal charge using the *Engel* criteria has underpinned a gradual broadening

[73] ECtHR (App Nos 5100–5102/71; 5354/72 and 5370/72) *Engel and others v the Netherlands*, 8 June 1976, para 82.

[74] ECtHR (App No 73053/01) *Jussila v Finland*, 23 November 2006, para 38.

[75] ECtHR (App No 26138/95) *Lauko v Slovakia*, 2 September 1998, para 58.

[76] ECtHR (App No 43509/08) *A. Menarini Diagnostics S.r.l v Italy*, 27 September 2011, para 40.

[77] ECtHR, Commission's Report, (App No 11598/85) *Société Stenuit v France*, 30 May 1991, para 62.

[78] '[E]xcept those which by their nature, duration or manner of execution cannot be appreciably detrimental', ECtHR, *Engel* (n 73), para 82.

[79] ECtHR (App No 14220/88) *Ravnsborg v Sweden*, 23 March 1994, para 35.

[80] ECtHR, *Jussila* (n 74), para 43.

of the criminal head to include cases not strictly belonging to the traditional categories of criminal law. Then the Court cited examples, such as administrative penalties, prison disciplinary measures, customs law, competition law and penalties imposed by a court with jurisdiction in financial matters. Consequently, according to the Court, 'the criminal-head guarantees will not necessarily apply with their full stringency'. Although the exclusion of competition law sanctions from the hard core of criminal law has not been explicitly confirmed by the ECtHR,[81] it is very plausible to consider that, as the Court cites competition law cases as not belonging to the traditional categories of criminal law, competition law sanctions are excluded from the hard core of criminal law.[82] The concept of a hard core of criminal law faced with the notion of general interests usually protected by criminal law makes the system established by the Court even more opaque. Indeed, the Court considered the preservation of free competition to be an interest usually protected by criminal law, but then cited competition law as not belonging to the traditional categories of the criminal law.

(ii) Nature of Competition Sanctions Examined by the CJEU

As the EU is not (yet) a signatory of the ECHR,[83] the case law of the ECtHR deals just with national competition law and has not examined EU competition law. However, the criminal character of competition law has also been discussed before the EU courts. The concept of a 'criminal charge' can be found, for example, in the reasoning of the EU case law. Indeed, the General Court, the Court of Justice and the Advocates General have had to examine the applicability of criminal law and procedural principles to competition law. Consequently, some EU court judgments mention the criminal character of competition law even if the EU jurisdictions do not always expressly refer to Article 6 ECHR.

Indeed, referring to the notion of a 'criminal charge' involves not only recognising the criminal character of competition law, but also referring explicitly to a legal instrument which has been formally incorporated into EU law. Thus, the EU courts have not easily applied the respect of fundamental rights of undertakings under the ECHR and have preferred to apply general principles of EU law instead.[84] Nonetheless, it should be recalled that the fundamental rights recognised by the ECHR constitute general principles of EU law (as laid down in Article 6(3) TEU), and the Charter of Fundamental Rights of the European Union contains rights which correspond to rights guaranteed by the Convention for the Protection of Human Rights and Fundamental Freedoms. As specifically stated in Article 52(3) of the Charter, the meaning and scope of those rights shall be the same as those laid down by the ECHR.

[81] Unfortunately, in *Menarini* (n 76) the ECtHR stayed silent on this issue.

[82] Nonethelesss, a contrary interpretation has been presented. For a presentation of the two interpretations, see T Bombois, *La protection des droits fondamentaux des entreprises en droit européen répressif de la concurrence* (Brussels, Larcier, 2012), 39 ff.

[83] Art 6(2) Treaty on European Union and Art 59(2) ECHR.

[84] See the examination of the different steps and strategies followed by the CJEU in the recognition of the respect of fundamental rights in Bombois, *La protection des droits fondamentaux des entreprises* (n 82), 64 ff.

It seems that Advocate General Vesterdorf was the first member of the Court of Justice to refer to the ECHR when examining fines imposed in competition cases.[85] Other Advocates General have followed his lead and even referred to the distinction made in the *Jussila* judgment between the 'hard core of criminal law' and those offences outside the hard core of criminal law, where criminal law guarantees provided for under Article 6(1) ECHR do not necessarily apply with their full stringency.[86]

The General Court and the Court of Justice have proved in their judgments to be more reluctant to recognise the criminal nature of competition law. One argument put forward explaining this reluctance is that 'the effectiveness of Community competition law would be seriously affected if the argument that competition law formed part of criminal law were accepted'[87] (even if this justification based on effectiveness is debatable).[88] However, it can be observed that the General Court and Court of Justice have softened their position somewhat in this regard. Indeed, the Court of Justice has made reference to the *Menarini* judgment of the ECtHR (albeit without explicitly deciding upon the criminal character of EU criminal sanctions).[89] Furthermore, the General Court acknowledged that:

> Given the nature of the infringements in question and the nature and degree of severity of the ensuing penalties [...] those penalties pertain to criminal matters for the purpose of Article 6 of the European Convention for the Protection of Human Rights and Fundamental Freedoms [...] as can be seen, inter alia, from the judgment of the European Court of Human Rights in *A. Menarini Diagnostics S.R.L. v. Italy*.[90]

(iii) Quasi-criminal Enforcement with a Quasi-criminal Protection

The purpose of the classification of competition law in the criminal sphere in the EU court cases is to apply the protective principles of criminal law to the procedure as well as to the sanction imposed. However, it turns out that these principles are not fully respected when applied to competition law cases but are nuanced. This can be reasonably explained by the fact that competition law does not belong to the hard core of criminal law but to another category of law, between administrative and criminal law.

[85] Opinion Advocate General Vesterdorf, *Rhône-Poulenc* (n 71).

[86] See especially, the Opinion of Advocate General Sharpston, *KME Germany* (n 67) ('If the fining procedure in the present case thus falls within the criminal sphere for the purposes of the ECHR (and the Charter), I would none the less agree that, in the words of the judgment in Jussila, (26) it "differ[s] from the hard core of criminal law; consequently, the criminal-head guarantees will not necessarily apply with their full stringency".'); Opinion of Advocate General Kokott in Case C-109/10 P *Solvay v Commission* EU:C:2011:256 ('It must also be borne in mind, with respect to competition law, that the ECtHR itself does not regard that area of law as a traditional category of criminal law; outside the "hard core" of criminal law, the ECtHR assumes that the criminal-law guarantees provided for in Article 6(1) of the ECHR will not necessarily apply with their full stringency'); Opinion of Advocate General Mengozzi in Case C-521/09 *Elf Aquitaine v Commission* EU:C:2011:89.

[87] GCEU, Case T-276/04 *Compagnie maritime belge v Commission* EU:T:2008:237, para 66, and Case C-338/00 *Volkswagen v Commission* EU:C:2003:473, para 97.

[88] Slater, Thomas and Waelbroeck, 'Competition law proceedings before the European Commission' (n 37), 20; Bailleux (n 13), 141–42.

[89] CJEU, Case C-501/11 P *Schindler v Commission* EU:C:2013:522, para 35.

[90] GCEU, Case T-9/11 *Air Canada v Commission* EU:T:2015:994, para 33.

This quasi-criminal law has also been named 'criministrative law'[91] where the rights and principles of criminal law are tempered ('"fairly fair trial" standards').[92] The case law of the EU courts illustrates the scope of the criminal law principles applied to competition cases: whereas some principles are strictly applied, others are done so in a looser manner.

For example, the application of the principle of non-retroactivity, which is a corollary to the principle of legality,[93] has been seriously tempered in competition cases. The EU courts have stated that

> the principle of non-retroactivity does not preclude the application of guidelines which, ex hypothesi, have the effect of increasing the level of fines imposed for infringements committed before their adoption, provided that the policy which they implement is reasonably foreseeable at the time the infringements in question were committed.[94]

Likewise, the application of the *lex mitior* has not been recognised as an obligation by the EU General Court (GCEU).[95] In addition, the respect of the principle of personal liability or principle that penalties must be specific to the offender and the offence[96] is also questionable in cases involving groups of undertakings[97] and in cases where an undertaking is liable for anticompetitive infringements committed by a predecessor undertaking.[98] The *ne bis in idem* principle is applicable in competition cases,[99] but is not applied in cases where the undertakings have already been sanctioned in non-EU countries[100] or by the national competition authority of a Member State (on account of the anticompetitive effects of a cartel in a Member State prior to its accession to the European Union).[101]

Concerning the procedure, the right against self-incrimination has been recognised[102] and undertakings fully benefit from the right to legal representation and the privileged nature of correspondence between lawyer and client[103] (although not with an internal lawyer).[104] Similarly, undertakings benefit from the right to the presumption of

[91] Bailleux (n 13).

[92] Ibid, 144 ff.

[93] Art 49 of the Charter of Fundamental Rights of the European Union and Art 7 of the ECHR.

[94] GCEU, Case T-138/07 *Schindler v Commission* EU:T:2011:362, para 143.

[95] GCEU, Case T-101/05 *BASF and UCB v Commission* EU:T:2007:380, para 234.

[96] '[A] natural or legal person may be penalised only for acts imputed to him individually […]; that principle applies in any administrative procedure that may lead to the imposition of sanctions under Community competition law', GCEU in Case C-122/07 *Siemens v Commission* EU:T:2011:70, para 122.

[97] L Bernardeau, 'Like mother, like daughter, (sauf) en droit de la concurrence?' (2015) 42 *Revue Lamy de la Concurrence* 74.

[98] For further details, see Bombois (n 82).

[99] The 'principle thus precludes an undertaking being found liable or proceedings being brought against it afresh on the grounds of anti-competitive conduct for which it has been penalised or declared not liable by an earlier decision that can no longer be challenged', CJEU in Case C-17/10 *Toshiba Corporation and Others v Úřad pro ochranu hospodářské soutěže* EU:C:2012:72.

[100] CJEU in Case C-231/14 P *InnoLux Corp. v Commission* EU:C:2015:451, para 75.

[101] CJEU in *Toshiba* (n 99), para 103.

[102] Recital 23 of Regulation No 1/2003 and CJEU in Case 347/87 *Orkem v Commission* EU:C:1989:387, para 35. Although its proper application has been questioned, see Bombois (n 82), 175 ff.

[103] CJEU in Case C-94/00 *Roquette Frères v Directeur général de la concurrence, de la consommation et de la répression des fraudes and Commission* EU:C:2002:603, para 46.

[104] GCEU in Cases T-125/03 and T-253/03 *Akzo Nobel Chemicals v Commission* EU:T:2007:287.

innocence,[105] the right to be informed,[106] the right of access to file,[107] as well as the right to be tried within a reasonable time.[108]

Importantly on this subject, the main and obvious feature which can distinguish competition law from criminal law and which exemplifies its administrative nature, lies in the fact that the sanctioning decisions are made by an administrative body (the Commission) and not by a court. The ECtHR and the Court of Justice are in agreement on this with the Court of Justice clearly acknowledging that the Commission cannot be described as a tribunal within the meaning of Article 6 ECHR.[109] However, the ECtHR has nonetheless judged that entrusting the prosecution and punishment of breaches of competition rules to administrative authorities is not per se inconsistent with the ECHR. This is so long as the person concerned has an opportunity to challenge any decision made against them before a tribunal that offers the guarantees provided for under Article 6 ECHR.[110] Consequently, the fact that the Commission is not a tribunal is not contrary to Article 6(1) ECHR in so far as the decision adopted by the Commission can be subject to subsequent review by a judicial body that has full jurisdiction. Such a review is certainly possible in cartel cases. The EU courts have unlimited jurisdiction under Article 31 of Regulation No 1/2003, in accordance with Article 261 TFEU, and are empowered to substitute the Commission's appraisal with their own and consequently may cancel, reduce or increase the fine or periodic penalty payment imposed.[111] Moreover, the TFEU allows a review of legality provided under Article 263 TFEU.

The multiple roles of the Commission acting as an investigating authority, a prosecutorial authority and a decision-making authority raise questions as regards impartiality. According to some authors, the conjunction of powers held by the Commission would lead to 'prosecutorial bias', 'i.e. the fact that a case handler will naturally tend to have a bias in favour of finding a violation once proceedings have been commenced' the impact of which on the outcome of decisions is impossible to measure and to correct by subsequent judicial review.[112] However, the EU courts have not judged the multiple functions of the Commission as being contrary to any principle of EU law.[113]

The repressive nature of competition law enforcement, therefore, has led to the creation of a quasi-criminal enforcement where criminal law appears to be a model for the establishment of a regime protecting the undertakings based on 'quasi-criminal principles' (criminal law principles not necessarily applied with their full stringency). The enforcement of EU rules against cartels has evolved from encouraging compliance with competition law through means characterised by flexibility ('"soft" law' control)[114]

[105] GCEU in Case C-199/92 *Hüls v Commission* EU:C:1999:358, para 150.

[106] GCEU in Case T-161/05 *Hoechst v Commission* EU:T:2009:366, para 163.

[107] Art 27.2 of Regulation No 1/2003.

[108] GCEU in Case T-213/00 *CMA CGM and Others v Commission* EU:T:2003:76, para 317.

[109] CJEU in Cases 209/78 to 215/78 and 218/78 *Heintz van Landewyck and Others v Commission* EU:C:1980:248, para 81.

[110] Case *Menarini* of the ECtHR (n 76) cited by the CJEU in *Schindler* (n 89), para 34.

[111] CJEU in *Schindler* (n 89), para 36.

[112] Slater, Thomas and Waelbroeck (n 37), 33.

[113] GCEU in Case T-348/94 *Enso Española v Commission* EU:T:1998:102, paras 56–64.

[114] Joshua and Jordan, 'Combinations, concerted practices and cartels' (n 62), 657.

to a mainly punitive form of enforcement. The severity of the sanctions imposed in cartel cases leads one to conclude that the sanction has become pivotal in this regulatory branch of law, as the penalty is in criminal law. Indeed, the 'duty to punish'[115] seems to have entered into competition law enforcement. Competition enforcement has therefore gone down the criminal law path. Consequently, the softening of criminal law principles when applied to competition law raises certain issues, such as the justification of this softening and the mitigation of criminal principles. The language of 'war against cartels'[116] has introduced a legitimacy to resorting to criminal law. The severity of the administrative sanctions and the will to stigmatise and to deter cartel behaviour has also led to the perception of the criminalisation of cartels as being justified. However, one fundamental question remains outstanding in this analysis: is cartel conduct really a form of criminal behaviour?

III. Is Cartel Conduct a Form of Criminal Behaviour?

The severity of administrative sanctions, the creation of a 'spiral of delinquency' where the cartelists try to hide their conduct,[117] the comparison with criminal offences like theft, all raise the question about the real nature of cartel conduct and the precise nature of the enforcement of the cartel prohibition. Indeed, despite the huge fines imposed penalising corporate entities, cartels are still being formed and are in operation. This leads to the question of whether or not administrative enforcement is the right way to tackle cartels.

In search of a strong answer to fight cartels and to sanction those responsible, the issue of cartel criminalisation – in particular prison sentences for individuals involved in cartel behaviour – has arisen in Europe. More than 10 years ago, a Commission official, Wouter PJ Wils, raised the question 'Is criminalization of EU competition law the answer?'.[118] He presented the use of criminal law as a solution to improve the effectiveness of competition law in the EU and in particular the use of jail sentences to combat cartels. At that time, the UK had just enacted the Enterprise Act 2002 introducing the cartel offence, and the OECD had published several recommendations encouraging countries to adopt individual and criminal sanctions to strengthen deterrence.[119] The fight against cartels remains a top priority of EU competition policy[120] but the

[115] AP Pires stated a methamorphosis of the right to punish ('droit de punir') in a duty to punish ('obligation de punir') in criminal law, see 'En guise de conclusion : un nœud gordien autour du droit de punir' in C Debuyst, F Digneffe et AP Pires (eds), *Histoire des savoirs sur le crime et la peine*, vol 2. *La rationalité pénale et la naissance de la criminologie* (Brussels, Larcier, 2008), 251 ff.

[116] Harding and Joshua (n 41), 278.

[117] Ibid, 51.

[118] WPJ Wils, 'Is criminalization of EU Competition Law the Answer?' (2005) 28(2) *World Competition* 117.

[119] OECD, 'Cartels: sanctions against individuals (Policy roundtables 2003)', 2005. For example, for Belgium, see OECD, 'Etudes économiques de l'OCDE: Belgique' (2009), 130.

[120] The current Commissioner for Competition, M Vestager, stated 'Breaking cartels remains a top priority for the Commission', European Commission, Press release, 'Antitrust: Commission fines car parts producers € 137 789 000 in cartel settlement', Brussels, 27 January 2016, IP/16/173.

EU does not have the competence to impose directly criminal sanctions.[121] Accordingly, the choice lies with the Member States as to whether or not to introduce criminal sanctions. In this regard, over half of the EU Member States have criminalised certain cartel offences,[122] whereas other Member States have rejected this approach[123] (section III.A). The heart of the issue lies in the justification for the use of criminal law sanctions against individuals who have been involved in cartels (III.B). The key question here is whether or not cartel conduct has the characteristics of, and constitutes, a criminal offence.

A. Criminal Enforcement in the Fight against Cartels

Over the past 20 years, the criminalisation of cartels has seen a revival of interest worldwide. More than 30 countries have criminalised some form of cartel conduct.[124] However, what has been described as a global trend towards the criminalisation of cartel behaviour covers a variety of different situations. The oldest laws of modern times sanctioning cartels emerged in Canada and in the United States at the end of the nineteenth century. Thus, section 1 of the US Sherman Act, adopted in 1890, laid down criminal sanctions for individuals and undertakings involved in a cartel. The choice of criminal sanctions was justified by the desire to fight against economic concentration amongst a few trusts belonging to the so-called Robber Barons, but also because at that time the modern administrative state did not exist and the way to fight against undesirable conduct was to make it criminal.[125] Since its adoption, the US criminal legislation has been strengthened to become a severe criminal form of enforcement, providing for heavy sanctions. Today, US criminal enforcement plays a leading role in the global trend towards the criminalisation of cartel conduct.

By contrast, in Europe, where there existed a certain culture of tolerance towards cartels until the first half of the twentieth century,[126] the introduction of modern rules governing competition has involved administrative sanctions and enforcement under the influence of the EU model.[127] The use of criminal enforcement is, however, present in some EU Member States and often co-exists with the administrative form of enforcement.[128] Without being exhaustive, criminal enforcement in EU Member

[121] On the possibility for the EU to criminalise competition law, see G Hapokian, 'Criminalisation of EU Competition Law Enforcement – A possibility after Lisbon?' (2010) 7(1) *The Competition Law Review* 157.

[122] GC Shaffer, NH Nesbitt and WS Weber, 'Criminalizing Cartels: a Global Trend?' in J Duns, A Duke and B Sweeney (eds), *Comparative Competition Law* (Camberley, Edward Elgar Publishing, 2013), 311.

[123] For example, Belgium made the choice of administrative fines against the individual since the adoption of the Law of the 3 April 2013.

[124] C Harding, C Beaton-Wells and J Edwards, 'Leniency and Criminal Sanctions in Anti-Cartel Enforcement: Happily Married or Uneasy Bedfellows?' in C Beaton-Wells and C Tran (eds), *Anti-Cartel Enforcement in a Contemporary Age. Leniency Religion* (Oxford, Hart Publishing, 2015), 233.

[125] DI Baker, 'Trying to use criminal law and incarceration to punish participants and deter cartels raises some broad political and social questions in Europe' in P Lowe and M Marquis, *European competition law annual 2011: integrating public and private enforcement, Implications for courts and agencies* (Oxford, Hart Publishing, 2014), 49–50.

[126] Harding and Joshua (n 41), 52–56.

[127] Decriminalisation of competition law, see Wils (n 118).

[128] L Idot, 'Le droit des Etats membres de l'Union européenne' (Colloque : La sanction pénale, l'article L 420-6 C. Com.) (2008) (1) *Concurrences* 14.

States can stem from a choice influenced by specific constitutional rules (eg Ireland), the relic of a law on pricing despite competition law being formally decriminalised (eg Article L.420-6 of the French Code de Commerce),[129] or the expression of a recent adherence to deterrence arguments in favour of the use of criminal law (eg the cartel offence in the UK).[130]

Dealing with criminal sanctions against cartelists requires an understanding of the specific features of cartels. Indeed, they involve a double dimension: a collective (corporate) and individual (human) dimension.[131] Thus, in the US, the Sherman Act imposes criminal liability on both. Targeting the corporation can be seen as a way to oblige it to monitor the behaviour of its employees.[132] In addition, in circumstances where the culpable decision is difficult to attribute to particular individuals, the company may be found liable.[133] However, it should be recalled that not all jurisdictions envisage the criminal liability of corporations. Imposing criminal liability upon individuals enables the law to focus on the human dimension of the practice and to individualise the problem.[134] Nevertheless, individual sanctions raise the issue of agency and the capacity to correctly target the person responsible.[135]

The focus on individuals is also an illustration of the influence of economic reasoning on criminal law where individual criminal responsibility constitutes a solution when fines are deemed insufficiently deterrent. Criminal offences aimed at individuals exist in the UK (under the cartel offence) and in France (not limited to cartels, but also applying to other anticompetitive practices), where they form complementary penalties (and secondary ones, because they are less often applied than the administrative infringement) to administrative enforcement, which is aimed against undertakings only.

The call for the use of criminal sanctions is also the manifestation of a need for security and for strong sanctions against cartelists. Citizens desire a social order to

[129] Art 419 of the French Criminal Code of 1810 introduced the collusion offence (*délit de coalition*). Subsequently, the Decree of 1953 (*décret du 9 août 1953*) criminally sanctioned anticompetitive practices. The legislative Order of 1986 (*Ordonnance du 1er décembre 1986 relative à la liberté des prix et de la concurrence*) empowered the Conseil de la concurrence (currently the *Autorité de la concurrence*), an independent administrative authority, to sanction anticompetitive practices, including cartels. The 1986 Order repealed the specific criminal penalities for competition law infringements, which is why it is considered to have decriminalised competition law. However, a legislative provision (Art 17 of the Ordonnance which became the current Art L. 420-6 of the French Code of Commerce) still enables criminal law sanctions to be imposed in cases of competition law infringements. See A Decocq and M Pedamon, 'L'ordonnance du 1er décembre 1986 relative à la liberté des prix et de la concurrence', *Encyclopédie du Jurisclasseur Concurrence-Consommation* (1987) Numéro spécial 1 bis Lexisnexis.

[130] Section 188 Enterprise Act 2002.

[131] Harding and Joshua (n 41), 258.

[132] B Wardhaugh, *Cartels, Markets and Crime, A Normative Justification for the Criminalisation of Economic Collusion* (Cambridge, Cambridge University Press, 2014), 52–88.

[133] A Jones and R Williams, 'The UK Response to the Global Effort against Cartels: is Criminalization Really the Solution?' (2014) 2(1) *Journal of Antitrust Enforcement* 100, 120.

[134] The call for individual sanctions (even if not criminal) can be observed in para 62 of the Report on the annual report on EU competition policy (2016/2100(INI)) of the EU Parliament where it 'calls on the Commission to consider the possibility of complementing cartel fines with personal sanctions aimed at company decision-makers, as well as individual penalties for those employees responsible for actually leading their company to commit a violation of competition law'.

[135] Harding and Joshua (n 41), 258 ff; C Harding and J Edwards, *Cartel Criminality, The Mythology and Pathology of Business Collusion* (Farnham, Ashgate Publishing, 2015), 194–95.

which they can relate and one which offers security and predictability.[136] In that context, the use of criminal law has been perceived as a solution.

However, the call for criminalisation must be respectful of the fundamental requirements of criminal law. As explained by one commentator on the subject of cartel criminalisation: '[i]f we are to use criminal law, we must abide by its conventions and justify our offence on its terms'.[137]

B. Justification of Cartel Criminalisation

The legitimation of the use of criminal law is central to the question of cartel criminalisation because the legitimacy of an offence justifies the encroachment upon the offender's liberty. In order to be considered as legitimate, the intervention of criminal law must be respectful of criminal principles, such as the principle of culpability or the principle of necessity. Indeed, as the most coercive form of social control, criminal law is a *droit de l'exception*: its use must be necessary. Therefore, it can be used only if all other responses have failed, as an *ultima ratio* or last resort.[138] Criminal law lays down the reaction of the state when a certain type of behaviour constitutes a real threat to the fundamental values of a society.[139] Thus, the state must protect essential values of a society when the violation of those values is serious enough. The seriousness of the fault committed can be determined by referring both to the behaviour adopted and to the harm committed (or consequences caused).

Two approaches justifying the use of criminal law have been developed in the cartel criminalisation debate. One approach is that criminal law can be justified independently of any effects resulting from the sanction due to the wrong that has been committed (see sub-section B.(i).). This justification of criminal law can be defined as retributive. It is anchored in historic legal theory and relies solely on the commission of a fault, following a Kantian approach of the sanction.[140] The other approach views criminal law as a means or a tool to achieve specific goals. In cartel criminalisation, criminal law has been justified as serving enforcement objectives, such as the enhancement of deterrence, the co-operation between countries in law enforcement (extradition) and the enhancement of leniency policies.[141] This justification can be described as consequentialist, utilitarian and instrumental (sub-section B.(ii)).

[136] C Beaton-Wells and F Haines, 'The Australian conversion: how the case for cartel criminalisation was made' (2010) 1(4) *New Journal of European Criminal Law* 499, 502–04.

[137] A MacCulloch, 'The Cartel Offence: Defining an Appropriate Moral Space' (2012) 8(1) *European Competition Journal* 73, 83.

[138] N Jareborg, 'Criminalization as Last Resort (Ultima Ratio)' (2004) 2(2) *Ohio State Journal of Criminal Law* 521.

[139] N Lacey, *State punishment. Political principles and community values* (London, Routledge, 1988), 100.

[140] W Naucke, 'Le droit rétributif selon Kant' in F Blondieau (ed), *Rétribution et justice pénale* (Paris, Presses Universitaires de France, 1983).

[141] Harding, Beaton-Wells and Edwards, *Leniency and Criminal Sanctions* (n 124), 238–39.

(i) Criminalisation Justified by the Act Committed and its Consequences

According to a traditional view of criminal law, the state can only deprive a person of the right to freedom if that person has committed a serious fault. This is consistent with the criminal law principles of necessity and culpability. The gravity of the fault can be assessed by reference to the harm committed to essential values protected by the state as well as by reference to the behaviour adopted.

Concerning the harm caused by cartels, the negative effects of cartels are well established and well recognised in economic theory. They produce both direct and indirect effects. The price increase resulting from a cartel harms consumer welfare by leading to a decrease in consumer surplus or consumer purchases. Moreover, the cartel members have fewer competitive constraints, leading in the long run to less efficient production and less innovation. Thus, cartels cause economic harm to consumers, suppliers, the market and even to society in general.[142] Even if the general consequences of cartels can easily be identified, it is more difficult to precisely quantify those negative effects. A comparison of different economic studies shows that the estimated price increase caused by a cartel can vary from 15 per cent to 53 per cent.[143] The European Commission has referred to an average overcharge of 20 per cent.[144] The quantification of the price increases is challenging and constantly leads to debates during private damages actions initiated by parties claiming to have incurred loss as a result of a cartel.

It is worth considering how those negative effects caused by cartels can be used to justify the criminalisation of the cartel infringement. In this respect, the notion of harm committed has been greatly used by those who believe in the deterrent effect of criminal sanctions.[145] However, it must be recalled that not all behaviour causing damage constitutes criminal behaviour. The reference to harm alone has also been rejected as a justification for the use of criminal law in cartel cases in the legal literature because of its nature (difficulties in agreeing on the identification and quantification of the harm).[146] However, the harm caused by cartels remains a pivotal argument in the legitimacy of the criminalisation of cartels. Different legal systems incorporate this same criterion. Thus, despite their differences, both the Anglo-American *harm principle* and the German *Rechtsgutstheorie* express the need for a certain type of harm to legitimise the creation of a criminal offence.[147] This is because the original aim of these theories was to protect the freedom of the individual by limiting the state's intervention to certain actions only.

[142] Wardhaugh (n 132), 7–11.

[143] E Combe and C Monnier, 'Les cartels en Europe, une analyse empirique' (2012) XXVII(2) *Revue française d'économie* 187, 208.

[144] European Commission, 'Commission staff working document, Practical guide quantifying harm in actions for damages based on breaches of article 101 or 102 of the Treaty on the functioning of the European Union', 11 June 2013, paras 142 and 143.

[145] A Stephan, 'Why Morality should be Excluded from the Cartel Criminalisation Debate' (2012) 3(2) *New Journal of European Criminal Law* 127.

[146] MacCulloch, 'The Cartel Offence' (n 137), 78.

[147] W Hassemer, 'The Harm Principle and the Protection of "Legal Goods" (Rechtsgüterschutz): a German Perspective' in AP Simester, A Du Bois-Pedain and U Neumann (eds), *Liberal Criminal Theory. Essays for Andreas von Hirsch* (Oxford, Hart Publishing, 2014).

It can be submitted that competition as a whole or the consumer in particular constitute the interests, values or legal goods that are protected by the cartel offence. Indeed, competition[148] (or competitive markets) can be described as an economic concept incorporating a range of different dimensions. Thus, in the US, great importance has been attributed to competition, where antitrust law includes not only an economic but also a philosophical and political dimension.[149] Likewise, Bruce Wardhaugh analysed in detail the harm resulting from cartels and highlighted the philosophical dimension of competitive markets. Using the work of John Rawl, the author concluded that cartelists harm the market as an instrument of distributive justice.[150] However, if US law has imposed the ban on cartels as a basic rule of business life and its violation triggers criminal sanctions, it is important to remember that the attitude towards cartels was less strict in Europe up until the 1950s.

Moreover, one can also submit that consumers constitute a legal good to be protected. Indeed, the often-made comparison of cartel behaviour with theft[151] suggests that the more tangible victim of cartels is the consumer. However, the protection by criminal law of such a legal good implies that criminal law offers protection against harmful behaviour that can be described as more diluted or diffuse than theft, given that it is primarily harmful to a group of consumers; the harm caused to individual consumers by cartels is often low (and indirect). In addition, the argument that cartels breach a consumer's right, such as the right to property, is debatable since it would imply that the market and not the legal process defines property rights.[152] Indeed, the consumer is not legally the owner of the consumer surplus, which is defined according to the market price.

Certainly, modern societies produce risks which require state intervention. Consequently, the values protected by criminal law are various in nature: from fundamental and personal rights linked to the life, health, freedom and property of an individual to more collective and diffuse values and non-personal interests, such as the environment or the economy. Using criminal sanctions to protect the values of competition or the consumer illustrates a tendency of criminal law to extend its application to interests which appear far removed from individual rights.[153] A more extensive approach to values protected by criminal law, coupled with a preventive approach to the sanction might lead to the criminalisation of behaviour that constitute abstract and anticipated dangers, far from actual violation of the fundamental and personal values traditionally protected by criminal law.[154]

[148] Which is not defined in legislation.

[149] G Amato, *Antitrust and the bounds of power. The dilemma of liberal democracy in the history of the market* (Oxford, Hart Publishing, 1997), 96 ff.

[150] Wardhaugh (n 132), 43–48.

[151] '[C]artels are the equivalent of theft by well dressed thieves', JI Klein, 'The War Against International Cartels: Lessons From The Battlefront', Speech, *Fordham Corporate Law Institute 26th Annual Conference on International Antitrust Law and Policy*, New York, 14 October 1999.

[152] See, Wardhaugh (n 132), 38–40.

[153] S Braum, 'Taking Chance on Per Se Cartel Crime?' (2012) 3(2) *New Journal of European Criminal Law* 113, 115.

[154] A Baratta, 'Les Fonctions Instrumentales et les Fonctions Symboliques du Droit Pénal' (1991) 15(1) *Déviance et société* 1, 12.

Beyond the consequences (ie the harm) caused by a cartel, the wrongfulness of the cartelists' behaviour must also be examined. As previously stated, the harmfulness of cartels, the fact that they are detrimental to consumers, and their secretive nature all lead to comparisons with established criminal offences like theft. This implies that there is an inherently criminal dimension to the behaviour of cartel members, going beyond looking solely at the negative effects of the behaviour. This in turn raises the question as to whether or not the legal prohibition on forming a cartel results from the inclusion in the law of an economic requirement (to behave autonomously in order to respect the functioning of the markets and the price-formation mechanism) or from a moral dimension, ie the cartel member violates a moral prohibition. Thus, the question addressed here is whether the cartel offence is *mala prohibita* or *mala in se*. In order to answer this question, commentators[155] have discussed whether participating in a cartel can be equated to stealing, deception or cheating.[156] It is submitted that the moral norm infringed by a cartel is most likely that of the subversion of the market and the competitive process.[157] This is in line with the view of Angus MacCulloch, who has written 'the wrong in the conduct is that the cartel members have chosen to break the rules of the game'.[158]

Beyond the issue of the justification of the use of criminal law, the wrongfulness is also relevant in the definition of the elements of the offence. In analysing the French and British offences, it is noticeable that the legislators insisted on the features of the behaviour adopted by the guilty individual in order to show its wrongfulness. This is demonstrated by, for instance, the individual who 'fraudulently takes a personal and decisive part in' the infringement under French Article L.420-6 of the Code de commerce,[159] who 'dishonestly agrees' with the arrangement under the previous UK cartel offence (prior to the Enterprise and Regulatory Reform Act 2013) or who kept the arrangement secret under the provisions of the current UK cartel offence. However, it is also noteworthy that the cartel behaviour in itself is not described in moral terms. Indeed, the French law refers to the articles prohibiting anticompetitive practices[160] and the UK law describes arrangements constituting cartels. Consequently, to be wrongful, it is sufficient for an individual to have committed, in a specific intended manner, the administrative offence. By contrast, in using the concept of conspiracy, the Sherman Act gave a more 'moral colour' to the prohibited behaviour. Consequently, the cartel offences in France and the UK appear to express the ancillary nature of criminal law and illustrate an 'administrativation' of criminal law.[161]

[155] Whelan, *The Criminalization of European Cartel enforcement* (n 22); MacCulloch (n 137); ME Stucke, 'Morality and antitrust' (2006) (3) *Columbia Business Law Review* 443; C Beaton-Wells, 'Capturing the Criminality of Hard Core Cartels: The Australian Proposal' (2007) 31(3) *Melbourne University Law Review* 675.

[156] Using the work of Stuart Green. See SP Green, *Lying, Cheating, and Stealing. A moral Theory of White-Collar Crime* (Oxford, Oxford University Press, 2006).

[157] MacCulloch (n 137), 87.

[158] Ibid. In French, Italian and also Spanish, Art 101 TFEU refers to 'the game of competition': 'jeu de la concurrence', 'il gioco della concorrenza' and 'el juego de la competencia'.

[159] On the implication of the terms used, see M-P Lucas De Leyssac and C Lucas De Leyssac, 'L'inquiétant article L. 420-6 du Code de Commerce et comment se rassurer' in F Alt-Maes, J-F Barbieri and P Bonfils (eds), *Les droits et le Droit. Mélanges dédiés à Bernard Bouloc* (Paris, Dalloz-Sirey, 2006) 651.

[160] Arts L.420-1, L.420-2 and L.420-2-2 of the Code de commerce. This cross-reference questions the respect of the principle of legality.

[161] Baratta, 'Les Fonctions Instrumentales' (n 154), 10.

(ii) Criminalisation Justified by the Consequences of the Sanction

The use of criminal law sanctions as an effective instrument serving competition policy has been widespread in the US. Indeed, the Antitrust Division of the Department of Justice has adopted an unequivocal position about the deterrent effect of criminal sanctions: 'the most effective way to deter and punish cartel activity is to hold culpable individuals accountable by seeking jail sentences'.[162] The US has encouraged the use of criminal sanctions against cartels within the OECD[163] and the International Competition Network (ICN).[164] The arguments based on deterrence have seduced some other legislators. Indeed, when the UK adopted the cartel offence, the main objective of the reform was to achieve deterrence through individual criminal sanctions.[165]

Deterrence is not a new justification for criminal law sanctions. Major European theorists of the Enlightenment, such as Cesare Beccaria and Jeremy Bentham, contributed to the renewal of criminal law by assigning to criminal sentences a consequentialist or utilitarian approach: the sanction has a preventative objective. The penalty aims at ensuring that potential offenders are deterred from committing an act which constitutes an offence. To that end, the legislator attributes a cost (jail, fines) to the commission of an act at a level where the cost exceeds the benefits obtained from the act. This relies on the assumption that individuals are rational and consequently that the threat of sanction should be enough to deter them.[166] More recently, law and economics authors have applied economic concepts to fields such as criminal law, which has given a new momentum to deterrence through criminal sanctions.[167] They influenced greatly the arguments in favour of jail sentences for cartel members. Their reasoning aims at demonstrating that the level of the fines imposed on corporate entities has been too low to deter cartel members.[168] In order to give the fines a deterrent effect, it could be possible to increase the probability of being detected and/or the amount of the fine. However, the harm done by cartels is so great and the probability of being detected so

[162] SD Hammond, 'The Evolution Of Criminal Antitrust Enforcement Over The Last Two Decades', Speech at *24th Annual National Institute On White Collar Crime*, 25 February 2010, Miami, Florida.

[163] The US influence in the writing of the OECD recommendation of 1998 seems clear, C Harding, 'Business collusion as a criminological phenomenon: exploring the global criminalisation of business cartels' (2006) 14(2) *Critical Criminology* 181, 196–97.

[164] Beaton-Wells and Ezrachi, *Criminalising Cartels* (n 48), 4–5.

[165] J Joshua, 'Shooting the Messenger: Does the UK Criminal Cartel Offense Have a Future?' (August 2010) *The Antitrust Source*; M Furse, *The criminal law of competition in the UK and in the US. Failure and success* (Camberley, Edward Elgar Publishing, 2012), 107. The UK Competition and Markets Authority has stated that: '[t]he criminal cartel offence was created by the EA02 (Enterprise Act 2002) with the intention of criminalising and deterring behaviour by individuals leading to the most serious and damaging forms of anti-competitive agreements, namely "hardcore cartels"', CMA, *Cartel Offence Prosecution Guidance*, March 2014, 3.

[166] E Gilardeau, *A l'aube du droit pénal utilitaire* (Paris, L'Harmattan, 2011); F Bonnet, 'De l'analyse économique du crime aux nouvelles criminologies anglo-saxonnes? Les origines des politiques pénales contemporaines' (2006) 30(2) *Déviance et société* 137.

[167] GS Becker, 'Crime and Punishment: An Economic Approach' (1968) 76(2) *Journal of Political Economy* 169.

[168] E Combe and C Monnier, 'Fines against Hard Core Cartels in Europe: The Myth of Overenforcement' (2011) 56 *The Antitrust Bulletin* 235, 267; MP Schinkel, 'Effective Cartel Enforcement in Europe', *Amsterdam Center for Law & Economics Working Paper No. 2006-14*; JM Connor and DJ Miller, 'Determinants of EC Antitrust Fines for Members of Global Cartels', (2013) wwwpapers.ssrn.com.

slight that the optimal fine would be beyond the ability of cartel members to pay.[169] It would have harmful consequences for the undertaking (risk of bankruptcy) and great social cost (for the employees, shareholders, customers, suppliers etc). Consequently, to avoid the effects resulting from large fines, it is argued that the penalty should involve the threat of imprisonment aimed at the individuals responsible who do not care about fines imposed on enterprises.[170] This economic reasoning has had a great effect on the arguments developed in the legal literature,[171] by governments (particularly the US)[172] as well as by the OECD[173] and the ICN.[174] Consequently, deterrence is the key underlying rationale for cartel criminalisation. It influenced the UK legislator, as shown by the genesis of the cartel offence in the UK, but also played a role in the retention in French legislation of the criminal offence sanctioning individuals involved in anticompetitive practices.[175]

Under this approach, criminal law is not aimed primarily at prohibiting and sanctioning a particular serious act (as examined above) but aims more at deterring its commission in the first place and in doing so it has to be efficient. It is a justification based on *performance*[176] which takes place in the 'Preventive State' dominated by a consequentialist mode of reasoning.[177] This type of justification raises many important questions.

First, it is difficult to assess with any precision what deterrent effect the threat of imprisonment can have upon individuals involved in cartels. Already, the elements for calculating the optimal fine are subject to debate and a source of contention.[178] The variables, such as the probability of detection, can be difficult to determine precisely.[179] Consequently, the anticipation of the costs and benefits and the risk of

[169] Wardhaugh (n 132), 95–97; Whelan (n 22), 52–53; GJ Werden and MJ Simon, 'Why Price Fixers should go to Prison' (Winter 1987) *The Antitrust Bulletin* 917.

[170] AM Polinsky and S Shavell, 'Should Employees Be Subject to Fines and Imprisonment Given the Existence of Corporate Liability?' (1993) 13(3) *International Review of Law and Economics* 239.

[171] See, eg, Wils (n 118).

[172] See the contribution of the US to the policy roundtable: OECD, 'Cartels: Sanctions against Individuals' Policy roundtables 2003, 99 ff.

[173] Ibid.

[174] ICN, *Defining Hard Core Cartel Conduct Effective Institutions Effective Penalties. Building Blocks for Effective Anti-Cartel Regimes* (Luxembourg, Office for Official Publications of the European Communities, 2005), Volume I.

[175] The so-called Coulon Report found that the criminal sanction against individuals should be maintained because '[l]a sanction pénale conserve ainsi un effet plus dissuasif à l'égard des personnes tentées de s'affranchir des règles de concurrence': *Rapport au garde des Sceaux, Ministre de la Justice, La dépénalisation de la vie des affaires, Groupe de travail présidé par Jean-Marie Coulon, Premier président honoraire de la cour d'appel de Paris* (Paris, 2008).

[176] Even if not specifically for criminal law, see François Ost and the concept of 'légitimation par la performance ou l'efficience', F Ost, 'La légitimité dans le discours juridique: cohérence, performance, consensus ou dissensus?' in F Ost and M Van De Kerchove (eds), *Jalons pour une théorie critique du droit* (Brussels, Publications des Facultés universitaires Saint-Louis, 1987), 179.

[177] A Ashworth and L Zedner, 'Defending the Criminal Law: Reflections on the Changing Character of Crime, Procedure, and Sanctions' (2008) 2(1) *Criminal Law and Philosophie* 21, 40.

[178] F Jenny, 'L'articulation des sanctions en matière de droit de la concurrence du point de vue économique', Colloque – Les sanctions du droit de la concurrence (2013) (1) *Concurrences* 1, 3.

[179] ICN, *Defining Hard Core Cartel Conduct* (2005) 74; K Yeung, *Securing Compliance, A Principled Approach* (Oxford, Hart Publishing, 2004) 72.

sanction in engaging in a cartel do not seem easy to assess, even for a rational individual. Moreover, the individual's rationality – on which the deterrence model is based – is questionable. This is even the case in cartels, which is a field belonging to white-collar crime where the rationality of the individual has often been considered as self-evident. Indeed, the decision-making process can be based on costs and gains but it is also influenced by other factors (sociological, psychological, situational) and depends on the individual's perception of the risks.[180] Therefore, the rationality of an individual is a notion that has to be put in perspective. In addition, scientific evidence of the effects of criminal sanctions, upon which preventative criminal law is based, is lacking.[181] A reliable empirical study has questioned the deterrent potential of criminal sanctions in cartel cases, since the pre-conditions for deterrence (namely, the knowledge of the law and its sanctions and the perception of likelihood of detection and prosecution) are difficult to assume.[182] The lack of evidence of the deterrent effect of criminal sanctions is an observation transcending the field of cartels[183] (but this has not stopped the proponents of deterrence from relying upon the 'self-evident' character of the deterrent effect).[184]

Second, the preventative use of criminal law can lead to a disconnection with traditional criminal principles. In itself, prevention through criminal law is not problematic. Indeed, with the legal theory of the social contract, the citizens conferred upon the state the duty to guarantee their security and protect their property. They have a legitimate right to be protected by the state even when the harm is merely potential. Thus, John Stuart Mill justified state intervention where the violation is current but also where there is a 'risk of damage'.[185] However, he was aware of the dangers threatening individual liberties and the necessity of limiting state intervention.[186] The state does not benefit from 'a *carte blanche* to exercise coercive powers in pursuit of its preventive function'.[187] Those limits to state powers are expressed in the principles governing criminal law.

The cartel offence in the UK illustrates the influence of prevention in the evolution of the offence in order to achieve a greater deterrent effect. The Enterprise Act 2002 required a specific notion in the moral element of the offence: the individual had to act dishonestly. This is a well-known legal notion in UK law that can be found in

[180] C Beaton-Wells and C Parker, 'Justifying Criminal Sanctions for Cartel Conduct: a Hard Case', (2013) 1(1) *Journal of Antitrust Enforcement* 198; C Parker, 'Criminal Cartel Sanctions and Compliance: the Gap between Rhetoric and Reality' in Beaton-Wells and Ezrachi (n 48) 239; C Parker, 'War on Cartels and the Social Meaning of Deterrence' (2013) 7(2) *Regulation and Governance* 174; ME Stucke, 'Am I a Price Fixer? A Behavioural Economics Analysis of Cartels' in Beaton-Wells and Ezrachi (n 48).

[181] P-A Albrecht, 'La politique criminelle dans l'Etat de prévention' (1997) 21(2) *Déviance et société* 123, 131.

[182] See the Cartel Project conducted in Australia at the University of Melbourne, Beaton-Wells and Parker, 'Justifying Criminal Sanctions' (n 180).

[183] Baratta (n 154), 14.

[184] 'Systematic empirical evidence to prove the deterrent effects of sanctions on individuals, and/ or to assess in a cost/benefit analysis whether such sanctions can be justified, is not available. Ultimately, countries have to consider whether they accept as self evident that individual sanctions, including imprisonment, can be a useful part of effective anti-cartel enforcement. There is a trend among OECD member countries to accept that view.': OECD, 'Cartels: sanctions against individuals (Policy roundtables 2003)', 7.

[185] A Ashworth and L Zedner, *Preventive Justice* (Oxford, Oxford University Press, 2014), 42.

[186] Ibid, 42–43.

[187] Ibid, 8.

the Theft Act 1968.[188] The concept was introduced in order to signal the seriousness of the practice.[189] However, the notion of dishonesty has been viewed as not being appropriate for cartel offences and liable to impede cartel prosecutions because of the difficulties for a jury to characterise the idea in cartel cases.[190] Consequently, the dishonesty element of the offence was removed from section 188 of the Enterprise Act on 1 April 2014. The justification given by the UK government was the need to improve enforceability and increase deterrence.[191] Consequently, the mental element of the offence is seriously diminished. The current offence is thereby mainly based on the material element: the offence does not require a specific mens rea anymore (and applies unless an exclusion or a defence stated in the law applies).[192] This is something which can be heavily criticised given the severity of the sanctions involved (a jail sentence).

Another influence of preventative criminal law lies in the possibility to sanction cartel behaviour that has not produced any harmful effects. It should be recalled that evidence of actual harm is not required for the commission of the infringement, as the cartel infringement is generally a 'by object' restriction under its administrative enforcement. There is a presumption that such an infringement produces anticompetitive effects.[193] The criminal offences under UK and French law do not mention the harm caused by a cartel as an element of the offence. It is possible, therefore, to sanction behaviour that has not caused any harm. Thus, under French law, a preparatory phase of the offence ('conception, organisation') could be sanctioned even if the anticompetitive practice is not implemented.[194] Similarly, under UK law, the offence does not require the arrangements to be implemented. It has been named an inchoate offence.[195] Consequently, as mentioned above, the principle of culpability (*nullum crimen, nulla peona sine culpa*) is weakened by the reduction of the moral element of the offence and also by the possible absence of any harm actually being caused by the infringing conduct.

[188] On the dishonesty test, see A MacCulloch, 'Honesty, Morality and the Cartel Offence' (2007) 28(6) *European Competition Law Review* 355, 356–58.

[189] A Stephan, 'How Dishonesty killed the Cartel Offence' (2011) 6 *The Criminal Law Review* 446, 447. See, Sir A Hammond and R Penrose, 'Proposed Criminalisation of Cartels in the UK – A Report prepared for the Office of Fair Trading' (OFT 365), November 2001, at section 2.5.

[190] A Stephan, 'The UK Cartel Offence: Farewell Dishonesty …', *Competition Policy Blog* (2012), www.competitionpolicy.wordpress.com. See also P Gilbert, 'Changes to the UK Cartel Offence – Be Careful What You Wish For' (2015) 6(3) *Journal of European Competition Law & Practice* 192.

[191] Department of Business Innovation and Skills (BIS), 'Growth, Competition and The Competition Regime: Government Response to Consultation', March 2012, at section 7.7.

[192] Jones and Williams, 'The UK Response' (n 133), 117.

[193] See the comparison between infringements of competition by object and risk offences: 'the prohibition on "infringements of competition by object" resulting from Article 81(1) EC is comparable to the risk offences (*Gefährdungsdelikte*) known in criminal law: in most legal systems, a person who drives a vehicle when significantly under the influence of alcohol or drugs is liable to a criminal or administrative penalty, wholly irrespective of whether, in fact, he endangered another road user or was even responsible for an accident. In the same vein, undertakings infringe European competition law and may be subject to a fine if they engage in concerted practices with an anti-competitive object; whether in an individual case, in fact, particular market participants or the general public suffer harm is irrelevant.': Opinion of Advocate General Kokott in Case C-8/08 *T-Mobile Netherlands BV* EU:C:2009:110, para 47.

[194] Lucas De Leyssac and Lucas De Leyssac, 'L'inquiétant article L. 420-6' (n 159), 658–59.

[195] Gilbert, 'Changes to the UK Cartel Offence' (n 190). See also, R Williams, 'Cartels in the criminal law landscape' in Beaton-Wells and Ezrachi (n 48), 303–04.

Another instrumentalist use of criminal law can be highlighted by its application for educative means. It has been shown previously that the identification of the moral wrongfulness of cartel behaviour can be found in the legal literature, but it is not obvious that the public perceives cartel conduct as inherently criminal and deserving of jail sentences.[196] Indeed, even if the public seems to regard cartels as wrong, even dishonest and deserving of individual sanctions, the support for imprisonment appears to be weak.[197] When it is not certain that an offence is *mala in se* or is not perceived by everyone as deserving the criminal qualification, the educational dimension of criminal law is often highlighted. However, if cartel behaviour is considered as morally neutral (*mala prohibita*), compliance with the law is less likely because people may not agree with the law and may not consider its enforcement as legitimate and fair.[198] In this way, criminal law is used not to express an existing and generally accepted prohibition but to create a consensus around a prohibited behaviour.[199] To fulfil this educational role, it has been affirmed that the criminal offence has to be enforced in order to raise awareness and create consensus within society.[200] However, recent empirical findings on cartels suggest that enforcement is of limited effect.[201] The instrumental use of criminal law can be criticised since compliance based on the fear of being sanctioned rather than on agreement with the law is not optimal and could be a sign of a malfunctioning society.[202]

IV. Conclusion

Cartel enforcement illustrates the interaction between administrative and criminal enforcement. Indeed, administrative enforcement of the cartel prohibition has become a quasi-criminal form of enforcement due to its severity, the coercive nature of the procedure and the inclusion of a moral feature. Consequently, the procedural protection afforded to undertakings involved in administrative enforcement has been raised to almost reach that existing in criminal proceedings. This contributes to the confusion of the traditional boundaries separating administrative law and criminal law. It raises the question as to whether, in the hierarchy of the 'odious',[203] criminal law is still the most severe or intrusive branch of law.

[196] Beaton-Wells and Parker (n 180).

[197] A Stephan, 'An Empirical Evaluation of the Normative Justifications for Cartel Criminalisation', (2017) 37(4) *Legal Studies* 621, 641; Opinion Poll for the Autorité de la Concurrence, '*L'Opinion des Français sur les cartels*' (2018).

[198] Parker, 'Criminal Cartel Sanctions and Compliance' (n 180), 257.

[199] JC Coffee, 'Does "unlawful" mean "criminal"?: Reflections on the Disappearing Tort/Crime Distinction in American Law' (1991) 71 *Boston University Law Review* 193, 223; JC Coffee, 'Paradigms Lost: The Blurring of the Criminal and Civil Law Models. And What Can Be Done about It' (1992) 101(8) *The Yale Law Journal* 1875, 1889; HV Ball and LM Friedman, 'The Use of Criminal Sanctions in the Enforcement of Economic Legislation: A Sociological View' (1965) 17(2) *Stanford Law Review* 197.

[200] Stephan, 'Why Morality should be Excluded' (n 145), 137.

[201] Stephan, 'An Empirical Evaluation' (n 197), 640.

[202] Harding and Edwards, *Cartel Criminality* (n 135), 237.

[203] See the observation on a muddling of the relationship between criminal and administrative sanctions under the influence of the ECtHR leading to the creation of a 'singulier brouillage des repères traditionnels dans la hiérarchie de l'"odieux"': M Van De Kerchove, 'Le principe de subsidiarité' in G Giudicelli-Delage and C Lazerges (eds), *Le droit pénal de l'Union européenne au lendemain du traité de Lisbonne* (Paris, Société de législation comparée, 2012), 33.

It can be also queried how this situation impacts the principle of the subsidiarity of criminal law. Indeed, the severity of the quasi-criminal enforcement of the cartel prohibition contributes to increasing awareness about the harmful nature of cartels but also confers upon the behaviour the attributes of criminal actions before even examining the justification in criminal terms. The recent criminalisation wave, dominated by arguments based on the deterrent effect or instrumental legitimation, seems to confirm the need to treat cartels as criminal. As a consequence, cartel behaviour is deemed a criminal offence submitted to an administrative enforcement, which consequently seems inappropriate.

As explained above, the justification based on the deterrent effect of criminal law can be questioned since the preventative approach of criminal law puts the respect of traditional criminal law principles at risk, such as the principle of culpability, and has lowered the requirements for the moral element of the offence, as is illustrated by the developments in UK law. As a consequence, the cartel offence is closer to the administrative infringement in decreasing the importance of the intent behind the actions concerned. The retributive justification for the use of criminal law deserves more attention and, with it, the issue of the criminal liability of the persons involved. Indeed, considering the complex functioning of cartels and the harm caused by them, formulating an offence that fairly targets the participant's actions causing the harm would certainly appear challenging for legislators but necessary in order to legitimise the use of criminal law.

11

Protection of Procedural Rights in Administrative and Criminal Proceedings: The Case of the Privilege against Self-incrimination in Belgian Customs Law

ANA LAURA CLAES AND MARIE HORSEELE

I. Introduction

This chapter focuses on the interplay between Belgian customs law and the privilege against self-incrimination (or *nemo tenetur*).[1] The first section will give an overview of the current legal framework of Belgian customs proceedings. Belgian customs law is characterised by a hybrid system of enforcement. The customs authorities are competent to conduct both administrative and criminal proceedings. The customs officials thus wear two hats. As a consequence, the pivotal point where the administrative proceedings become criminal is hard to determine. Moreover, the customs authorities can rely on the same set of investigative powers in either situation. These investigative powers are very broad and characterised by their repressive nature, often lacking sufficient procedural safeguards to protect the fundamental rights of the person who is subject to the proceedings.

One fundamental right that might clash with the Belgian customs proceedings is the privilege against self-incrimination. We will analyse this fundamental right in light of the case law of the European Court of Human Rights (ECtHR) as well as the case law of the Belgian Supreme Court (the Court of Cassation). For this analysis, we will apply the step-by-step reasoning of the ECtHR.

[1] This contribution is in part based on the findings of a Dutch article, which has not yet been published: AL Claes and M Horseele, 'Finding nemo (tenetur) – Een stand van zaken en de toepassing in het douanerecht' [2021] 16 *Nullum Crimen* (forthcoming).

The privilege against self-incrimination is particularly relevant for the Belgian customs proceedings with regard to its scope *ratione temporis* and *ratione materiae*. Firstly, due to the hybrid system, it is not clear when the privilege comes into play. Following the ECtHR case law, even certain administrative customs proceedings might be considered criminal, and thus have to abide by the privilege against self-incrimination. Within Belgian customs law, the classic distinction between '*criminal*' and '*non-criminal*' enforcement in this way becomes even more blurred.

Secondly, the case law of the ECtHR and the Belgian Court of Cassation leave room for a lot of debate on the scope *ratione materiae* of the privilege. Since customs proceedings rely to a large extent on the obligation for the taxpayer to cooperate and provide certain documents, the interpretation of the ECtHR and the Belgian Court of Cassation of what kind of evidence falls under the protection of *nemo tenetur* becomes important.

In the subsequent analysis of *nemo tenetur*, we will, with each step, infer conclusions about the part this principle plays in Belgian customs proceedings.

II. Customs' Legislative Framework

A. Europe

The 27 Member States[2] of the European Union constitute the EU Customs Union,[3] which is essentially created for the functioning of the single market. The latter can indeed not function properly without common rules at its external borders. To achieve this goal, national customs authorities act as if they were one.[4] The Union Customs Code (UCC)[5] provides for a comprehensive framework of rules and procedures applicable to trade in goods between the EU and third countries (non-Member States).[6]

[2] Since the UK left the EU.

[3] K Celis and J Verbeken, *Douane en accijnzen toegepast* (Antwerp, Intersentia, 2018) 5.

[4] European Commission, 'EU Customs Strategy': https://ec.europa.eu/taxation_customs/general-information-customs/eu-customs-strategy_en (accessed 20 December 2019).

[5] Adopted by Regulation (EU) 952/2013 laying down the Union Customs Code [2013] OJ L269/1. Amended by Regulation (EU) 2016/2339 amending Regulation (EU) No 952/2013 laying down the Union Customs Code, as regards goods that have temporarily left the customs territory of the Union by sea or air [2016] OJ L354/32; Regulation (EU) 2019/474 amending Regulation (EU) No 952/2013 laying down the Union Customs Code [2019] OJ L83/38; and Regulation (EU) 2019/632 amending Regulation (EU) No 952/2013 to prolong the transitional use of means other than the electronic data-processing techniques provided for in the Union Customs Code [2019] OJ L111/54. The UCC was further supplemented by the UCC Delegated Act, adopted on 28 July 2015 by Regulation (EU) 2015/2446 supplementing Regulation (EU) No 952/2013 of the European Parliament and of the Council as regards detailed rules concerning certain provisions of the Union Customs Code [2015] OJ L343/1.
The UCC Implementing Act, adopted on 24 November 2015 by the Commission Implementing Regulation (EU) 2015/2447 laying down detailed rules for implementing certain provisions of Regulation (EU) No 952/2013 of the European Parliament and of the Council laying down the Union Customs Code [2015] OJ L343/558, aims to ensure that all Member States implement the UCC uniform and apply the procedures in a harmonised way. The UCC Work Programme, adopted by Commission Implementing Decision (EU) 2016/578 establishing the Work Programme relating to the development and deployment of the electronic systems provided for in the Union Customs Code [2016] OJ L99/6, regards the electronic systems provided for in the UCC, that are laid down in the Implementing Regulation on technical arrangements relating to the UCC electronic systems.

[6] Celis and Verbeken (n 3) 14.

The UCC itself does not provide for a European enforcement system but obliges Member States to ensure that infringements of the UCC are sanctioned. Article 42 UCC prescribes that 'each Member State shall provide for penalties for failure to comply with the customs legislation. Such penalties shall be effective, proportionate and dissuasive'.[7] That Article also stipulates that administrative penalties can take the form of a pecuniary charge (including settlements that replace a criminal penalty) or the revocation, suspension or amendment of authorisations held by the person concerned. Apart from sanctions, Article 46 UCC provides that customs authorities can carry out any inspection measure that they deem necessary. A non-exhaustive list of possible measures is given, including inspecting goods, vehicles and luggage, taking samples, verifying the accuracy and completeness of information in a declaration, verifying the existence, authenticity and correctness of documents, and inspecting the accounts and other records.

The UCC does not contain any other provision on (administrative or criminal) enforcement, leaving this matter in the hands of the Member States.[8] Nevertheless, this enforcement power may only be exercised in compliance with Union law and its general principles. The CJEU will monitor whether the sanctions are 'effective, proportionate and dissuasive' (Article 42 UCC),[9] and whether the general principles, such as the legality principle, are respected.[10] Moreover, the Member States are held financially responsible for the collection of the customs duties, and thus for adequate enforcement.[11] National customs administrations thus play a key role in managing this liability of Member States towards the EU.

[7] The obligation for Member States to enforce EU law in general can also be found in Article 4.2 of the Treaty on the Functioning of the European Union (TFEU) which states that 'the Member States shall take any appropriate measure, general or particular, to ensure fulfilment of the obligations arising out of the Treaties or resulting from the acts of the institutions of the Union'. E Van Dooren, 'De bijzondere plaats van het Openbaar Ministerie in het Belgische douanestrafprocesrecht' in F Desterbeck (ed), *Het douanestrafrecht vandaag/Le droit pénal douanier aujourd'hui* (Brussels, Larcier, 2016) 45, 45.

[8] The Court of Justice of the European Union (CJEU) has reiterated on a number of occasions that, in the absence of harmonised European legislation on customs infringements, the Member States remain competent to determine the sanctions that they deem appropriate. See Case C-273/90 *Meico-Fell v Hauptzollamt Darmstadt* [1991] ECR I-05569. It should be noted, however, that the EU has taken certain steps towards EU-wide enforcement tools, with instruments like the European Investigation Order, the European Public Prosecutor's Office, and the European Anti-Fraud Office (OLAF). These instruments, although not specifically directed at customs law, may entail important consequences for the national enforcement mechanisms in customs law. However, they do not form part of this analysis.

[9] Case C-91/02 *Hannl & Hofstetter Internationale Spedition GmbH v Finanzlandesdirektion für Wien, Niederösterreich und Burgenland* [2003] ECR I-12077; Case C-213/99 *De Andrade v Director da Alfândega de Leixões* [2000] ECR I-11083; Case C-36/94, *Siesse – Solucoes Integrais em Sistemas Software e Aplicacoes Ltd v Director da Alfandega de Alcantara* [1995] ECR I-03573.

[10] Case C-546/09 *Aurubis Balgaria AD v Nachalnik na Mitnitsa Stolichna* [2011] ECR I-02531.

[11] Council Decision (EU, Euratom) 2020/2053 of 14 December 2020 on the system of own resources of the European Union and repealing Decision 2014/335/EU [2020] OJ L424/1, Art 9(1) provides that the Member State must transfer the customs duties to the EU. This obligation is further elaborated on in the Council Regulation (EU, Euratom) 2021/768 of 30 April 2021 laying down implementing measures for the system of own resources of the European Union and repealing Regulation (EU, Euratom) No 608/2014 [2021] OJ L165/1. If a Member State fails to comply with this obligation, it is obliged to reimburse the EU budget for the loss. In that case, the Commission can proceed under the infringement procedure laid down in the TFEU, Art 258. This is an objective procedure, meaning that the failure to comply with an obligation under European Union Law constitutes in itself a breach of law. Subjective elements such as negligence or error of assessment do not matter. At the same time, a sufficiently serious breach is required. The Member State must have manifestly

Of course, this does not alter the fact that the enforcement systems that Member States consider adequate can differ significantly. Within the European customs territory, an identical infringement of the customs legislation can be sanctioned in different ways. A distinction can be made not only with regard to the nature and the severity of the sanctions, but also with regard to the authority competent for sanctioning and the rules of procedure.[12]

The Belgian legislator has chosen to give preference to criminal enforcement of customs law.[13] The procedural provisions are of a particularly repressive nature. Moreover, the legislator indicated the customs administration as the competent authority to conduct this criminal enforcement. Customs officials thus wear two hats, namely one to carry out administrative proceedings and one to carry out criminal proceedings, depending on the case.

From a European comparative law perspective, this approach appears quite exceptional.[14] Most of the other Member States chose to keep the competences of the customs administration purely administrative. In the Netherlands, for example, only the public prosecutor's office is competent to actually criminally prosecute customs offences.[15] As far as we know, only Luxembourg has the same kind of hybrid system where customs authorities conduct both administrative and criminal proceedings. This comes as no surprise, because the law that governs this procedure is the same for Belgium and Luxembourg.[16] In the following subsection, an introduction to this unique enforcement system is provided.

B. Belgium

The Belgian customs enforcement system is mainly regulated in the General Law on Customs and Excise of 18 July 1977 (GLCE[17]). This law has its origins in legislation from 1822[18] and most of its provisions thus date back to the nineteenth century.[19]

and gravely exceeded the limits of its discretion. See the Opinion of Advocate General M Bobek of 6 February 2019 in Case C-391/17 *Commission v United Kingdom*, EU:C:2019:97. For more general information, see European Commission, 'Traditional Own Resources': https://ec.europa.eu/info/about-european-commission/eu-budget/revenue/own-resources/duties-and-levies_en (accessed 20 December 2019). P Van Nuffel and K Lenaerts, *Europees recht*, 6th edn (Antwerp, Intersentia, 2017) 654–60.

[12] E Van Dooren (n 7) 46.

[13] Nevertheless, a limited number of administrative sanctions are also available. See for example: General Law on Customs and Excise of 18 July 1977, *Moniteur Belge* 21 September 1977, 11.476, Art 266-2.

[14] E Van Dooren (n 7) 49.

[15] Note that this system also has its own problems. In the Netherlands, for example, customs officials cannot prosecute, but they do have a lot of investigative powers and can impose an out-of-court settlement ('*strafbeschikking*') which is criminal in nature (with the possibility to oppose the decision before the public prosecutor's office). As a consequence, it will also not always be clear when the administrative proceedings stop and the intention to impose a (criminal law) settlement or to transfer the case to the public prosecutor starts. See the General Customs law of the Netherlands of 3 April 2008, *Stb.* 2008, 111, chapter 10–11 *juncto* General Administrative Act of 4 June 1992, *Stb.* 1992, 315, art 5:44; Protocol of 1 July 2015 on the registration and settlement of tax offences and offences in the field of customs and surcharges, *Stcrt.* 2015, 17271.

[16] Act of 5 March 1922 approving the treaty of 25 July 1921 on the establishment of a Belgian-Luxembourgish Economic Union, *Moniteur Belge* 11 March 1922, 2.153.

[17] General Law on Customs and Excise of 18 July 1977, *Moniteur Belge* 21 September 1977, 11.476.

[18] General Law on Customs and Excise of 26 August 1822, *Stb.* 1822, 38.

[19] E Van Dooren, 'Modernisering door ongrondwettelijkheid. Effecten van constitutionele schendingen in de Belgische douanewetgeving' in J Rozie, F Deruyck, L Huybrechts and F Van Volsem (eds), *Na rijp beraad. Liber amicorum Michel Rozie* (Antwerp, Intersentia, 2016) 461, 461–62.

As indicated, the legislator focused on criminal enforcement. The idea was that customs fraud could generate enormous profits and that the chance of being caught was rather small. Offenders thus had to be treated ruthlessly and the customs administration needed considerable room for manoeuvre.[20] These ideas still dominate the current enforcement system that can be summarised in four main points:

(a) Any infringement constitutes a criminal offence;
(b) The customs officials wear two hats (administrative – criminal);
(c) The customs officials are vested with far-reaching investigative powers;
(d) The criminal procedure derogates to a large extent from general criminal law.

(i) Any Infringement Constitutes a Criminal Offence

First of all, every infringement of customs law constitutes a criminal offence. Customs law is packed with obligations to declare goods, provide documents or pay a certain amount of duties by a specified date. Failing to meet one of these obligations is criminally punishable either under the provision of a specific offence with a specific criminal penalty or, if no specific offence applies to the behaviour in question, under the so-called ancillary *catch-all* provision that criminally punishes any infringement of the customs law with a fine of 125–1,250 EUR[21] and a confiscation.[22] Examples of customs offences are: fraud relating to the movement of goods (smuggling),[23] failing to comply with transit requirements,[24] breach of seal,[25] supplying or using forged documents and declarations,[26] fraud relating to the quantity or nature of the goods,[27] and fraud committed with the aim of obtaining a preferential tax regime.[28]

(ii) Customs Officials Wear Two Hats

Secondly, as indicated, it is up to the General Administration of Customs and Excise (GACE[29]), as part of the Federal Public Service of Finance, to investigate and prosecute these offences.[30] This is an exception to the general rules of criminal procedure, where

[20] Ibid, 462.

[21] Due to inflation, Belgian criminal law currently has a rule to multiply all fines by 8. Criminal Fines Act of 5 March 1952, *Moniteur Belge* 3 April 1952.

[22] GLCE, Art 261.

[23] Ibid, Arts 220, 222 and 226–227.

[24] Ibid, Art 114.

[25] Ibid, Art 165.

[26] Ibid, Arts 259–260.

[27] Ibid, Arts 233, 234 and 236–237.

[28] Ibid, Art 256. It should be noted that Directive (EU) 2017/1371 on the fight against fraud to the Union's financial interests by means of criminal law [2017] OJ L198/29 has obliged the Belgian legislator to change some of the provisions of the GLCE regarding the offences and their penalties. The changes concern the following topics: the mens rea element, the criminal liability for attempt, and (higher) prison sentences. See the Law of 9 December 2019 amending the General Law on Customs and Excise of 18 July 1977 and the Value Added Tax Code transposing Directive (EU) 2017/1371, *Moniteur Belge* 18 December 2019.

[29] Abbreviation of the French term '*Administration générale des Douanes et Accises*'. In Dutch: '*Algemene Administratie der Douane en Accijnzen*'.

[30] GLCE Art 281 para 2; Belgian Court of Cassation, 26 November 1996, no P.95.0698.N; Belgian Court of Cassation, 11 March 1997, no P.96.0223.N; R Verstraeten, *Handboek Strafvordering* (Antwerp, Maklu, 2012) 87; E Van Dooren (n 7) 47.

investigative and prosecution powers normally fall within the competences of the public prosecutor's office. The GACE is therefore not only responsible for the administrative monitoring and sanctioning, but also for most of the criminal enforcement of customs law. Belgian customs law thus contains two types of enforcement procedures but only one authority to carry them out.

Generally, the GACE brings the case before a criminal judge. The recovery of customs duties is less likely to be brought before a civil court.[31] The problem, however, lies in that fact that GLCE does not make a clear distinction between the competences of the GACE in administrative or in criminal investigations. The pivotal point between the two types of proceedings in the pre-trial phase is hard to determine. As we will explain in this chapter, one of the consequences is that it is very difficult to determine when the right not to incriminate oneself will apply. The GACE might argue that it was wearing its '*administrative hat*', while in fact, it already planned on prosecuting.

There is one exception to the enforcement monopoly of the GACE, namely the competence to request a prison sentence. The legislator has determined that only the public prosecutor can file for a custodial sentence. The GACE can only seek the application of the non-custodial criminal sanctions enumerated by the GLCE, ie a fine, confiscation, the closure of an establishment, and professional disqualification.[32]

As a consequence of the prison sentence exception and the fact that the GACE is only competent to prosecute customs offences, a special interaction arises between the GACE and the public prosecutor's office. Different scenarios might arise:

- If the facts of the case constitute a customs offence that is only punishable by the enumerated non-custodial sanctions, only the GACE can prosecute.[33]
- If the customs offence is punishable with a prison sentence, only the public prosecutor can request it. The offence then leads to two different claims: one from the prosecutor and one from the GACE.[34]
- If the facts constitute a concurrence of offences, including a customs offence and a general criminal law offence (eg, cigarette smuggling by a criminal organisation), then the public prosecutor has the competence to bring the general criminal law offence before a criminal court, regardless of the intention of the GACE, and vice versa.[35] If both authorities bring their case before the court at the same time, the cases may be joined for the purposes of the proper administration of justice.[36]

[31] E Van Dooren, 'Iteratieve knelpunten van douane- en accijnsstrafrecht' in M Rozie (ed), *Actuele problemen van het fiscaal strafrecht* (Antwerp, Intersentia, 2011) 465, 465.

[32] Ibid, Art 281 para 2; Royal Decree no 22 of 24 October 1934 on the judicial prohibition of certain convicted persons and bankrupt persons from exercising certain functions, professions or activities, *Moniteur Belge* 27 October 1934, 5.768, Art 1 i); Belgian Court of Cassation 11 February 1997, no P.96.1031.N; E Van Dooren (n 7) 47.

[33] J Speecke, *Fiscaal Compendium – Fiscaal straf- en strafprocesrecht* (Mechelen, Kluwer, 2018) 5.

[34] However, only the GACE has the right to take the initiative to bring the case to court. The claim of the public prosecutor is thus ancillary to the claim of the GACE. GLCE, Art 281 para 3; G Steffens, 'Les diverses compétences des douanes' in F Desterbeck (ed), *Het Douanestrafrecht vandaag/Le droit pénal douanier aujourd'hui* (Brussels, Larcier, 2016) 15, 20; E Van Dooren (n 7) 47–48.

[35] GLCE, Art 282; Belgian Court of Cassation 16 May 2006, no P.06.0080.N; E Van Dooren (n 7) 48 and 52–54.

[36] E Van Dooren (n 7) 51–53.

(iii) Far-reaching Investigative Powers

Thirdly, the GLCE[37] confers a set of far-reaching investigative powers on the GACE, applicable in both administrative and criminal proceedings. The investigative powers include, inter alia: the right to follow goods;[38] the right to request (digital) documents and correspondence;[39] the right to search persons, goods and vehicles;[40] the right to search private or business premises;[41] the right to seize goods and documents;[42] the right to take samples;[43] the right to arrest people,[44] and the right to request all public services for information or documents.[45] Refusing to allow an inspection or a search, refusing to provide documents,[46] or hindering the customs authorities in any way in carrying out their duties is criminally punishable with fines.[47]

These powers are noticeably more extensive than the powers of other tax administrations, and sometimes even broader than the competences of the public prosecutor. A more elaborate analysis of three powers can highlight this special character: the right to search business and private premises (called 'visitation'), the right to request and inspect documents, and the right to seize goods and documents.

The visitation of private premises is subjected to different requirements depending on the circumstances. Within certain areas surrounding airports, harbours and borders, the customs authorities can search private premises without any judicial authorisation.[48] Outside that zone, the visitation of private (domestic) premises does require a judicial authorisation from the police court.[49] However, this authorisation is not needed in case of hot pursuit or if the resident gives permission to enter the premises. The visitation of business premises is always allowed without judicial authorisation (although other safeguards apply). The GLCE therefore allows for several searches without judicial intervention.[50] Moreover, the authorisation of the police court for the search of private premises outside the area surrounding airports, harbours and borders is not comparable to the search warrant provided by an investigating judge in general rules of criminal procedure.[51] The police court takes on a more passive role than the investigating judge and can only refuse to provide the authorisation if it suspects that the customs administration has no substantial reasons to conduct the house search.[52] This does not imply

[37] Together with the Law on Providing the Capacity of Officer of the Judicial Police to the Customs Officials, *Moniteur Belge* 8 May 2003, 2.4910.
[38] GLCE, Arts 175 and 224.
[39] Ibid, Arts 201 and 203.
[40] Ibid, Art 182; J Speecke (n 33) 5.
[41] GLCE Arts 173–175, 189 and 193–197.
[42] Ibid, Arts 221, 222 para 1, 224, 231, and 236–238.
[43] Ibid, Art 206.
[44] Ibid, Arts 247–252.
[45] Ibid, Art 210 para 1.
[46] Ibid, Art 201 para 3.
[47] Ibid, Art 329.
[48] Ibid, Arts 173–175.
[49] Ibid, Art 179.
[50] E Van Dooren, 'Het visitatierecht als onderzoeksmaatregel inzake accijnzen en douanerechten' [2006] 12 *Algemeen Fiscaal Tijdschrift* 18, 29–30.
[51] E Van Dooren, 'Douane & Accijnzen: visitatie' in *Strafrecht en strafvordering. Commentaar met overzicht van rechtspraak en rechtsleer* (Mechelen, Kluwer, 2018) 1, 45.
[52] GLCE, Art 198, para 3; Van Dooren (n 50) 30.

that the police court can only check the legality of the requested investigative measure,[53] but the judicial review remains more limited than in general criminal procedure.[54]

Aside from the visitation of private premises, the right to request and inspect documents is also quite broad.[55] The request can be aimed at anyone involved in the import or export process and applies to all kinds of documents and correspondence, including the accounts and documents kept on a digital device. Depending on the case, the person in question has to hand over the documents to the customs administration[56] or has to allow the administration to inspect them.[57] In the latter case, the customs official can still seize the documents or take a copy of them if they reveal indications of an infringement of the customs legislation.[58]

Adding to the previous measures, the seizure of documents[59] and goods[60] also has specific characteristics in customs law. The measure has a broad scope, applying to documents, transported or stored goods, and vehicles found through other investigative measures such as the visitation or request for documents. Once goods are seized, there is only limited possibility to lift the seizure. Article 275 GLCE provides that the seizure can only be lifted by paying a sum equal to the full value of the seized goods. The possibilities for recovery of seized goods that exist in civil proceedings or ordinary criminal proceedings are not applicable to customs proceedings.[61] On top of this, the owner of the goods is responsible for the costs of the seizure, whether or not he is implicated in the offence.[62]

All three measures can constitute problems when they are compared to the general criminal procedure and when they are analysed in light of fundamental rights (see below II.B.(v).).

It should be noted, however, that, regardless of this elaborate set of investigative measures, the GACE still has to request the help of an investigating judge[63] for some measures that are not included in the set, such as wiretapping. The request goes via the public prosecutor.[64] If a judicial investigation is needed, the investigative judge will then be in charge of the investigation. When the judicial investigation is finished, the case is sent back to the GACE, which will then decide on the consequences (eg, conducting further investigation or bringing the case to court).[65]

[53] Belgian Court of Cassation 27 March 2012, no P.11.1701.N.

[54] E Van Dooren (n 19) 475; A De Nauw, 'Overzicht van douanestrafprocesrecht' [2004–2005] 5 *Rechtskundig Weekblad* 921, 925.

[55] GLCE, Arts 201 and 203.

[56] Ibid, Art 201 para 2.

[57] Ibid, Art 203 para 1.

[58] Ibid, Art 203 para 2.

[59] Ibid, Art 189.

[60] Ibid, Arts 221–222.

[61] A Baert, 'De bevoegdheid van de rechter in kort geding bij aanhaling van goederen door de administratie der douane en accijnzen' [2013] 451 *Tijdschrift voor Fiscaal Recht* 925.

[62] GLCE, Art 275; Belgian Court of Cassation 14 December 2017, no C.17.0192.N; Baert (n 61) 925; E Van Dooren, 'Kostenperikelen bij douanerechtelijke inbeslagnemingen' [2018] 6 *Rechtspraak Antwerpen Brussel Gent* 514.

[63] Who will either start a judicial inquiry or intervene punctually via a mini-judicial inquiry. E Van Dooren (n 7) 58.

[64] GLCE, Art 282 para 2.

[65] E Van Dooren (n 7) 55–58; A Baert and L Gheysens, 'Douane- en accijnsstrafprocesrecht: een overzicht' in L Maes, H De Cnijf and L De Broeck (eds), *Fiscaal Praktijkboek 2013–2014 – Indirecte belastingen* (Mechelen, Kluwer, 2013) 293, 321–22.

(iv) Extensive Derogation from General Criminal Procedure

Fourthly, the GLCE contains multiple rules that deviate from the general rules of Belgian criminal procedure as determined in the Belgian Code of Criminal Procedure (CCP).[66] However, these general rules remain applicable for everything that is not regulated by the GLCE.[67] Apart from the hybrid system and the far-reaching investigating measures, two other examples can further illustrate the special character of the customs procedure.

First of all, the GACE has the competence to reach a settlement with the offender (usually in the form of paying a certain sum or waiving the right to the goods that were seized) in order to avoid prosecution.[68] This so-called 'transaction' is possible not only before legal proceedings are initiated, but also during the trial phase, until a judgment is rendered that has the authority of *res judicata*. A transaction is even possible after the Court of Cassation has overturned a judgment and has sent the case to another court of appeal for retrial.[69] Admittedly, in ordinary criminal proceedings, it is also possible to reach an out-of-court settlement while the case is already pending in court. But this out-of-court settlement is only possible until a first judgment is rendered,[70] since the legislator was of the opinion that the possibility of a settlement after a judgment could undermine the sense of justice because offenders could 'buy off' the conviction rendered by the criminal judge.[71] Moreover, according to the general rules of criminal procedure, the settlement is subjected to full judicial review, in order to make sure that the suspect acts freely with full knowledge and that the deal is not only legally possible, but also proportionate.[72] In our opinion, there is no convincing argument why similar rules should not apply to customs transactions.

The second example is that official reports drawn up by the GACE or documents they have obtained through investigative measures have a special evidentiary value. They are regarded as evidence until proven otherwise.[73] By contrast, under general criminal procedure, this is actually the exception to the rule.[74] The special evidentiary value can have enormous consequences, for example when using the competence to request documents under Articles 201 and 203 GLCE (see above II.B.(iii).). The GACE can request all documents and correspondence from the declarant, the importer, the exporter, the addressee of the goods, and all other stakeholders of the import or export process if it is necessary to check the declaration. If the GACE finds that the documents contain

[66] Code of Criminal Procedure of 17 November 1808, *Bull. Off.* 27 November 1808, 0.

[67] GLCE, Arts 281 paras 1 and 2.

[68] Ibid, Arts 263–264; E Van Dooren, 'Douanerechtelijk transigeren' in P Traest, F Deruyck, M De Swaef, J Rozie and M Rozie (eds), *De Wet Voorbij* (Antwerp, Intersentia, 2010) 495, 497.

[69] GLCE, Arts 263–264; Steffens (n 34) 20; Van Dooren (n 68) 500–501.

[70] CCP, Art 216*bis*.

[71] C Van den Wyngaert, P Traest and S Vandromme (eds), *Strafrecht en strafprocesrecht* (Antwerp, Maklu, 2017) 803.

[72] Belgian Constitutional Court 2 June 2016, no 83/2016.

[73] GLCE, Arts 205 and 272; A Baert, *Douane en accijnzen* (Mechelen, Kluwer 2017) 272–73; S Van Dromme, 'Douanerecht versus algemene beginselen van het strafrecht' in M Cornette (ed), *Douane.be: actuele problemen* (Antwerp, Intersentia, 2006) 75, 132.

[74] Belgian Court of Cassation 26 April 1926, *Pas.* 1926, 350; Belgian Court of Cassation 17 March 1952, *Pas.* 1952, 439.

inconsistent information regarding the purchase and sale of goods that are subjected to customs duties, it can rely on these documents as full proof of the fraud. It is up to the suspect to prove otherwise.[75] The burden of proof is thus reversed in customs criminal proceedings.

(v) Confrontation with General Criminal Procedure: Supreme Courts Favouring Customs Law

Finally, it should be mentioned that the special provisions relating to the investigation and prosecution of customs offences described above have been challenged multiple times for non-compliance with the provisions of general criminal law and with fundamental rights. This is possible via a preliminary ruling before the Belgian Constitutional Court.[76] Through such preliminary rulings, the Constitutional Court has the power to declare legislative acts that infringe upon certain provisions of the Belgian Constitution unconstitutional.[77] One of the constitutional rights is the principle of equality or non-discrimination, as provided by Articles 10 and 11 of the Belgian Constitution. Through this principle, the Constitutional Court is also competent to analyse Belgian legislation in light of the ECHR.

Regarding customs law, the argument presented before the Court was often that the difference in treatment of the suspect during customs proceedings compared to general criminal law proceedings was unjustified and thus constituted discrimination under Articles 10 and 11 of the Constitution. For example, regarding house searches,[78] the argument was raised that by eliminating a proper intervention by a judge, two fundamental rights were violated. On the one hand, the suspect is limited in his defence rights because he is refused access to an impartial investigating judge who searches for evidence *à charge* and *à décharge* (meaning inculpatory and exculpatory evidence). On the other hand, the visitation procedure seems to violate the right to respect for privacy and the home under Article 15 of the Constitution *juncto* Article 8 ECHR. In another preliminary ruling, the applicant had argued that the special evidentiary value of the documents obtained by the GACE, and thus the shift of the burden of proof to the suspect (in contrast with the general criminal procedure), was contrary to the presumption of innocence.[79]

Up until now, however, the Constitutional Court has not followed these arguments. Its rulings regarding customs procedural law have mostly been in favour of the customs authorities.[80] The Court has ruled several times that the differences from the

[75] Belgian Constitutional Court 15 October 2002, *BS* 4 February 2003, 4681; Belgian Court of Cassation 17 October 2001, *Arr.Cass.* 2001, 1700; Antwerpen, 13 February 2002, *Fiscale Actualiteit* 14 November 2002, 40/6; Baert (n 73) 263; A Baert and L Gheysens, *Douane en accijnzen* (Mechelen, Kluwer, 2013), 258; De Nauw (n 54) 5; Van Dooren (n 51) 5.

[76] E Van Dooren (n 19) 463.

[77] See: https://www.const-court.be/.

[78] Belgian Constitutional Court 14 February 2001, no 16/2001.

[79] Belgian Constitutional Court 15 October 2002, no 147/2002.

[80] While several provisions of substantive customs law have been tackled by the Constitutional Court, the Court of Cassation, and subsequently the legislator, the customs criminal procedure remains relatively untouched. Van Dooren (n 31); Van Dooren (n 19) 463.

general rules of criminal procedure do not create an unjustified difference in treatment and are therefore not in conflict with the principle of equality under the Belgian Constitution. According to the Court, the difference in treatment of the suspects in order to achieve the goal of creating a separate system of criminal enforcement is justified given the scale of the fraud in this technical and cross-border matter that is characterised by high mobility of goods.[81] Regarding house searches without judicial intervention, for example, the Constitutional Court has held that detecting and establishing customs offences is made more difficult due to the mobility of goods and that this mobility requires the customs administration to conduct immediate searches. The searches would lose a lot of their effectiveness if they were subjected to judicial authorisation. The derogation from general criminal procedure is strictly necessary to achieve the goal of a separate enforcement system to tackle the scale and frequency of customs fraud. The difference in treatment compared with persons suspected of a general criminal law offence thus rests on an objective criterion that is related to the goal of efficiently combatting fraud. Moreover, the visitation is subjected to sufficient safeguards to prevent abuse of power, so the legislator has found a balance between the rights of the suspect and the need for efficient enforcement.[82]

Similarly to the Constitutional Court, the Belgian Court of Cassation has, in turn, clarified that the mere fact that customs authorities have the competence to investigate and prosecute customs offences does not compromise the rights of the defence and does not give an impression of partiality, even though those authorities do not have the same degree of independence as the public prosecutor's office.[83] Furthermore, it has also ruled in favour of the customs enforcement regime on several other occasions.[84]

The Belgian Supreme Courts seem more lenient towards the needs of customs enforcement than the ECtHR. Regarding visitations, for example, the ECtHR has ruled that the elaborate seizures and house searches without judicial intervention provided by French customs law were disproportionate to their goal, namely the protection of the French economy, and thus in violation of Article 8 ECHR.[85] The analogy with the Belgian situation is manifest. The ECtHR in later cases similarly confirmed the importance of judicial authorisation or other safeguards against possible abuse of power.[86]

Moreover, the question can be raised whether customs offences are still so much more complex than, for example, cross-border fraud regarding other types of taxes,

[81] Belgian Constitutional Court 6 April 2000, no 40/2000, para B.19.4 and further; Belgian Constitutional Court 15 October 2002, no 147/2002, eg para B.7.2; Belgian Constitutional Court 20 February 2002, no 38/02, para B.17 and further; Belgian Constitutional Court 26 June 2002, no 108/02, para B.15 and further; Speecke (n 33) 456–59.

[82] Belgian Constitutional Court 14 February 2001, no 16/2001; Van Dooren (n 51) 31; Van Dooren (n 19) 475.

[83] Belgian Court of Cassation 16 May 2006, no P.06.0116.N.; Van Dooren (n 19) 464.

[84] Eg, Belgian Court of Cassation 17 October 2001, no P.01.1021.F.; Belgian Court of Cassation 16 September 2008, no P.08.0622.N/2; Belgian Court of Cassation 28 May 2019, no P.19.127.N.; Belgian Court of Cassation 5 November 2019, no P.19.0384.N. See also section IV below.

[85] *Funke v France*, App No 10828/84 (ECtHR, 25 February 1993).

[86] *Camenzind v Switzerland*, App No 21353/93 (ECtHR, 16 December 1997); *Stes Colas and others v France*, App No 3797/97(ECtHR 16 April 2002). Van Dooren (n 51) 45–46. However, until now, there were no cases concerning Belgian customs law.

drug trafficking, or cybercrime. These offences are prosecuted by the public prosecutor according to the general rules of criminal procedure. What makes customs criminal law so special that it deserves a separate type of procedure that does not give the same level of protection for the fundamental rights of the person concerned?[87]

As indicated, this chapter focuses on one fundamental right, namely the privilege against self-incrimination or *nemo tenetur*. The analysis of this right is most interesting in light of the overall research theme of this book because the customs authorities are able to conduct administrative and criminal proceedings and can choose from a broad range of investigative measures in both types of proceedings. It will be difficult to determine where the proceedings are still purely administrative and where they become criminal and thus when *nemo tenetur* comes into play.

III. *Nemo Tenetur* as Interpreted by the ECtHR

The *nemo tenetur* principle protects anyone accused of an offence 'against improper compulsion by the authorities and the obtaining of evidence through methods of coercion or oppression in defiance of the will of the accused'.[88] It includes the right to remain silent (by allowing the suspect to choose whether or not to respond to questioning) and the right not to contribute to incriminating oneself (by allowing the suspect to choose whether or not to collaborate in the production of evidence).[89] The ECtHR recognises that this principle, although not specifically mentioned in Article 6 of the European Convention on Human Rights (ECHR), is an international norm which lies at the heart of the notion of a fair procedure under Article 6. It contributes 'to avoiding miscarriages of justice and to securing the aims of Article 6'.[90]

[87] It should be noted the Luxembourgish (and Belgian) customs authorities requested an expert study funded by the European Commission to support the reform and modernisation of the current legislative framework, especially with regard to sanctions. This study was recently conducted by a team of the University of Antwerp. However, the results of that study have not yet been made public.

[88] *Allan v UK*, App No 48539/99 (ECtHR, 5 November 2002) para 50; I De La Serna, 'Le droit au silence' [2015] *Pli juridique* 3, 4.

[89] *Funke v France* is particularly important since in this case, the ECtHR made it clear for the first time that any accused person in a criminal case has the right to remain silent and not to contribute to his own conviction: *Funke v France*, App No 10828/84 (ECtHR, 25 February 1993) para 44. It is unclear whether the two are distinct concepts or whether one includes the other. The ECtHR is not very clear on this point. See, eg: *Saunders v UK*, App No 19187/91 (ECtHR, 17 December 1996) paras 68–69; De La Serna (n 88) 3.

[90] *Funke v France*, App No 10828/84 (ECtHR, 25 February 1993) para 44; *John Murray v UK*, App No 18731/91 (ECtHR, 8 February 1996) para 45; *Saunders v UK*, App No 19187/91 (ECHR, 17 December 1996) para 68; *Serves v France*, App No 20225/92 (ECtHR, 20 October 1997) para 46; *Heaney and McGuinness v Ireland*, App No 34720/97 (ECtHR, 21 December 2000) para 40; *Quinn v Ireland*, App No 36887/97 (ECtHR, 21 December 2000) para 40; *JB v Switzerland*, App No 31827/96 (ECtHR, 3 May 2001) para 64; *Allen v UK*, App No 76574/01 (ECtHR, 10 September 2002) para 1; *Allan v UK*, App No 48539/99 (ECtHR, 5 November 2002) para 44; *Weh v Austria*, App No 38544/97 (ECtHR, 8 April 2004) para 39; *Shannon v UK*, App No 6563/03 (ECtHR, 4 October 2005) para 32; *Jalloh v Germany*, App No 54810/00 (ECtHR, 11 July 2006) para 100; *O'Halloran and Francis v UK*, App No 15809/02 and 25624/02 (ECtHR, 29 June 2007) paras 46 and 52; *Shabelnik v Ukraine*, App No 16404/03 (ECtHR, 19 February 2009) para 55; *Bykov v Russia*, App No 4378/02 (ECtHR, 10 March 2009) para 92; *Zaichenko v Russia*, App No 39660/02 (ECtHR, 18 February 2010) para 38; *Krumpholz v Austria*, App No 13201/05 (ECtHR, 18 March 2010) para 31; *Pavlenko v Russia*, App No 42371/02 (ECtHR, 1 April 2010) para 100; *Gäfgen v Germany*, App No 22978/05 (ECtHR, 1 June 2010) para 168; *Brusco v France*, App No 1466/07 (ECtHR, 14 October 2010) para 44; *Chambaz v Switzerland*,

It is due to the case law of the ECtHR that *nemo tenetur* has taken up such a prominent role in criminal procedure. To fully understand it, we thus have to take into account this whole body of ECtHR case law.[91]

The ECtHR has handed down several judgments on *nemo tenetur*, also in a tax law context. In this chapter, we try to present the judgments that are most relevant to determining the application of the *nemo tenetur* principle in customs or other administrative proceedings. Although it is not always possible to draw a clear line within the case law of the Court,[92] three basic steps (including some intermediate steps) can be distilled:

1) Does the right to remain silent and not incriminate oneself apply *ratione temporis*?
2) Has the right to remain silent and not incriminate oneself been breached?
   a. Was there coercion?
   b. Is the obtained evidence incriminating?
   c. Does the right to remain silent and not incriminate oneself apply *ratione materiae*?
3) Has the right to remain silent and not incriminate oneself been breached in its essence (otherwise the violation will not be sanctioned)?[93]

Apart from these three basic steps, a fourth question could be raised, namely: 'Does the right to remain silent and not incriminate oneself apply to legal as well as natural persons?' Since customs proceedings will often involve corporate entities, the extent of the scope *ratione personae* is relevant. Questions can be raised not only regarding whether a legal person can enjoy the privilege, but also regarding who can invoke it on its behalf. This requires an extensive study, which has been conducted by other authors.[94] Therefore, we do not include this analysis in our study.

Especially the temporal and material scope of application of the principle raises a lot of questions. First of all, a lot of actors can be active in the field of law enforcement. In addition to the core criminal authorities – police, prosecutor, and judges – there are various administrative bodies that can, depending on the case, intervene administratively and/or criminally. The pivotal point between these two types of proceedings is, however, not easy to determine. Cases of a purely administrative nature can become criminal in nature at some point or the administration can

App No 11663/04 (ECtHR, 5 April 2012) para 52; *Navone and others v Monaco*, App No 32880/11, 62892/11 and 32899/11 (ECtHR, 24 October 2013) para 71; *Tarasov v Ukraine*, App No 17416/03 (ECtHR, 31 October 2013) para 82; *Ibrahim and others v UK*, App No 50541/08, 50571/08, 50573/08 et al (ECtHR, 13 September 2016) para 266; *Van Weerelt v the Netherlands*, App No 784/14 (ECtHR, 16 June 2015) para 54; *Kalnéniené v Belgium*, App No 40233/07 (ECtHR 31 January 2017) para 47; De La Serna (n 88) 4; C Conings and J Kerkhofs, 'U hebt het recht te zwijgen, uw login kan en zal tegen u worden gebruikt? Over ontsleutelplicht, zwijgrecht en *nemo tenetur*' [2018] 13(5) *Nullum Crimen* 457, 457 and 463; ECtHR, 'Guide on Article 6 of the European Convention on Human Rights: right to a fair trial (criminal limb)': https://www.echr.coe.int/Documents/Guide_Art_6_criminal_ENG.pdf (accessed 20 December 2019).

[91] S Lamberigts, *The privilege against self-incrimination of corporations* (KU Leuven PhD dissertation 2017) 63.

[92] As will become clear further on, the element of coercion, for example, pops up in several stages of the analysis.

[93] LCA Wijsman, *Nemo tenetur in belastingzaken – Nemo tenetur in tax matters* (Mechelen, Kluwer, 2017) 93.

[94] See for example: P Oliver, Fundamental rights of companies: EU, US, and international law compared (London, Bloomsburry, forthcoming March 2022); Lamberigts (n 91).

impose sanctions of a criminal nature.[95] This is problematic since the criminal law principle of *nemo tenetur* can coincide with the obligations to cooperate[96] that exist in administrative law. In customs law, the person in question must, in principle, cooperate loyally with the customs authorities. As such, they must make a declaration or provide answers to requests for information, produce books and documents, give the administration access to their professional and non-professional premises and so on (see above section II.B.(iii).). This contradictory legal position sometimes poses a serious dilemma for the person concerned: either refuse to cooperate during an inspection by the custom authorities and run the risk of being sanctioned for doing so,[97] or cooperate and potentially provide information that might demonstrate involvement in a customs offence (and thus incriminate oneself).

National legislators can determine that the defence rights, including the privilege against self-incrimination, in principle do not apply to what they consider to be purely administrative enforcement. In Belgium, this holds true for the Code of Criminal Procedure, where the Article that provides the right to silence (Article 47*bis*) does not apply to what the Belgian legislator identifies as purely administrative proceedings (see below section IV). However, the rules of the ECHR have direct effect and the ECtHR uses the autonomous concept 'criminal charge' to define the temporal application of *nemo tenetur* under Article 6 ECHR. It is possible that the person subject to an administrative inspection may in fact be regarded as a suspect in a criminal investigation. As will become clear, the ECtHR and the Belgian courts are not fully aligned in this respect. It is therefore necessary to look at both the ECtHR case law and the Belgian case law.

The second aspect is the material scope. It is not entirely clear what kind of evidence can be obtained under compulsion and what kind cannot. This is particularly relevant for customs proceedings, since often documents and accounts are requested by the customs officials. As we will explain below, the ECtHR has over time delivered diverging judgments on the protection of *nemo tenetur* with regard to documents.

A. Scope in Time

As mentioned above, the *nemo tenetur* principle is part of the legal protection under Article 6 ECHR and thus fundamental to the safeguarding of a fair trial. However, the ECtHR accepts that Article 6 ECHR need not be respected at every stage of the proceedings. The requirements of efficiency and flexibility may sometimes justify the prior intervention of administrative authorities, even if that intervention does not comply with the requirements of Article 6 ECHR. Indeed, *nemo tenetur* is in principle only applicable once the person is subject to a 'criminal charge' ('*une accusation*

[95] S Gnedasj, '[Verbod op zelfincriminatie] Wat zijn de gevolgen op fiscaal vlak als speurders het zwijgrecht miskennen?' [2014] 18 *Fiscale Actualiteit* 4.

[96] P Van De Weyer, *De rechterlijke toetsing van bestuursrechtelijke handelingen: een onderzoek naar de invloed van de vereiste van volle rechtsmacht in de zin van art. 6 EVRM* (KU Leuven PhD dissertation 2019) 149.

[97] For example, refusing to provide the documents is punished with a criminal fine of 25 to 250 EUR. See GLCE, Art 203 para 3.

en matière pénale').[98] Purely administrative investigations are not subject to the same requirements.

As indicated, the ECtHR has its own autonomous interpretation of what constitutes a criminal charge. The Court takes a substantive approach to answering the question of whether there is a criminal charge. Not only the formal notification of the charges can constitute a criminal charge, but also any measure that implies a suspicion and where the individual can reasonably expect that he will be the subject of a criminal prosecution. A person is criminally charged from the moment that his or her situation is substantially affected by actions of the authorities acting on a suspicion that a crime has been committed.[99]

Admittedly, determining *in concreto* when a person is criminally charged is difficult and a lot depends on the facts of a specific case. It is clear that a person who is the suspect in a criminal investigation *sensu stricto* has the right not to inculpate himself in the criminal investigation. As soon as a criminal prosecution has started, he should be able to invoke *nemo tenetur*.[100] It should be noted, however, that this only applies in the event that the criminal investigation is actually aimed at that person. It is possible that the authorities will only hear someone as a witness.[101] Nevertheless, if the authorities at some point suspect the person who was initially heard as a witness to have committed a criminal offence, then Article 6 ECHR becomes effective. If they continue to question that person as a witness, then these testimonies cannot be used against him in later criminal proceedings.[102]

Less clear is the situation where a person is coerced into cooperating during administrative proceedings (eg, by the customs authorities). When does the administrative inspection become a criminal charge? Purely administrative proceedings in principle do not have to fulfil the obligations under the criminal limb of Article 6 ECHR, and may thus contain obligations to cooperate that can be sanctioned in case of refusal.

[98] F Eerens, 'De vraag om inlichtingen: vraag maar raak?' [2015] 481 *Tijdschrift voor Fiscaal Recht* 386, 403.

[99] See for example: *Beuze v Belgium*, App No 71409/10 (ECtHR, 9 November 2018) para 119; *Ibrahim and others v UK*, App Nos 50541/08, 50571/08, 50573/08 et al (ECtHR, 13 September 2016) para 249; *Marttinen v Finland*, App No 19235/03 (ECtHR, 21 April 2009) para 62; *Serves v France*, App No 20225/92 (ECtHR, 20 October 1997) para 42; M-A Beernaert and F Krenc, *Le droit à un procès equitable dans la jurisprudence de la Cour européenne des droits de l'homme* (Limal, Anthemis, 2019) 57.

[100] This is the case in: *Heaney and McGuinness v Ireland*, App No 34720/97 (ECtHR, 21 December 2000); *O'Halloran and Francis v UK*, App Nos 15809/02 and 25624/02 (ECtHR, 29 June 2007); *Lückhof and Spanner v Austria*, App Nos 58452/00 and 61920/00 (ECtHR, 10 January 2008) (in contrast with the earlier *Weh v Austria*, App No 38544/97 (ECtHR, 8 April 2004)); *Pavlenko v Russia*, App No 42371/02 (ECtHR, 1 April 2010); *Gäfgen v Germany*, App No 22978/05 (ECtHR, 1 June 2010); *Zaichenko v Russia*, App No 39660/02 (ECtHR, 18 February 2010); *Navone and others v Monaco* App Nos 32880/11, 62892/11 and 32899/11 (ECtHR, 24 October 2013); *Tarasov v Ukraine*, App No 17416/03 (ECtHR, 31 October 2013); *Kalnéniené v Belgium*, App No 40233/07 (ECtHR, 31 January 2017).
Note on *Heaney and McGuinness*: In the *Weh* judgment (n 90), the ECtHR does not agree that the case of *Heaney and McGuinness* falls under this category (para 52): 'In Funke and in *Heaney and McGuinness* (both cited above) criminal proceedings were anticipated, though they had not been formally opened, at the time the respective applicants were required to give potentially incriminating information'.

[101] *Shabelnik v Ukraine*, App No 16404/03 (ECtHR, 19 February 2009) para 57; *Brusco v France*, App No 1466/07 (ECtHR, 14 October 2010) para 47; *Stojkovic v France and Belgium*, App No 25303/08 (ECtHR, 27 October 2011) paras 51–52; *Ibrahim and others v UK*, App Nos 50541/08, 50571/08, 50573/08 et al (ECtHR, 13 September 2016); *Weh v Austria*, App No 38544/97 (ECtHR, 8 April 2004) paras 52–53.

[102] *Shabelnik v Ukraine*, App No 16404/03 (ECtHR, 19 February 2009) para 57.

However, as can be deduced from the ECtHR case law, it is possible that there is a criminal charge during an administrative investigation (see below III.A.(i).). Furthermore, the ECtHR has ruled that legally obtained administrative evidence can constitute unlawful criminal evidence (see below III.A.(ii)..).

(i) The Administrative Investigation becomes Criminal in Nature

The administrative proceedings can, first of all, become criminal in nature when there are parallel criminal proceedings. The criminal proceedings then affect the administrative proceedings.[103] However, parallel criminal proceedings do not constitute a problem if it is guaranteed that the evidence from the administrative proceedings will not be used in the criminal ones.[104]

Second, the administrative proceedings can constitute a criminal charge when the criminal proceedings *sensu stricto* have not been started formally, but there is an intention on the part of the government to do so. This can be deduced from the fact that the administration suspects the person of an offence. The administration thus has a criminal charge in mind, one that is imminent, concrete, and not remote or hypothetical.[105] In a couple of judgments (see below III.B.(iii).), the ECtHR has, however, ruled that *nemo tenetur* also applies even if the government does not have any intention to start criminal proceedings, when the person who is requested to provide certain statements or material, cannot exclude that by cooperating, he might be exposed to a criminal charge.[106] In these particular cases, the scope was thus broadened from the intention of the government to start criminal proceedings to the fear on the part of the person who is requested to cooperate, that the government might form the intention to start criminal proceedings. This is not really reconcilable with the idea that *nemo tenetur* does not apply if the criminal charge is still remote or hypothetical. Yet, as will be indicated below, the Court has recently become more careful in awarding such broad protection to the principle.

Third, the administrative proceedings can constitute a criminal charge when the administration imposes or threatens to impose an administrative sanction of a criminal character.[107] The question arises, however, whether this applies to any type of administrative

[103] *Chambaz v Switzerland*, App No 11663/04 (ECtHR, 5 April 2012) para 55; *Shannon v UK*, App No 6563/03 (ECtHR, 4 October 2005) para 38; *Marttinen v Finland*, App No 19235/03 (ECtHR, 21 April 2009) paras 67 and further.

[104] If there is assurance that the evidence obtained will not be used in the criminal proceedings, the administrative proceedings remain purely administrative. See for example: *Van Weerelt v the Netherlands*, App No 784/14 (ECtHR, 16 June 2015); Van De Weyer (n 96) 153.

[105] *Weh v Austria*, App No 38544/97 (ECtHR, 8 April 2004) para 56.

[106] *JB v Switzerland*, App No 31827/96 (ECtHR, 3 May 2001) para 66: 'the applicant could not exclude that, if it transpired from these documents that he had received additional income which had not been taxed, he might be charged with the offence of tax evasion'; *Chambaz v Switzerland*, App No 11663/04 (ECtHR, 5 April 2012) para 54: 'le requérant ne pouvait exclure que toute information relative à des revenus supplémentaires de sources non imposées l'exposait à être accusé d'avoir commis l'infraction de soustraction d'impôt (JB c. Suisse, précité, para 65) et était de nature à compromettre sa position dans l'enquête pour soustraction d'impôts'.

[107] The ECtHR determines this on the basis of the so-called *Engel*-criteria (based on *Engel and others v the Netherlands*, App Nos 5100/71–5102/71, 5354/72, and 5370/72 (ECtHR, 8 June 1976) paras 82–83): (i) the classification of the sanction in domestic law; (ii) the nature of the offence, and (iii) the severity of the penalty.

sanction with a criminal character. After all, the administration is not only competent to sanction the underlying infringement that is subject to the administrative investigation, but can also impose sanctions for merely not cooperating during the investigation. For example, the tax administration can impose an administrative fine for the mere failure to submit a tax return. The ECtHR held in *King v United Kingdom* that this fine for non-cooperation does not violate *nemo tenetur*.[108] One could deduce from this judgment that any sanction for non-cooperation in the context of a routine check carried out by an administrative authority is not contrary to Article 6 ECHR. However, it is unclear whether the ECtHR would also apply this reasoning to other situations than a tax return.

The above-mentioned three scenarios involve a criminal charge in the context of an administrative procedure. Regarding tax cases specifically, we can conclude that the taxpayer will certainly *not* be criminally charged in the following two cases. Firstly, there is no criminal charge when the tax administration requests information that will only be used to levy the right amount of taxes, eg, customs duties (and not for the purpose of imposing tax fines or bringing a criminal prosecution).[109] This renders the procedure purely administrative. However, it is unclear what happens if the tax administration pursues a double objective, namely gathering information to levy the right taxes and at the same time sanctioning an underlying criminal offence, for example tax evasion.[110] In Belgian customs law, the customs administration can always pursue a double objective, since any violation of the customs legislation can result in a fine of a criminal nature.[111] Splitting investigative measures aimed at levying the right customs duties and those aimed at imposing a sanction for a previously committed offence does not seem possible.[112] According to Wijsman, *nemo tenetur*, then, always has to be respected.[113] Secondly, regarding tax returns, the tax administration will be able to impose sanctions for failure to file a complete or timely tax return.[114] As mentioned, in such cases failure to cooperate will be sanctioned, not any underlying infringement that could be revealed by the information contained in the tax return. The infringement of the duty

See, for example, *Janosevic v Sweden*, App No 34619/97 (ECtHR, 23 July 2002); *Vastberga Taxi A.B. and Vulic v Sweden*, App No 36985/97 (ECtHR, 23 July 2002); C Vanderkerken, *De fiscale strafvervolging: problemen van rechtsbescherming van de verdachte* (KU Leuven PhD dissertation, 2004) 453, para 735. The CJEU also recently confirmed that *nemo tenetur* must be respected in the context of procedures that may lead to the imposition of administrative sanctions of a criminal nature. In doing so, the Court also applied the *Engel* criteria. See Case C-481/19 *DB v Commissione Nazionale per le Società e la Borsa (Consob)* EU:C:2021:84 (CJEU, 2 February 2021) para 42.

[108] *King v UK*, App No 13881/02 (ECtHR, 8 April 2003) para 2; Vanderkerken (n 107) 461, para 745.

[109] *Van Weerelt v the Netherlands*, App No 784/14 (ECHR, 16 June 2015) paras 56–62; *Marttinen v Finland*, App No 19235/03 (ECHR, 21 April 2009) para 68; *Allen v UK*, App No 76574/01(ECtHR, 10 September 2002), paras 1–2. Similar reasoning for other administrations: (implicitly) *Saunders v UK*, App No 19187/91 (ECtHR, 17 December 1996) para 67; *IJL and others v UK*, App Nos 29522/95, 30056/96 and 30574/96 (ECtHR, 19 September 2000) para 100; *Fayed v UK*, App No 17101/90 (ECtHR, 21 September 1994) para 62.

[110] *JB v Switzerland*, App No 31827/96 (ECtHR, 3 May 2001); *Funke v France*, App No 10828/84 (ECHR, 25 February 1993); Vanderkerken (n 107) 462–63, para 746.

[111] GLCE, Art 261.

[112] Gnedasj (n 95); Vanderkerken (n 107) 462–63, para 746.

[113] Wijsman (n 93) 111–12.

[114] *Allen v UK*, App No 76574/01 (ECtHR, 10 September 2002); *King v UK*, App No 13881/02 (ECtHR, 8 April 2003); Van De Weyer (n 96) 149.

to cooperate can be sanctioned as there is no criminal charge for past behaviour.[115] Although the ECtHR until now has only applied this reasoning in relation to income tax cases, a similar approach could in theory be applied to customs declarations. However, customs declarations differ from income tax declarations. Unlike yearly income tax declarations, customs declarations are required for each customs movement. Because the customs declaration does not have to take place at fixed points in time, the infringement by merely not making a customs declaration will be less noticeable for the customs administration.

(ii) The Evidence is Used Later on in Criminal Proceedings

The *nemo tenetur* principle also applies when evidence obtained through coercion in the course of a non-criminal investigation (where no criminal charge is established) is used in subsequent criminal proceedings.[116] This is called the latent effect of *nemo tenetur*. The most important ECtHR judgment in this regard is *Saunders v United Kingdom*. Mr Saunders (director and chief executive of the Guinness enterprise) was questioned by inspectors of the Department of Trade and Industry (DTI) regarding alleged irregularities he committed in the acquisition by Guinness of the Distillers Company. At that time he was still a witness, not a suspect. Failure to cooperate was punishable by two years' imprisonment and therefore Mr Saunders made statements. After the investigation, criminal proceedings were started. The Crown Prosecution Service based its evidence to a large extent on the interrogations by the DTI. Mr Saunders received an overall prison sentence of five years. The ECtHR recognised that the guarantees of Article 6 ECHR do not, in principle, apply to the administrative investigation of the DTI.[117] However, Article 6 ECHR may apply in certain cases, ie if information obtained through coercion in the course of administrative proceedings is subsequently used in criminal proceedings.[118] Consequently a breach of Article 6 had occurred, and damages were awarded to Saunders. Legitimate administrative evidence may therefore constitute unlawful and thus inadmissible criminal evidence.[119] It is important to note that the Court of Justice of the European Union (CJEU) has also followed this case law on the latent effect of *nemo tenetur*. In its judgment of 2 February 2021, the Court considered that *nemo tenetur* must also be recognised in a purely administrative investigation (in which no criminal charge is established) if national law allows evidence obtained

[115] *King v UK*, App No 13881/02 (ECtHR, 8 April 2003); Van De Weyer (n 96) 149; Lamberigts (n 91) 74–75.

[116] *Saunders v UK*, App No 19187/91 (ECtHR, 17 December 1996) para 67. See also: *I.J.L. and others v UK*, App No 29522/95, 30056/96 and 30574/96 (ECtHR, 19 September 2000) paras 82–83; *Kansal v UK*, App No 21413/02 (ECtHR, 27 April 2004) paras 26–29; De La Serna (n 88) 7; F Kefer, 'L'employeur est-il tenu d'être présent et actif lors d'un controle social?' [2013] *Revue de Jurisprudence de Liège, Mons et Bruxelles* 1861, 1864; Lamberigts (n 91) 70; Van De Weyer (n 96) 153–55; Wijsman (n 93) 107 and 151–61.

[117] *Saunders v UK*, App No 19187/91 (ECtHR, 17 December 1996) para 67.

[118] The *Saunders* case concerns oral statements. Until now, this case law has not been confirmed by the ECtHR with regard to physical evidence, such as documents. There is, however, no reason to assume that this reasoning does not count for physical evidence.

[119] P Van De Weyer (n 96) 154.

Table 1 Scope of *nemo tenetur – ratione temporis*

Scope *ratione temporis*			
		Assurance that evidence will not be used in criminal proceedings.	
Criminal proceedings *sensu stricto* aimed at the person concerned.	Administrative investigation in three situations: (A) Parallel criminal proceedings concerning the same underlying infringement; (B) Criminal proceedings *sensu stricto* have not started but there is intention to do so or the person concerned cannot exclude it; (C) Administrative sanction with criminal character.	Purely administrative proceedings. BUT: cannot be used later on in a criminal investigation.	Criminal investigation (*sensu stricto*) but not aimed at the person concerned (*eg* a witness).
	During the investigative measure the person can become a suspect.		
		Cooperation obligations are allowed and can be sanctioned. ! As long as criminal proceedings are still '*hypothetical and remote*'.	
Criminal charge		*No criminal charge*	

in that investigation to be used subsequently in criminal proceedings against the same person to establish that he has committed a criminal offence.[120]

However, it is only the evidence that comes directly from those administrative proceedings that is potentially unlawful. By contrast, when that specific evidence is not used, but it forms the basis for criminal investigative measures that generate other evidence, then this does not constitute a *nemo tenetur* problem. The elements acquired during administrative proceedings may therefore be used indirectly as a basis for the criminal conviction.[121]

[120] Case C-481/19 *DB v Commissione Nazionale per le Società e la Borsa (Consob)* EU:C:2021:84 (CJEU, 2 February 2021) para 44.

[121] Van De Weyer (n 96) 156–57.

B. Has the Right to Remain Silent been Violated?

(i) Coercion?

The *nemo tenetur* principle does not preclude that the suspect provides incriminatory statements or evidence; it only protects against being obliged to provide evidence under pressure or coercion. Thus, before there can be a violation of the right not to incriminate oneself, coercion or pressure must be exerted on the person. The ECtHR easily accepts that coercion is present.[122] It should be noted that, in this step, the Court does not evaluate the extent of the coercion. This only comes into play later on in the analysis under the question whether the *nemo tenetur* right was violated in its essence (see below III.C.).

The ECtHR has accepted that coercion was present in at least the following types of situations:[123]

- Threatening the suspect with sanctions (including imprisonment, fines, and penalty payments) which results in the suspect either providing statements or evidence or being sanctioned for refusing to do so.[124]
- Deducing guilt from silence. This does not mean that no conclusions can ever be drawn from remaining silent. It simply cannot be the only or decisive proof of guilt.[125]
- Pressuring the suspect physically or psychologically, often in the form of (threatening with) an act in violation of Article 3 of the ECHR (torture and degrading or inhuman treatment).[126]
- Tricking, deceiving, or scheming. For example, training the cellmate of the suspect to trigger a confession.[127]
- Forcing the suspect to take an oath if, for the failure to do so, sanctions can be imposed.[128]

[122] Lamberigts (n 91) 70.

[123] *Ibrahim and other v UK*, App No 50541/08, 50571/08, 50573/08 et al (ECHR, 13 September 2016) para 267; ECtHR, 'Guide on Article 6 of the European Convention on Human Rights: right to a fair trial (criminal limb)': https://www.echr.coe.int/Documents/Guide_Art_6_criminal_ENG.pdf (accessed 20 December 2019); Wijsman (n 93) 95–100.

[124] *Saunders v UK*, App No 19187/91 (ECtHR, 17 December 1996) para 70; *Heaney and McGuinness v Ireland*, App No 34720/97 (ECtHR, 21 December 2000) paras 39 and further; *Weh v Austria*, App No 38544/97 (ECtHR, 8 April 2004) para 56.

[125] *John Murray v UK*, App No 18731/91 (ECtHR, 8 February 1996) para 47.

[126] *Jalloh v Germany*, App No 54810/00 (ECtHR, 11 July 2006) paras 104 and further; *Gäfgen v Germany*, App No 22978/05 (ECtHR, 1 June 2010) para 166; M-A Beernaert, 'La recevabilité des preuves en matière pénale dans la jurisprudence de la Cour européenne des droits de l'homme : nouvel état de la question' in I Bouioukliev and P Dhaeyer (eds), *La théorie des nullités en droit penal* (Limal, Anthemis, 2014) 80; Lamberigts (n 91) 70.

[127] *Allan v UK*, App No 48539/99 (ECtHR, 5 November 2002) para 50; ECtHR, 'Guide on Article 6 of the European Convention on Human Rights: right to a fair trial (criminal limb)': https://www.echr.coe.int/Documents/Guide_Art_6_criminal_ENG.pdf (accessed 20 December 2019).

[128] *Serves v France*, App No 20225/92 (ECtHR, 20 October 1997) para 47.

Moreover, when the suspect is in a weak position, for example because he is held in pre-trial detention, the threshold for the Court to establish coercion is very low. In Belgian customs proceedings, suspects are not often placed in pre-trial detention,[129] yet they might be in a weak position due to other factors. For instance, when the customs administration checks containers with perishable goods and requests more information, the person in question might feel obligated to provide the information in order to save the goods.

However, in *H and J v the Netherlands* the Court found no coercion. In this case, the suspects in criminal proceedings were confronted with statements they made during an asylum procedure. The Court reasoned that

> the applicants entered the Netherlands of their own accord, asking for its protection. For their entitlement to protection – in the form of safe residence on Netherlands territory (…) – to be recognised, they were required to satisfy the Netherlands Government that their stated fear of persecution was well-founded. Since they bore the burden of proof, the Court finds nothing incongruous in the Government's demanding the full truth from them. The suggestion that the applicants' statements to the immigration authorities were extracted under coercion is therefore baseless.[130]

The statements of the administrative investigation (asylum procedure) could thus be used in the subsequent criminal proceedings.

(ii) *Is the Evidence Incriminatory?*

To determine a violation of *nemo tenetur*, not only coercion is required, but also that the evidence is incriminatory in nature. The ECtHR ruled that not only directly incriminating statements (confessions), but also indirectly incriminating statements can lead to a violation of *nemo tenetur*. However, statements that have been obtained under duress and appear prima facie to be non-incriminatory – such as exculpatory remarks or mere information about questions of fact – can be used later in criminal proceedings to support charges. They can for example be used to contradict or question other statements or evidence of the accused or otherwise undermine his credibility. In each instance it must be examined, in concrete terms, whether the use of the evidence before the criminal court implied or promoted incrimination.[131]

[129] This probably has to do with the very specific rules that apply to pre-trial detention in customs law and the fact that not all offences are punishable with imprisonment. Moreover, the GACE prefers to work without interference by the investigating judge, and pre-trial detention requires the intervention of the investigating judge. See V Franssen and AL Claes, 'Enforcement of policies against illicit trade in tobacco products in Belgium' in J Vervaele and S Tosza (eds), *Combatting Illicit Trade in Tobacco Products. In Search of Optimal Enforcement* (Springer, *forthcoming* 2021).

[130] *H and J v the Netherlands*, App Nos 978/09 and 992/09 (ECtHR, 13 November 2014) para 75.

[131] *Ibrahim and others v UK*, App Nos 50541/08, 50571/08, 50573/08 et al (ECtHR, 13 September 2016) para 268; *Saunders v UK*, App No 19187/91 (ECHR, 17 December 1996) paras 71–72; *Zaichenko v Russia*, App No 39660/02 (ECHR, 18 February 2010) para 54; De La Serna (n 88) 7; ECtHR, 'Guide on Article 6 of the European Convention on Human Rights: right to a fair trial (criminal limb)': https://www.echr.coe.int/Documents/Guide_Art_6_criminal_ENG.pdf (accessed 20 December 2019); Wijsman (n 93) 101.

(iii) Even then: Does the Evidence Fall within the Material Scope of Nemo Tenetur?

(a) General: *Nemo Tenetur* is Inapplicable to Evidence that has an Existence Independent of the Will

If the situation entails a criminal charge and coercion, and the evidence is incriminating according to the ECtHR case law, *nemo tenetur* applies in principle. However, the material scope of this principle has been limited or extended by the Court on several occasions, in the sense that certain evidence may or may not be covered by the protection.

Indeed, the ECtHR accepts that the right not to incriminate oneself does not preclude an accused person from being obliged to produce (potentially self-incriminating) evidence where the existence of such evidence does not depend on the will of the accused person.[132] However, the meaning of the notions of 'will-dependent' and 'will-independent' evidence is vague.

(b) What is 'Independent of the Will'?

There is little discussion that statements (oral or written) are dependent on the suspect's will and therefore fall under the protection of *nemo tenetur* (see Table 2, category A).[133] The Court has ruled on several occasions that *nemo tenetur* guarantees in particular the defendant's freedom to remain silent in the context of an interrogation and thus includes the prohibition to force someone to make a statement.[134] *Nemo tenetur* thus offers first and foremost protection against forced incriminating statements,[135] since coercion is likely to influence the content of a statement and can lead to false confessions.[136] That being said, not only declarations fall under material dependent on the suspect's will. The difference between will-dependent and will-independent can therefore not be reduced to the difference between statements and all other kinds of evidence. Documents[137] and other types of physical evidence have been brought under the protection of *nemo tenetur*. In what follows, we will present the most relevant judgments on this account.

In *Funke v France*[138] the ECtHR ruled on the material scope of *nemo tenetur* for the first time. In this case, Mr Funke was obliged to produce bank statements for the

[132] *Saunders v UK*, App No 19187/91 (ECtHR, 17 December 1996) para 69; De La Serna (n 88) 7.

[133] Lamberigts (n 91) 73.

[134] See for example: *Jalloh v Germany*, App No 54810/00 (ECtHR, 11 July 2006) para 110: 'the privilege against self-incrimination is commonly understood in the Contracting States and elsewhere to be primarily concerned with respecting the will of the defendant to remain silent in the face of questioning and not to be compelled to provide a statement'; Vanderkerken (n 107) 457–58, para 739.

[135] *Saunders v UK*, App No 19187/91 (ECtHR, 17 December 1996) para 69: 'the right to not incriminate oneself is *primarily* concerned with respecting the will of the accused person to remain silent' (emphasis added).

[136] However, this does not mean that the litigant can 'abuse' *nemo tenetur* by refusing all cooperation with the authorities, for example by not showing up for a hearing or by using delaying tactics. Case C-481/19 *DB v Commissione Nazionale per le Società e la Borsa (Consob)* EU:C:2021:84 (CJEU, 2 February 2021) para 41.

[137] Meaning pre-existing documents (not including for example being coerced to fill in a questionnaire, which would fall under the category of a written statement).

[138] *Funke v France*, App No 10828/84 (ECtHR, 25 February 1993).

French customs authorities on pain of a fine and a daily penalty payment. It was important that the authorities only *suspected* that the bank statements existed. According to the ECtHR, this violated Mr Funke's right to not incriminate himself because he was convicted for the sole purpose of obtaining evidence of which the existence was uncertain. The ECtHR thus made clear that a defendant can also invoke *nemo tenetur* to refuse to hand over incriminating documents.[139] However, it remained unclear when exactly this could be refused.

In *Saunders v the UK*[140] the ECtHR tried to provide more clarity after *Funke*. The Court confirmed that *nemo tenetur* goes beyond mere statements. The Court ruled that 'the right not to incriminate oneself is *primarily* concerned [...] with respecting the will of an accused person to remain silent' (emphasis added), thereby implying that *nemo tenetur* can also apply to other types of evidence. Nevertheless, the Court went on to only specify what types of evidence certainly did not fall under the protection of *nemo tenetur*:

> as commonly understood in the legal systems of the Contracting Parties to the Convention and elsewhere, it does not extend to the use in criminal proceedings of material which may be obtained from the accused through the use of compulsory powers but which has an existence independent of the will of the suspect such as, inter alia, documents acquired pursuant to a warrant, breath, blood and urine samples and bodily tissue for the purpose of DNA testing.[141]

This reasoning was even more remarkable, given that the facts of the case concerned the use of statements, meaning that the Court did not even have to decide on this matter.

According to the ECtHR, there is thus no breach of the right not to incriminate oneself if the authorities forcibly collect evidence that exists independently of the will of the accused. However, the Court does not give a clear definition of this notion and does not provide an exhaustive list of examples.[142] The broader you interpret will-independent, the more limited the effect of the right not to incriminate oneself will be, since will-dependent evidence will then de facto only include statements. If one subsequently tries to reconcile Saunders with *Funke*, then requesting documents of which the existence is uncertain can be deemed as triggering statements about the existence of these documents (see Table 2, category B).[143]

In *JB v Switzerland*,[144] however, the Court created confusion with regard to the *Saunders* formula, since the Court provided three different considerations from which it ultimately deduced a violation of Article 6 ECHR. In this case, JB refused to provide the Swiss tax authorities with all documents concerning the companies in which he had invested money, and he was fined for this. First of all, the Court pointed out that JB could not exclude that the information arising from the documents would be used

[139] *Funke v France*, App No 10828/84 (ECtHR, 25 February 1993) para 44.

[140] See above III.A.; *Saunders v UK*, App No 19187/91 (ECtHR, 17 December 1996).

[141] *Saunders v UK*, App No 19187/91 (ECtHR, 17 December 1996) para 69.

In the *Quinn v Ireland* and *Heaney and McGuinness v Ireland* judgments the Court confirmed the general Saunders formula, although it altered it slightly. For example, the reference to 'pursuant to a warrant' is left out by the Court. *Quinn v Ireland*, App No 36887/97 (ECtHR, 21 December 2000), para 40; *Heaney and McGuinness v Ireland*, App No 34720/97 (ECtHR, 21 December 2000) para 40: 'material which had an existence independent of the will of the applicants such as, documents or blood samples'.

[142] Wijsman (n 93) 117–18.

[143] Wijsman (n 93) 121.

[144] *JB v Switzerland*, App No 31827/96 (ECtHR, 3 May 2001).

to establish tax evasion.[145] Second, the Court reasoned that the documents in question were different in nature from the examples of evidence enumerated in the *Saunders* formula. It did so in the following way:

> the present case does not involve material of this nature which, like that considered in *Saunders*, has an existence independent of the person concerned and is not, therefore, obtained by means of coercion and in defiance of the will of that person …[146]

The Court thus refers to *Saunders*, but at the same time it adjusts its formula from 'an existence independent from the will' to 'obtained in defiance of the will'. Furthermore, the Court does not explain why the requested documents in this case differ from the examples of will-independent evidence enumerated in *Saunders*, and thereby does not address the exact nature of the requested documents.[147]

These two arguments seem to add a new layer to the *Saunders* formula. Within the category of evidence independent of the suspect's will, one could make a distinction between evidence obtained independently of his/her will or requiring only passive cooperation (eg, evidence found with a search warrant) and evidence for which active cooperation is required (eg, providing documents). Following *JB* the latter category seems to have been brought back under the protection of *nemo tenetur*.[148]

Third, the Court was not convinced that the authorities were sure the requested information existed. In accordance with the *Funke* judgment, having to provide this information thus constituted a disguised declaration about the existence.[149] As a result of these three considerations, the Court determined that there was a violation of Article 6 ECHR.

In our view, the Court stirs confusion as it does not decide which of the three considerations is decisive. If the fact that the existence of the evidence was unsure was of overriding importance, then *JB* can be equated with *Funke*. However, with *JB*, the Court does seem to suggest a new criterion, namely 'material obtained in defiance of the suspect's will which could potentially contain some information about the offence'. In conclusion, in Table 2 a part of the category will-independent evidence (category D) would move to the other side of the scheme, namely the part for which some active cooperation is required. The distinction between will-dependent and will-independent evidence therefore suddenly appears to have eroded.

The new criterion of *JB* partly returns in *Jalloh v Germany*.[150] In this case, forced vomiting was used to retrieve drug beads that Mr Jalloh had swallowed after the police caught him distributing them. The Court again attempted to clearly outline the scope of *nemo tenetur*, and determined once again that it can apply to other evidence than

[145] *JB v Switzerland*, App No 31827/96 (ECtHR, 3 May 2001) para 66.

[146] Ibid, para 68. With *JB*, the Court thus seems to limit the example in *Saunders* of documents obtained through a warrant to documents obtained through search warrants. See Lamberigts (n 91) 77.

[147] *JB v Switzerland*, App No 31827/96 (ECtHR, 3 May 2001) para 68.

[148] EJ Koops and L Stevens, 'JB versus Saunders. De groeiende duisternis rond *nemo tenetur*' [2003] 33(3) *Delikt en Delinkwent* 281; C Van De Heyning and J Coppens, 'Het bevel tot medewerking van artikel 88*quater* Sv., het zwijgrecht en het verbod op zelfincriminatie' [2016] 3 *Tijdschrift Voor Strafrecht* 260, 263–64.

[149] *JB v Switzerland*, App No 31827/96 (ECtHR, 3 May 2001) para 69.

[150] *Jalloh v Germany*, App No 54810/00 (ECtHR, 11 July 2006).

statements.[151] First of all, the Court repeated the *Saunders* formula. The evidence in this case, ie the drug beads in the defendant's body, could be considered to fall under the category will-independent, and thus be allowed in criminal proceedings.[152] But, the Court continued, several elements distinguish *Jalloh* from *Saunders*. The Court reasoned that, similarly to *Funke* and *JB*, coercion was applied to the person in order to obtain 'real evidence in defiance of the suspect's will'. Furthermore, unlike the bodily material in the *Saunders* formula, the evidence did not require further forensic testing, eg testing the presence of drugs or alcohol.[153] The Court thus makes a distinction between direct real evidence (not requiring further testing) and indirect real evidence (which still requires forensic examination).[154] The Court continued that the degree of coercion exerted on Mr Jalloh is also different from the examples in the *Saunders* formula. To obtain the type of evidence mentioned in the *Saunders* formula, the defendant must only passively endure a limited interference or cooperate in the supply of material that arises from the normal functioning of the body (eg, a urine sample). In the case of *Jalloh*, however, the coercion constituted torture.[155] The Court therefore took into account the way in which coercion was exercised in order to determine whether *nemo tenetur* is applicable *ratione materiae*. Normally, however, the extent of coercion only plays a role at a later stage; more specifically it is a deciding factor in answering the question whether the violation of *nemo tenetur* is justifiable (see below section III.C).

In sum, the Court ruled in *Jalloh* that, despite the fact that the material in question was will-independent in the sense of *Saunders* (the drug beads existed independently of the suspect's will and there was no doubt about their existence on the part of the German police), there can still be a violation of *nemo tenetur*. This is the case when direct real evidence is obtained in defiance of the will of the person via a completely unlawful form of coercion (in this case a violation of Article 3 of the ECHR).[156] *Jalloh* thus constitutes a nuanced application of *JB*. In Table 2, this would mean that category D only partly comes back under the protection of *nemo tenetur*; more specifically, only direct will-independent evidence obtained in violation of Article 3 ECHR.

In *Gäfgen v Germany*,[157] the Court refined *Jalloh* to a certain extent. In this case, both statements and real evidence were obtained under the threat of torture. The Court made a distinction between obtaining evidence with the use of torture on the one hand, and through inhuman or degrading treatment on the other. If torture was used, the admission of real evidence always constitutes a violation of *nemo tenetur* under Article 6 of the ECHR. If inhuman or degrading treatment was used, however, the admission will only constitute a violation of Article 6 ECHR if it has been shown that this real evidence had a direct effect on the outcome of the case. However, if the outcome of the case is

[151] Wijsman (n 93) 122.

[152] *Jalloh v Germany*, App No 54810/00 (ECtHR, 11 July 2006) para 113.

[153] Ibid, para 113.

[154] In our view, this distinction seems artificial. Alcohol in a breath test can be detected in the blink of an eye, while drug beads can just as easily contain flour and therefore also require further investigation.

[155] *Jalloh v Germany*, App No 54810/00 (ECtHR, 11 July 2006) paras 114–115.

[156] ECtHR, 'Guide on Article 6 of the European Convention on Human Rights: right to a fair trial (criminal limb)': https://www.echr.coe.int/Documents/Guide_Art_6_criminal_ENG.pdf (accessed 20 December 2019).

[157] *Gäfgen v Germany*, App No 22978/05 (ECtHR, 1 June 2010).

based on other evidence, there is not necessarily a violation of Article 6 ECHR. In that case, the Court goes on to examine whether or not there is a causal link between this other evidence and the evidence obtained in violation of Article 3 ECHR.[158]

At last in *Chambaz v Switzerland*,[159] the ECtHR even went a step further. The first argument of *JB* sufficed to establish a violation of *nemo tenetur*, meaning that the suspect can refuse to hand over documents if he cannot exclude that the information arising from the documents would incriminate him.[160] Following this judgment, the tax administration can no longer force the taxpayer, by threatening a sanction, to provide certain documents. The whole category D in Table 2 would move back under the protection of *nemo tenetur*, without the need to prove a 'fishing expedition' (*Funke* and *JB*) or coercion amounting to a violation of Article 3 ECHR (*Jalloh* and *Gäfgen*). However, the taxpayer would still be obliged to provide access to his premises to allow the authorities to look for the documents themselves, because, in that case, he would not be obliged to contribute to his own incrimination and thus fall under category C in Table 2. In sum, potentially incriminating documents which the authorities cannot obtain without the active help of the suspect come back under the protection of *nemo tenetur* after *Chambaz*.[161]

The *Chambaz* case law has far-reaching implications. In Belgian customs law, any infringement of the obligations of the GLCE can be criminally punished.[162] Therefore, the taxpayer cannot rule out the possibility that any requested information relating to his customs duties could expose him to a criminal sanction. *Nemo tenetur* could thus be invoked for refusing any request for information or documents.

Judge Zupančič considered (rightly) in his dissenting opinion that this judgment could open Pandora's box. Every taxpayer could suddenly feel himself to be a victim of a violation of *nemo tenetur* just because he is obliged in an administrative investigation to provide certain documents that could possibly contain incriminating information. Moreover, with this judgment, the Court extends the material scope of *nemo tenetur* to all documents; nevertheless, the authorities could still obtain samples of DNA, blood or urine without any problem. One could wonder what the exact difference is between providing a DNA, blood or urine sample and providing documents. In other words, the distinction between evidence that requires none or only passive cooperation, like the collection of a DNA sample (see Table 2, category C), and evidence that requires active cooperation, like the production of documents (see Table 2, category D), becomes rather blurred.

[158] ECtHR, 'Guide on Article 6 of the European Convention on Human Rights: right to a fair trial (criminal limb)': https://www.echr.coe.int/Documents/Guide_Art_6_criminal_ENG.pdf (accessed 20 December 2019).

[159] *Chambaz v Switzerland*, App No 11663/04 (ECtHR 5, April 2012).

[160] *Chambaz v Switzerland*, App No 11663/04 (ECtHR, 5 April 2012) paras 53–58, specifically: 'La Cour observe, par ailleurs, que le requérant ne pouvait exclure que toute information relative à des revenus supplémentaires de sources non imposées l'exposait à être accuse d'avoir commis l'infraction de soustraction d'impôt (JB c. Suisse, précité, para 65) et était de nature à compromettre sa position dans l'enquête pour soustraction d'impôts'. See also: Wijsman (n 93) 127–28.

[161] Wijsman (n 93) 126.

[162] GLCE, Art 261 contains a catch-all offence, meaning that any violation of the Belgian customs legislation can constitute a criminal offence.

However, in the judgments *Van Weerelt v the Netherlands*[163] and *Kalnéniené v. Belgium*[164] the Court returned to the traditional *Saunders* formula, without any reference to the broad protection under *Chambaz.* Although these cases did not specifically concern the request to provide certain documents, the Court felt the need to reiterate its old *Saunders* reasoning. The Court thus seems more careful again and tends towards a restrictive interpretation of *nemo tenetur*.

(c) Conclusion

Following the case law of the ECtHR, we tried to deduce a step-by-step reasoning. Nevertheless, the exact material scope remains unclear and requires new case law by the Court.[165]

First of all, statements (oral or written) are dependent on the will and can be influenced by coercion. *Nemo tenetur* always applies (see Table 2, category A). Secondly, the results of a fishing expedition, which implies that the authorities are uncertain whether the evidence actually exists, are a statement in disguise (see Table 2, category B). The suspect declares whether or not he is actually in possession of the requested evidence.[166] Of course, states can avoid this situation to some extent by legally requiring citizens to keep certain documents or to register certain data.[167] Customs law, for example, requires taxpayers to keep documentary proof of origin, transport documents, import licences, customs value declarations … Thirdly, if the case does not constitute a fishing expedition, then will-independent evidence can be defined as everything that is not a statement and thus everything that exists at the moment the coercion is exercised. This includes physical will-independent evidence that requires the active cooperation of the suspect (see Table 2, category D) and physical evidence that can be obtained without or with only limited cooperation (see Table 2, category C).

Within the category of will-independent evidence, the Court has, however, sometimes brought a situation back under the protection of *nemo tenetur*. Following the *JB* and *Chambaz* reasoning, *nemo tenetur* also applies when evidence is obtained in

[163] *Van Weerelt v the Netherlands*, App No 784/14 (ECtHR, 16 June 2015) para 55.

[164] *Kalnéniené v Belgium*, App No 40233/07 (ECtHR, 31 January 2017) para 52.

[165] The reader should note that our digitised world is making this reasoning even more complex. Documents will now often be found in digital and encrypted format. The question then arises whether *nemo tenetur* is compatible with the suspect's obligation to decrypt the information. For a more in-depth study on this topic, see Conings and kerkhofs (n 90) 457–72.

[166] *Funke v France*, App No 10828/84 (ECtHR, 25 February 1993); *JB v Switzerland*, App No 31827/96 (ECtHR, 3 May 2001).

[167] For example, Belgian case law determined that authorities are always sure about the existence of the accounts. See Court of Appeal Antwerp 24 February 2009, *De Fiscale Koerier* 2009, 407; Court of Appeal Ghent 15 June 2010, *De Fiscale Koerier* 2010, 625; Court of Appeal Antwerp 20 March 2012, *Fiscale Jurisprudentie/Jurisprudence Fiscale* 2013, 10; Eerens (n 98) 406.

It is possible that the person concerned will then try to invoke the *Chambaz* case law in order to refuse to hand over these legal documents. If the ECtHR followed this argument, LCA Wijsman is convinced that the Court would then be more lenient towards the authorities in the next step, namely in determining whether the violation is justifiable. Requesting the handing over of legal documents is then less likely to be a violation of the essence of Art 6. Wijsman (n 93) 145 and 147.

Table 2 Evidence covered by the privilege against self-incrimination

Scope *ratione materiae*			
Will-dependent		Will-independent	
A. Declarations/statements	B. Evidence of which the authorities are not sure it exists (= statement in disguise)	C. All evidence that requires no or only passive cooperation	D. All evidence that requires active cooperation
COVERED BY NEMO TENETUR		NOT COVERED BY NEMO TENETUR	

JB + Jalloh + Chambaz

defiance of the will of the person, and the latter cannot exclude that it might lead to incrimination. This exception is also discussed in *Jalloh* (and *Gäfgen*), where the Court nuances the criterion, by adding that the evidence required no further forensic examination and that the coercion amounted to a violation of Article 3.

In our view, the case law of the ECtHR is thus far from bringing clarity about the scope of *nemo tenetur*. This holds especially for requests for documents, as will often be the case in customs proceedings. One should be cautious when drawing conclusions from it. According to *Chambaz* and (to a lesser extent) *JB*, anyone subjected to a customs investigation can try to seek cover under a broad protection of *nemo tenetur*. Two things should be kept in mind: (i) the Court seems to revive the original *Saunders* formula as it did in *Van Weerelt* and *Kalnéniené*, and (ii) even if the Court sticks to its broad interpretation of *nemo tenetur*, calling upon the right to remain silent might not always be in the best interest of the suspect. The customs authorities will then have to get the information themselves, for example through a search of the premises. They might thus resort to more intrusive methods. A search of the premises is indeed more intrusive than a formal request to hand over documents. This may sound a bit counter-intuitive. By protecting the *nemo tenetur* principle, the Court indirectly promotes the use of intrusive measures for the gathering of evidence. The reader should nevertheless remember that the suspect might be able to rely on other fundamental rights, such as the right to privacy, to defend himself when the authorities resort to these more intrusive measures. There remains, however, the question whether Belgian customs procedures meet these other procedural rights. You could, for example, wonder whether the possibility to search premises without a warrant is compliant with the right to privacy (see above section II.B.). This study, however, only looks at the application of *nemo tenetur*, leaving aside the analysis of those other fundamental rights.

C. Is the Violation Justifiable? Has the *Nemo Tenetur* Principle been Violated in its Essence?

An infringement of *nemo tenetur* leads to the exclusion of the evidence obtained through the infringement and could even mean that the criminal proceedings as a whole will be dismissed. However, these consequences are not absolute or applied unlimitedly. The ECtHR only sanctions the violation of *nemo tenetur* with exclusion if it is violated in its essence. The Court determines this on the basis of the following criteria:[168]

(i) Serious coercion[169] and extensive questioning. Serious forms of coercion (eg, threatening with imprisonment)[170] quickly lead to a violation of the principle at its core. The same applies to extensive questioning[171] or broad requests to provide evidence.[172] Limited requests are less likely to affect *nemo tenetur* at its core.[173]

(ii) The absence of relevant procedural guarantees. If there are no procedural guarantees that can mitigate the coercion, such as the possibility for the suspect to explain why he does not or cannot give certain information, or to challenge the use of the evidence obtained, the Court is inclined to establish a violation at its core.[174]

(iii) The decisive nature of the evidence obtained in violation of *nemo tenetur*. In contrast, if the evidence is only used to prove one element of the offence, the use is limited, and thus justifiable.[175]

[168] See for example: *Jalloh v Germany*, App No 54810/00 (ECtHR, 11 July 2006) para 101; *O'Halloran and Francis v UK*, App No 15809/02 and 25624/02 (ECtHR, 29 June 2007) para 55; *Bykov v Russia*, App No 4378/02 (ECtHR, 10 March 2009) para 92; *Zaichenko v Russia*, App No 39660/02 (ECtHR, 18 February 2010) para 38; ECtHR, 'Guide on Article 6 of the European Convention on Human Rights: right to a fair trial (criminal limb)': https://www.echr.coe.int/Documents/Guide_Art_6_criminal_ENG.pdf (accessed 20 December 2019); Wijsman (n 93) 94.

[169] Here, there is of course overlap between the scope criterion 'coercion' (see above section III.B.(i).) and the justification criterion 'extent of the coercion'. Without coercion, *nemo tenetur* does not apply, and without the coercion being severe enough, there is no violation of the privilege in its essence.

[170] *Heaney and McGuinness v Ireland*, App No 34720/97 (ECtHR, 21 December 2000) paras 53 and 55; *Saunders v UK*, App No 19187/91 (ECtHR, 17 December 1996) para 70.
A fine can also amount to a sufficiently high level of coercion: *Marttinen v Finland*, App No 19235/03 (ECtHR, 21 April 2009) para 73; *Lückhof and Spanner v Austria*, App No 58452/00 and 61920/00 (ECtHR, 10 January 2008) para 54; *King v UK*, App No 13881/02 (ECtHR, 8 April 2003) para 2; Lamberigts (n 91) 71.

[171] *Heaney and McGuinness v Ireland*, App No 34720/97 (ECtHR, 21 December 2000) para 24; *Shannon v UK*, App No 6563/03 (ECtHR, 4 October 2005) para 23.

[172] *Funke v France*, App No 10828/84 (ECtHR, 25 February 1993) para 30: 'production of papers and documents of any kind relating to operations of interest to their department'; *JB v Switzerland*, App No 31827/96 (ECtHR, 3 May 2001) para 39: 'documents etc. which might be relevant for the assessment of taxes'; *Chambaz v Switzerland*, App No 11663/04 (ECtHR, 5 April 2012) under 'Le droit interne pertinent': 'les livres, documents et pièces justificatives se trouvant en sa possession et qu'il remette des attestations et états présentant de l'importance pour sa taxation'.

[173] Having to provide the identity of the driver of a car on a specific date, on the penalty of a fine, only constitutes a limited request. See: *O'Halloran and Francis v UK*, App No 15809/02 and 25624/02 (ECHR, 29 June 2007); *Weh v Austria*, App No 38544/97 (ECtHR, 8 April 2004) para 54; *Lückhof and Spanner v Austria*, App No 58452/00 and 61920/00 (ECtHR, 10 January 2008) para 55. Criticised by Wijsman (n 93) 104 and 137. According to C Conings and J Kerkhofs, requesting the passwords of, for example, a mobile phone also constitutes a limited request. See Conings and Kerkhofs (n 90) 467. However, the information it gives access to is not limited at all. The authors make a distinction between giving the key and the information it protects.

[174] *Jalloh v Germany*, App No 54810/00 (ECtHR, 11 July 2006) paras 101 and 107; *O'Halloran and Francis v UK*, App Nos 15809/02 and 25624/02 (ECtHR, 29 June 2007) para 59; *Lückhof and Spanner v Austria*, App Nos 58452/00 and 61920/00 (ECtHR, 10 January 2008) para 57; Conings and Kerkhofs (n 90) 467–68.

[175] *O'Halloran and Francis v UK*, App Nos 15809/02 and 25624/02 (ECtHR, 29 June 2007) para 60. See in the same sense: *Bykov v Russia*, App No 4378/02 (ECtHR, 10 March 2009) para 103; *Gäfgen v Germany*,

In customs proceedings, the refusal to cooperate with the request to show the book-keeping or other documents is punished with a criminal fine of 25–250 EUR.[176] Although fines can constitute coercion, the low amount provided by the GLCE might not be severe enough to establish a violation of *nemo tenetur* in its essence.[177] Yet, as this power to request documents is far-reaching, in some circumstances, this might be considered a very broad and general request. Concerning the second criterion, the absence of procedural safeguards in general in customs proceedings might lead to the conclusion that *nemo tenetur* has been violated at its core. However, the Court especially focuses on the possibility for the suspect to contest the evidence and thus on the adversarial character of the proceedings. This safeguard is provided for the suspect in customs proceedings, as he has the right to contest evidence during the trial phase. Nevertheless, this possibility to contest the evidence is hampered by the special probative value of the records drafted by the customs authorities (see above section II.B.(iv).). Thirdly, the extent to which the customs authorities will rely on certain evidence depends on the facts of the case. In conclusion, it is not possible to determine with certainty whether customs proceedings will amount to a violation of *nemo tenetur* at its core.

If the Court does not establish a violation of the essence of *nemo tenetur*, then the violation can be justified by a public interest or the complexity of the offence.[178] For example, the compulsory identification of the driver in case of traffic offences can be justified by the public interest because when you go on the road, you are taking certain responsibilities.[179] In *Saunders*, the UK Government argued that the complexity of corporate fraud and the public interest in the honest conduct of companies and the effective fight against such corporate fraud justify a slight deviation from the fundamental principles of a fair procedure. This argument was, by contrast, not accepted by the Court.[180] When applying these examples to customs law, it is uncertain whether the Court would consider the violation of *nemo tenetur* justified and on the basis of which arguments. On the one hand, one could reason that if you import/export goods,

App No 22978/05 (ECtHR, 1 June 2010) para 186. For cases where the Court found that the conviction was based to a decisive extent on evidence obtained in violation with *nemo tenetur* see: *Zaichenko v Russia*, App No 39660/02 (ECtHR, 18 February 2010) para 59; *Yaremenko v Ukraine*, App No 66338/09 (ECtHR, 30 April 2015) para 66; *Jalloh v Germany*, App No 54810/00 (ECtHR, 11 July 2006) para 121; Conings and Kerkhofs (n 90) 468; ECtHR, 'Guide on Article 6 of the European Convention on Human Rights: right to a fair trial (criminal limb)': https://www.echr.coe.int/Documents/Guide_Art_6_criminal_ENG.pdf (accessed 20 December 2019).

[176] GLCE, Art 203 para 3.

[177] *Lückhof and Spanner v Austria*, App Nos 58452/00 and 61920/00 (ECtHR, 10 January 2008) para 54.

[178] If the Court does establish a violation of the essence, this cannot be justified by public interest concerns. *Saunders v UK*, App No 19187/91 (ECtHR, 17 December 1996) para 74; *Heaney and McGuinness v Ireland*, App No 34720/97 (ECtHR, 21 December 2000) paras 57–58; *Quinn v Ireland*, App No 36887/97 (ECtHR, 21 December 2000), paras 58–89; *Jalloh v Germany*, App No 54810/00 (ECtHR, 11 July 2006) para 97; *Bykov v Russia*, App No 4378/02 (ECtHR, 10 March 2009) para 93; *Marttinen v Finland*, App No 19235/03 (ECtHR, 21 April 2009) paras 74–75; *Zaichenko v Russia*, App No 39660/02 (ECtHR, 18 February 2010) para 39; Conings and Kerkhofs (n 90) 468; ECtHR, 'Guide on Article 6 of the European Convention on Human Rights: right to a fair trial (criminal limb)': https://www.echr.coe.int/Documents/Guide_Art_6_criminal_ENG.pdf (accessed 20 December 2019); Lamberigts (n 91) 80.

[179] *O'Halloran and Francis v UK*, App Nos 15809/02 and 25624/02 (ECtHR, 29 June 2007) para 57; *Lückhof and Spanner v Austria*, App Nos 58452/00 and 61920/00 (ECtHR, 10 January 2008) para 53.

[180] *Saunders v UK*, App No 19187/91 (ECtHR, 17 December 1996) paras 64 and 74; De La Serna (n 88) 7.

it is in the public interest that a number of obligations and rules are implied, including providing certain information. Nevertheless, taking into account *Saunders*, the Court might not consider the complexity of customs offences, the public interest in honest trade, and the effective fight against customs fraud as sufficient arguments to justify a violation of *nemo tenetur*.

IV. *Nemo Tenetur* in Belgian Case Law

In the Belgian legal order, the Belgian Court of Cassation[181] recognised *nemo tenetur* as a part of the rights of the defence in a judgment as far back as 21 February 1882,[182] and later also in the judgments of 13 May 1986,[183] 6 May 1993,[184] and 13 January 1999.[185] In contrast to the ECtHR, the Court of Cassation does not make a step-by-step analysis of all the conditions of *nemo tenetur*. The Court of Cassation mainly focuses on the temporal and material scope. Consequently, we have limited our analysis of the case law to these two aspects.

Since 2011,[186] following the ECtHR case law in *Salduz*,[187] the *nemo tenetur* principle can, inter alia, be found in Article 47*bis* of the Code of Criminal Procedure (CCP).[188] This legal provision has been amended in 2016 due to the so-called Salduz Directive of the EU and the evolving case law of the ECtHR.[189] Article 47*bis* CCP now provides that before any interrogation, in whatever capacity the person is heard,[190] it must

[181] This legal provision focuses on the relevant case law of the Court of Cassation. The Belgian Constitutional Court does not have extensive case law on the subject. The judgments reiterate general principles and the questions raised in this chapter are not dealt with in depth (see Belgian Constitutional Court 12 October 2017, no 116/2017, paragraph B.14.4; Belgian Constitutional Court 20 February 2020, no 28/2020, paragraph B.3.1). Secondly, the lower courts have very divergent reasoning. For example, the Court of Appeal in Liège seems to follow the *Chambaz* case law and thus interprets *nemo tenetur* very broadly, while the Court of Appeal in Ghent applies a more restrictive interpretation. See Eerens (n 98) 403.

[182] Belgian Court of Cassation 21 February 1882, *Pas.* 1882, 74.

[183] Belgian Court of Cassation 13 May 1986, no 9136.

[184] Belgian Court of Cassation 6 May 1993, no 6416.

[185] Belgian Court of Cassation 13 January 1999, no P.98.0412.F.

[186] Act of 13 August 2011 amending the Code of Criminal Procedure and the Act of 20 July 1990 on pre-trial detention in order to confer rights, including the right to consult a lawyer and be assisted by him, on any interrogated person and on any person deprived of his liberty (the Salduz Act), *Moniteur Belge* 6 September 2011, 56.347.

[187] *Salduz v Turkey*, App No 36391/02 (ECtHR, 27 November 2008).

[188] Code of Criminal Procedure of 17 November 1808, *Bull. Off.* 27 November 1808, 0.

[189] Directive (EU) 2013/48 on the right of access to a lawyer in criminal proceedings and in European arrest warrant proceedings, and on the right to have a third party informed upon deprivation of liberty and to communicate with third persons and with consular authorities while deprived of liberty [2013] OJ L294/1. Implemented by the Belgian law: Act of 21 November 2016 regarding certain rights of persons subjected to an interrogation, *Moniteur Belge* 24 November 2016, 77.974. See also P Monville and M Giacometti, 'Le droit d'accès sans restriction à un avocat dans les procédures pénales: (enfin) une révolution copernicienne?' in V Franssen and A Masset (eds), *Les droits du justiciable face à la justice pénale* (Commission Université-Palais Vol 171, Limal, Anthemis 2017).

[190] According to the ECtHR case law, witnesses normally cannot invoke *nemo tenetur*. Article 47*bis* CCP, however, does provide this right, and therefore goes one step further than the ECtHR. Nevertheless, the protection of witnesses is more limited than the protection of suspects. *Nemo tenetur* for witnesses is thus called '*nemo tenetur* light'.

be communicated to him that he cannot be obliged to incriminate himself.[191] However, the CCP is only applicable to what Belgian law considers to be criminal proceedings and a formal interrogation.[192] Regarding administrative proceedings or the protection against being forced to produce evidence outside the realm of a formal interrogation, the accused will thus have to invoke Article 6 ECHR before the Belgian judge.

A. *Ratione Temporis*

Above we discussed the different scenarios in which *nemo tenetur* can come into play according to the ECtHR. Quite logically, similar scenarios arise in Belgian case law. From the moment someone is criminally charged, he can benefit from the right not to contribute to his own incrimination. Whether a person is criminally charged depends on the facts of the case.[193]

First of all, *nemo tenetur* applies when a criminal investigation *sensu stricto* is being conducted.[194] This is also the case when the administrative authorities conduct investigative measures on behalf of the public prosecutor.[195]

Furthermore, in 2008,[196] the Court ruled that *nemo tenetur* applied when a criminal investigation was pending at the same time as the administrative proceedings. Similar to the ECtHR case law mentioned above (see above section III.A.(i).), the parallel criminal proceedings then have an impact on the administrative proceedings.

However, the analogy with the ECtHR case law does not go further than this. While the ECtHR also brings some other situations under the definition of criminal charge (see above III.A.(i).), the Belgian Court of Cassation remains more restrictive on the matter. What is even more remarkable, however, is that the Belgian Court of Cassation nowadays seems to contradict both the ECtHR's case law in *Saunders* and its own previous case law[197] according to which administrative evidence obtained

[191] The question can be raised whether Article 47*bis* CCP is elaborate enough to comply with the requirements of Directive (EU) 2016/343 on the strengthening of certain aspects of the presumption of innocence and of the right to be present at the trial in criminal proceedings [2016] OJ L65/1.

[192] According to the Court of Cassation, an interrogation within the meaning of Article 47*bis* CCP is a form of organised questioning by an authorised official about offences in the context of a (judicial) inquiry with the aim of finding the truth. That Article does, however, not apply to spontaneous statements or indications given by a person who is called to account for his behaviour by a competent official (for instance, a customs official), whose interpellation is only intended to get a correct picture of the facts. The fact that the information provided may indicate the existence of an offence is not decisive. See Belgian Court of Cassation 28 May 2019, no P.19.0127.N.; Belgian Court of Cassation 5 November 2019, no P.19.0384.N.

[193] Belgian Court of Cassation 29 November 2011, no P.11.0113.N., paras 27–28.

[194] See, for example, Belgian Court of Cassation 6 May 1993, no 6416; Belgian Court of Cassation 14 March 2017, no P.14.1001.N.; Belgian Court of Cassation 31 May 2017, no P.17.0388.F.; Belgian Court of Cassation 4 February 2020, no P.19.1086.N.

[195] Belgian Court of Cassation 19 June 2013, no P.12.1150.F.

[196] Belgian Court of Cassation 2 April 2008, no P.07.1744.F.

[197] In its judgment of 13 May 1986, the Court ruled that statements obtained before the actual criminal prosecution should be excluded as evidence. In this case, the tax administration conducted an interrogation, extracting declarations with misleading promises, and subsequently these declarations were used in criminal proceedings. Belgian Court of Cassation 13 May 1986, no 9136. In this context P Van De Weyer also refers to the judgment of 2008 (mentioned above). P Van De Weyer, 'Rechten van verdediging in een

without respect for *nemo tenetur* can constitute inadmissible criminal evidence (see above III.A.(ii).). By classifying proceedings as administrative, Belgian authorities can thus obtain evidence for the criminal trial without the need to respect *nemo tenetur*. Denying the latent effect introduced by *Saunders* definitely results in more narrow protection of *nemo tenetur*.

An example of the restrictive approach of the Court of Cassation is the case of 29 November 2011 about animal feed contamination.[198] The Ministry of Agriculture inspected an animal feed company in order to determine the origin of contaminated fat they had found in the animal feed that made the cattle sick. Their goal was to avoid further contamination. The representatives of the company were interrogated several times and requested to provide documents, more specifically a green diary. Following the Belgian Act of 11 July 1969 on Pesticides and Raw Material for Agriculture Horticulture, Forestry and Cattle Breeding, the representatives could be fined if they did not cooperate. The Court of Cassation confirmed in its judgment the reasoning of the Court of Appeal of Ghent that there was no suspicion during the entire administrative proceedings, since it was purely oriented at avoiding further contamination. Article 6 ECHR therefore did not apply *ratione temporis*.

In a second step, the Court of Appeal of Ghent had concluded that the declarations could be used in later criminal proceedings. The Court of Appeal thus went directly against the latent effect of *nemo tenetur* recognised in the *Saunders* case law. Although the *Saunders* reasoning was invoked again by the defence before the Court of Cassation, the Court avoided this argument and countered it by simply deciding that it was not incompatible with Article 6 ECHR to 'voluntarily' make incriminating statements during the interrogations of the Ministry of Agriculture. The duty to cooperate on the basis of Article 8 of the Belgian Act of 11 July 1969 did not impair the right not to incriminate oneself, as it did not *coerce* the person in question to make the statements.[199]

This counter-argument of the Court of Cassation was also considered in case law about the obligation to cooperate with an inspection conducted by the Labour and Social Security Inspectorate and the resultant criminal offence of refusing to do so, called obstruction of supervision. On 6 November 2018,[200] the Court of Cassation ruled that, although there was an obligation to cooperate, the person concerned was not obliged to provide the requested documents. It determined that simply refusing to provide the documents cannot constitute the offence of obstruction of supervision. Only knowingly and deliberately obstructing the inspection can do so. The Court thus allows a simple refusal to cooperate. Similarly to its judgment of 29 November 2011, the Court of Cassation limits the obligation to cooperate. In 2011, the case concerned an obligation to make statements, whereas in 2018 it concerned the obligation to hand over documents. Nevertheless, the Court is not always consistent on this matter. On 21 April 2015,[201]

administratieve sanctieprocedure bij de dienst voor Geneeskundige Evaluatie en Controle' [2018] 4 *Tijdschrift voor Gezondheidsrecht* 236, 241.

[198] Belgian Court of Cassation 29 November 2011, no P.11.0113.N.

[199] Oddly enough, the Court does not address all the contested investigative measures. It only refers to the statements made during the interrogation, while the Ministry also requested a diary (and thus a document).

[200] Belgian Court of Cassation 6 November 2018, no P.18.0339.N.

[201] Belgian Court of Cassation 21 April 2015, no P.13.1258.N.

the Court of Cassation ruled in the opposite direction. It considered that the deliberate failure to deliver certain data carriers (electronic or otherwise), which contain data that legally has to be retained, to a labour and social security inspector who has requested them can constitute the offence of obstruction of supervision. According to the judgment, it is not important whether the social inspector used his investigative powers. The Court of Cassation thus seems to assume that sanctioning the refusal is not contrary to *nemo tenetur*.

An even more striking example of the restrictive approach is the quite recent case of 20 November 2018.[202] In this case, the customs authorities checked several vehicles after receiving information from the police on heating oil fraud (constituting a customs offence within the competence of the GACE). They found tainted fuel in two vehicles. The Court of Appeal of Ghent considered that the initial police information was accurate and concrete and that it was at least partially confirmed by the inspection of the vehicles. According to the Court of Appeal, this inspection was, however, purely administrative and the relevant persons thus had to cooperate. It was only after the inspection of the books on pain of a criminal fine, which led to interrogations, that *nemo tenetur* applied. At the moment of interrogation, the suspect was reminded of his right not to incriminate himself. Every measure before that, the Court reasoned, did not entail a suspicion of a criminal offence. The Court of Cassation followed the Court of Appeal in this factual reasoning, disclaiming that it is not for the Court of Cassation to rule on the facts of the case. The Court merely checks whether the Court of Appeal justifies its decision according to the law.

In this case of 20 November 2018, the Court of Cassation also explicitly contradicted the latent effect of *nemo tenetur*, like the Court of Appeal in Ghent did in the case of 29 November 2011. According to the Court of Cassation, judges only have to exclude evidence obtained in violation of *nemo tenetur* when there was a criminal charge at the time of the investigative measure. Evidence obtained in purely administrative proceedings without respect for *nemo tenetur* can in any case be used in later criminal proceedings.[203]

If we try recapitulate the case law of the Court of Cassation and compare it to the case law of the ECtHR (see Table 1), we see that the Court of Cassation at least partially undermines the interpretation by the ECtHR of the concept of criminal charge. The Court of Cassation readily accepts that there is no intention on the part of the authorities to impose sanctions with a criminal character (either through criminal or administrative proceedings). The Court therefore categorises situations (B) and (C) of Table 1 as purely administrative proceedings. Since fewer situations will be characterised as criminal, the *Saunders* case law on the latent effect of *nemo tenetur* becomes

[202] Belgian Court of Cassation 20 November 2018, no P.18.0688.N.

[203] As we have already stated in fn 117, the *Saunders* case law only concerned the use of *statements*, obtained in administrative proceedings, in later criminal proceedings. The case law has not been confirmed with regard to physical evidence, such as documents. One could wonder whether this could be the reason that the Belgian Court of Cassation did not follow the *Saunders* case law. First of all, we do not see any reason why this case law should not apply to physical evidence. Second, there is no indication in the judgment that the Belgian Court of Cassation used this argument to disregard the *Saunders* case law.

Table 3 Scope of *nemo tenetur* – *ratione temporis* (Court of Cassation)

<table>
<tr><td colspan="4">Scope ratione temporis</td></tr>
<tr>
<td>Criminal proceedings sensu stricto aimed at the person concerned.</td>
<td>Administrative investigation in three situations:
(A) Parallel criminal proceedings concerning the same underlying infringement;
(B) Criminal proceedings sensu stricto have not started but there is intention to do so or the person concerned cannot exclude it;
(C) Administrative sanction with criminal character.</td>
<td>Purely administrative proceedings.
BUT: cannot be used later on in a criminal investigation.
During the investigative measure the person can become a suspect.</td>
<td>Criminal investigation (sensu stricto) but not aimed at the person concerned (eg a witness).</td>
</tr>
<tr><td colspan="2"></td><td colspan="2">Cooperation obligations are allowed and can be sanctioned.</td></tr>
<tr><td colspan="2">Criminal charge</td><td colspan="2">No criminal charge</td></tr>
</table>

even more relevant. However, the Court has already rendered several judgments in which it also has eliminated the latent effect of *nemo tenetur*. Overall, this results in the following adaption of Table 1 where categories (B) and (C) and the latent effect disappear. Irrespective of the inconsistency with the ECtHR case law, the current position of the Court of Cassation will probably be affirmed in future customs case law, since the most recent and relevant case (the judgment of 20 November 2018) concerned customs proceedings.

B. *Ratione Materiae*

Concerning the scope *ratione materiae*, the Court of Cassation started out with a fairly broad interpretation. In its judgments of 2 April 2008,[204] 8 September 2010,[205] and 19 June 2013,[206] the Court did not make a distinction between documents and statements, bringing both types of evidence under the protection of *nemo tenetur*. In fact, the Court seemed to apply a similar material scope to that applied by the ECtHR in *Chambaz*.[207]

However, in a judgment of 21 April 2015,[208] the Court deviated from the *Chambaz*-like reasoning because national legislation obliged it to do so. The Court decided that failing to submit requested documents can constitute the criminal offence of obstruction of supervision, formulated in Article 209 of the Belgian Social Criminal Code.[209] *In casu*, the requested documents contained data that the person in question was legally obliged to retain. Therefore, the authorities were sure the documents actually existed. The person concerned could therefore not refuse to hand them over. This reasoning is based on the distinction that the Social Criminal Code itself makes between the competence of the authorities to request legally required documents and the competence to request other documents. They can only sanction the refusal of the former. This distinction is inspired by the *Funke* judgment. The Belgian Social Criminal Code thus applies a more restricted material scope and so did the Court of Cassation by enforcing it. In conclusion, the *Chambaz* case law was not adhered to. In our opinion this is not necessarily problematic since the ECtHR itself seems to reconsider its *Chambaz* case law.

On 14 March 2017,[210] the Court of Cassation limited the material scope further by implementing the distinction between will-dependent and will-independent evidence from the *Saunders* case law. In the context of a house search, the suspect was asked to open a lockbox, which appeared to contain weapons. He was then asked if there were any more weapons in the house, whereupon he spontaneously indicated that he had other weapons in several locations. The Court of Cassation emphasised that the evidence was obtained in the context of a house search, in which there is no active obligation to cooperate, and that the investigators could have found the

[204] Belgian Court of Cassation 2 April 2008, no P.07.1744.F.

[205] Belgian Court of Cassation 8 September 2010, no P.08.1837.F.

[206] Belgian Court of Cassation 19 June 2013, no P.12.1150.F.

[207] It should be noted that the Court of Cassation in all three cases confirms the judgment of the Court of Appeal. In the first two cases, the Court of Appeal applied *nemo tenetur* to both documents and statements. The criminal conviction could nevertheless stand since the Court of Appeal based its judgment on other evidence. The Court of Cassation confirmed that the unlawful evidence was not decisive for the conviction. In the third case, the Court of Appeal had explicitly declared statements and documents obtained in violation of *nemo tenetur* inadmissible. The public prosecutor's office, which wanted to rely on this evidence, went to the Court of Cassation. The Court of Cassation, however, affirmed the judgment of the Court of Appeal. One can wonder whether the Court of Cassation would also have applied this broad *Chambaz*-like reasoning if the Court of Appeal had reasoned otherwise. The Court of Cassation would then have had to quash the Appeal judgment and send it to another Court of Appeal.

[208] Belgian Court of Cassation 21 April 2015, no P.13.1258.N.

[209] Social Criminal Code of 6 June 2020, *Moniteur Belge* 1 July 2010, 43.712.

[210] Belgian Court of Cassation 14 March 2017, no P.14.1001.N.

weapons themselves anyway without the indications given by the suspect. Therefore, the Court decided that there was no violation of *nemo tenetur*. In accordance with Table 2, and thus the case law of the ECtHR, the Court should have come to another conclusion regarding the material scope. Following the *Saunders* case law, the evidence obtained by opening the lockbox indeed does not fall under the material scope of *nemo tenetur*, but the statements made by the suspect should. In this case, however, the Court seems to bring both types of evidence under category C, since they were collected during a house search. Moreover, with this reasoning the Court seems to only focus on the material scope of *nemo tenetur*, whereas it also could have considered whether or not there was coercion.

In a judgment of 7 March 2018,[211] the Court of Cassation reaffirmed the *Saunders* case law. The Court determined that *nemo tenetur* does not apply to evidence (obtained under compulsion during a criminal charge) that exists independently of the suspect's will. The facts of this case were very similar to those of the judgment of 21 April 2015, since the authorities requested documents that the person concerned was obliged to retain. However, instead of only focusing on a reasoning similar to *Funke*, the Court now reiterated the *Saunders* formula on the material scope.

On 6 November 2018,[212] however, the Court of Cassation contradicted its previous case law in the sphere of labour and social security law. As mentioned above (see above IV.A), the Court ruled that simply refusing to provide employment or social security-related documents cannot constitute the offence of obstruction of supervision. Only knowingly and deliberately obstructing the inspection can do so. This case broadens the material scope of *nemo tenetur*, since documents that the person in question is legally obliged to retain no longer have to be provided as long as it is a simple refusal. The Court of Cassation therefore seems to pursue the *Chambaz* case law again. Nevertheless, it is unclear what the Court considers 'a simple refusal' and which kind of refusal is not allowed as it is not covered by *nemo tenetur*. In any case, by emphasising the type of refusal, the Court adds a new distinction that cannot be found in the case law of the ECtHR.

Finally, in a judgment of 4 February 2020 the Court again reiterated the classic *Saunders* formula.[213] The Court ruled that an investigating judge can oblige the suspect, on the basis of Article 88*quater* paragraph 1 CCP, to provide the password of a smartphone. Sanctioning the refusal to do so does not fall within the scope of *nemo tenetur*. According to the Court, having to provide a password cannot be considered to be providing statements. A password exists independently of the will of the person who has knowledge of it. The content of the evidence remains unaltered, irrespective of any imposed coercion. As a consequence, there is no risk of unreliable evidence.

The Court, however, did not explicitly specify whether the obligation to provide a password requires active or only passive cooperation and thus falls under

[211] Belgian Court of Cassation 7 March 2018, no P.17.0558.F.
[212] Belgian Court of Cassation 6 November 2018, no P.18.0339.N.
[213] Belgian Court of Cassation 4 February 2020, no P.19.1086.N.

category C or D of Table 2. It did emphasise that there is a distinction to be made between the password and the potentially incriminating information that can be found on the smartphone.[214] By stressing that they do not coincide since the authorities will still have to further examine the phone to find evidence, the Court implicitly seems to indicate that providing a password only requires little cooperation and would thus fall under category C.[215] Moreover, one could reason that the authorities can try to hack the phone themselves anyway (although they will not always succeed). However, the reasoning that providing a password requires only passive cooperation can be criticised. According to Article 88*quater* CCP, the authorities can punish the suspect for refusing to provide the password with a prison sentence of six months to three years and/or a fine of 26 to 20,000 euros. What then constitutes the difference between being sanctioned for not providing a password and being sanctioned for refusing to hand over certain documents? The obligation to provide documents has been brought under the protection of *nemo tenetur* by the case law after *Saunders*, namely *JB* and *Chambaz*, based on the argument that active cooperation was needed. Moreover, it is artificial to disconnect the password from the potentially incriminating information on the phone. The criterion of the need for further investigation does not seem tenable (see above section III.B.(iii)).

In conclusion, the case law of the Court of Cassation on the material scope of *nemo tenetur* is inconsistent. Depending on the facts of the case, the Court has applied different criteria to determine the material scope. Since the case law of the Court of Cassation is simply too fluctuating and unclear, we will not adapt Table 2 to it. A clear answer to the question of the material scope of *nemo tenetur* is nevertheless essential, since the request for documents (whether or not in digital format)[216] plays an important role in customs proceedings, as it is one of the predominant ways to gather evidence.

[214] The question arises, however, whether the password can be separated from the information behind it. The Court of Cassation seems to compare this situation with providing access to your home pursuant to a search warrant. As mentioned, the *Saunders* case law excludes all evidence found during a house search from the scope of *nemo tenetur*. The ratio behind this case law is that the authorities can also obtain the evidence if the suspect does not cooperate. During a house search, they can force entry. One could reason that the authorities can similarly force entry to a digital device through hacking and thus find the information without the password. Until now, however, the ECtHR has not ruled on this matter. It is possible that the Court will set different standards for gathering evidence in the digital world. Has the key to a digital device the same bearing as the key to the front door of a home?

[215] The Constitutional Court has followed this reasoning in its judgment of 20 February 2020, no 28/2020.

[216] GLCE, Arts 201 and 203 provide that the customs authorities can require that documents that are retained on a computer system have to be provided in a readable and understandable way. Moreover, Article 201 GLCE allows the authorities to request the importer/exporter/addressee to make a copy of the documents or even operate the computer himself. These cooperation duties are comparable to the obligation to provide a password in Article 88*quater* para 1 CCP, but require sometimes an even more active cooperation, such as operating the computer yourself. This more active cooperation is exactly what is excluded in a criminal investigation *sensu stricto* by Article 88*quater* para 2 CCP. Article 88*quater* para 2 CCP explicitly excludes suspects from the investigative measure that obliges them to operate the computer system. The legislator did so on the ground that this active participation would be in violation with *nemo tenetur*. Articles 201 and 203 GLCE thus seem to be incompatible with *nemo tenetur*, applying the case law of *JB* and *Chambaz*, since they essentially require you to hand over the incriminating documents. This reasoning, however, only holds true on the condition that a criminal charge is already established.

V. Conclusion

Belgian customs law establishes a hybrid enforcement system where customs officials have the competence to conduct administrative as well as criminal proceedings. The officials have far-reaching powers in both types of proceedings and the pivotal point where administrative changes to criminal is not clear. Furthermore, these powers often imply the obligation for the taxpayer to cooperate actively on pain of a criminal fine. By consequence these powers often clash with the fundamental rights, particularly with the right not to incriminate oneself. The fact that *nemo tenetur* is not interpreted in a clear and coherent way only adds to the complexity.

The right to silence and not to incriminate oneself generally allows the suspect during criminal proceedings not to cooperate. It remains, of course, possible for law enforcement authorities to resort to house searches and other more intrusive measures. These do not constitute a violation of *nemo tenetur* because in that case, the information is obtained independently of the will of the suspect. Of course, they may still constitute a violation of another fundamental right under the ECHR, such as the right to privacy, but these questions remain outside the scope of this chapter.

The first difficult question concerns the scope in time of *nemo tenetur*. According to the ECtHR a criminal charge might arise during administrative proceedings when there are parallel criminal proceedings *sensu stricto* concerning the same underlying infringement, when there is an intention on the part of the authorities to start criminal proceedings *sensu stricto*, or when the authorities (threaten to) impose an administrative sanction of a criminal nature. If none of these situations apply, the proceedings are considered purely administrative and the obligation to cooperate can thus be sanctioned. The ECtHR, however, gave *nemo tenetur* a latent effect with the *Saunders* case law so that *nemo tenetur* can also apply to evidence obtained during the purely administrative stage if it is later on used in criminal proceedings against this person.[217] Nevertheless, as we have seen above, the concept of 'criminal charge' is interpreted more restrictively by the Belgian Court of Cassation and the latent effect of *nemo tenetur* is even ignored in some case law.

The second difficult question concerns the material scope, which the ECtHR has sometimes limited and sometimes broadened. After *Chambaz* it seemed as though the taxpayer could easily refuse to give up any document. However, the Court has recently become more careful again in broadening the material scope, by referring to the old *Saunders* formula. It is therefore up to the ECtHR to develop a clear line in its case law. Furthermore, this seems absolutely necessary to also create more consistent national case law. For example, the case law of the Belgian Court of Cassation concerning the material scope of *nemo tenetur* is at the moment quite hard to untangle, which creates a lot of legal uncertainty.

It is thus not easy to discern the conditions for the applicability of *nemo tenetur*, particularly in customs proceedings. In such proceedings, a criminal charge can, in theory, be easily established according to the case law of the ECtHR. The customs

[217] De La Serna (n 88) 8; F Kuty, *Justice pénale et procès equitable* vol 2 (Brussels, Larcier, 2006) 286, para 1689.

administration mostly opts for criminal proceedings or a settlement to handle customs infringements and the intention to handle a case criminally might thus be established at a very early stage. However, in practice, at the moment of the investigative measure, it is hard to know which hat the customs authorities are wearing, since the pivotal point between administrative and criminal is not clear. Moreover, due to the restrictive interpretation by the Belgian Court of Cassation of the concept 'criminal charge', it will be hard to prove before this Court that the customs authorities were already oriented towards initiating criminal proceedings. The fact that in the past the Court of Cassation has in other matters often ruled in favour of the customs authorities only confirms our assumption.

In any case, regarding the material scope, one should be aware that the right to remain silent during questioning by the customs authorities is a fundamental human right and must be guaranteed when there is a criminal charge. Requests for (digital) documents, however, raise questions. It remains unclear to what extent suspects have to comply with these requests. If the ECtHR in fact keeps reaffirming the *Saunders* and *Funke* case law, documents of which the existence is certain, such as the accounts, must always be provided. Other requests might be considered a fishing expedition. This does, however, not prevent the customs authorities from obtaining these documents or other evidence themselves through more intrusive measures or via requests directed at third parties. The customs authorities can, for example, search business or private premises. Providing access cannot be considered as an obligation to cooperate actively, but as 'passive cooperation' not covered by *nemo tenetur*. The reader should nevertheless remember that the suspect might be able to rely on other fundamental rights, such as the right to privacy, to defend himself when the authorities conduct a search of the premises. The clash between the far-reaching investigative powers with limited procedural safeguards and other fundamental rights deserves further research, but does not fall within the scope of our chapter.

In conclusion, it is not easy to determine whether the ECtHR would rule in a Belgian customs case that *nemo tenetur* applies. And even if *nemo tenetur* applies, it will depend on the facts of the case whether the ECtHR would establish a violation of the right in its essence. If it does not establish a violation in the essence, it is also not clear from the case law whether the special characteristics of the Belgian customs criminal procedure will justify a deviation from the right to fair proceedings. The Belgian Constitutional Court has often ruled that because of the specific nature of customs fraud, the far-reaching powers of the customs administration can be justified. However, until now, this case law did not concern *nemo tenetur*. Since *nemo tenetur* is fundamental to avoiding miscarriages of justice and to securing the right to fair proceedings, the outcome in this matter might be different.

PART III

Toward a More Coherent Terminological Framework in Europe

12

Two Forms of Smudge: An ECtHR Perspective on the Blurring of Boundaries between Criminal and Administrative Law

KATJA ŠUGMAN STUBBS

I. Introduction

It is clear that in the life of law one comes across infractions (to use the most neutral term) of differing gravity. One of the most challenging legal questions is how to classify those offences into categories that make it possible to deal with them in a (procedurally) fair and sensible way.[1] By answering these questions we define the boundaries of a certain legal discipline. The problem is made more complicated by the various criteria different countries use to define what falls under the jurisdiction of criminal law and what is covered by that of administrative law. One would hope to find some guidance for solving these questions in the legal developments of the supranational entities: such as the Council of Europe or the European Union (EU). But sadly, it seems that the case law of the European Court of Human Rights (ECtHR) and developments in EU law have not provided an answer: if anything, the boundaries between the two domains are becoming ever more blurred.[2]

The aim of this chapter is to contribute to the debate on developments that are redefining the traditional concept of criminal law. In order to do this, we will move from the 'hard core' of the classical notion of criminal law – to adopt the language of a landmark judgment we shall examine in due course – and examine the periphery, the 'outskirts' of this legal field, and on to the area where criminal law merges with other legal disciplines;

[1] See, eg: D Husak, *Overcriminalization: The Limits of the Criminal Law* (Oxford, Oxford University Press, 2008).

[2] Vervaele, for example, discusses the emergence of EU administrative punitive sanctions: sanctions with mixed nature – criminal and administrative. See JAE Vervaele, *The Europeanisation of Criminal Law and the Criminal Law Dimension of European Integration* (European Legal Studies, 2005), 10, available at: aei.pitt.edu/44274/1/researchpaper_3_2005_vervaele.pdf.

especially administrative law. I will try to show that the boundary between the two disciplines is being smudged, blurred heavily, in (at least) two different ways, each of which has different consequences. I will then analyse the influence of ECtHR case law on this process of blurring and outline some of the dangers arising from this process as traditional criminal law loses its once relatively firm boundaries.

II. Attempts to Define the Differences between Criminal and Administrative Law

The division between the fields of administrative and criminal law has never been clear, neither in theory nor in practice.[3] Despite the fact that all categorisations, this one being no exception, are simplifications of reality and that,[4] luckily, life in its full richness cannot be perfectly classified by them, every legal scholar intuitively feels that there is and that there should be a difference between these two disciplines. If nothing else, administrative and criminal law are still taught as very distinct courses in universities, and the jurisdictions of law courts still follow the same division. A court must decide whether a case falls under its jurisdiction as an administrative or a criminal case. The distinctions therefore still serve some practical purpose.

Numerous definitions and various concepts have been developed in the attempt to define, at least at a theoretical level, this difference between criminal and administrative law.[5] It only seems logical that this division should be made by using some sort of balancing and gradation[6] according to the principle of proportionality: more severe offences require a different approach to those which are obviously less malign. The next questions are therefore: (1) what are the criteria by which we judge which infractions are mild and which severe,[7] and (2) what legal consequences follow from classifying

[3] As Advocate General Stick-Haxl pointed out specifically for penalties: '… a comparison of the legal systems of the Member States … reveals, in particular, that the boundary between criminal and administrative penalties is a fluid one'. See AG's Opinion of 27 November 2001, in Case C-210/00 *Käserei Champignon Hofmeister GmbH & Co. KG v Hauptzollamt Hamburg-Jonas* (EU:C:2001:645), [2002] ECR I-6456, at I-6468, para 46.

[4] M Damaška, 'Evidentiary Barriers to Conviction and Two Models of Criminal Procedure: A Comparative Study' (1973) 121 *University of Pennsylvania Law Review* 506, 577.

[5] Smith and Hogan, noting: 'the difficulty frequently encountered in defining the subject-matter of a particular branch of the law' go on to point out that: 'nowhere has this been more greatly felt than in the criminal law'. See JC Smith and B Hogan, *Criminal Law*, 7th edn (London, Butterworths, 1992) 15. Fletcher has come to a similar conclusion: 'Yet the truly difficult problems in determining the scope of the criminal law are left unresolved. We may share an intuitive sense that deportation, expatriation, tort damages, customs fines, and impeachment are not cases of criminal punishment, yet it is by no means easy to explain why'. See GP Fletcher, *Rethinking Criminal Law* (Oxford/New York, Oxford University Press, 2000) 412.

[6] Parker, discussing the idea of the optimal penalties, points out that: 'One of the virtues of optimal penalty theory, particularly as contrasted with a view of absolute deterrence or absolute "desert," is its consistency with this balancing principle that undergirds much of the criminal law'. See: JS Parker, 'Criminal Sentencing Policy for Organizations: The Unifying Approach of Optimal Sentences' (1989) 26(3) *American Criminal Law Review* 513, 569.

[7] Hart, for example, asks himself: 'What *are* the ingredients of moral blameworthiness which warrant a judgment of community condemnation?' See HM Hart, 'The Aims of the Criminal Law' (1958) 23(3) *Law and Contemporary Problems* 401, 412.

a certain infraction under a certain category? In other words: what exactly are we balancing and grading? The obvious answers which come to mind are: while with the increasing gravity of offence the state has a proportionately greater right to interfere, the people involved in those offences should also be protected by greater rights.[8] We should consider the overall fairness of the procedure and its effectiveness: maximum results for minimum 'investment' of resources. In an attempt to make things clear and transparent, great legal minds have constructed (at least) two different areas of law with two different kinds of procedure: (1) administrative law for dealing with milder offences, and (2) criminal law for dealing with the more severe offences which threaten the core of society.

Some sound theoretical concepts have been developed seeking either (1) to define the differences between the two disciplines: one tackling the most severe offences in the criminal law field and the other dealing with minor offences, or (2) to make at least an attempt to define the area of criminal law clearly and by this exclude all the other legal disciplines which might overlap with it. Without any pretence of offering an exhaustive discussion, I will set out a quick overview of a few potential criteria by which it is possible to tackle this question.

In his classic study on the subject, Herbert Packer offered the following criteria for deciding what conduct should be criminalised, rather than regulated by other fields of law:

(1) most people view the conduct as socially threatening;
(2) the conduct is not condoned by a significant section of society;
(3) criminalisation is not inconsistent with the goals of punishment;
(4) suppressing the conduct will not inhibit socially desirable conduct;
(5) it may be dealt with through even-handed and non-discriminatory enforcement;
(6) controlling the behaviour will not expose the criminal justice system to severe qualitative or quantitative strains;
(7) there are no reasonable alternatives to the criminal sanction dealing with it;
(8) the costs of enforcement are not prohibitive.[9]

Other authors have elaborated on elements of Packer's theory or focused on different factors. These include anything from philosophical categories, eg a harm principle,[10] harm to others,[11] infliction of deserved punishment on culpable wrongdoers,[12] moral condemnation of the community,[13] strictly legal factors (eg severity of infraction),[14]

[8] Hart, 'The Aims of the Criminal Law' (n 7) 411.

[9] HL Packer, *The Limits of the Criminal Sanction* (Stanford, CA, Stanford University Press, 1968). See also: A Ashworth, 'Is the Criminal Law a Lost Cause?' (2000) 116 *Law Quarterly Review* 225, 230–37.

[10] JS Mill, *On Liberty* (London, John W Parker, 1859) 21–22.

[11] J Feinberg, *The Moral Limits to the Criminal Law, vol 1: Harm to Others* (Oxford, Oxford University Press, 1984) 31–64.

[12] MS Moore, *Placing Blame: A Theory of Criminal Law* (Oxford, Oxford University Press, 1997).

[13] Hart, 'The Aims of the Criminal Law' (n 7) 405.

[14] It is well-accepted in criminal law theory that only the harshest infractions warrant criminal penalties and there should be limits to criminalisation; criminal law as *ultima ratio*. See, eg, Husak, *Overcriminalization: The Limits of the Criminal Law* (n 1) 54.

differences in liability,[15] procedural standards,[16] the nature and harshness of penalties,[17] and different goals[18] emerging from the idiosyncrasies of certain legal cultures in their criminal policies.[19] However, as pointed out above, the concepts are still far from clear.

III. Models of Criminal–Administrative Divide

A. An Ideal: A Clean-cut System

In an ideal world the fields of criminal and administrative law would be organised in a parallel, well-defined and well-run co-existence of criminal and administrative law. In such an illusionary world (1) the boundaries between the two disciplines would be well-defined and arranged, (2) the whole legal system would be meticulously planned in advance, and (3) in practice it would exist in a well-run co-existence. Minor or medium infractions in certain legal fields (eg, tax, environmental offences, market manipulation) would be processed through the administrative channel, and serious infractions through that of criminal law.

Such a model is simple and clear and there is a definite beauty to it: there are no overlaps in jurisdiction, the powers of different authorities are clearly defined, and problems with the transfer of evidence from one domain to the other are avoided, all of which leads to a clear and coherent system. For such a division to be successful, legislation would be needed to separate jurisdiction clearly between different authorities. In the most elaborate scenario, different cases would be handled by different authorities, leading eg to administrative infractions being investigated through inspections by relevant

[15] Fault in criminal proceedings and strict liability in administrative ones. See, eg, RA Duff, 'Perversions and Subversions of Criminal Law' in RA Duff, L Farmer, SE Marshall, M Renzo and V Tadros (eds), *The Boundaries of the Criminal Law* (Oxford, Oxford University Press, 2010) 103; P Cane, *Responsibility in Law and Morality* (Oxford, Hart Publishing, 2002) 40–53, 191–224.

[16] Faure and Heine report that in many countries there are specific features in the administrative procedure which are absent from that of criminal law (eg, administrative enforcing bodies possessing wide-spread powers to inspect while having authority to apply a sanction as well, far-reaching powers granted to enforcing administrative bodies even when there is no suspicion that an environmental crime has been committed). See M Faure and G Heine, *Criminal Enforcement of Environmental Law in the European Union* (The Hague, Kluwer Law International, 2005) 47, 49.

[17] Traditionally criminal law sanctions are considered denunciatory and educational, carrying moral outrage, whereas administrative penalties do not. See, eg, J Feinberg, *Doing & Deserving: Essays in the Theory of Responsibility* (Princeton NJ, Princeton University Press, 1970); RA Duff, *Trials and Punishment* (Cambridge, Cambridge University Press, 1986). Kelsen has also compared the sanctions of criminal and civil law: 'The difference between penal and civil sanction lies rather in its purpose. Civil sanction is to make reparation for the damage caused by the socially harmful conduct; penal sanction is retribution'. See H Kelsen, *What is Justice? Justice, Law and Politics in the Mirror* (Berkeley/Los Angeles/London, University of California Press, 1971) 247.

[18] Richardson compares the goals of criminal and administrative procedures. See G Richardson, 'The Legal Regulation of Process' in G Richardson and HG Genn (eds), *Administrative Law and Government Action, The Courts and Alternative Mechanisms of Review* (Oxford, Clarendon Press, 1994) 111.

[19] Theoretical attempts to distinguish between administrative and criminal law seem particularly difficult in common law systems, where the criminal law is still dominated by judge-made doctrines. Ashworth's observation to this effect is well illustrated by the fact that: 'there are probably more than 8,000 criminal offences in English law'. See A Ashworth, 'General Principles of Criminal Law' in D Feldman (ed), *English Public Law* (Oxford, University Press, 2004).

agencies, and criminal offences tackled by the police, public prosecutors and later on criminal courts. For such a solution to be effective, the investigative powers of administrative and criminal law authorities would be designed carefully to ensure that there was no overlap in their power to act. Ideally, the investigative powers of administrative authorities would be less invasive (eg, administrative search) as compared to those of criminal law investigators (eg, house search). Each procedure would also respect different procedural standards clearly based on the principle of proportionality: more invasive measures would be accompanied by stricter legal guarantees (eg, judicial order required for intrusive investigative acts in criminal procedure). By the same principle, administrative law sanctions would have limited reach (eg, fines up to a certain sum only, no deprivation of liberty) as compared to those of criminal law (eg higher fines, custodial sentences). There should be elaborated rules for evidence transfer between the administrative and criminal law channels. Even the most elaborate legislative division cannot prevent overlaps in practice; there would always be cases of a 'mixed' nature. The precondition for a clear and well-functioning system would therefore be efficient cooperation between all authorities involved. If a case is to be processed justly and efficiently, only collaboration at the outset can eliminate the problems of jurisdiction which might arise.

B. Overlapping between Criminal and Administrative Law

It is extremely difficult to bring about a completely clean-cut division in practice. Such a solution would have to be planned well ahead at the legislative level, making comprehensive use of realistic information on actual practice. Even then it would only be possible to imagine a given legal system achieving such a clear division within one certain legal domain or another (eg, tax law, environmental law). In reality most states have fragmented legislation adopted consecutively (through amendment) which is therefore 'fluid' rather than systematically pre-designed. It is also not impossible to imagine that the blurring of criminal and administrative boundaries would suit some political or at least crime policy purposes: some offences are much more conveniently processed if classified as administrative and others, no doubt for different reasons, as criminal.[20]

That being the situation, it is nearly impossible to design a transparent division that approaches the ideal. Since this ideal would require well-organised, well-meaning institutions communicating and collaborating openly and efficiently, reality might also often leave a lot to be desired. We can therefore conclude that there are many reasons why most legal systems, willingly or unwillingly, end up with some kind of parallel organisation with powers of administrative and criminal authorities overlapping[21] and have to cope with a more or less chaotic parallel arrangement, with the spheres of

[20] 'In the past, opaqueness in the qualification of sanctions served a purpose. Criminal law was not part of the competence of the [European Community], and therefore any hint that a sanction might be qualified as a criminal charge had to be avoided', see A De Moor-Van Vugt, 'Administrative sanctions in EU Law' (2012) 5(1) *Review of European Administrative Law* 5, 41.

[21] Faure and Heine point out that in the field of environmental law 'establishing a side system to criminal law, which allows different kinds of repressive sanctions by administrative bodies, is a European-wide tendency'. See Faure and Heine, *Criminal Enforcement of Environmental Law in the European Union* (n 16) 65.

administrative and criminal law working together as best they can.[22] I will try to show that there are at least two ways in which the blurring of those boundaries occurs, each of which brings different legal consequences.

(i) Two Clearly Defined Concepts Overlapping

The first kind of blurring occurs when two more or less clearly defined concepts overlap and the intersection between them can be dealt with either by a clearly defined administrative or clearly defined criminal procedure or, sometimes, both. This is a case in which national legislation in a given area of life causes segments of criminal and administrative law to interact or operate in parallel.

What is common to all such systems is the fact that they attempt to regulate this zone of overlap by applying either classical criminal or administrative concepts to it (and sometimes both). Some systems involving parallelism decide to solve the problem of possible overlaps by creating rules governing priority in cases where such overlaps might occur: eg, they enact the so-called *una via* mechanism by which it is predetermined at the legislative level that in a case where certain facts can be considered to constitute either a criminal offence or an administrative offence, one of the systems will take priority. Sometimes the same case can take the path offered by the other legal route if the first proves unsuccessful, for whatever reasons. If a criminal prosecution, for example, fails, the case can still be processed through an administrative procedure.[23]

Sometimes *una via* is not provided for by the legislation, but practice solves the problems of overlaps by creating a de facto *una via* solution. There is an explicit or tacit agreement among the authorities that certain cases will only be dealt with in a certain way (either administrative or criminal).[24] And sometimes case law decides this question. Such a solution can only work if the cooperation between different bodies and the feedback provided on the measures taken and the cases handled are of excellent quality.

Una via systems have some definite advantages over the more chaotic solutions. Overlaps are successfully resolved in a way that allows both legal fields to serve their purposes: minor infractions being dealt with by administrative authorities and more severe ones by criminal courts. Good cooperation and clear divisions also help to respect the *ne bis in idem* principle. Criminal courts are not overburdened with minor

[22] Widdershoven eg notices that in the Netherlands: 'there is a development where the administrative law and criminal law are slowly edging towards each other'. See R Widdershoven, 'Encroachment of Criminal Law and Administrative Law in the Netherlands' (2002) 6(4) *Electronic Journal of Comparative Law* 460.

[23] This is the case in Slovenian tax law. A tax levy procedure can be pursued in both the administrative and criminal court systems, with the criminal procedure always taking priority over the administrative one if a certain act constitutes both a criminal and an administrative offence. The administrative procedure is suspended until the criminal procedure is concluded. In cases where the criminal case is dropped, an administrative procedure may then be activated. In a case where an administrative procedure, for whatever reason, should be initiated first, a criminal procedure may still be pursued afterwards. See H Jenull, 'Uveljavitev načela ne bis in idem v prekrškovnem in kazenskem postopku' (2007) 28 *Pravosodni bilten* 99–113.

[24] Faure and Heine mention the German and Belgian example of administrative agencies having a legal duty to refer a serious environmental case to the public prosecutor, thus waiving their right to settle the case through an administrative procedure. See Faure and Heine, *Criminal Enforcement of Environmental Law in the European Union* (n 16) 65.

offences and can better serve their purpose of sanctioning the most serious offences (*ultima ratio*). Since administrative offences are handled by quicker and simpler procedures, more of them can be successfully processed, the result being that more wrongdoings are punished one way or another. Such a system also helps develop a better understanding of what is an administrative matter, on the one hand, and what is a criminal one, on the other.

It is much more likely, however, that such a system produces many problems, especially if it is accompanied by fragmented or obsolete legislation and poor levels of cooperation and feedback between different authorities.[25] The same case can be dealt with by different authorities, causing potential problems with the *ne bis in idem* principle;[26] on the other hand, some cases can be completely overlooked due to weak communication between the different bodies involved. As a result, such a solution tends to be unpredictable, unstable and does not provide for legal certainty or transparency.[27]

(ii) An Example of Solving the Overlapping Problem

To illustrate how these systems work, we can consider the model of parallel co-existence as it manifested itself in the Flemish Region of Belgium in its law against environmental violations. Until mid-2009 the system was rather disorganised, according to Raedschelders,[28] namely demonstrating most of the characteristics of a chaotic parallel system in which no authority is certain as to what its powers are. We can list the problems that arise from fragmented legislation and a lack of harmony between different enforcement actors – resulting from a lack of clarity as to which authority will be processing a given case[29] – as factors contributing to inefficiency in this field. Such a system could not provide equality before the law and legal certainty.[30] As a result of the confusion the system largely relied on public prosecutors, therefore using only criminal law as a means of fighting environmental violations.[31] A chaotic parallel system

[25] Faure and Heine report that in some countries: 'it has been well-documented … that there has been a kind of "civil-war" between the criminal prosecutor and the administrative agency in respect of the adequate kind of reaction in the case of environmental pollution'. See Faure and Heine (n 16) 65.

[26] Gorunescu reports such problems in the Romanian legal system. She notes that no clear criteria to distinguish between criminal offences and administrative infringements have been set either by legislation or jurisprudence. In her opinion the current vague legal regulation in Romania contradicts the *ne bis in idem* standard established by the ECtHR. See M Gorunescu, 'Considerations about overlapping criminal and administrative liability for the same offense' (2011) 1(1) *Challenges of the Knowledge Society* 169–75.

[27] S Raedschelders, 'Interrelations between Administrative and Criminal Sanctions in Environmental Law: New Legislation and Actual Practice in Flanders', Ninth International Conference on Environmental Compliance and Enforcement (20–24 June 2011, Whistler, British Columbia), 616, at 617, available at: inece.org/conference/9/proceedings/65_Raedschelders.pdf.

[28] Ibid.

[29] 'Enforcement was not evident and often no precedence was provided for the effective sanctioning of offences.' See (n 27) ibid.

[30] 'Moreover, there were significant differences in approach and prioritisation at the public prosecutor's offices of the various districts.' See (n 27) ibid.

[31] Watson describes a similar situation in English law in the field of environmental law infringements. The system relied on the use of criminal law to deal with environmental infractions, with the result that a vast number of wrongdoings were not punished at all. See M Watson, 'The enforcement of environmental law: civil or criminal penalties?' (2005) 17(1) *Environmental Law and Management* 3–6.

resulted in a de facto exclusion model, whereby criminal law basically took on all the cases.[32]

However, the Flemish legislator decided on a complete change of approach. With the introduction of the Environment Enforcement Act the option of a parallel system was chosen, whereby the criminal law system would handle only severe cases, while all the rest would be processed via the more efficient administrative approach. An attempt was made to organise a parallel system with clear divisions, by defining precisely the difference in (1) the legal definition of administrative environmental infringements, on the one hand, and criminal environmental offences, on the other.[33] This difference consequently determines (2) the type of sanctioning: administrative infringement can result in an administrative fine or deprivation of an advantage, while a criminal environmental offence can result in a criminal sanction being passed. Environmental offences may be sanctioned through criminal or administrative procedures. The fact of whether or not such an offence has been committed may be established by the police or even administrative supervising authorities, but the records are always handed over to the public prosecutor for assessment on how to proceed. The system therefore also established a clear division on (3) who makes the final decision on how a case should be processed: administrative cases are dealt with by administrative authorities and criminal ones by public prosecutors.[34] Interestingly, if the prosecutor does not start criminal proceedings, a procedure for imposing an alternate administrative sanction (eg, fine) must be initiated.[35] In this way, coherence and much greater efficiency were achieved.

For wrongdoings which can be qualified as environmental offences, the Flemish system obviously adopted the *una via* solution. The *una via* solution helped reduce double or even multiple conflicts of jurisdiction and solved the problem of priorities, avoiding the complications of cumulating sanctions and possible *ne bis in idem* conflicts. Despite the fact that criminal offences are (mostly) also established by administrative authorities, the legislator nevertheless decided that their assessments are to be reviewed later on by the public prosecutor. In the event that the Prosecutor deems a case to involve a criminal rather than an administrative offence, he must report this decision to the administrative authority, at which point any administrative fine already imposed must be cancelled: criminal charge and sanctioning take over. An administrative procedure is also prohibited in cases where the public prosecutor makes no decision at all. He can also decide not to insist on criminal prosecution and to refer the case back to the administrative authority, allowing them to go ahead and impose a fine.[36]

We can see from this example that overlapping was solved by applying either typical criminal law or characteristic administrative solutions to the 'grey zone', ie, by drawing a clearly defined line between the types of sanctioning, with clearly set authorisations

[32] In the exclusion model, infractions in a certain legal field fall under the exclusive jurisdiction of either the criminal *or* the administrative courts and are sanctioned by one or the other only; there is no co-existence. For more on exclusion models see: K Šugman Stubbs and M Jager, 'The Organization of Administrative and Criminal Law' in F Galli and A Weyembergh (eds), *Do Labels Still Matter? Blurring Boundaries Between Administrative and Criminal Law, The Influence of the EU* (Bruxelles, Institute d'etudes Europeennes, 2014) 155–69.

[33] Raedschelders, 'Interrelations between Administrative and Criminal Sanctions' (n 27) 618.

[34] Ibid, 618–19.

[35] Ibid, 619.

[36] Ibid, 620.

divided between the administrative and criminal law authorities. Raedschelders reports that the system works well: it has accelerated handling of cases,[37] and created a clearer and much more coherent structure.[38] What is of further interest for our discussion is that it elegantly used only the classic tools which belong to either of the two well-defined legal fields, which is a great illustration of how the problems addressed here can be solved when the two classically defined fields meet and indeed cooperate.

(iii) Criminal and Administrative Fields Merging into an Undefined Phenomenon

However, all the above-mentioned solutions stem from the presumption that differences between criminal and administrative law in certain legal systems actually *do* exist; that criminal justice is designed to fight crime and administrative justice is intended to handle administrative affairs and that they must try somehow to co-exist. However, experience shows that even these simple presumptions seem to be less and less true in many legal systems and at a supranational level.[39]

On the one hand, classical administrative bodies with their administrative powers based on administrative procedural solutions are increasingly being used to fight crime.[40] We can therefore observe the *over-extension* of some administrative law authorisations into areas which would traditionally be viewed as belonging to criminal law.[41] On the other hand, we are also witnessing the *downgrading of criminal law standards* to better fit a tendency for efficiency.[42] In such cases it is basically impossible to discuss the existence and co-existence of the two legal disciplines: it seems more adequate to understand the question as one of both disciplines *merging* into a new field altogether. This second type of blurring, therefore, occurs in systems which invent solutions that cannot indisputably be classified under one or other of these two categories. In other words, the boundaries between the two fields are becoming hazy, because they are starting to take on elements from each other, *creating a third kind of phenomenon*: a hazy grey zone of 'criministrative law.'[43]

[37] Ibid, 621.

[38] Ibid, 625–26.

[39] Vervaele, for example, discusses the emergence of EU administrative punitive sanctions: sanctions of a mixed nature – criminal and administrative. He mentions, furthermore, that the EU Commission's investigating powers of supervision over companies and third parties, namely the administrative inspection, strongly resemble the powers to search authorised under criminal law. It is, he concludes, 'apparent that the dividing line between administrative law supervision and criminal law investigation is beginning to fade'. See Vervaele, *The Europeanisation of Criminal Law* (n 2) 10.

[40] Faure and Heine point out that: 'as a result of the so-called administrative dependence of environmental criminal law it is often the administrative authorities that determine the content of environmental criminal law'. See Faure and Heine (n 16) 73.

[41] See Duff's idea on subversions of criminal law, which expresses something similar. He claims that the criminal law is subverted when conduct that should be dealt with by criminal procedure is dealt with by other modes of legal control. See Duff, 'Perversions and Subversions of Criminal Law' (n 15) 92–93.

[42] As Huisman and Koemans succinctly point out: 'New administrative sanctions have been created here as well, such as the administrative fine, but existing measures under administrative law are also used now for a new purpose: to fight crime'. See W Huisman and M Koemans, 'Administrative Measures in Crime Control' (2008) 1(5) *Erasmus Law Review* 121, 123.

[43] A Bailleux, 'The fiftieth shade of grey Competition law, "criministrative law" and "fairly fair trials"' in F Galli and A Weyembergh (eds), *Do Labels Still Matter? Blurring Boundaries Between Administrative*

In this state of affairs, we can no longer look for solutions from the discrete fields of criminal or administrative law, since the 'grey zone' is actually breaking down their traditional composition. As such, the situation calls for altogether different ways of dealing with blur and overlap, since the classical subject of criminal law is irreversibly dissolving.[44]

(iv) *Examples of Measures with Undefined Identity*

Without attempting to be exhaustive we will enumerate just a few examples of a mixed, criminal and administrative nature.[45] We can observe solutions which downgrade criminal law standards, pushing them closer to what were traditionally considered standards of administrative law. This trend is most clearly seen in simplified criminal or vaguely criminal procedures compensating for fewer rights with lower penalties such as petty offence solutions, out-of-court sanctioning (cautioning),[46] compounding (UK, France),[47] and the proliferation of the 'penal order' (*Strafbefehl* (German), *ordonnance pénale* (French), *kaznovalni nalog* (Slovenian)).[48] A good example of downgrading strict criminal law standards to a (near) administrative level of procedure is the mechanism of plea-bargaining, with its long tradition in common law countries and its extremely rapid adoption in the traditional continental European countries.[49]

and Criminal Law, The Influence of the EU (Bruxelles, Institute d'etudes Europeennes, 2014) 137, 139–44; P Caeiro, 'The influence of the EU on the "blurring" between administrative and criminal law' in F Galli and A Weyembergh (eds), *Do Labels Still Matter? Blurring Boundaries Between Administrative and Criminal Law, The Influence of the EU* (Bruxelles, Institute d'etudes Europeennes, 2014) 171, 171–76.

[44] Administrative law is by no means the only reason for this. There are other factors involved, eg, surveillance technologies, the fight against terrorism, creation of cyber space, etc. All such phenomena contribute to the break-down of the legal field of criminal law as it was classically conceived, either by putting the stress on prevention rather than reaction, intelligence rather than evidence, or by weakening the traditional concepts on which criminal law is based, eg, space, time, jurisdiction, etc.

[45] Damaška points out that most continental countries distinguish between criminal and non-criminal offences; the latter being handled by administrative agencies applying looser evidential rules. But even among criminal offences there are two distinctive categories regarding their gravity: 'The less serious the crime, the less elaborate the rules.' See Damaška, 'Evidentiary Barriers to Conviction and Two Models of Criminal Procedure: A Comparative Study' (n 4) 511.

[46] M Jasch, 'Police and Prosecutions: Vanishing Differences between Practices in England and Germany' (2004) 5(10) *German Law Journal* 1207–16.

[47] In France for example, compounding of tax cases is in the hands of administrative authorities which decide not to forward the case to the prosecution service if the investigated party agrees to pay a certain sum (usually a fixed tax levy, an administrative fee and a tax fine). As Vervaele points out, the decision not to prosecute is an administrative procedure which strongly resembles a criminal law decision, since it serves to disable both criminal and administrative procedures. In England and Wales extrajudicial disposal of tax cases is also possible in the form of compounding. This is a certain form of diversion: an administrative act under which further criminal prosecution is waived on the condition that a certain amount of money is paid. See ibid, 200–201, 231.

[48] A penal order is issued by a judge only on the basis of a file, without a trial. See J-M Jehle and M Wade, *The Rise of Prosecutorial Power across Europe, Coping with Overloaded Criminal Justice Systems* (Berlin, Springer, 2006) 74–75.

[49] As Wright and Miller succinctly wrote: 'We now have not only an administrative criminal justice system, but one so dominant that trials take place in the shadow of guilty pleas.' See R Wright and M Miller, 'Honesty and Opacity in Charge Bargains' (2003) 55(4) *Stanford Law Review* 1409, 1415. See also, eg, Lynch, who points out that the American criminal justice system has become an administrative system run by executive-branch officials, prosecutors. GE Lynch, 'Screening Versus Plea Bargaining: Exactly What Are We Trading Off?' (2003) 55(4) *Stanford Law Review* 1399.

On the other hand, the rising harshness of penalties issued and the increasing severity of infringements dealt with in administrative procedures shows the tendency to engulf an area previously reserved for criminal law. An example of this are the so-called punitive administrative sanctions, such as surcharge or exclusion of the producer from the benefit of the aid or scheme of aid for the marketing year following that in respect of which the irregularity was established. In case of surcharge a punished subject is required not only to reimburse the sum owed (eg, unduly paid or owed), but must also pay an additional charge which is obviously penal in nature.[50] Therefore, alongside a sanction's administrative feature (namely restitution), surcharge entails a punitive effect as well. Some countries also apply the so-called administrative detention: the classic criminal law practice of detention is adopted in those countries in administrative cases, following a procedure which does not satisfy the standards of criminal law.[51]

We can also observe the transformation of certain traditionally administrative bodies into institutions of a mixed administrative and criminal nature. A good example is offered by the case of the Dutch administrative authorities, sworn officials of the Tax and Customs Administration, who traditionally tackled customs irregularities. They acquired not only the power to conduct a criminal investigation following the standards of their Criminal Code in respect of all criminal offences in their jurisdiction, but even had these powers extended to enable them to order the detention of suspects in police custody.[52] The classical organisation of powers by which police, public prosecutor or a criminal pre-trial judge are the sole authorities with criminal investigative authorisations and especially the sole authority to infringe the right to liberty, was therefore completely lost.[53] A solution unthinkable even a few decades ago, of an administrative authority possessing the most essential invasive criminal law power, is therefore very much real and active at the present time.

The examples mentioned above illustrate how traditional legal concepts increasingly struggle or even fail to explain the nature of such newly invented bodies, their powers, and even the nature of evidence gathered in newly developed procedures.[54] We obviously need to create new concepts that will help us deal with the situation.

[50] See the case law of ECtHR regarding the question of when a surcharge requires the protection of article 6 rights in *Bendenoun v France*, App No 12547/86 (ECtHR 24 February 1994) Series A no 284 (1994) 18 EHRR 54 and *Jussila v Finland*, App No 73053/91 (ECtHR, 23 November 2006) (2006) 45 EHRR 39 § 3.

[51] 'Austria, after the criticism from the European Court has given up the possibilities of detaining offenders according to so-called administrative criminal law.' See D Van Zyl Smit and F Dünkel, 'Conclusion' in D Van Zyl Smit and F Dünkel (eds), *Imprisonment Today and Tomorrow: International Perspectives on Prisoners' Rights and Prison Conditions* (The Hague, Kluwer Law International, 2001) 816.

[52] This solution is utterly unacceptable in countries such as France or Slovenia because of the stricter separation of powers principle which their legal systems observe. Vervaele points out that in the French system the judiciary serves as a true counterweight for the executive, while in the Netherlands the primary consideration is the most effective cooperation between different authorities. See JAE Vervaele and AH Klip, *European Cooperation Between Tax, Customs and Judicial Authorities* (The Hague, Kluwer Law International, 2002) 77, 181 and PJP Tak, *The Dutch Criminal Justice System* (Nijmegen, Wolf Legal Publishers, 2008) 42.

[53] A similar phenomenon is evident in the USA: 'Although we have been discussing administrative inspections as if they were totally different from traditional searches by the police for evidence of crime, the reality is not so clear-cut.' See WF Funk and RH Seamon, *Administrative Law*, 3rd edn (New York, Aspen Publishers, 2009) 343.

[54] See different concepts of division between criminal and administrative investigation and the rules on the transfer of evidence between those two procedures in the Netherlands, Germany, France, and England and Wales in Vervaele and Klip, *European Cooperation Between Tax, Customs and Judicial Authorities* (n 52) 91–93, 163–68, 211–13, 235–39.

IV. The ECtHR and its Role in Blurring the Boundaries

A. Definition of 'Criminal Offence'

The trend for blurring of administrative and criminal law boundaries has also been supported by supranational entities, the Council of Europe (CoE) being no exception.[55] It has to be admitted that the earlier case law of the ECtHR ('the Court') contributed a great deal to a clearer supra-national and therefore autonomous[56] definition of a criminal charge with the purpose of establishing the scope of Article 6 protection. In its landmark case *Engel v The Netherlands*[57] and the numerous cases following it, the Court clearly wanted to achieve the goal of establishing a common, autonomous definition of what is a criminal case. And it succeeded in doing so. The famous *Engel* criteria are:[58]

a. Classification in Domestic Law

The first decisive criteria provides only a starting point in this exploration. If domestic law classifies a certain offence as a 'criminal offence', then it will be considered a criminal offence. If not, the Court will examine the other criteria.

b. Nature of the Offence

In evaluating the nature of the offence, the following factors can be taken into consideration:

- whom the rule is directed at: whether it targets a specific group or is of a generally binding character (*Bendenoun v France*);[59]
- who institutes the proceedings: whether it is, eg, a public body with statutory powers of enforcement (*Benham v United Kingdom*);[60]

[55] It seems that developments in EU law have not helped answer this question either: if anything, the boundaries between the two domains are becoming even more blurred. Not having criminal law competences, the EU searched extensively for ways of extending the legitimate administrative powers it did possess to the criminal law field, thus heavily contributing to the over-extension of administrative law solutions to what were traditionally considered matters of criminal law. The solutions yielded by this search include the EU Commission's extended investigative powers, the creation of so-called administrative penalties serving criminal law purposes, etc. See Vervaele, *The Europeanisation of Criminal Law* (n 2). De Moor-van Vugt eg analyses the emergence of the mixed-natured administrative sanctions introduced by the EU (eg, loss of a deposit, administrative fine, surcharge, exclusion from subsidies and blacklisting) which did not previously exist in Dutch law and examines their legal nature by applying ECtHR standards. See De Moor-van Vugt, 'Administrative Sanctions in EU Law' (n 20) 5–41.

[56] *Adolf v Austria*, App No 8269/78 (ECtHR, 26 March 1982) Series A no 49 (1982) 4 EHRR 313, § 30.

[57] *Engel and Others v The Netherlands*, App Nos 5100-5102/71, 5354/72 and 5370/72 (ECtHR, 23 November 1976) Series A no 22 (1976) 1 EHRR 647.

[58] Summed up with reference to European Court of Human Rights, *Guide on Article 6 of the European Convention on Human Rights, Right to a fair trial (criminal limb)*, at: www.echr.coe.int/Documents/Guide_Art_6_criminal_ENG.pdf.

[59] *Bendenoun v France* (n 50) § 47.

[60] *Benham v United Kingdom*, App no 19380/92 (ECtHR [GC], 10 June 1996) (1996) 22 EHRR 293, § 56: 'In addition, the proceedings had some punitive elements. For example, the magistrates could only exercise their power of committal to prison on a finding of wilful refusal to pay or of culpable neglect.'

- the purpose of the rule: whether it is punitive or deterrent (*Öztürk v Germany*,[61] *Bendenoun v France*);
- whether the imposition of any penalty is dependent upon a finding of guilt (*Benham v United Kingdom*);[62]
- what comparative aspect might be relevant: how comparable procedures are classified in other CoE Member States (*Öztürk v Germany*).

c. *Severity of the Penalty that the Person Concerned Risks Incurring*

The third criterion is determined by reference to the sanction which, by its nature and degree of severity, belongs in general to the 'criminal' sphere, and the maximum potential penalty for which the relevant law provides (*Campbell and Fell v United Kingdom*;[63] *Demicoli v Malta*[64]). It also considers 'the nature and purpose of the measure in question; its characterisation under national law; the procedures involved in the making and implementation of the measure; and its severity.'[65]

This definition has been conceived and refined with at least two purposes in mind, namely avoiding the idiosyncrasies of certain legal cultures and, even more importantly for our discussion, 'label-swindling'. This is by all means welcome. Different legal systems classify different offences under different categories and a supranational authority cannot adhere to such classification if it wants to assess different national cases with the same criteria. But more importantly, fixing such a universal measure of criminality is necessary to prevent domestic systems from cheating by classifying a certain offence as non-criminal in order to deny defendants the highest standard of legal protection afforded by criminal procedure, as set down by national law and in Article 6.

B. Is it Criminal or Administrative?

The Court has heard numerous cases in which it had to decide whether a certain offence can be classified as a criminal charge and therefore falls under Article 6 of the European Convention on Human Rights (ECHR). These particular decisions touch upon the core question of the boundaries of criminal law and blending of the criminal and administrative fields. The 'border zone' where the fields intersect is typically inhabited by relatively minor offences, which because of their mildness or numerousness[66] cannot be dealt

[61] *Öztürk v Germany*, App No 8544/79 (ECtHR, 21 February 1984) Series A no 73 (1984) 6 EHRR 409, § 53.

[62] An interesting illustration of the punitive element is found in *Benham v United Kingdom* (n 60) § 56: 'In addition, the proceedings had some punitive elements. For example, the magistrates could only exercise their power of committal to prison on a finding of wilful refusal to pay or of culpable neglect.'

[63] *Campbell and Fell v United Kingdom*, App Nos 7819/77 and 7878/77 (ECtHR, 28 June 1984) Series A no 80 (1984) 7 EHRR 165, § 72.

[64] *Demicoli v Malta*, App No 13057/87 (ECtHR, 27 August 1991) Series A no 210 (1991) 14 EHRR 47, § 34.

[65] *Welch v United Kingdom*, App No 17440/90 (ECtHR, 9 February 1995) Series A no 307-A (1995) 20 EHRR 247, § 28.

[66] In a scenario where all infringements are handled exclusively by the criminal law system there will either be an overburdening of the criminal courts with relatively minor criminal offences, or milder offences will go unpunished altogether due to protective mechanisms peculiar to criminal law (eg, the opportunity principle,

with appropriately within the area of criminal law. The criminal law system is more time-consuming and thus more expensive than the administrative,[67] and therefore any country's criminal prosecution service must set priorities in handling its caseload.[68] Disproportionate resources, meanwhile, can be lost by treating minor cases with the due care demanded by criminal law standards.[69]

A good example of such minor offences is violations of traffic law, since they fulfil both criteria: they are numerous and they are often manifestly non-heinous in nature (eg, not causing any harm, as in the case of a seatbelt left unfastened). Different national law systems use different solutions to classify such offences: some countries classify them as minor offences of a criminal nature, while some treat them either as purely administrative offences or a *sui generis* phenomenon (eg, regulatory offences). In the landmark case *Öztürk v Germany* the Court set important guidelines for assessing whether a minor offence of 'causing a traffic accident by colliding with another vehicle as a result of careless driving' falls under Article 6 protection or not. The first problem the Court faced while analysing whether those offences fall under its own definition of a criminal act was the diverse classification of traffic offences in national law. The German government claimed that the offence, since it had been decriminalised, was merely a 'regulatory offence' (german: *Ordnungswidrigkeit*). Such an offence, as they claimed, differed from a criminal offence both in its legal characteristics and consequences and thus in the procedure to be followed when it occurred. In this respect the Court noted that 'no absolute partition separates German criminal law from the law on "regulatory offences", in particular where there exists a close connection between a criminal offence and a "regulatory offence"'.[70]

Then it went on to examine the second, still more important criterion – the very nature of the offence. The court concluded that: (1) misconduct of this kind continued to be classified as part of the criminal law in the vast majority of the ECHR Contracting States, (2) the penalty in those cases retained a punitive character, which was the customary distinguishing feature of criminal penalties, (3) the rule of law infringed by the applicant had undergone no change of content, (4) the rule was directed not towards a given group possessing a special status, but towards all citizens in their

also called the principle of discretionary prosecution). One of the problems which arises with enlarging the scope of criminal law is a resulting problem of overcriminalisation; a phenomenon addressed by Kadish in the 1960s. See more in SH Kadish, 'The Crisis of Overcriminalization' (1968) 7 *American Criminal Law Quarterly* 17–34; and later works from JC Coffee Jr, 'Does "unlawful" mean "criminal"?' (1991) 71 *Boston University Law Review* 193–246; and: Husak, *Overcriminalization: The Limits of the Criminal Law* (n 1).

[67] Faure and Svatikova argue that it is more cost-effective too: 'complement criminal law enforcement by administrative law rather than to allow for a single (criminal) sanctioning instrument.' See MG Faure and K Svatikova, 'Criminal or Administrative Law to Protect the Environment? Evidence from Western Europe' (2012) 24(2) *Journal of Environmental Law* 253.

[68] In *Zumtobel v Austria*, App No 12235/86 (ECtHR, 21 September 1993) Series A no 268 (1993) 17 EHRR 116 the Court acknowledges this by saying: 'Regard being had to the respect which must be accorded to decisions taken by the administrative authorities on grounds of expediency …', § 32.

[69] With respect to this problem it is informative to consider law and economic studies on advantages of handling environmental infringements via both administrative and criminal law channels. See, eg, R Bowles and N Garoupa and M Faure, 'The Scope of Criminal Law and Criminal Sanctions: an Economic View and Policy Implications' (2008) 35 *Journal of Law and Society* 389–416.

[70] *Öztürk v Germany* (n 61) § 51.

capacity as road-users.[71] It concluded that the general character of the rule and the purpose of the penalty, being both deterrent and punitive, sufficed to show that the offence in question was criminal in nature in terms of Article 6. Most importantly, the Court argued that:

> it would be contrary to the object and purpose of Article 6, which guarantees to 'everyone charged with a criminal offence' the right to a court hearing and a fair trial, if the State were allowed to remove from the scope of this Article (art. 6) a whole category of offences merely on the ground of regarding them as petty.[72]

'The relative lack of seriousness of the penalty at stake cannot divest an offence of its inherently criminal character.'[73] The Court stressed, therefore, very firmly, that the pure fact that a certain criminal offence is minor or less serious cannot mean that it is any less criminal in nature; the same is true for the penalty it brings.

In *Schmautzer v Austria*[74] the Court had to decide whether Article 6 applied in cases where the offender was punished for not wearing a safety belt. In Austrian law this was classified as an administrative offence (in German: *Verwaltungsstraftaten*) and was dealt with in a special procedure – an administrative criminal procedure (*Verwaltungsstrafverfahren*). The Court stated

> although the offences in issue and the procedures followed in the case fall within the administrative sphere, they are nevertheless criminal in nature … the fine imposed on the applicant was accompanied by an order for his committal to prison in the event of his defaulting on payment … These considerations are sufficient to establish that the offence of which the applicant was accused may be classified as 'criminal' for the purposes of the Convention. It follows that Article 6 (art. 6) applies.[75]

According to the Court, traffic offences punishable by fines or driving restrictions, such as penalty points or disqualifications, can be considered criminal acts depending on the nature of the offence, the purpose of the rule at issue and the severity of the penalty, regardless of their classification in the domestic order. In *Lutz v Germany*,[76] the Court was very clear:

> The Court points out that the second and third criteria adopted in the judgments in the *Engel and Others* case and the *Öztürk* case are alternative and not cumulative ones: for Article 6 (art. 6) to apply in virtue of the words 'criminal charge,' it suffices that the offence in question should by its nature be 'criminal' from the point of view of the Convention, as in the instant case, or should have made the person concerned liable to a sanction which, in its nature and degree of severity, belongs in general to the 'criminal' sphere …[77]

[71] *Öztürk v Germany* (n 61) § 53.

[72] Ibid.

[73] *Öztürk v Germany* (n 61) § 54.

[74] *Schmautzer v Austria*, App No 15523/89 (ECtHR, 23 October 1995) Series A no 220 (1995) 21 EHRR 511.

[75] *Schmautzer v Austria* (n 74) § 28.

[76] *Lutz v Germany*, App No 9912/82 (ECtHR, 25 August 1987) Series A no 123 (1988) 10 EHRR 183, § 55. Mr Lutz was overtaking a car in an ambiguous traffic situation while riding a motor cycle and caused an accident. He was fined and claimed a breach of art 6(2) ECHR.

[77] See similar reasoning in support of the division between 'criminal' and 'disciplinary' in, eg, *Campbell and Fell v United Kingdom* (n 63) §§ 35–38, §§ 69–73.

C. What is a Criminal Sanction?

In *Malige v France*,[78] the Court had to decide whether the deduction of points from a driving licence is a sanction of criminal nature. It first decided that this penalty is criminal in nature and then concluded that:

> With regard to the nature of the sanction, the Court notes that points are deducted in the context of, and after the outcome of, a criminal prosecution … The sanction of deducting points is therefore an automatic consequence of the conviction pronounced by the criminal court.[79]
>
> The Court … infers that, although the deduction of points has a preventative character, it also has a punitive and deterrent character and is accordingly similar to a secondary penalty. The fact that Parliament intended to dissociate the sanction of deducting points from the other penalties imposed by the criminal courts cannot change the nature of the measure.[80]

In this respect, the Court decided that Article 6(1) did indeed apply. 'The Court reiterates that, where a penalty is criminal in nature there must be the possibility of review by a court which satisfies the requirements of Article 6 §1 …'[81] The same is true for minor offences such as committing nuisance or a breach of the peace.[82]

According to the Court's case law a procedure for tax surcharge could be classified as a criminal charge. It all depends on whether or not the *Engel* criteria are fulfilled. In *Bendenoun v France*,[83] for example, the Court weighed the different aspects of the French tax surcharge law and noted:

> the predominance of those which have a criminal connotation. None of them is decisive on its own, but taken together and cumulatively they made the 'charge' in issue a 'criminal' one within the meaning of Article 6 para. 1 (art. 6-1), which was therefore applicable.[84]

The crucial criteria were: the nature of the offence ('who the rule is directed at' – the surcharge covered all citizens in their capacity as taxpayers); the purpose of the rule (the surcharge was not intended as pecuniary compensation for damage but essentially as a punishment to deter reoffending, and thus was imposed with both a deterrent and a punitive purpose); and the severity of the penalty (the surcharge was substantial).[85] The criminal nature of the offence may suffice to render Article 6 applicable, notwithstanding the low amount of the tax surcharge (10 per cent of the reassessed tax liability in *Jussila v Finland*[86]).

[78] *Malige v France*, App No 27812/95 (1998) 28 EHRR 578.

[79] Ibid, § 38.

[80] Ibid, § 39.

[81] Ibid, § 45.

[82] *Lauko v Slovakia*, App No 26138/95 (ECtHR, 2 September 1998) (1998) 33 EHRR 40; *Nicoleta Gheorghe v Romania*, App No 23470/05 (ECtHR, 3 April 2012) §§ 25–26.

[83] *Bendenoun v France* (n 50) § 47.

[84] Ibid.

[85] As the Court concludes: 'Having weighed the various aspects of the case, the Court notes the predominance of those which have a criminal connotation. None of them is decisive on its own, but taken together and cumulatively they made the "charge" in issue a "criminal" one within the meaning of art 6 para 1 (art 6-1), which was therefore applicable.' *Bendenoun v France* (n 50) § 47.

[86] *Jussila v Finland* (n 50) § 3.

To avoid excessive detail, let us just mention that the Court reached the same conclusion in defining offences against social security legislation (failure to declare employment, despite the modest nature of the fine imposed (*Hüseyin Turan v Turkey*),[87] and the administrative offence of producing and distributing material promoting ethnic hatred, punishable by an administrative warning and the confiscation of the publication in question (*Balsytė-Lideikienė v Lithuania*).[88] Article 6 under its criminal head has also been held to apply to customs law (*Salabiaku v France*),[89] to penalties imposed by a court with jurisdiction in budgetary and financial matters (*Guisset v France*),[90] to certain administrative authorities with powers in the spheres of economic, financial, antitrust and competition law (*Lilly France v France*;[91] *Dubus SA v France*;[92] *A Menarini Diagnostics SRL v Italy*),[93] and even to certain offences against prison discipline (*Campbell and Fell v United Kingdom*, *Ezeh and Connors v United Kingdom*).[94] For example, as the Court made clear in *A Menarini Diagnostics SRL v Italy*, Italian antitrust fines are criminal sanctions despite the fact that they are applied by an administrative authority and, according to both Italian and EU law, are considered administrative in nature.

D. Milestone Case *Jusilla v Finland*

In all of the cases mentioned above the Court took considerable pains in deciding whether or not a certain case fell under the category of a criminal offence or whether a certain sanction could be classified as criminal. However, as soon as it reached an affirmative answer to both questions, the decision was (mostly) simple: Article 6 guarantees apply. For instance, in *Schmautzer v Austria* the Court stated: 'These considerations are sufficient to establish that the offence of which the applicant was accused may be classified as "criminal" for the purposes of the Convention. It follows that Article 6 (art. 6) applies.'[95] There is no doubt that the Court links the establishment of a certain offence as criminal (or a punishment, respectively) with the application of Article 6 rights.

Another question altogether is an assessment whether Article 6 was in fact violated. In this respect the case law of the Court has been far from consistent and predictable. As Goss points out in his critical book on the application of Article 6 in criminal cases, the case law reflects internal inconsistency as to how each specific tool and mechanism for assessing violation of Article 6 has been identified, explained and applied.

[87] *Hüseyin Turan v Turkey*, App No 11529/02 (ECtHR, 4 March 2008) §§ 18–21. The Court, again, concludes very firmly: 'En égard à ce qui précède, la Cour conclut que le requérant a fait l'objet d'une "accusation en matière pénale". L'article 6 de la Convention s'applique donc en l'espèce.' § 21.

[88] *Balsytė-Lideikienė v Lithuania*, App No 72596/01 (ECtHR, 4 November 2008) § 61.

[89] *Salabiaku v France*, App No 10519/83 (ECtHR, 7 October 1988) Series A no 141-A (1988) 13 EHRR 379.

[90] *Guisset v France*, App No 33933/96 (ECtHR, 26 September 2000) (2000) 34 EHRR 47.

[91] *Lilly France v France*, App No 53892/00 (ECtHR, 14 October 2003).

[92] *Dubus SA v France*, App No 5242/04 (ECtHR, 11 June 2009).

[93] *A Menarini Diagnostics SRL v Italy*, App No 43509/08 (ECtHR, 27 September 2011).

[94] *Ezeh and Connors v United Kingdom*, App No 39665/98 and 40086/98 (ECtHR [GC], 9 October 2003) (2003) 39 EHRR 1, § 82.

[95] *Schmautzer v Austria* (n 74) § 28.

Even more, he claims, those tools and mechanisms are deployed incoherently, with little explanation as to why a particular tool was used. He concludes that this level of incoherence generates uncertainty and unpredictability in the way in which the Court frames, explains and assesses Article 6 violations.[96]

However, *Jussila v Finland*[97] opened a new route of thinking. It brought a different understanding of two questions: (1) what is a criminal case? and (2) do the guarantees of Article 6 ECHR apply with 'full stringency' (to use the Court's diction) to all cases that are deemed 'criminal' within the autonomous meaning of the ECHR? In other words, a veritable Pandora's box was opened with respect to the scope of the rights pertaining to a certain criminal case.

The core question of the case was whether the procedure on tax assessment and the imposition of tax surcharges in Finland at the time fell within the autonomous meaning of Article 6 ECHR and thus whether the guarantees of Article 6 applied; in this particular case the right to an oral hearing was at issue. In paragraph 43 of the judgment the Court stated:

> While it may be noted that the above-mentioned cases in which an oral hearing was not considered necessary concerned proceedings falling under the civil head of Article 6 § 1 and that the requirements of a fair hearing are the most strict in the sphere of criminal law, the Court would not exclude that in the criminal sphere the nature of the issues to be dealt with before the tribunal or court may not require an oral hearing. Notwithstanding the consideration that a certain gravity attaches to criminal proceedings, which are concerned with the allocation of criminal responsibility and the imposition of a punitive and deterrent sanction, it is self-evident that there are criminal cases which do not carry any significant degree of stigma. There are clearly 'criminal charges' of differing weight. What is more, the autonomous interpretation adopted by the Convention institutions of the notion of a 'criminal charge' by applying the *Engel* criteria have underpinned a gradual broadening of the criminal head to cases not strictly belonging to the traditional categories of the criminal law, for example administrative penalties (*Öztürk*, cited above), prison disciplinary proceedings (*Campbell and Fell v the United Kingdom* …), customs law (*Salabiaku v France* …), competition law (*Société Stenuit v France*[98] …), and penalties imposed by a court with jurisdiction in financial matters (*Guisset v France* …). Tax surcharges differ from the hard core of criminal law; consequently, the criminal-head guarantees will not necessarily apply with their full stringency (see *Bendenoun* and *Janosevic*, § 46 and § 81 respectively, where it was found compatible with Article 6 § 1 for criminal penalties to be imposed, in the first instance, by an administrative or non-judicial body, and, *a contrario*, *Findlay*, cited above).

[96] R Goss, *Criminal Fair Trial Rights: Article 6 of the European Convention on Human Rights* (Oxford and Portland OR, Hart Publishing, 2016) 115–16.

[97] See as well the comment on the case in T Barkhuysen and M van Emmerik, 'Legitimacy of Europan Court of Human Rights Judgements: Procedural Aspects' in N Huls, M Adams and J Bomhoff (eds), *The Legitimacy of Highest Courts' Rulings* (The Hague, TCM Asser Press, 2009) 444. *Jusilla* was not the first case in which ECtHR relaxed procedural standards for minor offences: technically, the precedent was set by *Fejde v Sweden*, App No 12631/87 (ECtHR, 29 October 1991) Series A no 212-C (1991) 17 EHRR 14. This case was, however, essentially different to *Jussila v Finland* (n 50), since the Court only decided that the lack of an oral hearing at the appellate stage was not a breach of Article 6 since the applicant *did* have an oral hearing in the court of first instance and the applicant raised no questions of fact or of law which could not be adequately resolved on the basis of the case-file (*Fejde v Sweden* § 33).

[98] *Société Stenuit v France*, App No 11598/85 (ECtHR, 27 February 1992) Series A no 27.

It is worth analysing the whole paragraph just quoted, since it brings a new thinking into play concerning the application of Article 6 rights in criminal cases. The Court first explicitly states that the autonomous interpretation of the concept of 'criminal charge' stemming from *Engel* has gradually broadened the concept of 'criminal charge' to cases not strictly belonging to the traditional categories of the criminal law – administrative cases even being explicitly mentioned. Second, the Court claims, there are criminal cases of different gravity: hard core criminal cases and less heinous ones, and for the latter the criminal-head guarantees do not necessarily apply with their full stringency. And therefore, third, which is relevant to the specific case, in some criminal cases, depending on the nature of the issue, an oral hearing might not be necessary. The Court also decided accordingly, despite the fact that Article 6 did extend to the tax-surcharge proceedings, no breach of Article 6 was found to have occurred despite the lack of an oral hearing.

It is difficult to claim that the case law before *Jussila* was clear and consistent on the question of the full application of Article 6 rights. On the procedural side, the Court had already started to lower its criminal law standards. It admitted that, with regard to a large number of minor offences, states may have good reasons for introducing a system which relieves their courts of the task of dealing with the great majority of such relatively trifling cases. An offence of a minor nature (such as the possession of a rifle without the required licence) justifies the lack of an oral hearing before an appellate court (*Fejde v Sweden*),[99] and peripheral cases can be dealt with in the first instance by an administrative authority (*Lauko v Slovakia*).[100] Allotting the prosecution and punishment of minor offences to administrative authorities was therefore not inconsistent with the Convention even before *Jussila*, provided that the person concerned is afforded the safe guards of Article 6[101] by being able to bring any decision thus made against him before a 'judicial body that has full jurisdiction'.[102]

However, *Jussila* is still a milestone case for the different understanding of the criminal law field which it brought to the argument. What is interesting is the need of the Court to emphasise the existence of so-called 'hard core' criminal law in the first place. This is tantamount to admitting that there are some criminal law cases which are more essentially criminal than others, thus pointing out the non-exclusive nature of the division between the fields of criminal and administrative law.[103] At first glance, the position the Court adopted here seems more than reasonable, since it would seem absurd to put an act of genocide and a minor tax evasion on the same scale of justice. The problem lies with the lack of defined criteria for tackling cases that involve a less obvious disparity: distinguishing black from white is simple, but how are we to delineate the many shades

[99] *Fejde v Sweden* (n 97).

[100] *Lauko v Slovakia* (n 82).

[101] *Öztürk v Germany* (n 61) § 56. The so-called full judicial review which is to be afforded in order to *ex post* compensate for the omission of the semi-judicial administrative phase.

[102] Ibid.

[103] The judgment continues: 'What is more, the autonomous interpretation adopted by the Convention institutions of the notion of a "criminal charge" by applying the *Engel* criteria have underpinned a gradual broadening of the criminal head to cases not strictly belonging to the traditional categories of the criminal law …' *Jussila v Finland* (n 50) § 43. It seems like the Court is describing a phenomenon of over-extension of criminal law and tries to achieve the reverse effect with its decision.

of grey encountered by much legal practice?[104] As Judge Loucaides pointed out in his partly dissenting opinion:

> I find it difficult, in the context of a fair trial, to distinguish, as the majority do in this case, between criminal offences belonging to the 'hard core of criminal law' and others which fall outside that category. Where does one draw the line? (…) To accept such distinctions would open the way to abuse and arbitrariness.[105]

As the case law following *Jussila* showed, the Court had more than enough problems deciding the cases both at the 'core' and at the periphery of criminal law.[106] In *Marcello Viola v Italy*[107] the Court decided that the public interest in fighting organised crime justifies restrictions of rights covered by Article 6. In *Heglas v Czech Republic*[108] the Court points out that the general requirements of fairness laid out by Article 6 apply to all criminal proceedings regardless of the type of offence. However, when assessing whether the proceedings as a whole have been fair, the Court can take into consideration the weight of public interest in the prosecution of a certain offence.[109] There are also limitations of a right to be present at the hearing in cases concerning the process for imposing a penal fine (*Kammerer v Austria*).[110] However, the case law is far from being clear and consistent, thus contributing to the blurring of boundaries between the 'core' and 'periphery' of criminal law on one hand and of criminal and administrative law on the other. It is not too bold to claim that the resulting mix-up has contributed to the Court's case law being even more inconsistent, incoherent and arbitrary in this respect.[111]

V. Conclusion

The solutions downgrading criminal law and upgrading administrative law do serve some positive ends (eg, the aims of de-burdening criminal justice systems and improving their efficiency); however, the trends reviewed here have considerable negative side-effects.

[104] Bailleux traces the consequences of *Jusilla* distinction between the core criminal law and its periphery in EU law as well. See Bailleux, 'The fiftieth shade of grey Competition law, "criministrative law" and "fairly fair trials"' (n 43) 143.

[105] Judge Loucaides, partly dissenting opinion, *Jussila v Finland* (n 50).

[106] *Kammerer v Austria*, App No 32435/06 (ECtHR, 12 May 2010). In this respect see an excellent analysis of the application of ECHR standards to administrative procedures in De Moor-Van-Vugt, 'Administrative Sanctions in EU Law' (n 20).

[107] *Marcello Viola v Italy*, App No 45106/04 (ECtHR, 5 October 2006) §§ 7–77.

[108] *Heglas v Czech Republic*, App No 5935/02 (ECtHR, 1 March 2007) (2009) 48 EHRR 44. See similar reasoning in *Al-Khawaja and Tahery v United Kingdom*, App Nos 26766/05 and 22228/06 (ECtHR [GC], 15 December 2011) (2011) 54 EHRR 23 § 146.

[109] *Heglas v Czech Republic* (n 108), § 87.

[110] *Kammerer v Austria* (n 106).

[111] Goss concludes that the willingness of the Court 'to adjust levels of Article 6 protection in response to public interest consideration' after *Jussila* is radically different from its case law up to that point. See Goss, *Criminal Fair Trial Rights: Article 6 of the European Convention on Human Rights* (n 96) 187.

First, the traditionally designed boundaries between the criminal and administrative law disciplines are being eroded into an unrecognisable mess. Historically the concepts may never have been completely clear, and different minds have placed differing emphases on different aspects of the two systems. Nevertheless, history still suggests that the essential traditional distinctions between the administrative and criminal dimensions were well-grounded, and worked towards protecting and enacting higher principles of legal justice. The concepts were developed with a certain purpose in mind, and supported the protective effect of the principle of proportionality on human rights. New solutions downgrading criminal law, and others over-extending administrative authority, smudge the boundaries between the disciplines in ways that make widespread breaches of human rights entirely possible. It is no longer clear according to what standards and procedures different agencies of an uncertain legal nature will be acting. We are therefore witnessing a shift toward preventive strategies, administrative in nature, which bypass the criminal law standards. Is a certain sanction still a measure of criminal law, thus demanding all the required procedural standards previously guaranteed to accused parties (eg, a fair trial, the right to remain silent), or is it merely an administrative one, executed according to much looser principles? Is a particular authorised search one with criminal law objectives, and thus carrying an obligation to apply all the protective standards developed in criminal proceedings (eg, standard of proof, authorisation by judicial order) – or is it an administrative authorisation, which need only satisfy much lower safeguards? Can the evidence gathered in one procedure be produced in the other if a case is transferred? Procedural efficiency, if that is the priority, arguably *is* lowered if we continue applying the stricter criminal procedure standards in apparently 'milder' cases. But an incontrovertible hierarchy of values should tell us which danger is the greater, if change continues in the opposite direction: namely, if we continue introducing lower procedural standards to cases which would merit stricter regulation.

Second, such solutions extend the area of criminalisation. What at first glance seems a preventative strategy has hidden repressive effects.[112] It allows an invasion of lower (administrative) procedural standards into criminal law without the protection of criminal law guarantees.[113] As an end result we witness the *net-widening* of the criminal law,[114] namely a greater number of individuals being controlled by a criminal justice system partly disguised by widened administrative powers.

It is beyond the scope of this chapter to address in all their complexity the issues of what procedural rights should apply in all kinds of proceedings; it is, however,

[112] As Huisman and Koemans convincingly show by means of examples of the introduction of ASBO in Dutch law. Huisman and Koemans, 'Administrative Measures in Crime Control' (n 42) 142.

[113] Such as the privilege against self-incrimination, presumption of innocence, etc. As Duff and Green point out: 'Presumption of innocence has been progressively eroded by broad offence definitions, shifts in burdens of proof, and the use of strict liability …'. They also warn of various 'hybrid civil-criminal proceedings'. RA Duff and S Green, 'Introduction: Searching for Foundations' in RA Duff and S Green (eds), *Philosophical Foundations of Criminal Law* (Oxford, Oxford University Press, 2011) 11–12.

[114] 'Normalization of crime permits a routinization of crime control that licenses the removal of lesser offences from the hallowed bastions of the criminal trial to the instrumental channels of civil and administrative law.' A Ashworth and L Zedner, 'Defending the Criminal Law, Reflections on the Changing Character of Crime, Procedure, and Sanctions' (2008) 2(1) *Criminal Law and Philosophy* 21, 39.

instructive to witness the struggles supranational courts have faced in dealing with such questions.[115] The ECtHR *Jussila* case places an altogether novel and unwarranted distinction onto the classical scale by which criminal law has traditionally sought to find its requisite balances. The underlying meaning of the *Jussila* case seems to be that the full application of Article 6 rights to the over-extended concept of the 'criminal charge' has gone too far and we need to go back to distinguishing between the offences of different gravity. We can therefore interpret *Jussila* as a turning point which tries to 'correct' this excessive broadening. With the *Jussila* decision a way was opened to fixing the weight of a criminal charge according to 'case-sensitive' gradations, with subsequent logical adjustments to the procedural rights afforded to those facing such charges. The willingness of the Court 'to adjust levels of Article 6 protection in response to public interest considerations' after *Jussila* is radically different from its case law up to that point.[116]

This landmark judgment, moreover, exposed the very patchy and improvised nature of present arrangements. Part of the criminal law's traditional demesne is now assigned to administrative law (and other law domains, eg, civil law), with an attendant transfer of power, but there is more than a smudge or blur being made here *between* the two fields. The territory of criminal law *itself* is partly overtaken by a miasma, for we are now to understand that *within* criminal law there is something that should be considered a 'hard core', for which the old standards still apply; and since there is a core it follows that there is also a 'periphery' to which relaxed procedural standards are now appropriate. The Court itself has therefore created a ground for the 'grey zone' of 'criministrative' law. It is not clear either which offences should be placed in the peripheral zone of criminal law, nor is it clear which rights apply in this zone.

The fact is that in our understanding of the changing legal world we can no longer rely on the typology (however uncertain it was) that earlier theorists developed. This is not, I should stress, to concede that we should abandon the values and principles which that typology sought to support. The fight for definitions is once again taking place and new questions are being asked: what are the appropriate measures for those myriad cases filling the 'grey' areas between criminal and administrative law in their classic configurations; what authorities should deal with those cases; in what ways can we deal with evidence gathered in *sui generis* procedures, and what really constitutes a 'sufficient' instrument for the protection of rights in a given procedure? Undoubtedly we

[115] See, eg, highly elaborated discussions on a form of responsibility for administrative irregularities in the European Court of Justice (ECJ) Case C-210/00 *Käserei Champignon Hofmeister GmbH & Co. KG v Hauptzollamt Hamburg-Jonas* [2002] ECR I-6453. At the end of an extensive debate on the nature of sanctioning in criminal and administrative procedure, the Court decided that the general applicability of the fault principle to penalties of an administrative nature cannot be derived from the legal tradition of the Member States. See as well Case 137/85 *Maizena Gesellschaft mbH and others v Bundesanstalt für landwirtschaftliche Marktordnung (BALM)*, judgment of 18 November 1987, [1987] ECR 4587, para 13 deciding that the special arrangement involving advance release of security is not a criminal penalty, and Case C-240/90 *Germany v Commission* [1992] ECR I-5383, judgment of 27 October 1992, para 25, discussing exclusion and deciding that it is not a penal sanction. In the *Bonda* case a Polish court asked for a preliminary ruling on a question of the legal nature of the penalty provided for in art 138 of Regulation No. 1973/04, which refuses a farmer direct payments in the years following the year in which he submitted an incorrect statement. (Case C-489/10 *Lucasz Marcin Bonda*, judgment of 5 June 2012 (EU:C:2012:319)).

[116] Goss, *Criminal Fair Trial Rights* (n 96) 187.

must realise that the time in which crime was crime, and an administrative infraction was clearly something else, has now long passed. We find ourselves in an era that we could choose to regard as one of opportunity for reform and innovation, for new solutions to the ongoing puzzles of how to find fair and proportionate solutions for blurred zones in the law. It may well be time for a 'makeover.' But change will only be progressive if the values underpinning legal systems in their most serious operations – balancing human rights against retributive justice – are retained in the course of the overhaul.

13

The EU Legislature's Balancing Exercise between Practical Concerns and Conceptual Divisions

TAMÁS LUKÁCSI[1]

I. Introduction

From vengeance on the immediate offender to the unpaid work of removing graffiti, from 'expressive ritualism to managerial efficiency',[2] societies have invented various measures throughout history to sanction those who breach the law. We all begin with the 'hatred for anything giving us pain, which wreaks itself on the manifest cause, and which leads even civilised men to kick the door when it pinches his finger'.[3] Yet if we are truly civilised, we develop more sophisticated reactions.

Take the example of the *senatus consultum Macedonianum* in Roman law. Macedo, a golden boy with huge debts, killed his rich father in order to be able to pay those debts from his inheritance. Apparently, this was not an isolated event and the law-maker had to devise a measure to fight against the phenomenon. A civil law tool was invented which prevented creditors from suing on most of the loans given to spoiled heirs. Thus, in one fell swoop, the Senate could tackle both prodigal youth and their usurious creditors. If such cases were to happen nowadays, it would not be out of touch with reality to imagine politicians having the knee-jerk reflex of tweeting about the desperate and immediate need for a more draconian criminal law policy.

A community's response to criminal activity, the level and type of punishment is a mirror of the culture and standards of a society. As the German Federal Constitutional Court put it in its Lisbon-ruling:

> As regards the preconditions for criminal liability as well as the concepts of a fair and appropriate trial, the administration of criminal law depends on cultural processes of previous understanding that are historically grown and also determined by language, and on the

[1] The views and opinions expressed in this chapter are those of the author and do not necessarily reflect the official policy or position of the European Parliament. The author would like to thank Mirena Pencheva, Julianna Séllyei and the editors of this book for their valuable remarks.

[2] Nils Christie, *Crime Control as Industry* (London, Routledge, 2000).

[3] Oliver W Holmes, *The Common Law* (New Orleans, Quid Pro Quo Books, 2010) 11.

> alternatives which emerge in the process of deliberation which moves the respective public opinion.[4]

The supranational legislature of the European Union is not outside of that historical and cultural equation.

When it comes to the field of criminal law, mapping the balancing exercise of the EU legislature – and the European Parliament in particular – would, however, require an extensive monograph. What this chapter could possibly cover is no more than a glimpse of that landscape. The following chapter will give a brief summary of the EU legislature's conceptual framework: its cultural limits and constitutional constraints. The two are, of course, intertwined. Constitutional constraints on crime and punishment have also become part of our culture and civilisation. After all, ruling out destructive emotions is one of the key features of liberal constitutionalism.[5] In criminal law policy specifically, these constraints are put to the test by a tension between the *ultima ratio* principle and the popular push for criminalisation, fuelled by the fear that overcomes societies in times of economic or social turmoil.

At the EU level, I will argue, there are strong safeguards against overcriminalisation. Whilst in the pre-Lisbon case-law, criminal law – as the extended arm of internal market rules – seemed to gain some recognition, the Treaty of Lisbon somewhat reversed that tendency. I will study Articles 83(1) and (2) TFEU and examine how these legal bases constrain the exercise of criminal law competences, especially in the context of the 'different legal systems and traditions of the Member States' (Article 67(1) TFEU) and the general principles of proportionality and necessity.

The snapshot picture of primary EU law would not be complete without a description of the three main institutions' own guidelines for the exercise of their criminal law competences. This will lead to a brief overview of secondary substantive criminal legislation in the last 10 years. The word 'substantive' covers a choice that had to be made. When talking about EU criminal law competences, the definition of offences and sanctions comes to mind first. It should, nevertheless, not be forgotten that there are also procedural law competences in the Treaties. Notably, Article 82(2) points (b) and (c) TFEU allow for the adoption of directives establishing minimum rules for the rights of individuals in criminal procedure and the rights of victims of crime.

Parallel with the exercise of substantive law competences, the EU legislature adopted several acts on the procedural legal bases, such as the directives on legal aid,[6] procedural safeguards for children in criminal proceedings,[7] the presumption of innocence and the right to be present at one's trial,[8] the right of access to a lawyer in criminal proceedings,[9]

[4] BVerfG, judgment of the Second Senate of 30 June 2009, 2 BvE 2/08, § 253. English translation taken from the website of the Court.

[5] András Sajó, 'Emotions in constitutional design' (2010) 8(3) *I-CON* 354–84.

[6] Directive (EU) 2016/1919 of the European Parliament and of the Council of 26 October 2016 on legal aid for suspects and accused persons in criminal proceedings and for requested persons in European arrest warrant proceedings ([2016] OJ L 297, 4.11.2016, p 1).

[7] Directive (EU) 2016/800 of the European Parliament and of the Council of 11 May 2016 on procedural safeguards for children who are suspects or accused persons in criminal proceedings ([2016] OJ L 132, 21.5.2016, p 1).

[8] Directive (EU) 2016/343 of the European Parliament and of the Council of 9 March 2016 on the strengthening of certain aspects of the presumption of innocence and of the right to be present at the trial in criminal proceedings ([2016] OJ L 65, 11.3.2016, p 1).

[9] Directive 2013/48/EU of the European Parliament and of the Council of 22 October 2013 on the right of access to a lawyer in criminal proceedings and in European arrest warrant proceedings, and on the right

the right to information and the right to interpretation and translation,[10] and, last but not least, the rights of victims of crime.[11] These acts can be seen as part of the legislator's balancing exercise in a wider sense. As supranational criminal law advances and trickles down into national criminal law, procedural rights and safeguards flow from the same source and make sure that criminalisation goes hand in hand with the setting of minimum standards for procedural rights.

However, the procedural side of the balancing exercise cannot be discussed any further within the limits of this study. Therefore, my choice is to focus on substantive criminal law, through the study of one specific example. The EU legislation, published in 2017, on new psychoactive substances[12] raised an interesting question that encapsulates the balancing challenge with which the legislature is faced. This challenge consists in finding the right balance between criminal law as an extended arm of internal market creation and criminal law as a matter of national sovereignty, traditionally designed to prevent and punish behaviour that is disapproved of by society in a certain historical and cultural context. The case study will focus on this issue and will analyse how the legislator solved this particular challenge.

II. The EU Legislature's Conceptual Framework

A. *Ultima Ratio* or Overcriminalisation?

The principle of *ultima ratio* (*regis*) or last resort serves as a constitutional limit to the criminal legislative powers of all democratic political entities under the rule of law.[13] It 'demands that the national legislator take the path of criminalisation only when all else fails, and also that it considers alternatives to criminal law measures'.[14] This is desirable both because of the ideal of limited government powers, but also for practical reasons of enforcement possibilities.

However, this principle has been under pressure for a while: inflation in the economy has been on the leash in recent years, but inflation of criminal law is generally

to have a third party informed upon deprivation of liberty and to communicate with third persons and with consular authorities while deprived of liberty ([2013] OJ L 294, 6.11.2013, p 1).

[10] Directive 2012/13/EU of the European Parliament and of the Council of 22 May 2012 on the right to information in criminal proceedings ([2012] OJ L 142, 1.6.2012, p 1) and Directive 2010/64/EU of the European Parliament and of the Council of 20 October 2010 on the right to interpretation and translation in criminal proceedings ([2010] OJ L 280, 26.10.2010, p 1).

[11] Directive 2012/29/EU of the European Parliament and of the Council of 25 October 2012 establishing minimum standards on the rights, support and protection of victims of crime, and replacing Council Framework Decision 2001/220/JHA ([2010] OJ L 315, 14.11.2012, p 57).

[12] Directive (EU) 2017/2103 of the European Parliament and of the Council of 15 November 2017 amending Council Framework Decision 2004/757/JHA in order to include new psychoactive substances in the definition of 'drug' and repealing Council Decision 2005/387/JHA ([2017] OJ L 305, 21.11.2017, p 12).

[13] Cf especially the following references: Jannemieke W Ouwerkerk, 'Criminalisation as a last resort: a national principle under the pressure of Europianisation?' (2012) 3/4 *New Journal of European Criminal Law* 228, 229; Sakari Melander, 'Ultima Ratio in European Criminal Law' (2013) 3(1) *European Criminal Law Review* 45–64; Jacob Öberg, 'Do We Really Need Criminal Sanctions for the Enforcement of EU Law?' (2014) 5(3) *New Journal of European Criminal Law* 370, 383; Andrew Simester, Bob Sullivan, Graham Virgo and John Spencer, *Simester and Sullivan's Criminal Law – Theory and Doctrine*, 4th edn (Oxford, Hart Publishing, 2010) 652; Douglas Husak, 'The Criminal Law as Last Resort' (2004) 24(2) *Oxford Journal of Legal* Studies 207–235.

[14] Ouwerkerk, 'Criminalisation as a last resort' (n 13).

less so.[15] The reasons are manifold and it is not the aim of this study to analyse them. Suffice it to say that the inflation of criminal law may be partly due to the fear, which has become a 'normal' part of everyday life in the Western world living in the shadow of terrorism and the economic crisis. Beyond this, one has to take into account the political temptation rooted in the fact that criminal law is a popular measure and is not perceived to require significant additional budgetary resources.[16]

The result of all this is overcriminalisation, which dilutes the traditional moral authority of criminal law.

As far as the United States is concerned, in a study published in 2005, Eric Luna defines overcriminalisation as the abuse of the supreme force of a criminal justice system.[17] He refers to the existence of more than 4,000 federal offences beyond the offences defined by the various States. Some of these do not only fail at the last resort test, but also at the 'laugh test'. For example, Indiana bans the dyeing of birds and rabbits; Massachusetts punishes those who frighten pigeons from their nests. Until 2021 the federal government prohibited the unauthorised use of the US Forest Service characters 'Smokey Bear' and 'Woodsy Owl'. Moreover, innumerable local ordinances carry the possibility of criminal consequences, such as the jailable offence of failing to return library books in Salt Lake City.[18]

Compared to the somewhat entertaining nature of these examples, a book by Nils Christie on a crime control industry paints a darker picture of the phenomenon, succinctly captured by its subtitle: *Towards Gulags, Western Style*.[19] Indeed, Christie sees in the US crime control industry the seeds of totalitarianism.[20]

Naturally, this study cannot provide a full picture of the *ultima ratio* principle and the overcriminalisation phenomenon throughout the world. My task is to concentrate on the EU legislature's approach to the problem.

Despite the *topoi* of cheap press publications, to claim that the exercise of EU criminal law competences sows the seeds of totalitarianism does not hold water. It is true

[15] Nils Jareborg, 'Criminalization as Last Resort (Ultima Ratio)' (2004) 2(2) *Ohio State Journal of Criminal Law* 521, 523, but also Simester (n 13) 649; Jean Pradel, *Droit pénal comparé* (Paris, Dalloz, 2008) 800.

[16] See for this topic: Douglas Husak, *Overcriminalization: The Limits of the Criminal Law* (Oxford University Press, Oxford 2008) 231; Andrew Ashworth, 'Is the Criminal Law a Lost Cause?' (2000) 116(2) *Law Quarterly Review* 225–56; William J Stuntz, 'The Pathological Politics of Criminal Law' (2001) 100(3) *Michigan Law Review* 505–600.

[17] Erik Luna, 'The Overcriminalization Phenomenon' (2005) 54(3) *American University Law Review* 703–43.

[18] Luna (n 17) 704.

[19] Christie (n 2).

[20] It is interesting to note that concerns about the inflation of the criminal justice system are not only shared by academics, but Pope Francis also spoke in this sense in his 2014 address to the members of the International Association of Penal Law: 'In this context, a widespread conviction has taken root in recent decades that public punishment can resolve the most disparate social problems, as if completely different diseases could be treated with the same medicine. This is not so much about trust in some social function traditionally attributed to public punishment, as about the belief that it is possible that such punishment can obtain those benefits that would demand the application of a different type of social and economic policy as well as social inclusion. Scapegoats are not only sought to pay, with their freedom and with their life, for all social ills such as was typical in primitive societies, but over and beyond this, there is at times a tendency to deliberately fabricate enemies: stereotyped figures who represent all the characteristics that society perceives or interprets as threatening. The mechanisms that form these images are the same that allowed the spread of racist ideas in their time': https://w2.vatican.va/content/francesco/en/speeches/2014/october/documents/papa-francesco_20141023_associazione-internazionale-diritto-penale.html.

that the use of criminal law as a tool of market integration carries an inherent tension with the legitimacy of EU criminal law. However, I will argue that the EU legislature – since the Treaty of Lisbon – has found a balance, by no means unhealthy, between the popular pressure to criminalise anything that moves and the idea of a strictly limited supranational entity. This balance flows both from the Treaties – the constitutional charter of the EU[21] – and the practice of the EU institutions.

B. Primary Law

Before the entry into force of the Treaty of Lisbon, the area of freedom, security and justice (AFSJ) was part of a three-pillar structure. It was divided between Title VI EU (Third Pillar) and Title IV EC. In the third pillar, Article 31(1)(e) EU provided for the progressively adoption of measures establishing minimum rules relating to the constituent elements of criminal acts and to penalties in the fields of organised crime, terrorism and illicit drug trafficking.[22]

However, there was a controversy as to criminal law competence in the Community pillar, since there was no express Treaty reference to that competence. The legislative technique used to solve this problem was to adopt two measures: one, under the Community pillar dealing with regulatory issues and another, under the third pillar, containing criminal law measures. Nevertheless, the Court of Justice held that there was some criminal law competence even within the Community pillar. In *Casati*, the Court placed limits on national criminal law insofar as it might impede rules on free movement.[23] In the so-called *Greek maize* case, the Court encouraged the use of national criminal law as a sanction for breach of Community law, where it would be used at national level in analogous situations:

> whilst the choice of penalties remains within [Member States'] discretion, they must ensure in particular that infringements of Community law are penalized under conditions, both procedural and substantive, which are analogous to those applicable to infringements of national law of a similar nature and importance and which, in any event, make the penalty effective, proportionate and dissuasive.[24]

The Court accepted in the *Environmental Crimes* case an implied criminal law competence in the Community pillar.

> As a general rule, neither criminal law nor the rules of criminal procedure fall within the Community's competence. [...] However, the last-mentioned finding does not prevent the Community legislature, when the application of effective, proportionate and dissuasive criminal penalties by the competent national authorities is an essential measure for combating

[21] Case 294/83, *Parti écologiste Les Verts v European Parliament*, judgment of 26 April 1986, EU:C:1986:166, paragraph 23.

[22] Notable examples of adopted acts: Council Framework Decision 2002/475/JHA on combating terrorism ([2002] OJ L 164, 22.6. 2002, p 3); Council Framework Decision 2004/757/JHA laying down minimum provisions on the constituent elements of criminal acts and penalties in the field of illicit drug trafficking ([2004] OJ L 335, 11.11.2004, p 8); Council Framework Decision 2008/841/JHA on the fight against organized crime ([2008] OJ L 300, 11.11.2008, p 42).

[23] Case 203/80, *Criminal proceedings against Guerrino Casati*, EU:C:1981:261, paragraph 27.

[24] *Commission v Greece*, Case 68/88, EU:C:1989:339, judgment of 21 September 1989, paragraph 24.

> serious environmental offences, from taking measures which relate to the criminal law of the Member States which it considers necessary in order to ensure that the rules which it lays down on environmental protection are fully effective.[25]

This doctrine was reaffirmed in the *Ship-Source Pollution* case, but the Court specified that 'the determination of the type and level of the criminal penalties to be applied does not fall within the Community's sphere of competence'.[26]

The Treaty of Lisbon introduced a slightly different constitutional context. According to Article 83(1) TFEU, the

> European Parliament and the Council may, by means of directives adopted in accordance with the ordinary legislative procedure, establish minimum rules concerning the definition of criminal offences and sanctions in the areas of particularly serious crime with a cross-border dimension resulting from the nature or impact of such offences or from a special need to combat them on a common basis.

These areas of crime are the following: terrorism, trafficking in human beings and sexual exploitation of women and children, illicit drug trafficking, illicit arms trafficking, money laundering, corruption, counterfeiting of means of payment, computer crime and organised crime.

Article 83(2) TFEU, as a distant echo to the *Environmental Crimes* doctrine, sets out the following:

> If the approximation of criminal laws and regulations of the Member States proves *essential* to ensure the effective implementation of a Union policy in an area which has been subject to harmonisation measures, directives may establish minimum rules with regard to the definition of criminal offences and sanctions in the area concerned. Such directives shall be adopted by the same ordinary or special legislative procedure as was followed for the adoption of the harmonisation measures in question, without prejudice to Article 76 (emphasis added).

The main difference between the two criminal law legal bases is that in case of paragraph (2) there must be an already harmonised area where it proves to be 'essential' to adopt criminal legislation in order to implement those rules effectively. By contrast, in paragraph (1) the existence of a harmonised area is irrelevant; it is sufficient that the new criminal rules fall into one of the areas listed in that paragraph. Since that list contains areas where the use of criminal law is arguably not far-fetched by definition, such as terrorism or organised crime, paragraph (2) is more interesting from a theoretical point of view when it comes to examining the EU legislator's balancing obligation. Criminal law under paragraph (2) is geared in principle to ensuring or underpinning the efficiency of internal market rules; therefore the question whether or not to use criminal law or other forms of coercion through civil or administrative measures becomes highly relevant.[27]

In my view the word 'essential', read in its context and in the system of the Treaties, is the expression of the *ultima ratio* principle in the constitutional framework of the

[25] *Commission v Council*, C-176/03, EU:C:2005:542, judgment of 13 September 2005, paragraphs 47–48.

[26] *Commission v Council*, C-440/05, EU:C:2007:625, judgment of 23 October 2007, paragraphs 66–70.

[27] The *lex specialis* that Article 325 TFEU represents will not be examined in this chapter. It is a highly specific legal basis, never used for substantive criminal law.

EU. Beyond its dictionary meaning – absolutely necessary, basic or fundamental – the word 'essential' must be interpreted according to the system of the Treaties. According to Article 67(1) TFEU, in all AFSJ legislation – including criminal law – the 'different legal systems and traditions of the Member States' must be respected. This provision can be construed as a constitutional limit on EU criminal law competence, in the same vein as Article 5(4) TEU on the principle of proportionality and Article 5(3) TEU on subsidiarity (ie federal proportionality).[28]

Moreover, the use of the wording '*proves* to be essential' (emphasis added) includes, in my view, the EU legislator's obligation to be able to provide factual evidence as to the necessity of criminal law as opposed to other, lighter forms of coercion. I argued elsewhere that in case of a lack of such evidence, the validity of EU criminal law could be called into question by the Court of Justice on procedural grounds.[29]

However, despite the potential of this framework to limit the exercise of powers, it cannot be denied that there exists a tension between the effectiveness of internal market rules and the legitimacy of EU criminal law. As has been pointed out by Ester Herlin-Karnell, 'criminal law is fundamentally ill-suited for clear-cut analogies with the internal market'.[30] Nevertheless, the *Environmental Crimes* case-law seems to be based on the – in my view, erroneous – presumption that criminal law is effective per se. The pre-Lisbon use of 'effectiveness' as a constitutional principle can be seen as 'dangerously imprecise as a threshold for competence', just like the 'focus on security in combination with the effectiveness mantra constitutes a particularly dangerous combination'.[31]

I agree with these observations. At the same time, I believe that the Treaty of Lisbon has the potential to correct the mistake of the effectiveness mantra, and has reaffirmed the requirement of criminal law being 'essential' for underpinning market creation, to be read in the context of the principle of proportionality and the reference to Member States' legal traditions. Thus, the substantive criminal law competence of the EU, far from being an ancillary tool of market creation, is and should remain a measure of last resort.

Although this is my personal position, this reading seems to be confirmed both by the EU institutions' non-binding guidelines on the use of their criminal law competences and also by the practice of the institutions since the entry into force of the Treaty of Lisbon. The two subsections that follow will in turn examine these topics.

C. The EU Institutions' Position

(i) The European Parliament

When dealing with the position of the European Parliament, one could hardly avoid first mentioning the *Manifesto on European Criminal Policy* of 2011, drawn up by

[28] The term 'federal proportionality' is used by Herlin-Karnell, *The Constitutional Dimension of European Criminal Law* (Oxford, Hart Publishing, 2012) 111.

[29] Tamás Lukácsi, 'Az ultima ratio elve az Európai Unió jogában' (2015) 56(2) *Állam- és Jogtudomány* 20.

[30] Herlin-Karnell, (n 28) 18.

[31] Herlin-Karnell (n 28) 62, 85.

university professors.[32] It calls for a measured use of criminal legislation at the European level. It sports the *ultima ratio* principle at the top of its agenda. Indeed, since the EU places the individual centre stage, the European legislator may only demand that an act be criminalised if it is necessary in order to protect a fundamental interest, and if all other measures have proven insufficient to safeguard that interest. This is also due to the fact, according to the *Manifesto*, that criminal sanctions entail social stigmatisation which significantly affects citizens' rights, including the rights expressed in the Charter of Fundamental Rights. Furthermore, excessive use of criminal sanctions and criminalisation leads to a decline in the efficiency of criminal law.

The *Manifesto* adds a remarkable institutional argument to this picture: insofar as European instruments limit the freedom of the national legislator, the harmonised criminal law provisions cannot directly be justified on the grounds of democracy at national level. This makes it necessary to strengthen democratic legitimacy at the European level by a more active role of the European Parliament in the Union's legislative process. This argument reflects the institutional balance set out by the Treaty of Lisbon, according to which criminal law legislation entails a legislative procedure in which the European Parliament stands on an equal footing with the Council.

The *Manifesto* is echoed by the resolution of the European Parliament of 22 May 2012 on an EU approach to criminal law.[33] It is interesting to note 'EU' in the title which shows that the Parliament is not only defining its own approach, but an approach it deems valid for all EU institutions. However, the resolution is not a binding legal instrument according to Article 288 TFEU; therefore the Parliament may only be able to enforce this approach through its institutional leverage.

According to the European Parliament,

> in view of it being able by its very nature to restrict certain human rights and fundamental freedoms of suspected, accused or convicted persons, in addition to the possible stigmatising effect of criminal investigations, and taking into account that excessive use of criminal legislation leads to a decline in efficiency, criminal law must be applied as a measure of last resort (*ultima ratio*) addressing clearly defined and delimited conduct, which cannot be addressed effectively by less severe measures and which causes significant damage to society or individuals.[34]

[32] See www.crimpol.eu. The manifesto called for a more active role of the European Parliament in order to strengthen the democratic legitimacy of criminal law at the European level: 'Since criminal law is the most intrusive of the institutions of state control, in a democratic society it must be justified by reference to as direct participation as possible by the people in the legislative process. As long as, and to the extent that the EU has no competence to make supranational criminal legislation, the competence to adopt criminal law provisions remains the preserve of the Member States (i.e. their national Parliaments). Due to the fact that the European legislator can issue binding instruments which national Parliaments must comply with, constraints that impact on the freedom of national legislatures are placed on them. This means that even instruments of harmonisation must be justifiable from the point of view of democracy. As far as European instruments limit the freedom of the national legislator, the harmonised criminal law provision cannot be justified on the grounds of democracy at the national level. This makes it necessary to strengthen democratic legitimacy at the European level by a more active role of the European Parliament in the Union's legislative process' Point 4.c, subprinciple 3.

[33] [2013] OJ C 264E, 13.9.2013, p 7, also referred to as the De Jong resolution.

[34] Recital (I) of the Resolution.

The Parliament also emphasises that – in principle – 'it is not sufficient to refer to abstract notions or to symbolic effects, but that the necessity of new substantive criminal law provisions must be demonstrated by the necessary factual evidence'.[35]

(ii) The Council

The Conclusions on model provisions, guiding the Council's criminal law deliberations,[36] point to the same direction as the EP resolution, though with a slightly different emphasis, on the consistency of EU law. The *ultima ratio* principle finds its rightful place in point (1) of the Conclusions: 'criminal law provisions should be introduced when they are considered essential in order for the interests to be protected and, as a rule, be used only as a last resort'. After the enumeration of principles, the Conclusions indicate (point (3)) that

> when there seems to be a need for adopting new criminal provisions the following factors should be further considered, while taking fully into account the impact assessments that have been made:
>
> - the expected added value or effectiveness of criminal provisions compared to other measures, taking into account the possibility to investigate and prosecute the crime through reasonable efforts, as well as its seriousness and implications;
> - how serious and/or widespread and frequent the harmful conduct is, both regionally and locally within the EU;
> - the possible impact on existing criminal provisions in EU legislation and on different legal systems within the EU.

(iii) The Commission

The Commission's own guidelines are contained in a Communication published in 2011 under the title 'Towards an EU Criminal Policy: Ensuring the effective implementation of EU policies through criminal law'.[37] According to the Commission – and it is to be noted that the Communication addresses not only a Commission but an 'EU' policy – the EU legislator should follow two steps when taking a decision on criminal law measures aimed at ensuring the effective implementation of EU policies which are the subject of harmonising measures.

The first step should be a decision on whether to adopt criminal law measures at all. In this step, the *ultima ratio* principle again plays an important part. The Commission clearly sees this principle anchored in the Treaty, since it is

> reflected in the general principle of proportionality (as embodied in the Treaty on European Union and, specifically for criminal penalties, in the EU Charter of Fundamental Rights). For criminal law measures supporting the enforcement of EU policies, the Treaty explicitly

[35] Paragraph 3 of the Resolution.

[36] Draft Conclusions on model provisions, guiding the Council's criminal law deliberations, Council document 16542/2/09 of 27 November 2009: https://db.eurocrim.org/db/en/doc/1652.pdf.

[37] COM(2011) 573 of 20 September 2011.

requires a test of whether criminal law measures are 'essential' to achieve the goal of an effective policy implementation.[38]

Should step 1 demonstrate the need for criminal law, the next question is which concrete measures to take. Criminal law measures can be regarded as an element to ensure the effective enforcement of EU policies, as recognised by the TFEU. EU policies cover a broad variety of subjects, where common rules have been developed over the last few decades. These policy areas range from the customs union and internal market rules to the protection of the environment. In all these policy areas, Member States are obliged to ensure that breaches of EU law are to be sanctioned with effective, proportionate and dissuasive penalties. Member States can in general choose the nature of the sanction, which does not have to be criminal but could also be administrative.

D. Secondary Law

The constitutional framework that binds the hands of the EU legislature and the institutions' own non-binding guidelines, has resulted in a quite moderate output of new criminal rules since the entry into force of the Treaty of Lisbon. The number of new instruments at the time of writing is under 10. The number in itself, of course, does not allow for in-depth conclusions on EU criminal policy, but what it indicates is that even during a decade spent under the shadow of an economic crisis and terrorist attacks, the checks on EU criminal competence seem to work. The bulk of new laws were adopted anyway on the basis of Article 83(1) TFEU, which, by including a closed list of areas of serious crime, is less prone to lead to overcriminalisation than the more open Article 83(2) TFEU.

The first instrument to be mentioned is Directive 2011/36/EU on preventing and combating trafficking in human beings and protecting its victims.[39] This was followed by the adoption, in the same year, of Directive 2011/93/EU on combating the sexual abuse and sexual exploitation of children and child pornography.[40]

After 2012, a year without substantive EU criminal law, 2013 and 2014 saw the adoption of one new instrument each: Directive 2013/40/EU on attacks against information systems[41] and Directive 2014/62/EU on the protection of the euro and other currencies against counterfeiting by criminal law.[42] A hybrid (procedural and substantive) instrument should also be mentioned: Directive 2014/42/EU on the freezing and confiscation

[38] Paragraph 2.2.1 of the Communication.

[39] Directive 2011/36/EU of the European Parliament and of the Council of 5 April 2011 on preventing and combating trafficking in human beings and protecting its victims, and replacing Council Framework Decision 2002/629/JHA [2011] OJ L 101, 15.4.2011, p 1.

[40] Directive 2011/93/EU of the European Parliament and of the Council of 13 December 2011 on combating the sexual abuse and sexual exploitation of children and child pornography, and replacing Council Framework Decision 2004/68/JHA [2011] OJ L 335, 17.12.2011, p 1.

[41] Directive 2013/40/EU of the European Parliament and of the Council of 12 August 2013 on attacks against information systems and replacing Council Framework Decision 2005/222/JHA [2013] OJ L 218, 14.8.2013, p 8.

[42] Directive 2014/62/EU of the European Parliament and of the Council of 15 May 2014 on the protection of the euro and other currencies against counterfeiting by criminal law, and replacing Council Framework Decision 2000/383/JHA [2014] OJ L 151, 21.5.2014, p 1.

of instrumentalities and proceeds of crime in the European Union, which is based on the double legal bases of Articles 82(2) and 83(1) TFEU.[43]

Two years of break followed until 2017 when two new directives saw the light of day. Directive (EU) 2017/541 on combating terrorism[44] was adopted following the signature by the EU of the Council of Europe additional protocol to the Warsaw Convention.[45] It codifies the existing EU *acquis* in the field of combating terrorism and implements in EU law the specific preparatory acts defined by the additional protocol. In 2019 the so far latest act was adopted, which is Directive (EU) 2019/713 on combating fraud and counterfeiting of non-cash means of payment.[46]

For the purposes of this chapter, the most relevant act will be Directive (EU) 2017/2103 amending Council Framework Decision 2004/757/JHA in order to include new psychoactive substances in the definition of drugs and repealing Council Decision 2005/387/JHA.[47] I have chosen the legislative history of this act as a case study to give an insight into the practical challenges the EU legislature is facing in its balancing exercise.

Finally, it should be also mentioned that – however rare the phenomenon is and however unfortunate that rarity is – Article 83(1) TFEU also served as a legal basis for de-regulation, that is for repealing some obsolete acts.[48]

Turning to Article 83(2) TFEU, one could only wonder that such an open-ended legal basis has only been used once in the last decade. Despite all its potential to use criminal law as a customary tool for internal market creation – and scholarly literature does not fail to call to mind that danger[49] – the EU legislature has been careful with that legal basis. The only real example of using criminal law to enforce harmonised market rules is Directive 2014/57/EU on criminal sanctions for market abuse (market abuse directive).[50]

For the sake of being complete, it should be mentioned that formally Directive (EU) 2017/1371 on the fight against fraud to the Union's financial interests by means of criminal law[51] has also been based on Article 83(2) TFEU. However, I see that choice as problematic since there are no harmonised rules in that area in the sense of Article 83(2).

[43] Directive 2014/42/EU of the European Parliament and of the Council of 3 April on the freezing and confiscation of instrumentalities and proceeds of crime in the European Union, which is based on the double legal bases of Articles 82(2) and 83(1) TFEU [2014] OJ L 127, 29.4.2014, p 39.

[44] Directive (EU) 2017/541 of the European Parliament and of the Council of 15 March 2017 on combating terrorism and replacing Council Framework Decision 2002/475/JHA and amending Council Decision 2005/671/JHA [2017] OJ L 88, 31.3.2017, p 6.

[45] Council of Europe Convention on the Prevention of Terrorism, CETS No 196.

[46] Directive (EU) 2019/713 of the European Parliament and of the Council of 17 April 2019 on combating fraud and counterfeiting of non-cash means of payment and replacing Council Framework Decision 2001/413/JHA [2019] OJ L 123, 10.5.2019, p 18.

[47] Directive (EU) 2017/2103 of the European Parliament and of the Council of 15 November 2017 amending Council Framework Decision 2004/757/JHA in order to include new psychoactive substances in the definition of drugs and repealing Council Decision 2005/387/JHA [2017] OJ L 305, 21.11.2017, p 12.

[48] Eg Regulation (EU) 2016/95 of the European Parliament and of the Council of 20 January 2016 repealing certain acts in the field of police cooperation and judicial cooperation in criminal matters ([2016] OJ L 26, 2.2.2016, p 9).

[49] Herlin-Karnell (n 28).

[50] Directive 2014/57/EU of the European Parliament and of the Council of 16 April 2014 on criminal sanctions for market abuse [2014] OJ L 173, 12.6.2014, p 179.

[51] Directive (EU) 2017/1371 of the European Parliament and of the Council of 5 July 2017 on the fight against fraud to the Union's financial interests by means of criminal law [2017] OJ L 198, 28.7.2017, p 29.

Consequently, if it were able to set aside pragmatic political considerations, the legislature should have rather based that act on Article 325 TFEU.

This short enumeration of secondary law sets the scene for my case study. The quantity of legislation is far from being overwhelming, but it would still be impossible to analyse in detail the balancing exercise of the legislature in each individual act. Therefore, I chose one specific example where the daily challenges of the work with EU criminal legislation are faithfully, albeit incompletely, reflected.

III. A Case Study: Substantive Criminal Law on New Psychoactive Substances

A. The Context and Hidden Vice of the Proposal

The second longest lasting legislative procedure in the field of substantive criminal law, since the entry into force of the Treaty of Lisbon, concerned new psychoactive substances.[52] After the presentation of the proposals in 2013, it took four years to arrive at a result in this policy area which, paradoxically, is all about speeding up law enforcement reaction to new substances.

New psychoactive substances, also known as 'designer drugs' or 'legal highs' imitate the effects of substances scheduled under the UN Conventions of the 1960s and '70s,[53] but their chemical formula is different. These substances are emerging frequently and are spreading rapidly in the Union. Certain new psychoactive substances pose severe public health and social risks.[54] Case level drugs seizure data reported to the EU Early Warning System point to the continued growth of the new drug market. For example, in 2014, almost 50,000 seizures of new substances, weighing almost 4 tons, were made across Europe. Synthetic cannabinoids accounted for the majority of these, with almost 30,000 seizures, weighing more than 1.3 tons. New substances have been associated with a range of serious harms in Europe, including acute poisonings and deaths. There are also harms associated with patterns of drug injection. Mass poisonings, although rare, can place heavy demands on healthcare systems. In one such incident, reported in Poland in 2015, synthetic cannabinoids were linked to over 200 hospital emergency presentations in less than a week.[55]

Since the chemical composition of these substances is different from substances scheduled under the UN Conventions, Framework Decision 2004/757/JHA[56] does

[52] The EU PNR-Directive also took a long time to adopt, but that is not a substantive criminal law instrument.

[53] The existing EU legislation, ie Framework Decision 2004/757/JHA applies to the substances covered by the 1961 United Nations Single Convention on Narcotic Drugs, as amended by the 1972 Protocol, and to the substances covered by the 1971 United Nations Convention on Psychotropic Substances.

[54] See Recital (4) of Directive (EU) 2017/2103 (n 47).

[55] EMCDDA European Drug Report 2016: http://www.emcdda.europa.eu/system/files/publications/2637/TDAT16001ENN.pdf.

[56] Council Framework Decision 2004/757/JHA of 25 October 2004 laying down minimum provisions on the constituent elements of criminal acts and penalties in the field of illicit drug trafficking ([2004] OJ L 335, 11.11.2004, p 8).

not apply to them and, for this reason, they cannot be considered illegal drugs for the purposes of EU criminal law.

The challenge of the new legislation was to design a mechanism that makes it possible to bring within the scope of the Framework Decision these rapidly emerging and changing substances.[57] However, too rapid solutions are usually suspicious in criminal law, where safeguards and parliamentary involvement are traditionally important. How to balance these requirements? How to design a system that is rapid and efficient, but constitutionally sound at the same time? That was the challenge facing the legislator in this policy area. The Commission originally proposed a regulation and a directive, the logic of which was substantially changed during the legislative procedure.

The Commission proposal for a regulation of the European Parliament and the Council on new psychoactive substances[58] was based on Article 114 TFEU. The aim of the proposal was to establish rules for restrictions to the free movement of new psychoactive substances in the internal market. For that purpose, it set up a mechanism for information exchange on risk assessment and submission to market restriction measures of new psychoactive substances at Union level.

According to Article 13(1) of the proposal on severe risks and permanent market restriction,

> [t]he Commission shall, by means of a Decision, without undue delay, prohibit the production, manufacture, making available on the market including importation to the Union, transport, and exportation from the Union of the new psychoactive substance if, based on existing evidence, it poses, overall, severe health, social and safety risks …

The decision prohibiting the substance was proposed to take the form of a Commission implementing act adopted in the examination procedure. The proposal also foresaw a procedure to re-examine the level of risk as well as a provision on sanctions that the Member States would have to introduce for the infringement of the implementing decisions banning a substance. Let us take due note: those sanctions were not necessarily criminal penalties. Member States would have had the choice between criminal and administrative (or call them quasi-criminal) sanctions, on the condition that they were 'effective, proportionate and dissuasive'.[59]

It was therefore proposed that the Commission might impose a permanent market restriction on a new psychoactive substance by means of an implementing act, if it determined that the substance posed severe risks. The permanent restriction would be linked to the level of the risk which was assessed on the basis of non-exhaustive criteria related to harm to health, social harm and security risks. When the Commission imposed such a restriction, Member States would be obliged to lay down sanctions applicable to the infringements of the Decision imposing the restriction. If new information or evidence so suggested, the Commission would re-examine the level of risks that a new psychoactive substance posed.

[57] Despite the general invitation by the Intergovernmental Conference (IGC) to the legislature, contained in Declaration 50 annexed to the Treaties, the Framework Decision was only amended and not replaced, presumably because of the targeted nature of the amendment.

[58] COM(2013) 619 of 17 September 2013.

[59] Article 17 of the above-mentioned proposal.

The proposal for a regulation was coupled with a proposal for a directive. The interplay between the two instruments is worth examining and understanding as it reveals an important lesson to be learned about the balancing exercise of the EU legislature in the field of criminal law.

The proposal for a directive of the European Parliament and the Council amending Council Framework Decision 2004/757/JHA of 25 October 2004 laying down minimum provisions on the constituent elements of criminal acts and penalties in the field of illicit drug trafficking, as regards the definition of 'drug'[60] was based on Article 83(1) TFEU. It aimed to amend Framework Decision 2004/757/JHA, which sets out minimum rules obliging Member States to enact in their national law criminal penalties for the punishment of certain types of intentional conduct. The proposal for a directive is worthy of our attention because it was geared to underpin, by criminal law provisions, the permanent market restriction measures adopted under the concurrent proposal for a regulation.

The wrongful intentional conducts set out in the Framework Decision contain, among others, the production, manufacture, extraction, preparation, sale, dispatch, transport and importation of drugs.[61] The penalties required by the Framework Decision include imprisonment.[62] Notably, these sanctioning aspects were not to be subject to amendment by the proposal for a directive; it only aimed to amend the Framework Decision as to the definition of drugs.

According to Article 1(1)(b) and (c) of the proposal for a directive (together with its Annex), 'drug' means, among other things, any new psychoactive substance posing severe health, social and safety risks, subjected to permanent market restriction on the basis of the proposal for a regulation. Article 1(2) of the same proposal (amending Article 9 of the Framework Decision) set out that:

> In respect of new psychoactive substances subjected to permanent market restriction on the basis of … [Article 13(1) of the proposal for a regulation], Member States shall bring into force the laws, regulations and administrative provisions necessary to apply the provisions of this Framework Decision to these new psychoactive substances within twelve months after entry into force of the permanent market restriction.

Thus, any new substance that becomes subject to permanent market restriction under the proposal for the internal market regulation will automatically be included in the definition of 'drug'. Member States will have an obligation to implement that change and to enact the new element of the definition into their national criminal laws. Once the new substance is included in the definition of 'drug' in national law, certain types of intentional conduct in relation to that wider definition of 'drug' (like manufacturing, selling, etc that substance) will be punishable with criminal penalties, including imprisonment.

In my view, this system presented a serious challenge to the co-legislators. They were, in essence, asked to approve a mechanism whereby the Commission, through a chain of automatic references, would have been able to change Member States' national

[60] COM(2013) 0618 of 17 September 2013.
[61] Article 2(1)(a) of the Framework Decision 2004/757/JHA (n 56).
[62] Article 4 of the Framework Decision 2004/757/JHA (n 56).

criminal law by implementing acts adopted under an internal market legal basis. I will argue later that this solution could be problematic under EU law.

The European Parliament did not rise to the bait. But before telling that story, let us review the constitutional context.

B. The Constitutional Background and the Limits it Imposes

The competence of the Union in the area of criminal law is shared with Member States, according to Article 4(2)(j) TFEU. This means that national and Union law complement each other: the Member States shall exercise their competence to the extent that the Union has not exercised its competence; the Member States shall again exercise their competence to the extent that the Union has decided to cease exercising its competence.[63] The different legal systems and traditions of the Member States have to be respected in the exercise of competences relating to the area of freedom, security and justice.[64]

In addition, specific substantive safeguards apply to criminal law, in particular because of the stigmatising effect of criminal proceedings and the potentially harsh consequences of a conviction.[65] Criminal law, by its very nature, restricts human rights and fundamental freedoms of suspected, accused or convicted persons. Therefore, generally speaking, criminal law must be applied as a measure of last resort (*ultima ratio*), addressing clearly defined and delimited conduct that causes significant damage to society or individuals. Given the highly intrusive character of criminal law legislation, it must be considered as an *ultima ratio*, when all other legislative and administrative tools fail, or produce insufficient results of deterrence. A prudential argument also pleads in favour of this principle: excessive use of criminal legislation is prone to lead to a decline in efficiency.

The *ultima ratio* principle[66] is also a matter of proportionality. Pursuant to Article 5(4) of the TEU, the content and form of Union action shall not exceed what is *necessary* to achieve the objectives of the Treaties. Only if the condition of necessity has been satisfied can criminal law be in conformity with the principle of proportionality. Thus, I believe that to the extent to which the *ultima ratio* principle is an extension of the principle of proportionality, it is a legally binding principle under the Treaties.

Let us now examine, in light of these principles, the aforementioned proposals on new psychoactive substances, and especially one of their aims which is to create an automatic mechanism. According to that mechanism, when the Commission, under the proposed regulation based on Article 114 TFEU, imposes by means of an implementing act a permanent market restriction on a new substance, that substance will automatically be covered by the definition of 'drug' under the proposed directive based

[63] Article 2(2) TFEU.

[64] Article 67(1) TFEU.

[65] See Parliament's resolution of 22 May 2012 on an EU approach to criminal law, 2010/2310(INI), P7_TA-PROV(2012)0208, in particular Recitals I, J, K, L and paragraphs 3 and 4.

[66] See especially: Ouwerkerk, 'Criminalisation as a last resort' (n 13) 229; Melander, 'Ultima Ratio in European Criminal Law' (n 13) 45–64; Öberg, 'Do We Really Need Criminal Sanctions' (n 13) 383; Simester et al, *Simester and Sullivan's Criminal Law* (n 13) 652; Husak, 'The Criminal Law as Last Resort' (n 13) 207–35.

on Article 83(1) TFEU. Then, the modified definition of 'drug' will become part of the criminal law of the Member States through their obligation to implement the provisions of the Framework Decision as amended by the directive.[67]

The result of that mechanism is that the Commission's implementing acts – adopted under criteria from an internal market regulation and thus not necessarily fulfilling all criteria required by criminal law – would make their way into national criminal legislation. In substance, the Commission would be empowered to define by implementing acts certain elements of Union and national criminal law, without the Union legislature being able to revoke, or object to, that empowerment. Such an mechanism seemed to raise concerns as to its conformity with both primary Union law and general principles of law for the following reasons.[68]

First, the automatic self-transformation of internal market administrative measures into criminal law measures merges two different questions: *(a)* should a new substance be made subject to permanent market restriction in the internal market? and *(b)* should it be subject to criminal legislation? These two questions must be answered using two different tests. The necessity of administrative measures in the internal market and the necessity of criminal legislation are two distinct questions which should clearly be separated in Union law. The first test, to answer question *(a)*, can be defined by secondary legislation in the field of the internal market. The second test, to answer question *(b)*, should be defined under Article 83(1) TFEU and with regard to the above constitutional principles limiting the power to use criminal law.

What the Commission proposals suggested, in substance, is that the second test be subordinated to the first one. They suggested that whatever measure passes the threshold of the first test should be deemed, through a command of secondary law, to have passed the second test as well. Thus, the Commission would subordinate the criteria to be used for judging the necessity of criminal legislation under Article 83(1) TFEU to the criteria to be used for judging the necessity of administrative (quasi-criminal) measures in the internal market under the proposed regulation.

Moreover, the implementing acts foreseen by the proposal for a regulation would, through the mechanism described above, also implement the proposal for a directive. Under closer scrutiny, this also turned out to be a problem related to the legal bases. The legal basis of the proposal for a regulation limits the scope of acts implementing it to the area covered by Article 114 TFEU. However, those implementing acts would in reality also 'implement' the provisions of the proposal for a directive, which is based on Article 83(1) TFEU. Since the latter is a specific legal basis covering the area of illicit drug trafficking, and is not dependent on the necessity to implement another policy area of the Union, the proposed mechanism seemed to go beyond the limits set by the scope of Article 114 TFEU. While one can only agree with the aim of fighting against illicit drugs, the way the proposals were designed to tackle the problem contained a hidden vice, in the sense that the proposals would actually empower the Commission to circumvent a decision-making procedure established by the Treaty. Rules concerning

[67] See Article 288 TFEU, third subparagraph.

[68] It could also be noted that the chain of reference used in the two proposals (national criminal law referring to a directive, referring to a regulation, referring to an implementing act) does not serve the clarity of legislation.

the definition of criminal offences would no longer be adopted on the basis of, and through the procedure foreseen by, Article 83(1) TFEU, but on the basis of the proposal for an internal market regulation.

C. The European Parliament's Position and the Interinstitutional Negotiations

The above arguments found an echo within the European Parliament, and its first reading position changed the proposed mechanism. While the draft report[69] left the provision in question unchanged, at a later stage an amendment was tabled that introduced the idea of delegated acts for the purposes of placing new substances in the Annex containing the list of illegal substances. However, this amendment would have left the automatic link between the regulation and the directive untouched. The final report[70] adopted by the Committee on Civil Liberties, Justice and Home Affairs (LIBE) took on board that idea but developed it further. Amendment 15, reproduced below, ensured that the new substances that become part of the actus reus of the criminal offences defined in the Framework Decision are adopted by delegated acts under the criminal law instrument, and not by implementing acts under the internal market regulation.

Amendment 15

Proposal for a directive

Article 1 – point 2 a (new)

Framework Decision 2004/757/JHA

Article 9 a (new)

Text proposed by the Commission	*Amendment*
	(2a) The following Article is added after Article 9: ***'Article 9a*** ***Delegation of power*** ***The Commission shall be empowered to adopt delegated acts to amend the Annex to this Framework Decision, in particular to add to the Annex new psychoactive substances subjected to permanent market restriction on the basis of Article 13(1) of Regulation (EU) No …/… on new psychoactive substances.'***

Amendment 11 went even further: by deleting in the left hand column point (c) of the original Commission proposal, it cut the automatic link between the draft regulation

[69] Rapporteur: Teresa Jiménez-Becerril Barrio (EPP, Spain), PE519.605v01-00.
[70] RR/1023358EN, A7-0173/2014, 14.3.2014. https://www.europarl.europa.eu/doceo/document/A-7-2014-0173_EN.html.

and the directive, enabling thus the adoption of the above-mentioned delegated acts based on a separate assessment.

Amendment 11

Proposal for a directive

Article 1 – point 1

Framework Decision 2004/757/JHA

Article 1 – point 1

Text proposed by the Commission	*Amendment*
(1) In Article 1, point 1 is replaced by the following:	(1) In Article 1, point 1 is replaced by the following:
'"drug" means:	***'"drugs": shall mean any of the following substances:***
(a) any of the substances covered by the 1961 United Nations Single Convention on Narcotic Drugs (as amended by the 1972 Protocol) and the 1971 United Nations Convention on Psychotropic Substances;	(a) any of the substances covered by the 1961 United Nations Single Convention on Narcotic Drugs (as amended by the 1972 Protocol) and the 1971 United Nations Convention on Psychotropic Substances;
(b) any of the substances listed in the Annex;	(b) any of the substances listed in the Annex;
*(c) any **new psychoactive substance posing severe health, social and safety risks, subjected to permanent market restriction on the basis of [Article 13(1) of Regulation (EU) No .../... on new psychoactive substances];'***	*(c) any **mixture or solution containing one or more substances listed under points (a) and (b);'.***

This text was endorsed by the plenary of the European Parliament and thus became its official position in the first reading,[71] pursuant to Article 294(3) TFEU.

This first reading position kicked off the interinstitutional phase of the legislative procedure, which was then delayed in the Council for a long time due to disputes on the legal basis.[72] The file was thus blocked until 2016. Finally, the deadlock was broken by the fact that the Commission presented a new, less ambitious proposal for a regulation amending Regulation (EC) No 1920/2006 as regards the information exchange, early

[71] P7_TA(2014)0454 of 17 April 2014, at: https://eur-lex.europa.eu/legal-content/EN/TXT/?uri=CELEX%3A52014AP0454/.

[72] Some delegations could not agree with the use of Article 114 TFEU for the proposal for a regulation, because they thought that it would give the impression that the legislature is concerned with the free movement of psychoactive substances. Public health (Article 168 TFEU) was put forward as an alternative legal basis.

warning system and risk assessment procedures on new psychoactive substances.[73] The original proposal for a regulation was later withdrawn. The evaporation of the original proposal for a regulation, together with its implementing acts serving market bans, solved one problem: there was no longer a risk of an automatic link between the two instruments.

The dilemma that remained on the table was how to introduce, under the directive, new psychoactive substances into the list of illegal substances triggering criminal responsibility. Parliament, as we have just seen, opted for delegated acts. Another possible way forward would have been to leave it to the ordinary legislative procedure: whenever the Commission considers that new substances should be placed on the list, it should present a legislative proposal and the co-legislators would – in an expedited procedure – amend the Annex to the directive. This might be flawless from a constitutional point of view, yet it would be impractical because of the need to react rapidly to new substances that appear every month on the market. For this reason, this solution was not seriously considered. The third possible option was to use implementing acts pursuant to Article 291 TFEU. This was the solution preferred by the Council. The two opposing positions led to long negotiations between the institutions. The Parliament, by that time, was strongly supported by the Commission. After a U-turn on this matter, the Commission indeed also came to the conclusion that the use of implementing acts would be legally questionable.

The case-law of the Court of Justice provides useful elements for the delimitation of delegated acts (Article 290 TFEU) and implementing acts (Article 291 TFEU). On the one hand, as far as delegated acts are concerned, the Court made it clear that 'the purpose of granting a delegated power is to achieve the adoption of rules coming within the regulatory framework as defined by the basic legislative act'.[74] On the other hand, 'in exercising an implementing power, the Commission may neither amend nor supplement the legislative act, even as to its non-essential elements'.[75]

The Court also ruled that

> when the EU legislature confers an implementing power on the Commission on the basis of Article 291(2) TFEU, the Commission is called on to provide further detail in relation to the content of a legislative act, in order to ensure that it is implemented under uniform conditions in all Member States.[76]

However, such 'further detail' can only be added through an implementing act to the legislative act 'without its non-essential elements having to be amended or supplemented'.[77] As has been mentioned above, a specific substance that falls under the definition of drugs is one of the constituent elements of the criminal offences defined

[73] COM(2016) 547 of 29.8.2016. The aim of the proposal was, in particular, to define provisions concerning the early warning on new psychoactive substances, which should be strengthened. The procedures for drawing up an initial report and organising the risk assessment procedure should be made more efficient. Substantially shortened deadlines for all stages of the procedure should be set.

[74] C-88/14, *Commission v Parliament and Council*, EU:C:2015:499, judgment of 16 July 2014, paragraph 29.

[75] Paragraph 31 of the same judgment.

[76] C-427/12, *Commission v Parliament and Council*, EU:C:2014:170, judgment of 18 March 2014, paragraph 39.

[77] Paragraph 40 of the same judgment.

by the legislative act. For example, the 'production' of drugs is punishable as a criminal offence, when committed intentionally. This means that if someone is proven to have intentionally produced a substance that falls under the definition of drugs, that person will have to face criminal sanctions. By contrast, if that person produces a substance that does not fall under the definition of drugs, he will not be held liable for that offence. This flows from the principle of *nullum crimen sine lege*, contained in Article 49 of the Charter of Fundamental Rights of the European Union: a person cannot be held guilty of any criminal offence which did not constitute a criminal offence at the time when it was committed.

It has to be pointed out that the definition of drugs is a dynamic definition. New substances emerge on the market and if those substances are assessed as being harmful, they can be included in the definition of drugs. Such inclusion may be conceived as modifying the definition of drugs, because that definition would cover new substances that were not covered before. The consequence of such inclusion is that if someone commits an intentional offence concerning a new substance which was added to the list, that person will – in principle – face criminal penalties, including imprisonment. Therefore, it seemed to be advisable to consider that the list of illicit psychoactive substances falls within the regulatory framework of the legislative act, because a new psychoactive substance is a constituent element of the objective aspect (actus reus) of the criminal offence, defined by the legislative act. Adding a new substance to the list can be understood as modifying that regulatory framework, because intentional acts concerning that new substance will become criminal offences.

Moreover, it has to be recalled that the Court of Justice attaches great importance to the principle of legality of criminal offences.[78] According to the Court, the principle of the legality of criminal offences and penalties

> implies that Community rules must define clearly offences and the penalties which they attract. This requirement is satisfied where the individual can know from the wording of the relevant provision […] what acts and omissions will make him criminally liable.[79]

It is also established case-law that criminal law must be strictly interpreted and can be interpreted extensively only when applied to the benefit of the defendant. This 'is the corollary of the principle of legality in relation to crime and punishment and more generally of the principle of legal certainty' which 'is one of the general legal principles underlying the constitutional traditions common to the Member States'.[80]

In the light of these principles, it seemed to be preferable that the Annex to the directive setting out the list of illicit substances that form part of the objective aspect of the criminal offence is defined by the legislative act.[81] That solution would ensure that the

[78] C-308/06 *R (International Association of Independent Tanker Owners (Intertanko) and Others v Secretary of State for Transport*, EU:C:2008:312, judgment of 3 June 2008, paragraphs 69–71 and the case-law cited therein.

[79] Paragraph 71 of the same judgment.

[80] Cases C-74/95 and C-129/95 *Criminal proceedings against X* [1996] ECR I-6609, 6637, judgment of 12 December 1996, paragraph 25. See also judgments of the European Court of Human Rights in *SW v United Kingdom* (App No 20166/92) and *CR v United Kingdom* (App No 20190/92), 22 November 1995, Series A, No 335-B, paragraph 35, and No 335-C, paragraph 33 (1995) 21 EHRR 363.

[81] Ie a Directive.

provisions of the legislative act itself are sufficient to ascertain possible criminal liability. Nevertheless, updating the Annex that way would not be possible by implementing acts. According to the Court, even the addition of a footnote to the Annex of a legislative act may qualify as amendment of its non-essential elements.[82] In the light of the above legal arguments, the use of delegated acts in the context of the draft directive on new psychoactive substances seemed to be preferable.

D. The Outcome and its Assessment

The above arguments prevailed during the negotiations, and Directive (EU) 2017/2103 indeed provides for the adoption of delegated acts. Based on a risk assessment, the Commission shall without undue delay adopt a delegated act amending the Annex

> in order to add the new psychoactive substance or substances to it and provide that [they] pose severe public health risks and, where applicable, severe social risks at Union level, and that it is or they are included in the definition of 'drug'.[83]

The exercise of delegation is circumscribed by several criteria.[84] The power to adopt delegated acts is conferred on the Commission for five years, tacitly renewable in the event of lack of opposition by the Parliament or the Council.[85] The delegation of power can be revoked at any time by the European Parliament or by the Council. A decision to revoke puts an end to the delegation of the power specified in that decision. It takes effect the day following the publication of the decision in the *Official Journal of the European Union* or at any later date specified therein. However, for the sake of legal certainty, 'it shall not affect the validity of any delegated acts already in force'.[86]

The Member States' influence on the procedure is reinforced by the provision according to which, before adopting a delegated act, the Commission must consult experts designated by each Member State in accordance with the principles laid down in the Interinstitutional Agreement of 13 April 2016 on Better Law-Making.[87] As soon as it adopts a delegated act, the Commission must notify it simultaneously to the European Parliament and to the Council.[88] A delegated act will enter into force only if no objection has been expressed either by the European Parliament or by the Council within a period of two months from notification of that act or if, before the expiry of that period, the European Parliament and the Council have both informed the Commission that they will not object. That period will be extended by two months at the initiative of any of the co-legislators.[89]

[82] C-88/14, *Commission v Parliament and Council*, EU:C:2015:499, judgment of 16 July 2014, paragraphs 43–44.

[83] New Article 1a(1) inserted into Framework Decision 2004/757/JHA.

[84] New Article 8a inserted into Framework Decision 2004/757/JHA.

[85] Article 8a(2).

[86] Article 8a(3).

[87] [2016] OJ L 123, 12.5.2016, p 1.

[88] Article 8a(5).

[89] Article 8a(6).

The debate opposing delegated and implementing acts and opposing internal market and criminal law legal bases may seem to be too subtle, not to say pedantic. However, it reveals an important choice at the heart of the balancing exercise inherent in EU criminal law-making. It reveals the choice between, on the one hand, criminal law as an extended arm of internal market legislation, open to further – uncontrolled – extension by implementing measures of the executive, or on the other hand, criminal law as a core area of national sovereignty,[90] remaining even at the EU level under the control of democratically elected institutions.[91] The fact that powers are delegated to the executive branch acknowledges the need for rapid executive intervention to combat new psychoactive substances, but couples that need with the conditions under which the legislature can control and, in the end, may even revoke the delegation of power. Thus, it keeps in balance the traditional requirement of a *lex parlamentaria* in criminal law with the requirement of speed and efficiency.

IV. Conclusions

The European Union is in need of a 'constitutional compass'.[92] It is not by accident that this catchy image comes from an article on criminal law. The constitutional and criminal fields overlap to a great extent at the EU level. Even at national level, when the law-maker adopts texts that have the potential to take away liberty from fellow citizens, his hands should be trembling. At the supranational level, the question of responsibility and legitimacy – key concepts of any constitutional order – are all the more onerous.

In the above case study I tried to summarise one particular decision where a choice between implementing and delegated acts, and the interplay between internal market and criminal legislation, revealed to a certain extent the EU legislator's challenges when balancing various legal and policy options, in search for a responsible and legitimate solution. However, this is only one example and the criminal law domain is much larger than that. Similar – even more sensitive – decisions were required in the recent legislative procedure leading to the adoption of the Directive on combating terrorism.[93] There, the main challenge was to evaluate the necessity to criminalise behaviour that is distant from and preparatory to terrorist offences. When defining criminal offences, such as travelling for the purpose of committing a terrorist offence, glorifying terrorism, or training oneself on the internet in the use of weapons and explosives, there is also a delicate balancing exercise between the interest of the public to live in security and the interest to maintain human rights and freedoms that define our way of life.

All these choices and policy options raise different balancing questions and touch upon various interests. As I mentioned, it would be beyond the possibilities of this chapter to give a detailed insight into all these cases. Nevertheless, in the conclusions, I endeavour to weave together various threads that run through the text in order to

[90] See for example the Lisbon ruling of the German Federal Constitutional Court, 2 BvE 2/08, § 252 et seq.

[91] Cf Article 10 TEU.

[92] Ester Herlin-Karnell: 'European criminal law as an exercise in EU "experimental" constitutional law' (2013) 20(3) *Maastricht Journal of European and Comparative Law* 442–64.

[93] See above (n 43).

summarise the minimum legal requirements that the EU legislature should, in my view, respect in criminal law-making.

1. Appropriate legal basis. In accordance with the principle of conferral, there is no general criminal law competence at the EU level. The scope and arrangements for exercising the Union's competences shall be determined by the provisions of the Treaties relating to each area.[94] In other words, a specific legal basis is needed for the exercise of legislative competences. In the substantive criminal law area, those legal bases are Articles 83(1) and (2) TFEU and, in my view, there are no other sectorial legal bases that may serve for the adoption of substantive criminal law provisions.[95]
2. Criminal law as a last resort. The mere existence of a legal basis is not sufficient; the necessity of criminal law should also be demonstrated. In the case of Article 83(1) TFEU, the areas of serious crime contain an 'in-built' safeguard against frivolous law-making. In the case of paragraph (2), the word 'essential' serves as such a safeguard. In my opinion both provisions, read in the system of the Treaties, are subject to the last resort (*ultima ratio*) principle, according to which the legislator should take the path of criminalisation only when all else fails, and also, that it should always consider alternatives to criminal law measures. This interpretation is reinforced by Article 67(1) TFEU – according to which in all AFSJ legislation the 'different legal systems and traditions of the Member States' must be respected – and also by Article 5(4) TEU on the principle of proportionality and Article 5(3) TEU on subsidiarity. Although the final and authentic interpretation of the Treaties is a matter for the Court of Justice, the interpretation followed by the various institutions is not irrelevant, since constitutional interpretation should never be a monopoly of a single organ. In that regard, it is telling that the European Parliament, the Council and the Commission equally refer to the last resort principle in their guidelines governing criminal legislation.
3. *Lex parlamentaria*. It is a common tradition in the European concept of the rule of law that at least the core of criminal offences and penalties be defined by laws adopted by a legislative assembly. Article 49 of the Charter makes a clear reference to the principle of *nullum crimen sine lege*, which should be read together – as far as EU legislation is concerned – with Article 83(1) and (2) TFEU. Both of these legal bases provide for a legislative procedure[96] and allow for the adoption of directives, ie instruments that need further action by national law-makers on the occasion of their implementation. In principle, this means a double parliamentary intervention: first by the European Parliament, which represents citizens directly at Union level;[97] and secondly by national parliaments or – in exceptional cases – other instances (depending on the national constitution).

[94] Article 2(6) TFEU.

[95] For the very specific case of Article 325 TFEU see above (n 27) and text to n 51.

[96] Article 83(1) TFEU provides for the ordinary legislative procedure, while Article 83(2) TFEU provides for the 'same ordinary or special legislative procedure as was followed for the adoption of the harmonisation measures in question'.

[97] Article 10(2) TEU.

However, in certain fields, efficiency and the lack of specialised knowledge[98] on the part of the legislature plead for the use of lower level instruments. The typical example is the criminalisation of psychoactive substances, where it could prove to be too burdensome to require the legislator to muddle through, in a long procedure, a long list of obscure chemical formulas, only to observe to the letter the *lex parlamentaria* tradition. For these matters, delegated acts adopted by the Commission pursuant to Article 290 TFEU can be an acceptable solution. This allows for the EU legislative chambers to object to delegated decisions, to limit the time period during which the executive may exercise delegated powers, and to revoke the delegation if they no longer wish to entrust the executive with that responsibility. Moreover, delegated acts concern matters that come within the legislative framework. Therefore they do not risk – in contrast to implementing acts – detaching certain elements of the actus reus from that framework.

4. Evidence-based law-making. Article 83(2) TFEU allows for the adoption of criminal law in order to underpin the effective enforcement of harmonised internal market rules. This empowerment, in theory, risks turning EU criminal law into fuel for the engine of market creation. This risk is strongly mitigated, in my view, by criteria 1 to 3 as explained above. Nevertheless, a further mitigating factor is the wording according to which approximation of criminal law is only possible where it 'proves' essential to ensure the effective implementation of a harmonised Union policy. The term 'proves' refers to a certain form of factual evidence – eg impact assessment by the Commission – that should be considered by the legislature during the process.[99]
5. Autonomous evaluation. By this criterion, I would like to underline the specific nature of criminal law. It is not sufficient to respect criteria 1 to 4, but rather I think it is also important *how* they are respected. The decision on whether or not to criminalise a behaviour should always be based on an autonomous, separate assessment, which is different from the assessment conducted under sectorial policies. Automatic links between internal market and criminal law instruments look suspicious. If an offence is *formally* defined in a criminal law instrument, but that definition automatically depends on an instrument adopted under a different legal basis, then the policy decision to criminalise a behaviour was *in substance* made elsewhere than in criminal law. The example I analysed in the case study was that the criminal law definition of 'drugs' was open to amendment based on a provision of a criminal law directive, but that provision was nothing else than a dynamic reference to internal market implementing acts. In such cases, an autonomous evaluation of criminal policy choices becomes legally impossible and criminal law-making becomes practically outsourced to internal market decision-making entities. It is not a valid remedy if those entities are able to demonstrate that otherwise they have respected criteria 1 to 4. What they will not be able to demonstrate

[98] For example in the case of new psychoactive substances.

[99] Article 83(1) TFEU is a bit different in nature. Due to the closed list of areas of crime, it is less open to abuse, and while impact assessments are never useless, it would seem far-fetched to require the same level of evidence for the necessity of criminal law in the fight against terrorism or sexual exploitation of children, than for evaluating the necessity of the criminal enforcement of market rules.

is that they respected criterion 5: their policy choice cannot be an autonomous criminal policy choice, because they must have been acting under a different legal basis. This leads us back to my first point above, and thus the loop is complete.

Finally, I would like to add a consideration which is not strictly legal, and belongs rather to political legitimacy. If criminal law is special, it is special because we value our freedom, dignity and integrity and try to protect them against everyone, including public authorities. Apart from compulsory military service in war and licit martial arts, there is no lawful way for physical violence to reach us. Criminal law is the great exception to that rule. Therefore, policy choices as to how to punish and whom to punish are essentially different from decisions concerning the price of vegetables or the technical standards for manufacturing dustbins. When new criminal offences are created with one hand, I think it is a matter of political legitimacy to use the other hand in reinforcing or fine-tuning procedural safeguards.

At the EU level, this means that the balancing exercise of the legislator in substantive law-making should include, in the wider sense, continuous evaluation of how to exercise legislative competences relating to persons' rights in criminal proceedings and the rights of victims. Coupling substantive law provisions with meaningful minimum standards of procedural law reinforces the legitimacy of EU criminal law and helps to make sure that the 'constitutional compass' points in the right direction.

14

Criminal and Quasi-criminal Enforcement Mechanisms: Proposal for a More Coherent European Approach

CHRISTOPHER HARDING AND VANESSA FRANSSEN

I. Introduction

The underlying and main question for discussion in this collection has been the difference in contemporary legal systems between criminal law and other branches of law that are used for similar purposes or present other similarities.

As explained in the introduction of this book,[1] there was some dilemma in the choice of vocabulary at the start of this research. Upon reflection, preference was given to the term 'quasi-criminal enforcement mechanisms', first, because it most accurately describes the phenomenon under debate (ie, enforcement mechanisms that resemble or 'mimic' criminal law without formally carrying that label and that, depending on the legal system, may be referred to as 'administrative', 'civil', 'punitive administrative',[2] or, even more system-specific, 'secondary criminal law'[3] or '*Ordnungswidrigkeiten*'[4]) and, second, because its novelty reflects the absence of a well-grounded and systematic approach to the subject, as a matter of both wider European and comparative law. Indeed, when the question was posed how criminal enforcement could be systematically and empirically distinguished from quasi-criminal enforcement, no clear or easy answer seemed to be forthcoming. This confirmed the need for a more in-depth analysis of the phenomenon and that in turn served to justify this research project and its resulting discussion.

[1] V Franssen and C Harding, Introduction to this volume, section III.

[2] V Franssen and S Vandeweerd, 'General Nature, Characteristics, and Safeguards of EU Administrative Criminal Law' (2019) 90 *Revue Internationale de Droit Pénal* 13, 16 and the references mentioned there; A Weyembergh and N Joncheray, 'Punitive Administrative Sanctions and Procedural Safeguards. A Blurred Picture that Needs to be addressed', (2016) 7 *New Journal of European Criminal Law* 190, 194ff.

[3] N Zurkinden, Chapter 2 in this volume, sections II.C., II.D.(i). and III.C.

[4] D Brodowski, Chapter 3 in this volume, sections II and III.

Therefore, the overall ambition of this volume was to survey and analyse more fully and comparatively this legal phenomenon in a number of legal systems in Europe, to probe its nature and suggest a model for understanding better both theoretical classifications and practical differences.

This chapter will, first, provide a summary of the main findings of this collective research and, second, put forward a conceptual proposal for a more coherent approach toward criminal and quasi-criminal enforcement mechanisms at European level.

II. Main Research Findings

A. Surveying the Scene

A first task was to survey the landscape of alternatives to formal criminal interventions, comparatively across Europe, and to understand the underlying reasons for these alternative, quasi-criminal enforcement mechanisms.

It was already clear that the resort to 'administrative' procedures and sanctions was typically Continental European, while 'common law' systems used different concepts and formal rules and procedures to do anything similar, usually employing the term 'civil' rather than 'administrative'.[5]

The comparative survey has revealed, contrary to what one may have hoped for, that the resort to alternatives to legal control through formal criminal law – however they may be termed or classified in the legal system at hand – is prompted by quite diverging motivations. Indeed, reports in the present volume of what may be found in Nordic legal systems,[6] in Germany,[7] Switzerland,[8] the Czech Republic, Poland,[9] Belgium,[10] the UK[11] and the European Union (EU),[12] both in terms of historical background and recent developments, show a patchwork of policy and legislation, comprising a mixture of a (more or less) considered plan, unreflective reactive developments and, in some cases, constitutional or institutional limits. This results in piecemeal law-making and enforcement – '*à géométrie variable*', as the French would say – with diverging approaches across sectors and legal systems. EU 'punitive administrative law' is a prominent illustration of such sectorial law-making.[13]

Nevertheless, despite these differences, one may also conclude from this survey that, comparatively, there is an agreed sense that there may be something qualitatively different

[5] For a fuller discussion, see C Harding, 'The Interplay of Criminal and Administrative Law in the Context of Market Regulation: The Case of Serious Competition Infringements' in V Mitsilegas, P Alldridge and C Leonidas (eds), *Globalisation, Criminal law and Criminal Justice: Theoretical, Comparative and Transnational Perspectives* (Oxford, Hart Publishing, 2015), 119.

[6] R Lahti, Chapter 1 in this volume.

[7] Brodowski, Chapter 3 in this volume.

[8] Zurkinden, Chapter 2 in this volume.

[9] A Błachnio-Parzych, Chapter 4 in this volume.

[10] AL Claes and M Horseele, Chapter 11 in this volume.

[11] G Wilson and S Wilson, Chapter 5 in this volume.

[12] T Lukácsi, Chapter 13 in this volume.

[13] Franssen and Vandeweerd (n 2) 16.

about the regulation of competition,[14] transport and road traffic,[15] customs,[16] public health and safety,[17] environmental legislation,[18] financial conduct,[19] immigration,[20] or the recovery of illegally gained assets.[21] This justifies that the enforcement of such regulation is pursued, at least in some cases, through other means and kept outside the scope of criminal law – a point that was urged forcefully as a matter of theory and principle by the American scholar Sandford Kadish[22] already in the 1960s – or to use the language of the European Court of Human Rights (ECtHR), that it should be regarded as not belonging to the 'hard core' of criminal law.[23] Other scholars have referred to the distinction '*mala in se*' and '*mala prohibita*',[24] in a similar attempt to grasp the different nature of such regulation and enforcement.

This idea of privileging more efficient and less burdensome alternative enforcement mechanisms when the comparative benefits of criminal sanctions are not convincing enough can also be found in law & economics literature.[25] Yet, apart from the field of competition law and, to some extent, environmental law,[26] the impact of this literature is probably stronger in the Anglo-Saxon world (particularly the United States) than in Continental Europe.

In Europe, the impulse to do something different – whether that be a sub-categorisation of criminal law (like in Switzerland and the UK), or the full or partial adoption of 'administrative' procedures and sanctions (the other legal systems mentioned above) – seems to have varying historical triggers, sometimes even within one and the same legal system.

In this context, Germany historically has led the way, beginning some time ago with a well-considered distinction between 'criminal' and 'police', and a long

[14] See, eg, S De Sanctis, Chapter 10 in this volume; C Harding, 'The System of EU Antitrust Law: Characteristics, Safeguards, and Differences from Traditional Criminal Law' (2019) 90 *Revue Internationale de Droit Pénal* 85.

[15] See, eg, *Öztürk v Germany* (App No 8544/79) ECtHR, 21 February 1984, paras 52–53.

[16] Claes and Horseele, Chapter 11 in this volume.

[17] Including, eg, food safety. See, eg, M Simonato, 'The EU Dimension of "Food Criminal Law"' (2016) 87 *Revue Internationale de Droit Pénal* 97, 120–22 and 125–26; B van der Meulen and A Corini, 'Food Law Enforcement in the EU: Administrative and Private Systems' (2016) 87 *Revue Internationale de Droit Pénal* 71.

[18] See, eg, M Faure and F Weber, 'The Diversity of the EU Approach to Law Enforcement – Towards a Coherent Model Inspired by a Law and Economics Approach' (2017) 18(4) *German Law Journal* 823, 868–67.

[19] Wilson and Wilson, Chapter 5 in this volume; S Allegrezza, 'The System of EU Banking Regulation' (2019) 90 *Revue Internationale de Droit Pénal* 101.

[20] M Pichou, Chapter 9 in this volume.

[21] J Boucht, Chapter 8 in this volume.

[22] S Kadish, 'Some Observations on the Use of Criminal Sanctions in Enforcing Economic Regulations' (1963) 30 *University of Chicago Law Review* 423.

[23] *Jussila v Finland* (App No 73053/01) ECtHR, 23 November 2006, para 43.

[24] See, eg, C Harding, Chapter 6 in this volume, 120–22; C Wells, *Corporations and Criminal Responsibility* (Oxford, Oxford University Press, 2001) 7, noting that 'what appears to lie behind the "true" crime/"quasi" crime distinction is an unarticulated argument that, if an activity was not traditionally a matter for the criminal law, then it cannot achieve the status of the "true" crime. (…) The labelling of statutory offences as *mala prohibita* can be seen more as a reflection of the common lawyer's aversion to legislative creation than of any inherent distinction in relative harm. The use of regulatory enforcement should not be used as the basis for determining offence seriousness.' See also Khadish (n 22) 447, pointing out that 'it is an informal rather than an institutionalized distinction and lacks any clear meaning.'

[25] See, eg, R Bowles, M Faure and N Garoupa, 'The Scope of Criminal Law and Criminal Sanctions: An Economic View and Policy Implications' (2008) 35(3) *Journal of Law and Society* 389.

[26] See, eg, Faure and Weber (n 18).

tradition of agonising but, it seems, inconclusive scholarship attempting to justify and explain this distinction and to place it on a solid theoretical and policy footing.[27] Sure enough, Germany has evolved an impressive concept and legal infrastructure of *Ordnungswidrigkeiten*, which has been exported elsewhere and which has clearly influenced the ECtHR's case law concerning the notions 'criminal charge' and 'criminal penalty'.[28] In turn, the ECtHR's autonomous definition of these terms has had a significant impact on EU law and the case law of the EU Court of Justice (ECJ).[29] But at national level, that German development was actually the result of different successive motivations: rapid industrialisation and economic development in the later nineteenth century, denazification, decartelisation and decriminalisation.[30]

Should German decriminalisation be understood as something similar to Nordic depenalisation?[31] Not necessarily. In fact, there seem to be different motivations and ideas jostling together, even if heading broadly in the same direction. Yet most significantly, they do seem to share a genuine ideology of, in some sense, less severe sanctions, a wish *and need* to avoid an overburdening of criminal law systems, a search for more efficient as well as less burdensome and less resource-intensive methods of enforcement, or a pragmatic adoption of different forms when criminal law may be constitutionally unavailable.[32] A similar conclusion may be drawn from the Swiss approach.[33]

In some specific sectors, particularly in the field of economic and financial 'crime' (eg, competition law,[34] market abuse,[35] customs law[36]), the development of quasi-criminal enforcement has also been explained by the need for specialised investigating and prosecutorial authorities.[37]

In Central Europe, the development of quasi-criminal law was closely connected to political, social and economic developments, in particular the influence of Soviet law after World War II and the transformation process after 1989, and also translates the need for swifter proceedings and more specialisation.[38]

[27] Brodowski, Chapter 3 in this volume; D Ohana, 'Regulatory Offenses and Administrative Sanctions: Between Criminal Law and Administrative Law' in MD Dubber and T Hörnle (eds), *The Oxford Handbook of Criminal Law* (Oxford, Oxford University Press, 2014) 1064.

[28] *Öztürk v Germany* (n 15).

[29] See, eg, V Franssen, 'La notion "pénale": mot magique ou critère trompeur? Réflexions sur les distinctions entre le droit pénal et le droit quasi pénal' in D Brach-Thiel (ed), *Existe-t-il un seul* non bis in idem *aujourd'hui?* (Paris, l'Harmattan, 2017), 80ff; Franssen and Vandeweerd (n 2) 53ff.

[30] Ohana (n 27).

[31] Lahti, Chapter 1 in this volume.

[32] Brodowski, Chapter 3 in this volume. *Cf* EU competition law; see Franssen and Vandeweerd (n 2) 59 and 62.

[33] Zurkinden, Chapter 2 in this volume.

[34] De Sanctis, Chapter 10 in this volume.

[35] Wilson and Wilson, Chapter 5 in this volume.

[36] Claes and Horseele, Chapter 11 in this volume.

[37] See also International Association of Penal Law/Association Internationale de Droit Pénal (AIDP), 'Section III: Resolutions on Prevention, Investigation, and Sanctioning of Economic Crime by Alternative Enforcement Regimes', *Criminal Justice and Corporate Business*, 20th International Congress of Penal Law, Rome, 13–16 November 2019, available at: http://www.penal.org/sites/default/files/files/XX%20Congress%20Res%20Sec%20III%20EN.pdf (last accessed 23 July 2021), para C, point 1 (AIDP Resolutions Section III). For a good illustration, see S Blake, 'Strategy of Integrated Enforcement: The UK Competition and Markets Authority' in K Ligeti and V Franssen (eds), *Challenges in the Field of Economic and Financial Crime in Europe and the US* (Oxford, Hart Publishing, 2017) 265, 272ff.

[38] Błachnio-Parzych, Chapter 4 in this volume.

Consequently, rather than clearing the ground for a coherent overall jurisprudential basis for the quasi-criminal domain, the comparative analysis in this volume has complicated the picture by revealing a wide diversity of motivations and explanations.

B. Guidance from the European Level?

As indicated above when referring to the German example, the developments at European level (including both the Council of Europe and the EU) have been triggered, at least to a certain extent, by the evolutions and formal categorisations at national level. This also shows in the delimitation of the EU's competence to legislate in the field of criminal law, based on Article 83 of the Treaty on the Functioning of the European Union (TFEU). This competence is indeed defined in the light of what Member States consider to be 'criminal law'.[39] In sharp contrast with this formal approach, is the case law of the ECJ on procedural safeguards such as the principle of *ne bis in idem* in the field of tax law[40] or the privilege against self-incrimination in the field of EU competition law (with respect to legal persons)[41] and, more recently, market abuse (with respect to individuals or 'natural persons'),[42] which takes a more functional approach.[43] This dichotomy has, inevitably, contributed to a blurring of the boundaries between criminal law and (punitive) administrative law.[44]

Yet, as if things were not complicated enough, the influence has worked both ways. Indeed, as the analysis by Wilson and Wilson demonstrates, EU legislation on market abuse with its two-pronged approach has also impacted the way in which market abuse is regulated today in the UK.[45] The EU choice to criminalise certain types of behaviour also curtails national legislators in their options to decriminalise, even if such approach would be more coherent from a national perspective.[46]

The dichotomy between the formal and functional approaches, and the interaction between the national and European levels explain why, ultimately, the EU level is unable to provide much guidance when it comes to making a theoretically sound distinction between criminal and quasi-criminal enforcement mechanisms. At best, this distinction leads to a coherent combination of different, 'complementary' enforcement mechanisms

[39] J Blomsma, 'Challenges in the Field of Economic and Financial Crime from a European Perspective' in K Ligeti and V Franssen (n 37) 225, 230; *cf* Case C-43/12, *European Commission v European Parliament and Council of the EU*, EU:C:2014:298, 6 May 2014 (with respect to Art 87(2) TFEU).

[40] See, eg, Case C-617/10, *Åklagaren v Åkerberg Fransson* EU:C:2013:105, 26 February 2013.

[41] See, eg, Case 374/87, *Orkem v European Commission*, 18 October 1989, para 35; Case T-112/98, *Mannesmannröhren-Werke AG v European Commission*, 20 February 2001, para 67.

[42] Case C-481/19, *DB v Commissione Nazionale per le Società e la Borsa (Consob)*, EU:C:2021:84, 2 February 2021.

[43] For an analysis of this dichotomy, see Franssen and Vandeweerd (n 2) 57–58; Franssen (n 29) 89–90.

[44] See, eg, Weyembergh and Joncheray (n 2) 200–204.

[45] Wilson and Wilson, Chapter 5 in this volume, section II.B. *Cf* the more general assessment made by K Ligeti and V Franssen, 'Current Challenges in Economic and Financial Criminal Law in Europe and the US' in K Ligeti and V Franssen (n 37) 1, 13.

[46] V Franssen, 'EU Criminal Law and Effet Utile – A Critical Examination of the Use of Criminal Law to Achieve Effective Enforcement' in J Banach-Gutierrez and C Harding (eds), *EU Criminal Law and Crime Policy: Values, Principles and Methods* (Abingdon/New York, Routledge, 2016) 84, 106.

(which was the EU legislator's aim in the field of market abuse)[47] in conformity with the EU constitutional principles of subsidiarity and proportionality.

Yet, such coherent approach – which has been argued for by other scholars on several occasions[48] – is, considering the division of competences between the EU and its Member States, not always possible (eg, the EU legislator does not have the power to adopt minimum rules on criminal sanctions in the field of competition law, while it does in the field of market abuse). Moreover, the preference for criminal sanctions remains somewhat shaky, to the extent that it is largely guided by an effectiveness ('*effet utile*') logic[49] that does not square with more traditional conceptions of criminal law, based on impact assessments that are not necessarily convincing (eg, with respect to the adoption of minimum rules for criminal sanctions on market abuse), and/or lacks sound theoretical underpinnings.[50] Admittedly, the EU institutions have also insisted, in non-binding policy documents, that criminal law should be used as a last resort[51] – the reason why Lukácsi is optimistic that the Lisbon Treaty 'has the potential to correct the mistake of the effectiveness mantra'[52] – and in recent years, the EU legislature seems to have become much more selective in putting forward new criminal law initiatives.

The interplay between criminal and administrative enforcement may, however, be further complicated following the recent establishment of the European Public Prosecutor's Office (EPPO).[53] While the creation of the new 'judicial'[54] body of the Union[55] translates the explicit choice of the EU to push for criminal enforcement to fight fraud against the financial interests of the Union,[56] the EPPO will exchange information with other EU institutions, offices and bodies,[57] such as OLAF (ie, the EU's antifraud office, which has only administrative investigative powers),[58] and will have to cooperate

[47] Blomsma (n 39) 228–29.

[48] See, eg, European Criminal Policy Initiative, 'A Manifesto on European Criminal Policy' (2009) 4(12) *Zeitschrift für Internationale Strafrechtsdogmatik* 697, available at: http://www.zis-online.com/dat/artikel/2009_12_383.pdf, 709; P Asp, 'The importance of the Principles of Subsidiarity and Coherence in the Development of EU Criminal Law' (2011) 1(1) *European Criminal Law Review* 44.

[49] See, eg, E Herlin-Karnell, 'Effectiveness and Constitutional Limits in European Criminal Law', (2014) 5 *New Journal of European Criminal Law* 267.

[50] Franssen (n 46) 99–110; C Harding, 'Tasks for Criminology in the Field of EU Criminal Law and Crime Policy' in J Banach-Gutierrez and C Harding (eds), *EU Criminal Law and Crime Policy: Values, Principles and Methods* (Abingdon, Routledge, 2016) 111ff; Ligeti and Franssen (n 45) 14–15.

[51] See, eg, European Commission, *Towards an EU Criminal Policy: Ensuring the effective implementation of EU policies through criminal law*, COM(2011) 573, 20 September 2011, 6–7.

[52] Lukácsi, Chapter 13 in this volume, 373.

[53] Regulation (EU) 2017/1939 of the Council of 12 October 2017 implementing enhanced cooperation on the establishment of the European Public Prosecutor's Office (the EPPO), [2017] OJ L 283, 31 October 2017, 1. The EPPO launched its operational activities, with some delay, on 1 June 2021. Commission Implementing Decision (EU) 2021/856 of 25 May 2021 determining the date on which the European Public Prosecutor's Office assumes its investigative and prosecutorial task, [2021] OJ L 188, 28 May 2021, 100; Corrigendum to Commission Implementing Decision (EU) 2021/856, [2021] OJ L 190, 31 May 2021, 101.

[54] The EPPO will indeed be the first EU body endowed with autonomous (criminal) prosecution powers.

[55] Along with the adoption of the so-called 'PFI' Directive: Directive (EU) 2017/1371 of the European Parliament and of the Council of 5 July 2017 on the fight against fraud to the Union's financial interests by means of criminal law, [2017] OJ L 198, 28 July 2017, 29.

[56] For an early analysis, see eg V Franssen, 'Proposed Regulation on the European Public Prosecutor – Thinking Federal?', *European Law Blog*, 8 August 2013, available at: https://europeanlawblog.eu/2013/08/08/proposed-regulation-on-the-european-public-prosecutor-thinking-federal/ (last accessed 23 July 2021).

[57] See, eg, Arts 24(1), 43(2), 54 and 103, and recitals 100–101 of the EPPO Regulation.

[58] Art 101 EPPO Regulation. For an analysis of OLAF's powers and its cooperation with national authorities, see, eg, L Kuhl, 'Cooperation Between Administrative Authorities in Transnational Multi-agency

closely with national judicial *and* administrative authorities,[59] such as customs and VAT authorities, to conduct its criminal investigations.[60]

Neither does the ECtHR case law offer much conceptual stability. As Šugman Stubbs points out, it rather contributes to a further blurring of the boundaries.[61] This is because the Court's autonomous definition of the terms 'criminal charge' and 'penalty' is, obviously, founded on a case-by-case approach and the variable combination of the three *Engel* criteria,[62] with a whole subset of secondary criteria.[63] The obvious advantage of such approach is flexibility, enabling the Court to encompass the great variety of national situations. Yet, not surprisingly, the *Engel* criteria are also 'inherently vague'[64] and have been developed for a specific purpose: ensuring the overall protection of the safeguards laid down in the European Convention on Human Rights (ECHR), regardless of the national label attributed to the behaviour or the sanction. The gradual expansion of the scope of application of the notions 'criminal charge' and 'penalty' also confirms this.[65] For sure, the *Engel* criteria have not been designed to draw a clear conceptual distinction between ('hard core')[66] criminal law and other punitive enforcement mechanisms. Neither do they 'set standards for the development of guarantees for non-criminal law sanctions.'[67] Despite the Court's noble intentions, the impact of its case law on the distinction between criminal and quasi-criminal enforcement has been quite detrimental. To quote Šugman Stubbs, it has led to an 'unrecognisable mess', a 'downgrading' of criminal law safeguards and 'over-extending of administrative authority', making 'widespread breaches of human rights entirely possible' as it 'is no longer clear according to what standards and procedures different agencies of an uncertain legal nature will be acting.'[68]

The concern to develop adequate safeguards in the field of punitive administrative law is also at the heart of much legal debate at the EU level. When adopting such quasi-criminal enforcement mechanisms, the EU legislator has failed to develop a coherent, overarching framework of substantive and procedural safeguards.[69] Indeed, the task of clarifying the applicable safeguards has been largely left to the ECJ, which proceeds on a

Investigations in the EU: Still a Long Road Ahead to Mutual Recognition?' in K Ligeti and V Franssen (n 37) 135–55.

[59] In some legal systems, like Belgium and Luxembourg, there may even be one single national authority with both administrative and judicial/criminal enforcement powers. See Claes and Horseele, Chapter 11 in this volume, section II.B. For an analysis of the relation between the EPPO and the Belgian customs authorities, see V Franssen and AL Claes, 'Enforcement of policies against illicit trade in tobacco products in Belgium' in S Tosza and JAE Vervaele (eds), *Combatting Illicit Trade in Tobacco Products* (Berlin/Heidelberg, Springer, forthcoming 2021).

[60] Recitals 14 and 69 EPPO Regulation.

[61] K Šugman Stubbs, Chapter 12 in this volume, section IV.

[62] *Engel and others v the Netherlands* (App Nos 5100–5102/71; 5354/72 and 5370/72) ECtHR, 8 June 1976.

[63] For an analysis see Franssen (n 29) 64–76.

[64] AIDP Resolutions Section III (n 37), para A, point 3.

[65] Šugman Stubbs, Chapter 12 in this volume, section III.B.(iii); Franssen and Vandeweerd (n 2) 55–56.

[66] Indicative thereof is that ECtHR, since its *Jussila* judgment, has explicitly referred to this distinction only on a couple of occasions, while its case law applying the *Engel* criteria is vast.

[67] AIDP Resolutions Section III (n 37), para A, point 3. So far, it seems that the ECtHR only allows limitations to or 'deviations from' the procedural rights under the criminal head of Article 6(1) of the ECHR under 'exceptional circumstances'. A Bailleux, 'The Fiftieth Shade of Grey. Competition Law, "Criministrative Law" and "Fairly Fair Trials"' in F Galli and A Weyembergh (eds), *Do labels still matter? Blurring boundaries between administrative and criminal law – The influence of the EU* (Brussels, Editions de l'ULB, 2014), 139, 147.

[68] Šugman Stubbs, Chapter 12 in this volume, 363.

[69] Franssen and Vandeweerd (n 2), 69–71 and the references mentioned there.

case-by-case approach (eg, in the field of competition law)[70] and in response to specific questions raised by national courts in the context of a preliminary ruling (eg, with respect to the principle of *ne bis in idem*).[71] Moreover, in recent years, we have witnessed that the dialogue between the ECJ and the ECtHR is slow, can be quite confusing and may even lead, in some respects, to further doubts about the scope of application of certain procedural safeguards.[72] A recent example thereof is the ECJ's judgment on the right to silence of individuals in punitive administrative proceedings in the field of market abuse, where the Court granted wider protection to individuals than it has traditionally done to corporations (or 'undertakings') in the field of competition law.[73] The ECtHR has, to our knowledge, not (yet?) made such a distinction and treats individuals and legal persons alike.

At national level, the concentration of administrative and criminal investigative powers in one single 'Janus-faced' authority (eg, the UK Competition and Markets Authority,[74] the UK Financial Conduct Authority[75] or the Belgian customs authorities[76]) may also provoke tensions between different procedural safeguards.[77] Furthermore, the importance of substantive safeguards and subtle differences between traditional criminal law and quasi-criminal law, have been analysed extensively by de Jong in his chapter on the principle of individual culpability.[78]

In sum, contrary what one might have hoped for, the guidance coming from the European level is quite limited for a conceptual (*de lege ferenda*) approach, even if the legal developments taking place at that level are, of course, highly relevant for the interpretation of the present (*de lege lata*) legal framework.

III. In Search of a More Coherent Approach

As the above summary shows, the outcome of this research has been to confirm a sense of haphazard development and uncertain direction, of patchy attention and

[70] See, eg, Franssen and Vandeweerd (n 2), 72–75; Harding (n 14) 95.

[71] See, eg, A Weyembergh, 'Le *ne bis in idem* en matière pénale dans l'UE: de quelques développements récents et de quelques perspectives' in D Brach-Thiel (ed), *Existe-t-il un seul* non bis in idem *aujourd'hui?* (Paris, l'Harmattan, 2017), 195–212.

[72] For a general analysis, see, eg, Franssen and Vandeweerd (n 2), 79–82 and the references mentioned there; Weyembergh and Joncheray (n 2) 190. In particular, concerning the case law on the principle of *ne bis in idem*, see eg K Ligeti, 'Fundamental rights protection between Strasbourg and Luxembourg: Extending Transnational *ne bis in idem* Across Administrative and Criminal Procedures' in European Law Institute, K Ligeti and G Robinson (eds), *Preventing and Resolving Conflicts of Jurisdiction in EU Criminal Law* (Oxford, Oxford University Press, 2018) 160–81; M Luchtman, 'Ne bis in idem at the interface of administrative and criminal law enforcement – Sufficiently connected in substance, time and space?' (2019) 90 *Revue Internationale de Droit Pénal* 335.

[73] *DB v Commissione Nazionale per le Società e la Borsa (Consob)* (n 42). For an early analysis, see A Sakellaraki, '"You have the right to remain silent" during punitive administrative proceedings, CJEU confirms – Case C-418/19 DB v Consob', *European Law Blog*, 25 February 2021, available at: https://europeanlawblog.eu/2021/02/25/you-have-the-right-to-remain-silent-during-punitive-administrative-proceedings-cjeu-confirms-case-c%E2%80%91481-19-db-v-consob/ (last accessed 23 July 2021).

[74] S Blake (n 37).

[75] Wilson and Wilson, Chapter 5 in this volume, section II.A.

[76] Claes and Horseele, Chapter 11 in this volume, section II.B.

[77] Ligeti and Franssen (n 45) 11.

[78] F de Jong, Chapter 7 in this volume.

varying motivation. Neither national nor European legislative and jurisprudential developments give clear conceptual guidance on how to differentiate, in a forward-looking or structural manner, quasi-criminal enforcement mechanisms from criminal enforcement.

Still, this does not mean that those developments provide no useful elements whatsoever: quite the contrary. Moreover, as several contributions in this volume show, legal and other scholars have been reflecting for many decades on what makes criminal law so special. Many have also analysed, from various angles and using diverging terminology, the diversification of enforcement mechanisms and what distinguishes them from traditional criminal law. Together, these developments and scholarly analyses offer a rich source of inspiration for what could be future European-wide criteria distinguishing between criminal and quasi-criminal enforcement mechanisms.

In this section, we will draw inspiration from these and other sources to make a modest but firm proposal for a more coherent approach. Rather than taking the characteristics of quasi-criminal enforcement as the point of departure, we will now start from the distinctive character of criminal law, as there *seems* to be more consensus in this respect. Next, we will zoom in on four main factors that have affected the relation between criminal enforcement and its younger 'sibling' quasi-criminal enforcement, and that are important to keep in mind when searching for distinguishing criteria.

A. The Distinctive Character of Criminal Law

It may indeed be useful to proceed from some reflection of what we should understand by 'criminal' in exploring the nature of what is quasi or non-criminal. Even if a definition of criminal law is far from easy, there is a widespread acceptance of the special character of criminal law in general terms as a means of legal control.[79]

In the contemporary European context, this idea is encapsulated in the 2009 ruling of the German *Bundesverfassungsgericht* in the so-called *Lisbon* case:

> By criminal law, a legal community gives itself a code of conduct that is anchored in its values, and whose violation, according to the shared convictions on law, is regarded as so grievous and unacceptable for social co-existence in the community that it requires punishment.[80]

A few years later, in its criminal law policy guidelines, the European Commission echoed this case law:

> While EU criminal law measures can play an important role as a complement to the national criminal law systems, it is *clear that criminal law reflects the basic values, customs and choices of any given society*. The Lisbon Treaty accepts this diversity. For this reason, it is particularly

[79] C Harding, Chapter 6 in this volume; de Jong, Chapter 7 in this volume; Kadish (n 22); JH Langbein, 'Controlling Prosecutorial Discretion in Germany' (1973) 41(3) *University of Chicago Law Review* 439.

[80] BVergG, 2BvE 2/08, 30 June 2009, para 355. The Court had been asked to review, as a matter of German law, the compatibility of the Treaty of Lisbon with the German Constitution. While there is no written definition of 'criminal law' in the German Basic Law, the Court necessarily provided a constitutional elaboration of the concept.

important to ensure that EU legislation on criminal law, in order to have a real added value, is *consistent and coherent* (emphasis added).[81]

From that perspective, a resort to the quasi or non-criminal serves to reaffirm that special character and role of criminal law, or, in the words of Langbein, to 'rehabilitate' the criminal sanction.[82] Another way to express this line of argument is to assert its logically consequent principle: *ultima ratio*. Criminal law, as a legally and ethically precious and also very incursive form of sanctioning, should be used as a last resort.[83] In short, criminal law has a special constitutional and practical role in confirming the self-identity of a society.

This conceptualisation of criminal law is well supported in discourse, theory and literature, but not so much in formal constitutional texts. How may this paradox be understood?

It is notable and indeed rather strange that its explicit assertion and then discussion in the literature is most evident in American theoretical writing of some half century ago – by the like of such writers as Kadish,[84] Langbein and, of course, Packer.[85] This literature is still echoed in contemporary scholarship.[86]

Nevertheless, there has also been a failure to articulate more forcefully that earlier embedded expressive concept of crime[87] and symbolic nature of criminal law, resulting in a broad 'sense' that crime is important and distinctive but without explaining *why*, *how* and *when*.

For instance, if a criminal lawyer asks a criminologist: 'what, then, is your subject; how do you define crime and therefore your field of enquiry?', the latter will most likely refer to what is legally defined as crime, what is deviant, what is socially unacceptable, impermissible or damaging. While the lawyer will definitely be able to relate to the first reference, the subsequent descriptions do not necessarily coincide with the boundaries of criminal law. Therefore, rather than clarifying the subject of research, the question has tended to elicit a range of uncertainly grasped ideas.

[81] European Commission, *Towards an EU Criminal Policy: Ensuring the effective implementation of EU policies through criminal law* (n 51) 3. Nevertheless, at the same time, the Commission also stressed the need for effectiveness of EU law: 'Criminal law can play an important role to ensure the implementation of European Union policies. These policies depend on effective implementation by Member States. (…) In cases where the enforcement choices in the Member States do not yield the desired result and levels of enforcement remain uneven, the Union itself may set common rules on how to ensure implementation, including, if necessary, the requirement for criminal sanctions for breaches of EU law.' Ibid. This raises the question as to how the EU legislator can reconcile the essence of criminal law with the need for EU effectiveness. See also Franssen (n 46) 107.

[82] Langbein (n 79) 453.

[83] See also R Lathi, *Zur Kriminal- und Strafrechtspolitik des 21. Jahrhunderts. Der Blickwinkel eines nordischen Wohlfahrtsstaates und dessen Strafrechtgesetzreformen: Finnland* (Berlin, De Gruyter, 2019) 106–18.

[84] Kadish (n 22).

[85] HL Packer, *The Limits of the Criminal Sanction* (Stanford, CA, Stanford University Press, 1969), especially Part III, Chapters 13–17. Packer (1925–1972), who was a professor at Stanford University, is acknowledged as a highly influential writer on the subject. For a more in-depth analysis of Packer's theory, see Harding, Chapter 6 in this volume.

[86] See, eg, Šugman Stubbs, Chapter 12 in this volume, section II; JC Coffee, Jr, 'Does "Unlawful" Mean "Criminal"?: Reflections on the Disappearing Tort/Crime Distinction in American Law' (1991) 71 *Boston University Law Review* 193, 197–201.

[87] For a summary of expressive theory of criminal law and punishment, see DM Kahan, 'What Do Alternative Sanctions Mean?' (1996) 63 *University of Chicago Law Review* 591, 594–605; V Franssen, *European Sentencing Principles for Corporations*, doctoral dissertation (KU Leuven, 2013), 62–67.

Nor do lawyers seem to fare much better. For instance, a recent attempt by the International Association of Penal Law (AIDP[88]) to clarify and resolve the use of non-criminal law sanctions in relation to economic crime at its twentieth International Congress of Penal Law[89] again used the general concept of crime without explaining the meaning of the concept or the nature of the criminality under discussion. The focus of the discussion was the use of 'alternative' (non-criminal law) enforcement of what is taken as a given – crime, economic crime and sometimes serious crime without confronting the nature of this criminality or why indeed the conduct in question should be classified as criminal, especially if it is not actually dealt with as criminal in these other important sanctioning processes.[90] While it may be useful to delineate categories of enforcement as 'preventive administrative measures' and 'punitive administrative sanctions'[91] and say something about how these have come about, the discussion left aside the logical quandary that what is assumed to be criminal is not being dealt with as criminal.

There has been, in so much of the policy and discussion, an all too easy slippage from an idea of obvious and 'traditional' criminality into a wider labelling of conduct as criminal, although often under the descriptor of 'economic' or 'financial' crime – another notion that is challenging to define[92] –, but without justifying the view of such wrongdoing, rule-breaking or misconduct as a kind of 'crime'.[93]

The above 'classical' American theory on criminal law already warned against what we may now describe as regulatory and instrumental creep into the domain of criminal law. During the nineteenth and twentieth centuries, a growing concern regarding the perceived risks and potential harm of new technologies and economic processes – a fear of motor vehicles, large industrial units and complex financial processes, often associated with their more anonymous corporate control – provoked a craving for the regulation of risk and of potentially damaging outcomes. In legal terms, this shifted the preoccupation of legal control, from an expressive and indeed ethical concern with values, to a more preventive and predictive concern with risks. Risk, it was widely felt, should be controlled, at whatever cost. Dissuasion became regarded as crucial, at the cost of the expressive function of criminal law.

As the discussion in this book shows, there are indeed a number of explanations for the sanctioning and legal control of such conduct by alternative, non-criminal law

[88] This French abbreviation (*Association internationale de droit pénal*) is still much more commonly used than the English one, hence our preference for the former.

[89] AIDP, 20th International Congress of Penal Law, 'Criminal Justice and Corporate Business', Rome, 13–16 November 2019. This conference was preceded by a Preparatory Conference, organised by the AIDP and the Max Planck Institute in Freiburg, on 18–20 June 2018.

[90] See, on the other hand, the approach taken by Christopher Harding in: 'Building an Effective Control of Financial Crime? The Role of Criminal Law and Transnational Cooperation in the European Union' in R Pereira, A Engel and S Miettenen (eds), *The Governance of Criminal Justice in the European Union: Transnationalism, Localism and Public Participation in an Evolving Constitutional Order* (Cheltenham, Edward Elgar, 2020), 127. There the author explores the way in which the idea of 'financial crime' has developed and may be defined as a species of criminality.

[91] AIDP Resolutions Section III (n 37), paras II.B and II.C.

[92] Ligeti and Franssen (n 45) 1–5.

[93] For a more in-depth analysis of 'financial crime', from a UK perspective, see S Wilson, *The Origins of Modern Financial Crime in Britain: Historical Foundations and Current Problems* (Abingdon, Routledge, 2014).

methods, but they are usually not based upon a questioning of the nature of the conduct as criminal in the first place, even if this would be a more logical and sound approach from a theoretical perspective. In colloquial terms, this may be perceived as 'putting the cart before the horse'.

B. Understanding the Need for Quasi-criminal Enforcement Mechanisms

Overall, the quest for distinctive features of quasi-criminal enforcement mechanisms has been a bit disappointing, though not entirely unexpectedly so. What unites them, is that they have been created as an alternative for 'full-blown' criminal law, with all the protective procedures and high safeguards it brings, and that they mimic certain features or functions of criminal law. Apart from that, there is a lot of diversity among these alternative enforcement mechanisms. This, as such, is an important research result.

Therefore, instead of focusing on their apparent features, which are in any event confused and result in an 'undefined identity',[94] it is probably more important to explain and understand the *need* for such mechanisms.

Going back to the 2019 AIDP Resolutions, which focus on economic crime, it is noteworthy that their preamble asserts that 'in the global risk society, economic crimes are not only causing new risks but are also becoming more complex and transnational'.[95] This statement provides something of a clue about what is happening. In our view, there are four main factors that have affected and to some extent muddied the discussion on criminal and quasi-criminal enforcement:

(a) Perceptions of risk;
(b) Perceptions of complexity;
(c) A shift towards dissuasive and preventive methodology in legal control;
(d) The need for legal protection and defence.

(i) Perceptions of Risk

A very telling phrase in the recent AIDP Resolutions is the reference to the 'global risk society' and the assertion that economic crimes are causing 'new risks'. This statement is pregnant with easy assumption and masks a significant contemporary policy-making agenda which has driven an expansion of criminal law and regulation, and engendered a mindset of preventive need, based on loosely calculated prediction. Certainly, historical examination quickly reveals that the world has always been far from risk free, whether such risks arise from natural or human causes. On the other hand, it is not unlikely that relatively stable, affluent and comfortable Western society has become increasingly *risk averse* and that their populations expect governments and private insurers to protect them against a range of possible harms.

[94] Šugman Stubbs, Chapter 12 in this volume, 352.
[95] AIDP Resolutions Section III (n 37), Preamble, first note.

The pertinent question here – as we focus on conduct now often described as economic or financial crime and other activities deemed appropriate for regulation and attempted prevention by alternative methods of legal control which increasingly mimic the character of criminal law – relates to the nature of the risk, its impact and range of effects, indeed its reality in terms of existing or future harm. In some instances, there can be little doubt. For instance, there is no argument that the emergence of new and powerful transnational networks of organised crime, typically involved in trafficking activity and habituated to the use of violence, are squarely within the domain of traditional criminal law. Rather differently, there is empirical evidence relating to the possible *material* harm in relation to road traffic and other forms of transport or certain industrial processes, which enable some sensible calculation of both preventive strategies and assignation of responsibility. But when we enter the domain of economic and financial wrongdoing and rule-breaking, we find ourselves in a world of speculation, prediction and assumption. Moreover, it is conduct described as economic wrongdoing that has moved to the foreground of the quasi-criminal domain under discussion here.[96]

The heart of 'economic crime' in this context appears to be market behaviour which, particularly during the second half of the twentieth century, has emerged as objectionable as a matter of official policy and to some extent as a matter of public perception, and can perhaps be placed under two main headings: breaches of competition policy, and market manipulation. In relation to both there has been a significant expansion of official and legal intervention and regulation,[97] resulting in new criminal offences in national systems (for instance, engagement in anti-competitive cartels, insider dealing) and hard-hitting quasi-criminal enforcement at the EU level. But in relation to both, criminalisation and the actual enforcement of prohibitive rules have been contested.[98] Typically, such policies of legal control assume clear damage to the market and to consumer interests arising from such behaviour in the form of unjustified economic gain at the expense of a large number of other dispersed economic actors (for instance, a large number of individually unidentifiable consumers who pay a higher price for a product or service as the result of a price-fixing cartel). Yet this is a matter of predictive economic calculation, used to evidence an abstract market loss. In these contexts, the victimhood of the conduct is notoriously indeterminate: Which consumers definitely suffer a loss, of how much for certain, and in what way and with what consequences? This is far removed from the *determinacy* expected in a system of criminal liability and also any alternative system of quasi-criminal enforcement which seeks to mimic so much of criminal law.[99]

[96] See, eg, De Sanctis, Chapter 10 in this volume; Wilson and Wilson, Chapter 5 in this volume; AIDP Resolutions Section III (n 37), para I.

[97] De Sanctis, Chapter 10 in this volume.

[98] C Harding, 'Hard Core Cartel Conduct as Crime: The Justification for Criminalisation in the European Context' (2012) 3(2) *New Journal of European Criminal Law* 139; C Beaton-Wells and A Ezrachi, 'Criminalising Cartels: Why Critical Studies?' in C Beaton-Wells and A Ezrachi (eds), *Criminalising Cartels: Critical Studies of an International Regulatory Movement* (Oxford, Hart Publishing, 2012) 3–9.

[99] See also G Raitt, *The Metaphysics of Market Power: The Zero-Sum Competition and Market Manipulation Approach* (Oxford, Hart Publishing, 2019), who argues against liability for misuse of market power which does not meet legal determinacy requirements and rule of law concerns, as an approach that has been overtaken by economic theory.

(ii) Perceptions of Complexity

It has often been felt, with some justification, that economic and financial misconduct (and also other kinds of activity in the 'regulatory' sphere, especially depending on the application of standards) are matters of considerable technical complexity, requiring special expertise in any efforts of legal control. As such, it may be felt that such forms of conduct are not easily amenable to the processes of criminal law, designed originally to deal with human conduct which is more visible, accessible to the outside observer, and susceptible to judgements of right and wrong. We have already noted how the application and enforcement of competition policy has become a matter of economic judgement and prediction rather than assessment of human conduct.[100] In the European context, competition regulation has produced the model par excellence of specialist, non-criminal law enforcement now exported to so many other parts of the world, in the form of the competition authority, as typified by the European Commission at the supranational level and the *Bundeskartellamt* at the (German) national level – bespoke expert enforcers whose powers of investigation and sanctioning are considerable but decidedly not of a formal criminal law character. Market manipulation is also a subject which is not easily accessible to the lay external observer, as an area in which half-hidden financial procedures are described metaphorically with such vocabulary as 'laundering', or trading in 'futures' or 'derivatives'. The development of specialist or expert enforcement agencies has tended to muddy the overall field of legal control. Sometimes such agencies are still located within the field of criminal law (for instance, the UK Serious Fraud Office, or in the same system the Financial Conduct Authority which has both criminal law and civil or administrative powers). Sometimes they are creatures of the quasi-criminal domain (for instance, many competition authorities). The outcome has been generally messy, a matter of jurisdictional and procedural complexity, beset with a sense that there should be some move away from criminal law in its traditional form since criminal courts, lawyers and juries may not be judged competent to grasp the subject-matter, but coupled with a desire to retain the powers and force of criminal law.

(iii) The Rise of Dissuasive and Preventive Criminal Law

In its traditional form, criminal law is reactive: expressing disapproval of and sanctioning wrongs already committed. The act of censure is backward-looking and determinate, although in itself it will contain some element of dissuasion, a nod to the future, since the affirmation of values is necessarily educative as a matter of guiding future behaviour. But the assumption of harm as an abstract calculation referred to just above in the regulation of much economic crime bypasses imperatives of personal responsibility[101] and legal determinacy which underpin criminal law, and may result

[100] With the exception of US antitrust law, which has preferred to employ a clear criminal law model of enforcement by basing itself on a concept of conspiracy, coupled with a heavy reliance on guilty pleas which avoid the need for contested trials.

[101] de Jong, Chapter 7 in this volume section VII, concluding that there is a tendency in Western societies to disregard or even disparage the inner quality of conduct.

in exemplary sanctioning in the interest of prevention at any cost.[102] 'Prevention at any cost' is indeed a mantra of instrumental criminal law in a number of contexts, illustrated by the 'full panoply' argument of the Canadian representative at an OECD round-table meeting on anti-cartel enforcement, and more recently the unjustified EU accumulation of systems of sanctions to deal with market manipulation, requiring Member States to adopt *both* criminal law and administrative measures of control as necessary for sufficient control of such abusive conduct.[103] The risks for justice are then palpable: as Šugman Stubbs argues, 'new solutions downgrading criminal law, and others over-extending administrative authority, smudge the boundaries between disciplines (…). We are therefore witnessing a shift toward preventive strategies, administrative in nature, which bypass the criminal law standards.'[104] That in turn increases the clamour for a higher level of legal protection within the whole field, which further complicates the distinction between the criminal and non-criminal domains.

(iv) The Legal Protection Imperative

It is noticeable how in recent years the main legal site for discussion of the difference between the criminal and the non-criminal has been the associated question of the legal protection of those who are subject to these respective regimes of control – what may be termed the rise of the legal protection imperative. In the European context, much of this discussion has been at a supranational level, naturally enough in the case law of the ECtHR, as a destination for legal argument on questions arising at the national level, but also to some extent before the ECJ, mainly in the context of vigorous enforcement of competition rules from the 1970s onwards. The central question has been the classification of enforcement and sanctioning as criminal or otherwise, for purposes of determining the extent of rights of defence and the legal character of sanctions. It has then been a matter of deciding on the dividing line between criminal and the non-criminal or quasi-criminal, and what would be appropriate for either regime. The ECtHR has had frequent opportunity to consider a range of conduct, comprising diverse cases such as road traffic violations, tax surcharges and competition policy violations. Yet, as explained above, a clear and convincing solution to the dilemma of how to distinguish these regimes of legal control has remained elusive. The Court's established *Engel* criteria,[105] with a focus on the substance of the procedure and the sanction, in particular the form and severity of the sanction, have, it seems, given way to a different approach in the wake of the *Jussila* ruling,[106] emphasising the idea of public interest in the prosecution. However, it may be doubted whether this change of direction serves to help in the quest for a convincing boundary or for the appropriate level of protection.[107]

[102] Wilson and Wilson, Chapter 5 in this volume, section III.C.
[103] For a critical analysis, see, eg, Franssen (n 46) 95 ff.
[104] Šugman Stubbs, Chapter 12 in this volume, 363.
[105] *Engel and others v the Netherlands* (n 62).
[106] *Jussila v Finland* (n 23).
[107] Šugman Stubbs, Chapter 12 in this volume, section V.

As mentioned above, one consequence of this case law has been an expansion of the field of criminal law. A severe penalty in the non-criminal field has served to convert the matter into something criminal in substance, in order to ensure legal protection. This has been most obviously the case in relation to heavy fines imposed on competition violators, but even purely preventive measures may have a clearly punitive impact.[108] Shifting the focus of discussion to a 'public interest in prosecution' still begs the issue of how that interest is judged and determined, especially in the context of a 'global risk society'.[109] While the emphasis may no longer reside in the nature of the sanction, the matter may still remain hostage to variable perceptions of what is in need of regulation in the first place.

C. *Ultima Ratio* as Cornerstone of the Criminal/Quasi-criminal Enforcement Distinction

And so we return to the starting point: there is something special about criminal law and that in itself is a reason to use it sparingly. We certainly need to note the haphazard and different motivations and triggers for moving from criminal law to something non-criminal. While a considered attempt at systematic decriminalisation or depenalisation may explain what is happening in some instances, it may otherwise be a matter of wishing to save resources or unreflective following of fashion. In the meantime, other forces have also played a role, in particular the rise of an instrumental and preventive model of legal control and also a consciousness of the need to ensure legal protection. Both the latter, although springing from different and indeed opposed philosophies, have served to extend the ambit of criminal law and increase the degree of punitive content in non-criminal regimes.

If we leave aside the complicating factors, the main question, although not the answer, is disarmingly simple. What is appropriate for the 'core' of criminal law, and what is appropriate for non-criminal law (quasi-criminal enforcement and regulation)? It is easy enough to agree that the 'core' of criminal law, its very raison d'être, is the regulation of human interpersonal relations in order to affirm and protect the essential values of a society, and in that sense it has an enduring and pervasive character. In this regard, legislators at all levels 'should make more efforts to identify common core values which truly merit criminal law protection.'[110]

If pushed beyond those limits, criminal law would lose its essential character, as 'classic' American scholars, such as Kadish, Packer and Langbein, have already asserted. Put another way, if criminal law is then used as a response to other kinds of rule-breaking and wrongdoing, we enter the realm of over-criminalisation,[111] net-widening

[108] Wilson and Wilson, Chapter 5 in this volume, section III.C, discussing the case of Ian Hannam.
[109] AIDP Resolutions Section III (n 37), Preamble, first note.
[110] Franssen (n 46) 107.
[111] See, eg, Coffee, Jr (n 86).

and 'instrumental' and 'regulatory' criminal law and, at least in the European context, undermine the principle of *ultima ratio*. Therefore,

> the less frequently criminal law is used, the stronger the message of disapproval will naturally be. By contrast, if criminal law is instrumentalised for less important rules, resulting in an inflation of criminal offences, this threatens to undermine the expressive function of criminal law and punishment as a whole.[112]

So, what is the distinguishing feature of this residuum of rule-breaking and delinquency which should be dealt with in the quasi-criminal domain? Clearly, it comprises a broad field of conduct and agency (human and corporate), and is of great quantitative significance. But a common feature is that, unlike the core of interpersonal violence and serious damage to vital material interests, it comprises rule-breaking which comes and goes, according to time, circumstances, policy, ideology and culture, and in that sense is contingent,[113] even ephemeral, and its condemnation at a particular time may even be contested. This is, for instance, true of adultery, road traffic violations, anti-competitive business conduct and manipulation of markets, or the breach of professional codes.

The serious and considered project of codifying all of this under the German concept of *Ordnungswidrigkeiten* provides a valuable illustration of the range of, and the reasons for the 'quasi-criminal' and a model for where the dividing line between 'core criminal' and 'quasi-criminal' may be drawn. And when we approach the consequent questions of methods, procedures, authorities and sanctions, we should be wary of the tyranny of instrumental, over-dissuasive and sanction-led argument. Non-criminal law solutions *may* be punitive, preventive, dissuasive,[114] juridified and, in some respects, mimic formal criminal law, provided that it is remembered that there are differences. *Most importantly, there should be a qualitative difference in the kind of censure and resulting stigma and impact of any sanctioning.* And it is this difference in particular that should determine questions about the appropriate degree of legal protection. The latter may be guided by the application of well-established principles of proportionality, fair and equal treatment, and subsidiarity. Such an approach within the quasi-criminal field can then accommodate, for instance, concerns about personal responsibility in complex situations of agency, of the necessary degrees of evidence, of the judgement of specialist agencies, and the impact of different kinds and levels of sanctions.

In that way, we can avoid the agonising about importing criminal law standards into a non-criminal law domain, when it is accepted that it is something in some ways akin to criminal law, but different also in that it is performing a different role and function. Quasi.

[112] Franssen (n 46) 104.

[113] Harding, Chapter 6 in this volume, section V.

[114] This was already voiced by Advocate General Jacobs in the early 1990s: 'Criminal penalties, also, seek to dissuade; but it does not follow that every dissuasive sanction is penal.' Opinion of Advocate General Jacobs, Case C-240/90, *Germany v European Commission*, EU:C:1992:408, 3 June 1992, para 11.

INDEX

Lightning Source UK Ltd.
Milton Keynes UK
UKHW022230270522
403638UK00003B/153

9 781509 932863